Praise for *The Terrorist Next Door*

"Authoritative . . . chilling, detailed, and extensively documented."
—*Chicago Tribune*

"Perhaps most disturbingly, Levitas makes a strong argument that these groups have a broad-based 'weak sympathy' in numbers that far exceed their small active membership. He also shows how state and local governments have been reluctant to act against these groups, either out of sympathy or in an effort to keep the spotlight away from them. But as Levitas emphasizes, Oklahoma City and the hate groups' cheering for the September 11 attacks demonstrate that these groups will be ignored at our peril . . . [a] detailed, provocative examination."
—*Publishers Weekly*

"Levitas's research is exhaustive. . . . Admirable job . . . ominous message."
—*Kirkus Reviews*

"Detailed and groundbreaking research."
—*The Kansas City Jewish Chronicle*

"With unmatched investigative zeal and a multilayered knowledge of his subject, Levitas has now written the most comprehensive and (accurate) book on the Posse Comitatus, the militia movement and the rural radical right."
—*Searchlight*

"A well-researched, disturbing look at domestic terrorism."
—*Booklist*

"Daniel Levitas's well-researched book reminds us that the bizarre ideas of the radical right are not only dangerous in their own right, but in this fearful time, dangerously influential."
—William S. McFeely, Pulitzer Prize-winning author
of the biography, *Grant and Frederick Douglass*

"Despite Oklahoma City, few Americans have any real idea of the hate-filled minds in our country: anti-Semites and racists, people gripped by the belief that a Communist conspiracy has taken over the government. In *The Terrorist Next Door*, Daniel Levitas has written a detailed and gripping picture of these frightening groups. They are dangerous, and they have not gone away since September 11, 2001."
—Anthony Lewis, two-time Pulitzer Prize winner and
former *New York Times* columnist

THE TERRORIST NEXT DOOR

THE TERRORIST NEXT DOOR

THE MILITIA MOVEMENT
AND THE RADICAL RIGHT

Daniel Levitas

Thomas Dunne Books
St. Martin's Griffin ⚏ New York

To the farmers of Iowa and the memory of Dixon Terry

And to my friend and colleague Leonard Zeskind,
who got me started and helped me finish

THOMAS DUNNE BOOKS.
An imprint of St. Martin's Press.

www.stmartins.com

ISBN 0-312-29105-1 (hc)
ISBN 0-312-32041-8 (pbk)

First St. Martin's Griffin Edition: January 2004

10 9 8 7 6 5 4 3 2 1

CONTENTS

HELL'S VICTORIES

The raspy voice of "Reverend" William Potter Gale's tape-recorded sermon filled the airwaves over western Kansas on a summer night in July 1982. From the studios of country-music station KTTL in Dodge City, it carried into homes, diners, cars, and the cabs of combines that rolled across the last unharvested fields of winter wheat. Gale, a retired army lieutenant colonel, spoke in short, rapid-fire bursts:

> We've got a bunch of empty skulls in Washington, D.C. They're going to get filled up or busted—one or the other very soon. You're either going to get back to the Constitution of the United States in your government or officials are gonna hang by the neck until they're dead—as examples to those who don't. . . . These judges who are tearing this Constitution apart and these officials of government . . . are gonna return to the law of posse comitatus. . . . The law is that your citizens—a posse—will hang an official who violated the law and the Constitution.
>
> Take him to the most populated intersection of the township and at noon hang him by the neck [then] take the body down at dark and that will be an example to those other officials who are supposed to be your servants that they are going to abide by the Constitution. [A]ll the other things you do aren't going to be worth a hoot and holler.[1]

"Arise and fight!" Gale told his rural listeners. "If a Jew comes near you, run a sword through him."[2]

Like Gale's other speeches and sermons, this broadcast had a hate-filled theme: A satanic Jewish conspiracy, disguised as communism, was corrupting public officials and the courts, undermining the sovereignty of America and its divinely inspired Constitution. Gale, a self-proclaimed "minister" in the Christian Identity faith, believed that white Anglo-Saxon Christians were the true descendants of the Lost Tribes of Israel to whom God's covenant belonged. Jews were children of the devil, and the nonwhites that swarmed the planet were "mud people," incomplete renditions of the pure Aryan man that God created in Adam. Obsessed with maintaining white supremacy, Gale railed against all forms of "race-mixing" as a violation of "God's law."[3]

"How do you get a nigger out of a tree?" asked Gale in one 1982 broadcast. "Cut the rope." Other sermons warned of racial Armageddon, attacked Catholics and minorities, and advised listeners to learn guerrilla warfare so they could garrote people in their sleep.[4]

"You're damn right I'm teaching violence!" Gale acknowledged. "You better start making dossiers, names, addresses, phone numbers, car license numbers, on every damn Jew rabbi in this land . . . and you better start doing it now. And know where he is. If you have to be told any more than that, you're too damn dumb to bother with," he shouted.[5]

Gale's beliefs were rooted in a long history of radical right-wing thought in the United States. A decade before the Kansas broadcast, and almost twenty-five years before a pair of antigovernment zealots—Timothy McVeigh and Terry Nichols—bombed the Alfred P. Murrah Federal Building in Oklahoma City, Gale hoped to lay the groundwork for a violent revolution by creating a paramilitary group known as the Posse Comitatus. Latin for "power of the county," the term refers to the medieval British practice of summoning a group of men to aid the sheriff in keeping the peace by pursuing and arresting lawbreakers.[6] While the historic role of a posse comitatus had been to *aid* civil authorities in suppressing violence and vigilantism, Bill Gale's revision stood this ancient practice on its head—his posse was devoted to promoting armed insurrection. Under Gale's definition, *anyone* could call out the Posse, not just the sheriff, and if government officials attempted to enforce "unlawful" legislation the Posse could arrest and put them on trial with a "citizens' jury."[7] Although others later claimed the credit, it was Bill Gale who first developed and popularized the strategy. And it was Gale's encouragement that prompted right-wing militants to form local Posse chapters to mobilize against blacks, Jews, and other perceived enemies of the Republic, including government officials they said were subverting the intent of the Constitution. Building on the bigotry of Christian Identity theology and his involvement with the radical right after he left the army in 1950, Bill Gale popularized a set of ideas that have influenced anti-government activists to the present day. After founding the Posse Comitatus in the 1970s, Gale helped launch the Christian Patriot movement in the 1980s. And long before the first so-called "citizens' militias" appeared in the 1990s, Gale had introduced the concept of private armies and the "unorganized militia."[8]

Of course, there was nothing original in a right-wing group that cloaked itself in patriotism while instructing its followers to take up weapons, enforce white supremacy, root out communist subversion, and resist the evils of central government. But Bill Gale added a new and important twist that made his Posse Comitatus novel and attractive. His message was embellished with elaborate legalistic rhetoric that invoked, among other things, the Constitution, Magna Carta, and medieval principals of British law in order to legitimize his violent call to arms. Gale's Posse also was unique because it successfully bridged the gap between the anticommunist and segregationist movements of the 1950s and 1960s and the paramilitary movements of the 1990s. And during the early 1970s—when other right-wing organizations were collapsing—the Posse thrived by disseminating its ideas and spawning successive waves of violence. Unlike the paramilitary Minutemen of the 1960s, which was disabled after many of its leaders were prosecuted for illegal firearms possession, the Posse was largely unaffected by Bill Gale's death in 1988, seventeen years after its founding. Like children grown to maturity, the forces he shaped have fueled the radical right to the present day.

From Gale's original ideas and comparatively narrow base of tax protesters and Identity believers, the message of the Posse Comitatus has spread across America, spawning crime and violence and pushing seemingly marginal ideas into the mainstream. This book tells that story and unearths the roots of the Posse in its myriad and successive incarnations—from its origins in the era of Massive Resistance to racial integration in the 1950s and 1960s, to its birth in 1971; through its relationship with the right-wing tax protest movement in the 1970s, to its heyday during the Midwestern farm crisis of the 1980s; and its metamorphosis into the broader Christian Patriot and militia movements of the late 1980s and 1990s.

Undergirded by the twin pillars of racism and anti-Semitism, fear of communist subversion and advocacy of states' rights became the rallying cry of the radical right in the 1950s and 1960s. Part of the genius of Bill Gale's invention of the Posse Comitatus was the way in which he took these themes and repackaged them in pseudoreligious legalisms that emphasized individual and "natural rights." For decades, the Ku Klux Klan and its various allies had created social movements and sought political power based upon explicit appeals to racial purity and Christian Nationalism. Bill Gale was no less fanatical in his devotion to "white survival" or his denunciations of world Jewry. But Gale also fashioned an elaborate, American-sounding ideology that married uncompromising anti-Semitism, anticommunism, and white supremacy with the appealing notion of the extreme sovereignty of the people. By emphasizing the idea that white Anglo-Saxon Christians were joined together by natural and "lawful" rights that trumped those of a (racially) corrupt state, Bill Gale's Posse Comitatus reached a new constituency of conservatives who would have been reluctant to embrace an ideology that revolved solely around crude bigotry.

The continuing attraction of the ideas that Gale and others espoused, the criminal violence of their adherents, and the various opposition groups they encountered are among the main elements of this story. But examined here, as well, are deeper historical questions such as how and why congressional Democrats in 1878 outlawed the use of army troops to protect the rights of freed slaves by passing the Posse Comitatus Act. Although popular opinion holds that barring the military from enforcing civil law (except in unusual and extreme circumstances) is a hallmark of American civil liberties, the Posse Comitatus Act was motivated by obvious racism and voted into law without much genuine concern for the high ideals of Constitutional restraint on federal power. In this way, the 1878 Posse Comitatus Act was a precursor of Gale's belief that a group of private citizens was justified in arming themselves to resist federal laws they disliked, or in hunting down perceived enemies of the republic without "unlawful" interference by agents of the central government.

While this book recounts the birth of the contemporary Posse Comitatus and the development of the modern paramilitary right, it also explores the historical, social, and intellectual context for the ideas that motivated Bill Gale and fueled the movement he and others created. In short, it connects the Posse's ideas and values to centuries-old myths and prejudices, many of which survive to the present day. Although many pundits regard militia groups and their progenitors as fringe extremists, many of the core values and ideas that fueled such groups were shared by the majority of Americans until the middle of the twentieth century. It was not until the nation mobilized for war against Hitler's Germany, was compelled to assert moral superiority in the face of communism, and was challenged by the domestic conflict over civil rights, that it began the process of discarding the racial, religious, and nativist prejudices that had dominated its politics, society, and culture since before independence. And even today, millions of Americans still share the belief that the United States should be a predominantly Christian nation; that blacks breed crime and are innately less intelligent than whites; that interracial marriage should be against the law; that Jews are clannish, cunning, and too powerful for the good of the country (in addition to being Christ-killers). These and other essential themes of bigotry resonate well beyond the ranks of the far right. Added to this short list of prejudices is the vague but popular notion that makes millions of other Americans anxious about the future (despite the collapse of world communism): the idea that the nation is on the verge of relinquishing its sovereignty to a shadowy cabal of "globalistic" and "communistic" forces known as "the New World Order." And equally popular, if not more so, is the notion that citizens are obligated to arm themselves to prevent a tyrannical government from usurping their rights.

Gale's 1982 Kansas broadcast was carefully calibrated to appeal to farmers like Gordon Wendell Kahl, a sixty-three-year-old sometime mechanic and World War II veteran who was to become the Posse's most famous martyr. Wanted for violating probation in a 1977 federal income-tax case, Kahl responded with gunfire when U.S. marshals tried to arrest him outside Medina, North Dakota, on February 13, 1983. Two marshals were killed and three other lawmen were injured before Kahl escaped pursuers and disappeared into the right-wing underground. The first press accounts described Kahl as a "tax protester," but news stories soon reported that Posse and Christian Identity beliefs were behind his fatal run-in with the law. It took four months for the FBI to finally track him down in the hills of northern Arkansas where he was hiding out in the home of a fellow Posse member, Leonard Ginter. The Lawrence County sheriff, Gene Matthews, was killed in the gun battle that followed, as was Kahl, whose body was burned beyond recognition after law enforcement agents pumped tear gas and diesel fuel into the residence, sending it up in flames—not an uncommon tactic when lawmen finally catch up with a heavily armed cop-killer who refuses to surrender.

Because Kahl was outspoken in his beliefs, Bill Gale said he was killed "because he was teaching this law of posse comitatus, and [exposing] the banking system and the reasons for the foreclosures in the farms, the result of the Federal Reserve System."[9] Kahl's death gave rise to even stranger theories among his supporters, including claims that Kahl survived the shootout and was still in hiding. Official credibility wasn't helped by law enforcement spokesmen who denied that the Ginter home had been intentionally set on fire. When a *New York Times* reporter came to see what was left of the safehouse several weeks later and stumbled—literally—on the charred remains of Kahl's foot, the grisly discovery reinforced bizarre theories about his fate. According to Richard Wayne Snell, a Posse sympathizer who claimed to have been a courier for Kahl, Sheriff Matthews was killed because he had interrupted federal agents in the process of dismembering Kahl. "They cut off Kahl's toes and hands, torturing him to tell who had been harboring him," Snell declared. When Matthews told federal agents to stop torturing Kahl because they might have "the wrong man," they shot the sheriff thirteen times, Snell claimed.[10]

Enraged by Kahl's death, and inspired by frustrated farmers who set November 1, 1983, as the date for a symbolic protest against low crop prices, Snell decided to mark the so-called "farm revolt" by blowing up a natural-gas pipeline outside Fulton, Arkansas. He and two accomplices used two dozen sticks of dynamite, but the explosion only dented the pipe. Like Gordon Kahl, Snell was an Identity believer who used religion to justify his crimes. Ten days after the botched pipeline bombing, Snell robbed a Texarkana pawnshop. Snell often robbed pawnshops because he believed the owners all were Jewish and "deserved to die."[11] He would then deliver the stolen goods and money to a paramilitary compound in northern Arkansas dedicated to white revolution, The Covenant, the Sword, and the Arm of the Lord (CSA). According to James Ellison, leader of the Aryan encampment, Snell had been "sent by God to help the CSA by stealing."[12] In the Texarkana robbery, Snell killed the pawnshop owner, William Stumpp (an Episcopalian). The following year, on June 30, 1984, he killed Louis Bryant, a black Arkansas state trooper. Sentenced to life without parole for the Bryant murder, Snell received the death penalty for shooting the pawnbroker.

Snell's execution took place on April 19, 1995, almost twelve years after he killed William Stump and the same day as the blast that demolished the Alfred P. Murrah Federal Building in Oklahoma City. While most observers credit the burning of the Branch Davidian compound in Waco, Texas, two years earlier on exactly the same day, with prompting McVeigh and Nichols to bomb the Murrah building, some knowledgeable observers in law enforcement and elsewhere have speculated that Snell's 1995 execution also motivated the Oklahoma City bombers. In the months leading up to Snell's execution, his wife had pleaded with supporters to inundate Arkansas governor Jim Guy Tucker with clemency requests. Her appeals were circulated by right-wing groups across the country, including the Militia of Montana, which printed her entreaties on the front page of its December 1994 newsletter, *Taking Aim*. Under the headline "An American Patriot to be Executed by the Beast," Mary Snell's letter asserted that her husband's cold-blooded murder of Louis Bryant had been an act of self-defense. Three months later, as Snell's execution neared, the Montana militia group ran another communiqué from Mary Snell and highlighted the significance of the April 19 execution date. In its message, the militia underlined that Snell would be put to death on the anniversary of the "burning of Lexington [Massachusetts]" by the British and the incineration of the Branch Davidian compound at Waco.[13] Other right-wing activists later noted that exactly ten years earlier, on April 19, 1985, a large contingent of lawmen had commenced a siege of the CSA compound in Arkansas. In the militia newsletter, Mary Snell also made another calendrical connection: "April 19 is the first day of a weeklong sacrificial preparation for the GRAND CLIMAX ceremony celebrated by those who follow the Luciferian religion."[14]

In the days leading up to his execution, Snell spent considerable time with his spiritual adviser, Robert Millar, an Identity patriarch who presided over a 400-acre compound in eastern Oklahoma called Elohim City.[15] Snell did not believe in the existence of hell, and since killing Stumpp had been a righteous act, he expected to be eternally rewarded, not punished for it. Millar promised Snell that he would take his body back to Oklahoma and bury him there.

Prior to his execution at nine P.M. on April 19, 1995, Snell had been mesmerized by the images on the television monitor bolted to the wall outside his cell in Arkansas' Tucker Prison, according to Millar and others. Scenes of the smoking Alfred P. Murrah Federal Building in Oklahoma City flickered through the metal mesh covering the screen. Most of the building's nine floors had been sheared off by the explosion and what remained of the structure towered above a massive crater. One hundred sixty-eight men, women, and children were dead and hundreds more were wounded. Exactly twelve hours later, Snell lay prone on the execution gurney, his wrists and ankles restrained by straps, awaiting lethal injection. "Today is a very significant day," he had told one of his guards earlier.[16] Back in 1983, according to Snell's right-wing compatriots, he and others had been involved in a plot to attack the Murrah building.[17] Whether Snell's execution really played a part in the Oklahoma City bombing will probably never be known, but his last words were suffused with self-serving menace. As the fatal chemicals were prepared, Snell addressed his words to the Arkansas chief executive.

"Governor Tucker, look over your shoulder. I wouldn't trade places with any of you or any of your political cronies. Hell has victory. I'm at peace."[18]

Snell never knew who was responsible for the Oklahoma City bombing. Within ninety minutes of the blast, Timothy McVeigh was pulled over outside Perry, Oklahoma, by a highway patrolman for driving his 1977 Mercury Marquis without a license plate. A Gulf War veteran who quit the military after being rejected by Army Special Forces, McVeigh was arrested on traffic charges and for carrying a loaded semiautomatic pistol. Two days later, he was charged in the bombing. When FBI agents inventoried the contents of the car they found an envelope containing typewritten documents and copies of pages from right-wing books and magazines, including excerpts from *The Turner Diaries*, a futuristic novel glorifying a hoped-for racist revolution. Even before the FBI uncovered this evidence of McVeigh's motivation, watchdog groups were linking the *Diaries* and the bombing.[19] Initially, some terrorism "experts" and others in the media hyped the possibility of "Middle Eastern" terrorists, but they were quickly forced to backtrack when it became clear that McVeigh and his accomplice, Terry Nichols, were steeped in American right-wing ideology.

Two years before the bombing, Nichols had attempted to use a Posse-inspired "Certified Fractional Reserve Check" to pay off more than $17,000 he owed to the Chase Manhattan Bank. Nichols had obtained the check from a Tigerton, Wisconsin, group called Family Farm Preservation, run by a veteran Posse activist.[20] In 1993, Terry's brother James tried to beat a speeding rap in court by parroting Posse rhetoric, attempting to argue the case on his own and asserting his "sovereign" status before the judge. Like any faithful follower of the Posse Comitatus he claimed that the Constitution granted him a right to travel, so he needed no license to drive.

The framework for such "legal" theory was derived from Bill Gale's writings on the Posse Comitatus, which first appeared in 1971, more than twenty years before James Nichols got a speeding ticket. Gale published his material in *IDEN-*

TITY, the newsletter of his small congregation, the Ministry of Christ Church, based in Mariposa, California.[21] In his first article citing the Posse, Gale used the pen name "Colonel Ben Cameron," the pseudonym—appropriately chosen—of the leading character in D. W. Griffith's 1915 film, *Birth of a Nation* and *The Clansman*, the racist novel on which the film was based.[22]

Gale began his 1971 article by listing a "train of abuses" menacing America: submission to the United Nations Charter, unlawful taxation for the support of foreign governments, enactment of a "communist-inspired" income tax, and the passage of civil-rights legislation. "[The] Sovereign States have failed to repudiate the unlawful acts of . . . the federal government," he declared. The county should be recognized as the seat of power for the people, and the sheriff is to be the "ONLY LEGAL LAW ENFORCEMENT OFFICER IN THE UNITED STATES OF AMERICA!" All healthy men between the ages of eighteen and forty-five who are not in the military could be mobilized into a posse comitatus to redress their grievances, Gale explained.[23]

Although Gale initially relied on a network of Christian Identity believers and military veterans to spread the Posse message, he soon began promoting the idea among right-wing tax protesters as well. His suggestion to form local Posse units also was greeted warmly by members of the National Association for the Right to Keep and Bear Arms, and other groups devoted to "Second Amendment Absolutism," which interpreted the Constitution as conferring an unfettered right to gun ownership. And because many of these militant defenders of the Second Amendment also shared Gale's belief that America already was in the grasp of a communist dictatorship, they were eager to band together in preparation for all-out war. During the early 1970s, Posse groups spread rapidly from Gale's home state of California up the West Coast and then to the Midwest. In Idaho, Richard Butler (the future founder of the Aryan Nations) established the Kootenai County Christian Posse Comitatus and made headlines in March 1975 when he and fifty others tried to arrest a policeman who was about to testify against a Posse member accused of assault with a deadly weapon.[24] In Snohomish County, Washington, Posse activists delighted in frequent confrontations with just about anyone, especially county officials whom they threatened with citizen's arrest. They also crusaded against local restaurants that featured patriotic place mats they felt desecrated the American flag.[25]

From 1973 to 1976, Posse chapters spread to half a dozen counties in Oregon, where activists convened citizen grand juries, filed lawsuits against state officials, sent threatening letters to legislators, impersonated law enforcement officers, and campaigned vigorously against gun control, regional planning, and the IRS. It was also in Oregon that Henry Lamont "Mike" Beach, a retired laundry-equipment mechanic and salesman, plagiarized Gale's writings and pronounced himself national leader of the "Sheriff's Posse Comitatus." Although he lacked Bill Gale's charisma, Beach played a crucial role in spreading the Posse message across the nation. Thirty years earlier, Beach had been active in the right-wing Silver Shirt Legion of America and bringing Gale's idea of the Posse Comitatus to fruition was the realization of a lifelong ambition. From the offices of his Citizens Law Enforcement Research Committee in Portland, Beach disseminated thousands of copies of his pirated version of Gale's Posse manifesto, which he dubbed the Posse *Blue Book*. He also sold hundreds of "Posse charters" to eager activists for $21 apiece to be used by any group of seven white Christian men seeking to launch a local chapter.

By the mid-1970s, the Posse had leapfrogged across the Rocky Mountains and established a foothold in Wisconsin, where it gained notoriety for its aggressive encounters with the Internal Revenue Service and the state Department of Natural Resources. As the Posse spread, so, too, did Bill Gale's Identity message, sparking greater militancy. The resulting threats and violence prompted the United States Department of Justice to launch a full domestic security investigation of the Posse in 1976. The IRS also began a crackdown, targeting key tax-protest leaders affiliated with the Posse.

The Posse's base of support had always been predominantly rural, and in the late 1970s a devastating combination of high interest rates and low farm prices provided fertile ground for growth. Through newsletters, meetings, and hundreds of activists sprinkled across dozens of groups, Posse leaders broadcast their message to a growing audience of debt-ridden farmers, blaming an international Jewish banking conspiracy for the rash of foreclosures and business failures that ravaged the Midwest. The Posse's fanciful interpretations of the monetary and legal system caught on among some members of the fledgling American Agriculture Movement, which mobilized tens of thousands of farmers during several years of vigorous protest, beginning in 1977. Meanwhile Gale and other Posse leaders crisscrossed the heartland, telling farmers to prepare for the coming battle of Armageddon.

By the mid-1980s the Posse had metamorphosed again, becoming a national movement of some twelve to fifteen thousand hard-core activists and seven to ten times that number of more-passive supporters. Politically and demographically diverse—though still predominantly rural—it included farmers, laborers, small businessmen, and the unemployed, as well as former and current tax protesters, old-line Identity believers, hard-core Posse traditionalists, former Republicans and Democrats, longtime right-wing activists, and soon-to-be-indoctrinated fresh recruits. Violent incidents like the one involving Gordon Kahl and U.S. marshals in 1983 had prompted many to drop the Posse label and call themselves "Christian Patriots" instead. But the name change was purely cosmetic. The movement still embraced the Posse's extreme interpretations of the Constitution as well as its hatred of the banking system, the income tax, national government, and the welfare state. It focused on contemporary hot-button issues, like high interest rates and debtors rights, yet remained fixated on age-old myths about Jewish plots for world domination and the inherent supremacy of white Anglo-Saxon culture. Most of the movement's members shunned the overtly racist symbols and rhetoric of groups like the Klan, even as they embraced Identity theology and aspired to vigilantism. Klan politics had too much historical baggage and was more vulnerable to criticism. But the legalistic rhetoric of Christian Patriotism was intriguing and easier to justify.

Over the past three decades, the Posse has embraced Identity theology; preached its unique form of constitutional fundamentalism; opposed taxes, government, and gun control; promoted countless conspiracy theories; and reveled in all things racist and anti-Semitic. Unlike most other right-wing groups that shared similar beliefs, the Posse succeeded at joining its conspiracy theories, bigotry, and zest for violence to more mainstream issues, such as banking, land-use planning, environmental regulation, property rights, gun ownership, and race. The Posse also flourished by transplanting its ideology into many different groups that then spread Posse beliefs even further, creating a political climate that supported its future growth. This happened less by conscious design and more through a process of opportunistic evolution, with the Posse regularly adapting—and reinventing—itself to fit changing times and conditions. Its most recent incarnation has been through the militia movement of the 1990s, which attracted tens of thousands of followers by emphasizing mainstream issues like gun control and American sovereignty in a changing world. Attracting new followers became exceedingly difficult after the Oklahoma City bombing, but by then many of the ideas the Posse had promoted in the preceding decades had reached the mainstream.

Assessing the successes and failures of the movement that Bill Gale helped create also requires examining the resistance it encountered: from fellow far-rightists, opposition and watchdog groups, the media, law enforcement, and the courts. Factions, rivalries, and periodic prosecutions have weakened the movement. But it has been the opposition of activist organizations, everyday citizens, community leaders, and grassroots groups that has made the greatest difference. This was especially true during the farm crisis of the 1980s when liberal farm groups and their allies sustained a successful campaign to challenge the rural radical right.

The story of the Posse Comitatus does not begin with a litany of its failures and achievements, or with Oklahoma City, or with manifestos and sermons, or with violent altercations that made headlines and left lawmen and others dead. A more interesting and full account starts at a personal level, a century earlier, with the ancestors of William Potter Gale and their arrival in America. Like other nineteenth-century immigrants, they were fleeing tyranny and seeking freedom. First came Bill Gale's great-uncle and -aunt, Marcus and Rosa Gale, who were followed by his father Charles. Remarkably, the Gale family was Jewish.

2

FAMILY ROOTS

A large stand of cottonwoods towered over Painted Woods Lake on the east bank of the Missouri River, thirty miles or a six-hour ride on a good horse from Bismarck, North Dakota. It was from these trees that Painted Woods derived its name, for it was here that warring Sioux and Mandan Indians daubed the bleached wood of dead cottonwoods with symbols boasting of their victories and taunting their opponents. Today, much of the curiously curved, gourd-shaped lake is gone, its contents depleted by repeated drought, its outline shrunk by years of silt and nearby cultivation. But in 1883 the lake was full, the surrounding land was rich with game, and the promise of a government homestead beckoned many new arrivals, including Marcus and Rosa Gale, the uncle and aunt of Bill Gale's father. A decade later Gale's father, Charles, traveled the same route as he sought out Marcus and Rosa in North Dakota, only to find they had moved on to Portland. The family name had been Grabifker, but like countless other Jewish immigrants, Marcus changed the name—or it was changed for him—upon his arrival in the United States.

Both Marcus and Rosa were twenty-three when they came to Painted Woods with their infant daughter; part of the first wave of Jewish families drawn to the settlement established the year before by Judah Wechsler, an energetic Reform rabbi from St. Paul, Minnesota, more than four hundred miles away.[1] One of Wechsler's motives in setting up the colony was to relieve pressure on his struggling congregation of some fifty families who found themselves inundated by more than ten times that number of Eastern European refugees. Many of these recent arrivals were fleeing Czarist oppression but preferred St. Paul instead of congested urban centers like Chicago and New York. And for Marcus and Rosa Gale and others who chose to push on to North Dakota, there was the great lure of owning land—a freedom (along with many others) that had been denied to them and other Jews throughout Eastern Europe. Sometimes called Wechsler's Painted Woods, the colony also was dubbed "New Jerusalem," reflecting the hopes of its inhabitants.

With help from a successful St. Paul merchant, Wechsler secured a land grant on a partially wooded tract in Burleigh County.[2] The first families came in the summer of 1882, and by 1884 fifty-four households and some three hundred people, including the Gales, lived in the settlement. Shelter for many consisted of mud huts and other primitive structures. Luckily, fuel was plentiful, either in the form of lignite, dug from nearby creek ravines, or wood, which had to be cut. The colony had 1,400 acres under cultivation, of which Marcus and Rosa tilled fifteen; the remaining 145 acres of the couple's family homestead was listed in census records as "unimproved, including old fields and growing woods." With only a single team of oxen and two milk cows, they were engaged in what was barely subsistence agriculture. The Gales and their fellow colonists had fled Eastern Europe to escape anti-Semitism, only to encounter similar prejudice in North Dakota. One amateur historian's account of the colony summarized what probably were fairly common opinions about the settlers:

> "[T]hese refugees, were not the higher-type Jew, but were a poor, oppressed, ignorant peasant class, uneducated, inexperienced and utterly lost in their new freedom from serfdom. Without an overlord or master in charge, they did not seem to be able to care for themselves. They were an incompetent lot, to transplant in a new country, with its strange tongue and customs, and were pitiable indeed."[3]

The *Bismarck Tribune* was more sympathetic, reporting on June 6, 1882, that the settlement of twenty-two families would soon be growing and that its inhabitants had "taken claims, purchased railroad lands and will establish a village." The colonists were poor, but perhaps the newspaper believed the stereotype that all Jews were financially well endowed. "Russia loses $200 million by the exodus of the Jews whom she has oppressed beyond endurance," the *Tribune* explained.[4] Whether or not Marcus, Rosa, and their fellow settlers would ever have succeeded as farmers is hard to say. The first Jews arrived too late to plant a crop in July 1882, and survived the year on borrowed money and charity. The cost of settling a single family was substantial and Wechsler sought help anywhere he could. Contributors included the Hebrew Immigrant Aid Society and the renowned, Munich-born, Belgian Jewish financier and philanthropist, Baron Maurice de Hirsch, who donated $2,000 in 1883 from a $2.5 million trust fund he had established for Jewish immigrants.[5] The colony was supported enthusiastically by fellow Jews, but a significant number of the colonists' brethren, including communal leaders like Wechsler, also looked on the new arrivals with an ambivalence and paternalism that sometimes bordered on disdain. "The fact remains—they are among us. They are our kindred, and it is our duty to elevate them to a higher place to become good citizens of this country," Wechsler wrote in the *American Israelite* on March 9, 1883.[6]

Their means may have been meager, but whether the immigrants needed "elevation" is debatable. Few if any of the colonists were illiterate, and most, like the Gales, were proficient, if not fluent, in several languages, including Yiddish (their mother tongue), Russian, and English. "I have the satisfaction to say that I am not altogether an ignoramus, although I have spent my best years in the wild Western prairies," explained one of the settlers in a letter seeking employment in New York City after spending seven years in North Dakota. "I had the advantage of a good education in Russia and have graduated from a well-known business college in this country. For a period of four years I held the office of acting Justice of the Peace in the county I lived in. I am familiar with the English, German, French, and Russian languages and can make myself much useful in any line of business." The writer, A. Axelrod, was twenty-seven.[7]

Unfortunately, however, literacy and linguistic ability had little bearing on the colonists' ability to survive prairie fires, crop failures, and other hostile forces of nature. They also quarreled among themselves and with their neighbors. Eventually a combination of hardships, including a severe drought in 1886, overwhelmed Painted Woods. Despite the $30,000 Wechsler had raised and spent, New Jerusalem was more than $5,000 in debt. Unable to overcome either physical hardships or internal disputes, the colony failed. Dispirited, the rabbi resigned his post and headed for warmer temperatures in Meridian, Mississippi. Although most of the other colonists also left, Marcus and Rosa Gale remained until they received legal title to their homestead and had their third and final child. In 1889, after seven years on the land, they moved to Oregon where Marcus took up farming outside Portland.[8] Five years later, Marcus's oldest nephew, Charles—the future father of Bill Gale—fled the anti-Semitism of Eastern Europe, seeking freedom and opportunity in America.

Vilna Gubernia was one of fifteen Russian provinces in the Pale of Settlement, a vast area where the majority of Jews had been required to live—or forcibly resettled—since the end of the eighteenth century. Stretching from the Baltic Sea to the Black Sea, its abysmal confines had become home to three million of the four million Jews living in the Russian empire by 1881, including the ancestors of Bill Gale. The systematic persecution and grim poverty of the Pale grew markedly worse in the spring of 1881 after Jews were blamed for the assassination of Czar Alexander II who was killed by a group of Nihilists. Beginning in April, Russian peasants and workers, often with the blessing and assis-

tance of authorities, launched a series of pogroms in which mobs ransacked
Jewish homes, shops, and synagogues. Men were beaten, killed, tortured, and
humiliated by attackers who savagely tore off their beards. Women and girls were
assaulted and raped. Entire families were murdered. One hundred such pogroms
were carried out in the spring of 1881 and an estimated twenty thousand Jewish
homes were destroyed that year. One hundred thousand other Jews suffered major property losses.[9] While the new Czar found the condition of the Jews "la-
mentable," he said the events had been "forecast in the gospels." And he echoed
the views of many *pogromshchiki* when he wrote: "[I]n my heart I am glad that
the Jews are beaten."[10] The Russian interior minister, N. P. Ignatiev, expressed a
similar sentiment when he described Jews as "leeches who suck the blood of
honest folk."[11] Ignatiev blamed Jews for provoking the pogroms and proposed
the notorious May Laws of 1882 to further restrict their rights and activities.[12]
The stifling combination of mob violence and stepped-up persecution—along
with the quest for economic opportunity—prompted several million Jews to flee
Russia and Eastern Europe during the next twenty years.

Charles Gale was born about 1880, but unlike his uncle Marcus, who had
fled the Pale just two years after the start of the Pogroms, Charles's parents did
not leave Vilna Gubernia until 1894. By then there were six children: Charles,
four brothers, and an infant sister, Fanny, who played an important role when
she resurfaced decades later to remind Charles of his Jewish heritage.[13] The
family hoped to reach America, but made it only as far as Glasgow, Scotland,
where Charles's father and Bill Gale's grandfather (whom he would never meet),
Mayer Isaac Grabifker, became a drapery traveler, or cloth salesman. By all accounts, the elder Grabifker was not a likeable or successful man. "The older he
got, the meaner he got," Charles once said about his father whose abusive treatment of his sickly wife, Chaya Inda, disturbed the teenage boy.[14] Seeking to
escape poverty and his father's ill temper, Charles followed his uncle Marcus to
America.[15] Arriving in North Dakota in 1894, Charles spent the next several years
working as a farmhand and a laborer, although his aunt and uncle had moved
west to Oregon about five years before. Charles endured several years in North
Dakota, but prairie life was hard and in 1898 he went to Milwaukee and enlisted
in the army. The military was open to immigrants if they filed papers declaring
their intent to become citizens, but Charles hadn't bothered, so he simply lied
about his age (claiming he was twenty-two not eighteen) and said he was born
in North Dakota.[16]

Charles finished his first tour of duty with the First Wisconsin Volunteers—
an infantry regiment—in five months, but he reenlisted within days of his discharge. Although he sustained the lie about his place of birth, he honestly declared his Jewish heritage when he listed his parent's nationality as "Hebrew" on
his military papers. The term may seem peculiar by today's standards but it accurately reflected the sensibilities of a nineteenth-century Jewish immigrant who
preferred to assert his ethnic and religious heritage over that of Russia, which

he had fled. To complete his imperfect ruse about being American-born, Gale claimed Marcus and Rosa as his parents. A private in the cavalry, his second tour of duty was as brief as the first but when he reenlisted again he served three full years, and spent most of the time in combat in the Philippines.

The Spanish-American War had ended the previous year, but on February 4, 1899, just one month before Gale reenlisted, Filipino guerrillas launched a rebellion against U.S. forces in Manila. Their commander was Emilio Aguinaldo, a former American ally who had previously led revolts against Spanish rule. Charles Gale was among the seventy thousand American troops sent to put down "the Philippine Insurrection." He endured dysentery, malaria, dengue fever, and minor combat injuries while serving as a farrier, or blacksmith, in the Fourth Cavalry. His unit pursued guerrillas across the Philippine Islands until American forces captured Aguinaldo in March 1901. Hostilities ended the following month when the rebel leader took an oath of allegiance to the United States. Gale was discharged a year later.

Five years in the army had changed him significantly. He had originally joined to escape the hardships of prairie life and, like other immigrants, to acquire an American identity through military service. Although Gale had affirmed his Hebrew heritage in his 1898 enlistment form, by 1903 he was ready to transform himself into a full-blooded Anglo-Saxon native-born American, as well as an apostate. His first step was to omit any reference in his subsequent military papers to his Jewishness and to define his family nationality as "English."[17] Ironically, the civilian physician who examined the 5-foot 6-inch, 134-pound soldier observed in his medical report that Charles was circumcised, a fact that previous doctors seem to have overlooked.

Although American Jews certainly were free from the murderous depredations that had plagued them for centuries throughout Europe, the United States in the late nineteenth century was still a "full-fledged anti-Semitic society," according to historian Leonard Dinnerstein, in which attitudes toward Jews were strongly influenced by both religious and secular prejudices.[18] The former dictated the superiority of the Christian faith and taught that Jews were Christ-killers, while the latter held that Jews were unscrupulous, clannish, cunning, crude, and worse. Writing in *Harper's Magazine* at the end of the century, Mark Twain (who was not an anti-Semite) summarized these latter attitudes when he wrote that "the Jew . . . had a reputation for various small forms of cheating, and for practicing oppressive usury, and for burning himself out to get the insurance, and for arranging cunning contracts which leave him an exit but lock the other man in, and for smart evasions which find him safe and comfortable just within the strict letter of the law, when court and jury know very well that he has violated the spirit of it."[19] Besieged by such hostility, many Jews were eager to prove themselves to be upstanding citizens and to demonstrate their loyalty to America. Indeed, the Central Conference of American Rabbis reflected these anxieties when it resolved in July 1898 that it "rejoices in the enthusiastic participation of American Jewish citizens in the present [Spanish-American] war, which again evidences the fact that the Jew, in equal degree with his fellow citizens, is always ready to sacrifice life and fortune in defense of the sacred standard beneath which his fathers fought in the War of the Revolution, the Mexican War, and the Civil War."[20]

Gale's second step toward abandoning Judaism altogether came in 1905 when he married Mary Agnes Potter in St. Paul. Seventeen years old and fresh from her job as one of the first telephone operators in Minnesota, she was one hundred percent Anglo-Saxon. The daughter of William Potter, an English immigrant dairyman after whom Bill Gale was named, and Sara Pearson, his Illinois-born wife whose parents came to America from England and Ireland, she completed Charles's metamorphosis from a Yiddish-speaking immigrant to a full-blooded American.[21] Their first child, Charles Earl, was born April 25, 1906. Sisters Ruth and Beatrice followed, and next to last came William Potter Gale, on November 20, 1916. Their final child, Robert, was born in 1922.[22] Stout and hardworking with a forceful personality, Mary Agnes ensured that Charles would never return to the Jewish faith. Charles's decision to abandon Judaism was driven by the pressure to assimilate, but it almost certainly was influenced by his alienation from his father. By rejecting the religion of his birth Charles found a way to put the difficult memories of his youth behind him and establish an independent identity as an adult. Although Charles had had little contact with his siblings after first arriving in America, that soon changed.[23] One by one his four brothers came to the United States and landed directly in the welcoming arms of their uncle Marcus who took them in. So, too, did Charles's sister Fanny, the youngest of the Grabifker children. Though she hated Glasgow (and her father) she stayed on to care for her mother, who was ill with cancer. When Chaya Inda died in 1914, Fanny left.[24] She traveled the same route as her uncle and brothers before her, but stopped in St. Paul where she stayed with Charles—who by now was working as a mounted policeman—and Mary Agnes. It must have been awkward. The couple had been married for nine years and Fanny could see that the relationship had erased any sign of Judaism from her brother. Fanny remained in St. Paul for a year before moving on to Portland, Oregon, where relatives gladly received her. It was a world apart from the life led by Charles and Mary Agnes.

Marcus Gale had become a successful businessman whose vigorous faith made him a leader in the Jewish community. An active participant in one of the earliest Russian Jewish congregations in Portland, he served as president of Congregation Neveh Zedek off and on for twenty years until his death in 1945.[25] The congregation's impressive stone building was at the corner of Sixth and Hall Street in the heart of the Jewish neighborhood in south Portland.[26] By 1920, the Gale home at 835 Marshall Street was a typically bustling immigrant household. In addition to Fanny, who worked as a seamstress, two of the couple's grown children and two of Fanny's brothers shared the house.[27] Though he was generous, Marcus was not ready to take on the burden of caring for Charles and Mary Agnes who were preparing to leave St. Paul with their four children, including Bill who was four years old. Whether Charles left Minnesota expecting to get help from his uncle is difficult to say. Although he arrived in Portland carrying letters of introduction from the mayor of St. Paul saying he was "one of the best policemen we have had in . . . the past ten years," Charles ended up reenlisting in the army. The family later moved to Corvallis, eighty miles south of Portland, and it was there that young Bill was baptized in the Episcopal Church. More diligent in his new faith than his old, Charles Gale made sure the family regularly attended Sunday services, but all that time in the pew didn't help Bill make sense of his baptism. "My face isn't dirty," the perplexed child declared as the priest poured water on his head. But Mary Agnes soon decided the family should leave the Episcopal faith—she was convinced that certain church leaders were communists.

In 1922 the family moved again, settling this time in Monterey, California. Bill Gale was six and by his own account he had daily fistfights with the locals, whom he called "Monterey wops." When he wasn't fighting neighborhood boys or shining soldiers' shoes, young Bill earned dimes and quarters flashing his fists in boxing matches staged in the basement of the Monterey Presidio.[28] And when his younger brother Robert was old enough, the two often would duke it out—with and without gloves—in the backyard. These early experiences taught Gale that a bloodied nose was the best path to manhood for a young boy. It was a lesson he tried to teach his own son rather forcefully decades later, with sad results. Other aspects of his upbringing reinforced the same message of tough love. Charles and Mary Agnes were stern disciplinarians and both were equally capable with a left hook. But it was from his mother more than his father—along with the years he would later spend in the army—that Bill derived his domineering personality. Charles was a proud man whose erect posture and special ability for nonstop conversation made an impression on his son. Ultimately it was the combination of his mother's forceful character and his father's affable temperament that gave Bill Gale his charismatic personality. However, regardless of his parents' warmth, by the time Bill became a father himself he was capable of exhibiting only minimal affection toward his children.

Charles Gale finally retired from the army in 1927. After three decades of military service he had not advanced beyond the rank of private. But it was the skills he acquired as a farrier—and his lifelong love of horses—that gave him the greatest satisfaction. Only forty-seven years old, he suffered from chronic bronchitis and pleurisy, had almost no vision in his right eye, and was missing nearly all his teeth.[29] By 1932 the family had relocated to Los Angeles and was feeling the grip of the Great Depression. Conditions worsened when Charles's army pension was slashed from $50 to $15 per month. "It has been very difficult for me to make the payments on the home, the taxes, street improvements, insurance, etcetera, on such a small income, not mentioning food, clothing and necessities for my wife and two children," the retired soldier wrote the Veterans Administration in November. Mary Agnes remained her industrious self, but the family had difficulty getting by no matter how many jobs she worked. It took several years, and the passage of new legislation by Congress that aided Spanish-American War Veterans, before Charles's pension was partially restored. In the meantime, Bill Gale joined the National Guard Reserves. He was almost sixteen years old.[30] Two years later, after graduating high school, he enlisted in the army and was stationed at nearby Fort MacArthur. The army sent him to take additional courses in San Pedro and it was there that he met his future wife, Josephine Catherine Dvornich, the daughter of Yugoslavian immigrants who had prospered in the local fishing industry.[31] The two were married on June 7, 1937, just three days after Bill was honorably discharged from the army.[32] He was twenty and she was nineteen. The couple's first child, Geraldine, was born two years later.

Bill tried his hand at civilian life for several years, managing a small smelting and refining company in San Pedro. But he preferred more lucrative and independent work as the owner-manager of a small restaurant and bar on West Florence Avenue in Los Angeles, which he named Bill's Cafe and Cocktail Lounge. His mother cooked in the kitchen. Bill also enjoyed the restaurant hours, preferring to stay awake late and sleep most of the morning—a routine that became his habit later in life. In January 1941, Gale reenlisted in the National Guard Reserves and soon joined the regular army where he rose quickly to first lieutenant.[33] He was assigned to lead a detachment of the Filipino Battalion at Camp San Luis Obispo where he received high marks from his superiors, even though they also noted that the young officer was "inclined to argue." It turned out to be an indelible trait that only worsened with age.[34] Gale's early experiences with Filipino-American troops marked the beginning of a lifelong affection for the Filipino people, his later racist attitudes notwithstanding. And his role as a young officer at San Luis Obispo helped him construct the lie he would tell repeatedly years later: that he had trained and led Filipino guerrilla units during World War II.[35]

In September 1943, Gale was a young major just two months shy of his twenty-seventh birthday when he shipped out to Australia. A specialist in logistics, he had spent the preceding months in Washington, D.C., procuring tanks, trucks, and equipment for the war against the Japanese. Gale's role was to help supply American forces aiming to seize islands in the Central and Southwest Pacific, but he did not stay long enough to accomplish much. After just two weeks of duty he complained of liver trouble and jaundice and was hospitalized. Aside from a case of hookworm, his medical tests came back negative but he still spent nearly three months recuperating in the hospital. Not long after resuming his duties in early 1944, he complained again of jaundice. Though he may have had liver problems, army doctors were more concerned by the growing anxiety they observed in the young officer and they diagnosed Gale's condition not as hepatitis, but as "psychoneurosis . . . manifested by abdominal pain, indigestion, weakness, insomnia and fatigue."[36] Gale was flown back to the United States in April where he remained until a medical board let him return to the Pacific the following month. Despite the diagnosis of army doctors, Gale's superiors still considered him "a willing officer, anxious to learn and be of value," and dubbed him "exceptionally loyal."[37] In November 1944, Gale was appointed director of supply for the army's Pacific Section Headquarters on the northwestern coast of New Guinea. It was from this vantage point that Gale grandiosely claimed he spent the next six months planning "every operation in the Philippines," outfitting and training Filipino guerrilla units, and serving in combat on Leyte and Luzon.[38] These events are described in theatrical and overblown detail in a 1991 biography of Gale by Cheri Seymour, a California journalist who befriended the aging rightist shortly before he died in 1988.

"We took split bamboo and we put it in the grass off the trail, where we were going to set the ambush up," Gale recalled to Seymour. "Then, when a Jap patrol unit came down the trail, we would use firecrackers, anything we could find, to make the Japs think that we were there. . . . When they hit the ground, they would impale themselves on the split bamboo."[39] Gale also recounted how he and his Filipino unit allegedly ambushed three hundred Japanese troops after escorting them back to enemy lines during the siege of Manila. "We killed all three hundred. . . . No problem—we really had a ball. . . . We wiped 'em out quick! . . . That was a very interesting job. We were laughing about that pretty good!" he told Seymour gleefully.[40] Gale also claimed to have rescued thousands of American prisoners of war from behind enemy lines in daring operations at Los Banos and Cabanatuan in the Phillipines, but Gale's military records offer scant support for his version of events. In a further effort to embellish his war record, Gale said he had been shot in the shoulder, which simply wasn't the case. In fact, he was never wounded during the war and he received no medals for injuries suffered in battle.[41] Of the seven citations and awards he did receive, all but one were simply for military service during wartime in the Pacific theater, and none were given for having faced enemy fire.

By August 1945 Gale was back in an army hospital, complaining of jaundice, and the following month he was evacuated to the U.S. Gale later claimed he was so ill that the army had shipped him home with his coffin.[42] Meanwhile Josephine had given birth to a second child—a girl, Kathleen—and the couple's third child, Bill Jr., was born in October 1946, the same month Bill left for Tokyo. The family spent the next two years in Japan while Bill worked with the staff of General Douglas MacArthur, helping to supervise U.S. occupation forces in Japan.[43] It was Gale's most significant military assignment, and his family enjoyed the excitement and prestige of life overseas. Although Gale's superiors classified his performance as "excellent," they also commented on his lack of stamina, and in January 1948 Gale restated his habitual complaint of hepatitis.[44] However, as with his previous hospitalizations, liver tests showed no evidence of disease, again begging the question about his psychological state. By August he was back in California.

With help from Josephine's parents, the couple bought a large lot with a small wood frame house at 21137 Figueroa Street in Torrance. Gale was still in the army, but he was not adjusting well to his new post at Fort MacArthur, which lacked the prestige of Tokyo staff headquarters. Rather than report for duty at the reserve training center, Gale preferred to play golf or train boxers in the family garage which he had converted into a makeshift gym. Josephine filled in for him with excuses but Gale's superiors saw through the ruse. "[Gale has] considerable initiative in projects in which he is interested, like boxing, but he will not follow through on details and requires close supervision," noted one brigadier general. The couple's marriage also was beginning to erode, but it would be another fourteen years before they divorced. Josephine missed the cocktail parties and full-time household help that was a perk of being an officer's wife in Japan. By December 1948 she was pregnant again, but miscarried. Gale was hospitalized again in January 1949, citing fatigue as well as liver trouble, but showed nothing abnormal. Doctors speculated he might be suffering from mild yet chronic hepatitis but absent evidence of liver damage, also restated earlier suspicions of "a deep-seated psychoneurosis."

On April 25, 1949, Bill Gale's father died after an extended battle with cancer. He was sixty-nine years old. Several days later Charles's brother Jacob (another of Bill Gale's Jewish uncles), a Portland salvage dealer, died in Oregon.[45] When Charles died, he took with him the details of the Grabifker family's flight from Russia in 1894, the true story of his emigration from Scotland as a teenager, and his own explanation for abandoning Judaism. But the lies he told in life were partly unraveled with his death, and all of Charles's secrets did not remain hidden forever. His real father, Mayer Isaac, had passed away in 1924 in Glasgow, but Charles's uncle Marcus was the one listed on the death certificate as his father. Resting quietly on a Saturday evening in his Portland home just as the Sabbath was coming to a close, Marcus Gale, eighty-five, had died of a heart attack in 1945.[46] The last of Charles's siblings, Alex Gale, died in 1968 at the age of eighty, and was buried alongside Marcus in the cemetery of Congregation Neveh Zedek in Portland.

Charles had last seen Marcus eight years earlier, and the backdrop to their final visit was one of family tragedy. Bill's older brother had committed suicide in Seattle. Upon hearing the news, Bill, twenty-one, and Charles rushed to Washington State from California. On their way home, Charles who was jobless, battling failing health, and struggling to stay afloat during the Depression—decided to stop in Portland to ask his relatives for money. Years later in a letter to a niece, Bill's sister Ruth—a staunch partisan of her brother's right-wing misadventures—recalled the humiliating experience as it must have been told to her by Bill: "Not one even offered him ten dollars," said Ruth, who described the appeal for funds as a "test." Whether the two men, shocked and embarrassed by the family suicide, were snubbed in this way by Charles's Jewish relatives, we have only Ruth—an ardent anti-Semite—to believe. But with the exception of his sister Fanny—who lived in Los Angeles—Charles had nothing to do with his siblings and other Russian relatives after that. Fanny was a regular visitor to the Gale household, and a vocal reminder of Charles's Jewish roots. And so, between Fanny's constant presence and the visit with Charles's Portland relatives, there is little doubt that Bill knew his father's entire family was Jewish, and, by extension, that he himself had 50 percent "Jewish blood."

After Charles's death, Bill asked to be sent back to Japan but was denied and he remained at Fort MacArthur. In January 1950, in what was becoming an annual New Year's ritual, Gale again complained of jaundice. The following month, while on leave in San Francisco, he entered Letterman General Hospital. Doctors again conducted thorough tests, including two liver biopsies, but could find no evidence of disease. Based on this consistent medical evidence, it is almost impossible to conclude that Gale suffered from hepatitis.

Josephine was pregnant and remained in Los Angeles while Bill spent the next two months at Letterman, but she miscarried a second time. Three days after she lost the baby, Gale was brought before an army medical board and questioned by five doctors.

"Colonel, how were you able to do *any duty at all* during the past three years with all this hospitalization and sickness?" they pressed him.

"I have been trying," Gale answered weakly.

"Pretty hard?"

"Yes sir. I made it in Japan because General Eastwood . . . was more or less sympathetic and kept me on duty by letting me take it easy when I got sick," Gale confessed.

After twelve cumulative years of army service, Lieutenant Colonel William Potter Gale was pronounced permanently unfit for military service and classified as disabled due to hepatitis, despite repeated medical tests to the contrary.[47] Gale never disclosed the real reason for his forced retirement, and he lied when he said he'd left the army at the rank of full colonel—a claim he repeated incessantly until his death in 1988.

Gale was just thirty-three at the time of his retirement but he was about to face a midlife crisis. Late in 1951, an old army buddy recruited Gale to work at Hughes Aircraft, managing the company's property-control department. According to Gale, Hughes was owed the almost unbelievable sum of $1.3 billion in government contracts and it was his job to retrieve the money by properly accounting for all the inventory and costs involved. When Gale wasn't in the office barking orders, he was training boxers in the family garage, including his son Billy, whom he felt needed toughening up. But the small boy was five years old, and instead of hitting back, he cried and sought the safety of his mother's arms. Things went better with Gale's daughter Geri, probably because he waited until she was ten before he taught her to fight. Gale enjoyed his job at Hughes, but quit for unknown reasons after eighteen months and began to sell insurance without much enthusiasm. Nevertheless, he was good at it and between his disability and retirement pay, which totaled $436 a month, and the money he had earned at Hughes, the family was doing well financially. But Gale faced mounting tensions in his marriage and still complained of fatigue and liver pain. Unable to find steady work, he confided to his doctors that he suffered from a waning sex drive and complained he was the target of "innuendos" from his wife and mother-in-law who both doubted his medical disability.[48] Gale, who knew from past experience that liver tests would probably undermine his claims, refused to enter the hospital or undergo more laboratory tests, and the doctors grew skeptical of his condition.

Although he had dabbled briefly in the Republican Party, Gale now sought a more active distraction in politics. Within several years he assumed the chairmanship of the right-wing Constitution Party.[49] Chilled by the Cold War, right-wing meetings dwelled on poisonous talk of Jews and communists in Hollywood, and Gale often invited visitors to his home to discuss the topic late into the night. It was during one of these sessions, around 1953, that he embraced Christian Identity theology. The man who converted him was San Jacinto Capt, a former Klansman and Texas native many years his senior who had come to California decades earlier to work as a shipwright. "I got more knowledge of the Bible just listenin' to him than I'd ever had before," Gale once said of Capt, whom he also described vaguely as a "Baptist."[50] The two men further cemented their relationship when Capt persuaded Gale to enroll in a "study program" led by an anti-Semite Catholic priest known as Father Eustace.

The Gales enjoyed a financial windfall early in 1954, when they sold part of the property on Figueroa Street to make room for a new freeway that was planned to run through Torrance. With money from the sale and help from Josephine's parents they bought a comfortable home at 1842 Outpost Drive—a tony street lined with handsome two-story Spanish-style homes in West Hollywood—that reputedly had once been owned by the actress Lucille Ball. When the Gale kids mentioned the neighbor's swimming pool they got one, too.[51] The girls attended Hollywood schools where Kathy palled around with cast members from Walt Disney's hit television show, *The Mickey Mouse Club*. And John Wayne's son, Pat, would occasionally show up on the doorstep, fishing for a date with Geri, who was a gifted soprano. Both girls were as talented as they were attractive, and Josephine—always the hopeful stage mother—often gathered them around the piano when she wasn't shuttling them to dancing and singing lessons. The investment paid off. While still in high school, Kathy landed a plum spot as one of the dancers in the movie version of *The Music Man* and she danced for eight years on television's *Red Skelton Show* after graduation.

Despite the girls' success, the appearance of contented normalcy masked considerable marital strife and family stress. Young Billy's relationship with his father remained troubled throughout childhood and adolescence. And if the scrap wasn't between father and son, it was between Bill and Geri, his oldest. Of all the children, he was closest to Kathy, and each week they would huddle by the television to watch Tom Duggan, a conservative talk-show host, expound on politics and current events. "Well, he just thinks he's on the right track, but he doesn't *really* know the truth," Gale would growl self-importantly.

Gale rarely took part in family activities outside the home, choosing instead to pursue his "studies" with Father Eustace or with San Jacinto Capt. But it was Wesley Swift, an ordained Methodist clergyman–turned–Identity minister and leader of a dedicated congregation, who showed Gale the power of the pulpit and enticed him to build an Identity ministry of his own. Swift had joined the ranks of the radical right as far back as the early 1940s, when he embraced the Ku Klux Klan and launched an association with such national figures as the Reverend Gerald L. K. Smith.[52] A decade before the witch-hunt for Hollywood communists by congressional committees began in earnest, the anti-Semitism of World War II–era demagogues like Swift and Smith helped lay the groundwork for the blacklist of the 1950s. Along with other major "Christian Nationalists" of the period, like Father Charles Coughlin, the Reverend Gerald Winrod, and William Dudley Pelley, Swift and Smith planted and nurtured the seeds of a radical right-wing belief system that fueled the anticommunist, anti-Semitic hysteria that engulfed Hollywood and profoundly influenced Bill Gale. Charismatic zealots, intolerant in every sense—especially of rivals and subordinates—these men, like Gale, turned to various "ministries" as a means of personal and political salvation. They taught their followers to "keep the faith," but also, always, to keep a gun handy.

3

HOLLYWOOD BOLSHEVIKS

Early in their relationship, Wesley Swift was Bill Gale's mentor, and in 1956 he "ordained" Gale as an Identity minister. Eventually the friendship foundered on ego and rivalry, but not before Swift propelled Gale on an irreversible trajectory toward militant white supremacy.

Born in New Jersey in 1913, Swift was a Methodist clergyman by the time he was eighteen, but abandoned Methodism in favor of Identity soon after moving to the Antelope Valley outside Los Angeles in the early 1930s.[1] Swift became politically active in 1944, leaving his job as an auto-supply salesman to organize for the Ku Klux Klan the following year. In March 1946, Swift endorsed the Klan before an American Legion meeting in Big Bear Lake, a mountain resort town northeast of Los Angeles where there had been a rash of cross burnings.[2] "The Klan is here in Bear Valley to stay," he told the veterans' group. "We intend to form restrictive covenants, here and elsewhere, in order to hold the line of pure Americanism." Swift was especially fond of guns and he reportedly served as a shooting instructor for the KKK. His enthusiasm did not match his aptitude for safety, however, and he once shot himself in the hand with his .357 Magnum revolver while showing it off to friends.[3] The Klan provided an important outlet for Swift's bigotry, but it was through Christian Identity theology that he built a dedicated following and inspired men like Bill Gale.

A broad-shouldered man with a wide face, receding hairline, and cleft chin, Swift impressed audiences with his bombastic oratory and exceptional memory. With his thick lips pressed close to the microphone, Swift awed admirers by lecturing for hours without notes. Between 1946 and 1948, Swift established two organizations, the Great Pyramid Club, which he originally conceived as a screening body for the Klan, and the Anglo-Saxon Christian Congregation.[4]

The name of the former derived from Swift's belief in the pseudoscience of pyramidology that used mathematical calculations to correlate measurements of the Egyptian pyramids with biblical texts and prophecies. Swift told followers that the pyramids had been constructed by "Aryan" descendants of Adam. First developed in the mid-1800s, pyramidology had become especially popular in England and America late in the century. Leading pyramidologists included Charles Piazzi Smyth, the Royal Astronomer of Scotland, and David Davidson, a Scottish engineer and Identity believer.[5] One of the first self-taught experts was John Taylor, mathematician, editor of the London *Observer*, and author of the 1859 work *The Great Pyramid: Why Was It Built?* After investigating the passages and chambers of Egypt's Great Pyramid at Giza, Taylor concluded that its architect was "not an Egyptian, either by race or religion."[6] Critics called Taylor and his followers "pyramidiots." While the original intent of the Pyramid Club was to search out "strong" anti-Semites for Klan membership, the chief goal of Swift's Anglo-Saxon Christian Congregation was to build the Identity movement. By 1948, his preaching schedule took him throughout California, where he regularly addressed Identity groups.[7] About two hundred followers met weekly in Los Angeles as the innocuously named "Friday Morning Club" to hear Swift sermonize on his favorite themes. After explaining how to identify Jews by the shape of their noses, Swift urged their extermination. "Your destiny is not to absorb all these people, but to *destroy* them. They all deny Jesus Christ; they hate us. Therefore they must be destroyed before they destroy us," he said on February 13, 1948. Later that year, Swift made an ominous prediction: "I prophesy that before November 1953, there will not be a Jew in the United States, and by that I mean a Jew that will be able to walk or talk."[8] The creation of the state of Israel on May 14, 1948, gave Swift a fresh focal point for discussion. Labeling Zionists as communists, Swift called Israel "an outlaw state" and denounced President Truman for officially recognizing the new nation.[9]

Southern California had a lot of potential, Swift believed. The region had long been Spanish-influenced, but by the 1940s Los Angeles already had transformed itself into a city of many ethnic enclaves. It also had attracted a steady influx of Midwesterners whose conservative political culture made them receptive to the messages of right-wing ideologues. And remarks like Swift's at Big Bear Lake about enforcing restrictive covenants, played on the fears of residents who wanted to bar nonwhites and non-Christians from buying nearby homes. In an attempt to reach this broader audience, Swift began a morning radio show early in 1948. Called *America's Destiny*, the ten-minute broadcasts on Santa Monica's KOWL were tame compared to Swift's usual speeches, but he cleverly used the airtime to promote his other meetings.[10]

Swift's tirades caught the attention of Jewish leaders like Joseph Roos, a former motion-picture writer who had spent more than a decade tracking Nazi sympathizers on behalf of the Los Angeles Jewish community. Roos modeled his approach on the strategy developed by the Anti-Defamation League (ADL) in response to Hitler's rise to power in 1933.[11] Using undercover agents, he infiltrated and exposed fascist groups up and down the West Coast. One report described Wesley Swift as a "pistol-toting minister . . . proud of his gat."[12] The information Roos acquired about Swift and others was so thorough it was sometimes used by military intelligence and the FBI to identify and prosecute right-wing activists the government suspected of sedition and espionage.[13] Though beaten up several times by German-American toughs (the diminutive Roos was five feet one inch tall) he was relentless in pursuing anti-Semites. Roos' agents infiltrated Swift's organization, but the preacher somehow obtained copies of the detailed reports that informants had provided. With appropriate hullabaloo he announced that the documents proved that Jews were carrying on a "crusade against the white race of America," and denounced the ADL as a "Jewish Gestapo." The applause was tumultuous.[14]

Two men helped Swift connect with other right-wing groups and manage his legal affairs. One was San Jacinto Capt, the former Klansman and pyramidologist who converted Bill Gale to Christian Identity. The other was Bertrand L. Comparet, a Stanford-educated lawyer with an undistinguished former career as a San Diego assistant city attorney who later parted ways with Swift in favor of Bill Gale.[15] Gerald L. K. Smith, the well-known leader of the Christian Nationalist Crusade, was an even more important ally. The two met when Smith came to California in 1945 and Swift soon became a member of Smith's inner circle, helping to organize meetings and recruit supporters in California.[16] According to Roos, Swift became Smith's bodyguard and recruited other toughs from the ranks of the Klan as a protective cadre. Both men shared a love of guns, which they brandished to impress supporters, and they both enjoyed bullying their political opponents. Their friendship lasted nearly twenty years, during which time Smith—"the Dean of American anti-Semitism" according to historian Leo Ribuffo—gave Swift thousands of dollars, praised his speeches as a "thrill and inspiration," invited him to address meetings of the Christian Nationalist Crusade, and told Swift—who was fifteen years his junior—that he thought of him as a son.[17] Both men shared an interest in Identity theology and Smith praised Swift for identifying the "true Israel," and showing that "the crucifiers of Christ were apostates, sons of Satan, and the seed of Cain." But where Swift preached Anglo-Israelism from front to back, Gerald L. K. Smith tailored his theological message for broader public consumption and he held other religious beliefs that were not necessarily consistent with Identity doctrine.

Born February 27, 1898, Gerald L. K. Smith spent his early years as a Protestant preacher in the Christian Church (later the Disciples of Christ) and held pulpits in Wisconsin, Indiana, and Louisiana.[18] Around 1932, Smith left the Disciples to become an organizer for Huey P. Long's Depression-era scheme, "Share Our Wealth." When the Kingfish was assassinated several years later, Smith was prominent enough to deliver the eulogy to 150,000 mourners. Labeled the "high priest of prejudice" by biographer Glen Jeansonne, Smith formally joined the ranks of Christian nationalists in April 1937, when he inaugurated the Committee of One Million and regularly denounced Roosevelt and the New Deal as communist collectivism in countless radio broadcasts and rallies: One rally of supporters in January 1939 filled all 23,000 seats in Detroit's Olympic Stadium. Henry Ford, the anti-Semitic automotive titan, was one of Smith's backers.[19] In 1942, Smith launched *The Cross and the Flag*, dedicated to the proposition that "Christian character is the basis of all real Americanism."[20] The magazine promoted Smith's proposal to send blacks back to Africa, denounced "mongrelizers," and became infamous for its anti-Semitic diatribes.[21] Smith made a strong showing when he sought the Republican nomination for the United States Senate from Michigan in 1942, winning 109,000 votes in the September primary.[22] His political stock fell sharply two years later, however, when he ran for president on the ticket of the anti-Semitic America First Party and polled just 1,530 votes in Michigan and 251 in Texas, the only two states where the party appeared on the ballot.[23] In 1946 Smith started the Christian Nationalist Crusade and told the House Committee on Un-American Activities that Jews running Hollywood used movies to spread communism.[24]

Both Swift and Smith hammered away at this theme before an audience of 1,200 people in the auditorium of Hollywood High School on the afternoon of Sunday, November 14, 1948.[25] "This is a historic meeting," the thirty-five-year-old Swift told the crowd after presiding over the Pledge of Allegiance and prayers for miracles in the "great fight against the powers of Satan. . . . A startled American public is awakening out of its lethargy to see the deliberate plot to do harm to American traditions. We cry out against the domination and control of Hollywood by forces un-Christian and anti-Christian and anti-American." His voice rising, Swift picked up speed, each word nearly swallowing the next. "The motion-picture heroes and heroines are not only dope fiends and sex perverts, but are conscious agents of the Soviet Union." Movie-studio heads "lack faith in the Christian American way of life and are demonstrating it by their deliberate rehiring of the writers publicly branded as Reds." After railing against "racial mongrelization" as "unsound, unscientific, unscriptural, and anti-Christian," Swift brought Smith to the microphone. "There is no greater orator today . . . no greater authority on communism," he announced. Like Swift, Smith proclaimed himself in favor of "racial dignity and integrity," and he urged the crowd to support a constitutional amendment to enforce segregation and make race-mixing a crime. "I believe in keeping white white and black black!" he shouted.

America was a Christian nation and "war refugees"—anti-Semitic code for Jewish survivors of Nazi-occupied Europe—must be deported. "If such a move were enforced in Hollywood, you'd see names on theater marquees that you could read!" he declared. "Zionists work for World War Three, just as they instigated One and Two. As long as I am here, Christ-hating, preacher-killing revolution shall not succeed in America," Smith proclaimed to loud applause.

For Smith and Swift, communism was synonymous with Judaism, and Jews were the masterminds of a global conspiracy to undermine Christian civilization. "Do not call them Reds, call them Jews," Swift said.[26] Harangues like this were rooted in elaborate anti-Semitic theories that had originated in Europe and exploded in popularity during the first half of the twentieth century in America. More than anyone else, Henry Ford was responsible for their dissemination. In 1920, Ford published a series of articles in his newspaper, the *Dearborn Independent*, which targeted the "corrupting" role of Jews in all aspects of American life, from politics and entertainment to finance and morality. Most, if not all, of the articles were probably written by *Independent* editor William J. Cameron, a close associate of Ford's who played a leading role promoting the cause of Anglo-Israelism in the 1930s.[27] According to the articles, Hollywood movies were "psychic poison and visual filth . . . morally lawless[, and] the whole secret of the movies' moral failure [is that] they are not American and their producers are racially unqualified to reproduce the American atmosphere."[28]

"If you fight filth, the fight carries you straight into the Jewish camp because the majority of the producers are there," the *Independent* declared.[29] The articles appeared in ninety-one consecutive issues and were later compiled into four volumes and published by Ford as *The International Jew*.[30] Even the Ku Klux Klan reprinted its own bound edition. The series was little more than a reconstituted, Americanized version of *The Protocols of the Elders of Zion*, a notorious anti-Semitic work of the early twentieth century that purported to be the verbatim record of Jewish plots to accumulate wealth, destabilize aristocracy and authority, instigate war, control the press, promote economic chaos, undermine Christianity, destroy private property, and foment revolution so Jews could dominate the world. Ford's version of the *Protocols* attacked Jews on many fronts. At its core, however, was the assertion of the Jewish nature of Bolshevism, a theme ceaselessly repeated by Wesley Swift and Gerald L. K. Smith and some fifty years later by Bill Gale when he founded the Posse Comitatus.[31]

The *Protocols* had first appeared in Russia in 1903, and although exposed as a fraud in 1921 by *The Times* of London, it was widely embraced around the world.[32] Ford's version sold more than five hundred thousand copies in the United States and was translated into sixteen languages. (The myths and lies of the *Protocols* have survived to this day, recycled by generations of neo-Nazis, self-described Christian Nationalists, and other anti-Semites the world over.) The tract also won Ford the admiration of Adolf Hitler, who hung the automaker's picture on his wall and asserted in *Mein Kampf* that "only a single great man, Ford," had confronted Jewish power.[33] Hitler later told a *Detroit News* reporter, "I regard Henry Ford as my inspiration," a statement that reveals more about Ford's attitude toward Jews than it does about Hitler's."[34] Six editions of the German version of *The International Jew* were published between 1920 and 1922, until Alfred Rosenberg, the Russian-educated "philosopher" of the Nazi Party, produced his own edition of the *Protocols* in 1923.[35]

A potent anti-Ford boycott in the Jewish community and the debut of the competitive Chevrolet forced Ford to reconsider the economic wisdom of his bigotry and he later acknowledged that the *Protocols* were "gross forgeries."[36] In a June 30, 1927, letter to Louis Marshall, a leader of the American Jewish Committee whom he had previously attacked, Ford claimed he was "deeply mortified" and said he had been unaware of the contents of the *Independent*.[37] Eleven years later, and just months after Germany occupied Austria, Ford was awarded the Grand Cross of the German Eagle by Detroit's German Vice-Consul on the occasion of his seventy-fifth birthday. It was the highest honor that Hitler could bestow upon a foreigner and Ford did not refuse it.[38]

As Hitler rose to power in Germany, an array of American pro-Nazi groups capitalized on the same themes. The Reverend Gerald B. Winrod's Defenders of the Christian Faith, William Dudley Pelley's Silver Shirt Legion of America, and Father Charles Coughlin's Christian Front reached a combined audience of millions with the same mixture of anti-Semitism and anticommunism found in Ford's rendition of the *Protocols*.[39] Pelley attacked the "fleshpots" of Hollywood as "Oriental custodians of adolescent entertainment. One short word for all of it— JEWS!"[40] And Coughlin's weekly *Hour of Power* radio broadcasts—which reached between five and twelve million listeners—attacked "Reds" in Hollywood, "international bankers," and the supposedly Jewish financiers of the Bolshevik revolution.[41] In 1937, at the peak of his popularity, Coughlin's newspaper *Social Justice* reached 800,000 people and by 1938 the *Protocols* appeared in its pages.[42] And when Gerald Winrod campaigned for the U.S. Senate in Kansas in 1938 (critics called him the "Jayhawk Nazi"), his newsletter reached 110,000 subscribers and he polled 53,149 votes in a three-way Republican primary (and lost). Hollywood producers also were denounced by United States senator Gerald P. Nye, a Republican from North Dakota and staunch supporter of the isolationist America First Committee. Nye pointedly identified Hollywood producers as Jews and criticized them for "making movies designed to win support for American entry into the European war."[43] Once America entered World War II, federal authorities launched a vigorous crackdown on activists like Pelley, Coughlin, and Winrod, but even as the nation was mobilized for war against fascism, anti-Semitism reached an all-time high. In June 1944, 24 percent of Americans regarded Jews as a menace to the country, up from 15 percent two years earlier. And a year later, 58 percent said Jews had too much power, compared to 36 percent in 1938. Anti-Semitism began a slow decline starting in 1946, but by 1948 there still was plenty of anti-Jewish sentiment for demagogues like Wesley Swift and Gerald L. K. Smith to inflame and exploit.[44]

Support for racism and opposition to civil rights also was strong. President Harry S. Truman, a Democrat, enraged Southern members of his own party when he banned segregation in the military on July 26, 1948. A combination of factors was behind the president's decision: pressure from the NAACP; the need to reaffirm America's moral superiority in light of the Cold War to come (it was difficult to denounce the evils of communism while practicing apartheid at home); and the demands of African-American veterans who had just fought a war against fascism, only to return to segregated barracks and communities.[45] A splinter group of racist Democrats called "Dixiecrats" bolted from the Party and chose South Carolina governor Strom Thurmond as the nominee of their States' Rights Democratic Party. He went on to carry four Southern states and polled 1.1 million votes in the presidential election (and still serves in the U.S. Senate today). He did only slightly better than Henry Wallace, the former Secretary of Agriculture under FDR and a left-leaning Progressive Party candidate for president.[46] Earlier in 1948 a Gallup poll showed 68 percent of Southerners and 42 percent of Northerners thought the federal government should do nothing to end racial discrimination on the job.[47]

Right-wing groups like the American Council of Christian Churches (founded by the Reverend Carl McIntire in 1941 as a counterweight to the mainline National Council of Churches), exploited resistance to civil rights by denouncing proposed legislation as communistic. Full-page newspaper ads sponsored by McIntire's group in 1949 argued that Ohio's proposed Fair Employment Practices Code (FEPC) would encourage state socialism and "endanger national security through infiltration into vital industries of communists who supported FEPC."[48] (A decade later McIntire still had a vast audience of millions of radio listeners who heard his weekly message of apocalyptic anticommunism.)[49]

Arguments like these got a boost from news of communist advances abroad. The 1948 Soviet blockade of Berlin, the 1949 explosion of a Soviet atomic bomb, and the January 1949 communist victory in China all lent credence to dire predictions that America was in danger of succumbing to communist domination. These views were shared by the House Committee on Un-American Activities (commonly referred to as HUAC), which issued a steady stream of reports warning of growing communist influence in public life. HUAC had held hearings on suspected Hollywood subversion as early as 1940, but that effort went nowhere. Other attacks on Hollywood also met with opposition. When the Motion Picture Alliance for the Preservation of American Ideals was formed in 1944, critics denounced the group as racist, anti-Semitic, anti-immigrant, and antilabor. But with anticommunist sentiment mounting after the war, the congressional committee tried again. After HUAC zeroed in on the activities of a small group of Hollywood writers and directors known as the Hollywood Ten, the Motion Picture Producers Association capitulated and announced in November 1947 that members of the group had been suspended.[50] Grounded in decades of radical right-wing anti-Semitism that had ceaselessly linked Jews and Hollywood to communist subversion, the Hollywood blacklist had officially begun.

Hollywood was not the only place the nation looked furtively for "Reds," but it became an obsession for many anticommunists because of the longstanding myth that Jews were a corrupting moral influence and had assumed control of film and television to advance their culturally degenerate designs. It didn't matter whether someone consciously held these beliefs or not. The trope of Jewish Bolshevism had been repeated endlessly and often enough by American anti-Semites, that by midcentury it had seeped far into the mainstream.

Bill Gale was lured into the arms of the radical right in the 1950s by this same combination of anti-Semitism and anticommunism. His embrace of Christian Identity theology drove the point further home. Millions of other Americans would follow the same path, though not all of them denounced Jews as Satan's spawn or said they were the true descendants of the Lost Tribes of Israel. But one cannot divorce the explosion of anticommunism in the 1950s from the decades of Jew-hatred that preceded it, or from the anti-Semitism it helped engender. One of the chief architects of the era was a forty-one-year-old first-term senator from Wisconsin, Joseph R. McCarthy, who raised anticommunism to a national crusade, intimidating even the Republican White House of Dwight D. Eisenhower.

4

THE ENEMY WITHIN

I have here in my hand a list of two hundred five—a list of names that were made known to the Secretary of State as being members of the Communist Party and who nevertheless are still working and shaping policy in the State Department," announced Senator Joseph R. McCarthy at a dinner meeting of the Republican Women's Club in Wheeling, West Virginia, early in February 1950. The junior senator from Wisconsin repeated this accusation the following day in Salt Lake City and often thereafter, changing the number of communists each time.[1]

McCarthy's accusations inaugurated four years of anti-communist hysteria, the likes of which had not been seen since the Red Scare and the Palmer Raids of 1919–20. While McCarthy's charges were erratic and unsubstantiated, his timing was perfect. On January 21, 1950, Alger Hiss, a former State Department officer, was convicted of perjury and sentenced to prison for lying about his connection to a communist spy ring during the 1930s. "Hiss was the quintessential establishmentarian," according to historian David Bennett. "He was tall, handsome, well-groomed, and upper-class, a white Anglo-Saxon Protestant of impeccable credentials . . . The enemy within in 1949 was a new breed."[2]

Fear of the communist threat gained momentum on June 25, 1950, when North Korean forces crossed the 38th parallel and invaded South Korea. Two days later, the United Nations Security Council adopted a United States resolution calling for armed intervention, and President Truman dispatched American troops to the Asian peninsula. By winter the war was going badly, and Americans, who had hoped to see the conflict ended by Christmas, were forced to accept the reality that 300,000 Chinese "volunteers" had entered the conflict. The House Committee on Un-American Activities renewed its investigations of Hollywood in 1951, lending legitimacy to books like *Red Channels*, which claimed 151 Hollywood figures were "subversives."[3] McCarthy dropped another bombshell on June 14, 1951. In a landmark Senate speech, he viciously attacked former Secretary of State and World War II military hero George Marshall, accusing him of serving Soviet interests throughout his career. McCarthy also labeled Truman's Secretary of State, Dean Acheson, an architect of "the great conspiracy" that produced the 1949 communist victory in China. It was this "sellout" of China that had led to the disastrous situation in Korea, McCarthy argued.[4]

If the Hiss case convinced some Americans that a new breed of elite Bolshevik agents were at work, the espionage trial and executions of Julius and Ethel Rosenberg in 1953 confirmed the suspicions of anti-Semites who equated Judaism with communism. The Rosenbergs, a Jewish couple in their early thirties from New York, were accused of passing atomic secrets to the Soviet Union. They were arrested in July 1950 and convicted in March 1951. Two years later, after numerous appeals and protest rallies—the French philosopher Jean-Paul Sartre called it a "legal lynching"—the couple was put to death, the first civilians to be executed for espionage in the United States. Although historian Leonard Dinnerstein wrote that polls showed "the Rosenberg case did not significantly alter a declining trend in anti-Semitic expressions," nevertheless, rising anticommunist sentiment provided plenty of ammunition for professional anti-Semites.[5]

In 1951, a retired Army colonel, John O. Beaty, published *The Iron Curtain Over America*, an anti-Semitic, anticommunist polemic that professed to expose the role of "Judaized Khazars" in European and American history.[6] Beaty's work was heartily embraced by many Christian Identity proponents because it substantiated their belief that Jews were religious and racial impostors. A professor of English at Southern Methodist University, Beaty held a Ph.D. from Columbia University and had spent five years in army intelligence during World War II. As scholarship, the book was beyond fringe material, but it did much to popularize the "Khazar theory" among rightists—according to which the Jews of Russia and Eastern Europe (such as the ancestors of Bill Gale) were not "pure Semites" but had descended from converts to Judaism who occupied the medieval kingdom of Khazaria in Central Asia.[7] Originally a monarchy populated by non-Jews, the kingdom's royal family and nobles converted to Judaism in 740 A.D. and many commoners followed suit.[8] The story of the kingdom's mass conversion is true, but advocates of the Khazar theory added a twist: descendants of the converts eventually migrated westward and formed the nucleus of European

Jewry.[9] This idea not only delegitimized Ashkenazic (European) Jews as a people, but advocates of the Khazar theory also used it to attack the legitimacy of Israel by claiming Jewish war refugees had no claim to Palestine because they were a counterfeit race. According to Beaty, "Judaized Khazars" were "an indigestible mass [of Bolsheviks] in the body politic" of Russia who came to America and became a powerful but inassimilable minority of communists and atom spies.[10]

Beaty's book enjoyed no fewer than eighteen printings from 1951 to 1960. Both Gerald L. K. Smith and Gerald Winrod enthusiastically recommended it, of course. But so did Hedda Hopper, Hollywood's top gossip columnist, who called it "the most revealing and frightening book that's come to my desk in ages."[11] Though published only six years after the end of World War II, the book defended Germany as "the historic bulwark of Christian Europe,"[12] and waxed nostalgic about the author's visit there in 1936.[13] Beaty had a single, simple explanation for America's conflict with Germany: Khazars in the Democratic Party instigated the war to kill as many Aryans as possible.[14]

Not all attacks on Jews during this period were on the printed page. The screeds of Beaty and others encouraged bigots who preferred action to mere words. Eighteen bombs detonated in Miami in 1951 alone, destroying synagogues, Catholic churches, and black homes. The explosions were the work of Klansmen and others. Although anti-Semitism was on the decline overall, a 1951 confidential report prepared for the American Jewish Committee noted that "approximately fifty old-line anti-Semitic groups and leaders remain from the hundreds of units that flourished during pre–Pearl Harbor days, [and] they by no means constitute an index of the decline of anti-Semitic activity." Since 1946, the report noted, "a trend of infiltration of anti-Semites into conservative, patriotic, and other movements has become apparent."[15] Far-right groups had failed during World War II because they had too closely allied themselves with Nazis and other easily identifiable enemies of America, the report explained. "[But t]oday the situation is different. Communism is the enemy of America [and the new anti-Semitic strategy is] for demagogues to gain respectability by association with reputable causes, and respectable organizations and institutions, while at the same time publicizing the equation of Jews with communism."[16] The *New York Times* agreed: "One of the main objectives of the [anti-Semitic] movement is to penetrate United States and British democratic organizations by taking advantage of the rising tide of anticommunism."[17]

The process also worked well in reverse. Demagogues like Joe McCarthy often turned to established anti-Semites for help, hiring them as aides or relying on their "research" for his speeches and insertions into the *Congressional Record*.[18] After McCarthy was pressured to withdraw several items written by an anti-Semitic radio commentator, Upton Close, the senator wrote apologetically to Close that his "fight to clean communists out of our government was too important to get mixed up in anti-Semitic charges . . . regardless of how unjustified those charges might be . . ."[19] McCarthy reached the height of his power in 1953 but his downfall came soon thereafter when he used his Senate Permanent Subcommittee on Investigations to make outrageous charges of supposed communist infiltration of the army. In 1954 McCarthy was formally censured by the Senate for conduct unbecoming a senator and he died three years later of cirrhosis of the liver. He was forty-eight. McCarthy fell from favor, but the anticommunist climate he helped create fueled the growth of rightist groups that long outlived him.

In the presidential election of 1952 the choice was between Illinois governor Adlai E. Stevenson, a liberal Democrat, and Dwight David Eisenhower, a moderate Republican. The far right condemned both candidates with equal ferocity. Pundits like Close said Stevenson was allied with Alger Hiss and other planners of "dollar ruin, major war, or both."[20] Although Eisenhower was a popular World War II hero, he was attacked as "a coddler of Negro troops, a tool of Russia, a front for New Dealers, and a pal of Joe Stalin's. . . ."[21] Gerald L. K. Smith called the former five-star general a "Swedish Jew," and tried to derail his nomination. Almost nightly Smith drew thousands to the Embassy Auditorium in Los Angeles in January 1952. Smith told the crowd that Eisenhower was "the ADL candidate" and pledged to produce five thousand "fanatic Christian Nationalists" at the coming Republican National Convention in Chicago.[22] Smith gathered only three hundred volunteers but they inundated the three-day assembly with 150,000 pieces of literature.[23]

"Anti-Semitic animus against Eisenhower now appears to be almost on a par with, if not exceeding, that against Truman," observed the National [Jewish] Community Relations Advisory Council in July, noting that professional anti-Semites invariably referred to the two-term Democratic president as "Harry Solomon Truman."[24]

On the Republican side, rightists were split between supporting Robert A. Taft, the conservative Ohio senator, and General Douglas MacArthur; though support for Taft was lukewarm compared to their rampant enthusiasm for the general, who was not even running for president. In April 1951, President Truman had relieved MacArthur of his military command in Korea for trying to pursue more aggressive and direct military action against China; it was a course of action that Truman rightly feared could ignite a third world war.[25] MacArthur became a symbol of anticommunist resistance and ultranationalists launched competing third-party efforts to nominate him—in absentia—for president. Gerald L. K. Smith's Christian Nationalist Party won a spot for MacArthur on its ballot line in Texas and Missouri, prompting the *St. Louis Post Dispatch* to editorialize that MacArthur "ought to disassociate himself from that bunch, completely and immediately."[26] But despite these and other calls to repudiate bigotry, MacArthur's keynote speech to the Republican convention addressed the issue only briefly and obliquely. Ohio's Senator Taft was slightly more direct when he held a press conference prior to the convention and condemned the "smearing tactics" used against Eisenhower.

The most promising right-wing third-party effort was launched in the summer of 1952 by the Constitution Party, "an outright amalgam of blatant anti-Semites, highly placed socialites, and suave opportunists," according to the American Jewish Committee.[27] The party's founding convention in Chicago attracted nearly two hundred representatives from eighty right-wing groups and forty states. Republican congressmen Howard Buffett of Nebraska and Ralph Gwinn of New York addressed the group in a vain attempt to entice its supporters back into the fold of the Republican Party, but their plea was rejected.[28] Delegates denounced the two-party system and endorsed plans to run General MacArthur for president. Such agreement did not last long, however, as the party foundered over charges of religious intolerance not long after the convention ended.[29] Resigning her post as "temporary co-chairman" of the party, Suzanne Silvercruys Stevenson noted that some members of the National Committee had objected to her because she was Roman Catholic and foreign-born. "I will have no part of any movement which seems to me to be so steeped in bigotry," she announced.[30]

In the end, MacArthur's name appeared on three national ballots—Smith's Christian Nationalist Party, the Constitution Party, and the America First Party—but he received only 18,000 votes. Eisenhower swamped Stevenson with 55 percent of the 61 million votes cast. Like most other presidential campaigns launched by third-party candidates and movements, these results say more about the desire of voters to have their ballot count, than they do about the degree to which they identify with the platform of a candidate who has no chance of winning. Nor was MacArthur a willing contestant—had he actually campaigned on the platform of the far-right groups who urged his candidacy, he would have attracted many more votes.

Just one month after the 1952 election, the U.S. Supreme Court heard oral arguments in *Brown v. Board of Education of Topeka, Kansas*—a case that would forever change the political, cultural, and social landscape of America. *Brown* was the result of years of painstaking legal preparation to challenge segregation. Led by Thurgood Marshall, attorneys for the NAACP Legal Defense Fund had purposefully consolidated cases they had filed on behalf of black students and their families in several jurisdictions—including one brought by a group of thirteen parents and twenty children in Topeka.[31] The goal was to advance an inclusive vision of America where racial equality would achieve the status of a legal, political, social, and cultural norm, and all vestiges of slavery and Jim Crow—that uniquely American version of apartheid—would finally be abolished.[32] From a legal perspective that meant overturning the doctrine of "separate but equal" that had been the law of the land since 1896 when the United States Supreme Court rendered its decision in *Plessy v. Ferguson*, upholding racial segregation in railroad passenger cars. Near the end of its term in June 1953, the Supreme Court ordered the *Brown* case reargued. And the following year, on May 17, 1954, it handed down its unanimous decision.[33] Citing the detrimental effect of segregation, the court overturned fifty-eight years of precedent:

"We conclude that, in the field of public education, the doctrine of 'separate but equal' has no place," wrote Chief Justice Earl Warren, the former Republican governor of California. "Separate educational facilities are inherently unequal."[34]

Prior to the *Brown* decision the American far right had subsisted mainly on a noxious but nourishing brew of racism, anti-Semitism, and anticommunism. Other religious and nativist prejudices—like fear and hatred of Catholics and immigrants—also played a generous role. But coming during the intense anxieties of the Cold War, the *Brown* decision electrified the radical right and immediately fused a spectrum of bigots and vigilantes into a new common cause. It included Southern segregationists, garden-variety racists, professional anti-Semites, and everyday anticommunists. The result was the doctrine of "Massive Resistance" to integration and the birth of a dynamic social movement that would fuel more than twenty years of paramilitary violence, mainly in the South and West. Before the *Brown* decision, white supremacists had looked to the government to sanction, or at least ignore, de facto—and, better yet, de jure—discrimination. Now they saw themselves at war with the federal government. Like those Civil War partisans who insisted that secession was rooted in states' rights and had nothing to do with slavery, opponents of *Brown* couched their arguments in legalistic and constitutional terms. But regardless of their verbal invocations, resistance to *Brown* was rooted in the determination to preserve white supremacy at almost any price. Leading the charge were men like Mississippi Circuit Court judge Tom P. Brady, the vice president of the State Bar Association who compared blacks to apes and advocated aggressive political action (and worse) to resist integration. The former Chairman of the Speaker's Bureau for the States' Rights Democratic Party in 1948, and a graduate of Yale, Brady wrote a ninety-two-page booklet in 1954 titled *Black Monday* that launched the Citizens' Council movement and inspired scores of bigots not previously active in the racist movement to enlist in the cause.[35]

5

BLACK MONDAY

A blazing wooden cross nine feet high was jammed into a pipe sunk into the ground in front of Pensacola High School. It was just three days after the *Brown* decision had ruled segregation in public schools unconstitutional. On the same night, many miles across the state of Florida, on the Atlantic coast, another cross burst into flames. This one, wrapped in burlap and soaked with kerosene, was placed on a ridge overlooking the black section of Fort Pierce.[1] Thus began a fierce campaign of white resistance to integration.[2] While most Klan groups still relied on violence and the intimidating message conveyed by its flaming symbols, the newly formed movement of "Citizens' Councils" had another idea: use more "respectable" economic pressure against "agitators" who demanded desegregation.[3] The first Citizens' Council was formed in conservative, cotton-rich Sunflower County, Mississippi, inspired by Judge Tom P. Brady's hastily printed tract, *Black Monday*—the text of a speech he gave to the Greenwood, Mississippi, chapter of the Sons of the American Revolution a few months after the *Brown* decision.

Black Monday is a veritable encyclopedia of racist ideas. Though Brady prefaced his screed by stating that "the popular concept of a superior race has no place in this treatise," he went on to compare blacks to chimpanzees and refer to them as "beasts of burden . . . only one-half step from . . . primordial brute[s]."[4] To Judge Brady and his admirers, blacks were characterized by "abysmal vulgar-

ity . . . profanity . . . obscenity and depravity."[5] *Black Monday* proposed the creation of a forty-ninth state solely for blacks, and contained such lurid observations
as: "Whenever and wherever the white man has drunk the cup of black hemlock,
whenever and wherever his blood has been infused with the blood of the negro,
the white man, his intellect and his culture have died. This is as true as two plus
two equals four."[6]

One man heavily influenced by *Black Monday* was Robert B. "Tut" Patterson,
a former Mississippi State University football star, World War II paratrooper,
and the manager of a fifteen-hundred acre cotton plantation in Leflore County.
After reading Brady's remarks, Patterson called fourteen prominent businessmen
and civic leaders on July 11, 1954, to meet in Indianola, Mississippi. This meeting
was soon followed by a larger gathering of whites at the town hall, and the first
Citizens' Council was born.[7] Barely six months later, the newly formed State
Association claimed affiliates in thirty-three counties, with new out-of-state councils in Alabama and Georgia.[8]

Within a year, the movement boasted sixty thousand members in 253 Councils throughout Mississippi. Concentrations of Citizens' Councils often followed
the geographic and demographic pattern of late-nineteenth- and early-twentieth-
century lynchings in Mississippi, where racist violence was worse in counties
where blacks heavily outnumbered whites and whites had the most to gain by
dominating blacks, politically, economically, and physically.[9] Yazoo County was
typical. More than three-quarters of the population was black, cotton was king,
and by 1930 there had been almost one lynching every three years since 1882.[10]
The demographics of white domination had changed little by 1955, when the
county still was overwhelmingly black and more than 10 percent of Yazoo City's
eleven thousand people were Citizens' Council members.[11]

While the blood sport of racial violence never lost its appeal for some white
Mississippians, the Citizens' Council movement tried to cast itself as a law-
abiding entity. With only twenty-two thousand of the state's nearly one million
blacks registered to vote in 1952, the Citizens' Councils emphatically recommended that whites discourage Negro registration "by every legal means."[12] "If
necessary, organize a white private election within our group to combat the Negro bloc vote (as our old white primary)," one 1954 circular explained.[13] When
Citizens' Council delegates from eleven Southern states met two years later, the
movement claimed three hundred thousand members and they renamed themselves the Citizens' Councils of America.[14] Although the movement was careful
to heed Judge Brady's advice that Southern whites distance themselves from the
"nefarious Ku Klux Klans," the move was largely cosmetic.[15] An Alabama journalist claimed the Councils were nothing less than a "refined descendant of the
Ku Klux Klan." He wrote: "In place of bullwhips, the new 'citizen councils' have
substituted 'economic pressure' to handle what they term 'agitators'—both white
and Negro—who think the Supreme Court way rather than the Southern way
on segregation."[16] Still, the "refined" image of the Councils won the qualified

endorsement of FBI director J. Edgar Hoover, who ambiguously described them to President Eisenhower in 1956 as a movement that "either could control the rising tension or become the medium through which tensions might manifest themselves."[17] As for Council members themselves, many advanced the notion, as one put it, that "there will be no need for any 'hotheaded' bunch to start a Ku Klux Klan. If we fail, though, the temper of the public may produce something like the Klan."[18]

Although most Councilors, as they called themselves, regarded their lower-class Klan cousins with contempt, the movement was just as thoroughly racist. Seeking new supporters, Councilors conjured up terrifying images of race-mixing, warning, for example, that white girls would contract syphilis from integrated drinking fountains mandated by "the Supreme School Board," as they called the nation's highest court.[19]

"In general, the nature of the Negro is more primitive and childlike than the Whites, and his crimes are likely to be more savage and less sophisticated [sic]," wrote a prominent psychologist, Henry E. Garrett (a past president of the American Psychological Association), in one Council publication.[20] Such beliefs were commonplace among the elite that closed ranks with the Citizens' Councils and the South's leading politicians to oppose integration. Chief among the latter was Mississippi's senior senator James O. Eastland, who boldly declared: "The South will not abide by or obey, this legislative decision by a political court."[21] In 1956, Eastland was one of more than one hundred congressmen and senators from eleven states who signed a "Southern Manifesto" asserting the Brown decision and its legal progeny were unconstitutional.[22]

Speaking before two thousand Citizens' Council members and forty state legislators in Jackson, Mississippi, on December 1, 1955 (coincidentally the same day Rosa Parks refused to give up her seat on a public bus in neighboring Alabama), Eastland called the anti-segregation rulings "dishonest decisions . . . dictated by political pressure groups bent upon the destruction of the American system of government, and the mongrelization of the white race."[23] The Citizens' Councils did not confine their appeals to racism; they also embraced anti-Semitism. On August 31, 1954, one month after the Council's founding meeting, Robert Patterson circulated a reading list for new and prospective Council members. Included on the list were works by celebrated anti-Semites such as Gerald L. K. Smith and Gerald Winrod, along with less notable pamphleteers such as Mrs. Jesse Jenkins, leader of the Patrick Henry Society of Columbus, Georgia. Her organization's letterhead bore the imprint: "Communism is Judaism—Internationalism is Judaism—Judaism is Bolshevism."[24] Because integrationists were considered communists and Jews were seen as the principle agents of communist subversion, many hardline segregationists concluded that Jews were the driving force behind the civil rights movement. This theory had the added benefit of divesting blacks of intellectual and moral stature and reducing them to mere pawns in the struggle between devious Jews and the Christian defenders of white civilization. Bill Gale gave the same explanation for the civil rights movement, albeit in the vocabulary of Christian Identity: "[T]he Yehudi [Jews] and their agents . . . stirr[ed] up the Enosh [blacks] and demand[ed] that they be put in the same schools with Adam's young children in the Southern states. In this manner the Enosh [blacks] could be used to eventually destroy the Holy seed."[25]

One year after the *Brown* decision, on May 31, 1955, the Supreme Court issued an enforcement decree, ordering lower federal courts in Kansas, South Carolina, Virginia, and Delaware to implement its landmark ruling "with all deliberate speed," but the ruling had little immediate effect.[26] Despite the fact that the NAACP petitioned local school boards across the South to admit black students, most local officials ignored these demands. Worried Citizens' Council militants still sprang into action. In Selma, Alabama, more than half of those blacks courageous enough to support a desegregation petition lost their jobs within weeks of signing their names. In Mississippi, South Carolina, and elsewhere, Citizens' Council leaders began to aggressively implement the solution first proposed by Judge Brady in *Black Monday*: they activated his call for "a cold war and an economic boycott" against black agitators.[27]

"A great many Negro employees will be discharged," Brady predicted.[28] And they were. State legislatures also attacked black activists with new laws that especially targeted the NAACP. These wide-ranging and unconstitutional statutes required disclosure of NAACP membership rolls, demanded the dismissal of public employees who were NAACP members, and subjected the organization to investigations by state agencies and committees.[29] More disturbing than Brady's prescription for economic reprisal was his ominous forecast of violence. "If trouble is to come, we can predict how it will rise," Brady warned.[30] "The supercilious, glib young Negro, who has sojourned in Chicago or New York, and who considers the counsel of his elders archaic, will perform an obscene act, or make an obscene remark, or a vile overture or assault upon some white girl. For they will reason . . . 'We need but to assert ourselves and abolish every last vestige of segregation and racial difference.' This is the reasoning which produces riots, bloodshed, raping, and revolutions."[31]

Such were the circumstances—in the eyes of white racists, at least—that led to the lynching of fourteen-year-old Emmett Louis Till, on August 28, 1955. Till, a Chicagoan, was kidnapped from his grandfather's home in Money, Mississippi, after allegedly "wolf-whistling" at a white woman. When his beaten body was pulled from the Tallahatchie River, a 70-pound cotton-gin fan had been tied around his neck with barbed wire. Two men were arrested and later acquitted by an all-white jury. "The crowds are gone and this Delta town is back to its silent, solid life that is based on cotton and the proposition that a whole race of men was created to pick it," wrote Dan Wakefield in *The Nation* magazine.[32] From May 1954 until December 1955, the struggle between black civil rights activists and segregationists was generally limited to two issues: school integration and voting rights. But the situation changed dramatically when Rosa Parks refused to defer to local segregation codes in Montgomery, Alabama, on December 1, 1955. She was arrested and the subsequent yearlong bus boycott thrust Dr. Martin Luther King Jr., then a young pastor at Montgomery's Dexter Avenue Baptist Church, onto the national stage and fundamentally transformed the fight against segregation "from the courtrooms to the streets, from law libraries to the pews of churches, from the mind to the soul," wrote Lerone Bennett Jr.[33]

While King and the Montgomery Improvement Association were not the first to use nonviolent direct action to challenge white supremacy, the movement directed by King and others ultimately ended Jim Crow.[34] But the threat of such massive social transformation also invigorated countless racists and right-wing groups across the country. Committed to the lost cause of white supremacy, they couched their arguments in lofty rhetoric that extolled the honorable position of states' rights. Like the Southern partisans of a century earlier, they also looked to neutral-sounding legal doctrines to justify the continued subjugation of black America. The intimidation and violence of Massive Resistance could be criticized, but invoking the nineteenth-century doctrines of "interposition" and "nullification" lent an almost honorable gloss to their bigoted motivations.

6

PHILOSOPHER, STATESMAN, AND CHIEF

W e think the Southern states should carefully consider the doctrine and precedents that a State has the legal right of interposition to nullify, void, and hold
for naught the deliberate, dangerous, and palpable infractions of the Constitution
committed by the Supreme Court; infractions that are so great that our system
of government is threatened," wrote Judge Brady, Senator Eastland, and Mississippi congressman John Bell Williams in 1955.[1]

Although the idea of states' rights is commonly associated with the Civil War
and the segregationist campaigns of the 1950s and 1960s, the roots of the doctrine predate even the Constitution. And it is because the idea of states' rights
was so critical to the radical right, that it is essential to examine the original
arguments and circumstances surrounding the concept. The first major impetus
for states' rights came in 1798, when Federalist forces in Congress won passage
of the Alien and Sedition Acts.[2] Conceived as wartime emergency measures to
suppress American agitation in support of the French Revolution, these laws also
took aim at domestic political dissent, particularly the allies of Vice President
Thomas Jefferson and his vigorous and growing "Democratic societies," as these
local political groups were called. From his home in Monticello, Jefferson drafted
a manifesto arguing that the Alien and Sedition Acts were dangerously oppressive
and unconstitutional. Since the states were dominant over the federal Union, he
argued, they could "interpose" their sovereignty against a "usurpation" of federal

power. According to Jefferson there would be "revolution and blood" if the Acts were not repealed. Jefferson's text was quickly supported by the Kentucky legislature and Virginia followed suit.[3]

Two years later, Jefferson became president after defeating his former ally, the Federalist John Adams. But less than two months before Jefferson's inauguration, in a shrewd move that would sorely frustrate Jefferson, Adams appointed John Marshall as Chief Justice of the U.S. Supreme Court. Marshall was to emerge as a champion of the concept of a powerful federal government and it was against several landmark decisions of the Marshall Court that the battle for states' rights began to take shape.[4] Beginning in 1810, Marshall's rulings reinforced federal authority, restricted freedom of action by the states, and protected the national government from further anti-Federalist assaults.[5] It took twenty years for opponents of Federalism to develop a complete theory of state sovereignty, and to find a leader to press their cause. They found both in the doctrine of nullification and its author, John Caldwell Calhoun, the forty-six-year-old vice president of the United States under Andrew Jackson. An ardent defender of white supremacy and slavery, Calhoun laid the intellectual groundwork for Southern secession and the Civil War. Long after Calhoun's death his ideas were resurrected by segregationists and others intent on rehabilitating states' rights.

John C. Calhoun was born in 1782 on the South Carolina frontier. His Scottish-Irish immigrant father, later a county judge, was "one of the wiliest and most ruthless Indian fighters in the entire Southern backcountry," according to Pulitzer Prize–winning Calhoun biographer Margaret Louise Coit.[6] The elder Patrick Calhoun had led the battle, at gunpoint, for political representation for the Carolina up-country and was rewarded with election to the state legislature. He voted against ratification of the Constitution on the grounds that it permitted "other people" to tax South Carolinians.[7] When Patrick Calhoun died in 1796 he was a prosperous man, owning five farms and thirty-one slaves.[8] John C. Calhoun was much like his father in temperament and political disposition. After running the family's twelve hundred–acre plantation for eight years, Calhoun attended Yale, then law school in Litchfield, Connecticut. He was elected to the South Carolina Statehouse in 1808 and served one term before moving on to Congress in 1810. For the next twenty years he served as congressman, secretary of war under President James Monroe, and vice president in the administrations of John Quincy Adams and Andrew Jackson. Calhoun was an enthusiastic supporter of slavery, believing it to be a "positive good" and "the perfect foundation for a republican social order."[9] Underlying his admiration for human bondage was total contempt for the idea of equality among blacks and whites. According to Calhoun, the proposition that all men are born free and equal was "utterly untrue."[10] In 1874, Henry Wilson said of John Calhoun:

> While others, from indolence, greed of gain, and lust of power . . . eagerly clutched whatever the wicked laws of slavery gave them, Mr. Calhoun's

devotion to the system seemed to be the result of carefully studied and well-matured convictions. He was the acknowledged embodiment and exponent of the principles of chattlehood, its philosopher, statesman, and chief.[11]

Others simply called him the "Arch Nullifier" for his definitive treatise on states' rights, the *Exposition*.[12] Written anonymously in December 1828 as a report to the South Carolina Legislature in defense of states' rights, the essay expanded upon the doctrine of interposition articulated in Jefferson's Kentucky Resolution from thirty years before. Calhoun also outlined a comprehensive theory of state sovereignty, detailing how and why a state could supposedly make a federal law inoperable within its borders.[13] Calhoun expanded further on the concept of nullification (he preferred the term "state interposition") by criticizing what he called "majoritarian tyranny.[14] According to this idea, the South was an oppressed minority, and unless the "tyrannical" majority power of the North could be checked, the Union would be torn apart. Calhoun's "nullification" solution proposed transforming the minority status of the South by putting it on equal footing with the North. Calhoun termed this approach creating a "concurrent majority."

Calhoun biographer Margaret Louise Coit explained the process of nullification this way: "[It] did not suspend a law for the nation, but only within the state that protested. . . . It gave opportunity for three-quarters of the states in ['organic'] convention to determine whether or not to confer the questioned power upon the Union by constitutional amendment. The nullifying state would then have to obey or secede." The weakness of Calhoun's argument, according to Coit, was that if even as few as one-quarter of the states decided to nullify a law that was clearly constitutional, there would be nothing the other states could do.[15]

Legal strategies to interpose state authority against the federal government were critically important to the South, which was struggling to find ways to challenge steep federal tariffs on badly needed foreign imports.[16] In particular, Southerners focused their ire on the so-called 1828 "Tariff of Abominations," which they feared would undermine the slave economy by increasing the price of essential imports such as hemp, cotton bagging, and cheap wool needed for slave clothing. Calhoun and other defenders of slavery also worried that the tariff would invite retaliation from abroad, lowering the value of American cotton exports in Europe and thereby weakening the Southern plantation economy.[17]

If Southerners couldn't win the argument legally or politically, there were other options. By the time Calhoun wrote the *Exposition*, South Carolina was an armed camp, and militant pro-slavery leaders were calling for "rebellion, revolution, and forcible resistance to federal tariffs."[18] The crisis deepened in 1830, when the nullifiers won control of the state legislature, and when President Andrew Jackson signed legislation imposing new tariffs two years later.[19] The South

Carolina elections that year were "colorful, spirited, and often violent," according to Calhoun biographer and historian Charles M. Wiltse, and the nullifiers rode to victory.[20] They called a state convention, declared the federal tariffs of 1828 and 1832 unconstitutional, and warned that any use of force by the federal government would cause South Carolina to secede from the Union. Additional laws were passed to enforce their declaration—which they called an "Ordinance of Nullification"—including one saber-rattling measure that reorganized the state militia.

President Jackson responded firmly, alerting the federal forts in Charleston and threatening to use military force. On March 2, 1833, the military was authorized to collect tariff revenues. Armed conflict was ultimately averted, however, when Congress adopted a compromise and gradually phased out protectionist tariffs. Calhoun died in 1850, a decade before the South was inspired by his ideas to secede and start the Civil War.

Sympathetic biographers have argued that no violence was implied in Calhoun's doctrine of nullification and that it was "ingeniously derived" to "avoid either of the extremes of rebellion or submission."[21] These writers also maintained that Calhoun had the best interests of the Union at heart, and that the combined threat of interposition and secession was only a mechanism by which the (white Southern) minority could secure fair treatment from the (Northern) majority. But there was much more to it than that. At bottom, Calhoun's legalistic doctrine of state sovereignty was inseparable from his contempt for black equality and his support for slavery. And even if Calhoun's intentions were nonviolent, any attempt to implement his doctrine led inexorably to bloodshed. There was little practical difference between Calhoun's elaborately argued treatise on how to create a "concurrent majority" and the opinion expressed by then Mississippi congressman Albert G. Brown who bluntly told the South's opponents: "We ask you to give us our rights. . . . If you refuse, I am for taking them by armed occupation."[22]

Similar political violence and legalistic arguments favoring states' rights surfaced more than a century after Calhoun's death when governors in Alabama, Mississippi, and Arkansas stood in the schoolhouse door—sometimes figuratively and often literally—repeating Calhoun's mantra of states' rights while mobs of angry whites threatened violence and disorder. Such were conditions in Little Rock, Arkansas, one year after the *Brown* decision, where events would soon trigger the beginning of Bill Gale's reinvention of the posse comitatus and its rise to national prominence as the beacon of armed resistance to federal, state, and local authority.

7

THE LITTLE ROCK CRISIS

One year after the *Brown* decision, the school board in Little Rock, Arkansas, responded to a federal lawsuit filed by black students and approved a blueprint for school desegregation. It was 1955.[1] Attempts to execute the plan two years later prompted mob violence and a constitutional crisis that led President Eisenhower to federalize the Arkansas National Guard and mobilize army troops. The president's action marked the first time since Reconstruction that the commander in chief had used military force to protect the constitutional rights of blacks. The move horrified segregationists, who used the crisis at Central High School to muster support for Massive Resistance: the South's second great lost cause after the Civil War. The use of federal military force in Little Rock also triggered Bill Gale's first thoughts about the posse comitatus and started a process that was to establish him as one of the foremost influences within the radical right. And it was against the backdrop of the events in Little Rock in 1957 that Gale decided to run for governor of California on the right-wing Constitution Party ticket.

The Little Rock desegregation plan called for the gradual introduction of blacks into previously all-white public schools, beginning with the senior high school in 1957, and ending with the elementary school by 1962 or 1963. The resistance campaign, led by Citizens' Council activists, set about disrupting school board meetings, petitioning the governor, and taking out newspaper ads to manipulate white fears: "If you integrate Little Rock Central High . . . would the Negro boys be permitted to solicit the white girls for dances?" queried one broadside. Will "tender love scenes," in integrated drama classes, "be assigned to Negro boys and white girls?"[2]

Terrified by the prospect, Mrs. Clyde Thomason, a member of the newly formed "Mothers' League of Little Rock Central High School," sued and won a temporary restraining order against the desegregation plan.[3] The state chancery court based its decision on the testimony of Governor Orval Faubus who warned of the "probability of violence and civil commotion," falsely claiming that there had been an alarming increase in local gun sales.[4] Faubus was an unlikely champion of segregation. In 1954 he broke the color bar in Arkansas politics by appointing two blacks to the Democratic State Central Committee. Two years later he defeated his pro-segregationist opponent in the Democratic primary. It was not until Faubus used the National Guard to *block* black students from entering Central High, that he wholly abandoned his previous posture as a racial moderate—by Southern standards, at least.[5]

Unlike other places in the South, Little Rock had a local school board willing to pursue, rather than obstruct, integration. And so when Mrs. Thomason won her injunction, the school board turned to the federal court for relief. On August 30, 1957, Judge Roger N. Davies ordered desegregation to proceed, prompting Governor Faubus to call out the National Guard. Publicly the governor declared that the troops "will act not as segregationists or integrationists, but as soldiers called to active duty to carry out their assigned tasks." But his orders to the state militia said the opposite:

"You are directed to place off-limits to white students those schools for colored students and to place off-limits to colored students those schools heretofore operated and recently set up for white students," he told the head of the state militia.[6] As things heated up in Little Rock, the local Citizens' Council president, Robert E. Brown, urged Faubus to stand firm. "As the sovereign head of the state, you are immune to federal orders," Brown foolishly told the governor.[7]

On September 3, 1957, Judge Davies ordered school officials to proceed with integration, but Guard troops continued to prevent black students from entering the school. Although Faubus had promised the president he would allow the nine black students into Central High School, he reneged. This infuriated Eisenhower and his attorney general, Herbert Brownell, who concluded that Faubus's actions were nothing less than "an attempt to nullify the Constitution."[8] Faubus further enraged the president when he defiantly ordered the National Guard troops removed, relinquishing control of Central High to a seething segregationist mob. Rock-throwing and other violence led to scores of arrests by police. Despite disavowing violence, the Citizens' Council quickly established a "Freedom Fund" to help cover legal expenses for seventy-five people arrested during the fracas.[9]

Faubus's betrayal and the continued segregationist violence led Eisenhower to issue a formal proclamation on September 23, commanding "all persons engaged in such obstruction of justice to cease and desist therefrom, and to disperse forthwith."[10] Explaining that the situation was out of control, the mayor of Little Rock wired the White House with a desperate message the next day:

THE IMMEDIATE NEED FOR FEDERAL TROOPS IS URGENT. THE MOB IS MUCH LARGER IN NUMBERS AT 8 A.M. THAN AT ANY TIME YESTERDAY PEOPLE ARE CONVERGING ON THE SCENE FROM ALL DIRECTIONS MOB IS ARMED AND ENGAGING IN FISTICUFFS AND OTHER ACTS OF VIOLENCE.[11]

Eisenhower replied decisively, issuing an executive order federalizing the Arkansas National Guard and authorizing the Secretary of Defense to "use such of the armed forces of the Unites States as he may deem necessary."[12] On September 24, one thousand troops of the 101st Airborne in Fort Campbell, Kentucky, began to arrive in Little Rock.[13]

The following day the school's athletic field was transformed into a military command post, complete with field kitchens, tents, and trucks.[14] Outside Central High, soldiers lined the streets three paces apart, rifles and fixed bayonets at the ready.[15] The image appalled many Southerners; henceforth all Citizens' Council mail carried a stamp bearing the slogan "Remember Little Rock" and the image of a soldier holding a bayonet at the back of two white girls.[16] The troops were under the command of Major General Edwin A. "Ted" Walker, a forty-six-year-old decorated combat veteran of World War II and Korea.[17] Walker, a plain-speaking Texan, gathered the almost twelve hundred white students in a special assembly session and sternly warned them not to interfere with the orders of the federal court.[18] "I intend to use all means necessary to prevent any interference" with the execution of the integration plan, Walker told reporters.[19]

According to Harry Ashmore, executive editor of the *Arkansas Gazette*, Walker enforced his public duties as "a model of aloof correctness," and *Time* magazine put the general on its cover.[20] Privately, however, the general did not conceal his conviction that the troop deployment was part of a communist scheme.[21] After probing Walker's views and discovering the general's devotion to right-wing conspiracy theories and anti-Semitic tracts, Ashmore was so alarmed that he warned the Pentagon. Walker was "a public-relations time bomb," the editor told Washington.[22] Ashmore was right, but the general's fuse was slightly longer than Ashmore anticipated. Walker discharged his duties at Central High without incident. He resurfaced five years later, when James Meredith was seeking to become the first black student at the University of Mississippi. This time, instead of suppressing the riotous white mob, Walker rallied it.[23]

Although Eisenhower withdrew the 101st Airborne from Little Rock after about two months, federalized Guard troops remained until the following May[24] and became a focal point for segregationist rage and a recruiting magnet for the radical right. By May 1957, Bill Gale had become chairman of the right-wing Constitution Party of California and he saw the events in Little Rock as an opportunity to invigorate the Party and attract contributors to his campaign for governor. "I brought the Constitution Party out of the doldrums [when I was] elected state chairman," Gale later claimed. As part of his plan, Gale invited Mississippi judge Thomas Brady to address the group in Sacramento. "If something is not done, the power-mad Supreme Court can and will drive the people of this country over the cliff of constitutional government into the abyss of communism," Brady told Gale and 150 other Party stalwarts on December 8, 1957.[25]

As part of his campaign for governor, Gale announced the filing of a "criminal indictment" against Eisenhower for the "flagrantly illegal action [of] invading and occupying [the] sovereign State of Arkansas." Gale's "indictment" pronounced Eisenhower guilty of "high crimes and misdemeanors" and demanded the immediate arrest and trial of the president for violating the 1878 Posse Comitatus Act, which barred civilian authorities from using the U.S. Army to enforce domestic laws.[26] It was Gale's first recorded mention of the term in right-wing circles and predated his establishment of the Posse Comitatus as a right-wing group by nearly fifteen years. In tone as well as substance his "indictment" of the president contained the same mixture of vigilante action and twisted legalisms that would become the hallmark of the Posse.

While it is true that the 1878 Act forbids use of the army as a civil police power in most circumstances, Gale's interpretation was flat wrong and his criticism of the president was pure propaganda. According to the Act, the military *can* be used in a civilian context *if* doing so is "expressly authorized by the Constitution or by act of Congress." Congress had been silent on the matter, but the army troops that Eisenhower sent to Little Rock—and the Arkansas National Guard that had been called into federal service—clearly had been summoned pursuant to the president's constitutional authority to suppress insurrection.[27]

Although Gale was not alone in his criticism of Eisenhower for intervening in Little Rock, he was among the earliest opponents of desegregation—and perhaps the very first—to specifically cite the Posse Comitatus Act. It wasn't until six months later that Senator John C. Stennis of Mississippi made a similar point in a speech before the Mississippi State Bar Association: "There is a great similarity between the evil this statute [the Posse Comitatus Act] was written to prevent and the actual conditions which existed in Little Rock."[28]

Characterized by one federal judge as an "obscure and all-but-forgotten statute,"[29] the Posse Comitatus Act was an exceptionally significant piece of legislation. Its passage by a Democratic Congress in 1878 was designed to prevent federal marshals in the South from using army troops to protect the lives and rights of blacks after the Civil War. As such, the Act was a symbolic and actual triumph for defiant Southerners who sought to undermine black rights (especially those granted by the newly ratified Fourteenth Amendment), maintain white supremacy, overthrow Republican state governments, and establish "home rule," in the late nineteenth century.[30] From the moment General Robert E. Lee surrendered at Appomattox, many Southerners fought with ballots and bullets toward these ends, but there was always the chance that federal marshals backed by army troops would stand in their way. Passage of the Posse Comitatus Act was significant because it emasculated the marshals and gave white supremacists free rein. Its adoption coincided with the end of Reconstruction—the twelve-year period following the end of the Civil War and culminating in the election of President Rutherford B. Hayes. It was the beginning of a grim new era for African-Americans in the South, whose lives for most of the next century were ruled by Black Codes, lynch mobs, and Jim Crow until the *Brown* decision and the passage of federal civil rights laws in the 1960s.

While the Posse Comitatus Act of 1878 prevented the army from enforcing civilian law, its passage was not driven by any high regard for constitutional liberties, but by the Civil War–era legacy of states' rights and white supremacy. As such, the congressional debate that accompanied passage of the Act marked the symbolic—as well as the practical—resurrection of states' rights after the collapse of Reconstruction. Examining the arguments of those who supported the Act—as well as its actual effect—sheds important light on the paramilitary inclinations of those favoring states' rights, including Bill Gale, who first invoked the Act in 1957, and then later when he created the Posse Comitatus as a right-wing organization some fourteen years afterward. Analyzing Gale's obsession with the concept of posse comitatus—and his misinterpretation of the Act—also provides greater insight into the kind of racist society he sought to create.

Nineteenth-century supporters of the Posse Comitatus Act railed against the use of federal troops to defend the civil rights of blacks, in the same way as Bill Gale and others railed against President Eisenhower for using the army to accomplish the same goal some eighty years later. Ironically, however, the most notable use of federal forces as a posse comitatus prior to the Civil War came about when slave owners pressured the government to use army troops to capture escaped slaves. Those circumstances, and the events that followed, set the stage for repeated and bloody confrontations between federal authorities and local white supremacists—the echoes of which reverberate to the present day.[31]

8

VICIOUS AND DESPERATE MEN

On June 2, 1854, the largest posse comitatus in American history assembled in Boston to forcibly escort Anthony Burns, an escaped Virginia slave, to the ship that would return him to bondage. The posse numbered approximately sixteen hundred men—soldiers, marines, militia members, police, and others—and was arrayed against a huge crowd of fifty thousand anti-slavery protesters.[1] More than twenty years before adoption of the Posse Comitatus Act barred federal marshals from summoning army troops to protect blacks, United States Attorney General Caleb Cushing responded to the demands of Southern Democrats and authorized expanded use of the federal troops as a posse comitatus to pursue escaped slaves. The Cushing Doctrine—as it came to be known—was issued on May 27, 1854, at the height of the Burns Affair, and held that all able-bodied men above fifteen years of age, regardless of whether they were in uniform, could be used in a posse comitatus upon the request of a U.S. marshal. According to Cushing, no presidential approval was required because the men were performing a "citizen's duty regardless of their individual status, whether civilian, militia, or regular."[2] Though the doctrine was formulated to allow more aggressive enforcement of the 1850 Fugitive Slave Law, ironically, it was not widely employed until *after* the Civil War, when paramilitary resistance to Reconstruction forced federal marshals to use army troops to counter white-supremacist violence.

Armed vigilantism was widespread across the South, but the problem was especially severe in Louisiana, where thousands joined groups like the Knights of the White Camelia, the White League, the Ku Klux Klan, and the Regulators, to prevent newly enfranchised blacks from voting and to block Republicans from assuming office. Like the paramilitary rifle clubs of South Carolina, these roving bands of white supremacists specialized in political assassination, armed attacks on meetings, and wholesale massacres of blacks. Such violence produced more than one thousand deaths in Louisiana alone in the three months leading up to the presidential elections of 1868.[3] More carnage followed the elections of 1872, which produced rival contenders for local and state office, including the Louisiana governorship.[4]

This violence led Congressman Charles H. Joyce, a former Union Army officer and Republican from Vermont, to describe Louisiana as "cursed with a class of vicious and desperate men, who have kept society in a feverish and choleric state, filled the land with crime and violence, set at defiance the regularly constituted authorities of the government, and rendered life, liberty, and property unsafe and insecure."[5] When Congressman Joyce looked at Louisiana he saw sedition and insurrection and called for the army to restore order. But opponents of Reconstruction—which included many former Confederate soldiers and officers—still viewed the army as the despised enemy of all that they held dear: state sovereignty, home rule, and white supremacy. Despite the constant violence against blacks and white Republicans, the use of federal troops during Reconstruction was sporadic at best.[6] But the fact that troops were used at all to save black lives enraged ex-Confederates.

Such was the case in September 1876, when nearly one thousand armed and mounted Democrats went on a six-day rampage in Aiken County, South Carolina, long a stronghold of the Ku Klux Klan. In one incident, an army detachment arrived just in time to prevent scores of black Republicans who had been driven into a swamp from being murdered by hundreds of whites. "The members of the rifle clubs openly declared in the presence of the United States troops that it was their intention to have killed the last one of them, and they expressed the greatest disgust at the interference. . . ." recounted one congressional report, which also noted that after the clubs agreed to disperse, they "continued their murderous work upon the colored men on their way home."[7] These and other grisly events led South Carolina's governor, Daniel Chamberlain, to issue a proclamation on October 7, 1876, banning the rifle clubs and ordering their members to "retire peaceably to their homes." President Grant upped the ante ten days later when he, too, commanded "all persons engaged in said unlawful and insurrectionary proceedings to disperse. . . ."[8]

Clamping down on the rifle clubs was part of a larger Republican effort to deter violence and intimidation at the polls during the upcoming presidential election. On September 14, 1876, United States Attorney General Alfonso Taft had instructed federal marshals to monitor polling places if they suspected bloodshed. He also reminded them of their authority to form a posse comitatus of local civilians, militiamen, or federal troops if they felt it was necessary to enforce the law. Eventually seven thousand special deputy marshals were dispatched throughout the South to keep the peace that November.[9] Taft defended his orders by saying he was not authorizing domestic military action, but was simply enabling the marshals to use whomever they chose—including soldiers—to deter civil disorder.

"[It] does not assume to make any disposition of troops, but advises the marshal that if he has occasion to call out the posse, and soldiers are in his district, they may be embodied for the purpose," the attorney general explained. In reminding the marshals of their right to summon a posse of military men, Taft cleverly—and with purposeful irony—cited the 1854 Cushing Doctrine, which had been developed to allow army troops to pursue escaped slaves. "The present application of the principle is quite as legal and a good deal more humane," Taft observed in a speech in New York just two weeks before the presidential election of 1876.[10]

That contest pitted Republican Rutherford B. Hayes against Democrat Samuel J. Tilden and proved to be the most contentious election in American history. Hayes, a former U.S. congressman and three-time governor of Ohio, was so unremarkable a candidate that the writer Henry Adams described him as a "third-rate non-entity."[11] The Republican Party platform was so timid on Reconstruction and black rights that it inspired criticism from the great abolitionist Frederick Douglass. "Do you mean to make good to us the promises in your Constitution?" he thundered at the delegates gathered in Cincinnati that June.[12] Tilden, the governor of New York and one of the nation's richest men, was nominated at his party's convention of one thousand delegates that did not include a single black.[13]

Although Tilden emerged from election night with an overwhelming lead in the popular vote, he won only 184 electoral votes, one vote shy of the number needed to win the presidency.[14] Disputed returns for 20 electoral votes (exactly the balance Hayes needed for victory) were submitted from Florida, Oregon, Louisiana, and South Carolina. Ex-Confederates staged a near-coup in Louisiana and threatened one in South Carolina as a result.[15] But Southern Democrats were stymied by the threat of federal troops protecting Republican governors, and so they flexed their political muscle in Washington, D.C., where they held a seven-seat majority in the House of Representatives. Asserting that the 1876 presidential election had been stolen by the army, Congress demanded an account from President Grant. But the former army general staunchly denied the charges, submitting a lengthy report which said, in part: "The troops of the United States have been but sparingly used, and in no case so as to interfere with the free exercise of the right of suffrage."[16]

Southern Democrats were not impressed and made the absurd claim that troops had been sent to South Carolina to prevent blacks from voting Democratic or to shoot all those who attempted to do so.[17] Regardless of the role of the army in the election, ex-Confederates clearly understood that federal troops were preventing them from forcibly seizing power in key Southern states and thereby interfering with the ability of Democrats to influence the counting of the disputed ballots which would determine the outcome of the presidential contest. The president had authority over army troops, but the Democratic-controlled Congress held the purse strings. And so the Army Appropriations Bill, presented on February 23, 1877, instructed that no money be used "in support of the claims, or pretended claim or claims, of any State government, or officer thereof, in any State, until the same shall have been duly recognized by Congress." Violators risked five to ten years of hard labor.[18]

The sponsor of the Army Appropriations Bill was Representative John D. C. Atkins of Tennessee, a former lieutenant colonel in the Confederate Army and two-term representative to the Confederate Provisional Congress.[19] Rising before the House on March 2, Atkins denounced "carpetbag rule" and the Republican Party's "policy of vengeance and remorseless hate toward the conquered South."[20] He railed against large standing armies as "un-American and anti-Republican," as well as "European and monarchical." But the real issue was less the size of the army than *how* it allegedly had been used.[21]

"American soldiers, policemen! Insult if true, and slander if pretended to cover up the tyrannical and unconstitutional use of the Army. . . ." Atkins raged.[22] "I will never vote to appropriate money for the support of the army. . . . The people of Louisiana and South Carolina cannot be longer fettered by my vote; the army must be removed from their soil."[23] Congressional Republicans countered that restricting the army would produce anarchy and confusion, but the Democrat-controlled House passed the bill on a voice vote.[24] And the section barring use of federal funds "to maintain the political power of any state government" remained intact.[25] Ultimately, however, the House and Senate could not agree on language, no Appropriation Bill passed, and army troops went without pay until the following year.[26]

The conflict over army appropriations, although significant, paled in comparison to the larger political intrigue surrounding the disputed results of the November 1876 election. In late January 1877, a national commission was established to count the electoral votes and resolve the turmoil. The commission was composed of ten congressmen and five Supreme Court justices but its political balance became weighted in Republicans' favor by one vote and Rutherford B. Hayes was pronounced president. Tilden's Democratic supporters responded with talk of a filibuster that threatened to prevent Hayes's inauguration on March 4.[27] Eager to ensure that a Republican would take office, some of Hayes's supporters initiated talks with Southerners. The result was the historic Southern Compromise of 1877 in which Republicans agreed to recognize Democratic administrations in Florida, Louisiana, and South Carolina if Democrats agreed to accept Hayes as president. The deal also called for the removal of federal troops that had been guarding Republican governors in South Carolina and Louisiana.

By agreeing to return these troops to their barracks, Northerners conceded that the army would no longer be used to protect blacks and other Southern Republicans from those former Confederates and Southern whites who felt compelled to subjugate or attack them, no matter how viciously.[28]

"[This decision signified] the abandonment of the Negro as a ward of the nation, the giving up of the attempt to guarantee the freedman his civil and political equality, and the acquiescence of the rest of the country to the South's demand that the whole problem be left to the disposition of the dominant Southern white people," explained the distinguished historian C. Vann Woodward.[29] From the perspective of a black Louisianan, Henry Adams, the situation was clear: "The whole South—every state in the South—had got into the hands of the very men that held us as slaves."[30]

The constitutional crisis that produced the Southern Compromise formed the backdrop to the deliberations over the Army Appropriation Bill in March 1877. But it wasn't until the following year that Congress gave its final approval to legislation that would, once and for all, sharply limit use of the army as a posse comitatus and a force that could otherwise intervene in civil affairs.

9

LEGISLATING REDEMPTION: THE POSSE COMITATUS ACT BECOMES LAW

On Monday, May 18, 1878, Democratic representative Abram S. Hewitt of New York opened debate on the Army Appropriation Bill by asserting it was the responsibility of states, not the army, to suppress insurrection. The federal government should "give encouragement to rifle clubs, [and] sharpshooting clubs throughout the length and breadth of this land. . . . No citizen should be allowed to grow up in this country who cannot handle a gun," the congressman said, making a point that would still be popular a century later. "You never need fear disorders where the people bear arms."[1] Blacks in the South who were the target of armed Klansmen surely had a different point of view. Continuing the debate two days later, Democrat William Kimmel of Maryland ridiculed Rutherford B. Hayes as "this non-elected president," and denounced soldiers and standing armies that he said had "shielded . . . tyrants . . . obstructed the ballot [and] protected minorities in their usurpations."[2] The use of soldiers as a posse comitatus during Reconstruction had led to "military despotism" in the South where racial conflict had been nonexistent and blacks and whites "live in harmony," Kimmel claimed, preposterously.[3] He then introduced an amendment forbidding the military from acting as a posse comitatus:

> *Provided,* that from and after the passage of this act it shall not be lawful to use any part of the land or naval forces of the United States to execute

the laws either as a posse comitatus or otherwise, except in such cases as may be expressly authorized by act of Congress."[4]

Ultimately, Kimmel's posse comitatus amendment never came to a vote, and the task of limiting federal troops as a posse comitatus then fell to J. Proctor Knott, a lawyer and congressman from Kentucky. A onetime state legislator who became Missouri attorney general at twenty nine, Knott had been a pro-slavery Unionist living in Missouri when a Union Army colonel had him arrested in 1861 for refusing to take a loyalty oath supporting President Lincoln.[5] Knott was briefly imprisoned at the U.S. Arsenal in St. Louis, and the experience embittered him for life.[6] Like Representative Atkins of Tennessee—the former Confederate legislator and lieutenant colonel who had proposed the 1877 Army Appropriations Bill limiting use of the army—Knott hated the Union Army. "[The] most diabolical atrocities of the French Revolution pale with insignificance" compared to the crimes committed by federal troops, proclaimed Knott, who asserted that his Missouri political career had been "crushed by a set of thieving scoundrels under the guise of patriotism."[7] Seventeen years after Knott was released from Union Army custody, he drafted the Posse Comitatus Act.[8]

Appeals to states' rights and rhetoric about Southern sovereignty dominated debate on the Knott Amendment. Representative E. John Ellis, a Louisiana Democrat, former Confederate Army captain and prisoner of war, declared that "every Southern member on this floor" was aware of the "greatest abuses" of employing the army as a posse comitatus.[9] Alarmed by restrictions the Knott Amendment would place on the president as commander in chief, Republican Mills Gardner of Ohio denounced the measure saying, "Never, perhaps, in the history of the country has such extraordinary legislation been attempted."[10] These and other arguments didn't convince his colleagues, however. On May 28, 1878, the Posse Comitatus Act was approved as the twenty-ninth and final section of the Army Appropriation Bill, with 130 members (all but one of them Democrats) voting *yes*, 117 voting *no*, and 44 not voting. Hardly a Southerner could be found among those who opposed the Army Appropriation Bill and only five of the *no* votes were cast by Democrats.[11]

Even though rhetoric about the danger of standing armies was appealing to some, preventing military despotism never was the real issue. The prime motive of those who favored the Posse Comitatus Act was to secure Democratic (read: *white*) control of the South. The same motivations propelled debate on the Army Appropriation Bill one week later in the Senate, although language added there slightly moderated the effect of Knott's amendment.

On June 7, 1878, Senator Francis Kernan, Democrat of New York, added language permitting use of the army as a posse comitatus when expressly authorized by the Constitution; without his wording the measure permitted use of army troops as a posse comitatus only when authorized by Congress.[12] But Kernan also delivered pointed attacks on the Cushing Doctrine and, by extension, Attorney General Taft's 1876 reminder to federal marshals of their authority to muster army troops as a posse comitatus to halt election law violations.[13] After lengthy argument and parliamentary wrangling, the Senate let the language stand.[14] A conference committee was appointed and in its final form, the Posse Comitatus Act read:[15]

> From and after the passage of this act it shall not be lawful to employ any part of the army of the United States, as a posse comitatus, or otherwise, for the purpose of executing the laws, except in such cases and under such circumstances as such employment of said force may be expressly authorized by the Constitution or by act of Congress; and no money appropriated by this act shall be used to pay any of the expenses incurred in the employment of any troops in violation of this section; and any person willfully violating the provisions of this section shall be deemed guilty of a misdemeanor, and, on conviction thereof, shall be punished by fine not exceeding $10,000 or imprisonment not exceeding two years, or by both such fine and imprisonment.[16]

In triumphantly presenting his report on the committee's deliberations, Representative Hewitt did not speak of the need for more rifle clubs or state militias. Neither did he invoke apparitions of the governors of South Carolina and Louisiana who had been deposed by the Southern Compromise of the previous year. Gone was the sectional rhetoric of Maryland's Representative Kimmel and his utopian declarations of Southern "self-government" and attacks on the "usurpations" of blacks. Instead, Hewitt resorted to the smoke screen of civil liberties, declaring: "Thus have we this day secured to the people of this country the same great protection against a standing army which cost a struggle of two hundred years for the Commons of England to secure for the British people."[17]

It is easy to see the Posse Comitatus Act as a guarantor of civil liberties. After all, a strong case can be made against using army troops as a police power without specific authorization by Congress or the president. But Representative J. Proctor Knott and the 128 other Democrats who supported his amendment in 1878 did so because they wanted to *block* enforcement of the nation's new civil rights amendments and laws, not because they wanted to guarantee the liberties of America's black citizens.

As with Bill Gale's distortion of the ancient concept of posse comitatus, the effect of the Knott Amendment in the South was to permit violence and vigilantism, not obstruct it. Passage of the Posse Comitatus Act completed the work of the Southern Compromise of 1877 and was one of many signposts marking the restoration of white supremacy across the South.[18] From a legal standpoint, it prohibited the flexible use of federal troops by governors, sheriffs, and federal marshals, but its value to Southern whites was also largely symbolic. Like the Southern Compromise, it signified the erosion of a national political will to protect black rights. No matter what practical limitations the Act placed on civil rights enforcement in the post-Reconstruction South, white supremacy had triumphed, and the Southern states were "redeemed" by 1878.

Passage of the Posse Comitatus Act symbolically marked the political death of Reconstruction at the same time as it helped facilitate the restoration of white supremacy. After 1878 the federal government had neither the will nor the capacity for armed intervention in states of the former Confederacy and so it left the South free to oppress its black inhabitants through its viciously enforced customs of segregation and the laws of Jim Crow. As C. Vann Woodward observed, "racial ostracism" in the American South was all-encompassing and "extended to churches and schools, to housing and jobs, to eating and drinking . . . to virtually all forms of public transportation, to sports and recreations, to hospitals, orphanages, prisons, and asylums, and ultimately to funeral homes, morgues, and cemeteries."[19]

This was the world that the United States Supreme Court threatened to unmake three-quarters of a century later, with *Brown*. It also was a world that many white Americans were eager to fight to preserve. Initially Bill Gale thought politics might be the best arena to carry out this struggle, and so he decided to run for governor of California.

10

FROM JEW TO REVEREND GALE

On September 22, 1957, Bill Gale announced his candidacy for governor of California on the right-wing Constitution Party ticket, a group he chaired. "We must be able to stick our necks out and be able to take the attacks from the enemies of our republic. Without courage, we cannot win," he told two hundred Party delegates at Hollywood's Knickerbocker Hotel.[1] Gale campaigned on a platform demanding states' rights, abolition of the "Karl Marx–inspired socialist income tax," impeachment of Eisenhower and the Supreme Court, immediate U.S. withdrawal from the UN, an end to all foreign aid, and the use of only "gold and silver coin" to pay debts.[2]

On November 28, Gale went on television in Los Angeles to declare that the Constitution Party was only for Christians. Later that day, in Santa Barbara, he claimed that "Zionists" had become "corrupted" through intermarriage with "Babylonians." Jews were responsible for the communist revolution in Russia, Gale also said. These and other remarks won him the endorsement of the *Thunderbolt*, the mouthpiece of the racist, anti-Semitic, National States' Rights Party. They also briefly caught the attention of the American Jewish Committee.[3]

Gale's smorgasbord of right-wing rhetoric was driven by outrage over Eisenhower's use of troops in Little Rock and the president's support for a new civil rights act, which had passed Congress just one month before the troubles at Central High.[4] Although far from ideal, the bill was the first such legislation to pass Congress since Reconstruction and it won the endorsement of the young but influential Reverend Martin Luther King Jr. These developments galvanized Gale and others, but his candidacy was a lost cause from the start. When the Constitution Party failed to register the 50,000 voters necessary for his name to be placed on the ballot, Gale resigned as Party chairman and ran as a write-in candidate.[5] Initially his family greeted Gale's candidacy enthusiastically. Kathy, his youngest daughter, thought it was "good clean fun," and his wife Josephine fantasized about being California's first lady. "Jo has done a magnificent job" organizing the party's telephone committee throughout Los Angeles, crowed the Constitution Party's *Bulletin* in January 1958.[6] This was the first time Josephine was directly involved in Bill's political pursuits. It was also the last. Despite his eagerness for victory, Gale received just 1,073 write-in votes.[7]

Gale's defeat dampened his interest in mainstream politics and made him more disdainful of conventional conservatives who—according to Gale—refused to expose the "Jewish roots" of communism. Likewise, Gale's association with Wesley Swift and Gerald L. K. Smith made him a target for criticism by rivals in the Constitution Party.[8] Increasingly obsessed by the racism of his Christian Identity religion, Gale's worldview now mirrored the theology of his mentors, San Jacinto Capt, the former Klansman, and Wesley Swift. By the late 1950s Gale was leading his own weekly "Bible study" meetings in nearby Whittier. And he and Capt often traveled to Texas, where Gale taught "the Constitution and Bible," while Capt enlightened audiences about "pyramidology and Egyptology."[9] Gale called himself a minister and claimed he had been ordained in the Episcopal Church, but Josephine chafed at the thought. "He thinks he's an ordained minister, but it's a *lie*. He got his ministry through the mail," she told her daughter Kathy some years later.[10] Although Gale knew his credentials were a sham, he felt deserving of the title as a result of his studies in Christian Identity. At one point, Gale also claimed "credentials as a Doctor of Laws," though he never studied law, much less earned a degree.[11] Regardless of who actually "ordained" him—most likely it was Wesley Swift—Gale never received any formal religious training beyond what he learned from Swift's circle of believers.[12]

As devoted as Gale was to studying and promoting Christian Identity, it didn't pay the bills and so by 1958 he was selling insurance and securities for the well-established Hollywood firm of Waddell and Reed. By his account, he was number one in sales for five straight years.[13] Although Gale may have been exaggerating—as he often did—he had a genuine knack for making money. His good looks, charisma, and gift of gab were strong assets when soliciting clients, especially elderly widows. And when Gale found a customer he thought would be receptive to the Identity message, he would proselytize, and when he found an Identity follower who might be a likely customer, he sold them insurance.

By now, Gale's troubled military career was well behind him, along with his complaints of exhaustion, stomach pains, and jaundice. Apart from a brief hospital stay after a suspected heart attack in November 1955, which turned out to be nothing, his health was on the rebound. Gale's conversion to Christian Identity, and his involvement with other right-wing groups, seems to have cured him of both his imagined hepatitis and his previously diagnosed psychoneurosis. But Gale's devotion to his new religion set him on a collision course with his family.

Totally unrestrained in his anti-Semitism, Gale lectured everyone he met about the evils of race-mixing and the Jews. He also proselytized his siblings and converted his older sister, Ruth, by giving her a copy of the *Protocols of the Learned Elders of Zion*. "She couldn't sleep after that!" he declared, triumphantly.[14] Ruth reciprocated by vigorously defending him against criticism from any quarter. "They say he preaches hate. You bet he does," she wrote years later to a niece. "Hate the Devil and so did Christ. He does everything for Christ and anyone that don't like it can lump it. I have not found him wrong in anything he has told me since 1956. He is a Prophet or a Saint. . . . Those people in the Mid East are not Israel, they are yehuddin or offspring of Cain. Cain was of the evil one—Satan."[15]

But not all of Gale's preaching came off as well. He alienated his younger brother Robert and became estranged from his children. In 1957, Bill's oldest daughter, Geri, was approaching high-school graduation when she disclosed her plans to move to New York to pursue a singing career. Gale was outraged and did everything he could to dissuade her, calling it "Jew York" and threatening to disown her, which eventually he did. Gale also warned her to be on the lookout for Satan's children bearing horns and tails and so when she disembarked from her cross-country bus trip, the seventeen-year-old Californian surveyed the crowds warily for hidden appendages. Her father's attempts to indoctrinate her notwithstanding, Geri totally rejected anti-Semitism. Gale also tried, unsuccessfully, to convert his second daughter, who was still in high school. One day Kathy invited a Jewish friend to the house. His face contorted in disgust, Gale confronted the teenager and accused him of being a "false Jew." "I can smell a Jew," Gale growled at the startled visitor. "You're not Jewish. You think you are, but you're nothing but a proselyte Jew. A proselyte Jew is *worse* than a Jew. You're not Jewish because I can *smell a Jew* when they come in the door." Kathy was mortified. "Daddy! I can't believe you! How dare you?" she declared, her jaw dropping. "That's when I realized that my father had gone off the deep end and I decided not to ever bring anybody else over to the house," she recalled.[16]

Gale failed equally with his son. Billy was younger and understood less about his father's activities. But even as a child he felt uncomfortable in the presence of Bill Gale's colleagues and the hatred that accompanied them. "If anything, I learned the ill effects of prejudice from a unique perspective," he explained.[17]

The more Gale steeped himself in Identity doctrine, the more frequent his explosive arguments over race and religion became. One Jewish family in the neighborhood eventually moved as a result of his bigoted harangues. "Bill, you've got to stop," pleaded Josephine, who deplored her husband's habit of accosting visitors with lectures about religion and race. "You make these people prisoners. They want to leave the house, but you won't let them go," she explained. But Gale denied he ever brought the subject up. "My father would swear on a stack of Bibles that he never started any of these conversations. But this is really all he ever talked about to anybody, day and night," Kathy recalled. "It was just an obsession."

Initially family members found Gale's anti-Semitism peculiar, but when they recalled memories of Gale's aunt Fanny—his father's proudly Jewish sister—his bigotry became troubling and even more difficult to fathom. "Fanny insists that your family was Jewish," Josephine reminded Bill, but he just denied it angrily. "Oh, she thinks she's a Jew, but she's not! I went and looked up the family tree. She doesn't know what she's talking about. I have all the information," Gale said. But Bill's younger brother Robert, a navy officer, grew angrier the more he thought about how Gale had turned on their father through his anti-Semitic beliefs. In response, Gale and his sister Ruth developed an elaborate tale to deny their family heritage, calling it rumor and a "Jewish fable."[18]

"Nothing could be so false," Ruth asserted in a letter, responding to claims that her father, Charles Gale, was Jewish. "The apostle Paul thought he was Jewish, too, but he got the message on the way to Damascus," she wrote.[19] Charles was a Christian, she asserted, adding that both he and her mother, Mary Agnes, had been Identity believers. They were not. But Charles Gale had five siblings—all of them proudly Jewish—which required that Ruth and Bill devise a more elaborate tale. In an effort to explain how her Portland uncles were Jewish, Ruth claimed they had *married* Jewish women, but were not actually Jewish themselves. As for her father's sister, Fanny, whom she had first met in 1914 in St. Paul when she was just six years old, she had married a Jewish man: "When Fanny came over here, she started that Jewish business because she went to New York and got mixed up with them and became brainwashed," Ruth explained. "[Fanny] had one daughter and she married one—so that is where all that came in. The family on Dad's side was lousy with them. Dad used to get so angry with them. He never did forgive Fanny, even on his deathbed."[20]

Ruth claims Charles was angry with his sister, but unlike the estrangement Charles felt toward his Portland relatives, whom he had last visited eight years before his death in 1945, Charles saw Fanny frequently and the two got along reasonably well, in spite of Fanny's frequent, exasperated reminders to him that he had forsaken his religion. According to Corinne Rosenberg, Fanny's daughter, the two families got together in Los Angeles about once a month. In addition to fond memories, the gatherings prompted questions in her mind about her uncle's faith. Corinne was raised in a Jewish household, but it was evident that her uncle's home was not. "How can he deny his Judaism if he accepts you as his sister and they all know you're Jewish?" she asked her mother. "I don't know. It's crazy," Fanny replied with a resigned shrug. "He can do what he wants."[21]

If Bill Gale truly believed his father was not Jewish, it was a prodigious feat of self-deception. It is much more likely that he knew, and denied knowing. Bill was seventeen when his aunt Fanny moved to Los Angeles and became a constant reminder of his father's early faith. Four years later, he met his father's Jewish relatives in Portland. And when Bill Gale became an earnest anti-Semite in the 1950s, his wife reminded him of his father's background and his brother accused him of betraying their father's heritage. But Gale remained steadfast in his denials. After all, according to his own nazified standards, he was unquestionably polluted by Jewish blood. Bill Gale also idealized his father and choosing to become an anti-Semite may well have been his way of protecting the false genealogy his father had created to obfuscate the past.

Ironically, Gale did his best to hide the secret, even as he asserted that he *was* an Israelite—albeit a Christian one descended from the Lost Tribes of Israel—and preached to other Christians with no Jewish roots, that they were Jews. In short, Bill Gale was a Jewish anti-Semite who spent a lifetime trying to convince other anti-Semites that they, too, were Jews. As for his real Jewish identity, it was a secret Gale kept hidden all his life, for if it ever became known, his career as an Identity preacher and right-wing activist would have been over.

11

BIRCHERS AND MINUTEMEN

After Bill Gale left the Constitution Party in 1958 he launched a new, more militant organization with the help of his friend and Identity mentor, San Jacinto Capt. "The NAACP represents the [N]egro, the ADL represents the Jews; who represents you—the white Christian?" read the introductory mailing for the Christian Defense League. The effort was promising, but its success soon troubled Wesley Swift, who feared it would undercut his fund-raising and his congregation. To pacify Swift, Gale and Capt gave him $1,700 of the money they had raised and promised to discontinue their activities. The agreement didn't last long, however. Gale felt the need to strike out on his own and in 1960 he started the California Rangers.[1]

According to Gale, the inspiration for the Rangers came from a fellow veteran who asked for help forming a "volunteer civil defense organization." Gale claimed the group wasn't his idea, but he bragged he was the driving force behind it.[2] The California Department of Justice agreed. A 1965 state attorney general's report described the Rangers as "a secret underground guerrilla force" overseen by Gale, who used a "complex of organizations" to recruit members, including "militant-minded" racists.[3] Among those fitting that description was George Joseph King Jr., the son of a retired admiral who quit the John Birch Society because it moved "too slowly."[4] Gale also secured a position for King at his securities firm, Waddell and Reed, where he became King's supervisor. In 1963

King was arrested for selling a 50-caliber machine gun to undercover Treasury agents trying to infiltrate the Rangers. The incident exposed Gale's attempted recruitment of former servicemen through the American Legion and cost Gale his job.[5] The year before King's arrest, Gale had transferred his Legion membership to Signal Hill Post 490 in Los Angeles where he and King had sought support for the Rangers.[6] Publicity about King's arrest prompted an investigation by the Legion, which found that Post 490 was devoting its meetings to "the dissemination of anti-Jewish and anti-Negro materials." Legion officials revoked the Post's charter, negative headlines led to Gale's firing from Waddell and Reed, and the Rangers collapsed.[7]

For his part, Gale claimed the Rangers "never got off the ground" and asserted he had nothing to do with illegal weapons.[8] "At no time did I preach or teach anything about bearing firearms," Gale later said. "As a retired army officer, I would be called back instantly in case of war and would have scores of weapons and men at my disposal. Why should I create a private army?"[9]

Josephine had a good answer. "He needs to be the leader of the gang," she told her youngest daughter, Kathy. "He's still playing war. He's like a little soldier that can't adjust to peacetime because they no longer are important and so he needs to keep the antagonism and fighting and all of that around him because it gives him self-importance." Josephine, forty-five, had reason to be bitter. On December 4, 1962, Gale had filed for divorce.[10] After twenty-five years of marriage, Bill's interest in right-wing politics had become all-consuming. His immersion in Identity doctrine over the previous nine years and his strange houseguests and hate-filled diatribes had strained their relationship beyond repair. "That's all he lived, breathed, and ate. Just his hatred," Kathy said years later. Bill gave Josephine the house on Outpost Drive, the balance of the family savings account, and two of their four cars. Geri was living in New York and Kathy was dancing on Red Skelton's television show. Gale's relationship with his sixteen-year-old son, Billy, had been troubled for years and he readily relinquished custody.[11]

Gale divorced Josephine the same year he decided to run again for governor, though his previous difficulties with the Constitution Party probably influenced his choice to run this time as a Republican. In contrast to his previous bid, Gale's 1962 platform was relatively tame. Though he did declare himself "conscious of the Christian traditions of America" and a "devoted advocate of state sovereignty," Gale's twenty-point platform also whitewashed his opinions on Jews and the race issue, promising to support "realistic solutions to the race problem in the spirit of racial self-respect." With a straight face Gale denounced "racial demagoguery."[12]

Gale's campaign took him to San Diego, home of his brother Robert, who recently had retired from the navy. Gale's often-unannounced visits unnerved his brother and sister-in-law, as did the guests he occasionally brought along. "They stirred themselves up with different things that they interpreted in their Bible,"

Robert's wife recalled. "They were anti-Jew, anti-black, and anti-Catholic. They'd say the Jews were an inferior race and then, for some reason, that blacks weren't really blacks. It was all very confusing. But everyone just took him at his word, because he just kept talking and talking and talking."

"Frankly, I thought he was kind of goofy," Robert said matter-of-factly.

Though unintelligible to the uninitiated, Gale's religious rhetoric attracted a coterie of followers and his campaign for governor drew crowds that shared his political views. "If they come to collect my taxes, I'll meet them at the door with the butt of my gun," he told several hundred cheering white supporters in San Jose in 1962. Among those who heard him speak was Corinne Rosenberg, Gale's first cousin and the daughter of his Jewish aunt, Fanny. Gale greeted Corinne and her husband like the close relatives they were, but didn't modify his remarks on their account. The couple was appalled by the anti-Semitic inferences in his speech and by what they heard from the crowd. "The people who came to hear Bill didn't have on white sheets, but what came out of their mouths was awful. We just walked out. That was the last time I saw him," she said.[13]

Anti-communism was another constant theme of Gale's campaign. Among the threatening Bolshevik advances at the time were the 1959 victory of Fidel Castro in Cuba and the construction of the Berlin Wall in 1961. Further proof of creeping socialism was found in the victory of John F. Kennedy, a liberal Democrat and a Catholic, over Richard Nixon in November 1960. These developments spurred growth on the radical right. Of the approximately two hundred extreme conservative and far-right groups that existed in late 1961, nearly half were just two years old.[14] Fund-raising for anti-communist militants skyrocketed and subscriptions to right-wing publications soared. For example, subscribers to the ultraconservative weekly magazine *Human Events* increased from 13,502 in 1955 to more than 123,000 in 1962.[15] In 1959, groups such as the Reverend Carl McIntire's "American Council of Christian Churches," the Christian Anti-Communism Crusade of Dr. Frederick C. Schwartz—an Australian physician and the author of *You Can Trust the Communists (to Be Communists)*—and the Christian Crusade of the Reverend Billy James Hargis, commanded substantial followings.[16] In 1959, McIntire, Schwartz, and Hargis raised three-quarters of a million dollars for their political and religious projects. Three years later that sum tripled.[17]

Senator Joe McCarthy died of cirrhosis of the liver in 1957, yet he left behind a paranoid anti-communist political culture that spawned organizations and movements long after his death. Of this legacy, the most successful organization was the John Birch Society of Robert H. W. Welch. Like the organizations created by Wesley Swift and his contemporaries in the 1940s and early 1950s, the John Birch Society further shaped and defined Bill Gale's radical right-wing views, bringing him closer to establishing the Posse Comitatus.

Welch named his group in 1958 after a Georgia-born Baptist missionary who went to China in 1939, joined the U.S. Army, and became a captain in the

Intelligence Service, or so the story goes. According to Welch, Chinese communists killed John Birch in 1945, just ten days after World War II ended in the Pacific, because of the "powerful resistance" he would have inspired against the communists.[18] Welch memorialized the missionary-turned-soldier in his 1954 book *The Life of John Birch*, and he saw Birch's death as signifying "battle lines . . . in a struggle from which either communism or Christian-style civilization must emerge."[19]

Welch, fifty-nine, was a successful candy manufacturer and former board member of the National Association of Manufacturers when he retired in 1956 to devote himself to the anti-communist cause. Two years later, on December 8, 1958, Welch gathered eleven "men of industry" in an Indianapolis hotel and subjected them to a two-day monologue about the worldwide communist conspiracy.[20] "America," Welch began, had only a few more years before becoming "four separate provinces in a worldwide communist dominion ruled by police-state methods from the Kremlin."[21] In Welch's view, the Second World War had been caused not by Nazi aggression, but by "the worldwide diplomatic conniving of Stalin's agents," who sought to make Russia "a wartime ally of the Western nations."[22] The Kremlin would never take America by military conquest but would triumph by promoting subversion and instigating civil war.[23] As evidence, Welch pointed to the growing civil rights movement, saying "the trouble in our Southern states has been fomented almost entirely by the communists for this purpose."[24] Welch proposed a ten-point program to recruit one million followers to lance the "festering boil" of collectivism. He outlined the strategy in his *Blue Book*, a slim but widely read volume that became the program for the John Birch Society.[25]

Ideologically there was not much depth to Welch, although he did devote thirteen pages of his *Blue Book* to a tortured interpretation of Oswald Spengler's early twentieth century opus, *The Decline of the West*. Spengler, a German philosopher of history, was especially admired by fascists and other hard-core anti-Semites who used his analysis of the decline and advance of civilization to justify their own ideas about how Judaism, communism, and other "unclean elements" threatened the integrity of Western culture. According to Welch, Spengler's work proved how the "disease of collectivism" had infected America and Western Europe, and caused the degeneration of a formerly healthy, "organic" society.[26]

Like the Citizens' Council movement, the leaders of the Birch Society represented economic and social elites. The twenty-six members of the first Birch Council were wealthy and well established in their communities and included businessmen, bankers, lawyers, physicians, and retired military officers.[27] They endorsed Welch's plan of "dynamic personal leadership," and accepted the candymaker's self-nomination as a "hard-boiled, dictatorial, and dynamic boss."[28] Welch recommended (and they agreed) that the Birch Society remain unencumbered by either elections or democracy. The former was potentially divisive and the latter a "footstool of tyrants . . . a weapon of demagoguery [and] a perennial fraud," according to Welch.[29] Instead, the Society was to be a "monolithic body" operating "under completely authoritative control at all levels."[30] It was not democratic, but as a strategy for building a large and disciplined organization, it worked.

By late 1961, just three years after its founding, the Birch Society was spending $1 million a year and had at least twenty-four thousand dues-paying followers scattered across twenty-seven states and the District of Columbia, in local chapters of twenty members each. Headquartered in Belmont, Massachusetts, it had sixty-three full-time employees.[31] Welch's plan was grandiose, but unlike other right-wing groups that developed similar schemes, the John Birch Society was an organizational success: It genuinely recruited members at a grassroots level, nationwide; it generated dues on a consistent basis; it had an ongoing program of action and regular community meetings; and its local leaders usually were men of "status and financial solidity."[32]

Five years later, these same characteristics held true. Society membership had skyrocketed toward 100,000, staff numbered 220, the organization's budget had increased to $6 million, and the number of Birch Society bookstores stood at 340 in August 1965, compared to 225 eight months before.[33] Part of its success stemmed from mounting conservative frustrations in the wake of the 1964 presidential election.[34] After Republican Barry Goldwater was soundly defeated by Lyndon Johnson, Welch attracted a flood of new members with the slogan "*Now will you join the John Birch Society?*"[35] Presaging the successful strategy of the religious right by some thirty years, Welch urged followers to fight their political war on the terrain of public education by targeting Parent-Teacher Associations, school boards, and public libraries. The Society's shrill attacks on clergymen, educators, elected officials, and others it accused of being "communistic," made the group as effective as it was divisive. Amarillo, Texas (population 140,000), was a case in point. In 1961, the local Birch Society was led by the mayor and a retired Air Force brigadier general. After charging a local clergyman with being a communist sympathizer, they launched a campaign to purge area schools and libraries of "communist" literature. Nine books, including four Pulitzer Prize–winning novels, were removed. Teachers were accused of communist disloyalty and the town became riven by fear and suspicion.[36]

Although Welch avoided overt anti-Semitic ranting, he had a bad habit of gathering anti-Semites around him and recommending their publications to his members.[37] And when certain "patriots" were accused of anti-Semitism, Welch was either slow to criticize or quick to defend them. Speaking to his close-knit group of Birch Society founders in December 1958, Welch attacked John Roy Carlson, the pseudonymous author (his real name was Avedis Derounian) of *Under Cover*, a best-selling expose of the pro-Nazi movement in America during World War II.[38] Derounian's targets were many, including Coughlinites, the America First Committee, followers of Gerald L. K. Smith, and leaders of the thoroughly nazified German American Bund. But Welch preferred to ignore Derounian's evidence of the dangers posed by pro-Hitler groups, saying *Under Cover* "viciously smeared many good American patriots."

Officially Welch proclaimed bigotry unwelcome in the Birch Society, but the reality was that many local and national leaders were thoroughly steeped in gutter-level anti-Semitism or maintained close ties to those who were. Most notable was the columnist Westbrook Pegler, who was recruited to write a monthly column for Welch's *American Opinion* magazine in 1962, after he left Hearst Newspapers.[39] In one November 1963 column, Pegler declared himself a racist and wrote that it was the duty "of all intelligent Americans to proclaim and practice bigotry." Jews, he said, could not be the victims of persecution, because persecution "connotes injustice." They are, instead, enduring "retaliation, or punishment."[40] Pegler's stint at the Birch Society lasted more than a year before Welch finally dismissed him.

Like others on the right who sought to defend themselves from charges of bigotry, Welch sometimes did so by accusing Jews of *causing* anti-Semitism. "Malicious" and "unfair" charges of anti-Semitism provoke "anger against Jews in general," Welch warned in the April 1961 issue of the Society's monthly *Bulletin*."[41] Welch knew that accusations of bigotry could be damaging to the Birch Society, and he tried to give himself room to maneuver. "[The Birch Society has] a long past record of complete freedom of religious or racial bias," Welch wrote the ADL in May 1964. "We are not anti-Jewish. . . . We are not anti-Catholic, nor anti-Protestant, nor anti-Negro, nor anti-Mongolian, nor anti any member of any race or creed. We *are* anti-communist, to the extent of being anti *all communists*. . . ."[42] But Welch saw no contradiction between his proclamations of tolerance and his steadfast opposition to civil rights. In 1965 Welch announced that the "racial turmoil of the past several years . . . does not make sense unless you realize what the communists behind all of this agitation are trying to accomplish."[43] And Welch attacked Dr. Martin Luther King Jr. in a pamphlet titled *Two Revolutions at Once*, in which he referred to the civil rights leader as "a troublemaker pushing pro-communist programs."[44] The Birch Society printed 500,000 copies of this 16-page pamphlet, adding to its already impressive arsenal of anti–civil-rights propaganda.[45]

"Make yourself as much an authority on the whole 'civil rights' segment of the total conspiracy as you can . . . the *Civil Rights Drive* and the parallel *Negro Revolutionary Movement* constitute the most vulnerable point for attack. . . ." Welch advised in the Society's June 1965 *Bulletin*.[46] In opposing civil rights, the Birch Society did more than circulate paper tracts, it urged action. So-called TACT (Truth About Civil Turmoil) committees were established by Birchers throughout the country to recruit new members under the slogan "Support Your Local Police." This message played especially well among whites in the wake of the August 1965 Watts riots in Los Angeles. Thirty-four people were killed (most of them black civilians) and approximately four thousand arrested, in six days of violence that began when a white police officer stopped a black driver suspected of being drunk.[47]

Despite the hostility of the Birch Society toward the civil rights movement, its eager embrace of conspiracy theories, and the anti-Semitism espoused by many of its members and leaders, it was attacked harshly by the far right.[48] According to Wesley Swift and others, Robert Welch actually was a liberal and his close ties to the National Association of Manufacturers proved his loyalty to the establishment.[49] Notwithstanding Westbrook Pegler's yearlong sojourn in the pages of *American Opinion*, the Birch Society was considered too soft on the Jews; and to make matters worse, the Birch Society actively undermined the cause of anti-communism because it siphoned off recruits who would never learn the "truth" about the *real* forces behind Bolshevism. Bill Gale eventually joined the chorus of anti-Welch critics, but during his 1962 campaign for governor his literature made a carefully calibrated pitch to Birch Society followers: "Colonel Gale is not afraid to be known as an admirer of the American hero who was assassinated by a communist barbarian in China—the hero *John Birch*."[50]

While Gale and others criticized the Birch Society for being too tame (and worse), they welcomed the more militant politics and aggressive gunplay of another group, the Minutemen of Robert Bolivar DePugh. In contrast to the Birch Society, which emphasized political action, and was a large and highly structured organization, the Minutemen advocated the more daring and attractive avenue of clandestine guerrilla warfare.

Robert DePugh was a "deceptively ordinary appearing man" and the president of a small veterinary drug firm in Norborne, Missouri, outside Kansas City when he founded the Minutemen in 1960.[51] In June of that year, DePugh, thirty-seven, and nine fellow duck-hunters allegedly went on an outing and decided to prepare for the communist takeover of the United States. It is impossible to know the truth about the origins of the Minutemen, given DePugh's numerous obfuscations, but the basic outline of the story reads strikingly similar to Welch's account of the Birch Society's founding. According to various tales told by DePugh, he and a small cluster of enlightened followers began rapidly expanding their ranks in late 1960 by indoctrinating others about the "Communist Menace." It was an interesting course of action for a man who had confessed to being an admirer of Fidel Castro in 1958, two years before founding the Minutemen, but what probably attracted him to Castro more than anything else was the ability of the Cuban revolutionary to mount an effective guerrilla war against seemingly overwhelming odds.

From 1960 until his conviction ten years later for violating federal gun laws, DePugh and his followers trained in military maneuvers, infiltrated leftist groups, stockpiled illegal arms, and were frequently arrested. One confidential 1965 FBI report called the Minutemen "a tiny, paramilitary group of rabidly anti-communist vigilantes."[52] Like the leaders of other right-wing groups, DePugh greatly exaggerated the size of his following. But despite its relatively small membership (it probably numbered no more than a couple of thousand at its peak), the Minutemen made a lasting impact on the paramilitary right through its noisy campaigns against gun control and its success popularizing the idea that the Second Amendment right to "keep and bear arms" virtually compelled individual Americans to accumulate an arsenal to resist communist and internationalist subversion. Indeed, DePugh was one of the earliest activists on the right to make opposition to gun control a central part of his platform.[53] After DePugh's conviction on federal firearms charges in 1970, the Minutemen collapsed, but others—Bill Gale included—helped preserve its message, including the argument that the Constitution justified forming private paramilitary groups.

The Minutemen also drew predictable criticism from Robert Welch, who saw the battle against communism as a war "which is still political and educational rather than military."[54] But not all Birch Society members agreed. And when thousands of them later joined the ranks of Bill Gale's Posse Comitatus—or one of its many Christian Patriot descendants—their conservative pedigrees were often measured by how early they had chosen to disavow the Birch Society. However, with the Minutemen it was the opposite: Membership in DePugh's group conferred credibility and signified commitment.

Both the Birch Society and the Minutemen were fueled by the same potent mixture of anti-Semitism, anticommunism, and conspiracy-mongering that had dominated the radical right during World War II and the McCarthy era. But both groups were established *after* the *Brown* decision, and their success also was driven heavily by the fierce battle to dismantle segregation, for even if they were not explicitly racist like the Klan, issues of race took on enormous significance in the post-*Brown* era. The battle to preserve segregation also helped bind the cause of anti-federalism to race hatred with an intensity not seen since the Civil War. And when white racial fears of integration combined with anticommunism and anti-Semitism, right-wing organizing surged as a result. Millions of Americans, including FBI director J. Edgar Hoover, readily believed that civil rights activism was further evidence that communists were successfully boring through from within, weakening America's foundation and threatening the future of the Republic.

12

FLAGS, TENTS, SKILLETS, AND SOLDIERS

Segregation was dealt a fatal blow by the *Brown* decision and the civil rights victories that followed, but the struggle against black equality was still vigorous and violent a decade later. By 1964, America's leading right-wing and conservative groups were spending at least $14 million a year, not including $1.3 million that went to "an ignoble potpourri of anti-Semitic, racist, and other fanatical bodies," according to the Anti-Defamation League.[1] Klan groups experienced a dramatic revival immediately following the *Brown* decision, and by 1958 their membership stood at forty thousand.[2] This was a far cry from the Klan's three to four million followers in the mid-1920s, but it represented a dramatic revival for an Invisible Empire whose membership had been small and badly splintered in the early 1950s. By the middle of the decade the movement was large and militant enough to wreak considerable havoc. Sidestepping the supposed nonviolent posture urged by the Citizens' Councils, most Klan factions bombed, beat, and burned their way through the post-*Brown* era. Between January 1, 1956, and June 1, 1963, at least 138 dynamite bombings shattered black homes, churches, and integrated facilities across the South. Not to be spared were the homes of integrationist whites, as well as Jewish synagogues in Georgia, Florida, Alabama, and Tennessee, which also became targets in 530 acts of Klan violence from 1954 to 1959.[3] As the "respectable" tactics of the Citizens' Councils yielded fewer victories, these attacks became more frequent and aggressive. Frustrated by the failure of Southern politicians to reverse the *Brown* decision, Klansmen and freelance racists stepped up their night-riding and recruitment.

Although President Eisenhower had sent troops to Little Rock in 1957, civil rights activists received little protection from federal authorities in the several years that followed. The result was violence and bloodshed. It was not until the Freedom Rides of 1961 and the battles to integrate colleges in Mississippi and Alabama that federal marshals and troops were again called into action under the Democratic administration of John F. Kennedy. These conflicts heightened the intensity of the confrontation over states' rights, and segregationist enmity for the federal government rivaled hatred of the NAACP.

The showdown over college integration in Mississippi contained the same elements as the Little Rock crisis: a defiant and calculating segregationist governor who tried to outmaneuver the president and the courts; a handful of fearless black activists; mobs of whites bent on violence; and, ultimately, thousands of army troops. Events climaxed in September 1962 when Governor Ross R. Barnett refused to allow James Meredith to become a student at the University of Mississippi in Oxford. Barnett took the concept of state interposition personally, and on September 25, he physically blocked Meredith from submitting his school application.[4] Echoing the words of John C. Calhoun—and Thomas Jefferson decades before him—Barnett read a proclamation of "state interposition" under the glare of television lights on the tenth floor of the Woolfolk State Office Building in Jackson. Barnett then insulted the twenty-nine-year-old black Air Force veteran, rejected his enrollment attempt, and defied Meredith's two federal escorts.[5] Several days later, retired Major General Edwin Walker, who had ably commanded the 101st Airborne during the Little Rock crisis, arrived in Mississippi. His mission this time was not to lead federal troops but to oppose them. Walker had resigned from the army in 1961 after he was caught indoctrinating his troops with John Birch Society propaganda and disciplined for insubordination.[6] The following year, Walker confessed he had been "on the wrong side" of the Little Rock crisis and called for ten thousand volunteers to come to Mississippi.[7]

Walker arrived in Oxford on September 29 and promptly went on the radio to urge more segregationists to join the rapidly growing army of Klansmen and other thugs that were streaming into town.[8] "Barnett yes, Castro no!" the former army major general declared, praising the Mississippi governor. "Bring your flags, your tents, and your skillets! It is time! Now or never!" he exhorted.[9] While Governor Barnett publicly proclaimed his defiance of the federal courts—and his fealty to the "customs" of Mississippi—he tried to cut a deal with President Kennedy. But Barnett's offers to resolve the crisis were filled with half-truths and tactical feints buttressed by lies and false promises. After a week of fruitless conversations with Attorney General Robert Kennedy, the governor and the president agreed to a carefully scripted but fatally flawed plan: Federal marshals would sneak Meredith onto the Oxford campus on Sunday, September 30, and Barnett would announce the next day that he had been tricked. This would allow the governor to save face and would spare the president a military showdown that would further weaken his standing among Southern Democrats who were essential to his reelection plans. But from the moment Meredith arrived in Oxford at six o'clock that Sunday evening, events spiraled toward disaster.

As night fell, a crowd of more than two thousand students and segregationists laid siege to nearly three hundred federal marshals encamped at the university administration building, the Lyceum. Meredith remained hidden in a deserted dormitory across campus, guarded by a handful of marshals. Cheering, "Go to Cuba, nigger-lovers, go to Cuba!" the rioters raged at the marshals outside the Lyceum, attacking them first with rocks, bricks, and bottles, then with flaming Molotov cocktails.[10] Some witnesses placed former major general Edwin Walker at the head of the mob.[11] "Imagine that son of a bitch having been a commander of a division," remarked a frustrated President Kennedy, who huddled with his brother and other White House advisers to receive intermittent reports about the unfolding crisis. As the violence escalated, Kennedy tried to break the tension. "I haven't had such an interesting time since the Bay of Pigs," he quipped.[12]

The marshals tried to defend themselves with tear gas, but the crowd responded first by hurling iron spikes, then with gunfire. It was only after the marshals exhausted their supply of tear gas that the president called out the federalized Mississippi National Guard and dispatched army troops from Memphis. It took some twelve thousand soldiers to restore order, and eventually twice that number were briefly encamped at Oxford. At daybreak, 160 marshals lay wounded, 28 by gunfire, and two bystanders were shot dead.[13] Army soldiers detained Edwin Walker at gunpoint and turned him over to U.S. marshals who arrested him on charges of insurrection and sedition. "They don't have a thing on me," the retired general remarked to newsmen.[14] Southerners responded to the twenty-three thousand soldiers who invaded Oxford with outrage and bumper stickers proclaiming, "FEDERALLY OCCUPIED MISSISSIPPI" and, alluding to recent communist takeovers in Eastern Europe, "KENNEDY'S HUNGARY."

The battle to keep Meredith out of "Ole Miss" reached its climax exactly five years after Eisenhower had sent the 101st Airborne to Little Rock. In Arkansas, the governor's attempt to defy federal authority had been quashed by a decisive president who was not afraid to use military force. In Mississippi, however, a tentative and reluctant Kennedy tried relying on several hundred federal marshals to suppress a screaming mob ten times that number. It was a grievous miscalculation that resulted in considerable bloodshed. After the debacle at the Lyceum, the president gained a new appreciation for Eisenhower's resolve—and for the importance of using federal power to suppress racist insurrection.

Alabama crowded Mississippi from center stage the following year. Fearful that Governor George Wallace would use the National Guard against civil rights protesters, the president federalized the state militia and moved army troops into position. Then on June 11, 1963, members of the federalized National Guard were dispatched by Kennedy after Wallace defied the federal courts and prevented two black students from attending the University of Alabama at Tuscaloosa. It was another tense, highly theatrical showdown between a rabidly segregationist Southern governor and the president.

Standing at a lectern symbolically positioned behind a freshly painted white line, backed by a hundred and fifty state patrolmen in full riot gear, and flanked by four hundred reporters, Wallace denounced the "unwelcome, unwanted, unwarranted, and force-induced intrusion . . . of the might of the central government." In defying the president and the federal courts, Wallace was making good on his 1962 campaign promise to "stand in the schoolhouse door,"[15] and his January 1963 inaugural address, during which he infamously endorsed "segregation now, segregation tomorrow, [and] segregation forever" and assured "those of any group who would follow the false doctrines of communistic amalgamation, that we will not surrender our system of government, our freedom of race and religion."[16] This time Kennedy did not hesitate to act.[17] At three o'clock in the afternoon, one hundred troops of the newly federalized National Guard were minutes away from the Tuscaloosa campus, and Wallace retreated, vowing to "continue this constitutional fight."[18] The clash was less violent than the confrontations at Central High and Ole Miss, but the carefully staged conflict made Wallace the nation's standard-bearer for white supremacy—earning him nearly ten million votes for president in 1968. A bullet in his spine from a would-be assassin four years later cut short further attempts to ascend the national stage.

Throughout the closely scripted Tuscaloosa confrontation, the president had carefully avoided lofty pronouncements favoring civil rights and, instead, allowed Governor Wallace to frame the issue as one of federal versus states' rights. But the president struck a decidedly different tone in a speech that night in which he emphasized the importance of "equal rights and equal opportunities." In nationally televised remarks, Kennedy condemned segregation in the same starkly moral terms used by Dr. Martin Luther King Jr., and called for new federal civil rights legislation.

As with Little Rock and Oxford, the confrontation in Tuscaloosa once again reminded segregationists of the futility of relying on legal proclamations of interposition when faced with a president willing to call out the army to enforce civil rights. It also motivated some to choose another, more violent course of action. It was a little past midnight on June 11, 1963, only a few hours after the conclusion of Kennedy's televised speech, when Byron de la Beckwith hid behind a honeysuckle bush near the home of NAACP field secretary Medgar Evers in Jackson, Mississippi. Beckwith, a former Marine, was a fertilizer salesman and member of the Citizens' Council in Greenwood, Mississippi. Evers, thirty-seven and an army veteran, was arriving home late from a civil rights strategy session, when Beckwith gunned him down in the driveway. The single, high-velocity bullet fired from Beckwith's .30-.06 Enfield rifle smashed through Evers's back, ripped through his right lung, and exited his chest before penetrating a living-room window, an interior wall, and entering the Evers family kitchen. After bouncing off the refrigerator, the slug wound up on the kitchen counter. About twenty-five thousand people attended Evers's funeral at Arlington National Cemetery, but two all-white juries deadlocked on a verdict the following year, and Beckwith's crime went unpunished for more than three decades until February 5, 1994, when a multiracial jury in Hinds County Circuit Court convicted the seventy-three-year-old segregationist Christian Identity believer. Beckwith was later sentenced to life in prison.[19]

Byron de la Beckwith chose a bullet to deliver his message while others who aspired to build a mass following expressed their opposition to civil rights legislation in a manner they hoped would bring about political results. "If you want to serve nobody but a blue-eyed German at your place of business, that is your right," the Reverend Billy James Hargis told his audience of three hundred influential citizens in the small town of Borger, Texas, in November 1963.[20] Hargis, thirty-eight, was one of the nation's most successful right-wing evangelists and his Tulsa-based Christian Crusade generated an endless stream of anti-communist propaganda. His monthly magazine, *Christian Crusade*, boasted 130,000 subscribers, he had a staff of fifty, and his voice was heard on four hundred radio stations every day.[21]

Although Hargis claimed to disavow bigotry, his writings and remarks were anything but tolerant. In *The Truth About Segregation*, the portly Oklahoma minister wrote that ancient Israel's success was due to segregation, which was required by God and "one of nature's universal laws."[22] Although Hargis had been ordained in the mainline Christian Church (Disciples of Christ), he maintained close ties with Identity sympathizers like Gerald L. K. Smith and Gerald Winrod. And like Smith and Winrod, Hargis's message had considerable reach. In 1963 he organized a seventeen-state, twenty-seven-city speaking tour featuring himself and Major General Edwin Walker, who was now a segregationist hero for helping lead the mob at Ole Miss. Hargis's coast-to-coast tour was dubbed Operation Midnight Ride, and attracted forty thousand people.[23] The meetings helped build Hargis's following but did less for General Walker, who rambled at the microphone and was a terrible speaker. According to Paul Greenberg, a journalist who covered the civil rights movement and heard Walker and Hargis speak, the general had one of those military minds that would "put two and two together and get 666."[24] And so, too, did Bill Gale.

13

ANGLO-SAXONS TRIUMPHANT

In 1963, Gale moved to the Antelope Valley north of Los Angeles, to the desert town of Lancaster, where Wesley Swift also lived. It was the year of the confrontation in Tuscaloosa, the Medger Evers murder, and President Kennedy's assassination. Free from marriage and family obligations, Gale made his first attempt to set down in writing a thorough exposition of his religious beliefs—beliefs that would stand unaltered until his death in 1988. Gale's message emerged in a slim, 54-page volume titled *The Faith of Our Fathers*, published by his newly formed Ministry of Christ Church. Although the text never mentions the posse comitatus, portions of it clearly foreshadow Gale's more elaborate dissertation on the subject, which came eight years later. Gale's 1963 tract also provides insight into his view that the Constitution was inspired by God's desire to empower whites against the depredations of satanic Jews and so-called "pre-Adamic" non-white races.

The title of Gale's booklet is a play on words, referring to the purported faith of America's first colonists and "founding fathers," as well as the "faith" of the supposed ancestral white race. (No mention was made, of course, of Gale's father's Jewish roots.) Like all teachers of Identity, Gale emphasized the importance of the Genesis story. But Gale, like his mentor Wesley Swift, had a peculiar obsession with creatures from outer space, and his text included phantasmagorical theories about the role of otherworldly beings in establishing racial hierarchies on earth.[1] According to Gale, Adam and Eve and their descendants were celestial beings of "pure seed" whose Aryan character was demonstrated by their fair complexion and ability to blush, a trait absent from nonwhite races.[2] The racial prospects of the divine first family were shattered, however, when Eve was seduced by the devil and gave birth to Cain who then murdered his brother, Abel, and became the ancestral father of the Jews.

Gale's interpretation of the Book of Genesis contained a novel twist on the story of "original sin." According to conventional Christian theology, "the fall" of woman and man occurred when the serpent convinced Eve to eat from the Tree of Knowledge and Adam followed suit. While the causes and meaning of "the fall" have been debated for centuries, including its obvious sexual connotations, Identity believers like Gale were the first to define "original sin" as race-mixing.

In contrast to the pure offspring of Adam and Eve, Cain's children were the product of the sexual union of Eve and the devil, and as such were "a pollution of the Holy and Celestial seed." They also multiplied rapidly, "had no morals . . . and were evil."[3] To prevent further race-mixing, God instructed each generation of the Aryan descendants of Adam and Eve to separate themselves from Cain's offspring. Satan, on the other hand, was constantly luring them into the ranks of the "Enosh"—nonwhite, "kinky-haired," fallen angels who had originated on other planets and been brought to Earth by Lucifer after he was cast out of God's Kingdom.[4] According to Gale—who probably got these ideas from Wesley Swift—the arrival of the so-called Enosh predated the Creation of Adam and Eve by hundreds of thousands of years, hence their designation as "pre-Adamic" and essentially nonhuman.

"The angelic hosts came here on ships, when they lost the battle in the sky," preached Swift in Hollywood in 1963. "That is how the hosts of Lucifer and his fallen angels arrived here in the earth. They arrived because they were defeated in space and made this solar system their refuge."[5]

According to Gale's biblical genealogy, nearly all of Adam's descendants polluted their celestial bloodline by intermarrying with either the nonwhite Enosh or the satanic children of Cain. Enoch and Noah were the only exceptions—"righteous children" whose families renewed "the Celestial Family of Adam's seed"—but of Noah's three children only one, Shem, remained pure, as did his descendants, Abraham, Isaac, and Jacob, but not Jacob's twin brother Esau who took Satanic Canaanite wives. This, explained Gale, is why "many of Satan's children today appear on the surface to be of the Adamic race, while others have the appearance of the pre-Adamic peoples with whom they were mixed."[6] Gale's scheme of biblical racial classification translates thusly: The white, true Israelites of the Bible who mixed with the pre-Adamic Enosh transformed themselves into "non-white races," while the offspring of those who took Canaanite wives sometimes retained the appearance of Adamic peoples, but nonetheless acquired the satanic character of their Jewish ancestors. The true Israelites called the Canaanites and their descendants "Edomites" or "Yehudi," which translates simply as "Jews" in Hebrew but which Gale claimed means "the cursed ones."[7] It was the Yehudi, Gale wrote,

> . . . whom Jesus revealed hundreds of years later as the children of Satan. . . . He revealed their atheistic form of government as one we know today by the name of communism. These were the "Yehudi" in the days of Jesus and they are the "Yehudi" today. They are still doing the works of their father the Devil and it includes the efforts of Satan to mix the holy seed of Ad-am's family in order to destroy them, as Satan has tried to do since Adam and Eve came out of the garden.[8]

While the non-white Enosh were barbaric primitives and descendants of Luciferian aliens from outer space, and the Jewish Edomites were malevolent agents of the devil, the pure descendants of Adam were a master builder race who, among other things, used "atom-powered space vehicles" and "divine knowledge" to build the Great Pyramid of Giza.[9]

Viewed through the lens of Christian Identity, Gale saw all of history as a Manichaean struggle between white, divine, Anglo-Saxon Christians, and Satanic Jews. It was in Europe, Gale wrote, that the devilish Yehudi gained control of the wealth of the nations they invaded and acted as "destroyers from within."[10] America, in contrast, was a "New Jerusalem," divinely ordained to advance the interests of Aryan, "Adamic Israelites" through its thirteen colonies that were formed from the "thirteen tribes [sic]" of ancient Israel."[11] Echoing themes that would later become cornerstones of Posse ideology, Gale wrote that the American Articles of Confederation and the Constitution that followed were derived from the Bible and "Anglo-Saxon Law."[12] Likewise, the idea that America was founded by English immigrants fleeing religious persecution was "one of Satan's lies."[13] Gale even regarded the Boston Tea Party as an anti-Jewish protest, saying that those colonists who opposed the English stamp tax did so because they knew the tax would enrich the "money lenders" of England and Europe, who were children of Cain.[14] And repeating a long-standing anti-Semitic myth, Gale claimed that George Washington foresaw the invasion of America by "Cain's children" in a vision. This heavily recycled anti-Semitic canard was only one of many promoted by Gale. He also wrote that the Jewish celebration of Yom Kippur—the holiest day on the Hebrew calendar—disqualified Jews as American citizens. For Jews, the holiday emphasizes atonement, forgiveness, and self-improvement, but according to Gale, the observance proved Jews were dishonest and disloyal. That is because the traditional *Kol Nidre* prayer recited on the eve of the holiday asks that any impulsive and unfulfilled vows made during the previous year be nullified. Although the prayer refers only to pledges made between an individual and God, anti-Semites like Gale contended that it was a ruse to enable Jews to secretly renege on agreements with Gentiles.[15] And according to Gale's analysis of the Civil War, it was started by the Jews:

> The war was successfully started and brethren were fighting brethren. While brothers of Ad-am's family destroyed each other, the Yehudi sat back pulling the strings and lending the money to both sides. . . . The sons of Satan knew that they must bring about a mongrelization with the Enosh to effectively destroy the sons of God. Their land must be taken from them and their women folk subjected to the heathen.[16]

These ideas weren't limited to the self-published tracts of idealogues like Gale. In October 1958 the once-prestigious *American Mercury* magazine carried an article on "The Civil War Bankers," alleging that the Rothschild banking family of Europe "sent a twenty-one-year-old Jewish-German youth to the United States as their agent" to fan the flames of Civil War.[17] (Founded in 1924 by the journalist and critic H. L. Mencken, the *Mercury* had built its reputation on Mencken's biting satire and provocative brilliance. But Mencken left the magazine in 1933 and in 1952 it was acquired by J. Russell Maguire, a wealthy oilman and munitions magnate, who then filled its pages with hard-core anti-Semitic and right-wing propaganda. By 1964, circulation of the *Mercury* had fallen to twenty-seven thousand subscribers.)[18]

The Faith of Our Fathers championed states' rights by attacking the Fourteenth Amendment and repeating an argument popular among Southern segregationists—that the Amendment, which guaranteed equal protection under the law regardless of race, had never been legally ratified by the states. Gale also asserted that blacks were not citizens and therefore had no right to vote: "The States and ONLY the States have the right of qualifying their voters. . . . The federal government has no control over this whatsoever, not even by legislation, because legislation may not amend the Constitution."[19] Continuing in this vein, and foreshadowing the rhetoric of the Posse Comitatus, Gale also asserted that the post–Civil War Ku Klux Klan was based on the principle that lawmakers who passed legislation "outside the confines of the Constitution would be subject to arrest and removal from office for usurping powers not granted to them by the States or the people and for violation of their oath of office which required them to uphold, defend and protect the Constitution. Any act otherwise would be malfeasance and misfeasance in office and a criminal offense. . . ."[20]

If Gale regarded the "War of Northern Aggression"—as he and many white Southerners referred to the Civil War—as "hours of darkness" in America, then midnight came in 1913; the year Congress created the Federal Reserve System and the states ratified the Sixteenth Amendment, which established the graduated income tax. Like the income tax, the Federal Reserve Act of 1913 has long been a target of opprobrium for archconservatives who regarded the creation of the nation's first central banking system as an unconstitutional delegation of the congressional power to coin money and "regulate the value thereof."[21] But according to bigots like Gale, the creation of the Fed was part of a "Jewish plot to enslave America, pure and simple," and 1913 was the climactic moment that "the Yehudi" moved to destroy America.[22]

While it is true that the authors of the Constitution might not have foreseen the need to create a national bank, or anticipated the delegation of congressional power to it, they didn't include language in the Constitution forbidding it, either. What really concerned the nation's founders was the need to develop financial unity among the original states by ensuring that *no individual state* could issue its own currency. Hence the clause found in Article I, Section 8, that reserved to Congress the authority to coin money and regulate its value. But such economic and political considerations were lost on Gale, who saw nothing but Jewish machinations behind the creation of the Fed.

Gale further lamented the events of 1913 because that was the year the Anti-Defamation League of B'nai B'rith was established. Like the American Jewish Committee founded seven years earlier, the ADL was organized to counter anti-Jewish stereotypes and discrimination.[23] Brutal crimes like the 1915 lynching of Leo Frank in Georgia gave added impetus to both groups. But in the eyes of Bill Gale all the Jews ever did was engage in "publicity, pressure, deceit, lies, and all means of propaganda."[24]

The Faith of Our Fathers did not limit itself to exposing domestic Jewish subversion. It also described how the sinister Yehudi had undermined Christian civilization in Europe by orchestrating the Russian Revolution and the defeat of Germany in World Wars I and II. According to Gale, Germany was the single greatest obstacle to Jewish world domination and the Holocaust was a "cover story" for the Jewish invasion of America. The bodies of German victims of Allied air raids—not Jews—were the ones consumed by the crematoria of Auschwitz and other death camps, he wrote. Meanwhile, the "missing six million"— Gale called them "Yehudi criminals" and the "advance guard of Satan's government"—stole into America disguised as refugees, manipulated the next census count, and evaded deportation.[25]

Gale concluded *The Faith of Our Fathers* in a decidedly prophetic tone. The struggle for civil rights will prompt Adam's children to become "God's 'battle-ax' " against the "darkness of night" and to fulfill their duty to "cleanse the land," he predicted. Adam's children must "occupy the Earth" and "be brave enough to 'fight' and shed their blood in sacrifice if necessary. When they do that, Victory is theirs!"[26]

Gale's religious and racial theories may seem bizarre, but stripped of their futuristic fantasies about unidentified flying objects and devilish non-white aliens from outer space, his core beliefs were derived not from fringe theories, but from centuries of mainstream European and American theology, beginning with the notion that the covenant between God and the ancient Israelites belonged not to Jews, but to Christians. Of course, when presented pejoratively, the central tenets of Christian Identity theology can be made to seem like crackpot notions, but for centuries many Christians have been attracted by the thought of seizing— or at least joining in—the Hebrews' presumed special relationship with God.

The idea that the divine blessings bestowed upon the ancient Hebrews could be transferred to Christians dates back to the Middle Ages, when medieval historians, through legends, genealogies, myth, and error, traced the lineage of English kings directly to the biblical David and Shem. In 1649, John Sadler, a Puritan member of the British Parliament and friend of Oliver Cromwell, issued what may have been the first Anglo-Israelite manifesto, *Rights to the Kingdom; or Customs of our Ancestors*. Sadler argued that Anglo-Saxon laws were derived from Talmudic ones and mused about whether the Druids were Canaanites.[27] Nearly fifty years later, the famous Puritan cleric and colonial scholar Cotton Mather donned a skullcap, called himself "rabbi," and wrote his magnum opus, *Magnalia Christi Americana*—"Christ's Deeds in America." According to Mather, the Puritans were engaged in a divine mission to establish the "New Israel" in what would later become America.[28] While the Puritans didn't claim they were actual descendants of the ancient Israelites, they believed that they—not the Jews— were God's chosen people.

White Christians have not been the only ones to appropriate the promise of the Covenant. The Rastafarian movement was founded, in part, on the idea that black people are descended from the early Israelites. And while only a few African-American religious sects have claimed that blacks are the true Jews, the Exodus story has long held a special meaning for black Christians whose theology has emphasized a symbolic—if not an actual—kinship with the travails of the ancient Hebrews and their struggle for liberation from slavery.

If the idea that non-Jews might be heirs to the Covenant has been attractive to Christians well beyond the ranks of the radical right, so, too, has the notion that Jews are confederates of the devil and satanic killers of Christ. To say, as Bill Gale did, that Jews were the direct descendants of Satan, was merely a more explicit articulation of a concept that was popularized throughout Christian Europe for centuries: the idea that Jews, in spurning Jesus Christ as the messiah (and rejecting other aspects of Christian doctrine), were inspired or controlled by the devil himself.

Early advocates of British Israelism established their theology by building on the power of the Christians-as-Israelites idea and it wasn't until later that other advocates of the faith concluded that Jews were children of the devil. In the late eighteenth century, Richard Brothers, a Canadian, proclaimed himself a direct descendent of King David, and announced in London that the people of Europe and Britain were descendants of the Lost Tribes of Israel. Eventually, Brothers's messianic, millenarian delusions landed him in an insane asylum in 1795, where he spent the next 11 years.[29] Identity followers are naturally reluctant to acknowledge that Brothers contributed much to their faith, although they proudly cite the 1840 work of an Irishman, John Wilson, author of *Lectures on Our Israelitish Origin*.[30] And it was Edward Hine, one of Wilson's disciples, who in 1871 later published the best-selling *Forty-seven Identifications of the British Nation with Lost Ten Tribes of Israel: Founded Upon Five Hundred Scripture Proofs*. By the time Hine dedicated his book "to the (So-called) British People," Anglo-Israelism had spread throughout Britain.

The point here is not that the Covenant envy found in mainstream Christianity—and its various sects—is equivalent to that of Christian Identity. It is not. The Puritans may have seen themselves as inheritors of the biblical promise made to the Jews, but they did not see themselves as racial or ethnic "replacements" for the Jewish people. Besides, theories of racial origins were too poorly developed at the end of the seventeenth century to hold much interest for the Puritans. It was much easier to simply regard the Jews in the same way that Christians had for centuries: as a wayward people who had rejected Christ's promise and were, therefore, eternally damned.

In contrast to the Puritans and others, Identity believers who came later not only claimed the Covenant for themselves, but they explicitly usurped the identity of the Jews. And having done that, they felt compelled to ask the question, "Who, then, are those claiming to be Jews?" By the late nineteenth century the answer was plain enough: they were racial impostors. The development and refinement of this theologically racist idea was made possible by a large body of scholarly and scientific thought that advanced the longstanding notion of white, Anglo-Saxon, "Aryan" superiority.

As far back as 1734, the French philosopher and author Voltaire wrote that "bearded whites, fuzzy negroes, the long-maned yellow races, and beardless men are not descended from the same man" (although he later became a harsh critic of slavery). And twenty years later the Scottish philosopher David Hume opined that "the Negroes, and in general all the other species of men (for there are four or five different kinds) [were] naturally inferior to the whites."[31] Thomas Jefferson articulated similar thoughts in 1787, in *Notes on the State of Virginia*, which speculated "whether [blacks,] originally a distinct race, or made distinct by time and circumstances, are inferior to the whites in the endowments both of body and mind."[32] Notwithstanding the race prejudice of slave owners like Jefferson (who eventually modified his views), and the fundamentally white-supremacist worldview of many European philosophers, the egalitarian values of many of the Enlightment ideas they espoused eventually undermined the concepts of white superiority that they so readily took for granted (even if it did take centuries for the equality spoken of in Jefferson's Declaration of Independence to become enshrined in law).[33] And in Europe it was the Enlightenment that helped bring about an end to feudalism and serfdom and led to the emancipation of the Jews.

Assumptions about black inferiority were not limited to Enlightenment writers and philosophers or American patriots and statesmen. They became widely held scientific "truths." By the mid-1800s, the pseudo-sciences of craniology and phrenology—which used physical measurements of the skull and head to assess intelligence and classify "races"—achieved great respectability on both sides of the Atlantic. According to this popular discipline, the racial identity of non-Aryans could be established by measuring their heads, thereby proving their lesser intelligence, lower morality, and well-deserved position at the bottom of the human scale of evolution. Bolstered by such objective "evidence," the idea that white Anglo-Saxon Christians were a separate and innately superior race became thoroughly embedded in the American imagination by the mid–nineteenth century.[34]

Similar thinking prevailed in Europe with regard to the Jews. In 1844, Christian Lassen, a professor at Bonn (later the prestigious University of Bonn) in Germany, proposed a specifically *racial* distinction between so-called "Semitic" and "Aryan" peoples, where previously the distinction had been a linguistic one.[35] According to Lassen, history proved that "the Semites do not possess the harmonious proportion of all psychical forces which distinguishes the Indo-Germanics." And Ernest Renan, the distinguished head of the College de France, wrote that "Semites" were "an incomplete race," and inferior to the Indo-Europeans to whom belonged "almost all the great military, political, and intellectual movements of the history of the world."[36]

Just as many Christian theologians defined Jews as theologically inadequate (for rejecting Christ as the Messiah) *and* destructive (as agents of the devil), the racial schemes of most nineteenth-century Europeans and Americans classified Jews as both inferior and dangerously corrupting. In 1850 the German composer Richard Wagner, who regarded Jews as "plastic demon[s] of the decay of humanity," published his polemic, *Judaism in Music*, to explain the role of Jews in the downfall of Teutonic culture.[37] Shortly thereafter, the French writer and diplomat Count Joseph Arthur de Gobineau produced his *Essai sur l'Inégalité des Races Humaines* (*Essay on the Inequality of the Human Races*). Though not original, Gobineau's 1853 work systematized many of the central concepts about race that had been deeply rooted in European thought. To wit: humans were divided into a hierarchy of races, among which Aryans reigned supreme, and interactions among the different races explained all social and political phenomena.[38]

These ideas were further advanced with the appearance, in 1859, of Charles Darwin's *On the Origin of Species*. Though it was not Darwin's intent, his work gave additional impetus to the "science" of racism and was used—and distorted—by many who busied themselves with devising elaborate schemes to categorize human beings, including Jews, into separate and distinct "races." The emergence of explicitly racist aspects of Christian Identity during the mid–nineteenth century owes much to these developments, because the work of many scientists and scholars of the period legitimized or were appropriated to support such views.

As waves of nationalism swept across nineteenth-century Europe, scientific and social racism provided renewed justification for the persecution of Jews. (The term "anti-Semitism" was coined in 1879 by a German anti-Semite, Wilhelm

Marr, to describe the anti-Jewish movement that had arisen in Europe in response to the entry of Jews into non-Jewish society.) Scholars like Lassen and Renan had not explicitly defined all Semites as Jews, but by the end of the nineteenth century international scientific opinion had promoted the division between Jewish Semite and Aryan to "the status of an axiom," according to Leon Poliakov, author of *The Aryan Myth: A History of Racist and Nationalist Ideas in Europe*.[39]

Gobineau died in 1882, but his *Essay* profoundly influenced European racist thinking for more than half a century. Among those who embellished Gobineau's treatise was Houston Stewart Chamberlain, the son of an English admiral and the husband of Richard Wagner's daughter. In 1899, Chamberlain became one of the leading prophets of Aryanism with the publication of his 1,500-page *Grundlagen des Neunzenhnten Fahrhunderts* (*The Foundations of the Nineteenth Century*).[40] If the pessimist Gobineau saw Aryan civilization as doomed to decline because of the irreversible racial degeneration caused by race-mixing, advocates of Teutonic superiority like Chamberlain proclaimed the possibility of racial redemption through vigorous selective breeding. These ideas were later embraced and amplified by the Nazi propagandist Alfred Rosenberg and ultimately by Hitler himself. But the popularity of Chamberlain's ideas extended to many who were not fascists. Translated into English in 1911, *The Foundations* was praised by British newspapers and applauded even by the renowned Fabian-socialist playwright and critic George Bernard Shaw, who called Chamberlain's work an historical masterpiece.[41]

Chamberlain's book was warmly received by Americans like Klansman Lothrop Stoddard, a Harvard-educated lawyer and the author of nearly two dozen books, including *The Rising Tide of Color Against White World Supremacy*. Published in 1920, Stoddard's book significantly popularized antiblack racism and "racial anti-Semitism."[42] According to Stoddard, the concept of race was not an abstraction, but a "concrete fact, which can be accurately determined by scientific tests such as head formation, bodily structure, and color of hair, eyes, and skin."[43] Stoddard's arguments were based on the same flawed assumptions and pseudoscientific biology that informed the eugenicists' perspectives on race—namely, that the relatively minor genetic differences among people that produce visible (or "phenotypical") variations, such as skin color or facial features, are unmistakable markers of inborn differences in behavior, culture, character, and ability.

These ideas were equally popular among the nation's leading scientists, clergymen, social reformers, and politicians.[44] The famous American zoologist Louis Agassiz believed that blacks and whites had separate origins and that blacks were inferior to whites. His theories were given considerable credence by the work of another well-known scientist, the physician Samuel George Morton, who measured more than one thousand skulls to determine if there was a significant difference in brain size among the three "races"—Caucasians, Africans, and Native Americans. Morton filled the skulls with flaxseed, found huge differences in brain size, and pronounced Africans at the bottom, Native Americans in the middle, and whites on the top.[45] A few years later, the French scientist Paul Broca conducted similar experiments on male and female brains—this time "proving" the inferiority of women, whose brains supposedly were smaller.[46] In 1981, paleontologist Stephen Jay Gould reexamined the work of these men, remeasured Morton's skulls, and demonstrated the falsity of their findings as well as the prejudices—both conscious and unconscious—that had led both scientists to distort and manipulate their data. While the nineteenth-century arguments attributed both physical and mental inferiority to blacks, the debate later expanded to include arguments over presumed IQ differences between the "races." Despite shoddy science and the prejudices of their protagonists, books like *The Bell Curve*, which advance the same racist beliefs, continue to find many admirers.[47] However, rather than igniting fierce debate, as such ideas do today, the inferiority of the "lesser races" was automatically assumed by the majority of whites in early twentieth century America.

President Theodore Roosevelt maintained it was "the inescapable duty, of the *good* citizen of the right type to leave his or her blood behind him in the world,"[48] and gave Houston Chamberlain's racist book a mild endorsement, saying he saw no harm in its attacks on "egalitarian doctrines which were as false as they were pernicious."[49] And Madison Grant, chairman of the New York Zoological Society, echoed Chamberlain's thesis when he asserted in his 1916 book, *The Passing of the Great Race, or: The Racial Basis of European History*, that "the cross between any of the three European races and a Jew is a Jew."[50]

Thus, when Bill Gale wrote *The Faith of Our Fathers* in 1963, his racial theories rested on nearly two centuries of previously accepted myths and pseudoscience masquerading as fact. And Gale's propaganda about a supposed "international Jewish conspiracy," was marked by the same pseudointellectual deficiencies.

The belief that an all-powerful Jewish cabal is secretly behind world events was first popularized in the late eighteenth century when opponents of the liberal ideas of the Enlightenment and the French Revolution blamed the fall of the *ancien régime* on a plot of Freemasons, secret societies, and Jews. Like many myths, this one had a kernel of truth: Many Freemasons *did* support the ideals of the French Revolution. As nonsectarian Deists, they also favored faith in reason instead of divine decrees, trusted the ideals of fraternity rather than the whim of autocratic kings, and argued against papal infallibility. Freemasons also worked to improve schools and to abolish judicial torture and witchcraft trials.[51] Not surprisingly, Freemasonry was vigorously attacked, especially in Catholic countries such as France and Bavaria.[52] In 1738, Pope Clement XII threatened to excommunicate any Catholic who joined the Masonic order.

Freemasonry had much in common with another secret society that embraced humanist and rationalist beliefs, and one that was equally despised by the Catholic Church: the Order of the Illuminati. The group's founder was Adam

Weishaupt, a professor of canon law at the University of Ingolstadt in Bavaria. Established on May 1, 1776, the Illuminati was dedicated to promoting the utopian ideals of Enlightenment philosophy and challenging the entrenched power of conservative Jesuits in Bavarian society. Weishaupt found many recruits among the Freemasons and by 1784 his group numbered several thousand.[53] Although his plans emphasized a peaceful revolution of ideas, Weishaupt's movement threatened the established forces of church and state and he was forced to operate clandestinely. In 1787 the conservative ruler of Bavaria, Carl Theodore, issued an edict threatening Illuminati recruiters with death.[54]

Attacks on Freemasons and the Illuminati also took the form of popular pamphlets that supposedly exposed the dangerous machinations of both groups or featured false confessions of so-called "conspirators." Some were written by men like John Robison—individuals who were Masons themselves but who condemned mysticism and Illuminism for allegedly corrupting Masonry.

Robison was a Scottish mathematician and professor of natural philosophy at the University of Edinburgh and the author, in 1797, of an early and influential attack: *Proofs of a Conspiracy Against All the Religions and Governments of Europe, Carried On in the Secret Meetings of Freemasons, Illuminati, and Reading Societies (Collected from Good Authorities).*[55] According to Robison, the Masonic lodges in France were filled with "pernicious doctrines" that made society "a noisome marsh of human corruption filled with every rank and poisonous weed."[56] Robison's "exposé" benefited considerably from a trove of Illuminati documents that had been seized by Bavarian authorities during their crackdown on Adam Weishaupt in 1785–86. Among other things, the confiscated papers included scandalous letters from Weishaupt describing his search for someone to perform an abortion for his sister-in-law whom he had gotten pregnant while awaiting a papal dispensation to marry her following his first wife's death. Weishaupt's indiscretions lent color to the convoluted plots various writers attributed to him, but *Proofs of a Conspiracy* was more interested in assailing the underlying philosophies that had inspired the French Revolution of 1789.

This also was the goal of Abbé Augustin Barruel, a French Jesuit and the author of a five-volume work, *Mémoire pour servir à l'Histoire du Jacobinisme* (*Memoirs Illustrating the History of Jacobinism*). Published shortly after Robinson's book appeared, Barruel's *Memoirs* exposed the evil supposedly wrought by the medieval Order of Templars, a secret society that Barruel believed sought to depose the pope, destroy all monarchies, preach "unrestricted liberty to all peoples," and establish a world government.[57] According to Barruel, this ancient conspiracy had captured Freemasonry and used Enlightenment philosophy to promote rebellion and anarchy. Its ultimate goal was to undermine all religion. Barruel identified Weishaupt and his Illuminati as enemies of the human race, "sons of Satan," and the real forces behind the French Revolution.[58]

The works of Robison and Barruel arrived in America at the end of the eighteenth century and their sensational claims about European subversives prompted President John Adams and prominent members of New England's religious and political elite to issue frantic warnings about French plots to undermine the American Republic.[59] The resulting "New England Illuminati scare" planted the seeds for a vigorous anti-Masonic movement in America. Though the works of Robison and Barruel had originally been intended to serve the conservative interests of the Catholic Church, it did not take long, ironically, for the anti-Masonic myths they contained to be distorted to suit new American prejudices. "Anti-Catholicism has always been the pornography of the Puritan," wrote historian Richard Hofstadter in 1965, and the conspiracy theories of Barruel and Robison were quickly used to fuel anti-Catholic prejudices as American followers of the nineteenth-century anti-Masonic movement devoured alarming reports about the dual dangers of popery and Freemasonry.[60]

Events in Europe further fueled the anti-Semitism that grew out of the conspiracy theories of Barruel and Robison. In 1806 and 1807, the French emperor Napoléon Bonaparte called together rabbis and Jewish scholars in Paris to discuss the status of the newly emancipated Jewish populace and to ensure they would remain loyal citizens of France. Recalling the ancient Jewish council of elders, Napoléon called his meeting "the Great Sanhedrin." Although the Jews did not hesitate to pledge their allegiance to France, the event became a lightning rod for both anti-Semites and opponents of Napoléon, including the Holy Synod of the Orthodox Church in Moscow, which condemned the emperor as the Antichrist and a false Messiah for proposing to "reunite the Jews whom God's wrath had scattered over the face of the earth."[61]

The year 1806 was also when the earliest of a famous series of anti-Semitic forgeries appeared. The timing in conjunction with Napoléon's "Great Sanhedrin" was probably no accident.[62] This document was a fake letter, ostensibly sent from Florence, Italy, by an army officer, one "J. B. Simonini," to the French Jesuit, Abbé Barruel. Although it was a forgery, the "Simonini letter," as it came to be known, contained the seed of the whole myth of the Judeo-Masonic conspiracy. The scholar Norman Cohn, a foremost expert on *The Protocols of the Learned Elders of Zion*, summarized the myth as follows:

> [T]here exists a secret Jewish government which, through a worldwide network of camouflaged agencies and organizations, controls political parties and governments, the press and public opinion, banks and economic developments . . . in pursuance of an age-old plan and with the single aim of achieving Jewish dominion over the entire world.[63]

In the letter, "Simonini" claimed to have infiltrated the Jewish community and gained secret knowledge of Masonic symbols, Illuminati plots, and grand schemes for Jewish world domination. Among other things, the letter asserted that granting Jews citizenship was the first step to Christian slavery. Barruel's 1797 work had scarcely mentioned Jews, but he was receptive to Simonini's obsession, which appeared even more legitimate in light of Napoléon's "Sanhedrin."[64] Barruel circulated the Simonini letter widely, modified his own fantasies accordingly, and set to work on a manuscript that fully incorporated the anti-Semitic substance of the Simonini narrative. Barruel died in 1820, but it was largely through him that the modern myth of a Judeo-Masonic-Illuminati conspiracy was born.

One of the most significant versions of Barruel's "Jewish conspiracy" myth reemerged in 1868 with the publication of an anti-Semitic novel, *Biarritz*. The book contains a chapter—"In the Jewish Cemetery in Prague"—that luridly describes the fictional secret reunion of the Lost Tribes of Israel, who report to the devil on their progress in subjugating the Gentile world.[65] Various versions of this fictional story were excerpted and republished as pamphlets in Russia and elsewhere for the next twelve years. The text eventually came full circle, returning to France in 1881 not as fiction, but as supposed fact, in a manuscript called *The Rabbi's Speech*.[66] It took another twenty years for a full-fledged synthesis of these various fictionalized accounts to emerge. Concoted in the 1890s in Russia, one of the most popular early versions of *The Protocols of the Elders of Zion* appeared in 1903 in the pages of a St. Petersberg newspaper, *The Banner*. The forgery won its greatest audience after 1917–18, when the family of Czar Nicholas II was murdered by Bolsheviks early in the revolution and defenders of the Imperial family blamed Jews for their deaths. Anti-Semites on both sides of the Atlantic have since used the *Protocols* and their antecedents to "expose" the Jewish nature of Bolshevism and summon supporters to the barricades. Bill Gale followed in that tradition when he wrote *The Faith of Our Fathers* in 1963. The historical and theological pictures drawn in the pages of his tract bear no resemblance to reality, but the fact that these fictions have captivated audiences for centuries should serve as a clear reminder of the tenacious nature of popular prejudices, no matter how bizarre the ideas underlying them might seem to be.

14

THE MINISTRY OF CHRIST CHURCH

By 1965 Bill Gale was ready to remarry and start a new life. Fifteen years after being forced out of the Army, more than a decade after converting to Christian Identity, and three years after divorcing his wife of twenty-five years, Gale married Roxanne Lutrell. She helped him expand the Ministry of Christ Church and lay the groundwork for the establishment of the Posse Comitatus. None of Gale's family came to the couple's small wedding, though Roxanne was joined by Kitty, her teenage daughter. The couple's wedding photo shows Gale smartly dressed, his white "minister's" collar gleaming against his dark shirt and jacket, a small metal cross hanging from his left breast pocket. He embraced Roxanne, nine years his junior, as they posed, smiling, their hands joined to cut the cake on the table before them. Kitty stood alongside her mother, beaming. Both women were slim and attractive.

Gale was a handsome man, with penetrating eyes, high cheekbones, and dark hair that he kept closely cropped, revealing a receding hairline and well-tanned forehead. When Gale smiled, which was often, his cheeks displayed long, curved creases. At five feet six inches and 145 pounds, Gale was like his father: small but wiry and well-proportioned. Combined with his combative personality and tales of organizing Filipino guerrillas during World War II, Gale's taut physique lent credence to his claim that he was a man of action.

Roxanne had worked as an X-ray technician, but also taught a night course for medical assistants at a small private college on Magnolia Boulevard in Los Angeles. One of her students was a follower of Gale's and was intent on fixing the two of them up. Earlier that year the student had urged Roxanne to attend her wedding and meet her "minister." Soured on the Baptist Church, Roxanne wasn't interested in dating a clergyman. But after her student insisted, Roxanne agreed, though she planned to duck out after the first dance. The plan collapsed when she was seated next to Bill at the reception and found herself smitten from the start. The two talked and danced until Gale offered first to walk her to the door, and then to her car.

"Would you like to go out for a drink?" he asked. Roxanne was somewhat startled. *This preacher wants to have a drink? I'll bet I can drink him under,* she thought, bemused. After they arrived at the bar on Ventura Boulevard, Gale began to lecture her.

"You know, you're an Israelite," he told her.

"You've either had one too many or you've been using too much exotic rope," Roxanne retorted, never at a loss for words. "I am not a *Jew,*" she added, expelling the last word from her mouth as if it tasted unpleasant.

"I didn't say you were a *Jew,* I said you were an *Israelite,*" Gale replied.

"You're telling me that the Jews are not Israelites and that *I* am an Israelite?"

"That's right."

She stared at him, incredulous, but was hooked. The couple talked until four A.M. and when Roxanne got home she dusted off her Bible to see if what Gale was saying was true. They married shortly afterward.[1]

Gale had been fired from Waddell and Reed two years earlier, but his dismissal had neither reduced his earnings nor dampened his enthusiasm for the cause. In 1964 he opened his own securities and insurance firm in Glendale, on the northern outskirts of Los Angeles, and was doing well financially. He also ran unsuccessfully in the GOP primary for Congress in the Twenty-seventh Congressional District.[2] In addition to incorporating the Ministry of Christ Church, he tried to revive the dormant Christian Defense League.[3] This led to yet another high-profile arrest involving illegal weapons, similar to the incident with George King and the California Rangers the year before. On October 30, William H. Garland, a League member, was arrested at his home in Cucamonga, where police found eight machine guns and nearly one hundred other weapons. Gale's colleague, lawyer, friend, and Identity compatriot Bertrand Comparet handled Garland's defense.[4] Gale also began holding his own Sunday services at the Glendale Women's Club. This lasted until early 1967 when, he says, the ADL forced him to move. Eventually—and ironically—he found a new home at the local Masonic Hall.[5]

Around 1964, Gale's son Billy came to live with him in Lancaster, California. Josephine had given up trying to raise the troubled teenager and thought he might benefit from some of her ex-husband's rigid, military discipline. One day while rummaging through his father's closet he came across a Klan robe.

"Kathleen, you're not going to believe this," Billy told his sister on the phone. "I went into Daddy's closet and I saw a *white hooded robe!*"

"You're kidding!" she said, believing it was true but finding it difficult to accept. "Everything Dad was involved with was surrounded with hate. That four-letter word was just loud and clear all around him," she recalled. Whether it was Gale's hatred or, more likely, the tensions that had long plagued his relationship with his father, Billy didn't remain in Lancaster long. After returning to Los Angeles he joined the Army and was sent on the first of two tours of duty in Vietnam.

Earlier in 1964, Gale's mother, Mary Agnes, had passed away. She was seventy-six and lived the last year of her life in Lancaster, where Gale had moved her not long after his divorce.[6] Her death—and Gale's bigotry—prompted a final split between Gale and his younger brother, Robert. It happened on the day of the funeral while the family was gathered at the home of Gale's sister, Ruth.

"Black people have smaller brains," Bill told Robert, apropos of nothing in particular.

"Well, it isn't how big your brain is, it's how much of it you use that counts," his brother tartly replied. Bill's remark prompted Robert to recall the numerous times his brother had held his houseguests hostage to one racist rant after another. "Bill, if I had a black friend, for example, and that friend was in my house and you came over to visit, you would not have any right to insult him," Robert instructed his brother.

"Well, if that's the case, I'll never come to your house again!" Gale shouted gruffly.

"Fine!" Robert replied.

From that day on, the two brothers would have nothing to do with each another. With the exception of his sister Ruth, Gale's bigotry had created an insurmountable gulf between him and the rest of his family. Gale had become so distant from his own children, and so absorbed in his religious beliefs, that after his older daughter married a Jewish man and had children of her own, Gale refused to see them. To even acknowledge the existence of his grandchildren would be to compromise his religious beliefs, said Gale. "I don't care how many times she marries or how many Jew kids she has," he told Roxanne angrily.[7]

In November 1965, Gale published the first issue of his church newsletter, called *IDENTITY*. It contained articles on the Constitution, communist "brain-washing," race-mixing (misspelled "Miscegination"), and theology. "[T]he Israelites (NOT THE JEWS) are God's Chosen People," Gale wrote. "Hebrewism, NOT Judaism, is revealed as the parent religion of Christianity. The Bible is certainly NOT a Jewish book. Judaism is a cult based on materialistic laws of ancient Babylon, completely devoid of spiritual faiths and beliefs. Jews are not a race but a species of all races."[8]

Gale repeated these themes in the second issue that December but this time Roxanne added a "Women's World" section containing recipes for fruit-filled cookies, poppyseed cake, and cranberry relish. A "Poetry Corner" and "Children's Section" (not repeated in later issues) brought the publication to twenty pages. Consistent with the newsletter's holiday theme, it contained a foreboding essay about "Marxism in Christmas Cards," which warned that "the creative arts have been deeply penetrated by Marxist symbolism and crypto-communist messages."

"How much do you plan to spend this Christmas in support of the anti-Christ propaganda expressed in certain greeting cards?" the article (which supposedly had been republished from the *Daughters of the American Revolution Magazine*) began.[9] Later issues also addressed current events, such as the war in Vietnam, which Gale opposed, believing American involvement was masterminded by communists and Jews, working nefariously through the United Nations headquartered in "Jew York," as he liked to call it.

While Gale may have been genuinely worried about the communist content of holiday greetings, it was the adoption of federal civil rights legislation in 1964 and 1965 that caused him the most concern. "When will a GOVERNOR of one of the States or the LEGISLATURE of one of the States protect the citizens of their State by REPUDIATING such unlawful acts of the federal legislature and other branches of the federal government?" he demanded to know. "The federal legislation pertaining to the schools and the area of education is without question UNCONSTITUTIONAL, unlawful, illegal, and without legal effect."[10]

On March 7, 1966, the U.S. Supreme Court unanimously upheld the Voting Rights Act of 1965. Less than three weeks later, the high court declared poll taxes—which had barred blacks from voting in the South—unconstitutional. "The state laws that required a person to pass a simple literacy test before being registered as a voter have now gone 'down the drain,' " lamented one writer in Gale's newsletter. "When a nation allows the votes of morons and illiterates to equal those of educated informed persons the seeds of destruction have been planted and its fall is inevitable."[11]

Gale's theological musings had a limited audience, but his opposition to federal civil rights laws resonated with a much larger segment of the American public. In 1966, only 48 percent of whites approved of federal efforts to promote school integration, and that number fell to 36 percent in the next two years, and to just 20 percent in the South. The Civil Rights Act of 1965 had outlawed employment discrimination but when asked three years later whether the federal government should "see to it that black people get fair treatment in jobs, or leave these matters to the states and local communities," the overwhelming majority of whites (63 percent) endorsed states' rights.[12]

Favoring states' rights was one thing, but Gale demanded its enforcement. "If these local representatives of the people continue to fail in the performance of their duties in this regard, dire results will prevail."[13] Southern governors, Gale demanded, should declare martial law to enforce segregation. "In such instances, all officials of government including federal judges, federal defense department officials, justice department officials, and all others who violate the laws of the state or who violate the military oders [*sic*] of the Commander-in-Chief of the military forces of the State (the Governor), can be arrested either in person or in absentia. . . . It is a felony for anyone, including the President, to violate the U.S. Criminal Code," wrote Gale, who also took the opportunity to remind his readers of the restrictions placed on the military by the Posse Comitatus Act.[14]

In late 1966, Gale published a two-part article under the title *Racial and National Identity*, which he later reprinted as a separate booklet. Its religious content was similar to *The Faith of Our Fathers*, but the text emphasized Gale's ideas about constitutional government and brought him closer to assembling the doctrine for his Posse Comitatus.

"Having established the position that Jesus preached the Gospel of the KING-DOM, we should at this time emphasize the fact that Kingdom is a GOVERNMENT. [T]he Constitution of the United States is a Christian document based upon the Holy Scripture. The government of the United States is a Christian government known as a Constitutional Republic. [A]ll Anglo-Saxon and Christian Law [stems from the Bible]," wrote Gale.

Gale was not the first conservative to expound on the virtue of states' rights, or assert the supposed Christian roots of the Republic, but his articles on "Racial and National Identity" joined these themes to the militant race hatred and religious prejudice of Christian Identity and then dressed them all in an attractive gloss of invented and misapplied legal terminology.

"Because the Articles of Confederation had been adopted to be in effect 'forever,' it was necessary to adopt all of those provisions not picked up by the Constitution as Statutes known as the United States Code. Along with the Constitution, these Statutes became known as the Organic Law of the United States."[15] Since the Bible contained God's laws for government, violating any of these "Organic Laws" constituted an affront to God as well, Gale explained.

"If one believes that he can be in violation of God's laws and receive no punishment for such violation, then let the Supreme Court and the President and the entire Congress of the United States jump off the dome of the capitol building in Washington, D.C. They will receive their punishment when they hit the concrete below," he railed. "STAND UP for your God JESUS CHRIST and your NATION! Hang the TRAITORS to Christ and America. They are not thousands of miles away in Moscow. They are HERE amongst us!"[16]

15

THE CONJURER'S CIRCLE

In 1967 Gale began devoting the pages of *IDENTITY* to promoting the emerging tax rebellion movement and its leaders, including a convicted tax protester, Arthur Julius Porth.[1] A building contractor from Wichita, Kansas, Porth had been sentenced to five years in prison for refusing to file an income tax return or withhold taxes from his employees' paychecks. After exhausting all appeals, the nearly seventy-year-old tax protester was transferred to federal prison in Springfield, Missouri, for a psychiatric evaluation. Such a move was not uncommon when a judge was confronted by the insolence or inscrutability of a tax-protesting defendant—but the action sparked a right-wing outcry, and Bill Gale was among those who demanded Porth's release.[2] Gale's defense of tax protesters won admirers within the large and growing movement that both spread and became radicalized by his Identity and vigilante beliefs. Gale also recruited heavily from the ranks of the tax-protest movement to build the Ministry of Christ Church and, several years later, to launch the Posse Comitatus.

"As a clergyman, I am in a position to sense the attitudes of the people," Gale informed the federal judge who presided over Porth's case. Gale also claimed that Porth was a member of the Ministry of Christ Church. "Unless Mr. Porth is released at an early date, I fear that citizens will consider empanelling [sic] a Grand Jury under the authority of the Ninth Amendment, U.S. Constitution, for the purpose of indicting all officials involved. [This grand jury would] no doubt establish its rules . . . for the deputizing of its marshals for enforcement purposes," Gale threatened.[3]

Porth's legal problems were the culmination of a nearly twenty-year fight with the IRS, which started in the 1950s when he complained to the Truman administration that there was "fraud" in the Internal Revenue Service and the Federal Reserve.[4] Porth then sued the government, arguing that being forced to withhold money from his workers' paychecks made him an unpaid tax collector, which amounted to slavery and a violation of the Thirteenth Amendment. The lawsuit was dismissed and in 1957 the IRS ordered Porth to pay $4,000. Faced with a lien against his home, Porth paid part of the money and vowed to never do so again. After transferring his property to his wife's name, he embarked on a personal crusade against the income tax.[5]

In 1962, Porth began submitting incomplete federal and state tax returns, scrawling, "I plead the Fifth Amendment to the Constitution of the United States" across the top of his tax forms.[6] The declaration won him the support of the *Wichita (Kans.) Evening Eagle and Beacon*: "All Wichitans should offer their good wishes to A. J. Porth," editorialized the paper, which noted that Porth had a "unique rationale" for his actions. "If the Internal Revenue Service disagreed with the figures on his tax return, it could use them in a criminal case against him," the paper explained. "So Porth plans to fill in his name and address, leave the rest of the return blank, and stand on the Fifth Amendment guarantee against self-incrimination. . . . It cannot be prejudicial to suggest that Porth will lose his case; most protesters do. But at least he is making a run for it, as most of us never do. He deserves to be remembered for that. And if he won, wouldn't there be a scramble!" the newspaper happily observed.[7] Despite the paper's endorsement, federal courts rejected the scheme, which became popularly known as a "Fifth Amendment return."[8]

In praising Porth, the newspaper also recognized the efforts of the former governor of Utah, J. Bracken Lee. Lee, an archconservative, first spurned the IRS in the early 1950s, saying that taxes went to U.S. foreign aid, which supported America's enemies. Lee stuck to this argument throughout his twenty-year political career: first as governor, from 1949 to 1957, and then as mayor of Salt Lake City, from 1960 to 1972. The Wichita newspaper portrayed Porth and Lee as courageous iconoclasts whose acts of individual rebellion had a certain hapless charm, fated as they were for failure. Instead, there was a quietly growing tax-protest movement that would soon attract allies and followers in large numbers.

In 1952—the same year that Porth and Lee were starting down the road of tax resistance—Ralph Gwinn, a Republican congressman from New York, introduced the so-called "Liberty Amendment." Earlier opponents of taxation had focused on cutting local property taxes or putting a ceiling on federal income taxes, but Gwinn sought to abolish the income tax altogether by repealing the Sixteenth Amendment.[9] By 1964, seven states endorsed Gwinn's proposal—

Georgia, Louisiana, Mississippi, Nevada, South Carolina, Texas and Wyoming—but then it languished.[10]

By the mid-1960s, Porth was referring to himself as a "tax consultant," and he had broadened his arguments against the IRS. In addition to claiming that taxation was a form of slavery, Porth cited twenty-six other Constitutional provisions that he alleged were violated by the IRS. Among other things, he said the money he earned was not "income" because Federal Reserve notes were not redeemable in gold or silver.[11] Porth also claimed that the income tax violated Fourth Amendment prohibitions against illegal search and seizure, as well as the Fifth Amendment ban on taking property without due process and just compensation. While other tax protesters had pursued similar arguments, few did so as aggressively as Porth, whose battle with the IRS turned him into a right-wing celebrity. He cashed in on his status by publishing a manual for tax protesters and lecturing across the country. He also won fame as a tax rebel by his commitment to confrontation. Long before Bill Gale championed "citizen juries," Porth recommended arresting bureaucrats for violating the Constitution. He even drew up a form to be used on such occasions, Porth's "Official Warrant of Arrest," which he circulated widely beginning in the mid-1960s:

> For use by private persons making arrests when they have reasonable grounds to believe that the accused has committed treason, misprision of treason, conspiracy against rights of citizens, conspiracy to commit offence or to defraud United States, conspiracy to make false statements or entries generally, rebellion or insurrection, sedition, robbery, theft, blackmail, or any other felony.[12]

Porth was zealous in his attacks, but he also had a sense of humor. After advising the acting commissioner of the IRS to take a course in constitutional law, Porth requested a reward for reporting that the Federal Reserve had failed to pay income taxes since its founding in 1913—something the Bank was not required to do.

"Under Form 211 you pay informers," Porth wrote in May 1964. "I will fill this form out and hereby notify you that I wish a reward. . . . You may select your own firm of private CPA's [sic] to make the audit so I will be assured of the proper amount. However, I will wish to review their findings."[13] Later that year, Porth wrote a defiant 12-page letter to the IRS, demanding the government arrest him. It had been four years since he had filed his bogus Fifth Amendment Return.

"I do not pay Federal or State Income Tax," he wrote. "I want the Government to prosecute me for my willful failure to comply."[14] On October 21, 1965, a federal grand jury in Topeka obliged him with a five-count indictment.[15] Porth's lawyer was Jerome Daly, a fellow tax protester and soon-to-be-disbarred Minnesota attorney who also became his close friend and adviser. Daly filed his first protest return in 1965, listing only his name and occupation on the tax form and attaching a lengthy memo listing dozens of objections. Daly told the IRS he didn't understand what it meant by "income," and so couldn't pay taxes. "I'm stumped there," he claimed.[16] Daly relied on these and other arguments when he defended Porth in federal court, but the jury was unconvinced. Porth was convicted on all five counts, fined $50,000, and sentenced to thirteen years in jail.[17] The judge later canceled the fine and reduced the sentence to five years, but Porth's conviction made him a martyr in the eyes of right-wing tax protesters across the nation. While free on appeal in 1969, Porth explained his actions to an enthusiastic California audience:

"In spite of the fact that I have been defiant in not wanting to pay an income tax, it's not because I want to be a law violator. [But] I believe it became necessary to attempt to prove a point. And I believe that through the effort, people like you, people all over the United States are coming out where they didn't a few years ago and they're listening!"[18]

Porth judged correctly that his actions were helping the tax-strike movement grow, but both he and Daly wrongly predicted that the courts would vindicate them. "If people become knowledgeable of their constitutional rights and demand due process of law, the Internal Revenue Service can no longer seize a taxpayer's bank deposits. And I don't think it will be possible for the Internal Revenue Service to place a lien on someone's property," Porth predicted. Daly was even more optimistic. "As time has gone on and decisions have come out of the Supreme Court of the United States, and other Circuit Courts, I think our position has gotten better all the way along. . . . I think we've got 'em beat."

In 1969, the Eighth Circuit Court of Appeals ruled against Daly in a landmark decision invalidating the "Porth-Daly" Fifth Amendment return. In issuing its ruling, the court relied on a 1927 U.S. Supreme Court case involving a gangster, Manly S. Sullivan, who had refused to file his taxes because his income came from the sale of liquor during Prohibition and submitting the required form would have been tantamount to self-incrimination.

"[Sullivan] could not draw a conjurer's circle around the whole matter by his own declaration that to write any word upon the government blank would bring him into danger of the law," wrote Justice Oliver Wendell Holmes.[19] Citing this argument, the Eighth Circuit threw out Daly's claims, as the courts have ever since. Regardless of the ruling, tax protesters continued to rely on the Porth-Daly strategy. A decade after the Eighth Circuit invalidated Daly's arguments, the IRS received more than twenty thousand illegal tax-protest returns, nearly triple what it had received the year before.[20]

If Daly's arguments about "income" versus "property," or his invocations of presumed Fifth Amendment rights failed to derail the income tax, he had another recommendation: "I have been advising every citizen to obtain a high-powered rifle with a telescope sight on it and twenty-five hundred rounds of ammunition," he told one audience.[21] Daly was so enthusiastic about this idea that he printed it on the back of his letterhead. "I'd go to court and ask these judges that have read that on the back of the stationery and you'd be surprised at the soothing effect it has on them. It's good therapy for them," he said, only half joking.[22] With an attitude like that, it wasn't long before Daly's legal career was over. In stripping the tax-protesting attorney of his credentials, the Minnesota Supreme Court cited a number of frivolous documents Daly had filed in court, including one particularly colorful—and inflammatory—affidavit, in which he wrote: "This case involves a dispute with the Lutheran Church, Missouri-Synod, which is composed of preachers arrogating attributes of Deity to themselves in association with Papal-Jewish Hegemony, all of whom are in vortex with each other rotating and operating on a common axis sited in Hell."[23]

After Porth lost his appeals he was sent to jail in 1970. His supporters, including Bill Gale, held protest meetings, organized seminars, sent letters to the Kansas judge, and deluged the prison warden with phone calls. After serving only seventy-seven days of his five-year sentence, Porth was released on probation. Porth's actions set a new standard for militant opponents of the income tax and greatly energized the tax-rebellion movement. Prior to Porth's highly publicized battle, most tax protesters had been content to publish broadsides or agitate politically for tax repeal. But Porth established a much more personal and aggressive standard for tax resistance, and he inspired others to do the same. "Change is going to become effective when the people *demand* their rights. You're not going to get those rights by electing a new party, politically-wise. You're not going to get those rights by joining some group and all of you getting together and pushing the braver ones out to the front. You're going to get those rights when you as individuals demand your individual, constitutional rights," he said in 1969.

Porth made his demands on paper, but other tax-protest leaders preferred to do so face-to-face. Jim Scott was a Fresno, California, insurance agent and the founder of the national Tax-Rebellion Association. When IRS agents showed up at Scott's office in 1971, he met them with six witnesses, two tape recorders, a camera and a sawed-off, 12-gauge shotgun leaning against the wall. It was a story he recounted with glee. "So, all good citizens who want to avoid entrapment by these con-men, the masters of extortion, harassment, and intimidation, be counseled to use witnesses, tape recorders, camera, and visible weapons," Scott advised several hundred tax protesters meeting at the Disneyland Hotel in Los Angeles in February 1972.[24] Following Scott's advice and Porth's earlier encouragement to personally rebel, a group of tax protesters confronted a team of IRS agents in San Diego, California, several months later. Brandishing signs reading, STOP IRS TYRANNY, and shouting "America, Gestapo state!" warehouse owner John Heck and nine others were arrested after getting into a fistfight with federal agents that had seized control of Heck's warehouse.[25] The group was indicted on federal charges and became celebrated as the "San Diego Ten."[26]

In the summer of 1972, the *American Mercury* magazine devoted half of its seventy-page summer issue to "The Great Tax Strike." Although only 9,100 people subscribed to the right-wing quarterly—down from nearly 27,000 four years earlier—the *Mercury* was the voice of a much larger movement.[27] Its contributing editors included prominent racists like Henry E. Garrett, the Citizens' Councils supporter and past president of the American Psychological Association; the novelist Taylor Caldwell; well-known Holocaust denier Austin J. App; and other professional bigots.

"Mushrooming like an atomic explosion, all over the U.S. formerly-obedient tax slaves are rising in full revolt against their continued exploitation by the income tax," declared the *Mercury*.[28] "The morality and legality of the Tax Strike is beyond any question. It is made a moral imperative by the pages of time in the white man's long struggle to retain his liberty from the ambition of tyrants of all descriptions."[29]

Linking the "morality" of the Tax Strike to the "white man's struggle," the *Mercury* made explicit one of the driving forces behind the burgeoning tax-strike movement: white resentment over federal laws and programs perceived as benefiting blacks at the expense of whites. By 1968, it was obvious that Massive Resistance had failed and that the government was committed to dismantling segregation. Viewed through the eyes of white supremacists and ordinary bigots, the Civil Rights Act of 1964, the War on Poverty of the same year, and the Voting Rights Act of 1965 proved that the hard-earned tax dollars of whites would now be redistributed to blacks, whether through direct aid, political patronage, or both. The riots that rocked Los Angeles, Detroit, Newark, and other cities further solidified white resentment—and fears—about compensating blacks (legislatively or otherwise) for the ill-effects of segregation and discrimination. The declining white enthusiasm for civil rights could be measured in dwindling support for school integration and federal enforcement of nondiscrimination laws.[30] (A similar trend occurred two decades later, when racial prejudices and distrust of government led to the abandonment of the welfare state by a Democratic president and the Republican Party then succeeded in winning a majority in both houses of Congress during the 1994 midterm elections.)

Sometimes the attack on taxes openly stated these race-based concerns, and other times the arguments were camouflaged in general anti-statist, pro-constitutional rhetoric. One widely read archconservative who hammered on both themes was Martin Larson, an editorial board member of the *American Mercury* who chronicled the travails of tax protesters in his 1973 primer on the tax-resistance movement: *Tax Revolt, U.S.A.! Why and How Thousands of Patriotic Americans Refuse to Pay the Income Tax*, and its sequel six years later, *The Continuing Tax Rebellion: What Millions of Americans Are Doing to Restore Constitutional Government*.[31]

Tax Revolt, U.S.A.! was the first book to report in detail on the tax strike. Published by the far-right Liberty Lobby, Larson advanced antitax arguments in more or less populist, constitutional terms, but his opposition to the income tax was deeply rooted in his hatred of democracy, as well as his unwavering belief in white supremacy.

"The Negroes in the United States are increasing at a rate at least twice as great as the rest of the population," he warned in a 1967 article which asserted that the tax burden posed by blacks "unquestionably doomed [the] American way of life."[32] According to Larson, the majority of black women were prostitutes, whose "offspring ran wild in the streets, free to forage their food in garbage cans, and grow up to become permanent reliefers, criminals, rioters, looters, and, in turn, breeders of huge litters of additional human beings belonging to the same category."[33] Larson felt free to express these views in the pages of the *Mercury* in 1967, but when it came to churning out propaganda for a broader audience, he camouflaged his racism by focusing on the evils of central government instead.

"The federal government has become the enemy of the useful members of our society," wrote Larson in 1979. "It has degenerated into a vast system of extortion and bribery; and were it not for the fact that it transfers untold billions of hard-earned money taken by force from producers and given to many millions of non-producers and parasites, very few of the present members of Congress would or could be reelected."[34]

Such views—including veiled references to race—were firmly grounded in the ideological terrain of middle American radicalism, a phenomenon first identified by sociologist Donald Warren in his 1976 book, *The Radical Center: Middle Americans and the Politics of Alienation*.[35]

"[Middle American Radicals] are distinct in the depth of their feeling that the middle class has been seriously neglected," Warren explained, summarizing their perspective in the following statement: "The rich give in to the demands of the poor, and the middle-income people have to pay the bill.

"What this assertion implies is that there is implicit coalition, a kind of unholy alliance or, in the view of some, a conspiracy, in which groups who otherwise might seem to be at odds have joined together against the interests of the middle," Warren wrote.[36] This was exactly the thinking of the *American Mercury* in 1972 when it editorialized in favor of the tax-protest movement and declared, "The true purpose of government is *not* to plunder the productive middle class for the profit of the super-rich war criminals, the very poor welfare professionals, totally superfluous intellectuals, do-gooders and assorted leeches."[37] Larson emphasized this theme in his second book on the tax-protest movement. "The exactions demanded from the self-reliant and the largesse given the lazy, the incompetent, and the non-productive, cannot be an accident: all this MUST be the result of carefully constructed policy with long-range objectives."[38]

Such resentments gained further (and more mainstream) currency when the U.S. Supreme Court ruled in 1978 that the University of California–Davis medical school had unconstitutionally discriminated against a white student, Allan P. Bakke, because its admissions policy was designed to increase minority enrollment.[39] The decision heralded the beginning of a broadly based and powerful white backlash against affirmative action.

In addition to white resentment, the tax-protest movement derived much of its legitimacy from the delegitimation of government itself. America's failure in Vietnam and the Watergate scandal coincided with the first wave of tax protest, and both phenomena significantly eroded middle-class confidence in government and respect for political institutions. So, too, did the rise of the counterculture movements and the political left in the 1960s and early 1970s, which repeatedly emphasized distrust of government and the importance of challenging authority. The editors of the *American Mercury* made this point in 1972, but they used more colorful language. "[Left-wing] planners, plunderers and perverters . . . destroy[ed] the credibility of the government for the youth [and] for the taxpayer." This seemed ironic to the *Mercury*, which noted that young revolutionists who promoted "the putrid philosophy of the *untermenschen*" ultimately produced "a quite different philosophy in the productive, decent middle class of culture-bearers."[40]

Another dynamic driving the tax-protest movement was simple economics. By the late 1970s, spiraling inflation, sharply rising interest rates, and a deepening recession made millions of Americans anxious about their economic situation, and some found taxes an attractive target for their frustrations and fears. These concerns were manifest in many ways, but nowhere as dramatically as with passage, on June 6, 1978, of California's Proposition 13, which slashed state property taxes a whopping 57 percent.

While men like A. J. Porth preferred to make their pitch to Posse Comitatus activists and gun-toting militants, others, like Irwin Schiff, concentrated on spreading the same message to millions of Americans much closer to the political mainstream. Schiff, "America's leading untax expert," as he sometimes called himself, was a fast-talking insurance and financial consultant from Hamden, Connecticut, who parroted Porth's arguments about the Fifth Amendment and how paper money invalidated the income tax. "I only received Federal Reserve units, not dollars. I received no lawful money upon which a tax can be collected," he once told a judge.[41] In addition to his talents as an amateur magician, Schiff skillfully exploited the broadcast media's obsession for controversial content. His appearances on network television shows and radio broadcasts over the past twenty-five years have reached a huge national audience.

In 1976, Schiff, then forty-seven, wrote *The Biggest Con: How the Government Is Fleecing You*, and his second book, published six years later, *How Anyone Can Stop Paying Income Taxes*, earned him at least $135,000 in royalties over the next two years and another $85,000 in the decade that followed.[42] Schiff authored six other books, including his most recent, *The Federal Mafia and How It Operates*, which he wrote while in federal prison.[43]

As for who would join the struggle against the evils of federal taxation, Martin Larson said it would be middle-class radicals. "[T]he middle class can emerge victorious in its battle with the central, all-engulfing tyranny," he wrote in 1979.[44] At the head of that fight, according to Larson, were men like A. J. Porth, "America's best-known and most active tax-rebel;" Ardie McBrearty, founder of the United States Taxpayers Union; and Arizona patriot Marvin Cooley.

Cooley, a former melon farmer–turned–constitutionalist freedom fighter from Mesa, Arizona, had been an organizer for the John Birch Society until his tax-protest activities got him expelled. He once marched into the local IRS office and demanded to know the definition of a "dollar."[45] Cooley filled out his 1971 federal tax return as follows:

"I will no longer pay for the destruction of my country, family, and self. Damn tyranny! Damn the Federal Reserve liars and thieves! Damn all pettifogging, oath-breaking U.S. attorneys and judges. . . . I will see you all in Hell and shed my blood before I will be robbed of one more dollar to finance a national policy of treason, plunder, and corruption."[46] Cooley, a conservative Mormon and the father of ten children, had little formal education, but he wrote a right-wing best-seller. His 1972 book, *The Big Bluff*, which described the struggles of his fellow tax protester, W. Vaughn Ellsworth, and contained sample letters and copies of his tax returns, placed him in high demand on the far-right speaking circuit. Cooley's "tax avoidance" seminars were usually packed and he, like Porth, soon became a star in the protest movement. In December 1971, Cooley, forty-one, and a crowd of two hundred supporters shut down the court-ordered sale of a fruit stand that was being auctioned to pay delinquent taxes.[47] Wearing badges that read, NO WARRANT; NO TRIAL; NO JURY; NO COURT ORDER: JUST PLAIN TYRANNY! and singing patriotic songs, the protesters drowned out two sheriff's deputies who were calling for bids. Led by Cooley, they lectured the lawmen for forty minutes and threatened them with "citizen's arrest."[48] Although the crowd stopped short of taking the deputies into custody, they did block the sale.

"Cutting these legislative oath-breakers off at the hip-pockets by challenging their unlawful tax-collection procedures is going to do more to wake them up to the middle-class rebellion than would a million petitions and resolutions," said Cooley who was convicted and sentenced to prison for tax evasion in 1973, and again in 1989.[49] Cooley's book and lectures did much to push many former Birch Society members like himself further to the right, and he also helped plant the seeds for more violent activities through his association with Robert Jay Matthews, the founder of the neo-Nazi criminal gang, The Order.

In 1970, Bob Matthews was seventeen and still living with his parents in Phoenix when Cooley awakened him to the message of tax protest. Impressed with the young man's commitment—Matthews had purchased his first copy of Robert Welch's *Blue Book* when he was just eleven years old—Cooley made him sergeant at arms for some meetings.[50] Inspired by what he'd learned, Matthews listed ten nonexistent dependents on his W-4 tax form in 1973. This was a common tactic used by tax protesters to minimize withholding from their paychecks, but Matthews's scheme was destined to fail from the start, considering the fact that no teenager could have that many children. His tax form also showed that he was unmarried. Matthews was arrested, convicted on misdemeanor charges, and got off with just six months' probation. He then left Arizona and moved to Metaline Falls, Washington, a tiny town in the northeastern corner of the state, less than twenty miles from the Canadian border. Matthews may have departed the tax-protest movement, but it was an important stepping-stone in his political development, which ultimately led him to embrace hardened visions of right-wing revolution.

One year after Matthews took his young adopted son to be baptized by Aryan Nations leader Richard Butler, he founded The Order in 1983. Also known as the Brüders Schweigen (the Silent Brotherhood), its members robbed banks, counterfeited money, murdered critics and fellow white supremacists, and stockpiled an impressive arsenal of weapons, all in pursuit of Matthews's scheme to incite a race war and overthrow the government.[51] In early December 1984, federal agents tracked down Matthews and surrounded him at a remote hideaway on Whidbey Island, in Puget Sound, near Seattle. Unable to kill or capture him after a thirty-six-hour machine-gun battle, an FBI SWAT team lobbed flares and tear gas into the dwelling, setting it ablaze. Matthews was burned alive; his Brüders Schweigen medallion melted into his chest. It was December 8, 1984. Shortly before he was killed, Matthews wrote a four-page letter, summarizing his involvement in the radical right and his early experiences in the tax-protest movement.

> I left Arizona and the tax-rebellion when I was twenty. I left not out of fear of the IRS or because of submission to their tyranny, but because I was thoroughly disgusted with the American people. I maintained then as I do now, that our people have devolved into some of the most cowardly, sheepish, degenerates that have ever littered the face of this planet.[52]

Another tax protester who followed Matthews's path to armed radicalism was Ardie McBrearty. McBrearty also had once been enamored of Robert Welch, but by 1972 he, too, had become disillusioned with the John Birch Society. "The Tax Rebellion accomplishes two things that the JBS is incapable of with their present approaches," McBrearty wrote in an "open letter" to Robert Welch in the *American Mercury*. "(1) We get people involved by their commitment of the act of rebelling. . . . (2) We attract people of all persuasions because of one common bond, money. . . . To sign a membership application and mail twelve dollars is easy compared to signing a blank 1040 with protest and mailing it to the IRS bandits. Once a person has accepted our logic and has plunged into the rebellion, we have a dedicated and eager student activist; not just another timid patriot. . . . Our generation is getting older and fewer, so I say, 'If there is to be a battle sir, let it begin here.' "[53]

Two years later, McBrearty established the United States Taxpayers' Union, which was dedicated to repealing not only the Sixteenth Amendment but also the Occupational Safety and Health Act, consumer protection statutes, gun-control laws, and other "unconstitutional" legislation. Other founders of USTU, as its supporters commonly called it, included Francis Gillings, a California Posse militant whose armed skirmish with sheriff's deputies in 1975 brought him and the Posse both fame and ignominy. The Taxpayer Union's great expectations and exploits were thoroughly chronicled in the pages of *Tax Strike News*, a new publication that had displaced the *Mercury* as the voice of the movement. Published in southern California by A. J. Lowery and edited by his wife, Anita Kerns, the sixteen-page tabloid publicized the meetings and seminars of the tax rebellion, and recorded the legal problems of the movement's missionaries and believers in scrupulous detail. In addition to attacking the income tax, *Tax Strike News* criticized busing, the United Nations, and harmless attempts at improving government efficiency, like the system of Federal Regional Councils established by President Richard Nixon, which Lowery and Kerns viewed as part of the plot to impose "one-world government."[54]

But even this platform became too tame for McBrearty, who had become an Identity believer. In the early 1980s he was recruited by Bob Matthews to set up a security system for The Order. McBrearty, a construction engineer and electrician, used his skills to screen potential Brüders Schweigen recruits with "voice stress tests" he claimed he first developed to ferret out undercover agents when he was in the tax-protest movement.[55] McBrearty's enthusiasm for mayhem waned following Matthews's death in December 1984. He and twenty-three other Order members were indicted by a federal grand jury in Seattle on April 12, 1985, on charges of racketeering and conspiracy. McBrearty was the only defendant to testify against his fellow revolutionaries. Despite taking the witness stand, he was convicted and sentenced to forty years in prison. He and other members of The Order were subsequently indicted on charges of sedition but they were acquitted by a federal jury in Fort Smith, Arkansas, in 1988.

Men like Robert Matthews and Ardie McBrearty began their political journey as tax protesters and ended them as armed, right-wing revolutionaries, imprisoned or dead. But more than a decade before Robert Matthews and the crimes of The Order made headlines across America, right-wing activists were taking up Bill Gale's radical idea of the posse comitatus and planting seeds of hate and violence within the tax-protest movement.

16

VOLUNTEER CHRISTIAN POSSES

Bill Gale first raised the issue of the posse comitatus in his 1957 "indictment" of President Eisenhower, but a series of obstacles and distractions prevented him from elaborating on the concept for the next fourteen years. Immediately following the Little Rock crisis, Gale was consumed with his 1958 Constitution Party campaign for governor. After that defeat he focused his energies—again with scant success—on forming the California Rangers and the Christian Defense League. Divorce and remarriage followed, after which Gale devoted himself to building the Ministry of Christ Church and distributing his taped sermons. Finally, in an undated article in his *IDENTITY* newsletter, published during the first half of 1971, Gale resumed his interest in the posse comitatus. In an article titled "The Constitutional Republic," written under his pen name, "Colonel Ben Cameron," Gale observed that "[since] the Governors and Legislatures of the Sovereign States have failed to repudiate the unlawful acts" of the federal government, it was the duty of the people to form a posse comitatus. Gale's article took up eighteen of the newsletter's twenty pages, although it contained only twenty-seven lines specifically discussing the possse comitatus—the rest of the text was devoted to listing various government misdeeds that he said justified taking "vigilante action."[1]

Gale recycled the same ideas in the next issue, but he reorganized the text under the title "Guide for Volunteer Christian Posses."[2] The article began: "In the formation of this constitutional republic, the county has always been and remains to this day, the TRUE seat of the government for the citizens who are the inhabitants thereof. The County Sheriff is the only legal law enforcement officer in these United States of America." The sheriff could mobilize all men between the ages of eighteen and forty-five who were in good health and not in the military, while others could volunteer, Gale explained. "The title of this body is the Posse Comitatus."[3] And what if the local sheriff did not wish to form a posse? He simply would have no choice, declared Gale, who had little patience for lawmen who were "lackeys of the Courts." If a sheriff refused to protect citizens from unlawful government officials, "he should be removed from office promptly."[4] Alternatively, the citizens could form their own posse without the sheriff's help, Gale noted.

Gale cited four "major violations of the Constitution and Natural Law" which he said justified the formation of local posses. They were: (1) federal intervention in education and the schools; (2) the Federal Reserve System; (3) the graduated income tax; and (4) "unconstitutional" actions of the judiciary. Although Gale did not specifically mention integration or school busing, the racial imperative to maintain segregation was clearly implied. "County Sheriffs must be advised of the instances where unlawful acts of officials or agencies of government are committed in respect to education and the schools," he wrote. If the sheriff violated "Natural Law" or the Constitution, the posse had the right to take action, and to do so fully armed. "Arrests may be made," and the "criminal" handed over to the county sheriff for "trial by a Citizen Jury empaneled by the Sheriff from the citizens of the local jurisdiction. (NOT by the Courts as is current procedure . . . which has no basis under law)."[5] Like the bogus citizen's-arrest warrant developed by the tax-protest pioneer Arthur Porth, Gale suggested taking custody of government officials who violated the Constitution. Although Gale didn't explain how to put them on trial, he graphically described how to carry out their execution: " 'He shall be removed by the Posse to a populated intersection of streets in the township and at high noon be hung there by the neck, the body remaining until sundown, as an example to those who would subvert the law.' "[6] It was a phrase that would be cited often by law enforcement, the news media, and watchdog groups over the next twenty years, and did much to discredit the Posse Comitatus.

Gale called his article a "guide." But apart from recommending that all volunteers conduct research on the posse comitatus at their local law library, he didn't offer many practical suggestions for how to actually set up a local group. That help came when Gale officially announced the formation of "the United States Christian Posse Association" in 1972.[7]

"Upon application by a minimum number of seven Christian citizens, all of who [sic] must be residents of the County in which the Posses [sic] is to be organized, a Charter will be granted by the United States Christian Posses [sic] Association." Gale enjoyed impressing potential followers by sprinkling his blueprint with officious, military jargon: "[A]uthorized organizers" should elect a Posse "Commander" and "Assistant Commanders" in the areas of personnel, intelligence and investigations, operations and communications, and logistics and supply. "Detailed instructions pertaining to the duties of the above officers will be forwarded to all concerned by National HQ," promised Gale, who admonished members in advance that "no nonsense" would be tolerated. "Insincerety [*sic*] and trickery will be settled OUT OF COURT," he intoned.[8]

Gale's decision to launch the Posse Comitatus came less than a year after the death, in October 1970, of Wesley Swift who, at age fifty-seven, had collapsed in the waiting room of a Mexican clinic while awaiting treatment for kidney disease and diabetes.[9] Formerly friends, the two men had parted bitterly some five years earlier, and Gale's appraisal of his former colleague had grown harsher with time. Gale criticized Swift for his poor organizational abilities—although Gale's were far worse—and for what he said was Swift's lack of knowledge of the "money system," the Constitution and the law.[10] Gale had once hoped to acquire Swift's congregation, but he had so alienated Swift's followers (he referred to them derisively as "Swift-ites," and chided them for their "worship [of] a man rather than Jesus Christ!")[11] that they never would accept him. Instead Richard Butler seized Swift's pulpit in Lancaster. But the entertaining and bombastic Swift was a hard act to follow and, with the notable exception of Swift's daughter, the congregation dwindled to a coterie of Butler's friends and followers.

In 1974 Butler relocated his group to Idaho, where he purchased twenty acres of piney woods and a two-story farmhouse just outside Hayden Lake.[12] He constructed a chapel large enough to seat one hundred people and began holding regular church services. Within several years, the property was transformed into a compound and included a meeting hall, kitchen, office, printing press, several small cabins, a guard tower, and a trailer that was used as a school for young children. In 1977 Butler dubbed his acreage the national headquarters of the Aryan Nations, the political arm of his Church of Jesus Christ Christian.[13]

Butler's actions after Swift's death upset Gale, who felt he should have had first dibs on Swift's pulpit, and they, too, had a falling-out. Gale was especially perturbed because it was he who had recruited Butler into the Identity movement in the first place: It was about 1962 and Butler, then forty-four, was living in Whittier and working as an aeronautical engineer for Lockheed. An admirer of Adolf Hitler and Senator Joseph McCarthy, Butler became excited when California lawmaker Louis Francis proposed an amendment to the state constitution to bar communists from state jobs and elected office. Butler took up the cause and was invited to speak at American Legion Signal Hill Post 490 where Gale was busily recruiting for the California Rangers. Butler's speech wasn't a great success, but Gale invited him home for several all-night indoctrination sessions. "I gave him Identity—the Bible message," Gale declared proudly, who then took Butler and his wife to see Wesley Swift.[14]

In addition to the death of Swift in 1970—which may have spurred Gale to strike out on his own—there were other events that contributed to the emergence and growth of the Posse Comitatus. The 1970 conviction of Minutemen founder Robert DePugh on charges of illegal firearms possession left a void of leadership and a small but militant band of followers looking for a new organizational home.[15] Many of them found it in the Posse Comitatus. By the early 1970s, thousands of former and disaffected members of the John Birch Society also sought an outlet for their militant beliefs in the Posse. But beyond the inner circle of the Ministry of Christ Church, Gale's first Posse recruits came from the ranks of the tax-protest movement.

The first tax protester to invoke Gale's Posse Comitatus was George Lee Kindred, of rural Pinckney, Michigan, outside Ann Arbor. A retired farmer with silver hair and a ruddy complexion, Kindred had been a fan of President Franklin Roosevelt in his youth. As an adult, however, he joined the hard right, became an Identity believer, and signed up with the Minutemen in the 1960s.[16] In 1972, Michigan tax officials began investigating Kindred and a colleague, James W. Freed. When both men refused to produce their financial records, they spent six months in jail for contempt of court.

Kindred and Freed had a long history of involvement in right-wing causes, and the endorsement of paramilitary activism came easily to them. Disillusioned with the 1968 Wallace for President campaign, they became active in the Michigan Patriotic Party—the political arm of DePugh's Minutemen. By then DePugh was a federal fugitive, labeled "armed and dangerous" by the FBI, and Kindred's newsletter, *The Patriot*, carried letters written by DePugh while he was on the lam. Kindred's newsletter also advocated "Total Resistance" and he warned readers that black militants would send terror squads into white suburbs and rural areas to create chaos. "DO NOT REGISTER OR SURRENDER YOUR FIREARMS—REGISTER COMMUNISTS INSTEAD!" Kindred declared in October 1968. Following this advice, Freed soon found himself facing criminal charges for refusing to register his thirty-shot, .45-caliber, semiautomatic "Spitfire," which the Bureau of Alcohol, Tobacco and Firearms classified as a machine gun.[17]

After Freed and Kindred were arrested in 1972 on tax charges, supporters of the pair were inspired by Gale's Posse instructions and published notices declaring they had impaneled a grand jury "in accordance with the Law of POSSE COMITATUS and the CHRISTIAN COMMON LAW [*sic*]," and charged the state judge who had sentenced the two men with violating his oath of office.[18]

"The Citizen's Posse of Ingham County is hereby delegated as the lawful enforcement authority to insure compliance with this directive," their October 1972 call to arms commanded. Then, quoting directly from Gale's instructions, the group threatened to hang the officials responsible for Kindred and Freed's persecution.[19]

One month after Kindred's posse supporters issued their warning, *Tax Strike News* reprinted Bill Gale's "Guide for Volunteer Christian Posses," albeit without attribution. Underscoring Gale's recommendation for vigilante action, the article was accompanied by the silhouetted image of a dangling corpse.[20] Gale's "Posse" guide had been reprinted a year earlier by the *National Chronicle*—a tabloid read largely by Identity believers—but its appearance in *Tax Strike News* brought Gale's message to a much larger and more politically diverse audience.[21] Local Posse groups would soon spring up across the nation, catching the attention of local sheriffs, curious journalists, the public, and the FBI.

17

THE POSSE *BLUE BOOK*

In 1972, Bill and Roxanne Gale purchased one hundred acres in rural Mariposa, California, more than two hundred and fifty miles northeast of Los Angeles, on the outskirts of Yosemite National Park. They named their property "the Manasseh Ranch," after Gale's belief that America's Christian founders were descendants of the ancient Hebrew tribe of Manasseh.[1] The couple promoted the Mariposa compound pretentiously as both the national headquarters of the Ministry of Christ Church and the Identity movement, although Bill and Roxanne remained in Glendale where Gale preached regularly to his congregation.[2]

During one sermon, Gale spoke about his fight with local officials over whether the church property could be taxed (he had tried to claim a religious exemption) and urged his audience to "get ready for a declaration of war! . . . And if you don't have a gun, bring some rope! Because there's going to be one tax collector removed from office!" Taxes didn't pay the costs of government, Gale explained, but were instead used to redeem useless Federal Reserve notes. "In other words, turn it over to the international Jew bankers," he yelled. Attacking communists and tax collectors was par for the course, but Gale also had a bad habit of denouncing his fellow activists for rejecting the Identity message. He also refused to attend meetings of most other right-wing groups because— as he put it—they were led by people who were "blind."

"Let them come *here*," he hollered.[3] But few ever did, and Gale relied largely on his tape ministry to spread the word. Once every two weeks, Bill and Roxanne transferred his sermons to seven-inch reel-to-reel tapes and mailed them across the country.[4] It was in Portland, Oregon, among a small group of tax protesters and Identity adherents, that Gale's Posse message found its most energetic missionary and true believer: Henry Lamont "Mike" Beach, the former owner of a small company that repaired dry-cleaning equipment.

Beach, seventy, had been a leader of William Dudley Pelley's pro-Hitler Silver Shirt Legion of America during World War II, and his activities in Oregon had led to an investigation of him by the army. After dropping out of right-wing politics for the next three decades, Beach retired, sold his business, and latched on to Bill Gale's Posse Comitatus. By 1973, he had decided to devote himself full-time to the cause.

Beach stole the text of Gale's "Posse" guide and republished it as his own under the imprimatur of the Citizens Law Enforcement and Research Committee, or CLERC, a group he created out of thin air. Beach called his tract the "Posse *Blue Book*," perhaps hoping to capitalize on the Birch Society publication of the same name. But where Robert Welch's volume was more than 150 pages long, Beach's was just a slim sixteen. Small and oddly sized, at four by six inches, its cover featured a simple but compelling logo: the words SHERIFF'S POSSE COMITATUS, printed inside a circle superimposed over the outline of a five-pointed sheriff's star. Recognizing that tax protesters would be his most receptive audience, Beach printed the phrase *The United States of America was founded as a protest against taxation* on the inside of the back cover.[5]

The text of the *Blue Book* was lifted word-for-word from Gale's *IDENTITY* newsletter, beginning with the first article written by Gale in 1971.[6] Beach's publication exactly repeated Gale's definition of the posse comitatus, reiterated the list of government abuses that Gale said justified the formation of local vigilante groups, and attacked the courts for subverting the constitution. The *Blue Book* concluded with Gale's instructions for hanging public officials at "high noon."[7]

Under the heading "Posse Charter Information" the *Blue Book* explained that Beach's Citizens Law Enforcement and Research Committee was "in the process of organizing a Citizens Posse in every county in the United States, with every able-bodied patriotic male of good character, who is interested in the preservation of law and order, becoming a member." Beach offered to mail prospective members Posse charters requiring the signatures of "seven male Christians, interested in the preservation of our constitutional form of government."[8] Along with the charters he distributed, Beach circulated forms designed by Gale to gather information about law enforcement in counties where charters were requested, including the race and religion of the local sheriff.[9] Gale, his ministry, and his manifesto received no credit at any point. The plagiarism was total.

Gale's main goal was to spread the Posse message but Mike Beach was intent on merchandizing the Posse as well. He sold the *Blue Book* for twenty-five cents and asked for three dollars from each of seven charter Posse members. In one

"Dear Patriot" letter that accompanied these early mailings, Beach offered members a "CHARTER CERTIFICATE . . . 'suitable for framing,' " signed personally by Beach as "National Chairman."[10] Beach later sold car-door decals, Posse badges, and cassette tapes of speeches given by tax-protest leaders.[11] Although the charters were a moneymaking scheme, they caught on with rank-and-file members of the budding Posse. Ironically, though many of them despised the government, they desperately sought the legitimacy that they hoped would come with filing such officious-looking documents at the county courthouse.

Beach also instructed readers of the *Blue Book* to raise the profile of their new movement as much as possible: "Upon filing your charter, you should get out a news release and endeavor to get some publicity. [But d]on't expect too much from the newspapers," he cautioned. "Just remember, bad news is better than no news. It will make people aware of your existance [*sic*]."[12] One local Posse group that scrupulously followed his advice was in Lane County, Oregon, about one hundred miles south of Portland. With headquarters in Eugene, it became one of the first local chapters chartered by the Citizens Law Enforcement and Research Committee, in October 1973.[13] Its chairman was Dean Kennedy, a thirty-three-year-old former music teacher with a master's degree from the University of Oregon. A professed admirer of Hitler, Kennedy had been a member of the John Birch Society but dropped out after complaining that it had been infiltrated by the Illuminati.[14] True to Beach's instructions, Kennedy's Posse group filed its charter with the county recorder and paid the two-dollar registration fee using only "lawful money"—eight silver quarters.[15] Within days Kennedy was giving interviews, making his group's purpose known. Calling the Constitution "the embodiment of Anglo-Saxon common law," Kennedy told the Eugene *Valley News* that the Posse needed "a force of several hundred persons immediately."[16] Politicians who had gone astray would be arrested and turned over to the sheriff for trial, he warned. Kennedy also bragged that he had established a secret citizens' grand jury "to take sworn testimony pertaining to corruption and subversion by any agency of government or by individuals."[17] One instance that would merit the use of force by the Posse, Kennedy explained, would be if IRS agents entered a citizen's home without a search warrant.[18] In further fulfillment of Beach's instructions, Kennedy's group notified the county sheriff, David Burks, that he was the only legal law enforcement officer in the county and was bound by his oath of office to stop the IRS from enforcing the income tax.[19] The letter to the sheriff also contained the usual racist and (coded) anti-Semitic paranoia:

> The toadies that grovel at the feet of the parasitical banking fraternity occupy the seats of power in the land; in government, industry, and the academy. . . . They and their masters are PARASITES and must have a host to live upon. . . . Is it possible that we, men of the West, members of the only race that has had the intelligence and discipline to master

many of the powers of nature, [are] too stupid to preserve our race and civilization?[20]

Kennedy also headed the local chapter of the National Association to Keep and Bear Arms (NAKBA), a militant anti-gun-control group based in Medford, Oregon, which was quick to embrace the Posse cause. One month after setting up the Lane County Posse, Kennedy told readers of the NAKBA newsletter how to do the same.[21] The following issue of *Armed Citizen News* carried a banner headline—"NAKBA TO SUPPORT POSSE COMITATUS NATIONWIDE!"—and called for the "immediate organization of literally hundreds of citizen posses from coast-to-coast."[22] Like so many other articles in the right-wing press that promoted the Posse Comitatus, it relied extensively on the material originally written by Bill Gale, but was published entirely without attribution.[23]

Beach's rip-off and commercialization of the Posse annoyed Gale, who accused Beach of turning his idea into a "sideshow," but he also grudgingly gave his rival credit—though not by name—for spreading the word: "Some plagiarists up around Oregon, they stole the material and put some other material in with it—which was erroneous by the way—but at least it got it out."[24] Gale's wife, Roxanne, was angrier. "Beach snatched it up after Bill put it out there, just as soon as he saw it," she fumed, accusing Beach of just wanting to "make a buck." She added that Gale was aghast at Beach's instructions to Posse members that they print their names "plainly legible" and file their local charters at the county courthouse.[25] This suggestion also angered George Kindred, the Michigan tax protester whose experience with the Minutemen had taught him the importance of clandestine activities. "Anytime you have a national organization and they want to destroy it, they cut off the head!" Kindred told one meeting of Posse sympathizers. "Membership lists should *never* be published."[26] Kindred was right, of course, as the lists were a veritable treasure trove for the FBI, journalists, and others who were tracking the growing Posse movement.

Beach was not oblivious to the problem of government spying or agents provocateurs.[27] But from his experience as a right-wing Silver Shirt in the 1940s, Beach also understood the importance of building an influential and well-organized group. Thwarted thirty years earlier in his attempt to advance Hitlerism in America, Beach saw Gale's Posse Comitatus as a promising replacement. And if the effort provided him with fifteen minutes of fame, so much the better. Although Gale was justifiably angry with Beach for stealing his ideas, the fact is that Gale could not have popularized the Posse as successfully as did Beach. In addition to poor administrative skills—especially his lack of interest in maintaining membership lists and keeping track of money—Gale often treated his followers with condescension and contempt. Though Gale was amiable and charismatic (like his father), his arrogance often undermined his organizing efforts. Though Beach's involvement with the Posse lasted only a few years, he still played a critical leadership role in packaging and distributing Gale's ideas. And given his early political experiences, his attraction to the Posse Comitatus is easy to understand.

Like Bill Gale, Beach was greatly influenced by the anti-Semitic politics of 1940s-era fascists and Christian Nationalists. Thirteen years older than Gale, Beach had been directly involved in the struggles of pro-Nazi groups during World War II, while Gale did not begin his career until the height of the Cold War a decade later. Both men held unorthodox religious beliefs: Gale was a believer in Christian Identity, and Beach followed the personal brand of metaphysical spiritualism invented by William Dudley Pelley.

Beach was born in 1903, in western Nebraska, and arrived in the small settlement of Vale, Oregon, when he was five years old.[28] The oldest of three children, he spent the bulk of his childhood and teenage years in the sparsely populated "empty quarter" of southeastern Oregon. After completing all but six months of high school, he moved to the booming lumber town of Bend, but stayed only a year before settling in Portland.[29] By the time he was twenty-eight, Beach was married, the father of an infant daughter, and making his living as a mechanic, servicing laundry and dry-cleaning equipment. Eight years later and just two months after the Nazi invasion of Czechoslovakia, Beach joined Pelley's Silver Shirts and became a leader of the pro-Hitler group in Oregon.[30]

As the son of a New England Methodist minister, William Dudley Pelley was a somewhat unlikely candidate to lead one of the largest openly pro-Nazi groups in America. But he also became a Vermont newspaper editor, a novelist, a Hollywood screenwriter, and a well-known writer of pulp fiction before he experienced a "clairaudient" episode one night in May 1928 and reported conversations with the souls of the dead.[31] Metaphysical experiences over the next four years further "unlocked" Pelley's "mental powers," and led him to Asheville, North Carolina, where he promoted himself and his eclectic theology. On January 31, 1933, the day after Hitler became chancellor of Germany, he founded the Silver Shirt Legion of America.[32] Although Pelley claimed twenty-five thousand members and seventy-five thousand sympathizers, actual membership in the Silver Shirts probably never exceeded fifteen thousand. Pelley's avid followers wore shirts emblazoned with an oversized scarlet *L* across the left breast signifying *Love, Loyalty, and Liberation*, as they denounced President Roosevelt, calling him a Jew, and praised Hitler as an enemy of communism. The agitations of Pelley's group concerned government authorities and others who feared the Silver Shirts might emerge as a fascist fifth column in America. Pelley's rantings gave them good reason:

"I propose, from this date onward, to direct an aggressive campaign that shall arouse America's Gentile masses to a wholesale and drastic ousting of every radical-minded Jew from United States soil!" Pelley declared in 1938.[33] He also pledged to establish "the fullest and friendliest understandings and international relationships with all rightist and anticommunist nations abroad—particularly Germany, Austria, Italy, Spain, and Japan."[34] Silver Shirt membership was strongest in the Pacific Northwest, which was Mike Beach's territory, and Beach was proud of his involvement. "Nobody could join [in Oregon] without my permission," Beach bragged years later, alleging that federal officials had conspired unsuccessfully to have him lobotomized because of his political views.[35] The claim was untrue, of course, but the government did keep him under close surveillance.

Beach first caught the attention of authorities in 1941 when the Portland Police Department, suspecting wartime disloyalty, began to relay information to the FBI.[36] Later that year he applied for membership in the Guard Patrol, a volunteer civil-defense group organized by the Portland Police Department. Beach said he joined out of patriotism, but it is much more likely that he was following instructions that Pelley had issued, encouraging members of his paramilitary Silver Rangers to get themselves "sworn in as a deputy sheriff, deputy U.S. marshal, deputy constable, or special police officer."[37] Long before Beach became fascinated by the idea of organizing the Posse Comitatus—and stole Bill Gale's ideas—he had sought legitimacy and access to guns through an officially sanctioned group. At first Beach's application slipped through and was approved. But the Anti-Defamation League had pro-Hitler activists under observation and its complaints caused the Portland police to revoke Beach's credentials.

Pressure on American pro-Nazi groups intensified after the outbreak of war in Europe, and Pelley supposedly disbanded the Silver Shirts in 1940 to evade scrutiny, but neither Pelley's critics nor the government was fooled. After the Japanese bombed Pearl Harbor, army intelligence launched a thorough investigation of Beach and other leaders of the Silver Shirts whom they considered dangerous to military security. In May 1942, Pelley and two colleagues were indicted for sedition as a result of antigovernment statements that had been published in Pelley's magazine, *The Galilean*.[38] For example: "There is not the slightest enthusiasm anywhere in all America for this war—with the sole exception of the Jewish ghetto sections of our swollen cities. And those ghettos will not fight. Gentile boys from factory and farm must do the fighting." Of the British, Pelley said they had "indulged in a long line of retrogression and demoralization by Sodomic fornication with the Mongolic-Assyria-Jewish strain, and apparently are now paying the penalty for such violation of divine law."[39]

Regardless of the First Amendment, Pelley and his codefendants were convicted of sedition, and Pelley was sentenced to fifteen years in prison.[40] Like many Silver Shirts, Beach contributed to Pelley's defense, but he and other leaders knew the organization could not last much longer.[41] In the months leading up to Pelley's indictment, Beach established a new group in Portland with an innocuous-sounding name to promote Pelley's agenda and the Silver Shirt cause. He called it "the Research Club." Years later, when he promoted the Posse Comitatus, under the umbrella of the Citizens Law Enforcement and Research Committee, the name of this new group echoed his earlier effort.

Beach didn't get very far with the Research Club before he received an ominous notice from the army, threatening to banish him from the West Coast and notifying him that a special army panel—an Individual Exclusion Hearing Board—would consider his case.[42] Beach was among the first wave of approximately one hundred and fifty "pressure cases" brought by the army in August and September 1942 against individuals regarded as "important links in the chain of [pro-German and pro-Italian] subversive groups."[43] The authority for exclusion orders against individuals like Beach was grounded in the same executive order issued earlier that year by President Roosevelt authorizing the forced relocation of approximately 120,000 Japanese-Americans from California, Washington, and Oregon to ten concentration camps—benignly labeled "relocation centers"—in the western deserts of the United States.[44]

But Beach was a scrappy character. Angry at being booted out of the Guard Patrol, he became enraged by what he deemed government harassment. On February 13, 1943, Beach filed suit against the army, claiming he had been "deprived of his rights and liberties" and subjected to an "inquisition" by the Exclusion Board.[45] Although Beach was on shaky ground, given the wartime political and legal climate, it was a clever move and received prominent coverage in the Portland *Oregonian*.[46] Other lawsuits had been filed challenging the constitutionality of the detention of Japanese-Americans, but Beach's action was the first on the West Coast to specifically challenge the army's Individual Exclusion Order program.[47] Beach's lawsuit was dismissed on technical grounds, but he won his battle nonetheless. Although some army investigators argued passionately about the need to press the case, others in the chain of command concluded that a negative ruling by the courts would be worse than letting the matter drop. The fact that Allied forces were finally overwhelming their enemies also diminished the imperative to pursue suspected fascist agents. On March 17, 1943, Beach was notified that he would not be excluded inland. Although Beach had prevailed against the government, the experience left him fearful and bittered. He divorced, and retired from the movement. It took him thirty years to overcome his trepidations and rejoin the ranks of the radical right, but when he did, he did so with enthusiasm.

"We recommend that you hold weekly meetings for your members . . . then one meeting a month, leave open to the public. DO NOT CONDUCT POSSE BUSINESS AT THE PUBLIC MEETING!" Beach instructed his followers in 1974. "Never let it be known how many members you have. Twenty-five can be just as effective as five hundred when you keep them guessing. Not knowing how many of you there are, makes the TRAITORS more afraid of the influence you have." Beach did exactly this, telling conflicting stories and wildly exaggerating the size of his following. In interviews given less than two weeks apart in February 1974, Beach first said the Posse had one hundred thousand members in fifty states, and then revised the figure downward to thirty-six.[48] A year later he upped the membership numbers to five hundred thousand.[49] However, according to the FBI, the Posse had no more than ten thousand members at the time.

The Bureau had been keeping tabs on the Posse Comitatus since 1972, when its Portland office first noted the existence of an "organization calling itself Identity, or alternatively the Portland Posse Comitatus . . . [an] association of long-time Right Wing extremists . . . preaching hate against the Negroes and the Jews, and calling for the repudiation and overthrow of the existing law enforcement and judicial systems of this nation."[50] The FBI opened an investigation but concluded it eight months later, describing the Posse in curiously benign terms, saying Posse views on the constitutionality of law enforcement and the IRS were simply "unusual." "Group members not considered threat to community," concluded one report in April 1973.[51] A year later, the Portland FBI issued another classified report surveying Beach's Sheriff's Posse Comitatus, which it referred to in government shorthand as "the SPC." That June 1974 assessment noted that the Posse had grown to include six county chapters in Oregon, and others in at least eight states: Idaho, Michigan, Alaska, Washington State, Ohio, Wisconsin, Virginia, and Arkansas.

Describing the Posse as a "loose-knit, nationwide organization," the FBI labeled Dean Kennedy's Lane County chapter as the "most active to date."[52] But despite Kennedy's public statements and views—he told one newspaper that Hitler's *Mein Kampf* was one of his favorite books—the FBI report asserted that the Sheriff's Posse Comitatus was not "anti-semitic [sic] or anti-black in its pronouncements." Likewise, Beach's organization did not exhibit "any tendencies of following the Identity Group lead in getting arms and explosives or establishing an armed camp (Manaseh Ranch) [sic]."[53] While the FBI seemed willing to ignore evidence of racial and religious bigotry, it did worry that local groups would, "if they had the support [they] felt necessary, take such actions as the arrest and trial of federal agents and other citizens, and forcibly intimidate IRS officers."[54] And threats about arresting government officials and "removing them from office" constituted advocacy of "violence, terrorism, or intimidation of public officers," said the FBI.[55]

The Bureau's fears were realized two months later in Wisconsin, when a group of farmers and tax protesters assaulted and interrogated an IRS agent. It was the first of many confrontations between lawmen and Posse activists that would become increasingly violent. The architect of the incident was Thomas Stockheimer, a Korean War veteran, farmer, and the self-appointed leader of the Wisconsin Posse Comitatus.[56] In addition to orchestrating the assault, Stockheimer spread the Posse message to a broader constituency of rural conservatives, thereby planting the seeds for its future growth.

18

THE POSSE RIDES WISCONSIN

It was two o'clock on Friday afternoon, August 16, 1974, when IRS agent Fred Chicken arrived at the home of a farmer, Alan Grewe, outside Abbotsford, Wisconsin. Chicken, thirty-five, entered through the kitchen, past three women cutting sewing patterns, and was escorted into the living room, where he expected to review Grewe's tax records. Instead he encountered Thomas Stockheimer and a roomful of men. Five feet six inches tall and nearly 250 pounds, Stockheimer, forty-two, was large, trigger-tempered, and pugnacious.[1] Two years earlier, tax-protest leader Jim Scott had advised right-wing activists to use "witnesses, tape recorders, camera (sic) and visible weapons" when dealing with federal agents, and Stockheimer had all the gear on hand for his well-planned ambush of Agent Chicken.[2]

"These are some of my friends," said Grewe, but Chicken sensed a trap and turned to leave. "I'll come back later," he said. "No you are not," Stockheimer bellowed, first striking the IRS agent with his fist and then shoving him across the room. Chicken's briefcase flew out of his hand and glanced off the television set. Stockheimer forced him into a chair. "You didn't see me hit him, did you?" Stockheimer asked the others. "Oh no," came the chorus of replies. Then Stockheimer introduced himself and shoved a copy of the Posse Comitatus articles of incorporation into Chicken's hand.

It was a summer afternoon, but the drapes were tightly drawn and the living room was dimly lit. Rifles were stacked purposefully against a wall. Several men were seated on a couch opposite the shaken revenue agent. Others sat in chairs. A movie camera was trained on Chicken, its bright light shining into his eyes. One of the men whispered in low tones into a walkie-talkie, communicating with someone outside.

Stockheimer planted himself in front of Chicken. "What is your name? Where are your credentials?" he demanded to know. Fearful, Chicken pulled his identification card from his pocket and handed it to Grewe, who held it up to be filmed. "You are in violation of your sworn oath of office and are committing treason by enforcing the Internal Revenue Code," Stockheimer declared. After lecturing Chicken for several minutes about the Constitution, Stockheimer produced a copy of the *Communist Manifesto* and harangued Chicken about Marxist doctrine and the Sixteenth Amendment, which he said were one and the same. "I don't see any correlation," Chicken ventured. While Stockheimer paged through a stack of documents and droned on about "Christian common law" and complained about Nelson Rockefeller and the Jews, Chicken regained some composure. Luckily, the group didn't intend to inflict more serious harm. After about an hour, one of the men observed that Chicken wasn't paying much attention. "He's not listening," someone said. Chicken took this as his cue. "Can I go now?" he asked. "Yes," Stockheimer replied, adding "God bless you" as the revenue agent made for the door. Stockheimer was indicted and arrested the following week, on charges of forcibly assaulting a federal agent.[3]

According to the FBI, Stockheimer had hatched his plan to confront Fred Chicken while organizing a tax-protest rally in Oshkosh earlier that spring. But the FBI had wrongly assumed that the goal of the Posse was merely to "embarrass" the government, not assault federal agents. Alarmed by the ambush at Abbotsford, the Bureau stepped up its surveillance, but it did so with care.[4] Two weeks after the incident, FBI director Clarence B. Kelley told his Milwaukee office to ensure that agents handling investigations of Posse members "use caution and good judgement . . . in order to preclude any similar incidents. . . ."[5]

In addition to alarming the FBI, the assault on Fred Chicken provided journalists with the story they needed to illustrate the violent potential of the emerging Posse movement. It also helped secure Stockheimer's position as a Posse leader and marked the beginning of his descent into political criminality. A law-abiding Korean War veteran with no record prior to the Chicken assault, Stockheimer spent much of the next twenty-five years under the cloud of various indictments, or as a federal fugitive or in prison. Of all the early Posse leaders, he was the first to recognize the importance of broadening the rural base of the movement and reaching frustrated farmers—the group's most promising recruits. Stockheimer did this by expanding the focus of the Posse beyond its usual litany of conspiracy theories (which he enthusiastically endorsed) to include issues of more immediate concern to farmers and small-town residents, like land-use regulations and farm foreclosures. For Stockheimer and other early backers of the

Wisconsin Posse Comitatus, their first target became the Wisconsin Department of Natural Resources (DNR), whose efforts to enforce environmental laws ran counter to the idea of unfettered private-property rights that so many rural residents embraced.

Stockheimer was from Mosinee, in north central Wisconsin, and the founder, in January 1974, of the Little People's Tax Advisory Committee, a protest group that he quickly transformed into a launching pad for the Posse Comitatus.[6] Two months later he and six others chartered a Marathon County chapter under the auspices of Mike Beach's Citizens Law Enforcement and Research Committee.[7] Before taking on the DNR, Stockheimer's group issued a press release announcing their purpose: "[To] maintain our duly elected County Sheriff as the ultimate law enforcement official of this county, officers of the Federal Government, unconstitutional acts of the Congress and of the Legislature not-withstanding [*sic*]." Louis Gianoli, the veteran sheriff of Marathon County, was not impressed. "Those SOBs aren't going to come in here to do my job. And the first one of those guys who steps out of line will get his butt in jail," he told *Newsweek* magazine.[8]

But Stockheimer and his colleagues persisted in their efforts, and five counties had filed Posse charters by spring. Continuing talk of gunplay made lawmen fear that Stockheimer and his supporters might move from words to action.[9] "I want to know who are the main persons behind this Posse Comitatus, what is the purpose of the organization, and how active and volatile, etcetera, they are," ordered Frank Meyers, head of the Wisconsin Department of Justice Division of Criminal Investigation (DCI) in May.[10] Meyers's action marked the beginning of a wide-ranging investigation that used undercover agents, informants, sheriffs, district attorneys, former Posse members, and unwitting collaborators. State investigators culled names from local Posse charters and swapped information with the FBI and the IRS to build a comprehensive file on the group.

Stockheimer's effort to launch the Wisconsin Posse was helped by several men who were well respected in their communities. For some, highly publicized run-ins with authorities brought them greater legitimacy. For others, it brought them prison time and disrepute. Raymond J. Omernick, fifty, was a prosperous potato farmer from Shawano County, later the site of numerous standoffs between the Posse and authorities. A charter member of the Posse chapter in neighboring Marathon County, he ran for the legislature in 1974—the same year Fred Chicken was assaulted.[11] Omernick pulled 1,658 votes on the far-right American Party ticket, while the winning candidate, a Democrat, received 9,365.[12] Later, however, Omernick would win the post.

The American Party platform echoed the core themes of the radical right, declared busing a "needless safety hazard," and said it was "unalterably committed" to preserving local schools without "interference."[13] Its stand on the Second Amendment was also predictable: "Registering guns makes as much sense as the slogan Register Matches, Prevent Forest Fires."[14] Federal funding for local law enforcement was tantamount to supporting the "secret terrorist [arm] of dictatorial government," and "regional government" was an Illuminati-sponsored plot for world domination. Equal wages for women performing equal work was acceptable, but not "the militant feminists who would destroy the role of our wives and mothers as the anchoring and vital force in our family units." Naturally, the Party opposed abortion and family planning.

Omernick was defeated, but he kept himself in the news when he used armed men to resist state environmental officers. His defiance earned him credibility rather than contempt, and he became a municipal judge. Despite public disclosures of his links to the Posse, Republican voters gave Omernick nearly nine thousand votes in a 1978 primary and he went on to win the state assembly seat that year.[15] Omernick later said he dropped out of the Posse, but he still praised the group, saying he saw nothing wrong with building bunkers, buying weapons, and practicing paramilitary manuevers.

When Omernick first ran for office in 1974, he was among seventeen American Party candidates running in ninety-nine Wisconsin state House districts. The Party also fielded candidates in five out of nine U.S. congressional races.[16] Its standard-bearer for U.S. Senate, Gerald L. McFarren, polled 24,000 votes compared to 740,000 for the winner, Gaylord A. Nelson, the popular Democratic incumbent.[17] McFarren's tally was just 2 percent of the total, but he was more than a protest candidate. He received more than four times the votes of any other non–major party contender, and he mobilized thousands of dedicated supporters by publicly championing the Posse cause.[18] Further evidence of McFarren's right-wing base was found in those counties that had filed Posse charters, where he did two and three times better than in counties where no Posse groups were active.[19]

Like Ray Omernick, McFarren had been involved in a long-standing dispute with the Department of Natural Resources. In the late 1960s he had been accused of illegally dumping fill into a lake and his battles with the state over this incident had dragged on for years.[20] Now the Posse Comitatus rallied to his aid.[21] About three weeks after orchestrating the assault on Fred Chicken, Thomas Stockheimer drafted a stack of self-styled "subpoenas" charging the Wisconsin Department of Natural Resources with "abuses, harassments, usurpations, and violations of the constitutional rights" of McFarren, Omernick, and others. Stockheimer further demanded that state officials testify before a "Christian Citizens' Grand Jury."[22] He also led several hundred vocal supporters to disrupt a DNR hearing on the charges against McFarren.[23] Tax protester George Kindred came from neighboring Michigan for the event and was thrilled by the sight of Posse demonstrators chanting, "We want a trial by jury!" and confronting a "swarm of police . . . despite threats of jail with buses standing by to take them there." The ruckus ended abruptly when state officials called off the proceeding after they received a bomb threat.[24]

Stockheimer then seized the initiative and organized a grand jury of his own.

The meeting convened on September 12, 1974, in an innocuous setting: the University of Wisconsin Experimental Farm in Spooner. None of the subpoenaed officials showed up, but a pair of agents from the State Division of Criminal Investigation huddled on one side of a flimsy room partition, listening to Posse-men periodically shout the names of witnesses down the hallway in a lame attempt to imitate a legitimate proceeding. After the Posse cleared out, the agents scoured the trash for "items of possible interest."[25] The self-styled "inquiry" had run a day and a half, and the group had compiled a Christian Citizens' Grand Jury indictment targeting more than fifty state and local officials they accused of trampling their rights. In addition to pursuing justice for Omernick and Mc-Farren, the group sought to punish state officials for persecuting Donald Min-necheske, a Shawano County tavern owner. Like Omernick, Minnecheske was a popular local figure who had joined the Posse because of a series of run-ins with authorities. He had once been a town assessor, but was taken to court in 1971 by the state Department of Revenue for refusing to turn over the local tax rolls. Three years later the state filed liens against him for more than $10,000 in unpaid taxes. None of these problems prevented him from getting elected to the county board, however, which was then placed in the peculiar position of trying to garnish his per diem to pay an outstanding tax claim.[26] By 1976, licensing problems forced Minnecheske and his wife to close their tavern at Tigerton Dells. The couple then deeded 29 of their 577 acres in southwestern Shawano County to the "Life Science Church," a tax dodge set up by the disbarred tax-protesting lawyer Jerome Daly. The property later became an armed compound and the state headquarters for the Posse Comitatus. Ray Omernick succeeded in parlaying his resistance to state authorities into elected office, but Minnecheske eventually ended up spending nearly a year behind bars after he filed phony legal papers clouding the title to property worth $16 million that wasn't his.[27]

Just as Posse members sought legitimacy by filing their charters at the county courthouse, the group that convened in Spooner in September 1974 trooped down to the local courthouse to file their "indictment." Carrying tape recorders, walkie-talkies, and the seemingly omnipresent movie camera, about twenty Posse members demanded a judge's signature on their phony paperwork. When the judge refused, they indicted him as well.[28] After shadowing the Posse grand jury session, Wisconsin authorities made plans to monitor the next possible confrontation: a September 20, 1974, hearing in Eau Claire about McFarren's alleged environmental abuses. Fearing violence, and recalling the bomb threat that had canceled the earlier DNR proceeding, more than twenty police officers were placed on alert, helmets and riot batons concealed in the trunks of their squad cars, along with gas masks and other gear.[29] State police checked the building for bombs.[30] Posse supporters began arriving a little after eight A.M., and milled around outside the state office building, carrying signs supporting the American Party and McFarren. Sporting a blue plaid suit jacket for the occasion, Stock-heimer pinned a Posse badge to his chest.[31] The hearing room could hold about fifty people but the state police wanted full control of the crowd so they tried to close the building's front doors after only thirty-five of McFarren's supporters had been allowed in. As a result, McFarren and Stockheimer started a commotion on the street. "I want all of my friends with me when these commies try to hang me," McFarren protested. "They won't let anyone else in," he told the crowd. After several minutes of name-calling and shouting, McFarren stepped forward and forced open one of the outer doors to the building. A few people, including Stockheimer, shoved their way into the vestibule. "You have no authority in this building," Stockheimer told the guards, and pulled a canister of pepper spray from his pocket and discharged it at one of the officers, temporarily blinding him.

Chaos and confusion followed. One guard was thrown back; another was dragged into the crowd. Stockheimer sprayed this guard, too, holding the canister about five inches from his face. When more officers attempted to come to his rescue, someone in the crowd tore at one of the officers' ammunition pouches, spilling bullets to the ground. In an effort to drive Stockheimer and others out of the doorway, the guards themselves began to use mace. An acrid mist wafted into the building.[32] The melee lasted ten minutes. After the guards removed the last of the protesters from the entrance, they quickly chained and padlocked the doors. A plainclothes detective tried to relieve Stockheimer of his pepper spray but thought better of it when the crowd surrounded him.[33] At six o'clock that evening, the district attorney obtained a felony warrant for Stockheimer's arrest, charging him with battery, obstructing a police officer, and possession of tear gas.

These events prompted the DCI to put an undercover agent inside the Posse. The person they chose was Robert M. Ankenbrandt, a former police officer and member of the National Guard. Ankenbrandt, thirty-four, was clever and thorough; he reviewed files, spoke with his counterparts in other states, cross-referenced the names on Posse charters with the DCI database, and attended Stockheimer's October 8 hearing on the battery charges.[34] He also came up with an alias and a cover story: he would be "Ralph Anderson," a freelance land developer opposing the DNR because of zoning problems.[35] Raised on a farm in Sauk County, he had no difficulty playing the role. Ankenbrandt participated in dozens of Posse events for the next seven years (until he had to testify against a fellow Posse member on gun charges in 1981). The first major gathering he attended was the "Midwest-National Tax and Posse Comitatus Convention" in October 1974 in Milwaukee.[36] The event attracted about three hundred right-wing militants from more than a dozen states and featured an array of speakers, including the tax-protesting attorney Jerome Daly.[37] Fresh from a stint in federal prison and defiant as ever, Daly advised everyone to arm themselves with a "good pump-action twelve-gauge shotgun and a high-powered rifle."[38] A banquet was held in his honor.

Mike Beach spoke the following morning but he was less enthusiastically received. Beach began by claiming he had first lectured on the Posse Comitatus in 1937. The lie was loosely derived from his days in Pelley's Silver Shirts, and his failed attempt to join Portland's Civil Guard Patrol during World War II. The Posse Comitatus is "the sword Christ intended us to use," he said, warming to the crowd, only to backpedal, saying that citizen's arrests and other "militant activities" should be avoided. The Posse should concentrate instead on filing complaints against judges and overloading the courts with paperwork. Clearly this was the wrong message for such an audience. To make matters worse, Beach was long-winded, so the master of ceremonies cut him off.[39]

Also sharing the platform was W. Vaughn Ellsworth, a hero among tax resisters; Martin A. Larson, author of *Tax Revolt: USA*; George Kindred, "dean" of LEGAL, the "Layman's Educational Guild at Law"; Colonel Archibald Roberts, a veteran anti-Semite and the leader of the "Committee to Restore the Constitution"; and Gerald McFarren, who endorsed the Posse in his remarks. Thomas Stockheimer was one of the last to speak.[40] "You all know what we need to buy," he told the group. "Yeah. Gold and silver," someone called out. "No. Buy guns and bullets," he replied.[41]

Eight weeks later, on December 13, 1974, Stockheimer was convicted of assaulting Fred Chicken. While awaiting the jury's verdict at the end of the three-day trial, Stockheimer told one reporter that the Posse was "the only non-integrated fighting unit left" that was prepared to handle the race war and looting that would surely accompany the upcoming economic collapse.[42] Despite his conviction on a serious felony charge, Stockheimer got no more than a slap on the wrist—he was sentenced to only sixty days in prison—and he remained as defiant as ever.[43] "If assault had been my goal . . . Mr. Chicken wouldn't be around to testify, let alone file a report," he boasted.[44] The judge tried to justify the light sentence by saying that Stockheimer had no previous criminal record and there had been no illegal activity after the incident. This overlooked Stockheimer's mace attack on state police in Eau Claire, for which he was later convicted. The judge said he thought the sentence had "sufficient bite in it," but subsequent events proved it had no deterrent effect. After losing his appeal of the Chicken conviction in May 1976, Stockheimer jumped bail and became a federal fugitive.[45] He was arrested the following year in West Virginia and eventually was sentenced to another year in federal prison.[46] Stockheimer's criminal activities extended well into the 1990s, when he and eight associates were charged with mail fraud and conspiracy for selling bogus Posse money orders. One of Stockheimer's customers was the Oklahoma City bomber, Terry Nichols.[47]

Stockheimer emphasized the importance of militant action, and was among the first Posse leaders to focus on issues that were of day-to-day concern to farmers and rural people. But his greatest contribution to the movement, it turned out, came in 1975 when he recruited James Wickstrom—a heavyset, fast-talking tool salesman who later played a key role on the Posse Comitatus national stage, inspiring followers to murder and violence.

Born and raised in Michigan's Upper Peninsula, Wickstrom joined the army several years after graduating from high school. He avoided combat in Vietnam and served most of his two-year stint (he claimed it was six) as a warehouseman in Fort Lewis, Washington, and in Okinawa, Japan, before he was discharged in 1966.[48] By the early 1970s, Wickstrom was married and operating a service station in Racine, Wisconsin. But he quit when he couldn't make ends meet, and became a traveling salesman for Snap-On Tools. Several years later, Wickstrom moved to Marathon County, where he began attending meetings of Stockheimer's Little People's Tax Advisory Committee and quickly became a convert.[49] He quit his sales job, stopped paying taxes, and moved—on the advice of his new friends—to Schell City, Missouri, where he began working for the Church of Our Christian Heritage, an Identity congregation. Later named the Church of Israel, the group had been founded in 1973 by Daniel Lee Gayman, then thirty-six, a high-school principal and the publisher of a virulently anti-Semitic newsletter, *Zion's Watchman*. Gayman's church was on remote, heavily wooded property, about one hundred miles south of Kansas City. And by the mid-1970s it had become one of a growing number of paramilitary compounds in the Midwest favored by Identity believers and supporters of the Posse Comitatus.[50]

Wickstrom taught history and geography at Gayman's church school for about a year and then formed his own group—the Mission of Jesus the Christ Church—that he and his wife, Dianne, structured as a tax dodge. In 1977, Wickstrom declared his commitment to tax resistance in a seven-page statement he attached to his Wisconsin state income tax return and mailed from Missouri:

> [T]hese unconstitutional graduated income taxes are against God's law and the Constitution of the United States for harboring and aiding the enemies of our nation. The state and federal governments use our tax monies in the guise of foreign aid to build up our enemies, socially, economically, financially and in war materials. These same materials are then used to destroy our armed forces in times of war or conflict.[51]

In 1978 Wickstrom returned to Wisconsin, at the request of Donald Minnecheske, and began living on the property at Tigerton Dells that had been deeded earlier to the Life Science Church. The acreage was commonly referred to as "the compound" and was nestled in the timber and rolling, rocky farmland in a corner of a 570-acre tract owned by the Minnecheskes. It was a tranquil spot of northern hardwoods and green meadows, where children played among red rimrock boulders and the green pools of the Embarrass River. It was also here that Wickstrom "baptized" followers during paramilitary training sessions that attracted hundreds of people. But that came later. First, Wickstrom placed two fourteen-by-seventy-foot trailers side by side, removed the walls, and dubbed the structure "church property." The renovated trailer became his residence and the "Christian Liberty Academy," where he taught the children of Posse supporters.

When Stockheimer was released from federal prison on his bail-jumping charge in early 1979, he, too, moved to the compound. Eager to identify new leadership for the Posse Comitatus, he anointed Wickstrom, who promptly pronounced himself the "National Director of Counterinsurgency."[52] With his stocky build, bullet head, and rapid-fire delivery, Wickstrom quickly gained notoriety and a following, locally and nationally. One goofy but clever 1980 publicity stunt involved filing complaints with the FBI alleging that local and state authorities had committed treason by failing to maintain proper supplies of food and water in local bomb shelters meant to withstand nuclear attack. According to Wickstrom, the absence of sufficient provisions was part of a plot to impose martial law because the "starving masses" were sure to begin looting in the wake of a national emergency once they found that food supplies were unavailable as a result of "depleted and neglected Civil Defense Shelters." It was a fanciful allegation, but Wickstrom hardly cared; it earned him and the Posse prominent news coverage.[53] Wickstrom was artful at seeking publicity, but his most important activities at first went unnoticed. Beginning in 1980, Wickstrom crisscrossed the Midwest in earnest, driving thousands of miles to meet with financially strapped farmers in church basements, sale barns, and in their living rooms, promoting Christian Identity and the Posse Comitatus. It was an effort that would later yield bitter and murderous fruit.

But before Wickstrom and others seized on the farm crisis, the Posse turned its focus back West—toward Idaho, California, and Oregon—where many of its members also were gravitating toward gunplay as the preferred means of political expression. And, as in Wisconsin, they organized for action at the county level where, however sparse their numbers, they were sure to have the greatest impact.

19

THE POSSE AND THE FBI

Snow was gathering on the ground on a freezing January night in 1975 when Leonard Brabham, too drowsy to drive farther, parked his car at the Husky Truck Stop just outside Coeur d'Alene, Idaho.[1] After removing his artificial leg, Brabham, a fifty-two-year-old mill operator from nearby Athol, slipped into his sleeping bag. He was suddenly awakened a few hours later, his 1971 Datsun Coupe shaking violently from side to side. Although the windows were covered with frost he could still see the shadow of a man. Brabham reached down between the front seats and grabbed his .44-caliber Magnum revolver. "Lay off, you son of a bitch!" he shouted, pointing his gun at the door. When Brabham opened the window a crack, he saw a parked car fifteen feet away, its headlights glaring.

The man who had interrupted Brabham's nap was Roger A. Davis, a police officer from the local town of Post Falls who recalled that he came across Brabham's parked car in deepening snow. Concerned the occupant might freeze to death, he knocked on the window and shook the car. Brabham rolled down the window and handed Davis his driver's license, but then jerked the identification away, shoved his gun out the window, and threatened the officer. "I'll blow your head off," Brabham growled. The patrolman retreated, called for backup, arrested Brabham, and took him to the Kootenai County Jail where he was charged with assault with a deadly weapon. It was Monday, January 27, and Brabham spent the week locked up.[2] When he finally was released on bail, Brabham went to retrieve his car with a friend, Eldon Earl "Bud" Cutler, the future chief of security for Richard Butler's Aryan Nations.[3]

Butler had arrived in Idaho the previous year and it would be several more years before he formally established the Aryan Nations. In the meantime he gave himself the title of "Marshal" of the Kootenai County Christian Posse Comitatus, and recruited Brabham, Cutler, and several dozen other members.[4] Six weeks after the truck-stop incident, Butler and about fifty supporters tried to "arrest" Officer Davis at the county courthouse when he went to testify on the assault charge (Brabham was acquitted). As Posse militants jostled with a cordon of officers, one skittish lawman allegedly drew his gun.[5] Butler produced a sheaf of phony legal papers that demanded $10 million in damages and charged Davis with criminal conspiracy, assault with a deadly weapon, grand larceny, and other assorted crimes. According to Butler's vigilante logic, his attempted arrest of Davis was *lawful*, and the lawmen who protected Davis at the courthouse were criminals.[6] Butler also wrote to the Idaho attorney general and demanded he convene a "citizens' grand jury" and prosecute Kootenai County authorities.[7] The fracas at the courthouse led to a series of scorching editorials in the *Coeur d'Alene Press*, which compared Butler's Posse to the Ku Klux Klan and urged the arrest of Posse members. "Then they can judge the constitutional process from the inside," the paper observed.[8] Little did the newspaper editors know, but Butler's presence would haunt their community and state for the next three decades, bringing violence, hatred, and reams of bad press.

The events in Kootenai County came less than six months after the assault on Fred Chicken in Wisconsin, and the FBI was growing more anxious about the possibility of escalating violence.[9] The Bureau also had another concern: The Posse was growing rapidly and the Bureau was hard-pressed to catch up. In addition to its base in Wisconsin, the Posse had spread from California, up the West Coast into the Rocky Mountain states, and had secured scattered footholds in more than a dozen states across the country. The FBI had tracked Posse growth largely by compiling newspaper clippings and relying on other second-hand accounts. Soon it would shift gears and take a more aggressive approach, one that depended more heavily on undercover informants.

Two FBI agents had filed detailed reports on the Milwaukee Posse meeting in October 1974, and the Bureau was soon pushing its agents for accounts of events in their states. Similar gatherings took place in Seattle, Washington, Arkansas, and Colorado in early 1975 and were watched closely by the FBI. The Big Tri-State Tax and Law Rally in Eureka Springs, Arkansas, featured right-wing celebrities like A. J. Porth, Jerome Daly, and George Kindred and attracted militants from at least ten states.[10] Several hundred people attended the North-west Regional Posse Comitatus and Tax Convention in Seattle and heard Mike Beach and Colonel Archibald Roberts, both of whom had shared the podium in Milwaukee.[11] Beach and A. J. Porth also teamed up to address Posse members in Illinois where the founder of the DuPage County chapter was Julius Butler, a millionaire member of the John Birch Society whose brother was the founder of the Chicago suburb of Oak Brook.[12] "I don't recommend hanging [public officials]," Beach told his audience of about eighty people in a motel in Elmhurst in February 1975. "But a coat of tar and a pillow full of feathers would make an impression, and an impression would do good."[13] One month later, twenty Chicago-area Posse members demanded that lawmen arrest a judge who had ordered one of them to make alimony payments, and undergo a psychiatric evaluation. When their request was refused, a Posse "grand jury" indicted the judge.[14]

In March 1975, FBI director Clarence B. Kelley decided to act. He instructed the Bureau's office in Mike Beach's hometown of Portland, Oregon, to centralize and coordinate all information on the Sheriff's Posse Comitatus (SPC). As the "Office of Origin," Portland would be responsible for reviewing and analyzing reports about Posse activities from thirty-two "auxiliary offices" of the FBI.[15] The task involved massive paperwork and the special agent in charge tried to dodge the assignment. It made no sense to designate Portland as the Posse clearinghouse, he said, because Beach and Gale had "little, if any, national control or direction of the various Posse groups."[16] True, Posse chapters were largely autonomous, but that didn't alter the need to centralize the huge volume of information that was about to be gathered.[17] Washington ordered Portland to comply, and Portland instructed all FBI field offices to investigate every new Posse chapter in their area to see which ones were promoting violence.[18]

Fresh impetus for the probe came one month later when the Bureau office in Little Rock, Arkansas, sent an urgent Teletype to Washington warning of a possible threat against Vice President Nelson A. Rockefeller.[19] Rightists were always railing at Rockefeller, labeling him a Jewish agent of communist and capitalist subversion, and so it isn't possible to say whether the threat was real or exaggerated, but no arrests were made. Nevertheless, the Teletype was followed by an intensified government investigation. On April 21, 1975, four days after receiving news of the supposed threat, FBI headquarters issued a memo reiterating that every field office should ensure investigations were conducted "on all SPC leaders and known members." By June, the Bureau had examined known or suspected Posse chapters in fourteen states in the West, Midwest, and South since the beginning of the year.[20] One probe focused on the rapid spread of tax-protesting Posse groups in conservative west Texas. After opening files on four suspected chapters, the Bureau office in El Paso passed the information on to the IRS.[21] One of the Texas tax protesters was Gordon Wendell Kahl, the future Posse Comitatus martyr.[22] Foreshadowing Kahl's killing of federal marshals eight years later, reports the FBI filed on Kahl and his Texas compatriots contained the following warning: "Inasmuch as information has been received that members of the SPC are required to own firearms and since they have advocated violence, SPC members should be considered armed and dangerous."[23]

The same activities that caught the attention of federal agents prompted state officials to investigate. Wisconsin launched its investigation of the Posse in 1974 and Oregon followed suit the next year. The latter inquiry was triggered when Herbert S. Breed, chairman of the Klamath County Posse Comitatus, sent a raft of intimidating letters to state legislators. Breed, fifty-eight, had served on the board of directors of the National Association to Keep and Bear Arms before that group split over whether or not to embrace the Posse, and he took the side of the militants.[24] Breed's letters to legislators informed them that citizen's grand juries would try them for treason if they refused to repeal a landmark environmental law, the Land Conservation and Development Commission Act, or LCDC.[25] Passed in 1973, the law was despised by conservatives as a threat to private property. Like the attacks on the Department of Natural Resources in Wisconsin, the Posse in Oregon used the issue to spark its growth. Breed warned:

> We of the Sheriff's Posse Comitatus OPPOSE funding of LCDC, or ANY COUNTY, STATE or FEDERAL governmental agency that has the *same* or *simular* [sic] *purposes*. . . . The GOVERNMENT was created to PROTECT our GOD given RIGHTS, *not take them away*. . . . [I]f you vote to fund LCDC . . . and its illegal effects, we will take appropriate action. . . .

News of the letters spread quickly through the state capitol and appeared on page one of Salem's *Capital Journal*. The first to complain was state senator Ted Hallock, a Portland Democrat, who gave copies of the letter to the Klamath Falls district attorney, the state attorney general, and the FBI. Drawing attention to that section of the Posse *Blue Book* calling for the hanging of public officials, Hallock claimed Breed's letter was a death threat. "We must not let this go unchallenged," he told his colleagues on the Oregon Senate floor.[26] With appropriate historical perspective and a sense of humor, Oregon Secretary of State Cecil L. Edwards also asked the state attorney general to look into the matter.[27]

"You and your staff are too young to remember, but I recall when the Ku Klux Klan contributed substantially to the election of a governor of this state," wrote Edwards. "There were also alleged Ku Klux Klan members of the legislature. City officials were involved. Greasy bedsheets covered fuzzy brains in many parts of the state, but mostly in the southern and eastern counties."[28] Edwards's observation was accurate. With perhaps twenty thousand members, the Klan had indeed been a powerful force in the state in 1922 when it backed William Pierce—the successful Democratic candidate for governor—and received public recognition in exchange for its support.[29] Edwards also was correct about the concentration of the Klan in Oregon's southern and eastern counties. Fifty years later, Posse Comitatus chapters fared well in many of the same areas.[30]

In his letter to the attorney general, Edwards called Breed's threats "vigilante tactics," and asked whether the correspondence was illegal. The answer was "no." Breed's letters were "outrageous . . . distasteful and insulting," but they were protected by the First Amendment, the attorney general responded. He also offered some lame advice.[31] Legislators who received Breed's letters should simply reply saying they received a letter "under his signature which [they] assume is a forgery."[32] Although the attorney general declined to take any action against Breed, his Special Investigation Division did prepare a report on the Posse. The document concluded that the group was active in nine out of Oregon's thirty-six counties and had around two hundred members.[33]

Breed's letters may not have been grounds for prosecution, but they (and other threats) did provide justification for the ongoing federal probe. The FBI also put itself on firmer legal footing by offering a harsher assessment of the Posse. Investigations by the Portland office in 1973 and 1974 had reached relatively benign conclusions. But by 1975, when it ordered an expanded investigation, the Bureau cited the Posse's general propensity for violence, as well as the possibility that its members might attack blacks and Jews, as justification for the increased scrutiny. The Posse was now consistently classified as a "white hate group," flatly contradicting earlier assessments that it was not "anti-semetic [sic] or anti-black in its pronouncements."[34] And the fact that members of Gale's Ministry of Christ Church "advocated killing FBI agents and Internal Revenue Service agents as well as hanging certain judges," was offered as further justification for continued government surveillance.[35]

But the FBI's widening investigation of the Posse coincided with unprecedented disclosures about government intelligence abuses. With the death of FBI director J. Edgar Hoover in May 1972, the Bureau's illegal intelligence-gathering practices were finally coming to light. The emerging evidence shook popular perceptions of the probity, professionalism, and skills of the FBI. During Hoover's forty-eight-year reign, the Bureau had frequently treated political dissent as sedition: it spied on Americans who exercised their constitutional rights, disrupted political movements, committed political burglaries with no legitimate reason, blackmailed politicians, illegally tapped phones, and leaked derogatory information about political activists—especially civil rights leaders—to the press.[36] These activities multiplied in 1956, at the height of the Cold War and the beginning of the burgeoning civil rights movement, when Hoover launched the Bureau's Internal Security Counterintelligence Program.[37] Known as COINTELPRO, its goal was to disrupt and discredit the civil rights movement, leftist organizations, and, later, anti-Vietnam war-protest groups.[38] In 1964, Hoover expanded the program to include destabilizing the Ku Klux Klan.[39] While the Bureau had long spied on black activists, its decision to target white supremacists ended almost fifty years of a largely hands-off policy toward racist hate groups (with the exception of the role played by the Bureau in suppressing neo-Nazi groups during World War II).

After 1964, the FBI fomented discord within the Klan, using the same techniques it had mastered while undermining left-wing "subversives."[40] The Bureau stole membership records, planted rumors, leaked stories to the press, and employed hundreds of informants whose goal was to disrupt the movement, not just gather information.[41] Some of the tactics were juvenile but effective—like instructing informants to sleep with the wives of Klansmen in order to gather information and sow discord. Other tactics were blatantly illegal, such as when the FBI turned a blind eye to violence and failed to protect freedom riders from being ambushed and savagely beaten in Birmingham, Alabama, in May 1961.[42] Many critics had accused the Bureau of illegal conduct in the past, but the extent of FBI abuses did not become widely known until the early 1970s. Following news reports about COINTELPRO in 1974, Senator Frank Church, an Idaho Democrat, led a bipartisan investigation of the FBI and the Central Intelligence Agency.[43] Those hearings, and the report that it released in November 1975, led to new restrictions on government spying.[44]

Although the Bureau didn't use the same illegal tactics to disrupt the Posse, the radical right seized on revelations about past FBI misconduct to justify their fears of government persecution. "For twelve years *The Councilor* has told its readers that federal provocateurs had infiltrated political groups and were involved in criminal activity," reported the newsletter of the once-prominent Citizens' Council movement, in late 1974.[45] That statement was true enough, but according to *The Councilor* everything from the bombing of black churches to the murder of civil rights leaders had been orchestrated by the FBI to promote sympathy for blacks. Even the 1972 assassination attempt on presidential candidate George Wallace was viewed as part of a "hate assault" by federal agents who then protected Wallace's "real assassins." And true to the anti-Semitic bias of the Citizens' Council movement, *The Councilor* claimed to have "heard vague references to those crimes [committed by the FBI] under the term 'Operation Cohen' " and asked, "What part did the ADL play in all of this?"[46] And the National Alliance to Keep and Bear Arms warned in its newsletter, *Armed Citizen News*, that "[a]lthough COINTELPRO has been officially 'disbanded,' most of these . . . stool pigeons, infiltrators, and agents provocateurs are still being paid to continue their infiltration, harassment, and disruption of genuinely patriotic organizations."[47]

By January 1975, *Armed Citizen News* was in the hands of Robert DePugh, fifty-one, the former Minuteman who had served nearly four years of an eleven-year sentence for federal firearms violations.[48] DePugh was quick to point out that informants had splintered right-wing groups, but he was perfectly happy to drive a wedge of his own between two feuding factions of the National Association to Keep and Bear Arms. Around 1974, DePugh bankrolled NAKBA militants who seized the group's records, changed its name by substituting the word "Alliance" for "Association" in its title, and moved its headquarters from Medford, Oregon, to Norborne, Missouri, where he took it over, including its newsletter and mailing list. At its peak, the pro-gun group had been distributing as many as ten thousand copies of *Armed Citizen News* each month, and DePugh immediately began using the publication for self-promotion.[49] Ads for his

"VitaVim" tablets and "Minutemen Survival Tabs," as well as his 427-page prison memoir, *Behind the Iron Mask*, were prominently featured in each issue.[50]

DePugh also used *Armed Citizen News* to promote a new organization he envisioned as an all-encompassing radical right-wing coalition: the Patriots Inter-Organizational Communications Center. Barred by the terms of his parole from reactivating the Minutemen, DePugh launched the new group in September 1974. The inaugural meeting attracted two hundred participants from nearly one hundred groups and featured speeches by prominent white supremacists, tax protesters, Posse Comitatus advocates, and Second Amendment absolutists, including Robert Shelton, Imperial Wizard of the United Klans of America, and A. J. Porth. Needless to say, rivalries and faction fights doomed the concept from the start.[51]

In addition to his prodigious efforts at self-promotion, DePugh also published ads in the NAKBA newsletter for the Ku Klux Klan.[52] After receiving several letters a month from offended readers, NAKBA president Jack Marlow set the record straight:

> The Klan stands for the preservation of the white race which represents only sixteen percent of the world's population but produces seventy-five percent of the world's wealth and over ninety percent of its technical and scientific progress. The Klan stands for America first, the United States Constitution as originally written and intended, the free enterprise system, Christianity, the right of the American people to practice their faith including prayer in school, and the Second Amendment right to keep and bear arms.[53]

As proof of the Klan's patriotism, Marlow cited its persecution by the FBI. "Now, the truth has finally been brought out," wrote Marlow, referring to Senator Church's committee hearings. The FBI and other "government agencies have been conducting a massive hate campaign against the Ku Klux Klan."[54]

Following the highly publicized findings of the Church committee, the FBI made sure that its probe of the Posse was backed up by the necessary paperwork.[55] Every inquiry should be based on "information which indicates the SPC is engaged in activities which could involve a violation of Title 18, United States Code (USC), Section 1114 (Assaulting or Killing a Federal Officer), Section 2383 (Rebellion or Insurrection), Section 241 (Conspiracy Against Rights of Citizens), Section 245 (Federally Protected Activities), Civil Rights Act of 1968 or related Civil Rights Statutes," instructed the Bureau in April 1975.

The Bureau deepened its investigation the following month: "[Due to] an increase of vigilante-type activity coupled with an escalation of violent hate rhetoric," all field offices were ordered to "obtain in-depth coverage of each SPC group" using informants. Much of the information gathered by the Bureau up until then had been from newspaper clippings or other law enforcement agencies.

Now FBI director Clarence Kelley—himself a former FBI agent with twenty-one years' experience—demanded firsthand reports.[56] Secondhand sources like newspapers simply were "not acceptable."[57]

Although Kelley disdained news stories as insufficient from an intelligence point of view, one of the reasons why the Bureau racheted up its efforts was because of increased media coverage of the Posse. Mike Beach had once advised his followers that "bad news is better than no news," and that dictum certainly held true for the full-page article about the Posse that appeared in *Newsweek* on May 26, 1975.[58] Headlined "Return of the Posse?" the piece recounted a speech by Beach in Stockton, California, and described his "rapt" audience of eighty men and women as "a motley group . . . some in service-station uniforms and football jerseys, others in double-knit suits—most of them working-class Americans."[59] *Newsweek* said the Posse was "the newest—and fastest growing—of a seemingly never-ending stream of militant right-wing organizations," and repeated Beach's false claim that he had "founded the movement from his Portland, Oregon, home in 1968" and had half a million members. Like other articles catalogued by the Portland FBI, this one was copied and sent along to Washington, D.C.[60]

Bureau headquarters may have demanded increased vigilance, but the response of local offices was uneven and some agents simply tried to shirk Washington's directive. When the San Francisco FBI failed to develop informants and refused to interview one of the founders of the Sonoma County Posse, the agent in charge was reprimanded. Surveillance of the Posse "should be more extensive than the receipt of information of a public nature," explained Washington, D.C. And when the agent running the Butte, Montana, office reported that he didn't plan to interview any members of the Kootenai County Posse Comitatus, an irate Kelley chastised him for failing to place an informant in the group following the Posse attempt to "arrest" patrolman Roger Davis. "[A] Bureau-operated source must be developed in each SPC unit. [But your] files do not reflect source coverage having been obtained. . . . Promptly advise FBIHQ when such coverage will be obtained," Kelley demanded.[61]

Despite the push from Washington, many local offices discontinued their investigations of the Posse. In March 1975, the Portland FBI closed its probes of six chapters in Oregon, including the Lane County group led by Hitler enthusiast Dean Kennedy, saying some of the groups had "never established themselves as functional organizations" or that the investigations were not justified.[62] The Bureau may have been legally required to back off, but the decision was premature nonetheless. Fifteen months after the FBI closed down most of its inquiries in Oregon, a gang of seven heavily armed Possemen took over a wheat and potato farm in eastern Oregon. An eleven-hour standoff ensued before the group surrendered. The incident made national news and four of the men were later convicted on charges of burglary and riot.[63]

The basic radical-right complaint that it had been the target of COINTEL-

PRO abuses was justified, even, if the rhetoric used to denounce the government was steeped in bigotry and exaggerated claims. However, it is difficult to make the case that the Bureau's investigation of the Posse included illegal, COINTELPRO-style methods. Little evidence exists to support the charge, either in the Bureau's own records, in news reports, or from other sources. Unlike its treatment of dissident groups under J. Edgar Hoover, the FBI seemed to respect the constitutional rights of Posse members. Among other things, it closed investigations early—sometimes too early—as soon as it judged that the targeted individuals were engaged in constitutionally protected activity and were not planning any crimes. This was a far cry from the "anything goes" mentality of the Hoover era. A more serious problem stemmed from the on-again, off-again investigative approach taken by local offices where agents—out of laziness, sympathy with right-wing groups, or concerns for career advancement—did not appear to take the Posse Comitatus very seriously. The memos from Director Kelley may have clamored for more substantive information from the field, but investigating right-wing hate groups was not a path to promotion in the Bureau—that came more readily to agents who distinguished themselves by working "real" cases involving bank robbery, kidnapping, and murder. The consequences of this dynamic proved embarrassing two decades later when, in the wake of the Oklahoma City bombing, the Bureau had to scramble to get up to speed on right-wing hate groups because it had failed to devote sufficient resources to the problem much earlier.

In 1974, the Posse Comitatus made headlines when Tom Stockheimer assaulted Fred Chicken in Wisconsin. Escalating Posse activity and rhetoric, including larger meetings, a perceived threat to the vice president, letters to Oregon legislators, and more frequent near-confrontations—like the one with Leonard Brabham and, later, the attempted "arrest" of patrolman Roger Davis—prompted greater law enforcement scrutiny at the state and federal level. Before then, the Posse had confined itself largely to threatening words and gestures. Tempers had flared amid jostling and shouting, a few fists flew, but remarkably, no shots had been fired. That changed on September 2, 1975, in a tomato field near Stockton, California.

20

THE SPIRIT OF VIGILANTISM

Posse members began arriving several hours after midnight at Frank Ray's tomato farm outside Tracy, California, in the northern San Joaquin Valley. Summoned by Ray and other tomato growers, their goal was to block union organizers from entering the fields and recruiting workers.[1] Just before dawn, Francis Earl Gillings, forty-four, an unemployed service-station operator, Korean War veteran, and the "marshal" of the San Joaquin County Posse Comitatus, led about fifty armed men and women to the fields. Most sported large, chrome badges—a five-pointed star surrounded by a circle emblazoned with the words SHERIFF'S POSSE COMITATUS. The group bristled with pistols, shotguns, military and sporting rifles, pickax handles and chains. One reporter said he had not "seen so many guns on so few people outside a John Wayne movie."[2]

Several months earlier, a photo of Gillings had accompanied a full-page *Newsweek* article highlighting Mike Beach and the Posse Comitatus. Easily recognizable by his broad face, wide smile, and horn-rimmed glasses, Gillings had posed with a shotgun cradled lazily in the crook of his arm and a Posse badge pinned to his sport coat. "There is no greater law firm than Smith and Wesson, especially if it is backed up by a twelve-gauge injunction," he quipped.[3] Now, as he deployed Posse supporters around the two hundred–acre field, Gillings prepared to put his one-line axiom into action.[4]

It wasn't long before the reason for the Posse gathering arrived along Arch

Road: a dozen members of the United Farm Workers Union. Gillings called them "brown-bereted fascists" and was enraged that state labor officials recently had ordered growers to allow the UFW into the fields.[5] "You wouldn't want these people in your living room, and this tomato field is this man's living room," he said.[6] "We're armed and we mean business," added the local Posse chairman, Jim McDaniel, a Stockton electrician. "If they take away trespassing laws . . . we are in trouble in this country." Nearby, a teenage boy waved an M-1 carbine over his head.[7]

The UFW positioned itself opposite the tomato field while dozens of sheriff's deputies watched from a distance. After being turned back several times by the Posse, and refused protection by the deputies, the union organizers drove off.[8] About nine-thirty A.M., Gillings told his men to take a break. Most did, but a few remained close by, including Gillings's fourteen-year-old son, Steven, who wore a white, military-style helmet, and was armed with a semiautomatic rifle and a pistol. The teenager should have been attending his first day as a freshman at Tracy High School.

Several dozen lawmen in full riot gear suddenly approached the gate. "We have a warrant for your arrest," announced one of them, Sheriff's Inspector Daniel Delfatti, as he advanced on Gillings with three officers. But the warrant was something of a sham. Rather than take the political risk of arresting Gillings and his men for violating the order requiring growers to allow union organizers into the fields, the district attorney ordered deputies to arrest Gillings on a seven-month-old traffic warrant.[9] "Who do you want? Where is your warrant?" Gillings demanded to know as he quickly grabbed a twelve-gauge shotgun and racked the weapon. "Back me up! Back me up!" he hollered frantically as he retreated. "Back me up!"

"Drop the gun," Delfatti demanded.

"Kill the son of a bitch!" shouted a deputy from the other side of the fence.

"If you don't stop, I'll have to shoot," Gillings yelled. But the deputies kept advancing. When Delfatti got within five feet, Gillings stepped back and raised the shotgun. Meanwhile the Shasta County Posse chairman, Norman Brown, who was positioned behind the deputies, raised his rifle and took aim. "Drop your guns or you're dead!" he growled. Brown, fifty-seven, never pulled the trigger, but Gillings did. Eyewitness accounts differ as to how the gun went off: whether it discharged accidently as Delfatti grabbed the weapon and was struggling to bring Gillings down, or whether Gillings actually fired at close range. Either way, Delfatti was lucky. The shotgun pellets whizzed past his head, he wrenched the weapon from Gillings's hands, and threw him to the ground.

"Shots are being fired here!" shouted a newspaper photographer into his car radio. "Get pictures," his editors shouted back, but already he was gone, racing toward the field, camera in hand. As the other deputies rushed to Delfatti's aid, one put his knee on Gillings's neck, shoving his face in the dirt. Others quickly cuffed him. Seeing this, fourteen-year-old Steven racked a round into his rifle and dashed forward. "Stop!" shouted another deputy, but Steven wheeled and aimed at the officer who quickly dropped to one knee, raised his revolver, and ordered the boy to lower his weapon. Gillings strained to lift his head. "Don't do it, Steven!" he shouted, while pleading with deputies not to shoot. As Steven lowered the rifle, a deputy approached, but the teenager punched the lawman in the mouth, kicked him in the groin, and pulled him to the ground. Young Steven then reached for the pistol in his waistband, but deputies overpowered him.[10] Delfatti was escorting Gillings off the field when he suddenly collapsed in a wail of pain, clutching his head. The barrel of the shotgun had been close to his ear when Gillings's gun went off and the blast had delivered a powerful concussion.[11] The Posse claimed it was "the greatest piece of 'ham acting' ever seen," but Delfatti was hospitalized and couldn't work for a week.[12]

Like the assault on Fred Chicken in Wisconsin, and the attempted citizen's arrest by the Kootenai County Posse Comitatus, the September 1975 "tomato field incident," as it came to be known, was a watershed for the Posse Comitatus. Tough talk and belligerent threats were standard Posse fare, but the gunplay at Stockton signaled a new militancy within the movement. Gillings's weapon was the first to go off and it would not be the last.

After his arrest, Gillings predicted the Posse would become "twice as strong," but the shooting sparked dissension. Jim McDaniel, the local Posse chairman, was concerned about his group's image and ordered Gillings suspended, but forty-eight hours later it was he who had been ousted, when Gillings replaced him.[13] Similar tensions between Posse activists and more militant-minded colleagues drove others away from the movement, including Mike Beach.

The near shootout in Stockton reinforced the image of the Posse as a violence-prone band of right-wing extremists. In November 1975, the Anti-Defamation League's monthly *Bulletin* featured an article by its chief fact-finder, Irwin Suall. Headlined "The Vigilantes Are Comin' If You Don't Watch Out . . ." the piece described the Posse as "a strange new group of radical-right activists, gun-toters, and bigots" and predicted Posse members "may be counted on to provide local trouble if their numbers keep growing."[14]

Widely circulated news accounts described the "tense confrontation near Stockton," and quoted Gillings as saying "[t]here wouldn't have to be but one to three [hangings] in all the United States" to get public officials to obey the Constitution.[15] And while the *Stockton Record* did say that growers were "within their rights in denying entry to union organizers under the law of trespass," it denounced Gillings for taking the law into his own hands. "Posse members who talk so strongly in behalf of the law and order can best serve that cause by dispersing or becoming, simply, a club of men who enjoy firearms for target practice and hunting," the paper advised.[16] Negative publicity discouraged some Posse activists, but it strengthened the resolve of many others who looked forward to future confrontations. After all, the same actions that prompted criticism in the mainstream media earned lavish praise in the right-wing press.

The Posse Comitatus was "a heartening sign of public determination to see that law enforcement is restored and that no malefactor, just because he is a member of a 'minority' group . . . is allowed to escape responsibility for criminal acts," wrote the *National Spotlight* in the lead editorial of its inaugural issue on September 17, 1975.[17] The weekly paper was the house organ of the seventeen-year-old, multimillion-dollar Liberty Lobby, based in Washington, D.C., and its enthusiastic coverage in ensuing years helped raise the profile of the Posse and win it more recruits. In addition to praising tax protesters and Posse activists, the *Spotlight* claimed its goal was to satisfy "a growing hunger on the part of millions of Americans for old-fashioned truth and integrity in the press." In reality, it delivered a copious smorgasbord of racist propaganda and anti-Semitic conspiracy theories, thinly disguised as "anti-Zionism."[18] These themes were the consuming passion of the Liberty Lobby founder, Willis A. Carto, fifty-nine, a shadowy and highly influential far-right figure whose devotion to bigotry found outlets in a complex web of publishing houses and organizations, including the Holocaust-denying Institute for Historical Review he founded in Torrance, California, in 1979.[19]

In addition to its pro-Posse editorial, the September 1975 issue of the *Spotlight* included a full-page article describing a recent meeting between the U.S. Taxpayers Union—Ardie McBrearty's group—and the Sheriff's Posse Comitatus. Held in the woodlands of northern California, the meeting drew about one hundred people, including Shasta County Posse chairman Norman Brown.[20] Among other things, the group "discussed utilizing the Posse to protect citizens against illegal abuses by the Internal Revenue Service."[21] Other right-wing publications also got the word out, but the circulation of publications like *Tax Strike News* and the *American Mercury* was dwarfed by that of the *Spotlight*, which climbed to 315,000 subscribers from 1975 to 1981. (Circulation eventually declined to less than 100,000 by the mid-1990s, and in 2001 the Liberty Lobby closed its doors and discontinued the *Spotlight* after a lawsuit left it bankrupt.)[22]

The clash in Stockton produced accolades in the right-wing press, but it also prompted closer scrutiny by law enforcement, and more arrests. In a confidential memo to California's top assistant attorney general, one agency lawyer outlined the many laws under which Posse members might be prosecuted, including impersonating a peace officer, obstructing a peace officer, riot, and possession of a deadly weapon. The use of force by "a self-appointed 'posse comitatus' " had been repeatedly condemned and outlawed by federal courts, the lawyer reminded his boss.[23] Local authorities also moved against the Posse. After denouncing the group as "nothing but a bunch of vigilantes" and "probably the best argument in the world in favor of gun control," San Joaquin district attorney Joseph Baker charged Gillings and Norman Brown with felony assault.[24] Gillings was also accused of contributing to the delinquency of a minor—his son. And charged with resisting arrest was George Hill, forty-seven, a machinist with an eighth-grade education, a mop of curly gray hair, and a criminal record dating back to 1945.[25]

After Gillings ousted Jim McDaniel as the local Posse chairman, George Hill took his place. (Hill surfaced the following year in Oregon as part of another violent incident involving the Posse.)[26]

Gillings had the perfect pedigree for a Posse leader: he dabbled in politics as a candidate for Congress on the American Party ticket; he embraced tax protest, loved guns, hated busing, and was drawn to the notoriety of it all. And like so many others in his place, he used the Posse to both resolve his personal problems and to promote ultraconservative activism. The son of a sheriff and a native of South Dakota, Gillings was the father of five children and operated a gas station off the interstate near the town of Tracy. When he refused to collect sales tax in 1972 and 1973, local newspapers labeled him the "Tracy Tax Rebel."[27] When he ran for sheriff in 1974, he was depicted as a trigger-happy fellow who presided over "a small arsenal."[28] Gillings's election platform praised the "free enterprise system," pledged to defend the right to bear arms, and promised to uphold the Constitution. If elected sheriff—the "highest law enforcement officer in the land," Gillings said—he vowed to arrest "one or two federal agents and two or three bankers" and put them before a grand jury. Gillings came in a poor third in a three-way primary but still won 5,540 votes after openly campaigning as an extremist.[29]

Eager to keep his name in the news, Gillings filed a federal civil rights lawsuit against the Stanislaus County Board of Supervisors for flying the United Nations flag over the county library in Modesto. The U.N. was "dominated by anti-Christian, anti-American and pro-communist nations" intent on promoting "one-world government," and Gillings demanded $1.2 million in damages for the "cruel and unusual punishment" of being taxed to support the "anti-God, anti-freedom" U.N. flag. The lawsuit was filed in the name of the United States Taxpayers Union and Gillings threatened more lawsuits against those "attempting to force busing down our throats."[30]

Like many Posse leaders, Gillings launched his local chapter hoping it would help him fight his personal battle with authorities. Gillings announced the formation of the San Joaquin County Posse in 1975, after the Atlantic Richfield Company terminated the lease on his service station, and he threatened that its members would come to his aid.[31] The Possemen would be armed with badges, billy clubs, and sawed-off shotguns, Gillings warned, but the men never materialized and the eviction concluded without a confrontation.[32] Gillings also bragged that he made citizen's arrests of drunken drivers on the freeway, but there is no evidence such incidents ever took place.

True to his position as chairman of the local chapter of the National Association to Keep and Bear Arms, Gillings explained that the goal of the Posse was to prevent "officials from taking away our only means to resist tyranny in government—our guns." Gillings predicted his group would soon number in the hundreds, but the *Stockton Record* was not so sure. "We do not believe that public opinion in San Joaquin County will ever support the activity that he envisions," said the paper, which regarded the Posse as a "hazard to public peace."[33] The *Record*'s assessment of the Posse as a danger was right on target, but the paper missed the mark by underestimating its ability to appeal to growers' fears and hatred of the Farm Workers Union. Under the leadership of Cesar Chavez, the UFW had launched successful boycotts against lettuce, grape, and wine growers for their refusal to recognize the union; now tomato growers found themselves Chavez's target. (According to a Harris Poll, seventeen million Americans were boycotting grapes, fourteen million were boycotting lettuce, and eleven million were boycotting Gallo wines by 1975.[34]) And then there was the subtext of race. Tomato pickers were Mexican or Mexican-American and even though California agriculture would have been crippled without them, that had little bearing on the prejudice of many whites, growers and nongrowers alike. Gillings nodded subtly in this direction when he announced that private armed resistance to the UFW was essential because local law enforcement had allowed "alien Mexican communist–backed 'farm organizers' the 'RIGHT' to trespass on private property!"[35] And it was here, where the economic interests of growers and the bigoted, right-wing politics of the Posse converged, that an alliance was forged. According to both growers and the Posse, granting union organizers access to the tomato fields was legalizing trespass. "Where property rights are concerned, is there any difference between a farmers [*sic*] tomato field and his, or YOUR BEDROOM? [*sic*]" asked George Hill and Francis Gillings in a full-page ad that ran in *Tax Strike News* in November 1975.[36] At least one member of the California Supreme Court agreed.

"[T]he right to private property is protected against intrusion by one asserting his right to speech," declared Justice William P. Clark, Jr.[37] But Justice Clark's opinion was a dissent, and the court affirmed the First Amendment right of union organizers who sought access to growers' fields. Faced with the fact that the UFW would soon "intrude" upon their property, some growers vowed to break the law. "This is private property and they're not coming in here—not until we all go to jail," said one.[38] Others, like Frank Ray, called in the Posse.

About two weeks after his arrest, George Hill used the butt of his revolver to gavel to order a meeting of sixty Posse supporters. The two-hour session—part of a clever public-relations and political offensive staged by Hill and Gillings—included the induction of two new Posse members and was filmed by NBC television news.[39] Over the next several weeks, Hill and Gillings showered San Joaquin County officials with complaints, demanded the arrest of the district attorney and sheriff, and testified at the state capitol against gun control.[40] Addressing the Senate Judiciary Committee on a proposed handgun registration law in October 1975, Hill said: "I'm not advocating that we shoot every politician who disagrees with us. But there are certain rights I cannot give away, nor can they be taken away, and there comes a time when force of arms is necessary."[41] While Hill busied himself threatening lawmakers, Gillings's legal problems were mounting.

In addition to the pending criminal charges in San Joaquin County, a federal grand jury indicted Gillings and his wife in November for failure to pay income taxes in 1971 and 1972. As a founder of the United States Taxpayers Union, Gillings's vocal support of tax rebellion attracted the attention of the IRS.[42] If convicted, husband and wife each faced the possibility of $20,000 in fines and two years in prison.[43] Gillings was combative and loved the limelight and so decided to take advantage of both his troubles and his notoriety to seek funds and sign up new Posse recruits.

In a full-page ad in *Tax Strike News* in February 1976, Hill appealed for money and listed the concerns of the Posse: "fantastic sums of money 'stolen' from our paychecks by an income tax law illegally foisted on the American people . . . the great increase of crime . . . fast-decaying morals, drug use, pornography and permissiveness . . . socialist teaching in our schools . . . busing . . . the many needless and unreasonable controls placed on business by such acts as the Occupational Safety and Health and Environmental Protection Act . . . the far-reaching and determined drive by leftist groups to register and outlaw guns . . . our sellout to the Communists worldwide . . . [and] doctoring of news."

Gillings's fellow Posseman George Hill also pointed to "[r]apidly escalating inflation which is cutting our purchasing power and making it difficult to support our families [and] steadily increasing unemployment leading to more welfare, hardship, and worry." He added that the Posse was "well posted on who has caused these problems and why these conditions exist. They have been planned, promoted, financed, aided and abetted at every turn by a ruthless group of International Bankers and Industrialists" striving for world domination and plotting the "eventual takeover of the U.S."

These explanations echoed the tired rhetoric of Henry Ford's *The International Jew*, and the centuries-old Illuminati myth, but what Hill had to say about economic hardship was closer to reality. By 1975 the number of Americans living below the official poverty level had increased 10 percent over the previous year, to 25.9 million.[44] Unemployment, which had risen by half since 1974, stood at 8.3 percent.[45] And the Arab oil embargo of 1973–74, and the energy crisis that followed, spiked inflation to a postwar high of 12.2 percent by 1974, up 50 percent from the year before.[46] According to a nationwide survey by the *New York Times*, Americans were experiencing "a substantial decline in optimism about the future," and an erosion of "confidence, expectations, and aspirations." Apprehension about declining living standards was not why Francis Gillings and George Hill joined the Posse, but a shrinking economic pie did lend credence to the right-wing claims of Middle American Radicals who believed that the prosperity of the "productive" middle classes was being drained by "elites" from above and "parasites" from below.[47]

In June 1976, after a fifteen-day trial, Francis Gillings and Norman Brown were convicted of their role in the tomato field incident. Gillings was given a ninety-day jail term, a suspended sentence, and three years' probation. And the following year he was convicted of tax evasion. When he exhausted his appeals two years later, he was sent to federal prison.[48] He then got into further trouble with the law when he was released. None of this deterred him from continued activism.

Francis Gillings may have been invigorated by gunplay, but the tomato field incident—and others like it—left Mike Beach extremely uneasy and he tried to counsel restraint. In a December 1975 bulletin directed at Gillings, Beach criticized Posse members who engaged in "stupid actions and fighting with the Sheriff [because] [n]o Sheriff can be expected to become associated with a pack of hoodlums." Beach also complained about Posse leaders "making statements to the News [sic] media, throwing a bad light on the Posses [and pursuing the] misconstrued idea that the Posse can take over the law . . . leaving us wide open to the stigma of being called, 'Vigilantes.'"

Beach's criticisms were contained in a mailing titled *Posse Problems* and he noted that the most successful Posses were those that were quietly "fighting the battle in court rooms, keeping their membership secret, [and] avoiding unnecessary publicity, like wearing guns and improper use of the badge."[49] Beach also chastised Posse leaders who allied themselves with the tax-protest movement. To criticize Posse members who paid their taxes was "childish," he wrote, adding, "there are thousands who do." Beach drove himself further to the margins when he attacked those Posse members who advocated racism and anti-Semitism. Calling race and religion "the two most controversial issues," Beach said they should never be discussed in public. "Either issue will destroy your effectiveness and inhibit your growth" and weaken the Posse movement. Instead of getting on a "race kick," the Posse should be fighting "land use, zoning, Regionalism . . . Home Rule and un-elected officialdom." It was more than mildly ironic that a lifelong anti-Semite like Mike Beach chose to give such advice, especially when it alienated him from potential supporters in the Identity movement.

Shortly after issuing his December circular, Beach announced a new plan to reorganize the Posse. Local chapters should immediately drop any mention of the "Sheriff" in their titles and establish "a Citizens' Posse Comitatus" instead.[50] This would not lessen the authority of the Posse, but it would "do away with the friction we presently have with the Sheriffs." To advance his strategy, Beach filed articles of incorporation for the "Citizens' Posse Comitatus." And as part of his effort to further sanitize the image of the Posse, Beach began printing his infamous *Blue Book* without the controversial paragraph that called for public hangings. When questioned about the omission, Beach denied that the change had been initiated by him. "[A] few pantywaists felt [it] was going a little too strong," he said.[51]

Although Beach continued to be quoted frequently in the mainstream press—which persisted in crediting him and not Bill Gale with inventing the Posse Comitatus—whatever modest influence he once had within the movement plummeted. Beach produced fewer manifestos, chartered fewer Posse chapters, and became more disengaged. After he failed to file the required reports on his Citizens' Posse Comitatus, the Oregon Secretary of State dissolved the group.[52] In 1985, the eighty-two-year-old Beach looked back over his involvement with the Posse and called his former associates "idiots and half-wits." The Posse had been turned into a "radical group" and "destroyed" by members who joined "so they could shout and holler and do their dirty work," he said.[53] But along with condemning the Posse, Beach still praised William Dudley Pelley, his first hero. Admitting to his former role in the Silver Shirts, Beach said he would do it all over again if he had the chance.

Although Beach played an important role in popularizing the Posse Comitatus, it is surprising he didn't withdraw from the movement sooner. Apart from his time as a Silver Shirt, and the brief spark of resistance he displayed when he challenged the army during World War II, he was basically a coward. Though good at public relations, Beach was never really able to connect with his constituency, much less win their respect or admiration. And Beach was never indicted or even jailed for his beliefs, unlike more popular activists such as A. J. Porth and George Kindred, who made obvious sacrifices for the cause. Beach's *Blue Book* unequivocally condemned the income tax, but he never acted on its advice. He claimed to endorse the "power of the county," but he got cold feet when Posse rhetoric and actions drew fire from the county sheriff.

At the same time, whatever credibility Beach lacked among true believers, he more than made up for in chutzpah and merchandising talent. After stealing Bill Gale's writings and ideas in 1973 and making them his own, Beach spent the next three years marketing Posse paraphernalia and providing good copy for the press. In sharp contrast, Gale's disdain for the media virtually guaranteed that Beach would get the credit for originating the Posse Comitatus. Even the ADL, which prided itself on exposing key leaders of the radical right, described Beach as the group's "apparent founder," although it did acknowledge that Gale, whom it described as a "veteran anti-Semite," had established a "second home base" for the Posse in California.[54]

Beach's appropriation of credit for starting the Posse was so complete that even when he wasn't identified by name, the media invariably followed his script when describing the organization's roots. According to the *Washington Post* the Posse had started in Portland, Oregon, in 1968.[55] And according to a widely reprinted *Los Angeles Times* article about the "new vigilante group," Beach was "the man behind the movement [who] began chartering posses in 1969."[56] By 1976 erroneous descriptions of the origins of the Posse had appeared so frequently they were tantamount to historical fact. And with the exception of the ADL, which was aware that Beach had been a Silver Shirt, this important fact was almost universally ignored in media reports about Beach and the history of the Posse. Instead, reporters relied on Beach's innocuous descriptions of himself as a retired laundry-equipment salesman or a machinist.[57]

Although Beach contributed significantly to spreading the Posse message, credit for creating the movement still belongs to Bill Gale, who conceived and defined it as equal parts right-wing legalism, Christian Identity theology, militant tax protest, and armed vigilantism. And despite Beach's efforts to redirect the Posse toward tamer tasks, Gale's more violent ideology dominated the movement and defined the public's perception of it. Beach persisted in putting himself forth as the "national chairman," but the real leadership came from grassroots activists like Stockheimer, Gillings, and others who were not afraid to go to jail for their beliefs.

Recognizing that Beach had little to offer, a core of local Posse leaders and activists in Portland ousted him from any position of local influence. Presiding over this group of self-employed businessmen, laborers, retirees, and the unemployed, was a dapper and amiable seventy-two-year-old sign-painter, the "Executive Board Captain" of the Multnomah County Posse Comitatus, Sylvester P. Ehr.

21

BADGES AND STARS

The twelve-foot-long, bright yellow sign overlooking the parking lot outside the offices of Syl Ehr's West Coast Sign Company at 1021 Northeast Union Avenue in Portland carried a quotation he incorrectly attributed to Thomas Jefferson: "One man with courage is a majority."[1] Inside the building was the "Constitution Room," the regular meeting place of the Multnomah County Posse Comitatus. A long table ran down the center and shelves heavily stocked with right-wing literature lined the wall. At one end of the room stood an oversized podium bearing the insignia of the Multnomah County Posse Comitatus: a white, seven-pointed star set against a background of blue. Cigar, pipe, and cigarette smoke filled the air weekly, mixing with steam from coffee cups, when Posse members gathered to hear speeches and exchange information about their latest confrontations with authorities.

Syl Ehr supervised these meetings, jaunty and jovial, dressed in his signature oversized bow tie. The son of a hardware store and lumberyard owner from Moose Lake, Minnesota, Ehr was born in 1903—the same year as Mike Beach. When Ehr arrived in Portland in 1924 he found a job as an apprentice in a downtown sign shop before establishing a business of his own during the Depression.[2] After a wartime stint in the naval shipyards in nearby Vancouver, Washington, sign-painting became his lifelong career. Unlike Beach, Ehr and his followers relished tax protest, conflict, badges, and guns, and justified their illegal misconduct by citing the Constitution. Although the Portland Posse originally grew out of Bill Gale's tape ministry, most of its members avoided direct discussions of race, preferring to target judges, prosecutors, and the courts. Under Ehr's leadership, the group thrived on persecution and its actions produced the desired response. Many law enforcement officials would have preferred to ignore the Posse, especially its more bumbling antics, but Ehr's group was relentlessly provocative and the police had little choice.

In addition to the false quote from Thomas Jefferson, the sign outside Ehr's shop urged passersby to call "Paul Revere," Ehr's right-wing alias, "24 hrs. a day—7 days a week." Those who did heard a five-minute message that began with the spirited greeting, "Awaken, Americans! This is Paul Revere!" Ehr's taped bulletins chronicled his run-ins with bureaucracy; denounced judges as the "black-robed mafia"; assailed tax collectors and the courts; contained dire warnings about "the poisoning of public water supplies through fluoridation" and colorfully decried a large assortment of other, unnamed "plotters."[3]

Although he had both black and Jewish friends, Ehr's racist and anti-Semitic beliefs were deeply held. Ehr made occasional visits to the Aryan Nations compound at Hayden Lake, Idaho, hundreds of miles away, and in 1978 he self-published a 410-page, semiautobiographical novel, *Bearers of the Pall*, which romanticized the Posse Comitatus. Described by Ehr as "a sincere effort to bring to light the root of the evils that now engulf us as a nation," the book was filled with anti-Semitic stereotypes, and its characters referred to Jews as "Khazars," "sheenies," "kikes," "Yidds [*sic*]," and "Christ-killers" throughout.[4] Ehr favored repealing all constitutional amendments beyond the first ten and believed America was divinely ordained to be a Christian nation.[5] So obsessed with Jewish machinations were Ehr and his fellow Possemen, that they kept a lookout for six-pointed Jewish stars, which to them signaled the presence of The Conspiracy and all its malevolent intent.[6] Although Ehr's beliefs may have raised eyebrows among some of his fellow businessmen, that didn't prevent him from becoming a well-liked member of Portland's East Broadway Boosters and president of the Northeast Kiwanis Club. He was that curious type of bigot who readily embraced hateful ideas but whose prejudice never seemed to focus on individuals he met or knew.[7]

Like Mike Beach, Ehr was first introduced to the radical right through the writings of William Dudley Pelley in the 1930s and 1940s, but it wasn't until he joined the tax-strike movement in the early 1970s that Ehr committed himself to political action. In 1975 he was listed as the Portland "branch office" contact for *Tax Strike News*, and several years later he became one of seven "trustees" of the United States Taxpayers Union, along with California Posseman Francis Gillings.[8] Eventually Ehr was indicted for tax evasion, but a prosecution blunder caused a mistrial and the government dropped its case.[9] Some of Ehr's compatriots were not as lucky.

In April 1975, two prominent Oregon tax protesters, William M. Gardiner and Glen L. Lundy, were convicted on federal tax charges.[10] Just days before the trial, Lundy, a longshoreman, had appeared in court to ask that Syl Ehr and two of his fellow Possemen—Gilbert Meyer Jr. and La Verne Donald Hollenbeck— be allowed to assist him in court. Hollenbeck, forty-five, was an unemployed mechanic who sometimes repaired air conditioners for a living, but who spent most of his time writing letters to judges and bureaucrats that he signed "Counsel per Request," and "Court Strategist, 20th Century Non-Union Lawyer [and] member of the Sheriff's Posse Comitatus." Meyer, thirty-five, was the son of a service-station operator who also was a Posse enthusiast and Identity believer. Local sheriffs considered Meyer Jr. "a radical." Among other things he was known for having a live cougar as a pet, which he sometimes kept chained in the back of his pickup truck. Meyer also was belligerent, and when he came to court on Lundy's behalf he insisted on bringing a tape recorder. When he refused to shut it off it took three U.S. marshals to escort him out.[11] Four days later, a jury found Lundy guilty of filing a false tax-withholding certificate.[12]

When Lundy, forty-two, wasn't railing against the income tax, he was recounting his ongoing conflicts with police, judges, and the courts. During one Posse meeting he complained about an overtime parking ticket he had received and demanded that parking meters be abolished. "What they do is arrest the vehicle. It doesn't make sense," he claimed. Describing how, on another occasion, he had been threatened with legal action for removing his children from public school, Lundy claimed that he got even by simply arresting the judge. "That took care of that," he said. "Haven't been bothered since."[13]

In addition to denouncing parking meters and state-mandated automobile emissions tests, Posse spokesmen criticized Lee P. Brown, the African-American sheriff of overwhelmingly white Multnomah County.[14] More obsessed with the machinations of the Jews than the presence of blacks, the Portland Posse never publicly raised the issue of race as it related to the sheriff. Instead they groused about Brown because he had been appointed by the chairman of the county commission, not elected by the voters, and, more importantly, because he declined to issue permits for concealed weapons. Stymied locally, many Posse activists simply headed south to Klamath County where such permits were freely dispensed and could be used anywhere in the state.[15] Though the right to keep and bear arms was a popular topic at Posse meetings, the group preferred the subject of tax protest. According to Mike Beach, the talk sometimes turned ugly, as when some members of the Portland Posse allegedly plotted to kidnap a federal revenue agent. There is no evidence to support Beach's allegation, but it is the reason he gave for resigning from the group in late spring or early summer 1975. "The idea was too radical. I got the hell out," Beach said years later.[16]

The rift between Beach and the Portland group widened further when Syl Ehr and his followers filed their own articles of incorporation for Beach's Sheriff's Posse Comitatus and the Citizens Law Enforcement and Research Committee.[17] When he issued his 1975 letter on *Posse Problems*, castigating local activists for embracing tax protesters and trying to usurp the role of the sheriff, Beach had many local groups in mind, including the Multnomah County chapter. Portland was Beach's backyard, and it was there that LaVerne Hollenbeck drove around town with a pair of magnetic Posse Comitatus decals prominently fixed to his car doors. The large blue-and-white seven-pointed metallic stars were nearly identical to those used by the Multnomah County Sheriff's Department and it wasn't long before they caught somebody's attention.

On January 14, 1976, around eleven P.M., Sheriff's Deputy Russell Arsenault saw Hollenbeck's beat-up 1968 Plymouth cruising westbound on Southeast Division Street, on the eastern outskirts of Portland. After clocking Hollenbeck at nine miles per hour over the speed limit, Arsenault pulled him over. He then asked Hollenbeck about the sheriff's stars.[18] "I'm a police officer. I do the same job that you do," Hollenbeck replied, producing a distinctive seven-pointed gold star from his wallet that identified him as a "captain" in the Sheriff's Posse Comitatus.[19] Hollenbeck's false credentials ultimately landed him in jail and made his fight a cause célèbre in Portland Posse circles, but the brief story behind the badge he so proudly displayed involves a set of truly bizarre coincidences.

When the founders of the Portland Posse—Hollenbeck among them—decided to issue officious titles and badges to themselves, they went to Nudelman Brothers, the same company that provided the uniforms and other gear to law enforcement agencies in Oregon.[20] Not only were the Nudelmans Jewish, but the family's ancestors also had lived at the Painted Woods settlement in North Dakota along with Marcus Gale, the great-uncle of Bill Gale. After the colony failed, both families ended up in Portland where the Nudelmans went into the clothing business and eventually won the contract to supply uniforms and badges to the Multnomah County Sheriff's Department.[21] It is ironic enough that Bill Gale's father was Jewish, but the fact that his great-uncle's fellow settlers from Painted Woods ended up providing paraphernalia to the Posse Comitatus he created more than eighty years after they left North Dakota is almost unbelievable.

After Hollenbeck was convicted of impersonating a police officer—for which he was fined $100 and sentenced to thirty days in jail—some Posse supporters turned the facts upside down and blamed the Nudelman Brothers for Hollenbeck's troubles.[22] "LaVerne Hollenbeck BEARS HIS CROSS. Nudelman Brothers COUNT THEIR THIRTY PIECES OF SILVER," blared one anti-Semitic headline in *The Swinging Sword*, an irregularly published newsletter that championed the cause of the Portland Posse Comitatus.[23] The badge incident and other antics led to television and news reports, including one article in the *Oregon Journal*, which quoted Ehr as saying, "If we can put a few judges and the D.A. into the penitentiary, then we can get back our constitutional rights."[24] In spite of the veiled threats and bombast, law enforcement officials took the Portland Posse pretty much in stride, as they had the group under close surveillance.

Ehr's "Paul Revere" messages had first caught the attention of the Portland police and the Multnomah County Sheriff's Department in 1974 and both agencies planted informants in the group.[25] The Sheriff's Department's choice for the undercover assignment was John Osbourne, an aging former insurance adjuster who once had served eleven years in state prison for murder. Osbourne had always wanted to be a policeman, but he ended up sympathizing with the Posse instead. "I think we lost him after the second meeting," chuckled Marvin Woidyla, a Sheriff's Department deputy and one of Osbourne's handlers. "He provided us with just enough useful information to keep us off his back. . . . But the information he got back to us and the information we got from other agencies convinced me that we didn't have a whole lot to worry about. Our feeling was really that if they armed themselves they'd probably severely injure themselves before they got out of the room."

"If brains was gunpowder they couldn't blow their nose," added Woidyla's colleague, Macil Flye.[26] Although local authorities kept a close eye on the Portland Posse, the more they learned, the less concerned they became. "The problem here in the Portland area with the leadership of the Posse was they never had a defined goal," former deputy Woidyla explained. Sylvester Ehr "liked to talk." LaVerne Hollenbeck was "impressed with his badge" but "not very bright." The Meyer family were "radicals," but not necessarily violent. Sam Suwol, the Posse's attorney, had "the intellect of [a] candle." And Mike Beach was "one of these people who thought he could do something better and really wasn't a dangerous person." The meetings in the back room of Syl Ehr's sign shop were nothing more than an organized "mill-about," according to Woidyla. "If anything big was going to happen, it was going to happen elsewhere, [like] eastern Oregon." He was right.

On August 27, 1976, a group of seven Possemen, armed with pistols, rifles, clubs, and guard dogs, made national headlines when they seized a potato and wheat farm in Umatilla County in an attempt to settle a bizarre land dispute. Eight hours later the Posse group surrendered to a heavily armed contingent of Oregon state troopers and local sheriff's deputies. That incident, and the successful prosecutions that followed, further reinforced the Posse's reputation as a band of trigger-happy extremists and troublemakers. It also prompted a full-scale domestic security investigation by the FBI.

22

THE HOSKINS ESTATE

Umatilla County is in the northeast corner of Oregon's Columbia Basin, a sparsely populated broad plateau spanning five of the state's thirty-six counties. The powerful Columbia River flows into Oregon here from Washington State and continues on the final leg of its 1,240-mile journey from the interior of Canada to the Pacific Ocean. Umatilla County takes its name from an Indian word meaning "water rippling over sand," and the term aptly describes the many rivers that dissect the region. At thirty-two hundred square miles, the county is larger than Rhode Island and Delaware combined.[1]

When Sachiheko "Sach" Mikami and his brother Daniel purchased more than eight thousand acres in the early 1970s, the land was largely dry farm and pasture. But after they installed large-scale, center-pivot irrigation, the value of their wheat and potato farm skyrocketed. In 1974, Sach Mikami received a telephone call from a Posse activist, Everett Thoren. "I believe you owe us some rent because the property you are farming rightfully belongs to me," claimed Thoren, who suggested the two men meet. Mikami told him to call his lawyer instead.

Unbeknownst to Mikami, part of his property was the object of a long-running family dispute involving the descendants of J. T. Hoskins, a pioneer-era sheepman.[2] Unable to find a lawyer to press his case, Hoskins's elderly son Bill had enlisted Thoren's aid.[3] Thoren, fifty-three, was the father of eight children and a carpenter, not an attorney, but he had taken a year of law school night classes before dropping out. Six years earlier, Hoskins had pleaded with him for help but Thoren had said no. Then, in 1972, Thoren approached Bill Hoskins with an unusual proposal: If he and the other heirs would deed him their interest in the property, Thoren would pursue the claim of the defunct "Hoskins estate."[4]

"The only way I can do anything is if you sever complete interest in what you think you have," Thoren explained. In the end, he persuaded Bill Hoskins and several other elderly heirs to each pay him a dollar and sign paperwork he said would make him the legal owner of about half the Hoskins estate. Armed with the documents, Thoren called the Mikami brothers and began harassing neighboring farmers, insisting they were his tenants and owed him rent. Thoren even hired a surveyor and began trespassing on parts of the property, which got him arrested.

Thoren's pursuit of the Hoskins estate coincided with the arrival of the Posse Comitatus in Umatilla County, and he turned to the group for help. The presence of the Posse was formally announced in January 1974 in Pendleton, the county seat, by Samuel Mann Porter, a local right-wing activist whom state police had once termed "mentally disturbed," for his fanciful tales of welfare workers engaged in drugs and prostitution.[5] One month after setting up the Posse, Porter sent telegrams to the governor, warning that a two thousand–man Posse "committee" had been formed to arrest him.[6] Following the usual formula of overlapping organizational alliances, the National Association to Keep and Bear Arms soon appeared in Pendleton, with Herbert Breed, the NAKBA leader and Posse enthusiast from Klamath Falls, as the main speaker.[7] Porter recruited other militants, including Thomas R. Braun, a retired Marine Corps captain from nearby Hermiston, who stated the mission of the Umatilla County Posse clearly enough: "The aim of the Posse is to apprehend all public officials possible, elected and appointed, who receive and execute unconstitutional directives . . . charge them with violations of their oaths of office, and have them prosecuted."[8] In October 1975, Everett Thoren joined Braun, Porter, and nine other Posse activists to pursue an ambitious plan of action.

With paperwork drawn up by Porter, the group ordered Sheriff Bill McPherson to arrest three judges, County Attorney Jack Olsen, and two of Olsen's aides, on "charges" of treason.[9] "Failure to do so will authorize the Posse to act in your name to everyone's injury," they warned. But according to one local judge who spoke frankly to the newspaper, the Posse paperwork was "on its way to the waste can," and Porter, fifty-seven, was "a senile old man."[10] Further insults came from County Attorney Olsen, who called the Posse "a bunch of dingbats," and sent copies of Porter's legal threats to the state attorney general, suggesting it might constitute the crime of "simulating legal process."[11] The sheriff then issued a proclamation ordering the Posse to "cease entirely in it's [sic] operation,"[12] but the group was not easily dissuaded.

"[We] will hold those who participate in any violations . . . criminally responsible," Porter fired back in a typewritten memo that paraphrased Bill Gale's instructions: "Arrests may be made and the criminal remanded to sheriff's custody for trial by citizens' jury."[13]

In addition to wielding their pens, Umatilla County Posse activists relied on the occasional firearm to make their point. When police in Pendleton approached the home of Posseman Clifford Betz to investigate an alleged trespassing incident, Betz responded by firing his weapon through the front door, accidently killing the family dog. No lawmen were hurt, and Betz was charged with reckless endangerment.[14]

Such carryings-on worried even the ultraconservative John Birch Society, which was trying to drum up support for a new office in eastern Oregon. The Posse was "not acting in the best interest of the constitutional government," a Birch Society spokesman stiffly declared.[15] However, like most Posse militants, Sam Porter didn't care what the Birch Society said or thought; besides, it was his job to determine what was "constitutional" and what was not. In 1976, Porter announced he was "Chairman of the Legal (Judicial) Committee [of the] Oregon Association of Posse Comitatus," and he and Everett Thoren took their battle statewide. First Porter helped Posse members sue the Josephine County Commission for "counterfeiting" because the Commission accepted tax payments in paper money instead of gold.[16] Porter borrowed from Bill Gale's booklet, *The Faith of Our Fathers*, to make his case: "Six million Yehudis . . . Criminal Zionists . . . and foreigners with assumed names" were brought to the United States during World War II, he wrote in his "Affidavit Notice of Felony."[17] A second Porter lawsuit demanded $3.75 million in damages from various county officials.[18]

Meanwhile Thoren petitioned the state supreme court to remove the names of the Oregon Secretary of State and the attorney general from the statewide ballot. According to Thoren, both men had violated their oaths of office by failing to uphold "constitutional law." Only *he* had sufficient knowledge to determine which officials could enforce the Constitution, Thoren said. "That's a lot of power. . . . Even the old-time vigilantes had a better concept of government than that," editorialized the *Salem Oregon Statesman*.[19]

More Posse-inspired litigation followed, alleging similar complaints of conspiracy, fraud, counterfeiting, contempt of court, and additional unspecified violations of the Constitution. In April 1976, Porter and more than two dozen other Posse members filed a $150 million lawsuit against the governor, the state attorney general, and five of the seven justices of the Oregon State Supreme Court. Attached to their complaint was a demand that the sheriff arrest the Oregon Chief Justice, or "we the people shall bring [him] to justice under the law of Posse Comitatus." Like every other lawsuit Porter filed, it was thrown out of court.[20]

Porter's paper war infuriated Mike Beach. And so when Beach and other leaders of the Oregon Association of Posse Comitatus met in Klamath Falls on May 15, they expelled Porter from the group. (Of course, when Porter got the news, he sued them, too.) Beach's meeting concluded with discussion of plans for a Bicentennial Fourth of July outing near Beach's retirement home in Baker, about three hundred miles east of Portland. The group was instructed to bring dehydrated food, fishing tackle, shovels, tents, guns, and shooting targets. They were also told to study their army field manuals prior to the rendezvous. "[A] resistance movement must be the logical conclusion to the developing patriotic movement in the United States today. . . . The freedom of future Americans will depend on [it]," announced the group's secretary-treasurer, portentously.[21]

Meanwhile Everett Thoren planned to fight a different war, this one all his own. He decided to lay siege to the Hoskins estate. It was a battle launched by armed vigilantes, and the attention it received would lead the U.S. Attorney General to launch a nationwide offensive against the Posse Comitatus.

The summer wheat harvest was fast approaching when Thoren made plans to remove crops from land that had been planted by the Mikami brothers and surrounding farmers. His first step was to enlist several men from Portland, including Donald Allen Goodwill, forty-six. A part-time bartender with a drinking problem, Goodwill lived with his aging parents in northeast Portland.[22] He had known Thoren for only several months, but he was quickly impressed by the older man's apparent knowledge of the law.[23] Although he wasn't in the leadership of the Posse Comitatus, Goodwill was well acquainted with other members of the Multnomah County chapter, including Henry Richard Deering, a rifle-wielding Posseman who had recently got himself arrested for bringing a weapon to a land-use planning meeting.[24]

On July 19, a neighbor of the Mikamis, Jack Zabransky, found one of Thoren's men—a Portland security guard—standing alongside the road in his uniform. When asked what he was doing, the man said he had been hired by Thoren to guard grain that was being harvested.[25] No longer content to demand that the Mikamis and their neighbors pay him rent, Thoren had instructed Donald Goodwill to hire a custom harvester to cut Zabransky's wheat. As Goodwill and his men approached the grain trucks in the field, a state trooper appeared and warned they would be arrested for trespassing. The grain was removed to the local elevator and stored under Zabransky's name.[26]

Unable to stop the wheat harvest, Thoren hit upon a more dramatic plan: Take possession of Mikami Farms itself. According to Thoren's logic, half the property already was his, but since the Mikamis and others were farming it, he would have to break their "claim of adverse possession" by occupying Mikami farms for at least a day. But this scheme required a larger and more experienced group of men, so he turned to the San Joaquin County Posse Comitatus in California, whose showdown in the tomato field the previous year had earned the group widespread notoriety. Thoren first reached George Hill, the group's chairman.[27]

Born in Kansas in 1929, Hill had become interested in right-wing legal theories in the mid-1960s.[28] Neither he nor his wife held a job. Instead the couple and their five children survived, in part, on donations from people who requested "counseling" for their legal problems.[29] They also published a small right-wing newsletter, the *Citizen's News*. When Thoren outlined the situation with Mikami Farms, Hill likened it to the conflict between tomato growers and the farm workers' union.[30] Both cases involved defense of private-property rights, according to Hill, so he agreed to come to Oregon.[31] Hill recruited four other Californians for the seizure of Mikami farms: One was Robert David Cummings, thirty-one, a housepainter and laborer from Glendale, California, whom Hill had met at a tax-protest workshop in Arizona.[32] At six feet eight inches tall, and weighing 280 pounds, Cummings was rather intimidating.[33] Another recruit was Donald Ray Cooper, forty-two, a self-employed appliance repairman from Stockton and the husband of Hill's sister-in-law. Vernon Edwin Essig, a garageman from nearby Lodi, also joined the team. Essig, forty-eight, was an enthusiastic member of the National Association to Keep and Bear Arms and had signed the original San Joaquin County Posse Comitatus charter. The weak link in the chain turned out to be Essig's eighteen-year-old friend, Farrell Anthony Griggs. Griggs had been in the Stockton standoff with the UFW, but he ended up turning on his compatriots in Oregon.

On Wednesday, August 25, 1976, the five men crammed themselves into Essig's two-door Chrysler Saratoga, along with pistols, ammunition, and other equipment, and drove through the night to Oregon.[34] The group arrived in Portland late Thursday morning, and spent most of the day consulting with Everett Thoren, Donald Goodwill, and several others.[35] They also took time to fashion several homemade wooden clubs and buy extra ammunition. When they reconvened that night to polish their battle plans, they were disconcerted to discover that Thoren had a previous engagement: he had to be in Klamath Falls to attend his son's wedding rehearsal, or so he said.[36] The California Possemen hesitated, but Thoren convinced them to proceed with the plan and promised them $1,000 each if they did. About one A.M., the group departed for Umatilla County, a five-hour drive away. The Posse convoy consisted of three vehicles, eight men (five Californians, plus Donald Goodwill and two more Portland Posse reinforcements), and two guard dogs: a German shepherd and a nasty Doberman pinscher that belonged to Goodwill. Stopping briefly for a bite to eat, the group hurried on, eager to arrive at Mikami Farms before daybreak.[37]

23

SPUD SHED

Vern Essig loaded the magazine of his Browning 9-mm pistol with hollow-point bullets and returned the weapon to his holster in a "cocked and locked" position with a round in the chamber.[1] Although the group had agreed they wouldn't shoot unless fired upon, Essig, a Korean War veteran, wanted to be prepared.[2] He and his fellow Possemen had barely slept the previous two days, but they moved quickly to seize control of Mikami Farms. They took a pizza carton and scrawled, NO TRESPASSING, HOSKINS ESTATE, in large block lettering and hung it from a utility pole overlooking the farm entrance where Donald Goodwill had parked his beat-up 1966 Ford station wagon. Dressed in a blue suit and armed with a clipboard, Goodwill stood guard, his Doberman close at hand.

It was nearly daybreak, and workers—many of them Latino laborers—were beginning to arrive. Huge, threatening, and disheveled, Robert Cummings scared them off. Dressed in a green military field jacket and carrying a nine-shot, .22-caliber revolver on his hip, a seven-inch hunting knife in his belt, and brandishing a wooden club, Cummings walked among the potato storage sheds—buildings the size of football fields—gruffly informing anyone he encountered that they were trespassing and would be placed under citizen's arrest. To encourage their swift departure he added that "the cops might come and there might be some shooting." And if he thought the workers did not speak English he simply said, "Vamoose!" and put his hand on his gun. They did.[3]

When Sach Mikami arrived a little after six A.M. he found Goodwill's station wagon blocking the road. Cummings waved him off.

"What's going on here?" Mikami demanded.[4]

"We're taking possession of this property and if you try to enter, you'll be trespassing and we'll make a citizen's arrest on you," Cummings replied.

"Well, I own the property and I have business to do, so I am going in anyway," said Mikami as he started to pull his pickup around Goodwill's wagon, but Cummings stepped forward and put his foot on the truck's fender.

"You're not coming in. The rightful owners are repossessing the property." Mikami took stock of Cummings's six-foot, eight-inch frame, as well as the guns and clubs. He saw Goodwill's dogs straining at their chains. Realizing the Posse meant business, he put the truck in reverse. Looking to intercept his employees on their way to work, Mikami crossed paths with one of his foremen, Harvey Furukawa, and his wife. "We've got trouble at the gate," Mikami told them. "Try to go around through the field and come in from the rear to find out what's going on," he instructed. Then he sped off to call the cops.[5]

The Furukawas managed to sneak in the scale house where trucks loaded with potatoes and grain were brought to be weighed. The two of them quickly locked the doors and windows and radioed Mikami to report that as many as eight Possemen might be involved. (They were close. Eight men had arrived that morning, but only seven remained, as one of Goodwill's Portland buddies chickened out.) Now several of the men were approaching the scale house. "Don't confront them," Sach advised by radio. "Just stay inside and I'll get help as soon as I can." It was six forty-five A.M. and Mikami called the state police in Hermiston, ten miles away.[6] Inexplicably, it took more than an hour for the first lawman to arrive, and the Posse made good use of the time: They scared off more Mikami workers, cut telephone lines, disconnected the electricity, and removed the CB radio antenna from the roof of the scale house.[7] They also moved Goodwill's station wagon into one of the potato sheds and replaced it with a barricade of heavy metal pipes. Meanwhile George Hill was documenting the assault and vandalism with his Nikon Super-8 movie camera. Sach Mikami's brother Dan showed up and managed to find the Furukawas, but soon the Possemen came pounding on the scale house door. "You better let us in! Everybody better leave or somebody is going to get hurt," they shouted. Debbie Furukawa was terrified.[8]

A little after eight A.M., state patrol sergeant Amos Rasmussen finally arrived, sealed off the road, and approached the farm entrance where he saw Goodwill, Essig, and the dogs at the pipe barrier. Among the first things he noticed was Essig's pistol, cocked and locked.[9]

"Who is in charge?" he asked.

"I'm the chief of security," Essig replied importantly. Concerned about possible hostages, Rasmussen got the Posse to agree to let him enter the property so he could remove the Furukawas and other workers. But Goodwill and Essig wanted the lawman to first surrender his handgun. At six feet five inches and 250 pounds, the forty-year-old, seventeen-year veteran of the state patrol wasn't worried about a fistfight, but he was not about to abandon his weapon. "Look," he said, "if we get into a shootout, I'm not going down without taking a few of you bastards with me. And as for the dogs, if one of them even so much as looks like it is coming at me, I'm going to kill him, too." The tough talk added to the tension, but Rasmussen kept his gun and Goodwill and Essig led him to the building where the Furukawas were huddled. Fearful, they hesitated to leave with any of the Possemen nearby, but Rasmussen reassured them.[10] On their way out, one of the Possemen shouted to them with a surprising offer:

"We'd like to have you work for us as soon as we're all lined up here. We'll even think about giving you a pay raise, you know. You'll have really good bosses and you're just welcome anytime."

It struck Debbie Furukawa as completely bizarre. Earlier that morning she had been so scared she had vomited. Now the men who had terrorized her were offering her a job.[11] While Rasmussen rounded up a handful of other workers and escorted them to the front entrance, Essig explained the Posse position. "We are on the property legally and everyone else is trespassing. We are going to hold the property at all costs, until Everett Thoren tells us to leave."

"What force will you use if we try to remove you?" asked Rasmussen, an air force veteran who had served in the military police. "If you use your guns, we will, too," Essig replied. "We have a trunk full of baseball bats that we would rather use, but we'll use the firearms if we have to," he threatened.

"Well, how many men do you have on the property and how many guns?" Rasmussen queried, trying to appear nonchalant. "We have eight to eleven men," Essig lied. "[And] four pistols and two high-powered rifles and clubs," he further exaggerated, almost doubling the number of weapons they had brought. After clearing the farm of civilians, Rasmussen left and instructed a fellow trooper to retrieve several long-range rifles from his home. He also addressed the knot of reporters that had gathered at the roadblock. Negotiations would begin "at noon, or at one-oh-one," he told them, referring to the midday heat.[12] Then he left to retrieve more weapons from the state patrol office in Hermiston, as well as flak vests, radios, and binoculars.

Rasmussen responded to the unfolding crisis with professionalism and efficiency. Unfortunately, the local sheriff's department and the FBI did not. Had they done so, the standoff would likely have been averted. The day before the carload of Possemen departed California for Oregon, the Sacramento FBI had reported it was closing its file on the San Joaquin County Posse.[13] If agents had been watching the group more closely, they probably would have learned of its departure and had more time to plan ahead. Notwithstanding the blunder, the FBI in Oregon did find out about the Posse's plans, but quite late in the game, and they also fumbled their response. It was about eight P.M., the night before the farm takeover, when the Umatilla County Sheriff's Department received a call from the FBI man in Pendleton, Dan Jacobs. According to Sheriff's Department records, Jacobs explained that an informant had reported that eight members of the Posse were planning to leave Portland that night to take over property in Umatilla County owned by "Orientals." Jacobs named the men involved, described their three cars, and promised to call back to confirm if the group actually left Portland. Apparently he never did. And the Sheriff's Department did nothing to prepare.[14]

After returning to the farm with riot gear, Rasmussen set up four observation posts around the property, each with a team of men armed with high-powered rifles. He then returned to the farm entrance and asked Essig and Goodwill to surrender, but the two refused. "What will it take to convince you to leave the area and give up?" he asked.

"The only order we will obey is one from a federal court in Portland, or one from Everett Thoren," Essig replied.

"Well, I don't think that is going to be forthcoming. Is there anything else that will cause you to give up?" Rasmussen asked.

"If we were met with an overwhelming force," Essig replied.

"Well, what would you consider that to be?"

"When I was in the service in Korea, I was part of what was known as the 'frozen chosen,' and the odds were three hundred–to–one and we got out," Essig blustered. But Goodwill was having second thoughts and soon asked whether he could leave the property to call Thoren, since the phone lines had been cut by the Posse earlier. Rasmussen agreed. Around three P.M. Goodwill was escorted to state patrol headquarters while Rasmussen left one of his men in Posse "custody" to ensure Goodwill's safe return.[15] But Thoren was conveniently away in Klamath Falls (or so he said), and Goodwill had nothing to report.[16] Meanwhile Vern Essig said that if he could talk to an FBI agent, the Posse might consider giving up, so he and Dan Jacobs discussed arrangements for the group's surrender.[17] Around four P.M. Rasmussen gave the men a thirty-minute warning—he and others had decided they could not afford to let the standoff drag into the evening.

According to the terms that Essig and Goodwill had negotiated, the lawmen would advance on the property and into an open area between the potato sheds. The Posse would then relinquish its weapons. Rasmussen went over the plan with the Posse leaders. "You've got to go by what you say. If a shot is fired, we're going down and we're shooting," he told them. Twenty minutes after the deadline expired, Rasmussen ordered two dozen lawmen into action. With the "Code Blue" ambulance standing by and riflemen looking down their scopes, a phalanx of officers approached on foot and in thirteen patrol cars. Armed with revolvers, shotguns and batons, the men wore military-type flak vests and riot helmets with face shields. Despite the elaborate choreography, Rasmussen was on edge. He knew the Posse would have the first shot and chances were good it would take one of his men down. Then there was the problem of someone accidently firing a round. "If that happens, I'd better be watching for a place to dump into," he thought, scanning the wide-open farmyard with few places to hide.[18] Although the odds fell short of Essig's "three hundred–to–one," it was just the display of force the Posse needed to save face, and the men offered no resistance. Essig removed his pistol and handed it to one of the troopers. "There's a round in the chamber," he cautioned. The remaining Possemen were quickly disarmed and cuffed, their weapons inventoried and placed on the hood of Goodwill's station wagon to be displayed for police photographers and the news media.[19] There were three handguns and a Remington .30-.06 rifle—the latter weapon was capable of bringing down a man from up to four hundred yards away. All had rounds in the chamber. Boxes of ammunition, as well as baseball bats, wooden clubs, and other hazardous gear were found in the station wagon.[20]

Always conscious of the media, Goodwill and Essig had demanded access to reporters as part of the surrender agreement. Handcuffed and in separate squad cars, both men addressed a crowd of reporters at a roadblock. "These people have been fighting twenty-three years, the heirs of the Hoskins estate, to regain the land stolen and swindled by judges right here in the county," Essig announced. Goodwill, who shared the backseat with his German shepherd, also made a statement. "We proved our point. We took control of the property, and possession is nine-tenths of the law."[21]

Everett Thoren didn't arrive in Umatilla County until two days later, when he telephoned the jail at two-thirty Sunday morning and demanded to see "his men." When told that only attorneys could see prisoners outside regular visiting hours, he claimed he was "licensed by the Constitution to practice law."[22] Then he wrote Goodwill a note, encouraging him to tough it out behind bars: "I would like to have you all in the Hotel when . . . I go on national t.v. tomorrow . . . you can do more good where your [sic] at than free at this time." He signed it, "as ever your friend."[23] But by Monday, Thoren was back in Portland, camped out at the home of Multnomah County Posse "Captain" LaVerne Hollenbeck, fielding calls from the media and relatives of the jailed men. "My business now is finding missing heirs," Thoren told the Oregonian, bragging that he was helping one Portland woman retrieve a $50 million estate.[24]

The "potato shed" arrests made front-page news in the Stockton Record and the Lodi News-Sentinel in California. "Hang in there, things are popping," Velma Griggs wrote proudly to her son and the others who were still in jail. "You are the American patriot's [sic] of the hour. . . . This might be the start of the waking up of this nation."[25] Articles in the Oregon press prompted the Portland FBI to notify Bureau headquarters that the occupation of Mikami Farms was receiving widespread media attention.[26]

On Tuesday, September 7, an Umatilla County grand jury indicted the seven men on felony charges of burglary and riot. Cummings, Griggs, and Essig faced additional weapons charges.[27] When asked whether he understood the charges, George Hill emphatically replied: "I understand the charges are garbage," which earned him a rebuke from the judge. Two days after the indictments, the Portland FBI sent a twenty-two-page report on the Posse Comitatus to Washington, asking permission to initiate a full domestic-security investigation: "The movement's boldness and disregard for the laws of this country demonstrate great potential for violence," said the report, which also warned that Posse membership did "not appear to be declining." Seventy-eight chapters had been formed over the previous two years in twenty-three states, according to the Portland FBI, and California, Oregon, Wisconsin, and Illinois had the most local groups. And in places where state organizations had been formed, such as Oregon and California, "more cohesiveness and greater numbers of members . . . increases the likelihood that force and violence will occur." While the FBI derided Mike Beach's membership claims as "grossly exaggerated," it noted the exact number of active Posse members was unknown.[28]

The following week, news of the "potato shed" takeover made the *Washington Post*. "Frontier 'Justice' Rides in West," blared the headline of the page-one article, which quoted Umatilla County Sheriff Bill McPherson: "There's no way we're going to let them come in and play sheriff," he said. The news story was picked up on the wires and reprinted widely across the country. Not only did the "posse" theme conjure up colorful images of a Wild West showdown, but the characters also matched the script. The article described the Mikami Farms takeover, and cited Posse blustering in Portland, as well as the near-shootout in Stockton, California, the previous year.[29] It also hinted at a Posse plan to seize political control of rural Alpine County, California—a scheme in which the convicted tax protester Francis Gillings played a part. "[O]nce we get people up there then we'll elect our own sheriff and our own county council," bragged another well-known tax protester, Terrance Oaks. "We can get what we want then—mortars, machine guns, anything. Lord help the government agent who gets caught up there violating a citizen's rights. He might spend the rest of his life picking up trash along the highway."[30] As it turned out it was Francis Gillings who was convicted of a crime—he pleaded guilty to two felony counts of elections-law violations in connection with the scheme.[31]

On October 14, 1976, the U.S. Attorney General granted Portland's request and authorized a full domestic-security investigation of the Posse. The directive also gave permission for the widespread use of FBI informants. Probes of any person holding "local, state, or national office" in the Posse were permitted, as well as of anyone who had "engaged in activities which indicate he is likely to use force or violence in violation of federal law." Local agents were directed to immediately assess the propensity for violence of each new local Posse chapter. Oregon officials stepped up their inquiry as well.[32]

Meanwhile, Everett Thoren told Goodwill and the others that he was taking bold legal action on their behalf. But like his other lawsuits, the habeas corpus petition he filed with the state supreme court was gobbledygook and was swiftly rejected.[33] Of the seven Possemen indicted in the Mikami Farms takeover, four cases came to trial and were prosecuted by an assistant state attorney general, H. Robert Hamilton. While he acknowledged that some of the Posse's conduct was laughable, the confrontation at Mikami Farms had to be taken seriously. "It could have turned into a bloodbath . . . the likes of which the state has never seen," he said.[34]

Vern Essig was the first to go on trial. Security was tight, with armed guards posted at each courtroom door and an airport metal detector installed to screen visitors. Such precautions are standard in most county courthouses today, but in 1976 they were highly unusual.[35] Though there were no incidents in the courtroom, the FBI did report that three "explosive bombings" occurred in Hood River, just two weeks after the end of the trial, and an unexploded pipe bomb was found in the back of a pickup truck south of town.[36] After a three-day trial with two dozen prosecution witnesses, the jury deliberated less than two hours before convicting Essig of burglary, disorderly conduct, carrying a dangerous weapon, and unauthorized use of a vehicle.[37] While awaiting sentencing, Essig received a letter from his fellow Posseman, Don Cooper, lamenting their involvement in the potato-shed takeover, criticizing Thoren and citing Bible verses from the Book of Revelation that attacked "those who say they are Jews . . . but are the synagogue of Satan."[38]

Essig also heard from Ruth Gillings, who updated him on the latest Posse activities in California, including news of her pending trial for tax evasion. Gillings also wrote to Oregon authorities on Essig's behalf, praising him as "a model citizen" and a "true American Patriot of our time always working for better government."[39] Despite her pleas, Essig was fined $500, ordered to pay $1,500 in attorneys' fees, and sentenced to three concurrent, five-month jail terms and two concurrent five-year terms of probation.[40] Robert Cummings was next on trial and he, too, was convicted. Goodwill was next to last. The courtroom was packed the first day of the trial and the Posse had papered the building with leaflets that compared Goodwill to Jesus Christ, accused Judge William Dale of being "Pontias Pilot [*sic*]" and claimed that the arrests of the "Potato Patch Seven" were the result of FBI entrapment.[41] Goodwill also was convicted.

In July 1977, Everett Thoren became the fourth and final Mikami Farms defendant to go to trial. Acting as his own attorney, Thoren piled stacks of papers around the courtroom and tried the patience of the prosecutors and the judge. Predictably, he, too, went to jail. While Thoren was awaiting sentencing, a parole officer tried to interview him but Thoren claimed he was somebody else named "Gordon Grant." When he was finally forced to admit his identity, Thoren received three thirty-day jail terms, a three-year suspended sentence, and five years' probation.[42]

If Thoren's scheme to claim the Hoskins estate concluded as farce, his tax-protest activities more than fifteen years later almost produced a tragedy. The near-victim was Karen Matthews, a prim, attractive woman with dark, shoulder-length hair and wire-rimmed glasses, who was the elected clerk-recorder of Stanislaus County, California. Matthews's troubles began in November 1993, when several tax protesters appeared in her office in Modesto, demanding that she remove a $416,000 lien the IRS had filed against one of their members.[43] The group was called Juris Christian Assembly, and its founder and leader was none other than Everett Thoren.[44] When Matthews refused to remove the lien, the men returned to her office and attempted to file their own "common-law liens" against IRS agents. Matthews knew the paperwork was bogus and refused.

Members of the Juris Christian Assembly gathered in Thoren's mobile home to plot their course of action. They talked about how much they hated Jews and discussed whether Matthews should be killed. Within weeks, she began receiving threatening phone calls. "Do your job or something will happen to you," one anonymous caller told her. Matthews didn't take the threats seriously until a fake pipe bomb was found underneath her car and shots were fired through her office window. On January 30, 1994, as Matthews returned home after dinner at a local restaurant and entered her garage, she was knocked to the floor, beaten and slashed with a knife. Someone put a gun to her head. A voice addressed her: "This is a message to all recorders. If they don't do their job and record our documents, this will happen to them, too." Her assailant was Roger Steiner, whom Thoren had recruited all the way from Baker, Oregon, presumably because he had special experience in this line of work. In addition to his connections with militia groups, Steiner had been previously convicted of making death threats against two California state representatives who supported gun control. With the barrel of the gun close to Matthews's head, Steiner pulled the trigger, dry-firing the weapon several times. "Lady, you would be so easy to kill," he told her.

It took a yearlong investigation by the FBI, the IRS, and local law enforcement to track down Thoren, Steiner, and eight other accomplices. But just days before the government indicted them all, Thoren died in his home after choking on some food. An autopsy confirmed the cause of death was asphyxiation, but Thoren's family insisted the government had poisoned him. Before Steiner and the others went to trial, supporters of Juris Christian Assembly explained their beliefs: agriculture in California's central valley was being destroyed by weather experiments conducted by the federal government; the United Nations had caused a recent deadly air crash in Fresno; and Jews were responsible for America's ills. All nine were convicted in May 1997.[45]

Everett Thoren never paid for the crime of terrorizing Karen Matthews, and he barely paid his dues for masterminding the earlier takeover of Mikami Farms. But the ninety-day jail sentence he received in 1977 was the strongest that the prosecutor, Bob Hamilton, felt he could win. After Thoren's conviction, the state of Oregon decided not to bring the three remaining Mikami Farms defendants to trial. Moreover, by 1977, the scathing publicity from "the potato shed incident" had severely hurt the Posse. "We went to the mat on them. And there was a real lull in their activity as a result," Hamilton recalled.[46] The avalanche of bad press in Oregon quickly spilled over into California and the national media. And by the late 1970s the IRS had stepped up its prosecutions of tax protesters, too. Growing paranoia about government informants also created morale and re-cruitment problems for the Posse.

One year after authorizing its full investigation, the FBI reported "a marked decline of SPC chapters and membership and illegal activity." According to the Bu-reau, few Posse leaders were able to generate enough excitement to start a local chapter, or even to keep one going. Whereas the FBI had warned that state Posse organizations might prove to be an important organizational vehicle, the Bureau now found "no cohesiveness in the organization nationally, and little in local chap-ters."[47] The likelihood that Posse members would commit violence and illegal acts had "substantially declined," the threat of force was "primarily . . . rhetoric," and violations of the law by Posse members were "local in nature or related to income tax matters."[48] On October 5, 1977, the FBI director concurred with the recom-mendation of his Portland office and terminated the full domestic-security inves-tigation of the Posse.[49]

While the decision was not wholly without justification, the FBI assessment was flawed in several important respects: it underestimated the size and appeal of the tax-protest movement; it placed too much emphasis on the difficulties of local Posse groups—particularly on the West Coast—without recognizing the Posse as a national movement; and it failed to foresee the ability of the Posse to find new, receptive audiences for its message. The FBI also was misled by the prominent role assigned to Mike Beach by the national media. This led the Bureau to overlook the influence of Christian Identity theology and thereby pre-vented the Bureau from anticipating new outbreaks of violence. Even as the Justice Department was closing down its investigation of the Posse, the group was on the verge of finding a new and vigorous foothold in the farm protest movement that was simmering in the Midwest. And it was there, first in the wheat fields of Colorado and Kansas, that the virulent zealots and bigots of the Posse Comitatus would soon reappear and flourish as never before.

24

FARM STRIKE!

In addition to running a gas station, Alvin Jenkins farmed 320 acres of wheat and milo outside Campo, Colorado. It was all that was left of his four thousand–acre spread in dry, sparsely populated Baca County. When dwindling family income forced his son to leave the farm and go to college, Jenkins became even more frustrated. "I gave up my son. . . . Next I guess I'll be expected to give up my wife, who will have to move to some town where she can get a job," he said.[1] After reading about the 1977 farm bill pending in Congress, Jenkins, forty-three, met with friends over coffee to talk about low farm prices, rising costs, and the new legislation. They also received advice from friendly truckers who suggested they "go on strike." It was an alien concept at first, but the idea soon struck a chord.[2] Although farmers are usually known for being staunchly independent, the handful of men who met on September 6, 1977, set out to find others as angry as they were. When forty-one farmers turned out two days later in nearby Springfield, they named their group the American Agriculture Movement and pledged not to buy, sell, or produce any farm supplies or commodities until Congress raised farm prices. In the words of Eugene "Gene" Schroder—a veterinarian, third-generation rancher, and one of the group's founders—the strike would continue until farmers could bring their "prices up to the economy, or bring the economy down" to their prices.[3] The inner circle of AAM included several others who, like Schroder, would eventually be drawn closer to the ideas of the Posse Comitatus: Schroder's father Derral, rancher Jerry Wright, and Alvin Jenkins.[4]

Six feet tall and trim, Jenkins's good looks and slicked-back hair gave him the appearance of an aging doo-wop singer. He turned out to be the most charismatic of the early leaders of AAM and his speeches motivated thousands of farmers to join up. During the next two years, AAM evolved into a vigorous protest movement with hundreds of satellite offices and a presence in almost every state. Its "tractorcades" and rallies attracted national and international headlines. The protests were spirited, but AAM demands for higher prices ran into formidable opposition, and the movement was short-lived. Discouraged by unresponsive politicians, and pushed to bankruptcy by circumstances beyond their control, many AAM activists took up conspiracy-mongering. It was then that men like Jenkins used their personal magnetism and gift of gab to spread the right-wing constitutionalism invented by Bill Gale and other hateful believers of the rural radical right.

Since its founding in 1971, the Posse had grown by appealing to tax resisters, Identity believers, gun fanatics, and others on the right. Opposition to environmental regulations had also attracted new recruits. But by the mid-1970s, reams of bad press and the tax-evasion prosecutions of many Posse organizers had taken a heavy toll. The 1976 Oregon potato shed takeover—and other incidents of right-wing criminality—contributed significantly to the group's negative image and recruitment difficulties. Mike Beach had withdrawn from the movement and Gale was characteristically aloof, which didn't help. Fortunately for the Posse, the mounting farm crisis in the Midwest and the desperation of family farmers provided an ample pool of frustrated new activists.

The rebirth of the Posse also hastened the downfall of AAM, many of whose supporters already were bitter over their failure to win relief from Congress. As political paranoia and anti-Semitism found a more receptive audience, AAM's credibility declined and the once-vital populist organization split and floundered. Enter the Posse, whose most damaging effect—beyond the bigotry it preached— was the way it misled farmers into substituting dead-end conspiracy theories for the concrete reality of political action. Instead of sending telegrams, making phone calls, and lobbying Congress, more farmers began reading the *Spotlight* and other right-wing publications. Faced with foreclosure, desperate farmers were told to refuse legitimate legal advice and seek help instead from self-styled "advisers" who charged them thousands of dollars to teach them how to fight their cases in court *pro se*, without an attorney.

These scams proved disastrous for the farmers involved, though they did not go unchallenged. Even as some AAM activists and other farmers joined forces with the Posse and related right-wing groups, many farm and rural leaders, including some within AAM, denounced the trend and championed the cause of a more liberal farm movement which emerged as an effective obstacle to the rural radical right.

Alvin Jenkins and his friends were political conservatives, but their early approach to activism emphasized public protest and grassroots organizing, not gunplay and right-wing hype. The founders of AAM understood the complexities of federal farm policy and proposed a straightforward remedy that resonated powerfully among distressed farmers: "One hundred percent parity" for all commodities. "Parity"—a kind of cost-of-living index for farmers—is calculated by using 1910 to 1914 as its reference point. If the price of a commodity during this "base period" was sufficient to buy a certain quantity of nonfarm goods, then "100 percent parity" anytime in the future would purchase an equivalent amount. Using this yardstick, the parity price for wheat in December 1977 should have been $5.02 a bushel, instead of the $2.48 farmers were getting—far below their $3.41 cost of production.[5] According to AAM, federal price supports averaged 63 percent of parity, nationwide.[6] John Stulp, a Colorado veterinarian and AAM leader, put it another way. He calculated that he paid the equivalent of eight thousand bushels of wheat for his tractor in 1972, but would have needed nearly twice as many bushels just five years later to buy the same equipment. "There is no reason we should produce such a valuable product—food for people—and lose money," he told the *Washington Post*. If the federal government could impose a minimum hourly wage for workers, it could guarantee farmers a minimum price for their products, AAM argued. Economists countered by saying that parity was an outmoded concept that failed to account for technological advances and increased productivity.

"One hundred percent parity!" was a rallying cry that galvanized farmers, but it quickly was dismissed as unrealistic by Congress. So, too, was AAM's call for an immediate halt to all agricultural imports that undercut the price of domestic commodities.[7] To protest low farm prices, AAM announced that on December 14, 1977, farmers would quit selling commodities or buying supplies. If Congress didn't raise farm prices by March, farmers would act on the truckers' advice and refuse to plant next year's crop. In short, they would strike.[8] After confronting U.S. Agriculture Secretary Bob Bergland in Pueblo, Colorado, AAM organized a rally and tractorcade in Amarillo, Texas, that attracted thousands of farmers from more than half a dozen states.[9] Contributions from farmers, mainstreet merchants, and even a few local bankers kept ten phone lines buzzing in AAM's white stucco headquarters in a crop-dusting office in Springfield.

When the First Family traveled to Camp David to celebrate Thanksgiving in November 1977, thousands of tractors massed on the town square in Plains, Georgia, President Jimmy Carter's hometown.[10] In a coordinated protest thousands of miles away, hundreds of tractors gathered in Plains, Kansas.[11] AAM protesters taunted Agriculture Secretary Bergland, booing him loudly wherever he went. The former Minnesota wheat farmer responded shrewdly by praising farmers for their activism while promising them nothing.[12]

With the wind chill hovering near zero, hundreds of tractors, trucks, and other vehicles rolled into Washington, D.C., on December 10, 1977, four days before the strike deadline.[13] As farmers rallied near the Washington Monument, simultaneous protests converged on state capitals across the country.[14] Leading the ten-mile-long procession to Atlanta, wearing denims and a red, white, and blue cap, was Charles Thomas "Tommy" Kersey Jr., thirty-eight, a Georgia farmer with a disarming grin and down-home demeanor who would later turn to guns and Posse rhetoric when he became disillusioned with AAM. Kersey came from a wealthy family, and he and his brother raised peanuts, soybeans, corn, pecans, cattle, and hogs on six thousand acres that spread across three Georgia counties. He was college-educated and a sharp tactician whose swaggering bluster soon catapulted him into prominence within AAM.[15] News media estimated five thousand tractors in Atlanta, but AAM claimed that seventeen thousand vehicles and fifty thousand farmers showed up.[16] Regardless of the actual number, the caravan was impressive enough to tie up the interstate and win Kersey a thirty-minute audience with President Carter in Plains.[17] After meeting with farm-strike leaders the day before Christmas, the president told the men (and the media) that he sympathized with their plight but opposed 100 percent parity.[18]

The mounting farm crisis had its roots in a series of economic, technological, and political developments dating back to the Great Depression. In the aftermath of the farm foreclosures and bank failures of the 1930s, the Roosevelt administration had enacted legislation to protect farmers and consumers from the vagaries of nature and the volatile swings of the free market. Farmers were offered government loans in exchange for pledging their crops as collateral. If prices rose above a preassigned "loan rate," farmers could sell their crops and repay the government with interest. If prices remained low, the farmers kept the loan and the government retained the grain. The policy achieved two important objectives: farmers did not have to sell their crops at harvest, when prices were lowest, and the government was able to maintain stable reserves of grain to guard against future shortages. To prevent huge surpluses, farmers who wanted the price-support loans had to cut production. Others, who planted as much as they wanted, couldn't get the loans. As long as enough farmers signed up for the program (and they did), the combined effect of planting restrictions and government loans created a floor under commodity prices, and prevented farmers from becoming powerless price-takers in a marketplace dominated by a handful of large grain companies.[19]

Like many New Deal initiatives that interposed the force of government on behalf of working people, Roosevelt's farm program was harshly criticized by those who favored an unfettered free market. Attacks on New Deal agriculture programs gained momentum with the election of President Eisenhower in 1952, and the appointment of Ezra Taft Benson as Secretary of Agriculture. Benson was a hard-line advocate of free-market agriculture, who pushed for lower farm prices and expanded production during his eight-year tenure. But efforts to gut price supports met with stiff resistance in Congress, which still was heavily influenced by the rural vote. Conservatives renewed their assault under the administration of Richard Nixon, whose Secretary of Agriculture was Earl L. Butz. At fifty-six, Butz was a dean at Purdue University and a pugnacious protégé of Benson.[20] Two decades after his mentor famously remarked that farmers should "get big or get out," Butz told farmers to "adapt or die," and urged them to plant "fencepost to fencepost," as part of their obligation to feed the world regardless of low farm prices.[21]

Before his career ended in disgrace in 1976 for telling a racist joke (he later went to prison for tax fraud), Butz pushed to lower prices, slash production controls, and sell off thousands of government-owned storage bins across the country, which were an integral part of the government's supply management program.[22] These policies greatly benefited grain companies that favored overproduction and the resulting low commodity prices that brought them higher profits.[23] There were other advantages to encouraging all-out production. Large surpluses and low farm prices allowed the United States to export greater quantities of inexpensive grain to countries where food aid and cheap exports were used as an important Cold War weapon against the Soviet bloc.[24] But for farmers the policies spelled calamity and helped drive them into the arms of the radical right.

In 1973, net farm income had soared to a record $29.9 billion, but the huge surpluses that later accumulated drove prices way down.[25] By the fall of 1977, wheat brought only $2.20 a bushel, and farmers like AAM's John Stulp were losing more than half that amount with each bushel they sold.[26] Farmers also were faced with rising costs, and many producers felt they had to plant more to meet the demands of inflation. Benson's decades-old edict—"Get big or get out"—became the ethic of the era, and it was preached everywhere—from the bully pulpit of the U.S. Department of Agriculture and the lecterns of land-grant universities to the sprawling lots of agricultural implement dealers crammed with the latest four-wheel–drive machinery.

Of course, not all farmers swallowed the message of these "go-go years" or took on the heavy debt that came with planting fence row to fence row.[27] Some could not afford it. Others, especially older, more conservative farmers, were content to farm as they always had, without dreaming of buying their neighbor's farm or turning their hilly back-pasture into another bin-busting harvest of corn or soybeans. But many farmers had no practical alternative. Butz's mantra of planting fence row to fence row coincided with skyrocketing land values, and borrowing was just too easy. And it was only later, with skewed hindsight, that many agricultural economists scolded farmers for buying land that was now termed "overvalued," or for borrowing money to purchase the more powerful machinery they needed to farm their ever-growing operations. But these economists were conspicuously silent about the bankers who had encouraged such heavy borrowing to begin with. Some lenders even made house calls to push new loans, or they earned special bonuses based upon loan volume; others simply made next year's operating loan contingent on borrowing more money the year before.[28] "They almost hauled you in and stuffed the money down your shirt. [Then] prices dropped and interest rates went up and the money was gone," explained Michigan farmer Merrie Kranz.[29] Total U.S. farm debt skyrocketed as a result. From 1970 to 1984, debt increased more than tenfold, from $20 billion to over $220 billion, driving fully one-third of family farms into insolvency. Banks failed, small businesses closed as fast as shutters in a prairie storm, and massive unemployment swept agriculture-related industries.[30]

Nineteen seventy-eight was a midterm election year, and although the Democrats enjoyed a solid two-to-one majority in both the House and the Senate, the poor economy threatened to erode Democratic control of Congress.[31] In addition to a high trade deficit and rising inflation, the country faced mounting unemployment and declining productivity.[32] Farmers' grievances were real, even if their political demands were judged by many to be "unrealistic." The Carter administration struggled to find ways to appease AAM without actually acceding to its demands, but the strategy backfired because it set the stage for rising expectations which, when dashed, led to greater anger, and created an even wider opening for the right wing.

When Alvin Jenkins delivered a fiery speech before a packed meeting of the House Agriculture Committee on January 20, farmers were overflowing with frustration and anger. Hundreds leapt to their feet, clapping and cheering when he warned that those who refused to join the farm strike that was set for the spring might be "shot out of the cabs of their tractors."[33] But AAM underestimated the degree to which powerful congressmen—both Republicans and Democrats—were beholden to agribusiness. Multinational companies like Cargill and Continental Grain made generous political contributions to ensure that U.S. farm policy continued to favor overproduction and the resulting low commodity prices that brought them higher profits.[34] The Carter administration also had an interest in maintaining surplus production because increased exports offered some relief from a mounting federal trade deficit.[35] It mattered little to government economists that individual farmers lost money with every bushel they sold, as long as exports increased.

Farmers knew their economic problems were rooted in political decisions made in Washington and they understood their role as powerless price-takers in a marketplace dominated by a handful of huge corporations. Naturally they sought out new allies in their quest for political leverage. Many farmers who had criticized labor unions in the past now distributed food to striking coal miners, handed out sandwiches and pamphlets to truckers, and adopted the confrontational approach of groups they once reviled as "radical." On March 1, 1978, hundreds of farmers and their supporters blockaded a bridge on the outskirts of McAllen, Texas, to protest Mexican produce imports they said had been grown with illegal pesticides.[36] Police responded with billy clubs and tear gas, and the clash won a new round of media coverage for the farm strike, and energized

AAM. Two hundred and fifty farmers were arrested, prompting hundreds more to converge on the local jail.[37] The standoff ended after one angry farmer drove a tractor onto the steps of the jail. Police agreed to drop the charges and release the demonstrators so they could return to the bridge the next day. More than one thousand did, and that demonstration ended peacefully. One AAM newsletter feverishly described the events as "a turning point in American History," comparing it to the American Revolution and Christ's crucifixion.[38] Among the hundreds arrested was Georgia farmer Tommy Kersey. Although Kersey had been arrested for allegedly stopping trains in Georgia as part of the December 1977 farm strike, getting roughed up by police in McAllen radicalized him. "I used to think only Nazis and blacks were jailed like that," Kersey recalled. "I felt like going to Martin Luther King, digging up his grave, dusting him off, and shaking his hand to apologize."[39] He didn't say what for, but given his white rural Georgia roots, one could easily imagine what he might have said. Kersey now sought advice from Atlanta's first black mayor, Maynard Jackson, and Cesar Chavez, founder of the United Farm Workers Union, but he was hardly a convert to racial harmony.[40] Eight years later he defended the anti-Semitic tax protester Gordon Kahl, and mumbled faint praise about the Ku Klux Klan. When it came to the latter he observed mildly that the group looked "out for the well-being of the people, white and black, too, [although] they've been called kind of racist."[41] After McAllen, Kersey became even more influential within AAM, but he soon became enamored of far-right conspiracist Lyndon LaRouche, as did others in AAM.

Most AAM supporters were solidly conservative and, to justify their newfound activism, many turned to the ideology of agrarian fundamentalism. Like William Jennings Bryan, the 1896 Populist presidential candidate, AAM followers stressed the indispensable role of agriculture in the national economy—and they were right. "Burn down your cities and leave our farms, and your cities will spring up again as if by magic; but destroy our farms and the grass will grow in the streets of every city in the country," Bryan once said. In 1977 farmers sold more than $100 billion worth of goods and generated more jobs than food-processing, transportation, and retailing combined.[42] Machismo and agricultural fundamentalism peppered the pages of AAM newsletters: "Like the beard of Samson, the American family farm is the source and rootstock of America's strength. If our leaders have become so effete as to have lost touch with this source of strength, the nation is indeed in worse condition than we have realized."[43]

According to AAM, it mobilized fifty thousand farmers to lobby Washington during the winter of 1978 and turned out tens of thousands more in local tractorcades, rallies, and protests.[44] By spring, farmers were arriving in the nation's capital in shifts, not by truck and tractor, but by chartered buses, trains, and planes.[45] "We were like a swarm of ants who had located the spilled sugar," said AAM national "wagon master" Gerald McCathern.[46] In addition to their lobbying efforts, talk of a farm strike continued, though AAM had skillfully scaled back its demand to "50 percent no-plant."

On March 15, 1978, thousands of AAM supporters marched from the White House to Capitol Hill, accompanied by a stable of farm animals, including goats, roosters, guinea hens, and one Missouri mule. After dozens of goats were set loose, several were found capering in the office of South Carolina senator Ernest F. Hollings.[47] AAM lobbying helped win Senate approval for a farm bill that would have raised price supports for grains and cotton in proportion to the amount of land a farmer took out of production. According to the bill, written by Kansas senator Bob Dole, farmers who set aside half their acreage would be eligible to receive $5.04 a bushel for wheat—exactly 100 percent parity.[48] Though the measure was hardly a cure-all, it did fit neatly with the "50 percent no-plant" approach of AAM and reflected the common-sense realities faced by farmers, who had little incentive to plant more, but received less for their commodities.

After AAM deluged members of Congress with telegrams and phone calls, a House-Senate Conference Committee approved the measure and the final conference report passed the Senate, 49 to 41. But President Carter threatened a veto, objecting that the bill was both costly and inflationary. Although the measure had bipartisan support, the fact that its lead sponsor was a prominent Republican didn't improve its chances in the more heavily Democratic House. Hundreds of farmers watched from the gallery when the Majority Leader, Jim Wright (D-Texas), called the bill a "meaningless charade," and it was defeated: 268 to 150.[49]

The loss of the Dole bill was a watershed for AAM, with psychological as well as practical implications for farmers. For decades American farmers had been told they were the most efficient producers in the world. Many were fervently patriotic and, like Alvin Jenkins, military veterans. Others had sons who had volunteered to fight in Vietnam. AAM opened its meetings with the Pledge of Allegiance and its members could sing "The Star-Spangled Banner" without missing a beat. These were angry—not alienated—Americans, and they presumed their government would hear them out and respond; especially if they made the sacrifice to travel all the way to Washington, D.C. But the defeat of the Dole bill fueled cynical despair. Disillusioned by politics and the failure of the farm strike, some activists dropped out of AAM for good. Others vowed to continue organizing. And some did neither, but gravitated instead further to the right. These farmers would later coalesce into a faction led by a core group of AAM founders, including Jenkins, based in Campo, Colorado, that called itself Grass Roots AAM.

"A once-vital grassroots farm movement is now [perceived as] as an ultra-conservative right-wing group," lamented AAM founder Laurence "Bud" Bitner in July 1978. A member of the inner circle of AAM, Bitner, thirty-nine, was a rancher and local Democratic activist in Colorado.[50] Farmer John Stulp shared Bitner's concern. "We started getting that right-wing stuff right away," said Stulp, who remembered receiving letters from the Ku Klux Klan and the John Birch Society, offering to help farmers.[51] But for others in AAM the pamphlets, tape cassettes, and newsletter articles about the sinister machinations of shadowy elites took on new meaning. Admiration for labor unions and civil rights leaders gave way to attacks on gun control, the Trilateral Commission, and the proposed Equal Rights Amendment. AAM also got caught up in conservative passions provoked by President Carter's pledge to relinquish the Panama Canal—a move that deepened right-wing fears about American sovereignty abroad. Farmers who had once been roused by AAM's up-to-the-minute legislative bulletins now paid closer attention to announcements of tax-protest meetings and warnings about the impending takeover by "One World Government." The Springfield, Colorado, AAM office became a veritable fount of knowledge when it came to disseminating right-wing bugaboos:[52]

"The Chase Manhattan Bank, David Rockefeller, and the Council of Foreign Relations and international bankers have run this country long enough," fumed one AAM bulletin that also demanded the Carter administration restore "full U.S. constitutional government."[53] Farmers renewed their protests in 1979, but they received an even more hostile response on Capitol Hill. This intensified dissension in the ranks of AAM and widened the split that gave far-right militants the opening they needed to ratchet up their propaganda machinery and gain new recruits.

25

TRACTORCADE

The first of thousands of trucks and tractors converged on the nation's capital on February 4, 1979. However, unlike the generally sympathetic welcome farmers had received the previous year, politicians now made it clear they had little time for AAM. Within weeks of the farmers' arrival, Agriculture Secretary Bergland predicted that their chances of success were "from zero to nothing."[1] And according to the powerful House Agriculture Committee chairman, Thomas S. Foley (D-Washington)—a recipient of significant agribusiness largesse—legislating parity would simply make matters worse.[2] Farmers had scaled back their demand from 100 percent to 90 percent of parity, but it didn't make a difference.

When Bob Bergland testified before the House Agriculture Committee and announced that the president would veto any increases in price supports, he was loudly booed.[3] Bergland further angered protesters when he told the media that some farmers were motivated by "old-fashioned greed." AAM leaders demanded an apology and vowed to stay in the capital until the end of February.[4] With nearly one thousand tractors and other vehicles penned in on the capital Mall by a fleet of city buses, AAM settled in for a long siege.[5] For the month that farmers were in Washington, they lobbied Congress, protested at the Department of Agriculture, gave interviews, staged media events, and endured more bad press. One article in *Newsweek*, headlined, "A Harvest of Ill Will," pronounced the protests "a public-relations disaster," called parity "a fallacy," and asserted that "the average farmer is thriving."[6] Farmers temporarily redeemed themselves by plowing heavy snow off city streets, but whatever positive recognition they received was short-lived.[7] Unlike the year before, when the Dole "flexible parity" bill was moving through Congress, AAM's legislative demands went nowhere in 1979—a non-election year when legislators felt less pressure to consider farmers' pleas.[8] Right-wing ideas and rhetoric from both outside and inside the movement filled the vacuum.

Just before the tractorcade arrived, the *Spotlight* announced that thousands of farmers would be gathering in Washington to "protest the Trilateral Commission's continuing war against America's family farmers."[9] A month later, the *Spotlight* warned of "the complete takeover of the Agriculture Department by David Rockefeller's Trilateral Commission." And the February issue of the Birch Society monthly, *American Opinion*, praised AAM for "speak[ing] out against a conspiracy," but refused to endorse the group's demand for parity.[10]

On February 14, some AAM supporters presented Congress with a manifesto. Written in the pseudo-legal jargon of the Posse Comitatus, it accused Congress of crimes, "crass abuses," and usurping the "people's absolute right to govern themselves."[11] According to the document's tortured prose, the presidency had been turned into "a political Chancellorship under the detestible [*sic*] Civil Law of [the] long since defunct, putrified [*sic*] and fossilized Empire of Rome," and the United States had become "a perpetual debtors' prison [in which] the rule of ecclesiastical law masquerad[ed] as limited liability for the payments of debts." The homespun indictment demanded "the immediate suspension and repudiation of any and all mortgage foreclosures," but never mentioned parity. Instead, it attacked the Federal Reserve, denounced the income tax as "satanic," and called on Congress to reestablish the gold standard. The rambling text also parroted the coded anti-Semitic themes of other right-wing tracts and threatened to initiate a "quo warranto proceeding" if demands weren't met (the Latin reference was to an obscure legal mechanism which its promoters erroneously believed could revoke the authority of Congress and return the "legislative franchise" to the people).

Most AAM supporters probably never saw the broadside, much less endorsed it, but its distribution on Capitol Hill didn't help the farm group's credibility. Other Posse literature circulated among farmers, including a pamphlet by Jim Wickstrom—*The American Farmer: Twentieth-Century Slave*—which endorsed the AAM farm strike. Written in 1978, after Wickstrom returned to Wisconsin from Dan Gayman's Identity encampment in Missouri, the slim, fourteen-page booklet repeated all the anti-Semitic canards contained in *The International Jew* and *The Protocols of the Elders of Zion*.

According to Wickstrom, farm foreclosures were part of a scheme to nationalize agriculture. And just as "Jew money barons" had created the Depression, the same thing was happening again. Jews were "land-grabbing devils" intent on "financially and morally rap[ing] the WHITE CHRISTIAN AMERICAN PEOPLE." In endorsing the AAM farm strike, Wickstrom wrote that farmers should not give their "precious crops to the Jews so they can feed an army. . . . You will need your crops to EXIST ON in the hard times ahead," which he made clear would be a time of bloodshed. "Jesus REDEEMED OUR RACE with His blood, and the time is drawing near for us when we shall have the opportunity to follow Him in redeeming our beloved Christian Republic. We must establish this country under God's laws, even if it means losing our life for Him."[12]

Wickstrom sprinkled his pro-farmer propaganda with Christian Identity doctrine and denunciations of mainstream ministers. Jews, he wrote, were biblically cursed, and "a race of serpents." Ministers were "false prophets" for failing to warn their congregations about the anti-Christ nature of world Jewry and the planned takeover of America's farms. True to Posse dogma, his farm pamphlet attacked the income tax and asserted that America "IS AND ALWAYS HAS BEEN a Christian Republic."

Wickstrom's pamphlet became fodder for some AAM activists who commiserated late into the night during the winter of 1979. Vilified in the press, patronized by politicians, and frustrated on Capitol Hill, some farmers were an easy mark for right-wing activists and fellow farmers with right-wing views. Huddled over cups of coffee in their Winnebagos parked at the capital Mall, farmers analyzed each day's events and searched for explanations. In 1978 they had arrived in Washington with a single-minded focus on farm prices; now their conversations branched out more easily into discussions about the constitutionality of the income tax and paper money, the Trilateral Commission, America's declining position in the world, and, occasionally, "the Jews." Oftentimes what they heard sounded far-fetched and peculiar, but farmers were angry and eager for new information, and the nation's capital seemed like a good place to get it.

"There wasn't any major piece of legislation that had a shot at being introduced, let alone passed [in 1979]," recalled Gary Lamb, an Iowa AAM leader who opposed the radical right. "It was an atmosphere of confusion and frustration. People were all over the board. And a lot of times farmers just repeated things they were told without even understanding the dynamics of what was being promoted. And then there was always that percentage—those few—that grasped at any imaginary thing and rode that horse as long as it took 'em, until it fell over dead. AAM created this great network of people, but it also gave the right wing a toehold among farmers," Lamb explained.

On March 1, 1979, the last AAM tractorcade surrounded the Federal Reserve Building on Constitution Avenue.[13] Although the protest brought some enthusiastic waves from passersby, most Washington insiders took the opportunity to give AAM their version of a political kick in the pants. "They didn't accomplish anything [except] some high-visibility damage," said a spokesman for the powerful, business-oriented Farm Bureau, which took pleasure in the opportunity to disparage AAM. The feeling was mutual, especially among activists like Tommy Kersey, who had led thirty farmers in an egg-throwing protest at the headquarters of the Georgia Farm Bureau the year before.[14] Farmers were further insulted on their departure when officers with the capital's Civil Disturbance Unit, backed by two trucks and a hundred-man motorbike squad, marched through the AAM encampment, brandishing nightsticks to disperse any last-minute holdouts.[15] News stories followed for weeks afterward, assessing the political fallout as well as the cost to repair the capital Mall. When senators calculated the full price tag for the protests, they concluded that the District of Columbia had spent nearly $2.6 million in police overtime and other expenses, not counting half a million dollars in overtime paid to U.S. Park Police personnel.[16] Hostility toward farmers was so great that the government even considered, though abandoned, the idea of suing AAM to recover the money.[17]

After spring planting, AAM regrouped and decided to set up a national organization with a full-time staff in Washington, D.C. "There's an opportunity to have an awful lot of input on the next farm bill," Bud Bitner, the moderate, explained.[18] A majority of AAM members favored the move, but a core group of activists who were disgusted with politics and politicians vigorously opposed the idea.[19] This difference of opinion presaged a split that would later fracture the organization into two separate camps—AAM, Incorporated (AAM, Inc.), and Grass Roots AAM—and widen an opening for the Posse Comitatus.

Farmers may have been readying themselves for another policy fight on Capitol Hill, but their efforts meant nothing to Paul Volcker, the newly appointed chairman of the Federal Reserve Board. On October 6, 1979, Volcker unintentionally touched off a financial and stock panic when he announced the Fed was increasing the discount rate a full point, to 12 percent, and taking other equally drastic measures to fight inflation by tightening the nation's money supply. Banks followed suit, raising their prime lending rate to 14.5 percent, and by early 1980 many farmers were paying 20 percent interest and higher on their operating loans.[20] Inflation was "public enemy number one" in the eyes of the administration, only, unlike President Carter, Chairman Volcker was prepared to wage total war against it, regardless of the political (and human) casualties.

In simple economic terms, inflation is caused by "too much money chasing too few goods," and so the typical solution is to raise interest rates in order to drive up the cost of money, thereby limiting its supply. But as the Fed pushed interest rates higher, farmers were squeezed even more tightly between skyrocketing debt, rising costs, and low farm prices. For those driven to foreclosure and bankruptcy, the rhetoric of self-described "populists" and tax protesters had special appeal. Like the Posse Comitatus argument that taxes need not be paid because "Federal Reserve bank notes" weren't backed by gold or silver, farmers were told they should ignore their debts because bank loans were not "real money." But this argument ignored the fact that virtually *all* modern money consists of currency that has little or no intrinsic value, without which society would be reduced to bartering as the sole medium of exchange.

But logical reasoning didn't concern right-wing critics of the banking system, like "Pastor" Sheldon Emry, of the Lord's Covenant Church in Phoenix, Arizona, who did his best to convince farmers that the Fed was the fountainhead of their misery and all of America's ills. According to Emry, the Fed had erected "a complete and almost hidden economic and political colossus," which was responsible for "drug use, alcohol, racial intermarriage, sexual promiscuity, abortion, pornography, and crime."[21] A Christian Identity minister whose anti-Semitic and racist tirades were broadcast on dozens of radio stations across America, Emry distilled his critique into a thirty-page primer that became extremely popular among farmers: *Billions for the Bankers, Debts for the People: The Real Story of the Money-Control over America.*

Echoing the classic anti-Semitic image of the "Jew as octopus" that originated in Europe, Emry's booklet was filled with illustrations of a bearded, hooknosed banker whose tie clasp bore a not-so-subtle resemblance to a six-pointed Jewish star. Emry's shylock also had multiple arms that grasped rapaciously at factories, union halls, legislatures, and the Pentagon. Emry's thinly veiled anti-Semitic text carried the same prejudiced message as his cartoons: "Germany financed its entire government and war operation from 1935 to 1945 without gold and without debt, and it took the whole Capitalist and Communist world to destroy the German power over Europe and bring Europe back under the heel of the bankers."[22] Like the delusionary tracts of Henry Ford, Father Coughlin, Gerald L. K. Smith, and others who had attacked the "hidden hand" behind world finance, Emry was obsessed with the myth of Jewish world domination. It mattered little that Jews had been the victims of systematic employment discrimination in the American banking industry. The fact that Paul Warburg, a German-Jewish immigrant and member of the Kuhn, Loeb investment house, had been one of the principle architects of the Federal Reserve was enough to substantiate paranoid claims that a Jewish "money power" loomed darkly over America.[23]

According to Emry, the government should abolish the banks and issue "debt-free, interest-free money" instead. Such a move would not only provide relief for debtors, but also would bring about an end to unemployment, divorce, crime, juvenile delinquency, and mothers working outside the home.[24] Others predicted a similar, though less expansive, economic utopia by returning to the gold standard. Ironically, the right-wing advocates of this approach called themselves "populists" but their logic ran totally counter to the position of the original Populists of the nineteenth century.

"You shall not crucify mankind upon a cross of gold!" boomed the Nebraska Populist and presidential candidate William Jennings Bryan in 1896, criticizing the fact that the money supply was rigidly tied to the supply of gold—a "crown of thorns" pressing down upon "the brow of labor," he called it.[25] The result of such "tight money" was withering price deflation. It was only by *expanding* the money supply that farmers could be relieved of their economic woes, the Populists explained, hence their call for paper money backed by silver ("free silver"), as well as bolder plans for government-issued "greenback" currency—paper money that could be issued without the backing of mineral wealth. (A century later, right-wing activists turned economic logic on its head and pushed for a return to the gold standard, which would have shrunk the money supply and wreaked havoc with farmers and other debtors.)

Whether critics like Sheldon Emry preferred to highlight the diabolic effects of the "debt-usury system" or to denounce paper money, their purpose was the same: to redirect farmers' legitimate economic fears toward a fictitious international Jewish conspiracy. *Billions for the Bankers* did just this, by attacking the banking system, lobbing rhetorical grenades against the inherent worthlessness of money, and stoking popular resentment against those who loaned it for a price. While Emry's followers distributed literature at farm meetings, he bought advertising space in the *American Agriculture News*.[26] But conspiracy theories in the AAM newspaper were not limited to the classifieds.

In February 1980 the biweekly tabloid, which was published in Iredell, Texas, carried a Letter to the Editor asserting there was a "Federal-Israeli-Communist" scheme to control American farmland. Israelis, the Texas letter-writer warned, would soon be establishing collective farms in the U.S., patterned after "Marxist communes in Russia that were planned and directed by Jews, as were the Russian slave labor camps."[27] The allegation sufficiently impressed the editors of *AAM News*, Alden and Micki Nellis, that they went out of their way several years later to remind readers of the supposed plot. "It's likely the program just faded away. But has it?" they asked.[28]

In the early years of AAM, its newsletter preferred to discuss the real causes of farmers' problems: low prices, rising costs, high interest rates, and crushing debt. It proposed as solutions parity prices, commodity production controls, stricter regulation of the Fed, a moratorium on foreclosures, and urged the development and use of corn-based fuels like ethanol. However, by the early 1980s, *AAM News* had become an important and increasingly shrill mouthpiece for the growing right-wing faction within AAM. Disgusted with the Carter administration, most AAM supporters backed Ronald Reagan in the 1980 elections. But instead of relief, Reagan's election just brought worse farm policy decisions. While the AAM national office in Washington moved quickly to adapt to the new administration and the shifting dynamics on Capitol Hill, leaders of Grass Roots AAM, led by Alvin Jenkins in Campo, Colorado, lurched sharply to the right.

26

NO SUBSTITUTE FOR KNOWLEDGE

W e're preparing right now for the outcome of the battle that's being waged for control of this country by the Rockefeller cartel and the international Jew-Bolshevik cartel," AAM founder Jerry Wright announced in July 1982. "These Jews are not your Jew who lives next door. He's the international money changer who's been around forever, the one behind the scene. You have to expose them and they'll remove themselves from the scene, you know what I mean?"[1] Wright and others were preparing themselves with more than just pamphlets and speeches, however. In March, he and Gene Schroder had attended a three-day paramilitary training session in Weskan, a pinprick on the map in remote and underpopulated western Kansas.[2]

The gathering was held on land owned by another AAM activist, Leonard Cox, and was led by Bill Gale and James Wickstrom, the self-appointed "National Director of Counter-Insurgency" for the Posse Comitatus.[3] The session was billed as an "ecological seminar to clean up this land of ours" and one of the organizers, Wesley Ray White, forty-two, described it benignly as a "Bible study" session. But the program featured training in explosives, guerrilla warfare, knife-fighting, hand-to-hand combat, first aid, and "useable poisons."[4] Participants included men and women, farmers in seed corn caps and cowboy boots, AAM activists, Posse diehards in camouflage fatigues, and at least one undercover cop—a reserve police officer from nearby Colby, who took thorough notes.[5] After paying a $100 registration fee (women were charged $50, children, $35) and signing a form saying they worked for "no federal state, county, city, or foreign agency," the fifty-six participants were briefed by Wickstrom and Gale.[6] Additional instructors included supposed ex-military men, including one who claimed he was a mercenary and a Special Forces veteran who'd completed three tours of duty in Vietnam.

The participants divided into four groups and taught themselves the importance of "facial camouflage" by putting tear gas in their eyes. Then they learned how to make homemade explosives. They practiced setting up booby traps, land mines, and other "perimeter defenses," and learned how to distill poisons from venomous snakes and toxic houseplants. When darkness fell, some three dozen volunteers—accompanied by Jim Wickstrom acting "as corpsman in case of injury"—traversed roads and barbed-wire fences to practice night maneuvers. Navigating over rural terrain was apparently not a skill Wickstrom had learned while serving as an army warehouseman in Japan. He and another instructor soon led the group astray.

"Somewhere along the recon route we were supposed to be ambushed, exposed under an airiel [sic] flare and fired on with blanks to see what muzzle flash looked like at night. This never happened as [the instructor], being unfamiliar with the area, got us lost. . . ." reported the police reservist. Someone better-acquainted with the area led the would-be guerrilla warriors back to camp.

Instead of Sunday-morning worship, the Reverend Bill Gale taught a ninety-minute class in knife fighting. Sessions in hand-to-hand combat, paramilitary weapons, and wound treatment rounded out the day. At three-thirty P.M., Gale delivered a short speech, warned the farmers of "the upcoming disaster" in America and bid the group farewell. As far as the undercover cop was concerned, the three-day seminar was "a good learning experience."[7]

The curriculum for the Weskan training was the same that Wickstrom used in Wisconsin. Beginning about 1980, he and Thomas Stockheimer began holding "Posse Survival Seminars" at the compound near Tigerton, which attracted hundreds of participants.[8] And later that year, in September, he invited Gale to help conduct a three-day paramilitary training with some of the same instructors that led the group in Weskan. When Wickstrom wasn't training his Wisconsin followers in guerrilla warfare he was trying to get them to vote. In 1980 he ran for U.S. Senate on the Constitution Party ticket and won about sixteen thousand votes (out of two million cast). Gale returned to Wisconsin in 1981, to oppose legislation that would have outlawed paramilitary training. The sponsor of the bill was Mordecai Lee, a Milwaukee Democrat who happened to be Jewish. "I think you guys ought to hang that son of a bitch," Gale growled, within earshot of the media. Aware he might be quoted, the Posse founder backpedaled a bit. "I never threaten anybody. To hang that guy is too good for him," he said. Wickstrom offered a more thoughtful recommendation: "I believe we will have to have a citizens' grand jury . . . and hang him."[9] Similar talk of vigilante justice prevailed at Weskan the following year.

Weskan was less than five miles from the Colorado state line and the training there spotlighted the growth of the Posse Comitatus in Colorado as well as Kansas. Three weeks after Posse activist Wesley White helped organize the training, he drove to Colorado to deliver some explosives to Charles Norman Howarth, a tax protester and father of five who had once tried to unify right-wing activists under the banner of the Posse Comitatus before embracing the Ku Klux Klan.[10] Around 1980, Howarth drafted his own "Constitution" for the Posse Comitatus:

"Many Patriotic Constitutionalists have an almost morbid disdain for organization . . . but we must . . . have uniform rules—in short, [the Posse] must have A CONSTITUTION!" His twelve-page manifesto also called for a "National Assembly" of local Posse leaders, with elaborate policies and procedures. Membership would be forbidden to non-citizens, "homosexuals, pimps, and child molesters," as well as anyone who had ever "denounced Constitutional Republicanism . . . advocated the immigration of aliens . . . promoted State Welfarism . . . [or] been a member of a secret society . . . which practices a form of Satanism." Patriotic women were permitted to form special "auxiliaries" but forbidden to participate "in any action where the likelihood of physical danger is present."[11] Howarth's Posse went nowhere, and by 1982 he was hoping to jump-start the Colorado branch of Robert Shelton's United Klans of America—one of the most violent Klan groups.

Wesley White returned to Colorado Springs a month later to deliver fuse and explosive primer cord to the would-be Klansman, but the police were watching. About forty miles outside of town, officers pulled over White's cattle truck and arrested him and his wife. Police seized Howarth and another man in a restaurant parking lot the same day. Howarth had sold undercover officers ten pipe bombs for $1,000. Officers then raided Howarth's trophy monogramming shop and his home, arresting his wife and unsettling neighbors along the quiet, residential street where they lived. The raids uncovered bomb components, automatic weapons, ammunition, Klan robes, a library of Klan literature, and a list of fifty Klan and Posse members across the state.[12] According to newspaper reports, Howarth and White were among a group of tax protesters who were allegedly planning to bomb two federal judges and the Internal Revenue Service office in Denver.[13] Cornered by police informants and incriminating evidence, the two men pleaded guilty to felony explosives charges and went to jail.[14] The arrests sharply raised the profile of right-wing militants in Colorado, including men like Jay Ross, a fifty-year-old tax protester and owner of a roller-skating rink in Alamosa, who managed to outmaneuver local Democratic Party leaders to win the top line on the ballot in the primary race for county sheriff.[15]

Despite the increased police scrutiny that came with all these headlines, Gene

Schroder, Alvin Jenkins, and others in AAM continued to experiment with explosives. Five months after Wesley White's arrest, Schroder organized the first of two bomb-making seminars on his father's farm outside Springfield.[16] About twenty people from five states attended each gathering. Using an army demolitions manual, Schroder taught his fellow farmers how to make black powder by combining crushed charcoal and fertilizer with sulfur from a local drugstore. Although Schroder claimed the devices were just "large firecrackers," that wasn't the case; some were packed full of explosives.[17] The group tested their homemade bombs to see how much damage they could do. "We put a seven-pound charge under a tree stump out there about a mile and a half away. It split the trunk wide open," said Jenkins.[18] When reporters asked about the bomb-making sessions, Jenkins said they were "a very jolly, educational deal," but added ominously, "once you learn to use explosives, you can use it for whatever you want."[19] Schroder claimed the get-togethers were just "community seminars," but when asked why farmers had been taught to build bombs he didn't have an answer. "I guess a guy couldn't say. I just think there is no substitute for knowledge," he replied.[20]

Gene Schroder didn't want to talk explicitly about violence, but a Kansas farmer, Keith Shive, had no such qualms. "We don't want to perpetrate violence, but if we do, it'll be for a good cause," said Shive, sixty-one, a disgruntled AAM supporter who, in 1981, had started his own organization with a catchy name: the Farmers Liberation Army (FLA).[21] "We're not going to tell people they should plow under," he said, referring to the AAM "no plant" strategy of 1978 and 1979. "If they don't do it voluntarily, we'll do it for them," he said, hinting that his "Army" might have been responsible for a series of wheat-field fires outside Wichita in July 1982.[22] "[A] farmer who wants to save his farm from this damn government is going to have to be with us or against us," he declared.[23]

In one FLA position paper, Shive listed seventeen goals, highlighting three as most important: "[1] Get rid of the privately held Federal Reserve System . . . and its phony money. . . . [2] Adopt a sane U.S. monetary policy which eliminates interest payments to the International Bankers. [A]nd [3] Return our nation's court system to 'We the People.'" Copying from popular anti-Semitic tracts, Shive added:

> Meyer Amshel Rothschild [*sic*], the father of international banking, is credited with saying, "Let me issue and control the money of a country and I care not who passes the laws." With the Federal Reserve System in private hands, Rothschild's statement should tell you where the basic problem lies.

Not only is there no evidence that Rothschild ever made this remark, it is extremely unlikely that he would have said any such thing, since he never was involved in actually issuing or controlling a national currency, though he was a man of great financial influence. But the statement had long been accepted as true among anti-Semites because it reinforced the classic "Shylock" image of the disloyal and corrupt Jewish moneylender who holds himself above the law. And the fact that Rothschild and his family had created an international financial network made the comment credible to anyone who wanted to believe it.[24]

Keith Shive was hardly the first farmer to "quote" Rothschild to "prove" the falsehood that international Jewish bankers were exploiting agriculture. Famous nineteenth-century Populist orators, like Mary Elizabeth Lease of Kansas, frequently excoriated the Rothschilds and "British bankers" as the source of farmers' ills, thus feeding on the twin fears of Anglophobia and anti-Semitism. Famously remembered for saying, "Farmers should raise less corn and more hell," Lease campaigned for presidential candidate William Jennings Bryan in 1896, and often did so in an anti-Semitic vein.[25] For Shive, who frequently railed against the "eight Jewish families that own the Federal Reserve," the Rothschild canard was the least of his bigotry. He and others within Grass Roots AAM spoke freely about their anti-Jewish beliefs. "I'm not against all Jews," Shive told the Amarillo, Texas, *Daily News* early in 1983. "Jews who handle our clothing and our junkyards aren't necessarily bad. I'm against Jews who control our Federal Reserve System and the rest of our money . . . I don't know of any Presbyterians that are controlled by the Devil, and that's what Jews are—controlled by the Devil." Nevertheless Shive maintained that he would never consort with Nazis. "We're not for Hitler, even though he did kill a lot of Jews. We're just not for Hitler tactics," he said.[26]

Instead of criticizing Shive, the *AAM News* remained impassive. The actions of the FLA were "to be expected," said editor Alden Nellis matter-of-factly. And regardless of whether anti-Semitism, violence, or peaceful protest became the chosen route for farm protest, Nellis said, the publication would "be there to cover the farmers' efforts for a fair price in the marketplace."[27] The same edition of the *AAM News* that reported on the FLA carried a front-page article that pointedly noted that the Missouri farmer and AAM hero Wayne Cryts had suffered the indignity of having been forced to spend the weekend in an Arkansas jail cell with "Mexicans and Cubans [and] Blacks." Cryts's incarceration stemmed from a dramatic incident the year before, when he had led two thousand farmers to forcibly remove thirty-three thousand bushels of his soybeans from a bankrupt grain elevator in defiance of a court order. However, unlike some other leaders of Grass Roots AAM, Cryts publicly denounced anti-Semitism and the radical right. More editorials and skewed reporting in the *AAM News* prompted leaders of AAM, Inc., to push through a resolution at the group's national meeting in July 1982, rescinding the tabloid's status as the farm group's official publication.[28] This infuriated many Grass Roots AAM activists, including Leonard Cox, who spoke out against the move.[29]

The Weskan training and other activities prompted the Kansas Bureau of Investigation (KBI) to order its agents to gather more information on the Posse and report to Topeka.[30] Law enforcement concern increased that November when 105 Kansas sheriffs received a "Citizens' Grand Jury" indictment ordering them to arrest ten judges.[31] The poorly spelled notices threatened vigilante action if the lawmen refused.

> Any person attempting to interefear [*sic*] with the actions and determinations of said Citizens [*sic*] Grand Jury, will be subject to arrest and prossecution [*sic*] in accordance with the law of Posse Comitatus. . . . If county jails are denide [*sic*] by the county sheriffs for incarcerations of said outlaws . . . then said outlaws will be buried in potters field.[32]

The letters resembled the "indictments" handed down by the Wisconsin Posse in the mid-1970s, and given Jim Wickstrom's presence in Weskan, KBI agents suspected he was behind them.[33] Later that month, Wickstrom's voice was heard over Dodge City, Kansas, radio station KTTL:

> "The Jews are like a pen full of pigs . . .[34] You bring them into a country, it's just a matter of time, they eat everything up. . . . Who caused and planned the wars? Who passed all these abortion laws to kill our children? . . . These Jews didn't think they were going to drink of the cup of wrath. They're going to take a big swig, believe me. . . . [The Bible] didn't say you're gonna vote them out—it said, 'thus with violence shall that great city Babylon'—that international communist system—'shall be thrown down and shall be found no more' . . . and all the disco-bongo-congo from the [C]ongo is gonna be gone. All the nigger jive and the tootsie-wootsie is going to go!"

KTTL was one of four radio stations in Dodge City, a southwestern Kansas town of 18,000 people. Nellie Babbs, a forty-seven-year-old tax protester and silver-haired grandmother of six, and her husband, Charles, owned the station. The couple considered themselves "God's watchmen," whose duty it was to sound "a trumpet of warning." And so in June 1982, several months after attending the Weskan training, Nellie Babbs began nightly broadcasts of Bill Gale's taped sermons and speeches from the headquarters of "Cattle Country Broadcasting"—a corrugated sheet-metal building that doubled as her home. Wickstrom's speeches hit the air that fall, and the following year Babbs added new material she recorded from a weekly "Fed-Up Americans" telephone line operated by Wickstrom and the Wisconsin Posse Comitatus.[35]

Listeners heard the broadcasts across eastern Colorado, southwestern Kansas, and northern Oklahoma. "On many nights, KTTL could be heard for hundreds of miles," recalled Naomi Gunderson, an attorney and one of the few Jewish residents of Dodge City.[36] "At one hundred thousand watts, with a Class C license, it had one of the most powerful signals between Chicago and Denver."

"Yes, we're gonna cleanse our land. We're gonna do it with a sword. And we're gonna do it with violence," Gale bellowed in one January 1983 broadcast, titled *Victory with Jesus*.[37] The invective shocked Dodge City business and religious leaders, and especially alarmed the town's tiny population of blacks and Jews, who mobilized to respond. Led by Gunderson, local residents formed a group to apply for a competing license with the Federal Communications Commission (FCC) in an effort to force KTTL off the air. Meanwhile, local African-Americans formed a group to challenge the station when its license came up for renewal. "The American Jewish community did not sit idly by during the 1950s and 1960s when the civil rights of blacks were threatened. Nor will we sit idly by when Jews, or any other minority group, are threatened in the manner in which KTTL threatens them," wrote the group in its petition to the FCC. Although opponents of the station presented clear evidence that the station had repeatedly violated government broadcasting rules, the FCC stalled and then ruled that the broadcasts could continue. But by the time the FCC issued this final decision, the Babbses had divorced and the station was under new management.[38]

It was against the backdrop of controversy surrounding KTTL, the Farmers Liberation Army, and the Posse "indictments" of Kansas judges that several hundred AAM supporters gathered on the steps of the Baca County Courthouse in Colorado to protest the forced sale of Jerry Wright's farm on January 4, 1983. Worried about farmer militancy, the sheriff equipped extra men in riot gear. Wright owed more than $96,000 to the Federal Land Bank on his 320-acre farm and had been unable to make payments for several years. Tractors lined the streets of Springfield, and farmers from at least a dozen states—many of them veteran AAM protesters—gathered early to hear speeches by Alvin Jenkins, Gene Schroder, and others. "If there is any violence, it won't be started by farmers," declared Jenkins, adding that nobody was armed.

Flanked by Sheriff Willard Goff and two police officers, the county clerk emerged from the glass doors of the courthouse around ten A.M. to angry chants of, "No sale! No sale!" As the crowd grew louder, Wright shouted that his constitutional rights were being violated. Ignoring the protest, the clerk announced that the farm had been sold to the Federal Land Bank, which had arranged in advance to buy back the land. The clerk then scurried indoors. This infuriated the protesters who yelled that they, too, wanted to bid. When some of them tried to follow the clerk into the courthouse, lawmen blocked the way but several managed to get through. One was Kinan Burk, a balding, burly ex–army medic, and Wright's neighbor of twelve years. Once inside, Burk charged down the hall and into the treasurer's office before he was subdued. Blood flowed freely down his face after he collided with a filing cabinet. On the front steps, Sheriff Goff was exhorting his men to hold their ground as deputies maced and clubbed AAM supporters who clung to the doors or tried to force their way inside. A tug-of-war ensued as deputies attempted to drag some of the protesters inside to arrest them. The commotion continued until several tear-gas canisters were lobbed into the crowd from the upper floors of the courthouse. Meanwhile Burk and two other farmers were handcuffed and taken to the women's restroom. But Burke forced open a window and escaped, tumbling five feet to the ground outside. As television cameras rolled, a bloodied Burk defiantly raised his manacled hands above his head, recited the Pledge of Allegiance, and led the group in prayer until some enterprising Missouri farmers produced a pair of bolt-cutters and he disappeared into the crowd.[39] Although Burk and two other farmers were charged with assaulting police officers, a jury failed to convict them.

The melee in Springfield made national headlines and landed Jerry Wright a spot on *Nightline* and the *Today* show. The media treated the small riot like it was the first foreclosure protest of the 1980s, but it was not. Months earlier, more than one hundred farmers wearing red armbands had protested the forced sale of land, livestock, and machinery belonging to a Minnesota couple that had borrowed money from the Farmers Home Administration (FmHA), the government's "lender of last resort." Using a tactic from the 1930s called a "penny auction," the crowd intimidated would-be buyers with spirited bids of, "One penny!" and "No sale!" That protest had been the work of liberal advocacy groups that would soon come to play a major role in countering the rural radical right. Jerry Wright and his allies in AAM were copying those tactics that day in Springfield, but unlike the nonviolent protest in Minnesota—and another one that followed in Missouri—Wright and his cohorts resorted to fisticuffs in Springfield. And, while the "farm-gate defenses" devised by liberal farm groups were backed up by sophisticated legal advocacy, activists like Wright preferred to rely on the dead-end legal nostrums of the Posse Comitatus.

After Wright's farm was sold he asked the U.S. Supreme Court to void the sale on the grounds that it had been carried out pursuant to "admiralty or maritime law" (another tortured line of Posse reasoning that led nowhere). Predictably, the Court refused to hear the case. Then Wright filed a $100 million lawsuit against the Farmers Home Administration, to which he owed more than $172,000. Wright's complaint was filled with colorful invective: He referred to government officials as "a total package of maggots feeding on the most immoral and unethical line of human behavior that can only be described as a belch from a snake's belly."[40]

The Springfield protest, and everything that followed, exacerbated the feud within AAM. On one side were many—but not all—of the farmers who identified with Grass Roots AAM and preferred the freewheeling, right-wing politics of Gene Schroder, Alvin Jenkins, and the Campo, Colorado, office. On the other side were farmers who allied themselves with the Washington, D.C., strategy of AAM, Inc., and who realized the importance of repudiating violence and the Posse Comitatus. Such distinctions were not readily apparent to lawmen, however.

On February 9, 1983, several hundred law enforcement agents from six Midwestern states gathered in Salina, Kansas, to compare notes on the Posse. The daylong seminar was sponsored by the Kansas Bureau of Investigation and high-lighted events of the previous year: the Weskan training, the "indictments" of the Kansas judges, the arrests of Charles Howarth and Wesley White in Colorado, and the activities of Jim Wickstrom and Bill Gale.[41] "Essentially, what we're speaking about is groups that are based upon hate of some sort and have a philosophy of being anti-black, anti-Jewish, anti-Catholic, and in some respects, anti-government," explained the KBI director, Thomas Kelly.[42] Also participating was Baca County sheriff Willard Goff, who described the fracas at Jerry Wright's farm sale as "a Posse-staged incident."[43]

Goff was not entirely correct. The majority of AAM supporters who joined the protest had nothing to do with the Posse. But some of those who came to Springfield did, and among them was a tax-protesting farmer and sometime mechanic named Gordon Wendell Kahl.

27

TAX PROTESTER

The oldest of five children, Gordon Kahl was born January 8, 1920, and raised on a 240-acre homestead near Heaton, in central North Dakota.[1] Kahl honed his talents as a marksman while shooting gophers as a young boy, and the skill eventually landed him a position as a turret gunner on a B-25 bomber during World War II. Kahl reached the rank of sergeant and flew more than fifty combat missions, which earned him a fistful of medals, including two Purple Hearts and an assortment of shrapnel in his face and hip.[2] In 1945 he married Joan Seil, a hometown girl seven years his junior. Kahl added 160 acres to the family farm and tried to settle down, but he ended up taking a job as a mechanic at a farm-implement dealership instead. In 1948, Kahl moved his family to California on the first of many seasonal migrations. He still returned to North Dakota every spring and summer to farm, but winters in California were mild, and work as a mechanic was easy to find.

Kahl was introduced to right-wing conspiracy theories while serving as a gunnery instructor at the end of the war, but he didn't embrace Christian Identity until he began spending time in California in the 1950s.[3] Kahl had once been a Mormon, but he left after he became convinced that communists and Masons had infiltrated the Church.[4] Kahl's right-wing metamorphosis progressed, and by 1967 he was ready to renounce the income tax.[5] Vowing never to "give aid and comfort to the enemies of Christ," he wrote the IRS and declared he would no longer tithe to "the Synagogue of Satan."[6]

Like many others in the tax-protest movement, Kahl was a hard-core anti-Semite who believed—among other things—that World War II had been orchestrated by Jewish bankers who had "created" and backed Adolf Hitler in order to subjugate "the feisty German people." Concentration camps were "mostly work camps," where only fifty thousand Jews died, of starvation and disease, not extermination. And communism was "a smoke screen" for world Jewry, which used every tool at its disposal—including the Rotary and Kiwanis Clubs—to deceive and undermine Christians.[7]

Kahl may have been overflowing with hatred, but to his friends and relatives he was humble and quiet, a loving parent, a devoted and hardworking family man, and a zealous patriot who "refused to worship the government as God." He was a caring neighbor, an expert mechanic, and scrupulously honest. These virtuous aspects of his character did not extend beyond his small Anglo-Saxon circle, however. Kahl's world was divided strictly into opposites and he felt only murderous contempt for those who fell on the other side of the line—satanic Jews, nonwhites, and the Christian lackeys of the International Jewish Conspiracy. Chief among the last category were lawmen who did the bidding of ZOG—the "Zionist Occupied Government" of the United States. Of Kahl's six children, Yorie—his oldest son—was his favorite, and it was Yorie who shared his beliefs most deeply—beliefs that would lead both men to commit murder.

By the early 1970s, Kahl had abandoned California as a winter refuge in favor of the oilfields of west Texas. It was there, around 1973, that Kahl discovered the Posse Comitatus. Kahl and his family lived in a rented house in the town of Crane, and he soon became well known—like Portland's LaVerne Hollenbeck—for the Posse Comitatus decals he fixed to the doors of his pickup, and for refusing to register his vehicles.[8] But beyond spending several nights in jail for driving without a license, there were no arrests or confrontations.[9] After several years preaching the righteousness of tax protest to oil roughnecks and helping to lead late-night meetings in nearby motels, Kahl knowingly made a risky move: He went on television. In 1975, he and five fellow protesters went on the air in Midland, fervently declared their opposition to the income tax, and encouraged viewers to do the same. It had been eight years since Kahl first stopped paying taxes, and he had yet to be prosecuted. Kahl correctly anticipated his television appearance would change that. "We're finally getting a deal on TV. They're going to interview us on some of this tax stuff that's illegal," Kahl told a friend. "And when they do, that's when they're going to put the heat on me."[10] He was correct. Kahl was soon visited by a revenue agent, but the interview ended abruptly after Kahl lectured the IRS man about religion and told him he was "going to hell."[11] Kahl was indicted for not filing income taxes for 1973 and 1974 and arrested that December.[12]

"Do you understand the law and what you're being charged with?" Kahl was asked during his arraignment. "I understand God's law, but I'm not too good on Satan's law," he replied, declaring proudly that he hadn't *failed* to file his taxes, it was a deliberate act, done out of religious conviction. Kahl also refused to enter a plea and claimed the court lacked jurisdiction over him.[13] But these tactics didn't accomplish much. The judge was well known for his impatience with tax protesters, and ruled Kahl's Posse arguments irrelevant. The jury was not impressed, either. In June 1977, Kahl was convicted and sentenced to one year in jail, placed on five years' probation, and ordered to undergo a psychiatric evaluation at the federal prison hospital in Springfield, Missouri—the same fate that had been assigned A. J. Porth seven years earlier.[14]

Kahl was released on appeal after several months in prison, but he failed to overturn the conviction and spent eight more months in Leavenworth before he was released in August 1979. The experience reinforced his oft-stated belief that the *Communist Manifesto* had supplanted the Constitution. "It reminded me of some of the things you read about that happens in Russia and Red China," said Kahl. "It was a matter of getting us [tax protesters] out of circulation."[15]

As a condition of his probation, Kahl was ordered to pay his taxes, but refused. He also quit filing his required monthly probation reports the following year.[16] By November 1980, Kahl owed the IRS approximately $25,000 in back taxes, penalties, and interest. The government put a lien on eighty acres of his farm and seized the land in early 1981, in preparation for auction. Then an all-points bulletin was issued throughout North Dakota for Kahl's arrest for violating his probation.[17]

The task of bringing in the sixty-one-year-old tax protester fell to the North Dakota federal marshal, Harold "Bud" Warren, who first tried to negotiate with Kahl over the phone. Then Warren suggested a face-to-face meeting. Kahl agreed. "Believe me, if anybody is open for suggestions, I am," the marshal told Kahl when the two met.[18] But the dialogue went nowhere. "I was tried illegally, I was sentenced illegally, and as far as I'm concerned the whole thing was illegal from start to finish," Kahl replied. "I can't see any reason why I should go through that again. . . . When you become a Christian, you put yourself on the opposite side of the government. You cannot serve Satan and be a Christian at the same time," he said.[19] Warren then concluded that Kahl's probation violation was "hardly a serious crime," and decided to avoid a confrontation. Besides, he had been duly warned that Kahl was a "crack shot."[20]

The Kahl family migrated south again that winter, but this time they traveled to Arkansas, where Kahl attended tax-protest meetings and paid a visit to the paramilitary compound of the Covenant, the Sword, and the Arm of the Lord (CSA), tucked along the Missouri border. It also was in Arkansas that Kahl met up with Leonard Ginter, a carpenter with an eighth-grade education and former member of the Wisconsin Posse Comitatus, who would later hide him from federal authorities.[21] Kahl's legal and financial difficulties strained his marriage and his wife tried secretly to negotiate with the IRS—an action that resulted in her "Ex-Communication," from the "Gospel Doctrine Church of Jesus Christ," a family affair (and attempted tax dodge) established by Kahl and his favorite son, Yorie. "[Y]ou . . . have attempted to negotiate and compromise by paying tithes and other blackmail payments to the tithing collectors of the Jewish-Masonic Synogogue [sic] of Satan (also called Babylon the Great in the Scriptures) for the purpose of securing a more favorable treatment by Satan's servants in regard to certain church property," the twenty-three-year-old Yorie charged in a letter to his mother on August 27, 1982. "Should you see the error of your ways . . . we will be most happy to return you to full fellowship with the Saints who make up the body of Christ." Out of fear and frustration she eventually did.[22]

By 1982, Kahl was becoming more involved in efforts to recruit farmers to the Posse Comitatus. Accompanied by fellow Posse members from North Dakota, Kahl went to Kansas that November and met with the leader of the Farmers Liberation Army, Keith Shive.[23] Traveling with him was Scott Faul, twenty-nine, an organic farmer and tax protester, and Len Martin, the operator of a right-wing Christian school and the North Dakota "spokesman" for Shive's FLA.[24]

Martin, fifty-nine, had been raised on a farm just seven miles from the Kahl homestead. By coincidence he, too, had embraced Christian Identity and devoted himself to unmasking the International Jewish Conspiracy. In 1982, Martin put himself into the limelight by trekking across North Dakota with a stuffed-monkey doll clinging to his back, symbolizing how he felt about the IRS. The stunt attracted quizzical looks, feature-news coverage, and right-wing acclaim.[25] Later that year, while running the American Christian School in Ashley, Martin was introduced to Gordon Kahl. "Jews are now behind the theft of family farms in America; and their flunky Masons are involved in it up to their ears," Kahl told him.[26]

Martin was a prolific writer and had worked as a reporter for the *Spotlight*, in Washington, D.C., in the 1970s. He and Kahl spoke often and Martin turned their conversations into a booklet titled, *Why "They" WANTED! to Get Gordon Kahl*.[27] He later authored other tracts that helped elevate Kahl to martyrdom, including *The Truth About Gordon Kahl: Radical Tax Protester and Militant Posse Comitatus Member*.[28]

In January 1983, Kahl was accompanied by his son, Yorie, and Scott Faul, when he traveled to Springfield, Colorado, to spread the Posse and Identity message among farmers who had gathered to support Jerry Wright.[29] Kahl didn't stay for the protest, however. He returned to North Dakota, where he had plans to secure his independence from the government by organizing a Posse-controlled "township." The group often met in Medina, where Dr. Clarence Martin (another Posse supporter and no relation to Len Martin) hosted meetings at his medical clinic.

On February 13, 1983, about eighteen Posse members, including Kahl, his wife Joan, Yorie, and Scott Faul gathered at Martin's clinic. The men were heavily armed. Also in attendance were Len Martin, David Broer, forty-three—a self-employed carpenter and self-styled Posse paralegal—and Vernon Wegner. One week earlier, Wegner, twenty-five, had been fired from his job as police chief of the tiny town of Streeter, after he had made unauthorized purchases of mace, tear gas, and rubber ball grenades—some of the supplies were destined for members of the Farmers Liberation Army.[30] In discussing their plans to form a Posse township, the men had reached an impasse. Kahl insisted that only whites be allowed in, but Doc Martin disagreed. After several hours of wrangling, the meeting broke up.[31]

Medina was a small town of five hundred people, and Kahl's arrival had not gone undetected. Bradley Kapp, a twenty-six-year-old Stutsman County deputy sheriff, noticed Kahl's station wagon parked outside the clinic and remembered something about a federal warrant. He quickly notified the Marshal Service in Bismarck, about seventy-five miles away.[32] Bud Warren, the North Dakota federal marshal who had tried to negotiate with Kahl in 1981, was no longer in charge but his successor, Kenneth Muir, believed in a more aggressive approach. Since taking over Warren's post, Muir, fifty-three, already had tried to apprehend Kahl, but the wily farmer had evaded him.[33] Now Muir barreled down the highway with a deputy, Carl Wigglesworth, to a rendezvous with two other deputy marshals who had agreed to help bring Kahl in: Robert Cheshire Jr., thirty-two, and James Hopson Jr., fifty-nine.

Unfortunately, Kapp had been indiscreet in his surveillance and was spotted by some of the Possemen as they exited the clinic. Aware that an all-points bulletin had recently been issued alerting lawmen to be on the lookout for Kahl, David Broer called his friend, the local police chief, Darrell Graf, who had attended Posse meetings in the past. After Graf confirmed the APB, the men at the clinic devised a plan.[34] Switching cars and swapping caps and jackets, Kahl left the clinic with Broer around five-thirty P.M. while his wife, son, and two others took the Kahl station wagon. The ruse temporarily confused the lawmen, but hardly threw them off the trail. As Kahl and Broer crested a hill about a mile and a half north of Medina, they saw two vehicles with flashing lights.[35] One was a Medina police car driven by the deputy police chief, Steve Schnabel; in the other were Marshals Muir and Wigglesworth. Unknown to Kahl, the two remaining federal lawmen and Deputy Sheriff Bradley Kapp were closing in from behind in a Dodge Ram Charger. Both Posse vehicles turned off the pavement to the left and into a driveway that led to a trailer house alongside the road.

Kahl readied his Mini-14 rifle and instructed Broer to turn his brown AMC Hornet around. As he backed out of the driveway and turned south, the Charger skidded to a halt diagonally about twenty feet away, blocking Broer's car.[36] Kahl jumped out and pointed his rifle at the Charger. Meanwhile, Yorie and Scott Faul quickly got out of the station wagon, rifles drawn. Yorie took up a position behind a utility pole alongside the ditch while Faul took cover in the shelter of a belt of trees that surrounded the mobile home. The doors of the Charger flew open and Marshals Cheshire and Hopson took aim, ordering the Possemen to drop their weapons. Kahl and the others ignored the demand.

Seven months earlier, Bill Gale had anticipated a similar encounter. "If you come across a military road block, cause a disturbance so you can get the four or five cover troops distracted, get your sights on their riflemen and wipe them out," Gale had advised in one KTTL broadcast.[37] What happened next was a "Western-style standoff," according to James Corcoran, whose book, *Bitter Harvest: Gordon Kahl and the Posse Comitatus—Murder in the Heartland*, is the definitive account of the shootout and the life of Gordon Kahl.

The Ruger Mini-14 rifles carried by Kahl and his fellow Possemen were formidable weapons. Unlike the twelve-gauge shotguns held by the lawmen, the Mini-14 was a semiautomatic—each squeeze of the trigger discharged a powerful .223-caliber cartridge and deposited another round instantly in the chamber. Rugged and compact, the Mini-14 was popular among survivalists and tax protesters (so popular, in fact, that in 1980, the rifle had been the subject of a cover story in *Soldier of Fortune* magazine), who prized the Ruger's dependability compared to its more expensive rival, the military-style Colt AR-15, which had a bad habit of jamming when converted to semiautomatic.[38] Mini-14s were equipped with a single five-shot clip from the factory, but Kahl and the others had substituted thirty-round banana clips in their weapons.[39]

All in all there were six lawmen—four federal marshals and two local officers—and they had seven firearms between them: three shotguns, two handguns, and two semiautomatic AR-15s. It was approximately five minutes before six P.M. and the sun was setting in the chill air when the first shot was fired.[40] It isn't clear who got off the initial round, but in the thirty-second volley that followed, the three Possemen fired at least a dozen more, while the marshals and others managed only about eight. Three of the officers never discharged their weapons, but each time Kahl fired, he did so with deadly precision. At 160 pounds and five feet seven inches,[41] he wasn't physically formidable, but the sixty-three-year-old Kahl had no qualms about dying—or murdering—for his beliefs. Kahl's first two rounds wounded the sheriff's deputy, Bradley Kapp, and the Medina deputy police chief, Steve Schnabel. Kahl's third bullet struck Marshal Ken Muir fatally in the chest, shattering his sternum and filling him with shrapnel, but Muir still managed to get off a round in Yorie's direction. Luckily for the younger Kahl, he was wearing a .45-caliber pistol in a shoulder holster. Muir's bullet lodged there instead of his heart, sending fragments from the disintegrated pistol grip into Yorie's chin, turning his face into a bloody mess.[42] Deputy Marshal James Hopson Jr., who dove for the ground when the shooting started, suffered permanent brain damage when a ricocheting bullet drove a piece of asphalt into his skull, turning his right cerebellum into pulp.[43] Meanwhile a fusillade of bullets fired by Yorie and Scott Faul descended on the Charger, fatally wounding Robert Cheshire Jr.[44] Of the six lawmen, only one, Deputy Marshal Carl Wigglesworth, survived the gunfight unscathed.

Kapp had never before fired his gun in the line of duty, but before his trigger finger was severed by a bullet he managed to pump lead into Yorie Kahl's abdomen, kidney, liver, and lungs. After getting off four rounds, Kapp was unable to reload. His finger was hanging by a thread of flesh and so he did the only thing he could. He ran like hell.[45] When the shooting stopped, Kahl jogged over to Steve Schnabel, who had been shot cleanly through the back of the leg and taken cover in a nearby ditch. Thinking the twenty-three-year-old deputy police chief might still be in "fighting condition," Kahl readied his rifle. "Don't shoot me," Schnabel pleaded, surrendering his weapons. Kahl tossed them into the backseat of Schnabel's green Mercury police cruiser and slid behind the wheel.[46]

Kahl scrawled his version of events on a scrap of paper the night of the shooting and gave it to Scott Faul.[47] "I realize that being an enemy of the Jewish-Masonic-Communist-Synogogue [sic] of SATAN is not conducive to a long life, so I am writing this while I still can," the hastily written note began. "I am saddened by the fact that my hand had to be the instrument which sent these men to their reward, however they attacked us, and fired first, so I feel I was right, and justified in defending myself, and all those who were placed in this extreme danger with me."[48] Kahl elaborated on this theme of self-defense when he dispatched a longer, sixteen-page letter some three weeks later to journalists, Posse activists, friends, and family members. It isn't known who mailed the letter, but it carried a Texas postmark.[49]

"I, GORDON KAHL, a Christian patriot, and in consideration of the events which have taken place within the last few hours, and knowing to what lengths the enemies of Christ (who I consider my enemies), will go to separate [sic] my spirit from it's [sic] body, wish to put down on paper a record of the events which have just taken place, so that the world will know what happened," the handwritten letter began.[50] Kahl then recounted the events of February 13 in detail. But in an effort to exonerate his son and Scott Faul, whom he called "first-rate Soldiers of Jesus Christ," he took credit for all the fatal shots.[51] Kahl was proud of his marksmanship and courage under fire, but he purposefully did not recount his cold-blooded execution of Bob Cheshire Jr. When the shooting first started, Kahl saw Kapp and Cheshire firing from behind the Charger. Moments later Yorie was covered in blood. Kahl wanted revenge, but Kapp had fled the scene. According to author James Corcoran, the thirty-two-year-old deputy marshal was slumped halfway inside the Charger, defenseless and dying from one of Yorie's bullets that had shattered on his bulletproof vest, filling his face, neck, and shoulder with shrapnel. What was left of the round had penetrated downward, slicing through his upper chest, severing an artery. The wound would have been fatal, but Kahl then shot Cheshire at point-blank range, blowing apart his skull.[52]

In his letter about the shooting, Kahl claimed he "[took] no pleasure in the death or injury of any of these people, any more than I felt, when I was forced to bring to an end, the fighter pilots' lives who forced the issue during WWII. When you come under attack by any-one, it becomes a matter of survival." In biblical style, Kahl also encouraged his supporters to sell their "garment[s] and buy a sword, if you don't already have one, and bring His enemies before Him and slay them."[53] It was time to wage war against the Jews. Kahl explained:

> These enemies of Christ have taken their Jewish communist manifesto, and incorporated it into the statutory laws of our country, and threw our Constitution and our Christian common law (which is nothing other than the laws of God as set forth in the scriptures) into the garbage can. We are engaged in a struggle to the death between the people of the kingdom of God, and the kingdom of Satan. . . . We are a conquered and occupied nation; conquered and occupied by the Jews, and their hundreds or maybe thousands of front organizations doing their un-godly work. They have two objectives in their goal of ruling the world. Destroy Christianity and the white race. Neither can be accomplished by itself, they stand or fall together.[54]

After transporting the injured Yorie to Doc Martin's clinic in Medina, Kahl and Scott Faul fled in Schnabel's police cruiser, intently monitoring the police scanner.[55] Joan and Yorie were arrested that night at the hospital in Jamestown, where Yorie later made the mistake of talking to the FBI. "It could have been that I shot first. I can't remember much after that. I took some shots," he admitted.[56] Also arrested and charged with murder were David Broer, Vernon Wegner, and Scott Faul, who turned himself in the day after the shooting. Faul refused to say anything about Gordon Kahl's whereabouts, which remained a mystery after Schnabel's police cruiser was found abandoned about sixty miles northeast of Medina.[57]

Two days after the shooting, more than one hundred heavily armed U.S. Marshals, FBI agents, sheriff's deputies, and local police gathered in thick fog surrounding Kahl's small farmhouse outside Heaton. Agents surveyed the home warily from the safety of an armored personnel carrier provided by the National Guard before retreating to shout through a bullhorn for Kahl's surrender. Hearing no reply, they bombarded the house with tear gas and gunfire for nearly an hour before storming the residence, only to find it empty, except for an arsenal of two dozen fully loaded weapons, fifteen thousand rounds of ammunition, and a collection of Posse pamphlets and other right-wing literature.[58] So much gas was used that it was impossible to go inside without a mask for four months, and the house remained uninhabitable for nearly two years.[59] Law enforcement officials emphasized they were on the trail of a cold-blooded killer, but Kahl's family insisted he wasn't dangerous and lamented that the government was "hunting him like a dog."[60] Authorities managed to cajole Joan Kahl into appearing on television the next day. Distraught, she urged her husband to surrender. "Please, Gordon, please. I don't want you dead, too," she pleaded. "Please, I can't take it anymore. They won't hurt you."[61]

On Thursday, a sixteen-truck convoy descended on Ashley, about sixty miles south of Medina. Police sealed off highways and searched the homes of several tax protesters, including Len Martin and his Christian school.[62] The U.S. Marshal Service then announced a record $25,000 reward for information leading to Kahl's arrest.[63] Kahl had disappeared into the underground world of the radical right, and the FBI didn't have the faintest idea where to find him.

28

CIVIL DISORDER

On Monday morning, February 14, 1983, Kahl's bespectacled face was featured prominently on the front page of many major newspapers. In articles and newscasts the Posse Comitatus activist was usually described by the simple catch phrase "tax protester." Television news anchor Dan Rather went a bit further when he described Kahl as "a radical survivalist, a fanatic, [and] an ultrarightwing tax rebel," before adding—presumably for emphasis—that authorities were calling him "a killer." Early coverage of the shootout made little mention of the Posse Comitatus, or the Identity beliefs that motivated Kahl to commit murder, but the media soon found their man in Jim Wickstrom.

"The Posse in Wisconsin is on standby alert at this time. All communications are locked in," Wickstrom blustered, adding that the government had "declared war on the people of this country."[1] Posse leaders often exaggerated the size of their membership, and Wickstrom was no exception. He claimed three million members. According to the FBI, the figure was several thousand, but that was not accurate, either. Most people who considered themselves members of the Posse never filled out a membership card, signed a county charter, or sent in dues—they simply attended tax-protest meetings or participated in one of hundreds of "Constitutionalist" or "Patriot" groups that were scattered across the country. By the early 1980s, right-wing tax protest had become practically synonymous with the Posse Comitatus, and A. J. Porth's message of individual resistance had motivated tens of thousands to act. The IRS counted fifty-eight thousand illegal tax-protest returns in 1983 (*not* including other forms of tax fraud and evasion), up tenfold from five years earlier. The problem was so acute that the agency launched a special Illegal Tax Protester Program, and appointed special "tax-protest coordinators" to each of its district offices. Congress also raised the penalties for illegal tax protest. The movement was still enough of a concern two years later to prompt denunciations from IRS commissioner Roscoe Egger. "Self-proclaimed constitutional lawyers hold seminars across the country, while their only real goal is to help people falsify tax returns and line their own pockets," he said.[2] Filing an illegal return had serious consequences, and the fact that nearly sixty thousand tax protesters were willing to risk jail demonstrated the strength of the Posse movement. And for each of these committed protesters, there were at least several more eager supporters, even if they weren't willing—or able—to flout the law.

One measure of this broader constituency was in the popularity of the tax-protest book *The Miracle on Main Street*, which sold one hundred thousand copies from 1980 to 1982. The author of the slim, 160-page volume was Frederick "Tupper" Saussy III, forty-four, a musician, songwriter, artist, and advertising man from Nashville, Tennessee. Trim and balding, with gray-flecked temples, a caustic wit, and an easy smile, Saussy won right-wing stardom after his 1985 conviction for tax evasion and for publishing *Tennessee Waltz*, an autobiography of James Earl Ray, the assassin of Dr. Martin Luther King Jr. Convicted of a misdemeanor (and acquitted of two others) for failing to file his 1977 tax return, Saussy went underground and remained a federal fugitive for more than ten years. Arrested in 1997, he quipped, "I considered myself America's Least Wanted."[3]

Miracle on Main Street was wildly popular and so was the phony checkbook money that Saussy invented for tax protesters to pay their debts. Called "Public Office Money Certificates," they bore the following inscription: "This certificate is redeemable in dollars of the money of account of the United States upon an official determination of the substance of the money of account." Many others would replicate the idea in the years to come, from Midwestern con men who sold farmers false hope, to the more sophisticated and militia-oriented Montana Freemen who used laser printers to make their "checks" appear suitably authentic.

The FBI estimated only a few thousand Posse members, but more than one hundred thousand people read Saussy's book, and three to four times that number were regular readers of the *Spotlight*, which often touted the Posse cause and decried the attempts to arrest Gordon Kahl. In 1980, the conspiracy-obsessed tabloid had about 250,000 subscribers, of whom more than 4,000 were in Kansas, many of them farmers who were an easy mark for the Posse Comitatus.[4] Another measure of the potential audience for the Posse message was the success of more mainstream publications that echoed survivalist themes. After changing its name from *Shooter's Journal* to *Survival Guide* in 1982, that magazine's circulation tripled to 90,000. Although its articles about weapons, food storage, and outdoor lore did not reference the Posse, the magazine's popularity illustrates how attractive the idea of stockpiling food and weapons had become by the early 1980s. The readers of *Survival Guide* were 97 percent male, 76 percent married, and averaged thirty-four years of age. Contradicting the stereotype of the aging, unskilled, uneducated, and unemployed survivalist, the magazine catered to an audience of skilled workers with annual incomes of $25,000 or more.[5] The IRS reached similar conclusions about tax protesters. In one 1981 report examining the movement, the agency found that roughly half of all protesters had incomes between $15,000 and $50,000, and another 17 percent earned between $10,000 and $15,000. Examining illegal protest returns from three of its district offices in 1978 and 1979, the IRS found that 58 percent of the protesters were nonprofessional wage earners, 9 percent were doctors, 7 percent were teachers, and 6 percent were government employees.[6] While most subscribers to right-wing publications, or readers of tax-protest books and survivalist magazines, were *not* members of the Posse Comitatus, the group had more than just several thousand active supporters, contrary to the FBI's underestimate.

As with previous high-profile incidents, Kahl's murder of the marshals in Medina would prompt a law enforcement crackdown on the Posse, but not before Jim Wickstrom seized the opportunity to promote his movement. Disguising his far-out Identity beliefs and denying the Posse's affection for gunplay, Wickstrom decried violence and tried, instead, to focus the attention of would-be recruits on issues of banks and taxes.

"What we have here is a gentleman who is now being pursued in North Dakota on a setup to shut his mouth because the American people are waking up by the tens of thousands across this country, realizing that we have been duped by a private central bank," he told the *Milwaukee Sentinel* the day after the shooting.[7] And when Wickstrom appeared on the television talk show *Donahue* a week later, he told the nationwide audience that his organization "abhorred violence."

"My heart really goes out to the U.S. Marshals and the children of those marshals and their families," he claimed. And when Phil Donahue asked whether he would "join Mrs. Kahl in calling for Gordon Kahl to surrender," Wickstrom changed the subject, arguing that Kahl's civil rights had been violated and that the real issues were farm foreclosures, corrupt courts, the income tax, the Federal Reserve, unemployment, foreign workers, and (of course) the Jews.

Phil Donahue's dialogue with Wickstrom was oftentimes inane, and though he clearly didn't agree with his guest, he gave Wickstrom a tremendous platform to spread his ideas. This script is one that would be repeated often by other liberal media personalities who disdained the politics of hate (and hoped to increase their ratings) but wrongly assumed they could get the better of their right-wing guests by putting them on the air.[8] For his part, Wickstrom tried to translate his greater visibility into political candidacy when he ran for governor of Wisconsin a year later. He received only 7,721 votes, but considering the fact that he was campaigning as a criminal (he was convicted of impersonating a public official in 1983 and then served additional jail time for jumping bail), his showing was quite remarkable.[9]

In Kansas, the Kahl shootings prompted the highway patrol to ask the legislature for enough money to buy fifty Ruger Mini-14 rifles.[10] And all the talk about the Posse lent momentum to a bill to outlaw paramilitary training. Just days before the deaths in Medina, Representative Robert G. Frey, a Republican lawyer and chairman of the House Judiciary Committee, had drafted a bill to make it a felony to engage in paramilitary training with the "aim or intent of creating a civil disorder."[11] Frey drafted his proposal from a model statute written by the Anti-Defamation League. Six states had enacted the measure since 1981, and by 1983 the ADL was pushing it in six others: Kansas, Nebraska, Missouri, Idaho, Oregon, and Wisconsin.[12]

Despite the initial momentum in Kansas, the bill met stiff opposition from pro-gun groups and sportsmen, powerful constituencies in predominantly rural Kansas. The president of the state chapter of the National Rifle Association reminded lawmakers of this fact by testifying that his organization had thirty-seven affiliated shooting clubs. Frey's proposal was "an infringement on our individual rights to gather, even in our homes, for discussing and 'conversationalizing' on riflery of any kind," the NRA spokesman added.[13]

Support for Frey's bill came principally from law enforcement and the ADL. When the director of the Kansas Bureau of Investigation, Tom Kelly, testified before Frey's committee on February 21, 1983, he read excerpts from the undercover report detailing the Posse paramilitary exercise that had been held in Weskan the previous year. "I don't see any redeeming value in this type of training," he said. The Kansas National Guard, the state attorney general, and a Mennonite clergyman shared this view. "I believe the bill would help protect against communism," the clergyman added. Anti-Defamation League spokesman Allen Katchen said the same thing—presumably to curry support from conservative Kansas lawmakers—but it was nonsense nonetheless. According to Katchen, the ADL suspected, but had no evidence, that American paramilitary groups were "being furthered by the Soviet Union." He was closer to the mark when he compared the content of KTTL radio broadcasts to Nazism.[14]

Frey's Judiciary Committee also heard the Posse point of view from Thomas R. Wempe, forty-six, a self-employed salesman of livestock feed supplements who described himself as a "constitutional consultant." Wempe was the spokesman for "the Osage County Citizens' Union," and he mixed threats, right-wing rhetoric, and appeals to chivalry in his remarks: "Our forefathers were so adamant in their belief of civil liberties they charged us to take up arms against the civil servants who attempt to deprive our women and children of their mutual liberties and those who wish to enslave the people of this Republic." Five state troopers arrested Wempe for an outstanding speeding ticket immediately after he left the hearing room, no doubt adding to his fear of persecution.[15] More credible opposition came from legislators like Representative Dean Shelor, a Minneola Democrat, who accused Attorney General Robert Stephan of exaggerating the threat. The danger is "not the Posse Comitatus," he asserted. "[It's] the attorney general's inability to cope with a bunch of farmers who believe the Constitution is being challenged." Frey's measure failed, 67 to 42.[16]

If the Weskan training and other Posse activities (including the violence in North Dakota) was not enough to persuade Kansas legislators to ban paramilitary training, right-wing militants were sufficiently threatening in neighboring Missouri, home of The Covenant, the Sword, and the Arm of the Lord (CSA). The 224-acre CSA encampment was located on the shores of Bull Shoals Lake on the Arkansas-Missouri border. The property had been purchased in 1976 by James Ellison, a thirty-six-year-old former minister who had abandoned his mainstream Protestant theology in favor of Christian fundamentalism before converting to Identity. Initially, Ellison dubbed his settlement the Zarephath-Horeb Community Church, after the ancient city where the Hebrew prophet Elijah resurrected a widow's son from the dead, and Horeb, the biblical name for Mount Sinai.[17] But after receiving visions of a coming race war, he launched the CSA in 1978. Originally Ellison may not have conceived of his Christian commune as a paramilitary training ground for white supremacists, but by the time Gordon Kahl paid him a visit several years later, that is what it had become.

Ellison won a following with his detailed knowledge of Scripture, his claim to "divine revelations," and his talent at manipulating people. To many of his supporters, especially recovering alcoholics and drug addicts, Ellison's charisma and burly, bearded presence made him something of a father figure. Half the one hundred acolytes who lived in his compound were women and children, and Ellison's adult disciples were a cross-section of working-class America: high-school graduates and dropouts, mechanics and truckers, military veterans, housewives and waitresses, and a smattering of drifters, murderers, and thieves. Like most leaders of small religious sects, Ellison controlled his followers with a carefully calibrated mixture of threats and charm, punishments and rewards.

Ellison portrayed himself as a latter-day Elijah—a man of miraculous powers who was divinely ordained to confront the enemies of Israel. He preached that he was a direct descendant of the biblical King David and in 1982 he proclaimed himself "King James of the Ozarks." Ellison sought and received legitimacy for these beliefs from his spiritual mentor, Robert Millar.[18] A Canadian-born Mennonite minister–turned–Identity patriarch, Millar presided over a four hundred-acre settlement in eastern Oklahoma called Elohim City.[19]

Back when it was a Christian commune, Ellison's followers tried to make money logging cedar trees.[20] But as Ellison became immersed in Christian Identity, he directed his men to steal to support the CSA. To justify the thieving, Ellison cited the First Book of Samuel, which recounts how the ancient Israelites plundered the tents of the Philistines after David killed Goliath.[21] Among those who followed Ellison's instructions was Richard Wayne Snell, the Posse believer whose execution on April 15, 1995, may have influenced Timothy McVeigh to bomb the federal building in Oklahoma City.

As another fund-raising activity, the CSA manufactured machine guns, silencers, and explosives. And by the early 1980s the CSA machine shop was recognized in far-right circles as one of the best sources for illegally converted automatic weapons. The CSA found a market for its wares—and identified potential recruits—by selling survivalist paraphernalia at gun shows. Customers often were invited to attend the CSA "Endtime Overcomer Survival Training School" (so named because participants were taught how to prevail in the biblical "endtimes" to come). Marketed as "Holy Convocation[s] designed for the serious Patriotic Christian," the sessions took place at "Silhouette City," a surreal mock-up of urban America that resembled a low-budget movie set. There, camouflaged militants rappelled off buildings and darted through "streets" littered with wrecked cars and burning tires in preparation for the impending collapse of civilization.[22] In addition to the mock firefights at Silhouette City, Ellison's gatherings featured classes in weapons selection, first aid, natural childbirth, "basic rifle and pistol form," and Identity theology, but "foul language, alcohol, drugs, and illegal weapons" were forbidden.[23]

The CSA modeled its paramilitary curriculum after the highly successful "freedom festivals" organized by John R. Harrell, a sixty-one-year-old, Armageddon-obsessed multimillionaire from neighboring Illinois. Harrell also was the founder of the Christian-Patriots Defense League (CPDL). It was the activities of both groups that would give Missouri lawmakers the ammunition they needed to overcome the opposition of pro-gun groups, and outlaw paramilitary training.

Like William Dudley Pelley and other self-made men of the radical right, Harrell claimed supernatural visions had inspired his devotion to the cause. According to Harrell, he was thirty-seven years old and awaiting surgery for lymphatic cancer when the "presence of God," entered his motel room in Rochester, Minnesota, forced him and his wife to the floor, and "scooted [them] from one side of the room to the other," during a nine-hour ordeal which was repeated "night after night." The experience allegedly cured him of cancer and inspired his embrace of Christian Identity and violent rhetoric.[24]

"Buy yourselves a gun, and then buy some ammunition. If you don't get the ammunition you might as well get a club. It will be cheaper and you can beat them to death," he told one group of Klansmen in 1978.[25] Inspired by visions of a communist invasion and fears of the endtimes ahead, Harrell mapped out a twenty-state "Mid-America Survival Area," where he expected his cadre of trained patriots to gather. The scheme was grandiose, but Harrell had made millions selling mausoleums and agricultural real estate and he had ample resources to promote the plan. Harrell's twice-yearly, all-white "Freedom Festivals" drew large crowds to his fifty-five-acre farm outside Louisville, Illinois—one

1980 event attracted more than one thousand people and offered some fifty-five classes, including "Knife-Fighting," "Concealment of Valuables and Weaponry," and "Handgun Use for Personal Defense."[26] By the late 1970s and early 1980s Harrell's estate had become a popular destination for white-supremacist survivalists.

Harrell also had credibility in the movement because he had done hard time. Decades earlier, in the 1960s, he was imprisoned for sheltering an eighteen-year-old marine deserter who had read one of his pamphlets and felt compelled to fight the Jewish Conspiracy rather than report for duty. When lawmen came to seize the young soldier from Harrell's estate, Harrell resisted arrest and fled, evading authorities for eighteen months before he was captured in 1963 and served four years of a ten-year prison sentence on a variety of charges.[27]

Twenty years later, Harrell moved his paramilitary Freedom Festivals from Illinois to a 232-acre property in southern Missouri. Like the training sessions at the CSA, Harrell's events attracted right-wing criminals. One was Randall Radar, thirty, a former drug user and early disciple of Jim Ellison's who oversaw "military tactics" for the CSA. Around 1982, Radar left the CSA to direct weapons-training for The Order, Bob Matthews's group of Aryan revolutionaries.[28] In contrast to Harrell's financial independence, Jim Ellison always was struggling to make ends meet, and his insular, communal world often was inaccessible to outsiders. And unlike the massive resistance envisioned by the Christian-Patriots Defense League, Ellison conceived of his encampment as "an Ark for God's people during the coming tribulations" of race war. But despite their differences, Harrell was a strong supporter of Ellison's, and he often invited the men of the CSA to lead workshops at CPDL events, where they sold their wares and found new followers.

Prominent news coverage of the Missouri activities of the CPDL and the CSA helped pass an anti-paramilitary training bill in 1983.[29] Though the legislation caused John Harrell to cancel his 1984 Freedom Festival, it took another two years to shut down the CSA. Ellison's heyday ended on April 19, 1985 (another anniversary date of right-wing significance preceding the Oklahoma City bombing), when more than three hundred federal officers surrounded the CSA compound. After four days of negotiations the group surrendered. In addition to the usual illegal weapons and ammunition, investigators found grenades, dynamite, plastic explosives, blasting caps, homemade land mines, detonation cord, and one U.S. Army anti-tank rocket.[30] Ellison was convicted of conspiracy to commit arson, pleaded guilty to illegal firearms charges, and received a twenty-year prison sentence. Seven other men were convicted of CSA-related crimes.[31]

Despite his zeal, Ellison soon ratted on his former compatriots. After serving only a year in prison, and in exchange for a reduced sentence, he testified against an array of fellow white supremacists who were charged with plotting to overthrow the government, kill an FBI agent, and assassinate a federal judge. The trial was held in Fort Smith, Arkansas, in the spring of 1988, and the outcome was a stunning defeat for government prosecutors. The fourteen defendants included men like Richard Wayne Snell and the Aryan Nations chief, Richard Butler, but the government won no convictions; though some defendants—like Snell—already were serving lengthy prison terms for other crimes.[32]

In addition to passing in Missouri, anti–paramilitary training legislation won legislative approval in Idaho in 1983, over the protests of some lawmakers. "This bill speaks for minorities, not the majority," declared Representative Frank Findlay, an Idaho Republican who denounced the bill as "canned legislation."

"It's the ADL that's behind this. It's a foreign power that flaunts our laws," another legislator said. White supremacists and Posse members underscored their opposition to the bill with a cross-burning. "Cross-lighting is basically a warning. We're going to have our redress of grievances one way or another," explained the Aryan Nations security chief, Eldon "Bud" Cutler, another future member of The Order.[33]

The ADL model bill was also introduced in Nebraska in 1983, but it took three more years and two grisly Posse-related murders to convince legislators there to finally approve the measure.[34]

Banning paramilitary training gave some satisfaction to lawmakers and Jewish groups, but the effect of these laws was largely symbolic. Although John Harrell cancelled his CPDL gatherings after action by the Missouri legislature—and laws in other states likely discouraged similar sessions—the bans were extremely difficult to enforce. Prosecutors required hard evidence that the paramilitary training in question was part of a definite plan to commit civil disorder. Precise targets and dates, as well as reliable informants, were needed to secure an indictment, which explains why few if any cases have ever been prosecuted under these statutes. And as long as right-wing paramilitary enthusiasts didn't connect their training sessions to specific plans of action, they were free to run through the woods, their faces smeared with greasepaint, firing their Ruger Mini-14s without fear of prosecution. Indeed, a decade later, when the militia movement engaged in widespread paramilitary training, few if any of the movement's followers were charged under these old state laws, though many were arrested for other crimes. Federal laws that barred illegal weapons and explosives were much more of a threat, and federal agencies had more resources to investigate and prosecute right-wing groups—but such decisions were made all too sparingly until after the Oklahoma City bombing.

Although the threat of violence from paramilitary training sessions was real enough, the more substantial danger posed by the radical right in the Farm Belt was the spread of bigotry and the attraction of its dead-end solutions to desperate farmers. Ensnared in the rhetoric of the radical right, farmers with legitimate greviances lost credibility and found themselves divided, when they should have been uniting around more constructive efforts to pursue economic justice. Criminal prosecutions were a definite setback to the Posse movement—as were the reams of bad press and the various laws that were passed to prevent paramilitary training and the filing of bogus Posse paperwork. But none of these counter-measures were a substitute for what finally helped quash the rural radical right: a vigorous and well-organized social movement that was willing to confront the ideas and the bigotry of so-called "Christian Patriots," with both an alternative worldview and a concrete strategy to address farmers' woes.

29

AAM SPLIT

On February 9, 1982, a crowd of three thousand farmers and union members filled ten city blocks in Des Moines, Iowa, to protest the arrival of President Ronald Reagan. Braving a windchill of 41 degrees below zero, they demanded lower interest rates, an immediate moratorium on government farm foreclosures, and 100 percent parity. On the surface there was no difference between these demands and those of AAM. But in place of the conspiracy theories, constitutional fantasies, and anti-Semitic paranoia offered by the rural radical right, the policy agenda put forward in Des Moines contained a more sophisticated—and liberal—analysis of the farmers' plight. The newly formed Iowa Farm Unity Coalition, made up of mainstream farm groups, religious organizations, and labor unions, organized the protest. The coalition also included AAM, whose Iowa leader had rejected right-wing politics. In sharp contrast to Alvin Jenkins and others like him, the founders of the Coalition—and its counterparts in other states—were generally younger, and their views and values had been shaped by the civil rights and antiwar movements of the 1960s and 1970s.

Dixon Terry, thirty-two, was the driving force behind the Iowa Farm Unity Coalition and the energetic national movement that would soon shape the strategies and protests that put the farm crisis—and farmers' demands for economic justice—on the front page. A third-generation farmer, Terry had been a National Merit Scholar, the valedictorian of his 1968 high-school graduating class, and a philosophy major at Iowa State University. Then, disillusioned in part by the war in Vietnam, he dropped out and started a dairy farm with his wife, Linda, in the late 1970s. A prairie populist with fiery-red hair, wire-rimmed glasses, and a winning smile, Terry was forceful and articulate in presenting farmers' demands, which he always placed in the context of the need for broader social justice. A close adviser of the presidential candidate and civil-rights leader Jesse Jackson, Terry's opinions were frequently sought by politicians, journalists, and presidential candidates, even if the solutions he proposed were deemed "too radical" to enact into law. Although Terry and his cohorts never won the comprehensive overhaul of federal policy that farmers so desperately needed, they did secure legal and legislative victories that delayed foreclosures, gave debtors new rights, and saved tens of thousands of farms. They also dealt a damaging blow to the rural radical right.

Terry's politics were shared by men like the Reverend David L. Ostendorf, a United Church of Christ minister and the director of the Midwest office of Rural America, Inc., a nonprofit advocacy group that helped spark—and then staffed—the activities of the Iowa Farm Unity Coalition. Founded in 1975, Rural America had worked to promote a New Deal–style public-policy agenda for rural development. But since there was little hope of that happening after the election of President Ronald Reagan, the organization moved quickly to establish outposts beyond its headquarters in Washington, D.C. The Des Moines office opened in 1981 and was headed by Ostendorf, a native Midwesterner with experience organizing farmers and workers in the coalfields of southern Illinois. This author joined the staff the following year, serving first as an organizer and then as research director. It was Rural America and its allies in groups like the Iowa Farm Unity Coalition that would soon play a central role as farmers' advocates during the most severe agricultural crisis since the Great Depression—while also spearheading the fight against the rural radical right.

The Coalition and other groups established credibility and won legions of recruits by setting up telephone hotlines that dispensed much-needed legal and financial advice and acted as an antidote to the bogus instructions of Christian Patriot "advisers." The leaders of the progressive farm movement shunned right-wing rhetoric but were not shy about staging militant protests. "All lenders must negotiate in good faith with farmers and their representatives and keep them on their land and operating," the Coalition declared in its founding statement.[1] And for those lenders that did not deal with farmers fairly, there was always the threat of a well-publicized and dramatic "penny auction" protest. Such face-to-face confrontations between farmers and creditors became a media favorite and did much to generate sympathy for farmers' plight. The first round of these nonviolent "farm-gate defenses" took place in the fall of 1982, in Minnesota, Missouri, Illinois, and Wisconsin. Wearing red armbands and borrowing a tactic from the 1930s, the crowds intimidated would-be buyers at farm sales with spirited bids of, "One penny!" and "No sale! No sale!" While they received media attention, these first protests hardly won the publicity garnered by Jerry Wright and his friends in AAM during the melee in Springfield, Colorado, in January 1983.[2] And one month later, Gordon Kahl's violence in North Dakota blared from the headlines.

Unfortunately for AAM, the fatal shootout in Medina took place the same day as the *Denver Post* ran a front-page article exposing the alleged role of American Agriculture Movement leaders in bomb-making seminars and the Weskan training. The publicity further divided the already-fractured farm group and threatened to delegitimize the grievances of farmers. "Parity . . . was the rallying cry heard half a decade ago when American Agriculture was born in Springfield. But the word rarely is mentioned now in the organization's headquarters," wrote reporter William Ritz, who quoted Alvin Jenkins and Gene Schroder describing how they had constructed different explosives. In addition to recounting the details of how the leaders of Grass Roots AAM had drifted to the right, the *Denver Post* article noted that their Campo, Colorado, headquarters was stacked with anti-Semitic conspiracy literature.[3]

Coming on the heels of widespread news coverage of the melee at Jerry Wright's farm sale, the *Denver Post* article—and the reporting about Gordon Kahl—put AAM squarely on the defensive. "I am definitely not a racist—and as for bomb-making, I have never made a bomb or explosive in my life," said Jenkins, whose $5 million libel suit against the *Post* was later thrown out of court, after he failed to pursue it. "Furthermore, I have never attended a meeting of the Farmers Liberation Army or of the Posse Comitatus," he claimed.[4] Just days after the Medina shootings, the Kansas attorney general, Robert Stephan, had assailed the Posse's violent threats and racist rhetoric.[5] Stephan did not mention AAM, but the farm group's Kansas spokesman, Darrell Ringer, accused the attorney general of conducting a "witch-hunt."

"There is no Posse Comitatus that we know of and there are none of our AAM people who are a part of it," Ringer blithely asserted, though he knew better.[6]

In the wake of the *Denver Post* article, Alvin Jenkins tried to rehabilitate his reputation by meeting with civil rights leaders who were planning a march on Washington to commemorate the twentieth anniversary of the famous "I Have a Dream" speech delivered by the Reverend Dr. Martin Luther King Jr. The group included Coretta Scott King, the Reverend Jesse Jackson, singer Harry Belafonte, and Dr. Joseph Lowery, president of the Southern Christian Leadership Conference. "I feel there is an opportunity for us to become the leader in agriculture in the entire rural black community and to become known by the entire black population," Jenkins gushed in the *AAM News*. But he failed to explain why African-Americans would embrace an all-white group with no previous interest in civil rights, let alone a group tainted by allegations of bigotry and right-wing beliefs.[7] With exquisite timing, the same edition of *AAM News* that carried a picture of Jenkins and Dr. King's widow also contained a classified ad offering free copies of Sheldon Emry's anti-Semitic pamphlet, *Billions for the Bankers, Debts for the People.*[8]

While leaders of Grass Roots AAM issued defiant denials in response to the *Denver Post* article, spokesmen for AAM, Inc., in Washington, D.C., strongly condemned violence and distanced the organization from those who had attended "meetings or other activities which had as its purpose, avowed or secret, the use of violence, unlawful conduct, or illegal acts." AAM, Inc., also denounced the use of its "logo, stationery, and name by organizations and different groups for their own gain."[9] These and other statements were crafted by David Senter, a burly, cigar-chewing Texas cattleman who had come to Washington at the behest of AAM to work in the Texas Office of Federal–State Relations. When Senter's plain talk and no-nonsense attitude got him dismissed from that post, he was hired as national director of AAM. The *AAM News* had enthusiastically endorsed Senter in 1980, but by early 1983 it was attacking him fiercely.[10]

More than one thousand farmers attended the AAM national convention in Nashville that January, just weeks after Jerry Wright's farm sale. Armed guards flanked the doors, bickering marred the two-day proceeding, and right-wing activists managed to push through a resolution calling on AAM to protest the Federal Reserve as "illegal." The sponsor of the resolution was Patrick "Family Farmer" O'Reilly, a vocational instructor–turned–farmer and an ardent supporter of right-wing conspiracist Lyndon LaRouche.[11] In 1980, O'Reilly ran for Congress as a Democrat in Minnesota under the slogan, "You don't have to be gay and kill babies to be a candidate for the Democratic Party." Two years later, he ran on the LaRouche-sponsored National Democratic Policy Committee ticket. O'Reilly not only introduced the anti–Federal Reserve resolution at the Nashville convention, he arranged for LaRouche to address the group.[12]

Once a 1960s left-wing activist with a tiny band of followers, LaRouche was the paranoid leader of an anti-Semitic political cult with international neofascist connections. After breaking with the left in 1973, LaRouche had launched a dizzying array of publications and front groups dedicated to attacking David Rockefeller, the "Zionist lobby," British bankers, the Queen of England, and a host of other imaginary perils. LaRouche's elaborate conspiracy theories and dire warnings about global calamity helped reinforce the fierce loyalty of several hundred zombielike followers. To curry favor with a wider audience, LaRouche promoted nuclear energy, a "*Star Wars*" missile defense system, called for a "War on Drugs," attacked Jimmy Carter, and ran for president in the 1980 Democratic Party primaries. He also called for "parity" and demanded emergency relief for farmers.

"LaRouche targeted his message to conservative blue-collar and small-business voters whom he felt would support him as an alternative to the liberalism of the Democratic Party leadership," explained author Dennis King, an expert on LaRouche.[13] Although most Democratic officials dismissed LaRouche as a crank, he ended his 1980 presidential campaign with 185,000 votes, more than

$500,000 in federal matching funds—a first for an extremist candidate—and national name recognition.[14] (Democratic strategists and pundits were forced to rewrite their assessment of LaRouche six years later, when two of his supporters, Mark Fairchild and Janice Hart, stunned the political establishment by winning the Democratic Party nominations for lieutenant governor and secretary of state in Illinois.)

LaRouche's rantings about the British royal family and his technocratic ramblings about the marvels of nuclear fusion were hardly of interest to farmers. But his broadsides against the Rothschilds, the Rockefellers, and President Carter received a warm response. A clever opportunist, LaRouche linked AAM demands for parity to his attacks on the International Monetary Fund, the Federal Reserve, and the World Bank. In 1980, he tried to woo AAM president Marvin Meek as his vice presidential running mate. Meek declined, but LaRouche and his lieutenants dogged AAM followers at their meetings and national conventions. Soon Georgia AAM leader Tommy Kersey was being quoted in LaRouche's twice-weekly newspaper, New Solidarity. And by early 1983, a core of high-ranking AAM activists, including Kersey, had become key LaRouche supporters. One of them, AAM activist Billy Davis, a Mississippi lawyer and a cattleman, signed on as LaRouche's vice presidential nominee in 1984.[15]

After David Senter convinced the national leadership of AAM to repudiate LaRouche, he received death threats, which prompted him to send his wife and four children back to Texas for safety. He also sought help from the Washington, D.C., Capitol Police who provided round-the-clock security and advised him and Marvin Meek to wear bulletproof vests. And so when LaRouche supporters in AAM ran into difficulties organizing their anti–Federal Reserve protests in February 1983, it was only logical that they blamed David Senter.[16]

"The AAM, Inc., crowd is driving farmers out of its organization by its underhanded methods and slanders against the Grass Roots AAM in Colorado and supporters of Lyndon LaRouche," wrote Lawrence Freeman, a high-ranking LaRouche lieutenant, whose broadside was published in AAM News.[17] LaRouche's activities provoked tension within AAM, but the deeper conflict revolved around the Posse-oriented politics of the Campo, Colorado, faction and the attempts by Washington leaders to rein them in. Predictably, Farmers Liberation Army founder Keith Shive encouraged the split. "The only solution is for AAM Grass Roots to take the name AAM because it rightfully belongs to them. . . . Our problem with low farm income can never be solved in Washington, so why flirt with the enemy?"[18] Tired of issuing damage-control statements, Senter and others wrote new bylaws that permitted the expulsion of any state chapter that gave "express or tacit approval" to any activities "deemed unlawful by the appropriate civil authorities." This was the last straw, as far as many in Grass Roots AAM were concerned. In September 1983, the Kansas and Colorado chapters voted to withdraw from the national organization.[19] "There may have been a time when the rift could have been healed," wrote AAM News publishers

Alden and Micki Nellis. "[But] that time is now past. . . . Our hearts are not in supporting AAM, Inc., any longer." Alden Nellis also called on supporters to shut down the Washington office.[20] Leaders of Grass Roots AAM cast the split as a difference over money and political strategy—they criticized the expenditures of the AAM political action committee—but it really was a conflict over the ideology of the radical right.

When Alvin Jenkins started AAM in 1977, he was a conservative Republican. Although he never became a tax protester or Identity believer, or advocated violent confrontation with authorities, Jenkins eventually embraced elements of Posse ideology. His worldview was not that of a rabid anti-Semite like Gordon Kahl, but the conspiracy theories and right-wing views he advanced opened the door for others further to the right. "What are rights? . . . Are there really minority rights, civil rights, homosexual rights, women's rights, etc? Are rights whatever we want them to be?" Jenkins asked rhetorically in an essay in *AAM News*. "God and God alone is the source of rights. . . . No legislative body in the world has the right to make amendments and or statutes contrary to the law of God," he answered himself. Like many conservatives, Jenkins denounced "illicit sex," "lewd lifestyles," "homosexuality and lesbianism, " the absence of prayer in public schools, and the abandonment, by "unrighteous men," of their "God-ordained position of leadership in the home or in government." Of course these issues had nothing to do with low farm prices and the collapse of the rural economy, but Jenkins saw a connection. Any government that would legalize such "unlawful" behavior could not be trusted to enforce the Constitution. "Just because something is legal doesn't make it lawful," Jenkins explained, parroting a popular Posse line. "Six years ago we did not know what the problem was, but we do now," he added. And then, echoing the typically coded anti-Semitism of some rightists, Jenkins accused the "few families who own the Federal Reserve" of using grain companies as "pawns in a chess game . . . so that [they] can have billions of dollars." Faced with such a predicament, patriots had no choice but to act. "We cannot win overnight. If some go to jail, go in honesty and be proud of what you are doing."[21]

In addition to denouncing AAM, Inc., for "accomplishing nothing," Jenkins and the Campo faction staked their credibility on renewed calls for a farm strike, and set a date. "We must plow a new row. If this country was ever ripe for an agricultural strike, it will be about the first of November [1983]," Jenkins asserted.[22] But the planned "farm revolt" never materialized, at least not the one spearheaded by Jenkins. Instead, the rebellion would be led by liberal advocacy groups and progressive farmers, whose organizing efforts soon outstripped those of the rural radical right.

That task was made easier, in part, by the widespread condemnation of right-wing extremism that followed the killings of law enforcement officials by Gordon Kahl and his fellow Possemen. Although technically the farm crisis had little to do with the carnage in Medina—after all, Kahl had opened fire on the lawmen because he refused to be arrested for violating probation on tax charges—there was no better example to illustrate the deadly consequences of radical right-wing beliefs in the Farm Belt. For Christian Patriots, of course, the meaning of events in Medina was the reverse. Even though Kahl was dogged by income-tax liens and federal warrants, not bank loans and creditors, he was regarded as a symbol of broader rural resistance.

"You think some farmer is going to turn him in—him, a good neighbor? No way. Whoever collects that $25,000 [reward] isn't going to be around long enough to spend it," one North Dakota farmer observed.[23] The people who held such sentiments greatly aided Kahl, who vanished easily after the shootings and found seclusion with fellow Christian Patriots in Arkansas. Eventually, however, neither admiration for Kahl nor fears of reprisal were enough to prevent someone from coming forward to claim the reward: she was Karen Russell Robertson, the daughter of one of the Posse followers who had hidden Gordon Kahl on the outskirts of the Ozark National Forest.[24]

Marcus Gale, undated. After emigrating from Russia in 1881, the great uncle of Posse Comitatus founder William Potter Gale spent seven years farming in North Dakota before moving west and becoming a well-respected member of the Jewish community in Portland, Oregon. *Oregon Historical Society, Negative No. 103990.*

Chaya Inda Grabifker, undated. The grandmother of William Potter Gale fled the anti-Semitism of Eastern Europe and arrived in Glasgow, Scotland, in 1894 with her husband and six children, including Gale's father, Charles.

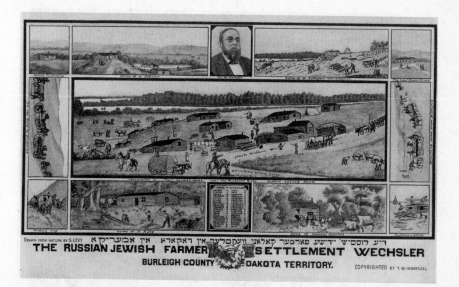

In 1884, the "Russian Jewish Farmer Settlement Wechsler," also known as "Wechsler's Painted Woods" or "New Jerusalem," was home to fifty-four households and about 300 people, including Marcus Gale and his wife, Rosa. *State Historical Society of North Dakota, C1480.*

Charles Gale, undated. After enlisting in the army in 1898, Charles Gale became a farrier, or blacksmith, and developed a life-long love of horses. Though he lied about his
age and place of birth on his October 24, 1898, military enlistment papers—claiming he
was born in the United States—Gale acknowledged he was Jewish, noting his parents
"nationality" as "Hebrew."

FORM FOR THE PHYSICAL EXAMINATION OF A RECRUIT.

Name, *Charles Gale* ; age, *22 ½* ; birthday *Mch. 2nd*

; birthplace, * *Bismarck Dakota*

residence, *494 S. Pierce St. Milwaukee Wis* Are you a citizen of the United States? * **YES.**

Have you made application for citizenship? If so, in what court? *

nationality of father, *Hebrew* ; of mother, *Hebrew*

State previous service (U. S. or foreign), and date of last discharge, with organization: *Served 5 m 21 day*
Co "L" 1st Wis Vol dis October 14 -98.

Have you applied before for enlistment; if so, where? **NO.**

If rejected, for what cause?

Have you given your true name and not an assumed one? **YES.**

Do you clearly understand the nature of the oath of enlistment, and are you fully determined to serve the

United States honestly and faithfully?

What is your object in enlisting? *To remain in the army*

Do you clearly understand the nature of the "Declaration of Recruit," connected with enlistment? **YES.**

Are you familiar with the Act of Congress approved June 16, 1890 (G. O. No. 68, June 27, 1890, from
the Adjutant General's Office), "to prevent desertions from the Army and for other purposes," as
amended?

Charles and Mary Agnes Gale and their five children, circa 1926. Top row, L to R, Ruth Jane, Charles Earl, Charles Sr., Mary Agnes. Bottom Row, L to R, William Potter, Robert Duane, Beatrice Ann.

William Potter Gale and Josephine Catherine Dvornich. The couple was married on June 7, 1937.

The Rev. Wesley A. Swift addressing the First Anglo-Saxon Christian Congress, June 11-13, 1948, in Los Angeles, California. Swift's bombastic oratory and racist, anti-Semitic theology attracted thousands of followers in the 1940s, 1950s, and 1960s, including Posse Comitatus founder William Potter Gale. *Jewish Federation Council of Greater Los Angeles' Community Relations Committee Collection, Urban Archives Center, University Library, California State University, Northridge*

Beginning May 22, 1920, auto-mobile magnate Henry Ford published a series of virulently anti-Semitic articles in ninety-one consecutive issues of his newspaper, the *Dearborn (Mich.) Independent*. The material was later compiled into the four vol-umes shown here and published by Ford as *The International Jew*. *Walter Bell*

Henry Ford, July 1938, being awarded the Grand Cross of the German Eagle, the highest honor that Adolf Hitler could bestow upon a foreigner. Shaking Ford's hand at left is Fritz Heiler, German consul in Detroit, while Karl Kapp, German consul in Cleveland, pins the medal on Ford. *AP/World Wide Photos*

James Proctor Knott (1830–1911), the sponsor of the Posse Comitatus Act of 1878. Knott had been a pro-slavery unionist and the attorney general of Missouri from 1858 to 1862, before becoming a Confederate legislator and lieutenant colonel in the Confederate Army. Knott then served six terms in the U.S. Congress, (1867–1871 and 1875–1883) before becoming Governor of Kentucky (1883–1887). *Kentucky Historical Society*

The intellectual architect of state's rights and Southern secession, John Caldwell Calhoun served twice as vice president of the United States (1828–1836). In 1828, Calhoun anonymously authored the *Exposition*, a groundbreaking essay that asserted that states could "interpose" their supposed sovereign power to resist the federal government. *National Portrait Gallery, Smithsonian Institution.*

Retired Major General Edwin A. "Ted" Walker (in hat) is arrested on October 1, 1962, after protesting the admission of James Meredith to the University of Mississippi in Oxford. Walker was charged with insurrection and seditious conspiracy, but a federal grand jury declined to indict him and the charges were dropped. *AP/World Wide Photos*

In the wake of fierce rioting by segregationists on September 30 and October 1, 1962, President John F. Kennedy deployed more than 23,000 troops to enforce integration at the University of Mississippi. The action sparked outrage among many white Southerners. *AP/World Wide Photos*

After President Dwight Eisenhower dispatched federal troops to Little Rock, Arkansas, in September 1957, to enforce the desegregation of Central High School, William Potter Gale used the right-wing press to publicize his filing of a bogus "criminal indictment" of the president for allegedly violating the Posse Comitatus Act. *Graphic by Walter Bell*

★ *Constitution*   ★ *Freedom*   ★ *Nationalism*

Patriot:
KNOW THYSELF!

RIGHT

They can only set free men free. And there is no need of that: Free men set themselves free.

A MONTHLY NEWSLETTER OF, BY AND FOR THE AMERICAN RIGHTWING

Mention of or summary on any group or activity absolutely must not be taken as indication of approval, either by the publisher or by any other group or activity. This publication is intended to give information only and not to do so in an unbiased manner, with no favoritism meant or implied to any particular group or activity.

No. 26. November, 1957.   Bradford Martin, Editor
P.O. Box 182, San Francisco

Single Copy, 25c
10 Copies, $1
92 or more Copies, 3c ea.

$3 per year

IKE IS INDICTED AS CRIMINAL

Col. William P. Gale, now stumping California as a candidate for Governor on the CONSTITUTION PARTY (269) ticket, is filing a criminal indictment in the name of the Party against Eisenhower for his flagrantly illegal action of invading and occupying Arkansas. Gale has discovered that on August 30, 1957 Congress re-affirmed the "Posse Comitatus Act" which specifically prohibits the use of the Army to enforce laws.

The CONSTITUTION PARTY demands the immediate arrest and trial of Eisenhower.

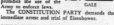

GALE

WHO RUNS RUSSIA?

One of the great questions about Russia has been who is actually running it. Some students of the question have asserted that there was a secret force standing behind the ostensible rulers which had the real power. This belief appears to be borne out by a detailed document from Sudeten German sources which has been presented to the House of Representatives by Rep. Timothy P. Sheehan (R, Ill.) in a August 5 speech.

The document charges that the Communist Security System (CSS) is the real power in Russia and the satellites and that this invisible government, through a wide range of methods, completely controls the entire Soviet system. Write Congressman Sheehan for a copy of his speech. House Office Building, Washington, D. C.

U. S. News & World Report in its August 23 issue carried an interesting quote from an unnamed

KNOWLAND DENIES "DEAL"

In an exclusive telephone interview with RIGHT, Senator William F. Knowland has denied increasingly-strong rumors that he has made a "deal" with the NAACP to put over a strong statewide FEPC in California, if elected Governor.

The rumored "deal" has been spoken of admiringly by some canny political observers as a masterstroke of politics. It would split Senator Knowland's opposition, the Big Labor-NAACP power bloc which until now has been supporting Governor Goodwin J. Knight. Thus, with the open support of thousands of California citizens who are fed up with the excesses of the Big Labor bosses and with the secret support of the ADL and the NAACP, Knowland would have comparatively easy sailing into the Governor's chair. These observers have pointed out that such a "deal" would fit in with Senator Knowland's demonstrated patterns of action and would solidify his standing with the NAACP, which he so devotedly served in the Senate.

Senator Knowland says he has no idea how the rumor started.

high official who deals with the Russians: "We are in the dark about who is really shaping Soviet policy. The Russians are running a big show . . . the Middle East, Europe, Asia, involving the most technical moves. . . We do not know who in Moscow has the time and skill to do the job that is well done and very fast."

Retired candy manufacturer Robert Welch, shown here in April 1963, founded the John Birch Society in December 1958. Fear of communism and opposition to civil rights spurred the group's rapid growth, from 24,000 members and a $1 million budget in 1961, to 100,000 members and a $6 million budget five years later. *AP/World Wide Photos*

Robert Bolivar DePugh (left) founder of the paramilitary group, the Minutemen, and Walter Patrick Peyson (right), on November 14, 1966, just after their conviction in federal court in Kansas City, Missouri, for violating the Federal Firearms Act. DePugh later went underground and became a federal fugitive for more than a year. *AP/World Wide Photos*

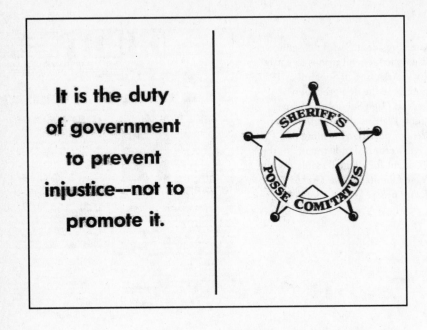

It is the duty of government to prevent injustice--not to promote it.

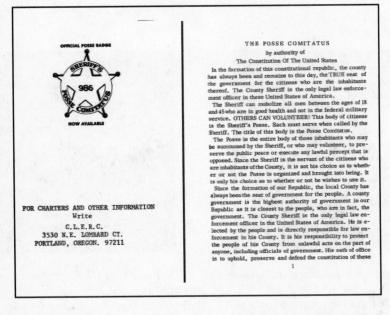

OFFICIAL POSSE BADGE

986

NOW AVAILABLE

FOR CHARTERS AND OTHER INFORMATION
Write
C.L.E.R.C.
3530 N.E. LOMBARD CT.
PORTLAND, OREGON. 97211

THE POSSE COMITATUS
by authority of
The Constitution Of The United States

In the formation of this constitutional republic, the county has always been and remains to this day, the TRUE seat of the government for the citizens who are the inhabitants thereof. The County Sheriff is the only legal law enforcement officer in these United States of America.

The Sheriff can mobilize all men between the ages of 18 and 45 who are in good health and not in the federal military service. OTHERS CAN VOLUNTEER! This body of citizens is the Sheriff's Posse. Each must serve when called by the Sheriff. The title of this body is the Posse Comitatus.

The Posse is the entire body of those inhabitants who may be summoned by the Sheriff, or who may volunteer, to preserve the public peace or execute any lawful precept that is opposed. Since the Sheriff is the servant of the citizens who are inhabitants of the County, it is not his choice as to whether or not the Posse is organized and brought into being. It is only his choice as to whether or not he wishes to use it.

Since the formation of our Republic, the local County has always been the seat of government for the people. A county government is the highest authority of government in our Republic as it is closest to the people, who are in fact, the government. The County Sheriff is the only legal law enforcement officer in the United States of America. He is elected by the people and is directly responsible for law enforcement in his County. It is his responsibility to protect the people of his County from unlawful acts on the part of anyone, including officials of government. His oath of office is to uphold, preserve and defend the constitution of these

1

The Posse *Blue Book* produced by Henry Lamont "Mike" Beach of Portland, Oregon, around 1973 (shown above), was entirely plagiarized from the writings of William Potter Gale, which Gale had published two years earlier in *IDENTITY*, the newsletter of his Ministry of Christ Church (see opposite page at right). *Graphics by Walter Bell*

IDENTITY
P. O. BOX 423
GLENDALE, CALIF.
91209

non profit org.

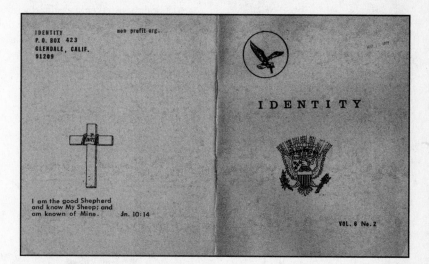

I am the good Shepherd
and know My Sheep; and
am known of Mine.   Jn. 10:14

IDENTITY

VOL. 6 No. 2

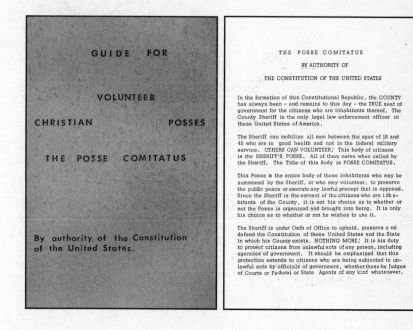

GUIDE   FOR

VOLUNTEER

CHRISTIAN   POSSES

THE POSSE   COMITATUS

By authority of the Constitution
of the United States.

THE POSSE COMITATUS

BY AUTHORITY OF

THE CONSTITUTION OF THE UNITED STATES

In the formation of this Constitutional Republic, the COUNTY has always been - and remains to this day - the TRUE seat of government for the citizens who are inhabitants thereof. The County Sheriff is the only legal law enforcement officer in these United States of America.

The Sheriff can mobilize all men between the ages of 18 and 45 who are in good health and not in the federal military service. OTHERS CAN VOLUNTEER! This body of citizens is the SHERIFF'S POSSE. All of them serve when called by the Sheriff. The Title of this Body is POSSE COMITATUS.

This Posse is the entire body of those inhabitants who may be summoned by the Sheriff, or who may volunteer, to preserve the public peace or execute any lawful precept that is opposed. Since the Sheriff is the servant of the citizens who are inhabitants of the County, it is not his choice as to whether or not the Posse is organized and brought into being. It is only his choice as to whether or not he wishes to use it.

The Sheriff is under Oath of Office to uphold, preserve and defend the Constitution of these United States and the State in which his County exists. NOTHING MORE! It is his duty to protect citizens from unlawful acts of any person, including agencies of government. It should be emphasized that this protection extends to citizens who are being subjected to unlawful acts by officials of government, whether these be Judges of Courts or Federal or State Agents of any kind whatsoever.

Henry Lamont "Mike" Beach, August 1976. Though mistakenly credited with founding the Posse Comitatus, Beach did play a significant role in the group's early growth. *AP/World Wide Photos*

Magnetic car decal used by members of the Multnomah County Posse Comitatus in Portland, Oregon, in 1975/1976. *Marvin Woidyla*

Return of the Posse?

They were a motley group, assembled in a modern Stockton, Calif., public meeting hall, some in service-station uniforms and football jerseys, others in double-knit suits—most of them working-class Americans. They milled around for some moments sipping instant coffee from Styrofoam cups, stood earnestly at attention for the pledge of allegiance and a prayer, then took their seats as a mild-faced man of 71 rose to address them.

The speaker's sandy-gray hair was slicked back, his mustache small and carefully trimmed. "Our Republic has already gone down the drain," said Henry L. (Mike) Beach. "Parasites have come in and destroyed our Republican form of government." As his audience nodded in agreement, Mike Beach outlined his personal scenario of what is happening in the United States. Vice President Nelson Rockefeller was the chief villain, as Beach told it: Richard Nixon, Spiro Agnew and President Gerald Ford had all conspired to set Rockefeller up for the Presidency. "He is the man," said Mike Beach, "who is going to be the dictator."

Charter: Beach's rapt audience of about 50 men and women, some accompanied by their children, was assembled for a meeting of an organization known as Sheriff's Posse Comitatus. "A member of the new-fangled revolvers conspicuously on their hips and wore silver imitation sheriff's badges on their chests. Card tables displayed "Genuine Citizen's Arrest Forms" and applications for a charter in the "National Christian Posse Association."

Posse Comitatus is the newest—and fastest growing—of a seemingly never-ending stream of militant right-wing organizations. Recently, Federal officials have begun to take keen interest in the Posse. They have found that its membership closely parallels the defunct paramilitary Sons of Liberty, as well as the National States Rights Party, which campaigns aggressively on an anti-black, anti-Semitic, anti-Federal platform. So far, Posse Comitatus seems to have found its most fertile ground in the Midwest and Far West. It has made little headway in the South, where the Ku Klux Klan carries many of the same ...

view of the law, which ranges from the inaccurate to the absurd. The group's literature insists that the Federal income tax is unconstitutional, that the county sheriff is the only legal law-enforcement officer in the U.S. and that county government is the highest authority in the Republic—on the ground that it is closest to the people. The Posse also proclaims that all firemen, land-use planning and gun laws are illegal.

The Bluebook that Beach distributes to his devoted followers once prescribed punishment for public officials who interfere with the Posse. The officer should be "... hanged by the neck ... at high noon ... on a busy intersection of streets in the township and at high noon be hung by the giants ..." Now, new editions of the Bluebook leave a blank space where that statement once stood; Beach simply says it was "too controversial."

So far, Posse Comitatus has only sporadic attempts to enforce its code. Last summer, Thomas F. Stockheimer, a Wisconsin Posse leader and unsuccessful American Party candidate for the state legislature, was convicted of assaulting an Internal Revenue Service agent and sentenced to 60 days in jail. In the fall, at a public hearing on land-use planning, Stockheimer, free on bond, was arrested for using Mace against seventy guards. In Kootenai County, Idaho, two months ago, a policeman was sent to serve a subpoena in a Posse syn-up dispute was "arrested" by Posse members. It took the sheriff and several deputies to "rescue" the officer from the shouting, milling crowd.

Jail: Usually, Posse efforts end in futility. In Du Page County, Ill., this spring, Posse Comitatus member was sentenced to jail for contempt of court during divorce hearing. A fellow-member possibly "indicted" the judge and demanded the he be arrested by the sheriff—who is noted them. In Spooner, Wis., last summer, a "Christian Citizens Grand Jury issued "indictments" against 43 state and local officials, including Gov. Patrick J. Lucey, for letting the state department of natural resources become too powerful. When Judge Allen Kinney refused to take any action on their indictments too ...

Despite the studied insults from law enforcement officials, thousands of Posse Comitatus members seem determined to save the country from the evil they see all around them—whether it country wants it or not. What hurts the most of all, though, is the abhorrence displayed by the elected sheriffs who a their supposed benefactors. Many sheriffs who have been harassed by Posse groups openly scorn the proffered assistance. "Those SOB's aren't going to run in here to do my job," says Louis Glaze the veteran sheriff of Marathon County, Wis. "And the first one of those guys w step out of line will get his butt in jail

—SUSAN FRAKER with WILLIAM J. COOK and other bureau reports

Gillings: Is Smith & Wesson a law firm?

...ment & Research Committee, he loudly mails out "Christian Posse" charters for $21 apiece and sheriff's badges for $6.50 each to charter members. Beach claims that chapters exist in every state except Hawaii and that membership is close to 500,000. The FBI scoffs at this figure, and the probabilities are that total membership so far is not much over 10,000. But the Posse seems to be growing, and its fondness for firearms is disquieting. "There is no greater law firm than Smith & Wesson," brags Francis E. Gillings, the Stockton Posse chairman, "especially if it is backed up by a 12-gauge injunction."

Posse Comitatus has its own special ...

Newsweek, May 26, 19

San Joaquin County, California, Posse Chairman Francis Gillings. A tax protestor and Posse militant, Gillings posed for this photo which appeared in *Newsweek* magazine, May 26, 1975, just months before he staged an armed skirmish with San Joaquin County sheriff's deputies in a tomato field ouside Stockton, California. The article, titled "Return of the Posse?" brought Beach right-wing notoriety and sparked greater interest in the group by the FBI. *Gillings photo by James D. Wilson*

54

Wisconsin Posse Comitatus founder Thomas Stockheimer, 53, on August 31, 1985, is escorted by U.S. marshals following his capture in Wisconsin four and a half years after fleeing a federal firearms indictment. *Milwaukee Journal Sentinel/Sherman Gessert*

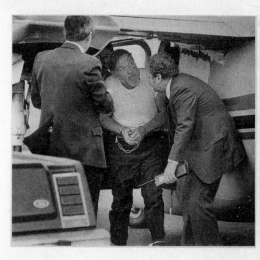

Right-wing tax-protest literature sold hundred of thousands of copies from 1975 to 1985 and is still popular today. In 1983, the IRS tallied 58,000 illegal tax-protest returns, ten times the number the agency received in 1978. *Walter Bell*

Arthur Julius Porth, November 6, 1970, after failing to overturn his conviction for tax evasion. Porth, a Wichita, Kansas, building contractor and tax-protest pioneer, inspired thousands of Americans to file illegal tax-protest returns. *Wichita (Kans.) Eagle*

Followers of the newly formed American Agriculture Movement join a "tractorcade" headed for Plains, Georgia, the hometown of President Jimmy Carter, to protest low farm prices on November 25, 1977. *AP/Wide World Photos*

A farmer and rancher from Campo, Colorado, Alvin Jenkins was one of the most dynamic of the founders of the American Agriculture Movement. Jenkins is shown here addressing a rally in Denver, on December 10, 1977, four days before the AAM "Farm Strike" deadline. Jenkins later turned sharply to the right. *AP/Wide World Photos*

David Goldstein, Executive Director of the Jewish Community Relations Bureau of Greater Kansas City, leads Jews at a protest in support of family farmers outside the office of the U.S. Department of Agriculture in Chillicothe, Missouri, on August 3, 1986. *Jewish Community Relations Bureau/American Jewish Committee of Greater Kansas City*

Former American Agriculture Movment leader Tommy Kersey (above) was jubilant after he and several dozen heavily armed men succeeded in preventing the foreclosure of Georgia farmer Oscar Lorick on November 15, 1985. *John Coley*

James P. Wickstrom, the self-appointed "National Director of Counter-Insurgency" for the Posse Comitatus, October 10, 1982. Beginning in 1978, Wickstrom targeted financially strapped farmers and other rural residents, preaching Christian Identity theology and the violent message of the Posse Comitatus. *Milwaukee Journal Sentinel/Jack Orton*

An accomplished con artist who targeted farmers with anti-Semitic propaganda and right-wing legal scams, Roderick F. "Rick" Elliott was convicted of theft and conspiracy by a Colorado jury on May 27, 1986, and sentenced to eight years in prison. *Reprinted with the permission of The (Denver, Colo.) Rocky Mountain News/David L. Cornwell*

Michael Ryan (right) being escorted into the Richardson County (Nebraska) Courthouse in 1985. Ryan was the leader of a Christian Identity encampment in Rulo, Nebraska, when he murdered James Thimm, 26, and Luke Stice, 5, in 1985. Sentenced to death for Thimm's murder, Ryan remains on death row. *Falls City (Nebr.) Journal*

Tax protestor and Posse Comitatus martyr, Gordon Wendell Kahl, following his arrest on April 15, 1977, in Midland, Texas. *AP/World Wide Photos*

Christian Identity believer and Posse Comitatus follower Richard Wayne Snell, 64, speaks at his clemency hearing in Tucker, Arkansas, on April 12, 1995. Snell was executed by lethal injection on April 19, 1995, exactly twelve hours after the bombing of the Alfred P. Murrah federal building in Oklahoma City. *AP/World Wide Photos/Bill McEntire*

The burned-out kitchen of the home of Leonard and Norma Ginter outside Smithville, Arkansas, where more than two dozen lawmen attempted to apprehend Gordon Kahl on June 3, 1983. Immediately before he was killed, Kahl fatally shot Lawrence County sheriff Gene Matthews. The residence was engulfed in flame after lawmen poured diesel fuel down a roof vent. *The (Walnut Ridge, Ark.) Times Dispatch*

William Potter Gale, September 1987. Defiant to the end, Bill Gale was convicted by a federal jury in Las Vegas, Nevada, on October 2, 1987, of conspiracy, attempting to interfere with federal tax laws, and mailing death threats to the IRS. He died six months later of complications from emphysema. *Las Vegas Sun.*

Militia Movement leaders address a U.S. Senate panel chaired by Senator Arlen Specter (R-Pennsylvania) in Washington, D.C., June 15, 1995. Right to left: Michigan Militia leader Norman E. Olson; Ohio Militia activist James Johnson; Michigan Militiaman Ken Adams; Militia of Montana spokesman Bob Fletcher; and Militia of Montana founder John Trochmann. *Jenny Warburg*

Karen Matthews, the Stanislaus County (California) recorder, testifies before members of Congress on July 11, 1995, about the threats and beating she received from members of a right-wing, tax-protest group in 1993 and 1994. *Jenny Warburg*

Following the Oklahoma City bombing in April 1995, 68 percent of Montana residents said they "actively opposed" the views of the Militia, but as many as 20 percent still declared their support. *Montana Human Rights Network*

Richard Butler at the pulpit in Hayden Lake, Idaho, October 2000. Converted to Christian Identity theology by William Potter Gale in the 1950s, Butler attempted to succeed his mentor, Rev. Wesley A. Swift, following Swift's death in 1970. Not long afterwards, Butler moved the dwindling remnants of Swift's congregation to Idaho where he established the Aryan Nations. The group was bankrupted in September 2000 when lawyers with the Southern Poverty Law Center won a $6.3 million judgment on behalf of a woman and her son who had been terrorized by guards at the compound. *Jenny Warburg*

Jenny Warburg

The terrorist attacks of September 11, 2001, prompted anti-Semitism as well as hate crimes against Arab Americans and immigrants. The neo-Nazi National Alliance organized a protest at the Israeli Embassy in Washington, D.C., on November 10, 2001 (above) while anti-Arab graffiti was scrawled in the dust near the site of the World Trade Center explosion at daybreak, September 12, 2001 (below). Incidents of anti-Arab and anti-immigrant vandalism, assaults, and murder rose sharply in the months following September 11.

AP/World Wide Photos

30

KAHL AND HIS COURIER

One month after the February 1983 shootout in North Dakota, Gordon Kahl arrived at the farm of Arthur Russell, near Mountain Home, Arkansas. Two days earlier, on March 11, a second federal warrant had been issued for his arrest for the murder of the two marshals in Medina. Though Russell was a right-wing patriot who lived less than thirty miles from Jim Ellison's CSA encampment, he was unknown to the authorities, and his property was an ideal place to hide the sixty-three-year-old tax protester. For the next two months, Kahl read the Bible, watched television, and befriended Russell's daughter, Karen, twenty-eight.[1]

While Kahl was in hiding, government lawyers prepared their case against his wife and son, and the other Possemen who had been on the road with him that day in Medina. The trial began under heavy security on May 12, 1983, in Fargo, North Dakota, and lasted two and a half weeks.[2] Gordon Kahl followed the proceedings from afar and made a special effort to make his presence known. On the last day of the trial, FBI agents received an anonymous phone call saying that Yorie Kahl's pistol could be found in a Fargo Dumpster.[3] Last seen in Gordon's possession, its whereabouts was the subject of considerable speculation. How the weapon found its way from Arkansas to North Dakota isn't certain, but it might well have been the work of Richard Wayne Snell, the Posse follower who claimed to have been a "courier" for Gordon Kahl. Now the jury learned that the bullet fragment found in the pistol grip didn't match any of the rounds fired by the defendants. This supported the idea that Yorie might have been shot at first. The appearance of the gun caught the prosecutor, Lynn Crooks, off guard, but he asserted that the evidence was irrelevant; after all, the lawmen were dead, the defendants were alive, and nobody could deny the Possemen had let loose a barrage of gunfire. The jury believed him. Both Yorie and Scott Faul were convicted of second-degree murder for the killings of Marshals Muir and Cheshire and received two concurrent life sentences. They also were convicted on half a dozen other charges. Though David Broer—who never fired a weapon—was acquitted of most of the charges against him, he was sentenced to two consecutive five-year terms for conspiracy and for harboring a felony suspect. Joan Kahl fared much better. The original murder charges against her, David Broer, and Vernon Wegner had been dismissed, and the jury acquitted her of the two remaining charges: conspiracy to impede the arrest of her husband, and harboring a fugitive.[4]

Two days after the verdicts were read in North Dakota, Gordon Kahl left the Russell farm with another Patriot couple, Leonard and Norma Ginter. After Kahl loaded his green duffel bag and Ruger Mini-14 into the backseat of the Ginters' car, the three drove about two hours over winding Ozark mountain roads to the tiny town of Smithville, population 113, some 125 miles north of Little Rock.[5] Leonard Ginter, sixty-one, was an unemployed carpenter from Wisconsin who once had filed articles of incorporation for his local Posse Comitatus in Grant County. In 1974 he ran for a state assembly seat on the right-wing American Party ticket, but received only seventy-five votes. That same year, Ginter, a Christian Identity believer, sued the governor for "conspiracy to deprive him of his Christian common-law rights, religious rights, and constitutional rights." Unsuccessful at sparking a right-wing revolution in Wisconsin, Ginter and his wife left the state in 1979 and moved to Arkansas, where they became active in the Association for Constitutional Enforcement, a Posse-type group.[6] Despite their contempt for the government, the couple received food stamps.

The Ginter home was in a remote area, some four miles north of Smithville. Built into a hillside that overlooked a creek near the bottom of a steep ravine, the house was made of concrete blocks. With entrances along just one side, it resembled a bunker. A vegetable patch and a chicken pen were nearby.

After Kahl left Mountain Home with the Ginters, Arthur Russell's daughter Karen called the FBI. The youngest of ten children, a high-school dropout and the mother of two, she was fearful that Kahl might return after committing further crimes.[7] She also wanted the $25,000 reward. Karen wasn't positive where Kahl had gone, but what she knew was enough to lead the FBI to the Ginter home. On June 3, 1983, FBI special agent James Blasingame gathered U.S. Marshals, local lawmen, and others at the Lawrence County Courthouse to plan the government's next move.[8] Since the Ginters had no phone, Blasingame and the Lawrence County sheriff, Gene Matthews, planned to drive up to the house and ask the Ginters to step outside. After removing them from the scene they would question the couple to confirm Kahl's whereabouts and then move in. Nearby roadblocks and a team of U.S. Marshals in the woods would prevent Kahl from escaping. At least that was the plan.

Twenty-eight law enforcement agents were involved: fifteen federal marshals, six FBI agents, three state police officers, and four county lawmen. After meeting all day, Blasingame gave the order to move out. Arriving outside Smithville shortly before six P.M., Blasingame had already started down the road toward the Ginter residence when he received word from an FBI spotter plane that a car had left the house and was headed in his direction. In it was Leonard Ginter with a cocked and loaded pistol in his lap and a rifle on the backseat. Blasingame and a small convoy of lawmen backed Ginter down the gravel road and ordered him out of the car. "Is Gordon Kahl in the house?" Blasingame and Sheriff Matthews asked, weapons drawn.

"No," Ginter lied.

"Who is?"

"Just my wife," he replied.

"Well, we need to talk to her," said Blasingame, who instructed Ginter to call her out of the house. It was the first of two fatal mistakes that lawmen would make. Five men followed Ginter up the concrete drive. When he got close to the house he yelled to his wife:

"Norma, come out. The FBI wants to talk to you," he said, emphasizing the letters "F–B–I" as loudly as possible. Ginter's wife came to the kitchen door and saw Sheriff Matthews by the garage. "Come out quietly," he ordered. With both Ginters out of the way, the sheriff abruptly decided to take matters into his own hands and entered the house through a utility room off the garage. The popular thirty-six-year-old sheriff was serving his first term in office, and he had a habit of placing himself in harm's way. Today it would lead to his death.

Matthews's move wasn't part of the plan, but a deputy U.S. Marshal, James Hall, and an Arkansas State Police investigator, Ed Fitzpatrick, followed the sheriff to back him up. By the time Hall and Fitzpatrick arrived in the doorway, Matthews was approaching the entrance to the Ginter kitchen. He continued into the room, walking briskly. Kahl had just finished dinner at the kitchen table. Alerted by Leonard Ginter's announcement, he crouched next to the refrigerator with his loaded Ruger Mini-14. Kahl probably saw Matthews first, but both men likely opened fire at nearly the same moment. A single high-velocity bullet tore through the sheriff's left arm, penetrating a seam in his bulletproof vest before entering his armpit and fatally ripping open his left pulmonary artery. Another round went through Matthews's right chest. But Matthews's shot struck Kahl in the head, killing him instantly. Confusion and a hail of gunfire quickly followed. Aware that Sheriff Matthews was severely wounded and thinking Kahl was still unhurt, the state police investigator, Ed Fitzpatrick, fired his shotgun around the refrigerator in Kahl's direction. He then ran outside and pumped four more blasts through the kitchen window. Number-4 buckshot sprayed the dining area, and raked the back of Matthews's bulletproof vest. Kahl's body was sprawled at the base of the kitchen counter and could not be seen. Matthews staggered back toward the utility room and collapsed into the arms of the federal marshal, who tried to drag him to safety, but got only as far as the garage.

Matthews was a large man, and bleeding heavily. He quickly collapsed. Several minutes later the stricken sheriff managed to drag himself to his feet and was carried to a nearby police cruiser. "I got him," he managed to say, before losing consciousness. But the lawmen had no idea whether Kahl was alive or dead, and they were not about to assume anything. The FBI let loose a barrage of gunfire. Tear gas filled the house and the acrid smoke wafted up the narrow gully. "Go get some gas so we can pour it down the top of the house and smoke him out," ordered James Handley, an FBI agent.

The Ginter home was built into a hillside and the roof was easily approached from the rear. After trying to knock off one of the roof vents by shooting at it, a state trooper dislodged it with a pickax while a local lawman dropped tear gas and a smoke grenade down the shaft. The canisters landed in one of the home's three bedrooms, spewing noxious smoke. Federal agents then instructed the lawman to pour diesel fuel down the opening, but when tear gas turned him back he simply set the can on top of the vent. A state trooper then shot it twice. After the contents poured out, a flaming paper bag was shoved down the hole. The combination of tear gas, smoke grenades, high-velocity ammunition, and diesel fuel erupted into an inferno. The fire burned intensely for hours despite driving rain from a summer storm overhead. Lawmen stopped firing their weapons but echoes of gunfire reverberated in the ravine as thousands of rounds of ammunition in the Ginter home exploded in the flames, and the noise merged with the sound of thunder.

When investigators finally entered the house they had to use oxygen masks and protective gear. They found nine firearms: six rifles, two shotguns (including one from the North Dakota shootout), and a revolver, along with plenty of spent ammunition. They also found what was left of Kahl's body on the kitchen floor. The bullet from Matthews's .41-caliber Magnum had struck Kahl above the right ear and blown off the top of his skull. It was fitting retribution for the manner in which Kahl had executed Marshal Robert Cheshire Jr. The spent round was in plain view, resting on a fragment of charred brain tissue. Burned beyond recognition, Kahl's remains had to be removed with a shovel and pitchfork.[9]

Coincidentally, Bill Gale and his wife Roxanne were vacationing in Harrison, Arkansas, at the time of the shooting. Reached by a *New York Times* reporter seeking comment on Kahl's death, Gale said that Kahl was killed for helping farmers and promoting the Posse Comitatus.[10]

Kahl's fiery death inspired others to act, including Kahl's self-described Posse "courier," Richard Wayne Snell, who told tales about how Sheriff Matthews had been killed by federal agents after Matthews interrupted them in the process of torturing Kahl. Snell was the son of a preacher and an ordained minister in the

Church of the Nazarene, but eventually he became disillusioned with Christianity and adopted atheism instead. Then, after twenty-eight years as a nonbeliever, he embraced Christian Identity. In 1982, Snell and his wife lived on an eighty-acre farm outside Muse, Oklahoma, where he made a living selling and trading army-surplus gear and spare parts that he salvaged from recycled junk and appliances. When this didn't bring in enough money, he supplemented his income by stealing.[11] He often delivered the proceeds from his robberies to the Covenant, the Sword, and the Arm of the Lord.

On November 2, 1983, five months after Kahl's death, Snell decided he would incite civil unrest by blowing up a natural-gas pipeline. The previous day had been designated as the start of a supposed nationwide "farm revolt" by protesting farmers affiliated with Grass Roots AAM. Armed with two dozen sticks of dynamite, Snell and two CSA accomplices drove to the banks of the Red River in southwest Arkansas. Under cover of darkness they wrapped the dynamite around the pipeline with medical tape, joined the charges with detonation cord, lit the igniter, and ran. Luckily the blast didn't rupture the pipe. In the event Snell came across suitable targets on other trips, he kept dynamite, fuse, igniters, detonation cord, and blasting caps hidden in the fender walls of his car.[12] Ten days after the failed pipeline bombing, Snell, fifty-three, and the same two men prepared to rob a Texarkana pawnshop owned by William Stumpp, an Episco-palian whom Snell wrongly assumed was Jewish.

Snell eased his 1980 blue Lynx station wagon across the alley and into the parking lot behind Stumpp's pawnshop. After checking to ensure his .22-caliber Ruger pistol was loaded and the silencer was screwed down tight, he closed his briefcase and got out of the car, leaving his CSA accomplices behind. Once inside, Snell distracted the pawnbroker by showing him a pocket watch with unusual markings. While Stumpp examined the watch and weighed it on a scale, Snell opened the briefcase and drew his gun. The homemade silencer had been man-ufactured at the CSA. Snell held the pistol to the pawnbroker's head and ordered him to open the safe. Then, when Stumpp turned his back and leaned forward into the safe's open door, Snell fired into the back of his head. Snell and an accomplice scooped up a wad of dollar bills from the register, grabbed a small box of handguns and several thousand dollars' worth of jewelry, and fled, leaving Snell's pocket watch on the scale. Stealing from the supposed Jew was an hon-orable crime, according to Snell, who gave the proceeds to James Ellison and the CSA.[13]

When Snell wasn't robbing pawnshops or attempting to foment civil disor-der, he hit the road in search of recycled junk that he could sell or trade. During one such trip, on June 30, 1984, he killed an Arkansas state trooper, Louis P. Bryant. Snell was headed home to Oklahoma, driving a cream-colored Ford van and hauling an eight-foot box trailer loaded with old washing-machine motors. Around four-fifteen P.M., about seven miles east of DeQueen, Arkansas, Trooper Bryant flashed his lights and signaled Snell to pull over. Snell had several outstanding warrants against him stemming from his refusal to make vehicle payments to a Texas bank, but Trooper Bryant hadn't had time to run a drivers'-license check.[14] As Bryant approached the back of the van, Snell exited his door and calmly shot the trooper in the chest and forearm with a .45 automatic pistol. Snell watched him crumple to the ground, got back in the van, and drove off, leaving Bryant, a thirty-seven-year-old father of two, in a pool of blood.[15]

"From my travels and experiences of over half a century, I have found that almost everyone is capable of killing, under certain circumstances," Snell later wrote.[16] In this case, the circumstances were simple enough: Louis Bryant was the first African-American state trooper hired in southwest Arkansas and had become well known in the area during his nine years on the force. Snell traveled the area frequently and was enraged by the thought of a black highway patrolman stopping whites. According to Mary Snell, her husband had once "reprimanded [Bryant] to think more highly of his own race than to continue such audacious behavior [as harassing] white women that he stopped during his day's work."[17] Snell also had other reasons for killing Bryant. All federal agents were tools of the Zionist Occupied Government of the United States. And state police, like Bryant, were acting outside their jurisdiction unless they were assisting local agencies. As a black man dressed in a uniform attempting to enforce the law, Bryant was seen as a fundamental threat to Snell's white-supremacist worldview.

Snell fled the scene of the Bryant shooting but was intercepted less than an hour later as he entered Broken Bow, Oklahoma. Two police cars forced Snell's van up a side street where the officers jumped out, guns drawn, and took cover behind the doors of their patrol cars. Snell had a thirty-round banana clip in his Ruger Mini-14, but the weapon was even more formidable than Gordon Kahl's, as it had been illegally converted to fully automatic. Snell came out of the van firing before darting behind his box trailer for cover. Luckily for the lawmen, Snell took the first round. After getting hit in the right shoulder, he pulled the .45 from his belt with his left hand and ran straight toward the officers, shooting over and through the police cruiser before he was hit in the ankle, knee, and stomach. The bullets missed his vital organs but shattered his bones.

"Lay down and drop your weapons. We don't want to kill you," the officers yelled.

"Kill me," Snell screamed.

"Drop your weapons. We don't want to kill you," the officers repeated.[18]

Snell collapsed and surrendered.[19] When police searched the van they found live grenades and the gun that had been used to kill William Stumpp the year before.[20] Sentenced to life in prison for killing Trooper Bryant, Snell received the death penalty for murdering the pawnbroker, and he was eventually executed on April 19, 1995, the same day as the Oklahoma City bombing.

31

SNAKE OIL FOR SALE

Joan Kahl received her husband's remains a week after his death and began planning for his burial in a small, tree-lined cemetery outside Heaton, North Dakota. She claimed that as an air force veteran Kahl was entitled to military honors, but was turned down.[1] It was hot and windy outside the Bowdon Country Seventh-Day Adventist Church on June 10, 1983, the day the church's pastor, Peter Dyck, eulogized his friend as a martyr, a patriot, and "a peaceful man."

"The only time violence came into play was when it was brought against him," Dyck told the crowd of more than 250 friends, neighbors, and family members. Kahl was a modern Paul Revere who traveled the country crying: " 'The tyrants are coming, the tyrants are coming,' " said Dyck. "Isn't this today evidence that the tyrants did come?" he asked, gesturing toward Kahl's casket, draped in an American flag.[2] An unofficial honor guard of several veterans pointed their rifles overhead and squeezed off several rounds in ceremonial salute before their guns misfired.

Six hundred miles away in Wisconsin, on the same day as Kahl's burial, Jim Wickstrom, forty, was convicted of impersonating a public official. The charges stemmed from documents Wickstrom had signed as the self-appointed clerk and judge of a Posse-created township in Shawano County. Wickstrom's so-called Constitution Township of Tigerton Dells spanned fourteen hundred acres and was home to some two dozen supporters. The goal of the township was to "remove" Posse members from government jurisdiction, thereby freeing them from their "illegal" obligation to pay taxes or follow state regulations. The scheme was identical to the one that Kahl and his compatriots had been discussing the day of the Medina shootings. According to prosecutors, Wickstrom's township was a "legal nullity," but the Wisconsin Posse leader insisted he was a legitimate elected official. "If he has a sincere belief that he is a public officer within the laws of the State of Wisconsin, I'm the Easter Bunny," prosecutor Douglas Haag told the jury of eight women and four men, at the end of Wickstrom's two-day trial in June 1983. Convicted on two counts, he was sentenced to a year and a half in jail, the maximum under the law.[3]

Kahl's funeral sparked a flurry of news articles recounting the shootings, his subsequent disappearance and fiery demise, and the appeals made by the Posse Comitatus to farmers. But just days after Kahl's death, the *New York Times* took note of a different kind of farm protest movement. Headlined "Farmers and Unions Joining to Fight Economic Hardship," the front-page article highlighted the activities of groups like the Iowa Farm Unity Coalition, and noted the creation of a new, national coalition of rural activists: the North American Farm Alliance (NAFA). Formed in April 1983 by farm leaders from twenty-three states and Canada, the Alliance reflected the populist politics of men like Iowa's Dixon Terry. Alliance leaders called for parity and a moratorium on forced farm sales, but they also embraced Jesse Jackson's platform, proclaimed their allegiance to civil rights, called for "full employment for all working people," and pledged to work nonviolently for "a new prosperity based on peace through social and economic justice."[4] Several weeks after Kahl's death, a Nebraska farmer and the chairman of the North American Farm Alliance, Merle Hansen, sixty-three, addressed a group of AAM supporters and others in Hico, Texas. Unlike his audience, which included a smattering of Posse partisans and LaRouche supporters, Hansen's politics were decidedly left-of-center. Using a barbecue grill as a makeshift podium, Hansen linked the farm crisis to various forms of discrimination.

"Corporate America not only wants to buy raw materials for nothing, they want to hire labor for nothing. That is also the reason for discrimination against women. It is an economic thing. Women earn only fifty-nine cents on the dollar," he told the crowd. "If we work together, maybe all we'll lose is our prejudice," he said.

While Alvin Jenkins and Grass Roots AAM proclaimed their nationwide "farm revolt" starting November 1, 1983, NAFA and other liberal groups staged their own events emphasizing "farmer, labor, and community solidarity." In Waterloo, Iowa, more than two thousand farmers and unemployed members of the United Auto Workers union gathered for speeches, soup, bread, and coffee. Using meat from hogs donated by farmers, members of the United Food and Commercial Workers Union processed eleven thousand pounds of sausage to be distributed for free to the hungry and the unemployed.[5] A month later, Jesse Jackson packed a community college auditorium in Great Bend, Kansas. Jackson had declared himself a candidate for the Democratic presidential nomination and his pitch to farmers stressed the theme of urban-rural, black-white cooperation. "What is news today is not that your farm is in trouble, what is news today is that we might come together and do something about it," Jackson told the cheering, nearly all-white crowd of eight hundred and fifty on December 10. "I submit to you that when the national debate begins in January, the plight of the poor farmer, the poor urban dweller, the unemployed, the handicapped, the young, these people will be on the front burner of the American agenda this time around."[6]

Despite its embrace of Posse politics, the *AAM News* reported enthusiastically on Jackson's overtures to farmers. Then it closed its doors. On December 27, 1983, Alden and Micki Nellis sorrowfully announced that they were discontinuing publication. With only twenty-eight hundred subscribers left, the tabloid's circulation had fallen sharply during the previous two years. "If the newspaper were vitally necessary, more people would feel they had to have it. In short, a product which is not in demand should not exist," the couple explained. The couple blamed dwindling subscriptions on farmer apathy, rather than the newsletter's strident conservatism. When the *AAM News* had started six years earlier, it focused on issues that had mobilized hundreds of thousands of farmers: parity for agriculture and the prospect of legislative reform. But from the day the newsletter carried its first classified ad for Identity minister Sheldon Emry in 1980, its focus had gradually narrowed toward right-wing and sectarian concerns. By late 1983, the *AAM News* was publishing right-wing treatises on the Federal Reserve and promoting the legal nostrums of Posse patriots who claimed they could stop farm foreclosures.

But Alden and Micki Nellis denied any mistakes. "We have not compromised our beliefs in order to attract money. . . . We have been proud of the *American Ag. News* and are still proud of it," the couple wrote in their farewell column. Micki Nellis encouraged readers to transfer their subscriptions to *Life in the Heart of Texas*, a folksy magazine she promised to publish that would include book reviews, recipes, and portraits of small-town life. But Alvin Jenkins wanted more robust political fare. He recommended an altogether different publication, the *Primrose and Cattleman's Gazette*. It was a telling endorsement.[7]

The *Gazette* was the brainchild of Roderick F. "Rick" Elliott, fifty-six, a career con artist and anti-Semite based in Brighton, Colorado, who capitalized on the rhetoric of the Posse Comitatus to recruit and defraud farmers. Among his staunchest supporters were activists associated with Grass Roots AAM, including Derral Schroder. Elliott had a criminal record stretching back to 1949, when he was first arrested, at age twenty-two, for impersonating a federal officer. He was arrested at least ten more times during the next two decades and charged with passing bad checks, perjury, unlawful flight to avoid prosecution, and selling securities without a license. In 1962, Elliott served two years in the Utah State Penitentiary and was rearrested in 1965 for violating parole.[8]

Elliott's publication, the *Primrose and Cattleman's Gazette*, had appeared around 1974. At first glance, the weekly tabloid seemed like any other homespun rural paper: it was crammed with livestock sale notices, miscellaneous farm news, ads from agriculture implement dealers, and canned dispatches from politicians and local county fairs. To add pages and boost advertising revenues, the *Gazette* relied on plenty of filler: sports commentaries, free recruitment ads for the U.S. Marines, recipes, preprinted columns, and material copied from other publications of interest to farmers. It isn't certain when the first hate literature appeared in the *Gazette*, but by 1981 the practice attracted the attention of the Anti-Defamation League. The catalyst for ADL scrutiny was a six-part series that Elliott offered as "firsthand evidence" of the Jewish plan for world domination. Titled *The Hidden Tyranny: The Issue that Dwarfs All Other Issues*, the text was a supposedly "confidential interview" with Harold Rosenthal, a twenty-nine-year-old administrative assistant to U.S. senator Jacob Javits of New York. Originally written by Mrs. Opal Tanner White, an elderly associate of the anti-Semitic minister Gerald L. K. Smith, *The Hidden Tyranny* first appeared in 1978, two years after Rosenthal was killed by Arab terrorists who were attempting to hijack an Israeli jetliner in Istanbul.[9] Since Rosenthal was dead, White was free to attribute anything she wished—however scurrilous or hateful—to the onetime Javits aide.

In addition to attacking Jews, the *Gazette* demanded "100 Percent Parity!" and supported the AAM call for a farm strike. "[T]his action would take just one short week before the entire problem would be corrected. . . ." Elliott wrote in November 1982.[10] About the same time, Elliott launched a new enterprise to supplement the *Gazette*: the National Agricultural Press Association, or NAPA. For $20 in annual dues, members were promised a "framed, sealed membership certificate, a press card with accompanying coat pocket wallet calendar, a car window press sticker, and other associated products used by the press media." Presumably to curry favor with bigots and some farmers from the South, NAPA's promotional announcement included a full-page photo of the Confederate flag.[11]

Dressed in a western string tie and signature suit jacket with his name and the NAPA logo monogrammed across his left breast, Elliott hit the road selling bigotry and false hope alongside his NAPA wares: nonexistent low-interest loans and prepackaged Posse-style lawsuits. Tall and balding, with a large head, bushy eyebrows, and a belligerent demeanor, Elliott opened his meetings with patriotic-sounding prayers. And like others on the rural speaking circuit, he also liked to start with a joke. One of his favorites played on anti-Jewish stereotypes and ended with the punchline, "Iceberg, Greenberg, Goldberg, what the hell's the difference?" Speaking to farmers at one meeting in Wisconsin, Elliott had this to say about the Jews: "I don't have to get up in the morning and look at the crucifix and feel sorry—I didn't put the nails there."[12] Addressing another group of farmers, Elliott called Japanese-Americans "slant-eyed buggers," and vilified Cubans and Mexicans.[13]

Beyond his racist remarks, Elliott skillfully pandered to farmers' economic fears and presented himself as their champion. Like other accomplished con artists, his pitch contained just the right amount of down-home aphorisms and brazen pronouncements.[14] According to Leonard Zeskind, a veteran expert on the far right and the first to sound the alarm about Posse organizing in the Farm Belt, Elliott was nothing more than an old-fashioned snake-oil salesman, whose cures offered patients the illusion of fast relief, but left them in far worse condition once he was safely down the road. The National Agriculture Press Association was a "combination medicine show and fascist organizing project," Zeskind explained.[15]

Elliott solicited written contributions from *Gazette* subscribers but he preferred to publish articles written by men like William Pierce, the chairman of the neo-Nazi National Alliance.[16] In October 1982, Elliott serialized *Who Rules America?*—an infamous anti-Semitic "exposé" that had first appeared in Pierce's glossy publication, *National Vanguard*.[17] Other selections from the *Gazette*'s menu of anti-Semitic propaganda included a six-part "Open Letter to the Goyim (Gentiles)," which promised "a 'crash course' on Jewish-Communism . . . the 'International Jew' and his Satanic plans to rule the world"; praised the *Protocols of the Elders of Zion*; and lauded Nazi Germany for "rising up against Jewish control." The piece was authored by NAPA "International Director," Colonel Francis P. "Bud" Farrell, a retired air force officer from Pennsylvania whose name appeared at the top of the *Gazette* masthead.[18] According to Farrell, "Jews use their awesome financial power to: enrich themselves, create depressions, create wars, take over governments and government jobs, impose oppressive taxation, establish government snooping and controls, destroy economies, and create chaos among the people."[19]

By 1983 these and other statements had attracted the attention of Alan Berg, a well-known talk-show host with KOA radio in Denver, whose no-holds-barred style with guests was popular with many listeners.[20] Berg also was Jewish and he relished attacking anti-Semites on the air, so he invited Bud Farrell and Rick Elliott to be interviewed. On June 15, 1983, he and Elliott clashed.

"You are accusing the Jews of a world conspiracy to take away your Christianity. That is not exactly like a love affair with the Jews, is it?" asked Berg, baiting him.

"What's wrong with being a Christian?" Elliott shrewdly replied. The banter continued until the two began to argue about American aid to Israel and the extent of the Holocaust. Then Berg lost his temper: "Everything you have said is a lie. . . . You have it made up . . . like all fanatics—like John Birchers, like Klansmen, like all those folks."

"You're crazy," said Elliott.

"I'm crazy, sir—you're a healthy person? . . . It's kind of sickening. It really is," Berg replied.[21]

A year later, on June 18, 1984, Berg's body was riddled with automatic gunfire in the carport of his Denver home. He had been assassinated by Bob Matthews and members of the Order.[22] Five months later Matthews was dead and two dozen of his followers were subsequently arrested and convicted on racketeering charges for bank robbery, counterfeiting, and murder, including the killing of Berg. During the group's trial in Seattle, government prosecutors argued that Berg's on-air quarrels with Rick Elliott had precipitated his murder. It was a plausible theory because one of Berg's killers and Elliott were linked.

David Lane was a Denver-area Klansman, NAPA member, and Aryan Nations supporter who had worked as a night watchman at Elliott's NAPA office in Brighton (on the outskirts of Denver) at the time of the KOA broadcasts. And it was Lane who later joined The Order and drove the getaway car after Berg was shot.[23] One month before Elliott was interviewed by Berg on KOA, Lane paid for a full-page ad in the *Gazette* promoting the Aryan Nations.[24] Titled "The Death of the White Race," the ad proclaimed: "YOUR FIRST LOYALTY MUST BE TO YOUR RACE WHICH IS YOUR NATION."[25] The same issue of the *Gazette* carried the first installment of Gordon Kahl's sixteen-page letter giving his one-sided account of the North Dakota shootings.[26] And later that month, Elliott ran an excerpt from *The International Jew—The World's Foremost Problem*, Henry Ford's notorious rewrite of the *Protocols*.[27]

By the fall of 1983, the farm crisis was worsening. With harvest in full swing—and annual operating loans coming due—thousands of farmers packed school auditoriums, sale barns, and church meeting halls to hear what Elliott had to say. "FARMERS: Are Your Lenders Deciding Your Destiny?" advertised one hand-lettered sign, inviting anyone with "sleepless nights, no living funds, complicated legal problems [and] no operating capital" to the middle-school auditorium in Cameron, Missouri. A week later Elliott joined Tommy Kersey, Gene Schroder, and Lyndon LaRouche to address more than one hundred supporters at Kersey's headquarters in Unadilla, Georgia.[28]

For a $500 application fee, Elliott promised cash-strapped farmers low-interest loans while dispensing bogus advice culled from the Posse Comitatus, including instructions for filing "common-law liens" against creditors. Elliott also told farmers that every loan they had signed since 1974 was "null and void" because the contracts didn't comply with the federal Truth in Lending Act.[29] Like his other legal advice, this was wrong, too, as agricultural loans were explicitly exempted from the Act. But because Elliott told farmers to shun lawyers, those who listened to him rarely learned that simple truth until it was too late.[30] Relying on Elliott's boilerplate lawsuits, many farmers fell victim to foreclosure after they missed deadlines for filing important legal papers. Others were assessed fines for clogging the legal system with frivolous lawsuits. One Nebraska federal judge dismissed more than forty NAPA-style lawsuits over the course of two years.[31]

By June 1984, Elliott was claiming twenty thousand members in about forty states and boasting that the circulation of the *Gazette* had risen to sixty-eight thousand—a fourfold increase over the seventeen thousand subscribers he had claimed just nine months earlier. These figures were undoubtedly inflated, but hard times and his knack for scams had dramatically boosted Elliott's audience and the number of his supporters. And it certainly didn't hurt that he had won the endorsement of Alvin Jenkins, who had become a NAPA member.[32] In addition to taking in thousands of contributions, and an untold number of $500 "loan application fees," Elliott borrowed money from a small circle of NAPA "investors" whom he promised to repay but never did. By far his most generous backer was the AAM activist Darrell Schroder, who gave Elliott almost $100,000 over six months. Schroder first gave Elliott $20,000 to make overdue mortgage payments on the NAPA office building in Brighton. Then Elliott convinced him to part with $57,000 more so he could redeem his home from foreclosure. More cash payments followed, including $10,000 that Schroder asked his son Gene— also a NAPA member—to contribute so Elliott could supposedly buy an airplane.[33] Despite his affinity for Schroder's money, Elliott held AAM in contempt. "What the hell do they do but they want to take tractors and drive them across the country? That's the worse thing that could have ever happened to the American Agriculture family [sic]," he told Alabama investigators.[34]

In addition to bilking farmers, Elliott took tens of thousands of dollars from other supporters, including Bud Farrell, NAPA's Jew-hating "International Director." All in all, Elliott took in more than $230,000 in "loans" from at least nine people across four states that he never repaid.[35] Spurred by news about Elliott's promise of low-interest loans, Colorado authorities finally opened an investigation and began interviewing disgruntled NAPA associates. The information they compiled led to a nineteen-count indictment on September 17, 1984, charging Elliott and his wife, Karla, with theft and conspiracy.[36] Negative media coverage dogged Elliott before and after his indictment, but he continued to draw large crowds and new supporters, some of whom opened satellite offices across the Midwest. One July 1984 letter to area farmers from the NAPA "regional office" in Rushford, Minnesota, began:

Dear American farmer: You had assistance with legal preparation pertaining to your mortgages and notes—you may have answers and questions. You may have neighbors, friends, or relatives, who might need assistance—let them know about NAPA . . . please call for an appointment. . . . Schedule of Rick Elliott speaking to follow.[37]

Among those who responded to a similar invitation—and whose involvement with Elliott and the radical right would lead to his tragic death—was Nebraska farmer Arthur Kirk. After joining NAPA in 1984, Arthur Kirk, forty-nine, became convinced that his financial problems were caused by an international Jewish conspiracy.[38] Early in the afternoon of October 23, 1984, three sheriff's deputies came to Kirk's Cairo, Nebraska, farm with papers demanding repayment on an overdue loan. Unless Kirk could come up with $100,000, he would be forced to liquidate his crops, livestock, and machinery. According to law enforcement officials, Kirk waved a .41-caliber revolver and ordered the deputies off his farm, gesturing toward a Posse sign he had posted that he believed barred government officials from his property. Kirk then pointed the long-barreled gun at the head of one of the deputies from just five feet away. The lawman responded by drawing his own weapon and telling Kirk he was under arrest. But when Kirk turned and ran, the deputies withdrew rather than start a shootout. Kirk returned to his chores and grimly contemplated the prospect of financial ruin while the sheriff obtained a warrant for his arrest.

Lawmen surrounded the farm that evening, preventing Kirk's wife, Deloris, from returning home. As night fell, a state SWAT team moved into position. Negotiators contacted Kirk by phone around eight-thirty P.M., but most of what they heard was anti-Semitic ranting. One psychiatrist, who reviewed tape-recordings of the negotiation session, described Kirk as undergoing "a serious mental breakdown." That may have been the case, but the conversations also reveal a man who had read too much of the *Primrose and Cattleman's Gazette*.

"Damn fucking Jews. Destroyed everything I ever worked for," Kirk raged over the phone. "Who's got the power in the world? Who runs this world? The fucking Jews. By God, I ain't putting up with their shit now! . . . There's a big move on to try and subvert the Constitution, change the whole thing. Communism! That isn't communism, it's Judaism." After an hour of shouting, Kirk announced that agents of the Israeli secret police—the Mossad—were hiding outside his house.[39]

"I'm going out and clean the goddamn bushes out!" he shouted before bursting out the back door. His face blackened, Kirk was wearing a crash helmet. When a SWAT team member shouted for him to "Freeze!" Kirk turned and opened fire with his illegally converted, fully automatic AR-15 rifle. He managed to squeeze off only two shots. It had been outfitted with a massive, seventy-five-round drum magazine and jammed on the third round. The SWAT team returned fire in the darkness, striking Kirk in the shoulder and thigh. By the time they recovered his body ten minutes later he had bled to death.[40]

Kirk's death was further evidence of the potential for violence in the Farm Belt. Like Gordon Kahl, Kirk soon became a powerful symbol for the movement and his widow, Deloris, crisscrossed the Midwest, sharing her version of the tragedy with farmers and tax protesters.[41] Among those who helped her spread the right-wing message and reinforce the martyrdom of her husband was the evangelist Larry Jones, founder of the $30 million-a-year television ministry Feed the Children.

"SWAT TEAM KILLS FARMER!!!" screamed one fund-raising letter issued by Jones that solicited money to "help other Arthur Kirks." In addition to claiming that Kirk was "anything but a violent man," Jones repeated right-wing rumors that the SWAT team had mutilated the Kirk family cat. "There are farmers all across our Nation who are today being threatened by extinction. . . . A good man is dead!" wrote Jones. Noticeably absent from the letter was any reference to the two dozen weapons and reams of Posse literature found in Kirk's home, or his anti-Semitic rantings. Jones paid to broadcast two video segments over nearly one hundred television stations that showed his sanitized version of the incident.[42]

Deloris also turned to Rick Elliott for support, appearing alongside the Colorado flimflam man in Omaha that winter to receive a NAPA award. Joining the two of them was a Nebraska state senator, Ernie Chambers, the sole black member of the legislature. Chambers was a frequent critic of the police and he saw the Kirk incident as an opportunity to put Nebraska law enforcement and the state's governor, Bob Kerrey, on the defensive. Chambers quickly demanded a grand jury investigation. To deflect criticism about Kirk's death, Governor Kerrey appointed a respected retired judge, Samuel Van Pelt, to look into the matter. Trim and bespectacled, the thoughtful jurist interrupted his midlife sabbatical to produce a lengthy and balanced assessment of the death of Arthur Kirk. Van Pelt's report weighed in at more than six hundred pages. Initially bewildered by Kirk's references to the Mossad, Van Pelt concluded that anti-Semitic appeals were gaining substantial ground among some farmers. "It's the exact same approach used in Germany fifty years ago when Hitler blamed the Jews," said the judge. "[Rural America] might now be fertile to sprout the same kinds of hate."[43] But not all Nebraska lawmen shared Van Pelt's concerns. Some chose to look the other way when it came to the Posse Comitatus, and they did so with deadly consequences.

32

JIM WICKSTROM'S MAIN MAN

On August 17, 1985, Nebraska authorities unearthed two badly decomposed bodies from unmarked, muddy graves on an eighty-acre farm occupied by Christian Identity believers outside Rulo, Nebraska, a tiny town on the banks of the Missouri River. The victims, five-year-old Luke Stice and twenty-six-year-old James Thimm, had been brutally tortured.[1] The murders were the work of Michael Wayne Ryan, thirty-seven, a former Kansas truck driver and Identity believer. Ryan also was an avid disciple of James Wickstrom, and he convinced his followers that he spoke directly to God. Eager to believe Ryan's warnings of imminent Armageddon, his victims joined him in Rulo, where he promised them paramilitary salvation.

The son of a telephone repairman, Ryan dropped out of high school less than two credits shy of graduation and tried his hand at various jobs before he took up trucking.[2] Ryan was living with his wife, Ruth, and their three children in a dilapidated farmhouse outside Whiting when he first met Wickstrom in May 1982. It was just a few months after the paramilitary training session in Weskan and Ryan was one of many followers that Wickstrom was cultivating across the state of Kansas.[3] "Arm yourself and prepare for war," Wickstrom told him. "The main battle will occur in Kansas, 'the Battle of the Wheat Fields.' "[4]

Inspired by Identity theology and Wickstrom's images of the endtimes, Ryan took up stealing to supplement his welfare check and build an arsenal. Kansas lawmen first took note of Ryan when he was named as a suspect in the theft of several firearms from a small department store in his hometown of Anthony.[5] Then, in March 1983, Ryan and his brother-in-law—who also was a Posse member—tried to obtain weapons from the Kansas National Guard.[6] The incident prompted the Kansas Bureau of Investigation (KBI) to gather more information about Ryan, which they shared with federal agents. After talking with the Bureau of Alcohol, Tobacco, and Firearms, Kansas investigators felt confident that federal authorities would initiate an undercover investigation. Unfortunately, they were wrong.[7]

One of the most substantial leads about Ryan's criminal activity came a year before the murders of Stice and Thimm. In May 1984, the KBI obtained a startling confession from a twenty-six-year-old Posse militant, Donald E. Zabawa.[8] A former prison guard from Minnesota, Zabawa had been involved with the Covenant, the Sword, and the Arm of the Lord in Arkansas where he had taken part in mock attacks on law enforcement officers and expressed a desire to "kill cops for the cause."[9] After moving to Kansas in 1983, Zabawa visited Keith Shive, founder of the Farmers Liberation Army, who showed him his weapons and spoke of blowing up grain elevators and "wanting to kill judges, lawyers, and bankers." Like most of what Shive said, it was idle talk.[10] This was not the case with Mike Ryan.

"Mike Ryan is Jim Wickstrom's main man in Kansas," explained Zabawa in an eighteen-page handwritten statement he gave to authorities after his arrest for shooting up a police car to protest the arrest of two fellow Posse members. In addition to recounting his first meeting with Ryan in early 1983, Zabawa's statement detailed the alleged activities of about twenty men whom he accused of stockpiling illegal weapons and explosives, manufacturing pipe bombs, threatening judges, planning several robberies, and even murdering a sheriff. "Ryan's group has vowed not to be taken alive. They don't believe in a lot of paperwork. They just want to kill Jews, people against the movement," he said.[11] Zabawa gave his statement as part of an anticipated plea bargain, but when the deal fell through, he recanted. Still, most of what he said about Mike Ryan turned out to be true.[12]

After a year of viewing Wickstrom videos and attending survival seminars, Ryan had formed his own group of Identity followers and was readying them for Armageddon. He also prepared his family. Among other things, Ryan gave his teenage son Dennis an AR-15 semiautomatic rifle, telling him that the weapon would be needed in the upcoming war against the Jews and the forces of Satan. Previously, the boy had enjoyed baseball and saxophone; now he was focused, like his father, on the coming Apocalypse.[13] Beliefs such as these isolated the Ryans in the small town of Whiting, so they left Kansas for the farm at Rulo in June 1984. Ryan also wanted a more secure base of operations for his stealing and other crimes.[14]

The farm was operated by Rick Stice, one of Ryan's followers, and consisted of eighty acres of wooded, hilly terrain bordering the Missouri River. The property contained two mobile homes, an aluminum-shingled house, and a hog shed.[15] From June 1984 until it was raided the following year, the farm housed about twenty-one people—slightly more than half of them were children.[16] Though many of Ryan's followers had been farmers, they now shunned pork because they considered themselves true Israelites. They also stockpiled vitamins and truckloads of ammunition. To compel their loyalty, Ryan convinced them that he knew the will of God. Like his mentor Jim Wickstrom, Ryan "proved" this with the "arm test." It worked like this: While a follower extended his or her right arm, Ryan would pose a question to Yahweh while pushing down on their wrist. If their arm held steady or went up, God was answering yes. If it dropped, the answer was no. It was a simple parlor trick, but to those who believed, it was totally convincing.

Ryan also manipulated his followers with menacing belligerence and shrewd insight into their weaknesses and insecurities; alternately awed and terrified of Ryan, and obsessed with doing "God's will," they readily followed his commands. After the murders were uncovered, some of Ryan's followers rationalized their obedience by saying they had been the victims of "mind control." There was some truth to this, but if Ryan's group was a cult, it was a highly political one, and the motives and decisions of its members were based heavily on anti-Semitic conspiracy theories and religious beliefs, not just the fear and admiration they felt for Mike Ryan.[17]

Many of Ryan's followers had been lured to the Posse by easy explanations for the farm crisis. But not everyone who signed up was going broke. Some, like Timothy Haverkamp, twenty-two, came from economically stable, well-educated families.[18] And Haverkamp's cousin, Cheryl Gibson, was attracted to the radical right not by financial problems, but by family members and Christian Identity theology. Cheryl, twenty-eight, came from a family of devout Catholics. But early in 1984 she embraced Christian Identity at the urging of her mother and younger brother, James Haverkamp. Her father and sixteen-year-old sister also fell under Ryan's spell. Instead of attending church, Cheryl began listening to audiotapes of Jim Wickstrom. True to her new Identity faith, she abandoned pork and attended Bible study sessions on the new Saturday Sabbath. Led by Mike Ryan, these discussions were heavily laced with apocalyptic images from the Book of Revelation and predictions of a coming communist invasion. Cheryl and her husband had been married eleven years, but on May 12, 1984, she took their five children—ages twenty months to nine years—and went to stay with Mike Ryan in Whiting. Two weeks later she filed for divorce and vanished.[19]

James Thimm—one of the murder victims—was an unlikely candidate to join a paramilitary group. He had been an above-average high-school student in Beatrice, Nebraska, and his boss at the local lumberyard found him outgoing and well-liked. But after five years on the job the young man became obsessed with the Posse and he was fired from work.[20] He ended up at Rulo, as did his friend David Andreas—who would later participate in his brutal murder. Andreas and Thimm had met in 1977 and were members of the same Mennonite congregation. When Andreas ran into financial trouble managing his family's 170-acre farm he went to an American Agriculture Movement meeting in Lincoln, Nebraska. It was January 1982, and it was there that he first heard Jim Wickstrom speak. Later that year he met Mike Ryan.[21] Like James Thimm, Andreas, thirty, also earned decent money from a job in town. But Ryan told him that he would be condemned to eternal damnation unless he came to Rulo, so in August 1984, Andreas hurriedly packed his bags and vanished, leaving only an ominous note. "Don't look for me," he wrote.[22] Andreas's parents were bewildered, but he had once been a member of the popular British Israelite sect, the Worldwide Church of God, whose followers kept kosher, observed the Saturday Sabbath, and celebrated Jewish holy days. Andreas had left the Church in 1977, but there may well have been something in Wickstrom's "Old Testament" Identity message that resonated with Andreas's previous religious beliefs.

Other Ryan recruits, like Rick Stice, joined the group seeking solace from emotional and financial ruin. In 1982, Stice and his wife, Sondra, were struggling to make ends meet. Victims of drought and flood, the young farm couple had canceled their health insurance just one month before Sondra was diagnosed with cancer. Overwhelmed by his wife's illness as well as the burdens of farming, Stice began attending Posse seminars led by Jim Wickstrom, where health topics and alternative "healing" were often discussed. Stice soon joined the group, which helped him take his ailing wife to see a Posse "doctor" in Wisconsin. But the "cure" had no positive effect and she died in April 1983.[23] Although Rick Stice had dutifully helped transform the Rulo acreage into a Christian Identity encampment, he fell into disfavor with Mike Ryan after he got Cheryl Gibson's sixteen-year-old sister Lisa pregnant. Ryan had "married" the couple, but he was jealous of Stice nonetheless. Furious at Stice, Ryan "annulled" the "marriage," took Lisa as his own, and demoted Stice to the status of a "slave" within the group.[24] By January 1985, James Thimm also had incurred Ryan's wrath and both men were ordered to move into the south trailer on the compound.[25] Ryan was growing increasingly abusive, but his followers maintained their obedience, living in fear and denial, believing his predictions about Armageddon. To further control and intimidate Rick Stice, Ryan targeted Stice's youngest son for horrific abuse. Towheaded and blond, the once-spirited five-year-old Luke was called a "mongrel" and "Satan's child." Citing the "beast" in the Book of Revelation, Mike Ryan scrawled the numbers 666 in red marker across the child's forehead. But instead of protecting his son, Stice participated in the boy's abuse, which included beatings, whippings, plunging his head under cold water, forcing him to exercise to the point of exhaustion, and rolling him in the snow.[26] Late one night in mid-March, after Dennis Ryan threatened to shoot him, Rick Stice fled the farm. But instead of reporting the abuse and rescuing his three children, Stice returned to the farm after just a week.[27]

Forced to sleep outside on the porch, and chained at night so he could not escape again, Stice was ordered to sexually abuse his own son. He complied. Ryan also ordered James Thimm and Rick Stice to sodomize one another.[28] Then, one day in late March, Ryan struck Luke Stice in a rage and broke his neck, killing him. It was not until a week or so later, after Mike Ryan forced him to dig his son's grave, that Rick Stice mustered the courage to escape again.[29] Although his two other children remained on the farm, Stice still didn't go to the authorities. In fact, he didn't reveal anything about his son's death until months later, when he became a paid FBI informant. The former hog farmer was pathetic but hardly pitiable when he eventually took the witness stand to testify against Ryan and other Rulo defendants. Never indicted for any of the abuse he had perpetrated against his son, Stice pleaded guilty to only one charge of interstate cattle theft. Asked whether he did anything to stop his son's torment, Stice replied, "I thought that was what was to be done. . . . I didn't do nothing." And despite all that had transpired, Stice testified that he still believed Wickstrom's teachings.[30]

Rick Stice managed to flee the horrors of Rulo, but the agony continued for James Thimm. Shortly before Stice managed his second escape, Thimm was shot in the face by Ryan's teenage son Dennis. The bullet entered Thimm's left cheek and exited near his right eye, but he miraculously survived the wound only to die several weeks later after enduring gruesome torture. Accused of doubting the existence of Yahweh, he was chained to a farrowing crate in the hog shed and ordered to have sex with a goat. The next day Ryan, Dennis, and the other men— Timothy Haverkamp, James Haverkamp, and David Andreas—raped him repeatedly with a shovel handle coated with axle grease, tearing his bowel. "I ought to shove this thing up to your heart," Ryan growled.[31] The men also whipped Thimm hundreds of times. The brutality continued the following day until Ryan ordered the men to shoot Thimm's fingertips with a .22-caliber pistol. He then kicked Thimm in the arm, breaking it.[32] On the fourth day, both of Thimm's legs were broken and the skin was flayed from his leg.[33] His torment finally ended when Mike Ryan kicked him in the head and stomped on his chest, crushing it. "Things will go better now," he announced.

Ryan supervised Thimm's burial in an unmarked grave, and instructed Timothy Haverkamp to shoot the corpse in the head. "That way, if the body is accidentally exhumed, say one hundred or two hundred years from now, it will look like he was executed."[34] Medical experts were not so easily fooled when they examined the body some four months later, but Thimm's injuries were so extensive (and his remains so badly decayed) that it was impossible to determine an exact cause of death.[35]

News of the horrible murders was bad enough, but the fact that there had been numerous reports of illegal activity surrounding Mike Ryan and his activities in Rulo raised questions about whether the deaths could have been prevented. At the center of the controversy was the local sheriff, Cory McNabb, whom Cheryl Gibson's husband, Lester, accused of protecting the Posse Comitatus. But McNabb was not the only one in law enforcement who allegedly failed to act. There were others who were said to have turned a blind eye when it came to Rulo, and this compounded both the horror and the tragedy.

33

A DOMESTIC DISPUTE

As early as March 1983, two years before the deaths of Stice and Thimm, Kansas authorities had tried to interest the Bureau of Alcohol, Tobacco, and Firearms in pursuing Mike Ryan, but their leads were ignored. The Zabawa statement came one year later, and that, too, was dropped. Ryan and his group might have made their move to Rulo entirely unobserved had it not been for Lester Gibson's efforts to locate his five children after Cheryl disappeared in May 1984. The saga of the missing Gibson children and Lester's tireless efforts to find them became a prominent subplot in the Rulo tragedy and highlights the numerous failures by law enforcement to take the threat of right-wing violence seriously.

During the year his family went missing, Lester Gibson distributed stacks of leaflets, spent thousands of dollars on private detectives, and constantly nagged officials for help. Locally his efforts led to the appointment of a special county prosecutor, Pam Fahey, who secured felony arrest warrants against Cheryl for interfering with her husband's visitation rights. But beyond this move by the county, Lester's efforts were met largely with denial and resistance.[1] In January 1985—around the time that both Rick Stice and James Thimm had been designated "slaves"—Fahey took her file and the felony warrants to the FBI, but she was rebuffed. "I kept telling [them] that it was more than just a domestic dispute, but you just couldn't get anyone interested in it," she complained.[2] Federal agents weren't the only ones who dropped the ball. Not long after Ryan established the Rulo compound, an investigator with the Nebraska State Patrol looked into reports of automatic-gunfire on the farm, but he came away empty-handed. The officer didn't follow up until ten months later, but by then Luke Stice and James Thimm were dead.

After Cheryl disappeared, Lester hired Dennis Whelan, a chain-smoking, hard-drinking private investigator from Omaha, who uncovered key evidence linking Ryan and Rulo to the Posse. Combing through the trash at the abandoned Ryan farmhouse in Whiting, Whelan found receipts for huge quantities of ammunition. He hired a private plane to fly over Rulo and saw "tons of stolen farm machinery and equipment."[3] He dug up intelligence reports like the Zabawa statement and distributed them to anyone who would listen, including U.S. senators and federal agents in several states. But the FBI treated the information about suspected paramilitary activity at Rulo like "a joke," said Lester Gibson.[4]

After the death of Arthur Kirk in Nebraska, Whelan and Gibson went to see Judge Sam Van Pelt. After conducting his investigation into Kirk's death, the judge was alert to the threat of the Posse and he quickly arranged for the men to meet Governor Bob Kerrey. He also contacted investigators with the Nebraska State Patrol. But according to Whelan, the Nebraska lawmen didn't want to get involved. "It was all too political, they told us; especially after that big blowup in Cairo[, Nebraska,] with Arthur Kirk, and with Senator [Ernie] Chambers trying to convene a grand jury to investigate the cops," Whelan recalled.[5] These encounters were disturbing, but Whelan and Lester Gibson were even more alarmed by reports they received about local authorities who were supposedly sympathetic to the Posse.

When Cheryl Gibson first went into hiding, Lester had no idea where she had gone. But numerous rumors eventually led him to Rulo and so he went to see the Richardson County sheriff, Gene Ramer. Kansas lawmen had no authority to follow Cheryl across state lines, so Lester asked Ramer for help. The sheriff was not entirely unsympathetic, but he still chose to see things as a run-of-the-mill domestic dispute. Plus, Ramer was ill with cancer and so he delegated most of the investigation to an uncooperative deputy, Cory McNabb, who soon took over Ramer's post. Once he became sheriff, McNabb refused to move against Mike Ryan and his followers, even after warrants were issued in Kansas for Cheryl Gibson's arrest and rumors had mounted about illegal activities at Rulo. And in the end—even according to McNabb—it was a quirk of fate, not good police work, that led lawmen to the bodies of Stice and Thimm.

In the early morning hours of June 25, 1985, McNabb supposedly received word that suspected "cattle rustlers" might be coming his way from nearby Kansas. Scouting for the suspects in his patrol car around two A.M., he pulled over two of Ryan's followers in Salem, Nebraska. James Haverkamp and David Andreas weren't rustling cattle but they were driving suspiciously, had an expired license plate, and were towing a weed sprayer with no lights. It turned out the sprayer was stolen and the men were heavily armed.[6]

A contingent of lawmen from three states descended on the Rulo farm later that day with a search warrant and uncovered five truckloads of stolen farm equipment, fourteen illegal weapons, numerous semiautomatic rifles and large-caliber handguns, and about 150,000 rounds of ammunition—enough to fill two delivery vans.[7] The probe spread to Kansas several days later, where a dozen of Ryan's followers had relocated. There they found a concrete bunker with its own power supply, 80,000 rounds of ammunition (some of it armor-piercing), an assault rifle, thousands of gallons of water, and crates of food. The farm's owner denied involvement with Ryan's Posse group. "I'm just a farmer. I'm just trying to survive," he said, explaining that the bunker was a "fallout shelter" to be used in the event of nuclear attack.[8]

According to McNabb, the early morning arrests of Haverkamp and Andreas were precipitated by a mysterious phone call about suspected cattle rustlers. Whether that was the case, or whether McNabb had finally decided he could no longer ignore the encampment (Whelan had uncovered ample evidence of widespread thieving and all of it pointed to Rulo, and other law enforcement agencies were beginning to ask questions), the arrests marked the beginning of the end of the macabre events at Rulo. Removed from the encampment and feeling safer in their jail cells, Haverkamp and Andreas compared notes and decided to confess. They tried to get word to McNabb through their lawyers, but Rick Stice—who was now a paid informant for the FBI—spilled the news first, telling agents where they could find the remains of his son. But Stice knew nothing of the murder of James Thimm—he had fled the compound before that murder—and so it was left to Andreas and Haverkamp to lead authorities to his shallow grave.

Throughout these investigations, Sheriff McNabb showed remarkable disinterest in the Posse Comitatus. After the June raid revealed an arsenal of about sixty weapons (the bodies were not found until two months later), McNabb allowed Cheryl Gibson and her children to remain on the farm overnight, even though they were wanted in Kansas. Fearful that his family would be spirited away once more, Lester kept an all-night vigil with Dennis Whelan in a van outside the farm entrance. An angry McNabb confronted them at sunrise. "You didn't think the law could handle it or what?" the sheriff snarled. "This thing has nothing to do with the Posse," he continued, launching into a tirade denying Ryan's links to the radical right.[9] McNabb later justified his actions, saying Ryan's group was merely "reclusive" and posed no threat. "Their primary aim as far as I can tell, was to be left alone."[10] The county prosecutor, Douglas Merz, made the same lame assertions. "I have no idea what their affiliations are," he said of Ryan and his group. According to McNabb, nobody had been able to substantiate "that any such [illegal] activity was going on" at Rulo.[11] But the Kansas prosecutor, Pam Fahey, had a different explanation: "My feeling was that they were either afraid of the Posse or in sympathy with them," she said.[12]

These suspicions were reinforced when National Public Radio correspondent Frank Browning sought interviews with Mike Ryan and Cheryl Gibson after the June raid. Sheriff McNabb escorted Browning to the farm gate but when he didn't like the direction the interview was going, he soon broke in, telling him to shut off the tape recorder. "I wouldn't want Cheryl to get in trouble just because I'm good enough to let you come out here," he said. And the retired Nebraska judge, Sam Van Pelt, who also had gone to Rulo to investigate, was unnerved by Ryan's praise of McNabb. According to the judge, Mike Ryan had told him "what a great man Sheriff McNabb was, how well he handled the whole thing, and how the people of Richardson County really ought to get behind him when he comes up for election."[13]

Other disclosures cast a shadow over the county prosecutor, Douglas Merz. According to the *Hiawatha Daily World*, Rick Stice had been introduced to James Wickstrom by the prosecutor's uncle, a retired Nebraska state senator and farm-implement dealer.[14] Though the elder Merz denied it, his interest in the Posse was not a secret. In April 1983, the retired senator gave a copy of Gordon Kahl's letter detailing the Medina shootout to a local journalist. And later that year he allegedly attended a meeting in Omaha sponsored by Rick Elliott's National Agricultural Press Association, where Deloris Kirk and Senator Ernie Chambers received awards.[15]

Questions about the loyalty and effectiveness of law enforcement angered Nebraska governor Bob Kerrey, who denied there was any need to examine whether the murders of Stice and Thimm could have been prevented, or whether lawmen had waited too long to move against Rulo. "The State of Nebraska does not respond to 'coffeehouse' rumors," he told journalists in a huff. "I think it is offensive that you ask the question. . . . The last thing on my mind is the need to examine it," he said.[16]

Ryan already was facing federal weapons and theft charges when he appeared in court on August 21, 1985—heavily guarded—to be arraigned on charges of first-degree murder. The bodies had been discovered four days earlier. Eventually convicted of second-degree murder in the death of Luke Stice (Ryan pleaded no contest), he received the death penalty for killing James Thimm and remains on Nebraska's death row. Also convicted (and given life imprisonment) after pleading guilty to second-degree murder for killing Thimm, was Timothy Haverkamp, twenty-three, Cheryl Gibson's cousin. James Haverkamp and David Andreas both were sentenced to twenty-six years in prison for torturing Thimm and other crimes. The men pleaded guilty, testified against the other Rulo defendants, and were released in November 1999 after serving thirteen years.[17] As for Cheryl, she reconciled with her husband and testified against Mike Ryan and other Rulo defendants (though in 1999, she and Lester divorced). "I don't know whether any crime in Nebraska was ever this horrible," said Richardson County district judge Robert Finn, who presided over the eighteen-day trial in the death of James Thimm in 1986.[18]

Unlike the 1983 murder trial of Yorie Kahl and Scott Faul in North Dakota, where federal prosecutors downplayed the religious and political beliefs of the accused, the Rulo proceedings featured ample testimony about Christian Identity theology. Taking the witness stand during her second day in court, Mike Ryan's thirty-five-year-old wife Ruth explained how the six million Jews killed during the Second World War weren't really Jews.[19]

After murder charges were filed against Mike Ryan and the others, Governor Kerrey downplayed the activity of right-wing groups. "I'm not concerned that Nebraskans are buying the extreme arguments that are being presented by these people," he asserted, consistent with his earlier posture of denial.[20] State lawmakers were less sanguine. Prompted by Omaha senator Jerry Chizek, the State Judiciary Committee held hearings on hate-group violence, and the legislature finally gave its approval to an anti-paramilitary training statute in 1986.[21] First introduced in 1983, it took the death of NAPA follower and Nebraska farmer Arthur Kirk and the murders of Luke Stice and James Thimm to force passage of the bill.

34

NEOCONSERVATIVES AND THE GRAND WAZIR

The gruesome discoveries at Rulo came just two days after the national broadcast of an ABC-TV *20/20* investigative report detailing the growth of the rural radical right. Titled "Seeds of Hate," the twenty-two-minute segment featured a breathless Geraldo Rivera chronicling the death of Arthur Kirk and the exploits of the Order, and exposing the scams of Rick Elliott and others of his ilk. Zeroing in on right-wing appeals to farmers, Rivera paid special attention to those he called "the ministers of hate": Jim Wickstrom, Richard Butler, and Bill Gale, whose voice was heard in the opening minutes of the broadcast.

"Those who hate our God, Jesus Christ, are before us today. Kill 'em all! Wipe 'em out! There's a war coming!" Gale is heard to say in a voice-over accompanying video footage of Aryan Nations members using posters of the Israeli prime minister Menachem Begin for target practice.[1] Elsewhere in the broadcast, Wickstrom is seen delivering his Identity spiel to a group of farmers: "You wonder why you're losing your farms and ranches and businesses out there? Because your minister has lied to you concerning a bunch of international communist Jews that have stripped your wealth and your land."[2]

While some of the on-air ranting seemed downright bizarre, Rivera's interviews with several Nebraska farmers were entirely down-to-earth and much more disturbing. With American Agriculture Movement caps perched on their heads, the men calmly explained the International Jewish Conspiracy to Rivera and expounded on their biblical beliefs. "A Zionist Jew is nothing but pure evil," said Dan Hawkins. "And yes, they have designs on my farm, my neighbor's farm. They have designs on the whole earth." Asked by Rivera if they would be prepared to take up weapons "when the time comes," the farmers thoughtfully replied in the affirmative.[3] For mainstream leaders of AAM who had long battled to distance themselves from radical right-wing rhetoric, it must have been excruciatingly painful to watch.

Rivera did not even pretend to be objective. For farmers whose backs are to the wall, "sometimes even stupid ideas start making sense," he announced.[4] Like Denver talk-show host Alan Berg, Rivera was combative and relished confrontation. However, unlike Berg's radio interviews, the *20/20* segment was seen by millions of people. It also was painstakingly researched. The producer, Bob Lange, had traveled through the Midwest for months, pursuing leads, developing sources, gathering confidential law enforcement documents, and convincing bigots to go on camera. And in spite of Rivera's hyperventilating delivery, the facts of the broadcast were correct: farmers *were* being recruited by the rural radical right, which *was* part of an increasingly violent movement that was heavily influenced by militant Christian Identity beliefs. Rivera's final message to viewers was on target as well: "Add stopping the ministers of hate to all the other more compassionate reasons we should be helping America's family farmers."

Despite its accuracy, the broadcast and the issues it raised ignited fierce controversy among Jewish groups, within farm organizations, and among media commentators. Some critics disagreed with the fundamental premise of the broadcast—farmers were *not* falling prey to the radical right, they said—while others denounced ABC for airing the segment at all. And television critics, many of whom passionately disliked Rivera anyway, quickly seized on issues of personality and style to attack the segment. "Geraldo Rivera . . . the grand wazir of the gonzos, goes a-flailing on a special segment of *20/20* tonight," announced Tom Shales in the *Washington Post*.[5] Others savaged the broadcast, calling it "inflammatory reporting" and "recklessly rendered, machete journalism."[6] And because the broadcast challenged the long-standing assumption that hate groups appealed only to a "lunatic fringe," it was met with derision and disbelief.

"Just dealing with this subject seems a tainting, demeaning experience, something to be approached with utmost caution," wrote Shales, who criticized ABC for "bringing it all up on network television and thereby granting it wildly amplified circulation." Shales also attacked Rivera for making what he said was barely a token effort to examine the roots of farmers' frustrations or ask why they might be susceptible to conspiracy theories laced with hate.[7] And the fact that ABC had mixed footage of peaceful, yet spirited, farm-sale protests with reports about the murderous exploits of The Order (overlaid by Bill Gale's threatening rant and the staccato of weapons fire) angered many rural Americans, who understandably became defensive at what they heard and saw. Dixon Terry, president of the Iowa Farm Unity Coalition, commented in this vein when he said, "A glaring inadequacy of the *20/20* piece is that it failed to acknowledge the peaceful organizing efforts of grassroots groups."[8]

Not all the criticism was grounded in genuine concern for farmers, however. "What was the key information Rivera omitted from his exercise in left-wing McCarthyism?" asked the *Spotlight*. "Simply the most obvious, overwhelming source of the farmers' anger: that the American government is subsidizing the foreign nation of Israel with billions of taxpayer dollars while denying desperately needed credit to U.S. farmers."[9] Then there was Rick Elliott, whose tortured grammar and garbled prose made his tirade against ABC a parody of itself:

"Admittedly your reporter did find some of the low-class idiots that ravish this nation," began Elliott in a letter to ABC president James Duffy. "But strangely he failed to look at a mercenary which is main-stream information in today's *Denver Post* who has far more cause for the story you televised than half-baked broke farmers that were interviewed and exposed in a very uncouth manner." In addition to assailing the network for "nit-wit statements ... yellow journalism, slander and liable [*sic*]," Elliott took a swipe at the pope: "Pertaining to me, your pack of lies perfectly exemplifies exactly what you attempted to expose and it would seem that any Papal compensation should be directed towards your absolute responsibility to American history and heritage. ABC certainly will never be found on the granite walls of Mt. Rushmore.

"Your courtesy would sincerely be appreciated to rectify the shallow responsibility you hold to the history of the American press," his letter concluded.[10]

Protests from Rick Elliott and the *Spotlight* were to be expected, but the broadcast also fueled a debate at the opposite end of the political spectrum, between activists associated with PrairieFire Rural Action (formerly the Midwest Office of Rural America) and the North American Farm Alliance (NAFA).[11] Though both groups were strong allies on many issues, they had strategic differences when it came to responding to the rural radical right.

Disturbed by the breadth and depth of Posse activity, PrairieFire had been gathering information and sharing it with journalists, law enforcement agencies, and others since 1983. Through its farm-survival hotline and grassroots contacts in the countryside, the organization was in a unique position to obtain firsthand information about right-wing organizations and their leaders. PrairieFire believed it had a moral imperative to attack the bigotry of the rural radical right, but it had another reason for deciding to aggressively oppose the Posse and others: As the sponsor of countless grassroots meetings of farmers, the organization was determined to prevent its gatherings from becoming forums for conspiracy theories and anti-Semitic ideas. Among other things, PrairieFire's goal was to teach farmers how to legally block or delay foreclosure and to lobby effectively for political relief. Posse activism directly interfered with these objectives, and PrairieFire resolved to take the initiative to discredit the radical right. Adding to

PrairieFire's concern was its assessment that the radical right had gone largely unopposed since the mid-1970s and a concerted attempt at counteraction was long overdue.

In November 1984, PrairieFire was cited in a six-part newspaper series detailing right-wing organizing in the Farm Belt. Published in the *Rochester (Minn.) Post-Bulletin*, the articles helped lay the groundwork for additional media exposure of the radical right, including the *20/20* investigation the following year. Then, in April 1985, the Iowa Farm Unity Coalition approved a resolution drafted by PrairieFire's minister-leader, the Reverend Dave Ostendorf, which read:

> We deplore and reject the extremist philosophies and actions of those individuals and organizations that promote violence, anti-Semitic, or racist responses to the farm crisis, and reaffirm and recommit our efforts and energies to building a constructive, progressive, nonviolent farm movement that is committed to justice for all people of this nation and the world.

This declaration became the blueprint for dozens of similar statements that would be issued by farm, rural, and religious groups over the next several years, including the influential National Council of Churches.[12] Soon afterward, PrairieFire disseminated the first in a series of "confidential memorandums" to hundreds of key contacts across the country.

"Despite the many constructive, community-based efforts . . . to help farm and rural families and communities cope with [the farm crisis,] extremists have skillfully been able to use and manipulate the financial insecurities of farmers in order to promote their own propaganda of hate," PrairieFire warned in June 1985.[13] "The strategy of 'quarantine'—that is, of disregarding and isolating extremists by deliberately not responding to their activities [is] no longer effective."

In contrast to this strategy, the North American Farm Alliance and some other farm activists feared that an aggressive effort targeting the radical right might overshadow the larger and more important issue of the crumbling rural economy and farmers' legitimate demands for relief. After all, commodity prices were still well below the cost of production, and nearly one out of five of the nation's farms were in severe financial distress, including ninety-three thousand that were technically insolvent, holding a whopping $47 billion in debt.[14] And the crisis was affecting more than farmers. Nationally, two thousand farm-equipment dealers had gone out of business in 1983 and 1984, and without legislation to increase farm income, Wharton Econometrics predicted a loss of 270,000 non-agricultural jobs by 1985.[15]

While leaders of the Farm Alliance despised the radical right, they also worried that more publicity along the lines of the *20/20* segment would give farmers a bad name, something they could ill afford, especially while they were lobbying politicians for help. Many Americans were inclined to see farmers as hardworking and underpaid, but NAFA felt it was unwise to highlight the embarrassing spectacle of farmers getting suckered by hate groups, as the *20/20* segment had done. These sentiments were voiced articulately by one Nebraskan who wrote an angry letter to the *Omaha World-Herald* criticizing the *20/20* broadcast:

> The farmers of Iowa, Nebraska, and the Midwest were made out to be a radical paramilitary mob, anti-Semitic and racist—armed to the teeth, ready like SS troopers to spring up and kill all who are against them. . . . An ineffective farm program by the government, bungling politicians, bad banking practices, dwindling markets, and low prices were carefully omitted, leaving us Geraldo Rivera, with his voice pitched half an octave too high . . . pointing a finger at struggling farmers who are losing their farms, livelihoods, future, and the very nature of an American lifestyle.[16]

Instead of PrairieFire's countercampaign, some Farm Alliance leaders preferred to concentrate on building support for the Reverend Jesse Jackson, whom many farmers viewed warmly as a champion of the underdog. And in place of the confrontational approach advocated by PrairieFire, NAFA urged a different strategy: Farm groups should "out-organize" the radical right and win away its base of support with an alternative political message. *Why alienate potential recruits by disparaging some of their ideas?* NAFA reasoned. *Let's win them over with our politics, instead.* How this was to be done without criticizing right-wing conspiracy theories and offending farmers who believed them, was not explained. The debate continued, but PrairieFire forged ahead.

In November 1985 the organization began holding training sessions to build an extensive grassroots network to expose and undermine the radical right. Through dozens of meetings held over the next several years, more than one thousand farmers, clergy, union members, hotline operators, lawyers, state officials, and others became closely involved in the effort to counter the radical right. In developing its curriculum and strategy, PrairieFire received considerable help from the Center for Democratic Renewal, an Atlanta-based watchdog group that had been formed six years earlier as the National Anti-Klan Network. Led by charismatic civil rights activists like the Reverend C. T. Vivian (a top lieutenant to Reverend Martin Luther King Jr.), and experts on the radical right like Leonard Zeskind, CDR helped shape PrairieFire's thorough and aggressive approach. The campaign dealt a major setback to the radical right, but not without encountering resistance from another quarter: the Anti-Defamation League of B'nai B'rith.

The *20/20* segment had come as an unwelcome surprise to the ADL, which received telephone calls from startled supporters and Jewish leaders across the country. The agency had thirty regional offices, but few contacts in rural communities and little firsthand information about how troubled farmers were responding to the appeals of right-wing groups. The organization had done an excellent job of tracking anti-Semitism in the pages of the *Primrose and Cattleman's Gazette*, but it lacked a firm grasp on the extent to which Rick Elliott had truly penetrated the Farm Belt. While the ADL often received valuable information from undercover operatives and informants in other hate groups, it had failed to cultivate reliable sources inside the *rural* radical right. Instead its staff relied heavily on hearsay reports from journalists and law enforcement agents to find out what was going on.

The fact that nobody from the ADL had been invited to appear on camera for the *20/20* broadcast—or was even cited as an authoritative source—reinforced the agency's anger. For a national television network to broadcast a major exposé on hate groups without citing "the world's leading organization fighting anti-Semitism" was a huge blow to the credibility of the ADL. Rather than acknowledge that the broadcast was accurate, which risked begging the question *Why, then, was the ADL not interviewed?* the agency decided to attack ABC instead.

"We have received considerable response to ABC's *20/20* segment, entitled 'Seeds of Hate,'" wrote Justin J. Finger, the ADL civil rights director, to ABC the day after the broadcast.

> The ominous tone of the telecast and its conclusion that desperate farmers are turning increasingly to violent hate groups have combined—not surprisingly—to alarm some of our constituents who watched the program. We thought you should be aware that [o]ur field investigations have yielded scant evidence to suggest that farmers are turning in significant numbers to extremism. . . . Although the potential clearly exists for some future success by groups fishing in the "troubled waters" of the farm crisis, there is no reason to ring any alarm bells at the present time.[17]

In addition to minimizing the threat, the ADL asserted that "farmers have overwhelmingly, like the vast majority of Americans, rejected groups that spread bigotry and divisiveness." On the surface it seemed a simple-enough assessment, but the statement was rhetorically complex. No one—not even Geraldo Rivera—had alleged that the *majority* of farmers had joined the radical right or were even likely to do so. But by presenting the issue this way, the ADL discredited claims that *some* farmers were. The statement also reinforced another pillar of ADL belief: Americans were decent and tolerant, always inclined to choose diversity and pluralism over bigotry and discrimination.

The ADL had several reasons for promoting this message and minimizing the right-wing threat. For one thing, such arguments helped bolster its claim that racism and white supremacy were "extremist" notions that lacked a mainstream following and a significant social base. This was important to the ADL because it undermined the credibility of right-wing groups, even if it wasn't necessarily true. For example, while numerous studies had revealed a marked decline in some aspects of anti-Semitism, negative stereotypes about Jews as unethical, dishonest, aggressive, pushy, clannish, and conceited were still widely held among approximately one-third of Americans in the 1960s. And as many as 51 percent of Americans in 1964 agreed with the statement that Jews should "quit complaining about what happened to them in Nazi Germany." Anti-Semitism continued to decline after 1964, but could hardly be regarded as "marginal." One study by the American Jewish Committee in 1981 found anti-Semitism to be a "serious social problem," with nearly one in four respondents agreeing with the statement that Jews have "too much power in the United States." And a comprehensive national survey conducted by the ADL itself in 1992 found one in five American adults—between thirty-five and forty million people—holding unquestionably anti-Semitic views.[18] Nevertheless the ADL insisted that bigotry wasn't a problem in the Farm Belt: Posse groups were having *no* success, and the *vast majority* of farmers rejected both the organizations *and* their ideas.

The ADL had not always downplayed the threat of the radical right. In fact, for most of the agency's seventy-year history it had issued frequent and strongly worded warnings about the popularity of right-wing causes as well as the dangers posed by smaller bands of racists and anti-Semitic militants. But with the rise of neoconservativism in the Jewish community in the late 1960s, some of those in the ADL leadership chose to pursue the more narrow cause of Jewish self-interest in place of continued alliances with blacks and broader support for civil rights. Neoconservatism became the lens through which many in the ADL—and other Jewish agencies—interpreted events and planned their strategies on behalf of the Jewish community.[19] It also profoundly distorted the ADL's assessment of the dangers posed by the radical right and others whose agendas also smacked of anti-Semitism.

For example, during the late 1970s, neoconservatives used the issue of Israeli security to justify forming alliances with some evangelical and fundamentalist Christians whose interpretation of the Book of Revelation led them to support the Jewish state because they anticipated its imminent destruction. According to these beliefs, the Second Coming of Christ will be preceded by several key events, including the return of the Jews to biblical Palestine; their destruction by the Antichrist's armies; and the final conversion to Christianity of those Jews who remain. In his 1990 book *The New Millennium*, Christian Coalition founder Pat Robertson laid out this same interpretation: Israel is destined to be destroyed and then, writes Robertson, "according to the Bible, the Jews will cry out to the one they have so long rejected."[20]

Not all Christians with whom the ADL and other Jews built alliances shared this reading of the Bible, but many did. And there was still the thorny problem of maintaining relationships with Christian groups that supported Israel but demanded prayer in school or otherwise backed initiatives that threatened the wall of separation between church and state and, even further, to "Christianize" America. The ADL was not the only Jewish group that sought allies among evangelical and fundamentalist Christians who supported Israel, but the ADL's approach was the most aggressive, and the ADL appeared less concerned with unraveling the many contradictions inherent in the relationship. Most American Jews had misgivings over the political agenda of fundamentalist Christians—especially those who sought to convert them ("complete" them, in evangelical terms) or those who accused them of "killing Christ." Their anxieties were greatly reinforced by statements like those of the Reverend Dr. Bailey Smith, president of the sixteen-million-member Southern Baptist Convention, who announced in 1980 that "God Almighty does not hear the prayer of a Jew."[21] Despite the obvious insensitivity—and outright anti-Semitism—of many conservative Christian groups, neoconservatives sought them as allies, choosing the false promise of Israeli security over the need for domestic pluralism and civil liberties. They also tried their best to stampede the rest of the Jewish community toward the same direction.

"Why should Jews care about the theology of a fundamentalist preacher?" asked Irving Kristol, a Trotskyist turned leading neoconservative, writing in *Commentary* magazine in 1984. "What do such theological abstractions matter as against the mundane fact that this same preacher is vigorously pro-Israel?"[22]

The neoconservative movement gained considerable momentum in the wake of the 1967 Arab-Israeli war, which led many liberal churches and secular leftists to criticize Israel. Passage of the 1975 U.N. resolution equating Zionism with racism prompted even more concern inside many Jewish agencies, whose leaders resolved to put their doubts aside and develop ties with conservative Christians. Evangelical and fundamentalist support for the cause of Soviet Jewry during the 1970s and 1980s further solidified the alliance. And so when Jerry Falwell's Moral Majority and other groups pushed heavily for the election of Ronald Reagan in 1980, the neoconservatives were close at hand; among them, men like Nathan Glazer, Irving Kristol, Norman Podhoretz, and Nathan Perlmutter, who was executive director of the ADL from 1979 until his death in 1987.[23]

In 1982, Perlmutter wrote *The Real Anti-Semitism in America*, which argued strongly in support of a Christian conservative–Jewish alliance.[24] Another neoconservative driving force within the ADL at the time was Irwin Suall, the head of the agency's fact-finding division. The former national secretary of the Socialist Party–Social Democratic Federation and the onetime treasurer of the anti-communist Young People's Socialist League, the combative Suall had carried the conflicts of the sectarian left of the 1930s, 1940s, and 1950s into the ADL. Throughout his long tenure as fact-finding director, from 1967 to 1987, Suall continuously sought to do battle with the ghosts of Stalin on the American left, while turning an increasingly blind eye to the thuggish cadres of the paramilitary right.[25]

"The principal struggle in defense of Jewish security in the United States today does not concern the radical right. The greatest threat to the fabric of democracy comes from the left," Suall told me when I visited the ADL's New York headquarters in 1986. Perlmutter had echoed these sentiments a couple of years earlier when he said he was more concerned by lack of support for Israel than he was "with some Klansman in a cow pasture in central Missouri."[26] By the time of the farm crisis, the viewpoint of Suall, Perlmutter, and others was firmly entrenched at the ADL.

In addition to the politics of neoconservatism, the ADL was driven to downplay Farm Belt anti-Semitism because of its rivalry with other Jewish groups and its fear of being upstaged by organizations like PrairieFire and the Center for Democratic Renewal. Prior to the *20/20* broadcast, PrairieFire had been in contact with leaders of the American Jewish Congress and the American Jewish Committee (AJC). Both groups were prominent in the Jewish community and more inclined than the ADL to pursue coalitions with minorities and non-Jewish groups, including farmers.

Within weeks of the *20/20* broadcast, Rabbi A. James Rudin of the AJC was in Iowa on a fact-finding mission. "A quarantine approach is no longer adequate or appropriate," he told the leaders of the Des Moines Jewish community. "A more visible and vigorous strategy should be adopted." A native of Pittsburgh, Pennsylvania, Rudin had joined the national staff of the AJC some fifteen years earlier, and was now its director of interreligious affairs. A modest man with a slight build and a receding hairline, Rudin's assessment of the Midwestern situation was motivated as much by his compassion for farmers as by the evidence of anti-Semitism that he saw. "The current plight of the family farmer cannot be exaggerated," Rudin wrote in a report to colleagues in September 1985. "It is reliably estimated that some 30 percent of Iowa's 113,000 farmers will lose their land within the next twelve to eighteen months, while another 30 percent will barely survive. The destructive political and social consequences from such massive dislocation will be staggering." On the issue of anti-Semitism, Rudin was quick to note that the radical right had made "significant gains among some of the economically distressed farmers."

"It is impossible to estimate with accuracy the precise number of farmers who have accepted the message of hate and violence. . . . However . . . the threat is real and growing and . . . a comprehensive campaign is needed *now* to prevent the pathology from spreading."[27] The American Jewish Committee quickly publicized its concerns at a press conference in New York on September 20, 1985, and invited a contingent of Iowans to participate.

Dixon Terry had criticized the *20/20* broadcast for having "failed to acknowledge the peaceful organizing efforts of grassroots groups," but he nevertheless welcomed the opportunity to denounce the radical right: "Farmers are victims of the hate propaganda and phony schemes of a surprisingly strong, organized right-wing element," he explained. "I have seen good intelligent Iowa farmers waste hundreds of dollars they couldn't afford on phony seminars to teach them bogus legal remedies for their problems when they've reached the end of their rope. Deceiving farmers, diverting them from real solutions, milking them of their money—this is probably the most common damage done by the right wing."

Joining Terry at the podium was the Roman Catholic bishop of Des Moines, Maurice J. Dingman. "The rhetoric of those who hate is to utter base falsehoods. High in their arsenal of arguments is a simple lie. They will say: 'The Jews are out to get your land,' " he said.[28] The American Jewish Committee also released a report by Leonard Zeskind which estimated there were between two thousand and five thousand "hard-core activists," and between fourteen thousand and fifty thousand "sympathizers" of the radical right in the Midwest. "Extremists in Farm Belt are Assailed," was the headline in the *New York Times* the next day.[29] Coincidentally, on the same day as the news conference, Irwin Suall had been quoted in the *Times*. "Although there has been very intense effort on the part of the extreme right trying to fish in troubled waters, they aren't catching any fish," he said.[30]

Three weeks later, more than two dozen Jewish leaders from the Midwest met in Kansas City, Missouri, to examine the issue more deeply. The group included Sheldon Filger, director of the Omaha ADL, who argued unsuccessfully that the problem of Farm Belt anti-Semitism was overblown. Filger suffered further damage to his credibility a couple of months later when he tried to make the same point in a similar meeting but was confronted by colleagues who brandished copies of full-page ads the ADL had placed in Jewish newspapers, soliciting money to fight the threat of rural anti-Semitism. "Anti-Semitic Activity Rising in Midwest; Jews Prime Target for Hate," read the headline of one ADL appeal in the *Kansas City Jewish Chronicle*.

On the other side of the argument was David Goldstein, the director of the Kansas City Jewish Community Relations Bureau and a veteran of the fight to shut down KTTL radio in Kansas. "Our task is to prevent the radical right from winning the hearts and minds of rural society," he told the group of Jewish leaders who gathered in Kansas City in October 1985. "We must find ways to prevent those who are becoming soft on anti-Semitism from going over the line." Goldstein proposed a simple, direct solution: Jews must develop working alliances with Christian clergy and liberal farm organizations.[31] Not only did his colleagues agree, they concluded that the threat posed by the rural radical right was real.

From the perspective of the ADL, the situation was snowballing toward organizational disaster. Headlines in the *New York Times* citing other Jewish groups that contradicted the ADL's assessment of anti-Semitism was embarrassing enough, but now dozens of local Jewish leaders seemed poised to reject its expertise. To repair its sorely damaged credibility, the ADL seized on a time-honored political solution: it commissioned a poll. But like other efforts to bolster its weak position vis-à-vis the farm crisis, this backfired, too.

The ADL survey of rural residents of Iowa and Nebraska was conducted by veteran pollster Lou Harris in January 1986 and was designed to test respondents' "latent attitudes" toward Jews, and their beliefs about the causes of the farm crisis.[32] Among the six hundred people questioned, 35 percent put heavy blame for the farm crisis on "an international communist conspiracy" and 28 percent blamed the Trilateral Commission—both persistent bogeymen of the far right. Twenty-seven percent agreed (as did 31 percent of farmers) with the claim that "farmers have always been exploited by international Jewish bankers who are behind those who overcharge them for farm equipment or jack up the interest on their loans." Harris's interpretation of the results was straightforward and disturbing. He wrote:

> [I]t must be pointed out that any phenomenon which affects over one in four residents must be viewed as a mass phenomenon, even if it is not massive. Put another way, one does not have to venture far into either state to find an abundant number of people who are prepared to lay some of the real blame for the plight of farmers on international bankers, and many of these clearly are thought to be Jewish.[33]

Because ADL director Nathan Perlmutter wasn't about to acknowledge that the poll directly contradicted his agency's previous assertions, he distorted the findings with dizzying spin. "These results clearly show that the American farmer, although hard-hit economically, is decidedly not as vulnerable to bigotry as those who shrilly cry wolf about anti-Semitism would have us believe," Perlmutter announced.[34] This contradictory packaging of the Harris Poll results marked a new and more desperate stage in the ADL's campaign of denial. Instead of debating whether right-wing groups were capitalizing on farmers' distress, the ADL now had succumbed to belittling the American Jewish Committee and PrairieFire, accusing them of "exploiting" the issue and "crying wolf."

"Since last year's ABC-TV *20/20* segment on anti-Semitism in the Farm Belt, its scary message . . . has been the subject of concerned press conferences and meetings. Regrettably, the exploitation of the subject exceeded by far a studied assessment of it," Perlmutter told his national commission in a memo. "The results confirm that charges of anti-Semitism in our farm lands were grossly exaggerated." To prove his assertion, Perlmutter selectively cited the responses to some Harris Poll questions but did not disclose the answers to others that measured the most negative attitudes toward Jews. According to his memo, 24 percent of respondents affirmed anti-Semitic stereotypes, like: "Jews are irritating because they are too aggressive," and 30 percent said "The Jewish lobby in the United States is far too powerful for the good of this country." But Perlmutter left out even worse results: Fully 42 percent of respondents agreed with the view that "Jews should quit complaining about what happened to them in Nazi Germany," and an equal number believed that "when it comes to choosing between people and money, Jews will choose money." There were more glaring omissions. The ADL press release announcing the poll stated that "anti-Semitic sentiments are more frequently encountered in the over-sixty-five age group and among those with less than a high-school education," but the ADL did not highlight the fact that two groups—"farmers" and "conservatives"—also were among those *most inclined* to hold anti-Jewish beliefs. Like all polls, this one contained questions designed to elicit particular results. So when Harris asked farmers whether they had been to any meetings of, or belonged to, groups like the National Agricultural Press Association, the vast majority—98 percent—predictably responded no. Such a finding appeared to support the ADL's oft-stated assertion that the radical right was winning few adherents. In reality, if even 2 percent of the region's farmers had actually attended right-wing meetings as the data did suggest, that would have amounted to tens of thousands of people. But when asked whether they had heard of, or were familiar with, NAPA, a startling 50 percent said yes. Twenty-nine percent said they had heard of the right-wing Populist Party, and 24 percent were familiar with the Posse Comitatus. According to the ADL analysis, this finding was somehow reassuring: "[C]omparatively few farmers are even aware of the major extremist groups seeking to exploit the situation," the ADL falsely declared. And ADL's statement that "[d]irect involvement by farmers with extremist groups . . . has been 'minimal and minute' " flatly contradicted Harris's own analysis that the messages of hate groups in the region "have been anything but minute and small."

The ADL's skewed interpretation of the poll data quickly provoked criticism. "I draw very little comfort when one out of four farmers responded with anti-Semitic comments . . . and neither do I think the Jewish community should," explained Rabbi Rudin of the American Jewish Committee. And the director of the Chicago office of the AJC, Jonathan Levine, pointed out that even relatively small numbers of anti-Semites might have a disproportionate impact in underpopulated rural communities. "It seems to me that when you're dealing with a dispersed rural population . . . that we not minimize the potential danger and our risk," he said. Criticism by Jewish leaders who had previously been at odds with the ADL was perhaps to be expected, but the most stinging rebuke came from Lou Harris himself: "Farmers are being told their trouble is being caused by bankers, which means the Jews. . . . Anyone who thinks [anti-Semitism] is not there, is kidding themselves," he said.[35]

The ADL hoped the Harris Poll would reestablish its credibility on the subject of Farm Belt anti-Semitism, but it also had another goal in mind: to provide cover for its Republican allies and the Reagan administration, which faced mounting criticism about the deepening farm crisis. The ADL sought to minimize reports of Farm Belt anti-Semitism because images of gun-toting farmers recruiting their desperate neighbors reinforced concerns about the crumbling rural economy and thereby fueled doubts about Republican farm policy that was contributing greatly to economic distress in the countryside.

As further justification for its assertion that PrairieFire and others were "crying wolf," the ADL argued that the arrests of right-wing leaders had "virtually crippled their recruitment efforts." As a reference to Bob Matthews (who was dead) and the incarcerated members of The Order, the statement was correct. But this wasn't true for right-wing scam artists like Rick Elliott, who continued to draw large crowds and new recruits, despite his indictment for theft and conspiracy. Elliott was eventually convicted, but he still had a mailing list of five thousand supporters scattered among thirty-seven chapters in about a dozen states when he was sent off to jail.[36]

35

SOFT-PEDALING HATE

The ADL chose to see the Posse "glass" as less than half-empty, but in reality the challenge posed by the rural radical right was growing, as an array of Christian Patriot groups emerged that skillfully employed Posse rhetoric while cleverly dodging the Posse's explicitly violent image. Leonard Zeskind called this development the rise of "the soft Posse."

Beginning in 1983, the Medina gunfight, the deaths of Kahl and Kirk, the Rulo murders, and the collapse of Wickstrom's Wisconsin Posse compound that followed, all helped prompt the emergence of a broader Christian Patriot movement. And it was this development, in turn, that laid the groundwork for the formation of militant militia groups in the 1990s.

Indictments, arrests, and negative publicity can affect a social movement in a variety of ways: they can crush it, drive it underground, increase its appeal, or cause it to camouflage its message so it is less vulnerable to criticism. Whether by choice or chance (or a combination of the two), the Posse took the latter route and underwent a metamorphosis that allowed it to disguise its hard-core rhetoric and broaden its appeal. The Posse was able to do this and survive because its main strength had always been its philosophy and ideas, not its status as an organized group. Other organizations, like the Ku Klux Klan and the John Birch Society, that were more heavily invested in building membership and promoting their organizational identity, were less flexible about setting aside their institutional interests in favor of spreading their ideas. The Posse was not.

While Posse activists had long referred to themselves as "Christian Patriots," the term became even more useful in the post-Kahl, post-Kirk era. For diehard Posse supporters, the "Christian Patriot" label said who they were without exposing them to quite as much criticism or surveillance. Yet to themselves and others in the know, they were still Identity believers, tax protesters, and armed opponents of the government. And for those newer to the struggle, who were not quite as obsessed with preparing for the endtimes or acquiring bulk quantities of armor-piercing ammunition, being a "Christian Patriot" still identified them as dissidents willing to fight for the Constitution, as well as for their farms.

There had been a similar transformation in the movement a decade earlier, when Bill Gale's Posse first gained momentum and recruits by penetrating the much larger tax-protest movement and radicalizing it with racist theology and guns. And the tax protesters, in turn, helped the Posse grow by adding their colorful, convoluted rhetoric to the pantheon of Posse grievances. The Posse changed again several years later, after it was hit by bad press, indictments, and low morale in the wake of the potato-shed takeover in Oregon and other failed showdowns. Then it found cover and new support among distressed farmers in the Midwest and South. Like its infiltration of the tax-protest movement, the Posse penetration of AAM in the late 1970s was not the result of grand strategic thinking, but stemmed from a combination of coincidence and opportunity. And regardless of the cause or motive, the Posse succeeded marvelously in hoodwinking frustrated farmers by adapting its message to new circumstances and constituencies.

By the mid- to late 1980s, another transformation was under way and it involved an array of individuals and groups that skillfully packaged key elements of Posse rhetoric and belief and delivered them to farmers in distress. Many of these groups were led by men like Rick Elliott—con artists with ugly politics who cashed in on the travails of others by using bigotry and doggerel to enhance their pitch. Others were more committed to the politics of the movement, but had learned to carefully calibrate their message, in both style and content. They conveniently borrowed pieces of Posse ideology while disguising (or ignoring) others—especially open discussions of Identity theology and explicit appeals to violence.

Gone, largely by the mid- to late 1980s, were the days when Jim Wickstrom would pack meeting rooms with evangelical appeals to Jew-hatred and impassioned visions of the coming race war. Instead, the disquisitions were more technical and legalistic, with politics and religion occupying smaller and more confidential corners of the discussion. And explicit mention of the Posse—which had become a public-relations and law enforcement lightning rod—was reserved for quieter conversations. Despite the sanitized message of these "softer" groups, their activities actually broadened the appeal of the Posse and ensured the survival of its ideas, albeit in a new and different form.

The Christian Patriot movement continued to draw supporters, generate money for its leaders, and spread its ideas. Both new recruits and hardened followers attended house meetings, evening lectures, and weeklong seminars on "Christian Common Law" where they were indoctrinated further into the Posse worldview. Convinced the government was in Satan's thrall, and frustrated by their unsuccessful attempts to challenge the system, many Christian Patriots tried to sever themselves from it. Armed with do-it-yourself "status packets," they "rescinded" their "contracts with state," believing the government would no longer have jurisdiction over them. By shredding his driver's license, automobile registration, Social Security card, and birth certificate, a farmer could become a "freeman," a "constitutionalist," and a "sovereign citizen." More than a handful of farm wives found themselves speechless and confused when their middle-aged husbands, who had only recently been proud to celebrate decades of marriage, explained that renouncing their marriage certificates was part of the plan to save the farm.

Out of genuine support, ignorance, or both, a handful of government officials supported these pitiful protests even though they often violated state and federal law. Arizona state senator Wayne Stump was among the most agreeable. In a December 1985 letter he sent from his state capitol office to police chiefs and sheriffs across Arizona, Stump, a chiropractor, wrote:

> It has come to my attention that numerous individuals in our state have rescinded all of their contracts with the United States federal government, the state of Arizona, and each of its political subdivisions, establishing themselves as freemen under the organic national Constitution of the Republic of the United States of America. Consequently, they may be driving without auto registration, driver's license, or any other evidence of contract.
>
> [I]nasmuch as this procedure is entirely appropriate when properly carried out . . . I am requesting to be notified of the names . . . of participants of any such confrontations arising from the exercise of a person's freeman status in order to evaluate the outcome of properly rescinded contracts.

It is doubtful that Stump's opinion had much impact on law enforcement, but Posse activists and other Patriots readily brandished copies of his letter to convince others that their arguments had merit. If "asseveration" was the shield by which righteous patriots might keep the beast of government at bay, "common-law liens," "land patents," and "Fractional Reserve Checks" were their paper swords. Like other twisted principles of Posse jurisprudence, the concept underlying the common-law lien had some legitimacy; in this case it was the law that allowed skilled workers to file a mechanic's lien against any customer who failed to pay their bill. But unlike a bona fide mechanic's lien, the purpose of the "common-law lien" was not to secure compensation for services rendered; rather, its goal was to harass the person against whom it was filed by clouding title to any property they owned.

According to Christian Patriot logic, bankers had bilked farmers by loaning them phony paper money not backed by gold and silver and so farmers were entitled to payment for the losses they incurred when they couldn't satisfy their debts. Rather than pursue these claims as civil suits in court (where they would be thrown out) Christian Patriots took the shorter but equally futile route of simply adding up the damages and filing liens against creditors, judges, and anyone else who had the bad luck to serve as cogs in the tragic machinery of debt collection. Because it took several years before states outlawed the practice, county clerks felt obliged to record the phony liens. Though the documents were worthless, they still entangled their victims in a web of paperwork that made it nearly impossible for them to sell their homes or other property until they got the liens removed. In other instances, Christian Patriots persuaded farmers to engage in a series of sham transactions, including the filing of common-law liens against the indebted farm, which would thereby cloud the title and supposedly discourage foreclosure. The nuisance tactic sometimes won a small delay, but it never worked and nearly always ended up costing the farmer more in the end.

Another worthless but convincing scheme involved the use of "land patents." Issued by the federal government in the nineteenth century, the patents gave individuals clear title to public land that the government made available for settlement. Two hundred years later the documents were suitable for nothing more than framing, but the Posse claimed that land patents were powerful legal documents that automatically overruled any existing title, mortgage, or lien. Farmers were instructed to write to the federal Bureau of Land Management to obtain a certified copy of the original patent for their parcel of land and then file it at the county courthouse. Like so many other Posse stratagems, the land patent relied on elaborate but irrelevant legalistic incantations. " 'Exhibit A' Allodium Freehold Title Deed at 'Common Law.' PRIMARY GRANT, ABSOLUTE, AND PERFECT TITLE . . ." read one distressed farmer's courthouse filing that accompanied his patent. In reality the patent was nothing but a temporary illusion and, like a cheap magic trick, the flaw was readily revealed.[1] One of the first to definitively demystify the ruse was a federal judge from Indiana, William C. Lee.

"The court cannot conceive of a potentially more disruptive force in the world of property law than the ability of a person to get 'superior' title to land by simply filling out a document granting himself a 'land patent' and then filing it with the recorder of deeds. Such self-serving, gratuitous activity *does not, cannot* and *will not* be sufficient by itself to create good title," Judge Lee wrote in a landmark opinion invalidating the use of land patents. Courts elsewhere looked to Judge Lee's ruling to craft their own decisions, including one Illinois judge who bluntly referred to land-patent filings as "nothing more than a compilation of disjointed and nonsensical claims and legal conclusions totally unsupported by citations on the record or relevant legal authority."[2]

When Christian Patriots tried to enforce their land patents and common-law liens in court, most insisted on doing so pro se—without an attorney. And like the leaders of the tax-protest movement of the 1970s who did the same thing, they almost always lost. One of the most vigorous promoters of these maneuvers was George Gordon, founder of the Missouri-based "Barristers Inn School of Common Law." A California native, Gordon had been active in the radical right in Idaho before leaving there in 1984 and setting up shop in southern Missouri.

Gordon charged desperate farm couples $50 per day and $225 per week for seminars that featured topics such as: "Eighteen Alternatives to Stopping Fore-closures Other than Bankruptcy"; "Are Banks Loaning You Money or Are They Loaning You Credit?"; "Who Rules the World and How They Achieved It"; "Are You a Practicing Communist?"; and "Marriage—Privilege by License or Right by God?"[3] But these sessions were merely loss leaders for Gordon, a former dairyman with a high-school equivalency certificate who charged up to $1,000 for a week of "private counseling" and $3,500 for 110 hours of his "training materials" in "basic courtroom strategy and procedure," featuring videotapes and audiotapes and reams of prepackaged paperwork.

Gordon said he preferred payment in gold, but he really didn't care. "The cost of these semi-private classes is 2 ounces of gold with gold at $500 spot, $200 in junk silver (with junk silver at $5 × face), Russian rubles . . . Czechoslovakian hellers [sic] . . . Mexican pesos, or 1,000 Federal Reserve notes." And for those short on currency (foreign or domestic) he generously offered to accept a range of goods, including tractors and other farm implements, in exchange for his "services."[4]

"Spending what you have even on a wild scheme is better than doing noth-ing," Gordon claimed, but some of his bankrupt farm clients who had trouble buying groceries after they paid thousands of dollars for his worthless advice probably would have disagreed.[5] By 1986, Gordon boasted that he had spoken to more than fifty groups in thirty-five states and produced hundreds of hours of lessons on videotape. Given the level of farmers' desperation, and the strength of the Christian Patriot movement, the claim was probably true.[6] Although the bulk of his lectures focused on legal issues and Posse-style interpretations of the Constitution, Gordon also was a Christian Identity believer who tried to feed his farmer clients racism and anti-Semitism along with his other advice.[7] Like Mike Ryan's followers, who avoided pork and thought they were descendants of the biblical Hebrews, Gordon insisted that the "common law" required observance of "Passover and the Feast of Unleavened Bread" (as he called it), and his cir-culars were careful to note the weeklong Jewish harvest festival of Succoth. Gor-don said he was opposed to violence and told audiences that "you have to have a place to go other than to the gun barrel," but he invoked the names of Kahl and Kirk as martyrs to the movement and said they had been "forced" to use their weapons.[8]

Another prominent and energetic huckster, who offered a similarly bountiful array of useless Posse tactics laced with anti-Semitism, was Conrad LeBeau. A former carpenter who made a living selling quack health remedies, LeBeau's attention was drawn to the plight of farmers when he protested high interest rates outside a Milwaukee bank in 1981. In addition to his hatred for what he called "this great Whore of Babylon—the money and banking power," LeBeau was motivated by what he thought was an excellent marketing opportunity: right-wingers were particularly susceptible to his brand of medical chicanery.[9] Armed with the mailing list of another right-wing group, LeBeau quickly launched a newsletter of his own; after several name changes it became the *Patriots Information Network Report*.[10] LeBeau was a frequent writer of letters to the editor and he extolled the virtues of Laetrile (an ineffective cancer treatment) and the evils of the Federal Reserve with equal vigor. His *PIN Report* became an excellent outlet for both his musings and his remedies. Mailed from a post-office box in a Milwaukee suburb, the newsletter contained do-it-yourself legal forms, instructions for filing common-law liens and land patents, and testimonials about the miraculous powers of hydrogen peroxide—"an immune system booster, germicide, fungicide, viricide, anti-carcinogenic . . . and may even stop AIDS."

LeBeau said he got his political views from his father—a fan of the Depression-era radio priest, the Reverend Charles Coughlin—but whatever tutoring he got, LeBeau's worldview was terribly confused. He criticized what he called the "single conspiracy theory . . . dogma of the political right," which held that Jews, international bankers, and communists were forever one and the same; yet he praised the rabidly anti-Semitic Identity minister Sheldon Emry for carrying out "Christ's mission on earth."[11] He attacked the tax-protest tabloid, the *Justice Times*, for being on a "hopeless trip [and] married to a lifelong battle with the IRS," yet he readily tilted at the windmills of paper money and the Federal Reserve. LeBeau claimed he wasn't prejudiced, yet he promoted anti-Semitism and his byline occasionally appeared in the *Spotlight*.[12]

"Most international bankers are Jewish but not all Jews are international bankers," was his common refrain, to which he often added that he felt "no resentment to Italians because some are members of the Mafia."[13] Like Bill Gale, LeBeau advanced the bogus notion that Jews might be unfit to hold public office because the *Kol Nidre* prayer said on Yom Kippur—the holiest day of the Jewish calendar—proved that Jews "serving in either the Federal or State Courts may in fact have secretly renounced their oath to uphold the Constitution."[14] And LeBeau proudly claimed that a later effort he organized called the Christian Credit Society was endorsed by Eustace Mullins, a lifelong anti-Semite and Holocaust denier.[15]

During the seven years that LeBeau crisscrossed the Farm Belt, he made a special point of promoting funny money of his own design. Called "Fractional

Reserve Checks," or FRCs for short, he claimed that his privately created "check-book money" could be used to "pay off bank loans of any kind."[16] LeBeau's idea was a rip-off of the "public office money certificates" invented by the tax protester Tupper Saussy III.[17] Like Saussy's certificates, LeBeau's checks were worthless, but they caught on with Christian Patriots who believed that debtors had the right to issue their own homemade currency to repay loans that banks had "cre-ated out of thin air."[18] LeBeau had his pitch down pat:

> Under natural equity, we return to a lender exactly what he loaned us. If a lender loans us apples, we return apples to him, if he lends us silver, we pay him in silver, if he lends us cash, we pay him cash, and if he lends us credit/checkbook money/book entries which he creates out of nothing, then we have equal and sovereign rights to pay him back with credit/checkbook money/book entries which we also create out of nothing.

This message was well received by anxious farmers who paid LeBeau $65 for his "Foreclosure and Legal Karate" kit, which promised to explain how "nearly every bank loan in the United States can be legally voided."

LeBeau was a one-man show but he built a following with the help of others who had a larger following and who should have known better. Such was the case with Charles Walters Jr., editor and publisher of the monthly tabloid *Acres U.S.A.* First published in 1970, *Acres* was considered eclectic but well respected by many organic farmers who enjoyed its practical, how-to columns as well as Walters's iconoclastic essays attacking misguided government farm policies. But by the early 1980s, Walters was pandering to the radical right. He ran full-page ads for George Gordon's "School of Common Law," pushed land patents, pro-moted racist books, whitewashed the bigotry of Arthur Kirk, published interviews with Posse con artists, and promoted the scams of flimflam men like Conrad LeBeau. Born into the Kansas dust bowl in 1926, Walters attended Creighton University in Omaha, and the combination of his Depression-era upbringing and his progressive Catholic sensibilities led him to identify with the underdog. But Walters also had a graduate degree in economics from the University of Denver and he fell in love with the mythical mathematics of agricultural fundamentalism. Well-read and blessed with an excellent memory, Walters was an opinionated curmudgeon whose entertaining diatribes—whether delivered in print or from the podium—often lapsed into hyperbole and paranoia. He once compared American farm policy to Stalin's liquidation of the Kulaks and he accused the liberal farm group PrairieFire of being an "Eastern establishment front organi-zation" whose purpose was to "stage an ineffective fight for the family farm," as a cover for "the real agenda [which] calls for elimination of that same family farm."[19]

Walters was content to criticize those who were genuinely dedicated to help-

ing farmers but he preferred to encourage bona fide scams such as those promoted by Common Title Bond and Trust, a right-wing group with links to Bill
Gale. Initially based in Nevada, Common Title was the creation of Roger Elvick,
a Gale associate. The scheme Elvick promoted was simple, but it involved just
enough convoluted paperwork to have the appearance of a legitimate financial
fix. At its core were so-called "sight drafts"—worthless checks modeled after
Tupper Saussy's funny money and Conrad LeBeau's "Fractional Reserve Checks."
Elvick and his cronies sold the drafts to farmers, saying they could be used to
pay debts. Then, when a bank tried to collect payment from Common Title by
submitting the draft it had received, it got a bogus document called a "bill of
exchange" in return. This piece of paper was supposedly "redeemable at any
Federal Reserve institution," but its real purpose was to buy Elvick and his promoters more time. It also made the paperwork more convincing. Elvick fran-
chised his con among more than two dozen right-wing activists across twenty
states, but many of his advance men quickly found themselves in trouble with
the law. After one Ohio patriot gave his bank a sight draft for more than $100,000
to satisfy a lesser debt, he walked away with a check for the $5,065 balance and
was promptly indicted. And another longtime Posse activist in South Dakota,
Byron Dale, was sentenced to five years in prison after being convicted of grand
theft for buying farm machinery at an auction using sight drafts.[20] According to
Chuck Walters, Dale was given a bad rap.

While groups like Common Title Bond and Trust cashed in financially on
farmers' economic woes, some right-wing politicians used the same issues to
propel them electorally to higher office. One legislator who made it all the way
to Congress by attacking the Federal Reserve was a Washington state senator,
Jack Metcalf. A schoolteacher for twenty-nine years, Metcalf was the national
cochairman of the anti-Fed group Redeem Our Country, and he spent the mid-
1980s touring the nation, speaking to farmers, tax strikers, *Spotlight* readers and
Posse diehards about the evils of America's central bank. These meetings helped
Metcalf build a national base for his successful congressional campaigns a decade
later. Defeated the first time he ran for Congress in 1992, Metcalf won 54 percent
of the vote in 1994, and went on to serve three terms in Washington, where he
promoted a long list of far-right causes before he retired.[21]

As a state senator, Metcalf's presence on the leadership roster of Redeem
Our Country lent important legitimacy to the group, which was riddled with
bigots and Christian Identity believers. According to Jim Townsend, the group's
founder, the sinister forces behind the Fed were "foreigners . . . all eight of them,
[who] have their fingers in just about every large financial deal in the nation. We,
The People, are only pawns in their game." Townsend's fictional list of Fed
"owners" included "the Rothschilds of London and Berlin . . . Lazares Brothers
of Paris . . . Israel Moses Seaf [*sic*] of Italy . . . Kuhn Loeb and Company of Germany and New York . . . Warburg and Company of Hamburg, Germany." [22]

Although he was called "a kook" by the majority leader of the Washington

State Senate, Metcalf shepherded an anti-Fed resolution through the National Conference of State Legislatures, authored at least seven pieces of state legislation attacking the Fed, and convinced the Washington State legislature to authorize a 1987 voter referendum on whether or not the state should sue the Federal Reserve.[23] Metcalf also wooed the powerful Washington State Building and Construction Trades Council to promote this effort. Referendum 41 failed at the polls, but not before winning 36 percent of the vote.[24] Metcalf also traveled frequently to meet with fellow legislators in other states to encourage them to introduce similar bills of their own attacking the Fed.

When Metcalf stumped across the Midwest in 1985 on behalf of Redeem Our Country and his own group, Honest Money for America, his meetings were organized by men like Fred Carpenter, the chairman of the Populist Party of South Dakota. The deceptively named Populists were actually an amalgam of rightists, Klansmen, racists, and neo-Nazis created by Willis Carto and the Liberty Lobby. But in addition to its race-driven politics, the group had a platform and the ability to attract the interest of some farmers. And like many marginal third-party efforts, its goal was less about winning votes than about selling its ideas. The group made a good audience for Metcalf and he, in turn, lent credibility to their beliefs.[25] His 1985 four-day, three-state speaking tour filled meeting halls with hundreds of farmers. The gatherings were well publicized and Metcalf and his audiences delighted in the media attention that magnified their message.[26] Some of his forays into the Farm Belt were a bit more clandestine, however. Addressing one group in September 1984, Metcalf cautioned supporters to camouflage their rhetoric:

"I'm going to give you a little lesson in practical politics. And I really think we in this movement should think about this. . . . If you talk about a conspiracy coming to Congress—and we all know it was a conspiracy . . . the average person is going to turn that off. He's heard it, he doesn't really know if he believes it or not, but you're going to turn him off."[27] Metcalf's advice was not very profound, but he chose an important venue to deliver it: the Heritage Library of Lawrence Lewis Humphreys Jr., a multimillionaire and right-wing paramilitary enthusiast from southwestern Oklahoma.

36

THE DEADFALL LINE

Larry Humphreys inherited millions of dollars in cash, property, and oil wells while still a teenager when his father—a wealthy Oklahoma banker and oilman—died in 1970. Sent to a New Jersey prep school after he dabbled in drugs, Humphreys then dropped out of the University of Oklahoma and ran a bar in Vail, Colorado, before returning to Texas. It was in Houston in the late 1970s that he first read about the Illuminati-Freemason plot to control the world and adopted Christian Identity as his religion. Humphreys soon moved to his family's 300-acre ranch outside Velma where he created the Heritage Library as a "research center dedicated to the preservation of our Christian Heritage and Constitutional Republic [and] document[ing] that the Anglo-Saxon, Celtic, Germanic, and kindred peoples trace their ancestry through the Caucasus mountain area back to the captivities and migrations of Israel in the seventh century B.C."[1]

The 7,000-square-foot circular building, constructed in 1983, resembled a small town library, but its 25,000 books on Anglo-Israelism, pyramidology, and other esoteric topics were far more controversial.[2] The library also reportedly contained the books and papers of the World War II–era fascist Ralph W. Townsend. Senator Joe McCarthy's former secretary worked on the library staff, and the group's trustees included two prominent right-wingers: the tax-protesting patriarch A. J. Porth, and Donald Gayman, brother of the Missouri Identity minister, Daniel Gayman.[3]

An ardent fan of Jack Metcalf, Humphreys sent letters to all fifty governors in December 1985 urging them to contact the Washington state senator to discuss the adoption of "a uniform state currency" in preparation for "the generally predicted banking collapse or debt repudiation."[4] Humphreys also was a tax resister and by 1984 he owed $200,000 in unpaid taxes and other debts and was ready to put his Posse beliefs into action.[5] After racking up ten speeding convictions over two years—and getting his driver's license suspended—he announced he was "a private, natural person, without a franchise from any state," and mailed a notarized statement to the county courthouse that read: "I hereby cancel, revoke, rescind, and otherwise render null and void for any and all purposes, any and all applications for a drivers' [sic] license and any and all licenses subsequently issued to me." Humphreys made more than twenty thousand copies of the document and distributed it as a flyer.[6] Not long after he declared his sovereign right to travel, Humphreys was stopped by a Velma police officer for driving without a license plate (he had put an American flag in its place). Tried by a jury of his peers, he was convicted of five misdemeanors, sentenced to thirty days in jail, and fined $850. His thirty-one-page appeal did not impress the judge, who reminded the youthful multimillionaire that "the operation of a motor vehicle on a public highway 'is not an absolute right.' "[7] Frustrated by the judicial system and angered by his encounters with the law, Humphreys made a videotape explaining his beliefs and mailed it unsolicited to several hundred rural and right-wing activists. Among those who received a copy was Tommy Kersey, the onetime American Agriculture Movement leader from Unadilla, Georgia.[8] Kersey had recently launched his own organization with a cryptic acronym: the National Farm Products Minimum Pricing Union, or NFPMPU. Flush with cash from the sale of his 5,000-acre farm, he had big plans to reinvigorate the farm protest movement.[9] Grandiose in his rhetoric and in his intentions, Kersey said he would sign up one hundred thousand farmers in twenty states by the end of 1985. But Kersey had soured on legislative answers to farmers' plight and the best he could come up with was a rehash of the old AAM 50 percent "no-plant" scheme—with a twist. He told farmers to plant half their crops and use the savings to buy commodities futures on the Chicago Board of Trade. On the one hand the plan accurately reflected farmers' reality: If the cost of producing a crop far exceeded the price a farmer received, it didn't make much sense to operate at a loss. Why not plant less and invest the savings, like other speculators who seemed to be getting rich playing the markets? And besides, if enough farmers did the same thing and produced less, prices were sure to go up. Despite a certain attractive, easy logic, Kersey's plan was destined to fail. Farmers were shrewdly attuned to commodities markets and were not going to transform themselves into grain traders overnight. And it was impossible to convince even a small number of them to voluntarily cut production in exchange for speculative returns.[10]

While Kersey pushed his plan, progressive farm groups were mounting a large-scale lobbying effort to pass the Farm Policy Reform Act—a liberal overhaul of national farm policy—on Capitol Hill. Unfortunately, it never even came close to winning approval in Washington. During the winter of 1985, progressive groups like Minnesota Groundswell drew fourteen thousand protesters to the state capitol in St. Paul and the Iowa Farm Unity Coalition helped attract an equal number to a national rally in Ames. But fewer than fifty farmers joined Kersey when he called for a rally in Atlanta that February.[11]

Kersey disliked groups like PrairieFire, whom he called "squeamish" for ruling out violence, but he still followed their lead by organizing several "singsong" foreclosure protests (as he disdainfully called them) of his own.[12] With the farm crisis mounting, Kersey was becoming even more eager to insert himself on the stage of rural protest. Always the swaggering showman, he invited Larry Humphreys to help lead a paramilitary show of force in Georgia.

On November 15, 1985, the two men organized several dozen heavily armed supporters to prevent the eviction of Oscar Lorick, a farmer in Bleckley County, Georgia. They draped a huge American flag over the garage of Lorick's modest brick ranch home, daubed LIVE FREE OR DIE on a farm silo, and hung a banner from the front porch proclaiming, OSCAR STAYS, BANKS GO! Other signs denounced ZOG, and the Federal Reserve.[13] "This country is in trouble because of the Federal Reserve system and the bank fraud it perpetrates," explained a neighboring farmer, who brandished a revolver and a semiautomatic rifle. "Sooner or later they're going to come after the rest of us."[14]

Armed with an arsenal, Lorick's supporters divided themselves into two groups: one barricaded the property with hay bales while the other waited on a nearby farm as backup.[15] To quash any doubts about their commitment to violence, the men used the hay bales for target practice and let loose a barrage of bullets into the nearby woods.[16] Wielding a Heckler & Koch 91 semiautomatic rifle, and equipped with a gas mask, one of Humphreys's three Oklahoma compatriots gestured toward a length of string linking the hay-bale perimeter. "This is the deadfall line. They ain't coming across it," declared Doug Giesbracht, a gunsmith.[17] Giesbracht had chosen his weapons wisely. His HK-91 was modeled after a fully automatic military weapon and came with a flash suppressor, collapsible stock, pistol grip, and a twenty-round magazine. The rifle was menacing enough to fall under a federal assault-weapons ban several years later. Giesbracht also was a self-proclaimed Christian Patriot, and he didn't hesitate when asked to list his grievances and demands, none of which had anything to do with higher farm prices: abolition of the Federal Reserve; direct coinage of money by Congress; an end to the "unconstitutional tax on wages"; stopping foreign aid "to communist or anti-American governments"; cancellation of debts; and withdrawal from the "pro-communist" United Nations.[18]

The local sheriff believed Kersey's strategy was to provoke a "Kent State" incident that would catapult him into public view. It was a potential death trap

the sheriff wisely decided to avoid. Arriving unarmed, the sheriff calmly negotiated a temporary truce to give Lorick time to file a lawsuit to stop the eviction.[19]
The Lorick standoff closely followed the script laid down by Posse activists a
decade earlier in Stockton, California, and during the Oregon potato-shed incident that followed: a gang of armed men inside a fortified perimeter asserting
their version of private-property rights while staring down the barrel of a gun.
But the Kersey-Humphreys group was far larger and the arms they mustered
were far more lethal than anything the Posse had previously assembled. It was a
truly massive show of force.

Lorick, sixty-six, was a well-chosen candidate for this particular media circus.
Two months earlier, he had been one of five struggling farmers featured in *People*
magazine. Heavyset, jowly, and soft-spoken, Lorick had the quiet disposition of
a hapless victim. He also was hardworking, and black. Lorick began farming with
a mule at the age of five after his father died. His family had once owned 2,000
acres, but like most black landowners in the South (and elsewhere), those hold-
ings had been whittled away to nearly nothing. All that remained was Lorick's
79-acre vegetable tract (which had been in his family since the Civil War), and
his home, both of which the bank already had purchased at a foreclosure sale for
$20,000 less than the $112,000 he owed.[20] "Don't know what I borrowed or what
the bank did, either. I couldn't read the papers," the illiterate father of five told
reporters matter-of-factly. "Folks have done me unfair."[21]

The event won Humphreys and Kersey front-page publicity, and led to a
series of bizarre events that ultimately helped Lorick save his farm. At first a
Miami woman who said she read about the protest in the newspaper announced
that she and her husband would buy the property for $75,000 and lease it back
to Lorick for $1 a month. But the deal fell through after her husband was arrested
on unrelated charges of check forgery and theft.[22] Days later, a mysterious Atlanta
man wearing a ski mask and identifying himself only as "A. N. American," announced he would come up with $100,000. "Personally, I'm nobody. . . . But if I
can be known as 'A. N. American,' I can represent anybody," he explained. It
smelled like a hoax, but unlike the false hope offered by the Florida couple, the
relief promised by the anonymous benefactor was real: he gave Lorick an $8,000
Rolex watch, plunked down $7,500 to buy the farm, and agreed to pay the re-
maining $67,500 within sixty days. The Good Samaritan turned out to be an
established businessman, Frank Argenbright, the owner of the national security
company of the same name, and the president of the American Polygraph Association. (Argenbright's company came in for criticism decades later, after the
terrorist attacks on September 11, 2001, focused national attention on the poor
training and low pay received by airport security workers such as those Argenbright employed.)

"It doesn't make sense when you have a commodity as valuable as food and
people can't make a living growing it," Argenbright explained. Lorick's land was

saved, but he soon abandoned farming anyway. Then tragedy struck a half a dozen years later when two of his sons drowned in a boating accident.[23]

Predictably, the media focused on the Humphreys-Kersey gunplay and the drama of mysterious benefactors coming to the rescue, but it overlooked the important role played by African-Americans who also helped Lorick save his farm. The NAACP hired Lorick's attorney, who handled all the negotiations with the bank, and Lorick received important advice from the Federation of Southern Cooperatives, a preeminent organization of black farmers.[24] Kersey said his choice to defend Lorick had nothing to do with race, because "this is a problem that affects everybody," but the move shrewdly insulated him from criticism that he was a bigot, and provided much-needed cover for the caustic racism of Humphreys's Christian Identity views. According to Humphreys, segregation was biblically ordained, Jews were "a rod of chastisement" used by God to punish Christians for disobeying divine law, and Native Americans should be "repatriated" to Israel because they were descendants of "Hebrew Phoenecian peoples."[25]

Oscar Lorick commended Humphreys and Kersey for stopping his eviction. However, being illiterate, he could not read Humphreys's newsletter, which stated that white workers were treated worse than blacks had been under slavery. Nor was he aware of Kersey's stand toward the Ku Klux Klan. "I never been a member but I got no problem with them," said Kersey, adding, "I knew Gordon Kahl, talked to him many times. He was set up. . . . The media is trying to slant public opinion against these people. What they really stand for is protecting us from an oppressive government," said Kersey, who kept a small flag and handwritten note bearing Kahl's name pinned to a wall map of the United States in his office.[26]

Thrilled by their newfound fame, Humphreys and Kersey were eager to re-create the Lorick standoff at the epicenter of the farm crisis, in the Midwest. "I want to pick the right spot, get it lined up, and bring in enough men to throw the county into a state of insurgency," Humphreys explained, claiming that SWAT teams are "scared to death of the idea of twenty-five or thirty [men] holding a place . . ." Kersey agreed. What he wanted was a "show of force. . . . Not singsongs and all that stuff, but whatever it takes."[27]

In January 1986 the men brought their message of "Christian economics" and armed resistance to the Farm Belt. "A lot of organizations . . . draw a line before they start," Kersey told farmers in Northeast Iowa. "[But] when you tell a person how far you are willing to go, that's just like playing football and telling the man you'll never cross the five-yard line."[28] When challenged about the potentially deadly consequences of the Georgia standoff, Humphreys turned the question on its head and asserted that he had *saved* Lorick's life, because without his help, Lorick would have gotten killed trying to stop the eviction.[29] Furthering this twisted logic, Humphreys cited the law of posse comitatus to justify his actions. "The common-law rule to 'come out bearing arms at the hue and cry of a neighbor in distress' was being applied [in Georgia]," he said. Of course,

Humphreys overlooked the fact that it was the job of the sheriff—not the citizens—to empower a posse.[30]

In preparation for their January 1986 Midwest tour, Humphreys was interviewed by the *Spotlight*. "What we see today is nothing more than a rerun of the age-old struggle between the moneylenders and their Bolshevik allies and the family farmers in communist Russia," he explained. "If this doesn't work, we're going to see armed resistance on a grand scale, all across the land."[31] Beginning in southern Minnesota, Kersey and Humphreys held eight meetings over several days that drew one thousand enthusiastic farmers.[32]

Dressed in camouflage fatigues, with guns bulging under their jackets, Humphreys's men patrolled the halls while he railed about the need for a "land sabbath" to forgive farmers' debts and warned—in a reference to Gordon Kahl and Arthur Kirk—that police and sheriff's deputies planned to "kill people off their land."[33] Kersey was advertised as the "number one national farm leader," and he gave instructions on filing land patents and how to use Tupper Saussy's phony certificates to pay off debts. Loans are created out of "thin air," Kersey told farmers, "So pay 'em back with credit." When lenders return the public office money certificate "not knowing what to do with it, stamp it 'PAID' and send it back again. Just like they do," he chuckled.[34] This was standard Posse fare, but a more elaborate sales pitch was given by a Kersey associate and former Baptist minister from Macon, Georgia.[35] Denouncing "bankster gangsters," the Reverend Paul Davis advised farmers to pay him $750 so they could deed their property to an offshore trust that he would then "manage" for a fee. Davis also promised to file a common-law lien against the farmer's property, clouding the title and hopefully complicating the anticipated foreclosure. Kersey praised Davis as "the only preacher I know with guts enough to stand with farmers who have taken up arms," and his endorsement helped Davis bring in hundreds of thousands of dollars during this Midwest tour. The minister was bold to conduct such a brisk business, considering he had been indicted seven months earlier by a federal grand jury in North Carolina for similar activities. Midwestern authorities were unaware of those pending charges, but after hearing Davis's pitch they quickly obtained injunctions barring him from promoting the scheme in their states. Later that year, after the evangelist was convicted on multiple counts of fraud and helping others to commit tax evasion, Kersey claimed that he, too, had been duped.[36] "I take part of the blame," he confessed to farmers back in Georgia. "If you can't believe a Baptist preacher, who can you believe?" he whined.[37]

Unlike earlier right-wing forays into the Farm Belt, the 1986 Humphreys-Kersey tour met with significant opposition. Led by PraireFire and the Center for Democratic Renewal, a growing number of farm, rural, and religious groups went on the offensive. The results were not immediate, but PrairieFire's campaign marked the beginning of the end of Posse influence in the Farm Belt. Prior to 1986 only a handful of liberal organizations had issued public statements denouncing anti-Semitism and the rural radical right.³⁸ But the large audiences attracted by the Humphreys-Kersey tour prompted more groups to step forward.

"The [National Conference of Christians and Jews] will oppose any group that fosters and builds hatred and distrust within a community and within our society," announced the NCCJ.³⁹ Half a dozen Iowa religious leaders chimed in, declaring their opposition to "anti-Semitism, racism, and violence as explanations and as solutions [to the rural crisis]."⁴⁰

Public statements denouncing right-wing tactics and rhetoric had impact, but PrairieFire preferred to more directly challenge the organizing efforts of the rural radical right. It had done this with Rick Elliott, disseminating information about his criminal record and anti-Semitic statements to journalists, sending farmers to his meetings to pose as willing dupes to gather information, and organizing grassroots opposition whenever the National Agricultural Press Association medicine show rolled into town. These activities stigmatized Elliott and severely undermined his organizing efforts, while all the negative publicity encouraged authorities to pursue legal action against him. Steady leaks from infiltrators and disgruntled former supporters also eroded Elliott's confidence, and further obstructed NAPA recruitment.

PrairieFire applied the same strategy to Kersey and Humphreys, and when the two men arrived in Iowa they received a chilly welcome. Unable to find a place to meet in Sioux City, they were forced to move the event to nearby Cherokee County only to find their audience of two hundred people shut out of the local community center in the bitter cold.⁴¹ One small-town paper criticized the lockout, but most of the media, including Iowa's flagship daily, the *Des Moines Register*, waved them off. "So we say to you, Tommy Kersey . . . we don't want your brand of armed radicalism in Iowa," the *Register* declared.⁴² PrairieFire also enlisted the help of prosecutors and law enforcement to expose the bogus nature of the remedies that Kersey and Humphreys proposed. In Jamestown, North Dakota, the men were boldly confronted by Sarah Vogel, an assistant state attorney general, who denounced common-law tactics as self-defeating and worse. She had good reason to know. Just two years earlier, Vogel and a team of lawyers had won a major class-action lawsuit against the Farmers Home Administration, halting tens of thousands of government foreclosures, but not before some of her clients went astray and paid money to right-wing hucksters. Ignoring her advice, some lost their farms. Humphreys called her "an agent of Satan."⁴³

The Humphreys-Kersey tour culminated on January 25, when several hundred farmers and right-wing enthusiasts braved 35-mph winds to huddle in a dimly lit, freezing metal storage shed two miles north of Kearney, Nebraska. There they heard speeches exhorting them to Christian Patriot resistance. "Christ told us he didn't come to bring peace, but to bring us a sword," Humphreys told the crowd in one of his oft-repeated refrains.⁴⁴ Dubbed the "Farm and Urban Economic Crisis Convention," the meeting was advertised as having the "tentative sponsorship" of the local chamber of commerce, but the opposite was true. A group of local ministers denounced the gathering and the Nebraska Conference of the United Methodist Church took out a large ad in the Kearney newspaper, criticizing "the extremist philosophies and actions of those individuals and organizations that promote violence, anti-Semitism, sexism, or racism as responses to the Rural Crisis."[45] Then Humphreys's group was booted from its reservation at the local Holiday Inn because of "security concerns."[46]

Forced to relocate to the outskirts of town, the participants heard from Christian Patriots, Identity proselytizers, and Posse "pro se" advocates. Also on the agenda was Ernie Chambers, the black Nebraska state senator who had championed the cause of Arthur Kirk. Calling the Cairo farmer's death "a setup from the beginning," Chambers provided the right-wing gathering with much-needed political cover from charges of racism.[47]

The first to speak was Richard Kelly Hoskins, a self-styled investment adviser from Virginia, and the author of *War Cycles Peace Cycles* and other conspiratorial tracts. Hoskins's book was a cheaply typeset, self-published work that called the Holocaust a hoax, said the Jews were a counterfeit race, and purported to explain the racial roots of usury. Hoskins had a decades-long, hate-filled pedigree (he wrote *Our Nordic Race* as early as 1958), and when he took the stage in Kearney he fed his audience of eager farmers from the standard menu of "international banking conspiracy" fare.[48] Hoskins also informed them that integration was "illegal" and that the end of white rule in Rhodesia/Zimbabwe was "against God's law."[49]

Unfazed, Senator Chambers followed Hoskins to the podium. Chambers was a frequent critic of police misconduct and his affinity for antiestablishment politics already had led him to share the platform with professional anti-Semites like Rick Elliott and others. Now he was getting deeper into the Posse and he relished defending his actions. "I've been told that some of the people out here are anti-Semitic, anti-black, and so forth," he said. "We have to look past all those convenient labels and slogans and look at the fact that some people in this state are facing desperate circumstances."[50] When questioned by the media about Hoskins's racist remarks, Chambers said they were no worse than the actions of teachers who opposed divestment of Omaha School District funds from companies that did business in South Africa.[51] And Chambers received some of the most vigorous applause of the day for his condemnation of the shooting of Arthur Kirk. "Violence is as American as cherry pie," he told the all-white audience, affirming Kirk's right to defend his farm with a gun.[52] Chambers's interest in the Posse wasn't just a passing phase. Two months after the Kearney meeting, he addressed one hundred supporters of the Iowa Society for Educated Citizens; an amalgam of Aryan Nations enthusiasts, broke farmers, and militant tax strikers. The speaker the previous month had been Delores Kirk.[53]

One of the last to take the stage at Kearney was George Gordon. The Missouri "barrister" got the attention of his audience by calling them "practicing communists" while he extolled the virtues of Christian Common Law. It was quintessential Gordon—part folksy humor, part right-wing diatribe, part self-promotional con—right down to his mismatched tie and pinstripe shirt. Also addressing the crowd was Everett Sileven, a Baptist minister and Nebraska gubernatorial candidate. Sileven's long-running battle with state authorities over his unaccredited Christian school had landed him in jail, won the support of Moral Majority leader Reverend Jerry Falwell, and made Sileven a minor celebrity in right-wing circles. Stumping for votes, Sileven promised that if elected governor he would reform the monetary system and make farmers' 160-acre homesteads exempt from foreclosure. He also promised to fire the state troopers who circled the parking lot recording license plate numbers.[54] Sileven placed fourth out of eight candidates in the 1986 GOP primary that spring, winning 4,281 votes, while the successful GOP nominee, Kay Orr, went on to become the nation's first female Republican governor.[55]

Sileven also campaigned out-of-state. One network that helped him was the American Coalition of Unregistered Churches, a loose-knit group of preachers who refused to comply with state licensing requirements. Like the Posse "citizens' grand juries" of the 1970s, Sileven and his cohorts convened a "Court of Divine Justice" to come to the aid of pastors who insisted on defying state authorities. Writing in the *Justice Times*, Sileven recounted the results of one session held to support a pastor in Texas who had refused to license his boys' home:

"In less than forty-eight hours . . . Fort Worth was hit with the largest tornado ever in the history of the city. A few days later the sheriff was riding a horse that bucked him up in the air and he came down on the saddle horn, injuring him severely. . . . Another victory for the Lord!" Nebraska's would-be governor proclaimed.[56] After losing the GOP primary, Sileven stayed on the national circuit. On one visit to Iowa he told Christian Patriots that "sodomists should be executed," the Christian right "has a duty to protect America from the incursion of Mexicans," and elected officials in Nebraska should be "removed from office."[57]

All of the hubbub surrounding Kearney marked the beginning of a downhill slide for the remnants of the Posse Comitatus and its allies in the rural Christian Patriot movement. Kersey and Humphreys had drawn large and enthusiastic crowds across five states in January 1986, but the several hundred people who turned out in Kearney were far below their expectations.[58] When Kersey visited Iowa several months later, he drew no more than ten people at each of half a dozen stops. Largely gone was his talk of armed resistance, but Kersey's immersion in right-wing politics already had put him far out of touch. A veteran of the "100 percent parity" campaigns of AAM, the issue of farm prices had all but vanished from his agenda. "Monetary reform is the only real solution . . . it's not the price of corn. It's the price of money," he declared.[59] Unfazed, he returned to Georgia and called for a "Great American Money Rally . . . to receive the official opinion of Georgia's attorney general, Mike Bowers, concerning constitutional, congressional, and state government accountability for the U.S. Federal Reserve banking system through which 'debt' is both generated and resolved."[60] Though Kersey predicted between twelve and fifteen thousand people would show up, fewer than thirty attended, hardly enough to cheer him on. A year later, Kersey, forty-eight, closed his farm-protest office and moved on to selling insurance.[61]

By midsummer 1986, Humphreys's star also was beginning to wane. He filed for Chapter 7 bankruptcy to avert a sheriff's sale and he lost the 265 acres surrounding the Heritage Library to foreclosure the following year. Although Humphreys blustered about making a show of armed resistance if "at least seventy-five men" came to his aid, only a handful of supporters did, and of those, four were stopped on traffic complaints and arrested on weapons charges. To make matters worse, Humphreys faced charges of assault and battery brought by his wife.[62] These troubles didn't prevent the former millionaire from seeking the Republican nomination for Congress that fall. Describing himself as a "student," the clean-cut and boyishly handsome thirty-three-year-old declared his intention to unseat Representative David McCurdy, a popular Democrat. Humphreys campaigned against taxes, attacked the Federal Reserve, renewed his call for a land sabbath, and received 28 percent of the vote in the general election.[63] His showing was comparable to that of other GOP nominees in Oklahoma congressional races who stood no chance of winning, but the fact that nearly thirty thousand people voted for him at all reveals much about the blind loyalty of Republicans in heavily Democratic districts, the ignorance of the Oklahoma electorate, and the right-wing sympathies of at least some of those thirty-thousand voters.[64]

In May 1986, Rick Elliott was convicted by a Colorado jury on fourteen counts of theft and one count of conspiracy and was sentenced to the maximum of eight years in jail (his wife received a deferred sentence in exchange for an earlier plea bargain).[65] Elliott had been represented by a public defender at the trial, but he turned to a fellow anti-Semite for help with his appeal. Newly graduated from the University of Wyoming College of Law, Roger Elletson was the author of a rambling twenty-nine-page tract entitled *Highlights of the Power Parameters of Money*. According to Elletson, Karl Marx was a "talmudic sage"; America was "saturated with debt and racial aliens"; the Russian Revolution was orchestrated by Wall Street; and "the Oppenheimer-Rockefeller-Rothschild cabal" was intent on achieving "the total annihilation of the Aryan race and every vestige of Christian Civilization in South Africa."[66] Elletson's love for the Aryan race notwithstanding, Elliott's conviction was upheld and the Colorado con man was finally sent to prison where he served four years.

The high point for the right wing in 1986 came on March 18, when two LaRouche followers, Mark Fairchild, thirty-one, and Janice Hart, twenty-eight, stunned the Illinois political establishment by winning the Democratic Party nominations for lieutenant governor and secretary of state. Though Party officials painted the upset as a fluke, the Fairchild–Hart victories owed much to the concerted appeals they and other LaRouche candidates had made to blue-collar workers, farmers, and other disenfranchised voters. Campaigning in the state capital, Fairchild had called for a halt to farm foreclosures, a freeze on farm debt, and higher commodity prices so farmers could make "an adequate profit." LaRouche-sponsored candidates did particularly well in downstate Illinois, an area hard-hit by the farm crisis. Illinois was losing more than five thousand farms a year, and congressional estimates predicted the number of farms would shrink 40 percent nationally over the next fifteen years.[67] There was clearly a link between the Fairchild–Hart victory and the plight of rural voters, and this prompted groups like the Illinois American Agriculture Movement (which was not allied with the Grass Roots faction) to express concern:

> The AAM cautions all farmers to be wary of political recruiters for extremist groups who may canvass rural Illinois, inspired by the recent Fairchild–Hart Democratic primary victory. . . . This is not the time to submit to extremism and demagoguery. Rural Illinois' problems will be solved within the mainstream.[68]

Illinois law required candidates for governor and lieutenant governor to run on the same ticket, and the Democratic Party gubernatorial nominee, former U.S. senator Adlai E. Stevenson III, refused to run on the same ballot as Fairchild. Calling LaRouche supporters "neo-Nazis" and "adherents to an extremist philosophy steeped in violence and bigotry," he hastily organized a third party bid but was defeated that November.[69]

"I'm going to revive the spirit of Abraham Lincoln and General Patton. We're going to roll our tanks down State Street," Hart had proclaimed wildly the day after the primary. In spite of this bizarre statement she pulled 478,000 votes in the general election—100,000 *more* than she had won in the primary. Although there would be no tanks rumbling through Chicago, Hart and other LaRouchies had the satisfaction of delivering the Illinois statehouse to the GOP. In addition to putting LaRouche's name on the front page of daily newspapers around the nation, the fiasco heightened awareness about the vulnerability of rural residents to right-wing appeals.[70]

Though media attention focused on Fairchild and Hart, other LaRouche candidates did surprisingly well, including two who ran unopposed (in GOP-dominated districts) and won Democratic nominations for Congress (but were defeated in the general election). One primary winner was William Brenner, an organic farmer and the former president of the Iroquois County National Farmers Organization (NFO). The group advocated collective bargaining as the route to higher prices and was generally thought of as a liberal farm organization; however, unlike AAM, Inc., it had yet to publicly denounce the radical right.

Parroting what he had learned from LaRouche and other right-wingers, NFO's Brenner claimed that the International Monetary Fund and the Federal Reserve were responsible for America's problems. A smattering of other NFO leaders did the same, including the state treasurer of its Missouri chapter."[71]

LaRouche was back in the news later that year, but not to celebrate. In October, a federal grand jury in Boston handed down the first of a series of sweeping indictments charging ten LaRouche activists with fraud and obstruction of justice involving two corporations, three campaign committees, and more than $1 million in unauthorized charges to the credit-card accounts of more than one-thousand people. A subsequent federal indictment issued in Virginia charged LaRouche and others with conspiracy and more than $34 million in loan fraud.

A federal raid on the group's headquarters in Leesburg, Virginia, threw the LaRouche operation into temporary disarray. Unlike other right-wing groups, however, LaRouche's highly disciplined and well-financed organization withstood much of the pressure. LaRouche operatives returned to the Farm Belt in September 1988 with a cleverly packaged organizing drive they called "Food for Peace." The name was chosen because it was easily confused with the U.S. government overseas aid program by the same name. Like previous LaRouche pitches to farmers, this one demanded parity prices, a moratorium on farm foreclosures, extolled the unlimited virtues of technology, and attacked progressive farm groups. According to LaRouche, PrairieFire was in league with the Anti-Defamation League, the Israeli secret police, and the Soviet KGB as part of a "vast gang-countergang scenario . . . with the purpose of turning small numbers of economically distraught farmers into 'suicide terrorists' patterned on Gordon Kahl and Arthur Kirk."[72] Adding further detail to these delusions, LaRouche said progressive farm groups were controlled by an international oligarchy operated by Benedictine monks headquartered in Collegeville, Minnesota.

As many as four hundred people from thirty states and ten countries came to Chicago to applaud Food for Peace, and local meetings were held in fifteen states and Canada that fall. The effort finally stalled after LaRouche and six aides were convicted of conspiracy and loan fraud in December 1988.[73] Farm issues remained high on the LaRouche agenda during the five years he spent in federal prison from 1989 to January 1994, but he never duplicated his success of the late 1970s or the mid-1980s.[74]

Farmers had always paid a price for embracing the radical right, and by the late 1980s the costs of doing so were becoming much more apparent. PrairieFire and its network of supporters worked hard to highlight this fact, emphasizing the practical as well as the moral, ethical, and legal liabilities of becoming involved with both the hard Posse and its softer variants in the Christian Patriot movement. PrairieFire did this, in part, by helping orchestrate denunciations of the movement and by regularly supplying the media with the inside information it needed to publish exposés about the radical right. The resulting bad press both dampened Christian Patriot morale and encouraged more aggressive prosecutions, thereby further depressing recruitment. And in place of bigotry and agricultural fundamentalism, PrairieFire and other farm groups emphasized the importance of building coalitions with city dwellers, blacks, Jews, and others in support of political demands for farm relief. It was a sound strategy, but it was not enough to deflect the economic juggernaut bearing down on rural America.

37

FARMERS ABANDONED

In October 1986, Jewish groups and farm organizations announced a nationwide petition drive calling for a moratorium on farm foreclosures, "fair prices for farm products that cover the cost of production," and emergency assistance for farm and rural families. "We in the farm community are proud to stand arm-in-arm with the Jewish community," announced American Agriculture Movement executive director David Senter at a press conference in New York. A leader and veteran of the battle to keep LaRouche followers and the Posse out of the ranks of AAM, Senter understood the importance of standing publicly with Jewish groups. Speaking alongside him at the Manhattan headquarters of the Union of American Hebrew Congregations was David Goldstein, the director of the Kansas City Jewish Community Relations Bureau. The petition drive had grown out of Goldstein's efforts to bring Jews and farmers together to fight both anti-Semitism and farm foreclosures.[1] "For the security of the Jewish community, we felt it necessary to combat this flaring-up of anti-Semitism," Goldstein explained. "And in keeping with our religious tradition and social values, we determined that we must come to the aid of our rural brothers."[2] Inspired by his words and his example, other Jewish groups took similar steps, but not the Anti-Defamation League, which still insisted on downplaying both the rural crisis and threat of the radical right.

While Jewish organizations reached out to farmers, so, too, did the Reverend

Jesse Jackson, who emphasized the importance of white farmers and urban blacks joining together in pursuit of their mutual interests. On April 6, 1986, Jackson rallied with hundreds of farmers in Chillicothe, Missouri, to protest Reagan administration farm policies. "To see us seated at this table represents the answer to many prayers and much prophecy," said Jackson, whose Midwestern farm protest appearances were an integral part of his strategy to seek the 1988 Democratic presidential nomination. In contrast to the Posse-oriented audiences Jackson had addressed in Kansas two years earlier, the farmers who gathered in Chillicothe in 1986 had more progressive politics. "I wouldn't have been here ten years ago," admitted farmer David Arensberg. "But then, I wouldn't have marched on Selma, either. Today I'd be tickled to death to do something like that," he offered. "Jesse Jackson speaks the farmer's language because we've become the new poor," added Arensberg's wife Roberta.[3]

Led by David Goldstein, Jews from Kansas City traveled to Chillicothe, too. Their presence outside the Farmers Home Administration office that summer (Jews made up the majority of the one hundred protesters) was an impressive show of solidarity. "[We are both] minorities who suffer and deal with the pain of being misunderstood. . . . We need each other. We need to be friends. And we need to work into a coalition," Goldstein declared.[4]

Protests like these did not bring about the comprehensive federal relief that farmers truly needed, but they made headlines and exerted pressure on politicians—especially those who already felt they were on shaky ground. In Iowa the collapsing rural economy had delivered the state legislature to the Democrats in 1982, and President Reagan barely carried the state two years later, despite his national landslide. And in 1984, Iowans sent Tom Harkin, a liberal Democrat, to the U.S. Senate.[5] In October 1985, the Iowa Farm Unity Coalition forced Governor Terry Branstad, a conservative Republican, to declare a statewide economic emergency, triggering a limited moratorium on farm foreclosures. The proclamation was a sweet political victory for activists who had worked for three years to force the governor's hand, and it had the added benefit of discrediting those pundits who claimed that only "poor managers" were being driven out of agriculture.

In addition to pressuring politicians, liberal farm groups continued their direct-action campaign to stop farm foreclosures. The presence of burly (but nonviolent) union members made such penny-auction protests particularly successful and attractive to the media. With agricultural-implement manufacturing hard-hit by massive layoffs, members of the United Auto Workers Union were among farmers' strongest allies. Farm leaders helped cement farmer–labor ties, organizing food drives for union members, recruiting farmers to walk picket lines, and persuading farmers to support union-backed political candidates. The effect of this cooperation was both concrete and symbolic. After four hundred Iowa activists attended a March 1986 "farm-labor-citizen" lobby day, they won new state laws requiring mandatory mediation and the separate sale of farm homesteads as part of the foreclosure process, and funding for free legal aid to help struggling farmers fight creditors. Subsequent lobbying expanded farmers' rights to buy back their lost homesteads at fair market value (regardless of their actual debt); placed stricter limits on the amount of land certain kinds of corporations could own; and ensured continued funding for mediation and legal services. Although the latter programs were desperately underfunded, they saved countless farms and served as a powerful antidote to the lure of right-wing hucksters. Farmers also won additional relief at the federal level with the adoption, in 1986, of a novel bankruptcy provision for farmers. The new Chapter 12 filing was less complicated and costly than other forms of bankruptcy, and thousands of farmers immediately took advantage of it. The response was so enthusiastic— and economic conditions so grim—that Congress had to find $34 million just five months after the law went into effect, to fund fifty-two new federal judgeships.[6] But farmers were less interested in going bankrupt than they were in getting paid fairly for their products. So they and other disaffected rural voters flexed their political muscle and helped return the U.S. Senate to the Democratic Party in 1986, ending six years of GOP rule.[7] The following year, farmer advocates and their lawyers pushed through the Farm Credit Act of 1987 and secured strong protections and new rights for Farmers Home Administration borrowers. Other gains came through the courts.

In May 1987, lawyers with the Minnesota-based Farmers Legal Action Group won a far-reaching federal court injunction stopping all government foreclosures. With about one-third of all FmHA borrowers behind in their payments, and two thousand in actual foreclosure, the injunction was nothing short of a miracle. These gains stood in sharp contrast to the steady stream of legal setbacks that plagued the rural radical right. By 1987, land patents had been ruled useless in five Midwestern states and con men like Conrad LeBeau were announcing their departure from the movement.[8]

"After being in the forefront of the battle for honest money for several years . . . I have concluded that none of the existing avenues being pursued by any or all of the many sincere leaders has little more than a ghost of a chance at success," wrote LeBeau with bitter disappointment. "The public is so preoccupied in its struggle for survival that it cannot see its own way out of this debt-usury jungle."[9] A December 1987 article in the *New York Times* contributed to LeBeau's frustration. Headlined "Economics, Hate, and the Farm Crisis," the article described LeBeau's seminars as part of a larger movement of right-wing and anti-Semitic groups, including the Aryan Nations.[10]

"The article contained mostly inaccurate quotes and libelous statements. What else should one expect from a banker-owned publication?" the former carpenter complained.[11] LeBeau was disillusioned by the movement and troubled by bad press, but the driving force behind his departure was financial. After seven years of selling farmers false hope, his strategies had been debunked and not enough people were buying. Faced with a dwindling subscriber base and increasing criticism, he departed the scene.[12] Though he returned to selling unproven remedies ("perfect stool health" being yet another of his peculiar obsessions) the government eventually won a permanent injunction barring him from marketing half a dozen products that he claimed were treatments for cancer, AIDS, emphysema, diabetes, multiple sclerosis, parkinsonism, Alzheimer's, and arthritis.[13]

By the late 1980s, farmers may have had to worry less about getting duped by men like LeBeau, but they still remained under enormous financial strain. Nearly 200,000 out of 1.5 million farms surveyed in January 1986 were "very highly leveraged" with debt-to-asset ratios greater than 70 percent.[14] (Estimates varied, but a farm was being lost every four to seven minutes across the nation.)[15] And the Farm Credit System (FCS), which held about 25 percent of the $176.3 billion in farm debt, was hemorrhaging $1 billion to $2 billion per year. Approximately one-quarter million FCS borrowers already had been eliminated, leaving the system holding some 2.2 million acres of land valued at nearly $1 billion. Adding insult to injury, much of the property was sold to investors at a fraction of its original price.[16] The Farmers Home Administration (FmHA) and its borrowers were no better off—the agency was left holding properties valued at $833 million, representing an area larger than Rhode Island. Farm losses also had a devastating effect on rural communities. Sales of tractors and harvesting combines were 57 percent lower in 1987 than they had been three years earlier and UAW members still were reeling from massive layoffs.[17]

Farmers used to joke that they were "land rich and cash poor," but plummeting real-estate values depleted them on both fronts, making it even harder to borrow the seasonal loans they needed to plant their crops. This burden fell especially hard on FmHA borrowers, 85 percent of whom were highly leveraged and had nowhere to turn. Denying credit for spring planting was tantamount to an economic death warrant, but that didn't stop the Reagan administration from shutting down "the lender of last resort," as FmHA was known. Seven hundred million dollars were slashed from the $2 billion originally budgeted for farm-operating loans in 1987. This decision had both an economic and a human cost—the latter most commonly represented by an increase in farm suicides and marital strife.[18] Millions of Americans unfamiliar with rural life had seen these phenomena vividly brought to life several years earlier in the feature film *Country*, starring Jessica Lange and Sam Shepard. The movie was about the impact of the farm crisis on an Iowa family and revealed the stark indignity of foreclosure and the callousness with which government loan officers forced farmers off the land. The final scene of the movie was of a successful penny auction and the film ended with a real-life postscript informing audiences that a federal class-action lawsuit had temporarily halted all government foreclosures. But despite the promise of hope offered by the judge's ruling (in both real life and the film's conclusion), the decision did not remain in place forever and farmers still couldn't get a decent price for their product. Bankruptcy and foreclosure continued to swallow families whole, even as activists pressed harder for relief.

As the farm crisis intensified and protests generated headlines, more money flowed to groups like the newly formed National Family Farm Coalition, in Washington D.C., that coordinated most of the lobbying for federal relief. About eighty thousand people had attended the first Farm Aid Concert in 1985, raising more than $7 million. Future concerts organized by the musician Willie Nelson brought in millions more. Groups like PrairieFire and the Iowa Farm Unity Coalition used their share of the proceeds to fund hotlines and send farmers to Washington to lobby for the 1987 Farm Policy Reform Act, a bill sponsored jointly by Representative Richard Gephardt (D-Missouri) and Iowa senator Tom Harkin. And once again, representatives of the liberal segment of the Jewish community endorsed farmers' call for justice. In March, Rabbi David Saperstein, director of the Religious Action Center for the Union of American Hebrew Congregations, testified before the House Agriculture Committee and endorsed the Harkin–Gephardt bill. Limiting production and increasing prices paid to farmers was "the fairest and best way to raise net income . . . allowing most family farmers to remain on the land and to begin to repay their stagger-ing debts," said Saperstein, speaking on behalf of eight hundred Reform Jewish congregations and their 1.2 million members.[19] The push for Harkin–Gephardt infuriated right-leaning ideologues like Charles Walters Jr., publisher of *Acres U.S.A.*, who called the bill "worthless legislation" and lambasted Willie Nelson for funding groups whose "real" purpose was to "[stage] an ineffective fight for the family farm [and] to keep under-the-gun farmers from becoming too rest-less," instead of telling them "how to fight back judicial tyranny [*sic*]."[20] Walters railed against the Harkin–Gephardt bill because it promised only 70 percent parity, but any legislation that aimed to set commodity prices even close to cost-of-production levels was virtually doomed from the start. And so, too, was the Harkin–Gephardt bill.

By 1988 the National Family Farm Coalition had nearly doubled, to forty-six groups in thirty-two states. And according to the *New York Times*, the "150 small activist groups across fifty states," that made up the progressive farm move-ment were the contemporary "heirs of the agrarian populist movement." Like their nineteenth-century forebears, these groups also sought to influence who might be president. During the 1988 Democratic primaries, liberal farm activists strategically fanned out within the campaigns of all the Democratic contenders. Ultimately, and unfortunately, they were forced to pin their hopes on the party's nominee, Michael Dukakis, the governor of Massachusetts who delivered an ex-ceptionally dismal performance in the general election. George Herbert Walker Bush's victory extinguished any hope for federal relief, and the free market–oriented farm bill adopted by Congress two years later spurred yet another round of low prices and farm losses.

But even before Bush's 1988 victory, farmers and their supporters had be-come financially and psychologically drained. Foreclosures and bankruptcy had removed many committed leaders and left fewer foot soldiers at the front lines.

Farms and marriages failed, activists moved on or decided to hunker down and work "harder" to get out of debt, though this approach rarely worked. And some leaders who were indispensable to the movement were tragically killed in farm accidents, like Dixon Terry, who was struck by lightning in the spring of 1989 while putting up hay on his farm. His death, and those of others, left a huge void. By the end of the 1980s, financial support from liberal foundations and other funding sources (including Farm Aid) was drying up, as more headlines declared that the farm crisis was finally "over." It wasn't, but with so many farmers already driven out of agriculture there were fewer foreclosures and bankruptcies to report. Hundreds of thousands of Midwesterners had fled the region, including 140,000 Iowans who left the state during the 1980s. Rural population declines continued into the 1990s, as an average of one out of five of the nation's 3,141 counties lost people at a time when the country's overall population grew 13 percent. Heavily agricultural states like Texas, Oklahoma, Iowa, Nebraska, Kansas, Minnesota, and the Dakotas were hardest hit.[21]

PrairieFire had played a major role in quashing right-wing recruitment, and the collective efforts of the progressive farm movement had saved thousands of farms, but this was not enough to overcome the accumulated burden of more than a decade of low prices, high interest rates, and falling land values. Both the progressive farm movement and the Christian Patriot movement collapsed. And they did so, coincidentally, at the same time as the imprisonment and death of Bill Gale.

38

AN ENEMY GOVERNMENT

On October 23, 1986, federal agents seized Bill Gale, sixty-nine, at his ranch outside Mariposa, California. In a ten-count indictment issued in Nevada, he and seven other men were charged with conspiracy, attempting to interfere with federal tax laws, and mailing death threats to the IRS. After initially denying his identity, Gale was hauled to a Las Vegas jail where he spent four months awaiting trial while his health deteriorated from worsening emphysema. The indictment stemmed from Gale's association with the Committee of the States (COS), an organization he had launched in 1982. Like the Posse Comitatus, Gale's Committee was geared toward violence and vigilantism and both groups embraced the bigotry of Identity beliefs. Gale and others harassed tax collectors by mailing death threats called "constructive notices." They targeted a black Nevada judge, Earl White, whom they accused of subverting the Constitution by his rulings in local traffic court. "Let's hang the nigger," one indicted coconspirator had proclaimed.[1] And when Committee members mailed death threats to an IRS supervisor, they emphasized that the "unlawful" income tax was invented by "the son of Jew rabbi [sic] . . . Moses Mordecai Levi, also known as Carl Marx [sic] . . . the author of the *Communist Manifesto*." A copy of the latter document was thoughtfully enclosed. "Communism is the avowed enemy of this Christian Constitutional Republic and any person who supports it is herein declared to be a traitor," committee members proclaimed. To maximize the intimidating effect of their threats, Gale's Nevada patriots sent their notices to the judge's home address, warning that he might face the death penalty for "interfering" with members of the Committee of the States.[2] According to federal prosecutors, the message was clear: "Back off or die."[3]

The origin of Gale's indictment lay in the federal crackdown on The Order, Bob Matthews's group of Aryan revolutionaries. After a string of spectacular crimes committed by Matthews and his followers, including a $3.8 million armored-car heist in July 1984 and the murder of Alan Berg in Denver the month before, the Justice Department launched a series of investigations targeting rightwing groups. In addition to the two-year probe of the Committee of the States that led to Gale's 1986 arrest, the FBI singled out the Arizona Patriots, a Posse-style group that had modeled its planned activities on the exploits of The Order. Gale's arrest triggered a small wave of violence.

On December 1, 1986, David John Moran, the "National Education Chairman" of the Committee of the States, committed five armed robberies in a triangle of towns between San Francisco and Sacramento. An accomplice was arrested but Moran eluded capture. "The arrests of William P. Gale and others by the agents of ZOG is the proverbial straw that broke the camel's back," Moran wrote before he robbed a series of liquor and convenience stores. "Thus I, like the members of the [Order], have declared war. . . ." Moran, thirty, had renounced his Social Security number—his "slave number," he called it—and canceled his bank account in an effort to opt out of the system, but that had not deterred the collection efforts of the IRS. Frustrated by his continued "persecution," inspired by fond memories of Bob Matthews, and driven by rage over the crackdown on the Committee of the States, Moran decided to replicate the hit-and-run tactics of The Order, albeit on a smaller scale. One week after his daylong crime spree, Moran was fleeing north on California Highway 101 at about nine P.M. with a companion, when the couple was stopped for driving with a faulty headlight. Surrounded by fog and redwoods, Moran leapt from the car, firing a 9-mm pistol. He managed to hit one officer in the flak jacket before he was killed.[4] It was December 8, 1986, and by an odd coincidence, Moran's death occurred exactly two years to the day that Bob Matthews had died in a firefight with FBI agents on Whidbey Island, Washington.

Several months after Moran was killed, while Bill Gale was still in jail in Las Vegas, a bomb attack was launched at the federal building in Laguna Niguel, about fifty-five miles southeast of Los Angeles. On March 2, 1987, nine crudely made homemade mortars—the projectiles resembled pipe bombs—were fired at the building in broad daylight; five missed their target and started a grass fire nearby, while four unexploded charges scattered across a parking lot and an open field.[5] Just as Gale had recommended how to respond violently to a law enforcement roadblock—and Gordon Kahl had, coincidentally, followed his advice—

Gale also drew the attention of Christian Patriots to federal buildings as possible "enemy" targets when he delivered his original sermon proposing the Committee of the States:

"You've got an enemy government running around. You've got a criminal government running around the land. And its source and its location is Washington, D.C., and the federal buildings they've built with your tax money all over the cities in this land." Similar thinking led Timothy McVeigh to destroy the Oklahoma City federal building eight years later.

Though Gale denied he played a prominent role in the Committee of the States, he invented it and inspired its members to plot violence. Gale inaugurated the Committee on September 6, 1982, with a sermon from the pulpit of the Ministry of Christ Church, explaining how and why patriots should take control of the federal government.[6] Like his original Posse manifesto, The cornerstone of Gale's plan was an "indictment" charging that Congress had "unlawfully" delegated power to the Federal Reserve; "treasonously" appropriated money "towards the support of alien and foreign governments"; and unconstitutionally ordered American troops into battle on behalf of the "International Jewish Banking Conspiracy." After detailing these and other transgressions, Gale presented his solution:

> [Members of Congress] are employees on the public payroll . . . therefore they are subject to dismissal and removal from office and replacement by a Committee of the States as provided for in Article Five of the Articles of Confederation and Perpetual Union. . . . This removal from office and replacement by a Committee of the States is hereby recommended and authorized!

The reasoning was sophomoric, but Gale's belligerent charisma and his pretended rank of full colonel in the U.S. Army made his assertions appear credible—at least to those Patriots who wanted to believe anything he said. Gale correctly assumed that the government would take notice of the commitee's threats and so he instructed his followers to form a citizens' posse in every county. "Anybody who tries to interfere with the lawful operations of the Committee of the States should be faced by that armed posse and be declared outlaws and be apprehended upon sight." Later versions of this advice instructed that the death penalty be imposed. Like the Posse Comitatus he announced in 1971, Gale manufactured the Committee of the States using equal parts vigilantism, historical misinterpretation, and outright fiction—all papered over by a meaningless legalistic gloss.

In his sermon launching the Committee of the States, Gale claimed decades of "knowledge [from] studying constitutional law, Bible law, divine law, and the organic law of this Republic," but his understanding of the Articles of Confederation was fatally flawed. Drafted one year after the Declaration of Independence and ratified in 1781, the Articles provided for "a firm league of friendship" between the original thirteen states and established Congress as the national legislature, with selective powers of national defense and other functions. But the nation's early leaders soon realized that the Articles were fundamentally inadequate to the task of binding the states into a coherent Union. It wasn't until the nation's founders held their Constitutional Convention in 1787, and appended the Bill of Rights two years later, that the United States fashioned a workable document to fully unify the new nation. Gale asserted that the Articles of Confederation remained in effect to the present day, but such reasoning defied logic, reality, and the Constitution itself.

Gale had proposed his Committee of the States in 1982—in part—as a remedy to the farm crisis then unfolding in the Midwest. He opened his sermon by denouncing sheriffs, lawyers, judges, and bankers for "conspiring" to force farmers from the land. That same year, Gale had helped lead the paramilitary training session in Weskan, and for the next two years he and Roxanne toured the Midwest in their motor home, promoting the Committee of the States to farmers and Christian Patriots across the country. During one such trip in May 1984, Gale stopped midway between Dallas and Fort Worth and met with Randall Ray Reineking, a Posse activist from Sheboygan, Wisconsin. Like others on the right-wing circuit, Reineking hopscotched from state to state, running into problems with the law. "We're going to meet this summer in Mariposa," Gale told Reineking, inviting him to come.[7] It was a fateful encounter. Reineking became the "clerk" of the Committee of the States, but he later turned on Gale as a witness in federal court.

Just days after meeting with Gale, Reineking was arrested in Kansas after concocting a scheme to help a troubled farmer, Emil Wiley, whose tractors had been confiscated to satisfy a debt. Reineking and Wiley drew up a bogus legal document in a lame attempt to get the local sheriff to retrieve the machinery, but the lawman saw through the ruse. And it was that incident that led to the arrest of Donald E. Zabawa, the Posse militant, who gave Kansas investigators his lengthy statement detailing the criminal activities of Mike Ryan and his followers.[8] Eventually Wiley and Reineking were convicted of forgery, but not before the two men attended the founding convention of the Committee of the States at Gale's Manasseh Ranch over Fourth of July weekend in 1984. It was there that they and forty-two others signed a declaration proclaiming themselves "the Lords and Masters of this self-governing Republic known as the United States of America," and ordered the dissolution of Congress. The Committee also charged that government officials had misappropriated public funds to support "alien and foreign governments"; unlawfully delegated powers (to the Federal Reserve); and committed troops to "acts of war on foreign soil without a formal constitutional Declaration of War."

"Public Servants have committed acts of SEDITION . . . and are as insolent as those of the Roman government in the days of the Apostle Paul," asserted the group's manifesto. The July 1984 declaration also delivered a stern ultimatum: All members of Congress who did not immediately resign would be put on trial by the Committee of the States. And, like the "constructive notices" that Committee members would later mail to IRS agents and the Nevada judge, the declaration stated that any attempt to interfere with the Committee would result in death.[9] In addition to claiming the authority of the United States Congress for themselves, Gale's followers were equally brazen in demanding additional rights and remedies. A fifteen-point "Declaration of Alteration and Reform" summarily announced the repeal of all international debts and obligations; the abolition of all departments of government "not functioning in pursuance [sic] of the Constitution"; an end of the income tax; and the creation of a national bank. The Committee accused Congress of sedition, and arrogantly decreed that it would now assume "all functions of the Department of Justice [and] the Department of Defense."

While Gale and his bill of particulars professed concern for family farmers, his solution would have been disastrous for agriculture and the economy. Among other things, Gale favored repeal of the Federal Deposit Insurance Act, which would have bankrupted the depositors of failing banks, and he suggested printing enough money to liquidate all national and foreign debts, which would have produced runaway inflation and worldwide economic chaos. The latter course of action was absurd for many reasons, not the least of which was the fact that it directly contradicted another central Posse demand: the immediate guarantee that all paper money be "redeemable in gold and silver."

As the duly appointed "clerk" of the Committee of the States, Randall Reineking presided over the signing of the document while Bill Gale stood in a kitchen doorway and watched. For all his confrontational bluster, Gale refused to sign his name, claiming that the Articles of Confederation barred retired military officers who received government pay from serving as delegates. It was a self-serving and specious argument but so was most of what Gale said. Gale withheld his signature but implicated himself nonetheless when he signed other paperwork for the group's "unorganized militia" as its "chief of staff." When asked whether the militia would make good on its threats, Gale told the group, "Yes indeed, the militia will carry it out. That's not a threat, that's a promise."[10] And earlier, in his 1982 sermon announcing the Committee of the States, Gale had emphatically declared that his "solution" would have to be carried out "in a hard manner." "It's not nice," he growled.[11] To ensure this was the case, Gale helped organize paramilitary training sessions at the Manasseh Ranch featuring lessons in ambush techniques, explosives, knife-fighting, and nighttime raids.[12]

Among the forty-four people from a dozen states who signed Gale's declaration were Richard Butler, the Aryan Nations chief; a smattering of Midwestern farmers (including Reuben Leimer, a Populist Party activist and a fan of Jim Wickstrom's who had been interviewed on ABC's 20/20); Arthur Stigall, an activist from California whose manual, How to Form a Common-Law Grand Jury, would surface a decade later in the ranks of the militias; and several members of the Arizona Patriots. One of the Arizona men was Richard Van Hazel, a Vietnam veteran and onetime police reservist from Flagstaff, whom Gale appointed "chief marshal" of the "unorganized militia" of the COS.[13] Another was Norman Kuhman, a newspaper publisher and self-styled savior of family farms who signed up with the Arizona Patriots in the early 1980s after financial difficulties forced him into bankruptcy.[14]

Like countless other Posse offshoots, the Arizona Patriots first came to the attention of authorities when its members began filing pro se lawsuits challenging state motor vehicle laws.[15] But the Patriots stood out from other groups because of the involvement of former film and television actor Ty Hardin. A native of New York City, Hardin had acquired modest celebrity and a Texas accent in the late 1950s when he played the cowboy character "Bronco Lane" on television. After twenty years of acting, Hardin reportedly became disgusted with "Zionist control of Hollywood" and left California. He reappeared in the late 1970s in Prescott, Arizona, where he sponsored workshops on Christian Common Law, published the *Arizona Patriot*, and helped activists like Kuhman wage their own personal paper war. Several years of fighting Satan in traffic court led Hardin and his followers to hunger for more. Just weeks before Gale's July 1984 meeting in Mariposa, ten members of the Arizona Patriots reportedly met in the foothills of the Bradshaw Mountains to discuss blowing up bridges and killing Arizona governor Bruce Babbitt. (None were charged with a crime in connection with this alleged meeting.) Talk like this got the attention of law enforcement and the following year the FBI placed an informant in the group, who recorded hours of Patriot scheming using a secret microphone concealed in his boot. Eighteen months later, on December 15, 1986, federal agents rounded up eight people, four of whom were charged with plotting to rob an armored car loaded with casino money so they could build a white-supremacist training camp. The group also discussed bombing a Phoenix synagogue and an IRS office complex in Ogden, Utah.[16] Much of the planning for these crimes took place at a 320-acre ranch in northwestern Arizona. The remote property near Kingman was owned by Jack Maxwell Oliphant, sixty-two, a one-armed right-wing activist who had lost his limb in a firearms accident years before. Oliphant's compound lacked water and electricity and was strewn with evidence of the group's survivalist maneuvers: thousands of spent rifle shells and hundreds of empty crates that once contained rocket ammunition. Other evidence uncovered there that invited further comparisons with The Order included detailed blueprints of the electrical systems of two major dams that were found inside a cardboard barrel.[17]

A handful of the Arizona Patriots who had attended Gale's July 1984 meeting in Mariposa, including Richard Van Hazel, joined Gale two weeks later to help promote the Committee of the States at the Aryan Nations annual conference in Hayden Lake, Idaho.

Van Hazel was a big man, six feet three inches tall and 250 pounds. He was also a lumbering windbag who bored even the Aryan Nations assembly with a lecture about the evils of Social Security numbers and by boasting about his assortment of homemade driver's licenses. Roger Elvick, the "Speaker" of the Committee of the States, made a much better impression. A self-described "expert" on British common law, Elvick spoke for half a day about Posse legalisms and Magna Carta—the historic thirteenth-century document that proclaimed the privileges of feudal English barons (and the selective rights of others) and which helped lay the foundation for portions of the American Constitution and the Bill of Rights.[18] Like Bill Gale's theories about the Articles of Confederation, Elvick's strained interpretation of Magna Carta was grounded in misunderstanding and exaggeration—but to him and other Posse enthusiasts the medieval text offered instant and unimpeachable justification for violent rebellion.[19] Although some essential concepts contained in Magna Carta have indeed been preserved and modified by centuries of legal rulings and legislative acts (both British and American), Elvick spoke about the document as a living thing which conferred specific and immediate rights, which it did not. The convoluted reasoning of Elvick and Gale both excited and confused their audience of Klansmen, neo-Nazis, and Christian Patriots, prompting one FBI informant to complain that a person "almost had to be a 'Philadelphia lawyer' to understand what was being said." But the infiltrator still was impressed. Elvick was a "brilliant individual . . . an exceptionally good speaker," and Gale won high marks, as well.[20] The FBI took particular note of the implied threat of violence contained in Gale's assertion that members of Congress who refused to yield to the Committee of the States would be indicated and removed from office.[21] But Gale's comments were mild compared to the speeches that followed.

The day after Gale's presentation, Louis R. Beam Jr., the Aryan Nations' "world ambassador," took the podium. A Vietnam veteran and former Grand Dragon of the Texas Knights of the Ku Klux Klan, Beam was a hardened bigot. In the late 1970s, he had trained and led a paramilitary army of more than 2,000 men that he called the Texas Emergency Reserve. And in 1981, he used the group to terrorize Vietnamese refugees fishing in the Gulf of Mexico until a lawsuit filed by the Southern Poverty Law Center prompted a federal judge to disband the group. Addressing his audience at the Aryan Nations compound, Beam joined several others who discussed guerrilla tactics and explained how sabotage, booby traps, and explosives could be used to start urban riots as part of a larger plan to foment white revolution. According to an FBI informant, Beam explained how these activities "would be centered in large metropolitan areas [with] a large black population."

By destroying public facilities such as utilities, cities would be left in darkness, prompting looting, according to Beam. "[This] would create an emergency situation [requiring] the police, fire departments, and National Guard to quell the problem, leaving the city unguarded," Beam explained, adding that at this point, "the operational units" could then begin killing federal judges.[22] Like the men of The Order who had just killed Alan Berg—and were busy planning the armored-car robbery that soon would net them $3.8 million—Beam drew inspiration from *The Turner Diaries* and its clandestine plans for white-supremacist revolution.

Published in 1978, *The Turner Diaries* "recounts" the fictional future thoughts and actions of thirty-five-year-old Earl Turner, a white racist who joins a neo-Nazi group called "the Organization" and later becomes a member of its inner circle: the Order. The book describes the "Great Revolution of 1991–1999," as seen through the eyes of its pseudonymous author, Andrew Macdonald.[23] In real life, Macdonald was William Pierce, the founder and leader of the National Alliance, one of the nation's most militant neo-Nazi groups. A former assistant professor of physics at Oregon State University, Pierce was once the editor of *National Socialist World*, the flagship publication of George Lincoln Rockwell's American Nazi Party. After Rockwell was assassinated in 1967, Pierce became a leader in the Nazi Party and then, in 1974, went on to establish the Alliance. Prior to 1978, *The Turner Diaries* was serialized in the National Alliance magazine *Attack!*[24] Before his death in July 2002, Pierce worked from out of a 346-acre compound outside Hillsboro, West Virginia, where he managed a network of propaganda outlets, recruited new supporters, and promoted violence. In addition to his 1999 acquisition of the "White Power" music label Resistance Records and its companion magazine by the same name, Pierce's weekly radio program, *American Dissident Voices* (which was heard over satellite, short-wave, and AM radio), his Internet broadcasts, telephone message hotlines, and e-mail alerts reached a growing audience of would-be racist "revolutionaries" worldwide.

In the future world of Earl Turner created by William Pierce, America is a vast police state bent on persecuting gun owners and white racists; Jews are "arrogant aliens . . . the ferment of decomposition of races and civilizations to be roast[ed] . . . over bonfires at every street corner in America"; black men are "cannibalistic animals," and "swarming hoarde[s] of indifferent mulatto zombies threaten to leave Earth, God's great Experiment . . . devoid of higher man." Predictably, Turner and his fellow revolutionaries refer to Adolf Hitler as "the Great One" and commemorate his birthday by leveling the Israeli embassy with explosives.[25]

Turner's fictional diary begins in September 1991, two years after "the Cohen Act" outlaws private ownership of guns. Responding to police raids spearheaded by blacks, Turner joins a four-person revolutionary cell based in Washington, D.C., and is soon assigned the task of blowing up FBI headquarters. Unable to locate sufficient dynamite for the task, Turner relies on a mixture of fertilizer and fuel oil, the same components as Timothy McVeigh's Oklahoma City bomb. Pierce, a physicist, provides detailed instructions for assembling the device. The carnage from the explosion is immense and, like McVeigh (or vice versa), the fictional Turner concludes that there is no way to end the "racially destructive philosophy" of the federal government without killing innocent people and shed-

ding "torrents—veritable rivers—of innocent blood."[26] Turner and his fellow revolutionaries then raid government armories, attack newspaper offices, launch a
mortar attack on the U.S. Capitol, and shoot down an airliner bound for Tel
Aviv.[27] After helping conquer Los Angeles and seize a cache of nuclear weapons,
Turner assists with "the Day of the Rope," in which tens of thousands of supposed "race traitors" are hung from lampposts, power poles, and trees with plac-
ards around their necks confessing their racial sins.[28] Although Turner and his
compatriots rejoice in the expulsion of "non-Aryans" from the "liberated zone"
of southern California, they see the rest of America as a "Jewish pigsty [and] a
cesspool of mongrels [and] sick, twisted white liberals."[29] This problem is solved,
however, when Turner and others initiate a near-complete nuclear Armageddon
by launching nuclear missiles against New York, Israel, and Russia, prompting
massive retaliation. A nuclear bomb planted by Turner in Baltimore leaves sixty
million more dead. The diary ends with Turner carrying out one final mission:
he flies a single-engine crop duster over the Pentagon and detonates a 60-kiloton
nuclear warhead. An epilogue by the fictional Macdonald concludes the book by
describing the food riots, black cannibalism, and bloody race war that follows,
but the white race finally triumphs by launching a massive chemical, biological,
and nuclear attack against China that "sterilizes" sixteen million square miles of
the planet.[30]

When *The Turner Diaries* was first published it drew little attention outside
of a relatively small circle of national socialists. But men like Louis Beam and
Robert Matthews took its fictional message seriously and promoted it as a blueprint for their planned takeover of America. Even the name Matthews chose for
his group—the "Order"—was taken directly from the pages of Pierce's *Diaries*.
And when it came time for Louis Beam to write his own guidelines for revolutionary violence, he echoed Pierce's message about the need to eliminate white
race traitors:

> We must begin the preparations necessary to retrieve our country from
> the hands of the enemy which now controls it. It should be plain to everyone
> what is needed: knives, guns, and courage. . . . [Race traitors] are the ones
> . . . whose blood must flow between our fingers before our land will be safe.
> . . . They are the ones who are guilty. . . . [31]

Beam's instructions appeared in *Essays of a Klansman*, a hundred-page booklet
that he published from Hayden Lake in 1983, the same year Bob Matthews
founded The Order. The highlight of Beam's tract was a diagram outlining how
"Aryan Warriors" could earn "points" for murdering judges, law enforcement
agents, civil rights activists, elected officials, and other political targets. According
to an FBI informant, Beam presented the chart at Hayden Lake in July 1984
along with the following advice:

"I'm not telling you to go out and commit acts of terrorism, but . . . you need to decide whether you want to act on your own or whether you prefer to recruit a few people to work with you. It is best to work alone, but small groups of up to five individuals can be effective."[32] Former KKK Grand Dragon Robert Miles of Michigan addressed the group and concurred. A convicted felon, Miles had served more than half of a nine-year sentence in Marion Federal Prison for firebombing ten empty school buses in 1971 to protest school integration.[33] Hard time had no rehabilitative effect. Writing from his cell in 1977, Miles extolled the virtues of violence:

> Words alone have not unseated one tyrant in history. Legal measures alone have not turned back one wave of oppression anywhere, at any time. Action, acts, deeds, and defiance in physical manifestations alone are the lifeblood of rebellion. . . . "March separately, but strike together" is good logic . . . and the adage applies in this race war. It applies to the hundreds of white racist groups who make up our army as regiments and corps. We have many leaders, but our objective is one and the same: white power! Our race is our nation.[34]

And not long after his release from jail, Miles announced that he would not rest "[u]ntil every single Federal swings legally from a hanging tree."[35]

If Aryan Nations chief Richard Butler was seen as the aging patriarch of the movement, he also was perceived by many as doddering and nearly senile. Miles, on the other hand, was regarded as shrewd, and many listened to what he had to say that day at Hayden Lake:

> Join the National Guard, or at least recruit somebody who can. . . . Get to know all the law enforcement officers that live within fifty miles of your home. . . . Find out where they live. Identify all the communist front groups and their members, including the rabbis and the Jews. Write the information down on three-by-five index cards or put it on a computer. Gather as much information as you can.

But Miles admonished the group to be careful. "Do not discuss anything illegal with anyone," he warned.[36] Miles dispensed similar advice in the *Inter-Klan Newsletter and Survival Alert*, a publication he produced jointly with Louis Beam. It was in 1983, in the very first issue, that Beam advanced the concept of "leaderless resistance." He wrote:

> The orthodox scheme of organization is diagrammatically represented by the pyramid, with the mass at the bottom and the leader at the top. . . . In the "pyramid" type of organization, an infiltrator can destroy anything which is beneath him. . . . In order to get around the obvious problem . . . the cell system developed . . . in [which] numerous cells are created which

operate completely isolated from each other . . . but are orchestrated together by "headquarters." The entire purpose of Leaderless Resistance is to defeat state tyranny.[37]

There was nothing new in this elementary strategy for subversive violence—in fact, Beam credited one Colonel Ulius Louis Amoss with first writing about Leaderless Resistance in 1962—but Beam was single-mindedly dedicated to promoting it. [38] Just as the grandiose fictional exploits described in *The Turner Diaries* helped give birth to the sprawling criminality of The Order, Beam's point system and guidelines for smaller-scale rebellion introduced the concept of Leaderless Resistance that helped propel a generation of racist revolutionaries into violent clashes with the government.

Beam also sought to apply the latest technology to advance the cause of white revolution when he announced at Hayden Lake that the Aryan Nations would soon be establishing its own computer bulletin-board system. Called Liberty Net, Beam promised it would be linked to a system set up months earlier by the neo-Nazi activist George Dietz.[39] Though computer bulletin boards like these are hopelessly outdated by today's standards, Liberty Net was far ahead of its time.

More than one hundred people came and went during the weeklong gathering at Hayden Lake in July 1984, including Bill Gale and other supporters of the Committee of the States. Of the nearly sixty or so listed by name in classified FBI reports, at least ten soon came under indictment for various crimes, eight of whom were convicted. The list included men like Randolph Duey, a former postal clerk who would be sentenced to one hundred years in prison for his crimes associated with The Order; Eldon "Bud" Cutler, the Aryan Nations' "security chief" who would be convicted for trying to arrange the murder of a government informant; and David Tate, a teenager raised at the Aryan Nations compound who went on to shoot and kill a Missouri state highway patrolman in 1985. The list of attendees was a virtual who's who of the white-supremacist movement, but it also included lesser-known figures such as Colonel Francis P. "Bud" Farrell, the "international director" for Rick Elliott's National Agricultural Press Association.[40]

During a break in the proceedings, Gale and Butler made small talk with several men and their wives. Alan Berg had been murdered by The Order less than a month earlier, and mention of the killing prompted smiles and a joke. "Wasn't it nice how all those empty cartridges fell in a neat twelve-inch-diameter circle?" one of the men remarked. "Oh, [David] Lane would never do anything like *that*," added another sarcastically. [41] They were correct. Lane had driven the getaway car. It was Bruce Carroll Pierce who had unloaded twelve rounds from a MAC-10 automatic pistol into Berg. The weeklong gathering ended with church services and a nighttime cross-burning on July 21. Beam was either drunk or careless during his final speech when he told the group that Berg had been shot because he had "ridiculed one of our leaders. . . . We no longer have time for prayer or negotiations. The time has come to fight the race-mixers!" [42] Beam didn't say whether the person Berg supposedly insulted was Rick Elliott or another anti-Semite who had been skewered by Berg (there were several), but according to government prosecutors, Berg's interview with Elliott and other bigots on the air may have been what prompted David Lane and others to kill the Denver talk-show host. The fact that Lane was employed as a part-time security guard at NAPA headquarters also made it more likely that he took note of Elliott's interview on KOA.[43]

Despite their common hatred for the government, Gale left Hayden Lake reportedly disgusted by all the "Nazi crap." In fact, tensions were common between self-proclaimed Patriots who draped themselves in the American flag and genuine Hitler worshipers who preferred the boldness of the swastika and its explicitly genocidal intent. After leaving Hayden Lake, Gale stayed in touch with his Nevada followers and urged them to act on behalf of the Committee of the States. A spate of threatening letters to IRS agents and others followed. Rehearsing what they had learned at Gale's ranch in Mariposa, the men practiced garroting their enemies with piano wire. One participant defended these practice sessions by claiming they were just "picnics on the mountain," but a federal prosecutor later dryly suggested calling the outings "piano-wire picnics" instead.[44] The activities of the Committee of the States prompted closer scrutiny by federal authorities that by now were using their Arizona Patriots informant to gather information about Gale's group. When members of the Committee of the States were subpoenaed to appear before a federal grand jury in the spring of 1986, Richard Van Hazel (the "unorganized militia" leader) said he planned to "bury them in bullshit and shut this thing down."[45] Gale urged his followers to destroy incriminating evidence. "I have burned all communications; keep no records of any kind," he advised them. But it was a nearly impossible instruction to follow, given the Posse obsession with paper. When Las Vegas police arrested Committee members George R. "Mike" McCray and his brother Pat in September 1985 on misdemeanor traffic violations, they found each had a briefcase full of incriminating evidence. As the "chairman" of the Nevada Committee of the States and the "commander" of its "unorganized militia," Mike McCray's briefcase included letters from Bill Gale, copies of threatening "constructive notices," and application forms for Identity meetings in Mariposa. The police made copies of the paperwork and passed them along to the IRS, who then gave the material to federal prosecutors. The documents made up a large portion of the 450 exhibits that the U.S. attorney planned to submit at Bill Gale's trial, which began in Las Vegas on September 15, 1987.[46]

Gale was in a wheelchair, dressed in a black shirt with small white polka dots, and clutching a cane as he was introduced by his lawyer, Thomas F. Pitaro. The evidence would show the defendant's military record was "heroic," Pitaro told the jury, asserting that his client had retired due to disabilities "incurred in combat" and deserved the "title and respect of Colonel Gale." Given the fact that Gale was only a lieutenant colonel with minimal (if any) combat experience and had a history of repeated diagnoses by army doctors of "psychoneurosis," this account of Gale's military background was wholly inaccurate.[47]

The October 9, 1986, indictment of Gale and his compatriots had named eight defendants, but two pleaded guilty and agreed to cooperate with the government. A third defendant would plead guilty before the trial was over.[48] This left five core defendants, including Gale: the McCray brothers, Fortunato "Slim" Parrino, and Richard Van Hazel. Parrino was a fifteen-year veteran of the Los Angeles County Sheriff's Department and the assistant minister of Gale's Ministry of Christ Church. He also was the "chief marshal" of the California Unorganized Militia.[49] In his opening statement to the jury of seven women and five men, Assistant U.S. Attorney Richard J. Pocker referred to the facts of the case as "a bad Grade B movie," but he cautioned that it was "a serious situation" and described Gale as "a charismatic angry man."

"Contrary to what you might hear later, this is not strictly a case about unpopular beliefs," Pocker explained.[50] Defense lawyers countered by arguing the importance of freedom of speech and they tried to downplay the alleged offenses. Nine out of the ten charges involved "just five pieces of paper," one lawyer said. "The 'constructive notice' is a joke," Pitaro flatly stated.[51] The government spent the next ten days presenting its case. One of the first witnesses was Randall Reineking, the former "clerk" of the Committee of the States, who took three days to detail Gale's role as the founder of the group. His testimony, along with that of William Sivils, the principal FBI informant, and several others who had been close to Gale, painted an overwhelmingly negative picture of the defendants. Gale's lawyer and attorneys for the others took only a day and several witnesses to present their defense, reasoning that more time going over the same material might only reinforce the worst about their clients. In closing arguments more appropriate to the prosecution's summation, Slim Parrino's lawyer dwelled on the peculiar motivations of the indicted men:

> I find it ironic that . . . these people want to be everything they hate. . . .
> That which they hate, attorneys, they want to be. That which they hate,
> judges, they evidently want to be. Banks, they don't like bankers, they create
> their own bank. . . . Jews, they don't like Jews, yet they say they are the true
> Israelis [sic] and they would steal from the Jews their designation of God's
> chosen people.

The lawyer, Frank J. Cremen, also tried to convince the jury that the Committee of the States was nothing more than a figment of Bill Gale's imagination. According to Cremen, Gale knew the group was just "a theory," because he had said: "We ought to get that phony government Justice Department to go out and prosecute all of those people who killed Christ and have them hung."[52]

Thomas Pitaro, Gale's lawyer, seemed to be fishing for a mistrial when he reminded the jury of his client's incendiary rhetoric and then praised them for remaining impartial:

> After hearing the religious views of Reverend Gale . . . not one of you people has come forth and said, "I can't perform my function anymore." [But] what if . . . Reverend Gale . . . insulted, or abused or provoked this honest juror. . . . Only you would know if you would violate that oath by having a decision based upon the passion and prejudice because you disagree vehemently . . . with the religious and political views expounded by this man.[53]

Nobody took the bait, and when the jury rendered its verdict on the thirteenth day of the trial, it found Gale and his four codefendants guilty on all counts.[54] As if to suggest something sinister, Roxanne Gale pointed out that both Gale's arrest in 1986 and his trial a year later had been held during Rosh Hashanah, the Jewish New Year. And, coincidentally, the trial verdict was read just hours before the beginning of Yom Kippur. "The Jews forgot to brag about the defendants being kidnapped by IRS SWAT teams one year ago during the Jewish New Year," she wrote in a letter to supporters. "I guess it's called twice the fun for once the price. May Jesus Christ reward them on their timing," she sarcastically observed.[55] Predictably, U.S. Attorney Bill Maddox had a different point of view. "The verdict is a victory against bigotry," he declared.[56]

On Friday, January 15, 1988, Gale and his fellow defendants appeared for sentencing.[57] Severely weakened by emphysema, Gale remained in his wheelchair while Pitaro wagged a finger at the judge, lest he send a man of Gale's distinguished military background and flagging health to prison.[58] Immune to Pitaro's scolding, the judge sentenced Gale to three one-year concurrent terms in prison, followed by five years' probation and a $5,000 fine. All but one of Gale's codefendants fared worse; they drew prison sentences ranging from thirty months to seven years, long probations, and $5,000 fines.[59] Slim Parrino, Gale's presumed successor to the pulpit of the Ministry of Christ Church, stunned his mentor and former coconspirators by delivering a tearful apology and proclaiming his "divorce" from the Committee of the States. The performance earned Parrino a reduced sentence to time served plus five years' probation.[60] Richard Van Hazel received the longest prison sentence, of seven years—but it only seemed to harden him. Eleven years later, Van Hazel and an accomplice were arrested in a Detroit suburb for the attempted kidnapping of an accountant whose court testimony had helped convict an Arizona chiropractor for tax evasion. According to sheriff's deputies, the men had a wealth of incriminating evidence in their car:

guns, rifles, knives, tear gas, components for making explosive booby-trap devices, and a fake letter that read like a suicide note. Posing as U.S. Marshals, Van
Hazel and his partner allegedly planned to kidnap and murder the accountant
and make it look like a suicide.[61]

For decades Bill Gale had escaped responsibility for inciting violence, but
organizing and leading the Committee of the States finally brought about his
demise. Indicted, arrested, convicted, and freed on bail pending his appeal, Gale
died of complications from emphysema on April 28, 1988, at Castle Air Force
Base in Merced, California, three months after he was sentenced. The convictions
of his codefendants were upheld. Unlike Gordon Kahl, the combat veteran and
murderer of federal marshals whom the air force denied a military burial, Gale's
funeral on May 2 was held at Riverside National Cemetery in California. His
coffin was draped with an American flag, though Gale had recently been convicted of threatening federal employees with death. Six army pallbearers stood
erect in full dress uniform and saluted the casket. One of them was black. None
of Gale's three children attended the funeral, but a small group of fellow rightists
and racists did, including members of the Committee of the States.[62]

Gale's death made headlines and prompted reverent eulogies from fellow
activists, but like many in his movement, Gale had lived a life of lies, and died
a coward. His father was a Jew—as were half his ancestors—who had fled the
anti-Semitic marauders of the Pale. And though he was undeniably a Jew by his
own racial standards, Gale hid his heritage and encouraged the murder of his
family's descendants.

Many of Gale's relatives recalled that he could be charming and warm, but
he also was a failure as both a husband and a father. He disowned his eldest
daughter for moving to New York City, where she landed a successful career in
show business and married a Jew. Determined to "make a man of his son," Gale
assaulted him physically and emotionally and set him fleeing from home to enlist
in Vietnam—not once, but twice. And after divorcing Josephine, his first wife,
Gale rebuilt his life on a solid foundation of hate and then married Roxanne
Luttrell.

Starting in the mid-1950s, Gale faked his theological credentials and
preached the need for violence, but he never had the courage to even wave a
weapon at the legions of enemies he denounced as traitors to the Republic. Decades in uniform had given Gale a genuine military bearing, but it was the exaggeration of his rank and nonexistent army exploits that gave him credibility,
not his real accomplishments in uniform, which were mainly bureaucratic. Gale
was financially independent—thanks, largely, to his army pension and a natural
talent for selling insurance to elderly widows. He also was totally dedicated to
"the Cause." Gale also had ample charisma—and bombast. But even these considerable assets were diminished by Gale's coarse, combative personality that in-
cited him to relentlessly attack fellow rightists and belittle his own followers.

For the first fifteen years of his political life, Gale worked jealously in the shadows of Wesley Swift and other more prominent anti-Semites. After converting Richard Butler to Christian Identity, Gale took him to meet Swift. But not long afterward, Gale became Swift's rival, and when Swift died it was Butler, not Gale, who inherited the remnants of Swift's congregation, on which the Aryan Nations was built. Gale tried his hand at launching paramilitary groups like the Christian Defense League and the California Rangers, but he was an incompetent organizer and neither group got off the ground. In fact, Gale's organizational limitations were so great that although he invented the Posse Comitatus, he was unable to translate its appeal into institutional success. The Posse's novel and powerful blend of theology, law, and vigilantism attracted followers magnetically, but they preferred the plagiarist Mike Beach, or the sermonizing Jim Wickstrom, rather than dealing directly with the arrogance of Bill Gale. And so when Gordon Kahl became the first full-fledged Posse Comitatus martyr in 1983, it was Wickstrom—and even Beach—who got most of the credit, despite the fact that Gale was nearly as responsible for the carnage in Medina as Kahl himself.

Gale embarked upon his right-wing career in the early 1950s, when anticommunist paranoia and the racist backlash against civil rights defined conservative politics for much of the era. He was in good company, since millions of Americans, including many powerful politicians, rejected the very notion of black equality and were fearful of communist world domination. But the Massive Resistance pursued by segregationists had proved an utter failure by the mid-1960s. And though the Cold War persisted for decades, conspiracy-obsessed groups like the John Birch Society lost ground to the civil rights movement and the antiwar protests that followed. By 1970 the most prominent figure on the paramilitary right—Robert DePugh—was in jail, and many of the leading right-wing groups of the post–World War II period were in disarray. Conservatives triumphed with the election of Richard Nixon in 1968, and George Wallace demonstrated the broad appeal of white racism when he won nearly ten million votes running for president the same year. But by the end of the 1960s a large portion of the radical right had lost vitality. And so it was by accident rather than any orderly political design that Bill Gale stepped forward in 1971, brandishing his tract about the Posse Comitatus Act and the Organic Law of the Republic. Unlike the garden-variety bigotry and Cold War rhetoric that flourished in the wake of the *Brown* decision, Gale's political beliefs were rooted in a theology that justified murder, even if Gale himself was too cowardly to kill. Before the arrival of the Posse Comitatus, a stream of British Israelism had run through the American right, but Bill Gale imaginatively diverted it into new and wider tributaries that reached a broader audience of tax protesters, Second Amendment fanatics, and farmers in distress.

Over time Gale's message has resonated with many right-wingers whose targets of hate included federal authority in all forms, taxes, bankers, civil rights, leftists, blacks, and Jews. Conversely, they frequently endorsed appeals to "law and order," states' rights, and the notion that the Constitution could be readily invoked in defense of their unlawful acts. And because the assassinations of Dr. Martin Luther King Jr. and Robert Kennedy gave new impetus to gun control, Second Amendment activists loved the Posse, too. There was nothing new about vigilantism in defense of segregation, but Gale's arcane invocations of Christian Common Law made his message about the "lawful" mechanics of the Posse Comitatus seem fresh and authoritative. This only heightened the appeal for gun-toting racists who saw themselves as patriots. And though Gale was not the first person to claim erroneously that the authority to raise the "unorganized militia" rested with common citizens, he paid special attention to the topic and promoted it heavily within the Committee of the States, thereby helping spawn the militia movement that followed.

Most rightists reserved a special hatred for the Federal Reserve System as well as the IRS, but it was Bill Gale's Posse Comitatus that joined both of these themes under the banner of Identity theology and invoked divine authority for armed resistance to Satan's armies and his agents in the federal government. Aided by an energetic, sometimes incompetent, and often dangerous cadre of zealots, the Posse message of armed vigilantism has reverberated throughout America since Gale circulated his first treatise on the subject more than thirty years ago. The message has reached hundreds of thousands of right-wing supporters through the movement's pamphlets, newsletters, video and audiotapes, and radio broadcasts. More recently, the Internet has provided another forum for disseminating these ideas. Millions more heard the Posse line—usually critically presented—through the media megaphone as each violent confrontation sparked another headline or televised tragedy. Of course, the vast majority of Americans rejected the Posse message outright, but the movement still gained recruits, especially when it targeted the tax-protest movement of the 1970s, the farm crisis of the 1980s, and the militia movement of the 1990s. And it was through these dynamic social movements that Bill Gale's simplistic yet elaborate framework of ideas has won a substantial following these past three decades.

Gale never fired a gun in defense of his beliefs, but his mouth and his pen inspired considerable violence. His entire political life was a rage against ethnic pluralism and representative democracy. Without Bill Gale there never would have been a Posse Comitatus or a Christian Patriot movement. And just as the ideas espoused by William Pierce and Louis Beam helped shape The Order, Gale's Posse manifesto fed and nurtured the American militia movement—including, in part, the ideology that motivated the Oklahoma City bombing orchestrated by Terry Nichols and Timothy McVeigh in 1995.

39

MILITIA MADNESS

Beginning in 1992, a series of events resurrected the ideals and beliefs of the Posse Comitatus and sparked the formation of right-wing citizens' militias. First was the lethal 1992 standoff between federal agents and the family of Randy and Vicki Weaver at their home on Ruby Ridge, in remote Boundary County, Idaho. Second was the fiery death of scores of Branch Davidians in their compound in Waco, Texas, the following year. Third was the passage of federal gun-control legislation in 1993 and 1994. Convinced the government was at war with its own citizens by simultaneously trying to kill and disarm them, a broad spectrum of right-wing activists coalesced around the notion that it was time for paramilitary rebellion. Rather than declare themselves outlaw revolutionaries like Bob Matthews and the Order, militia organizers defined themselves according to the language of patriotic constitutional vigilantism that had been popularized by Bill Gale. Theirs was a *lawful* movement, grounded in centuries of divinely inspired jurisprudence; a *defensive* movement to *protect* American values and ideals; and a *deliberative* movement composed of men arranged in hierarchies governed by order and legitimacy. In reality, the militias were nothing of the sort. Most were patently illegal or tutored their followers in a litany of crime. Rhetoric about "defending" America was nothing more than a smoke screen for offensive action against agents of the supposed New World Order and other perceived enemies of the Republic. And as for their obsession with order and discipline, the militias were just as anarchic as the Posse had ever been. The only difference was that the militia movement was much larger and involved many more would-be guerrilla warriors, some of whom were eager for violence.

The militias had many facets—its links to hate groups, its embrace of Christian Common Law, its obsession with states' rights—but the movement had one overarching goal in mind: to create private armies to resist enforcement of gun-control legislation. Like the early days of the Posse Comitatus, the militia movement gained momentum and recruits by joining its cause to that of gun fanatics and other believers in the absolutism of the Second Amendment for whom the incidents at Waco and Ruby Ridge were clear examples of federal tyranny. The tragedy at Waco began with an attempt by the Bureau of Alcohol, Tobacco, and Firearms to arrest the Branch Davidian leader, David Koresh, for illegal firearms possession. And in the case of Randy Weaver, federal marshals were attempting to bring him to court after he had failed to appear on charges linked to the sale of a sawed-off shotgun. Both events set the stage for the emergence of militias and planted the seeds of destruction in the mind of Timothy McVeigh.[1]

Randy and Vicki Weaver were Christian Identity believers who had fled to Idaho from Iowa in 1983 in anticipation of the endtimes foretold in the Book of Revelation. After hanging around the fringes of the Aryan Nations, Randy Weaver got in trouble with the law for selling two sawed-off shotguns to a government informant in 1989. When he refused to become an informant himself, he was arrested on gun charges in January 1991. Released on bond, he skipped his next court date. For months, the U.S. Marshals Service conducted surveillance of the Weaver's remote cabin on Ruby Ridge in the Selkirk Mountains to figure out how best to take him in. On August 21, 1992, one of their carefully planned scouting missions went bad. Fourteen-year-old Samuel Weaver was killed in a shootout that also took the life of Deputy William Degan, one of the most highly decorated marshals in the service.

Vicki Weaver, forty-two, was killed the next day, half her head blown off by a bullet fired from two hundred yards away by Lon T. Horiuchi, a member of the FBI's elite Hostage Rescue Team.[2] Unbeknownst to the FBI sharpshooter, she was holding her infant of nearly nine months in her arms. Kevin Harris, a family friend, was severely wounded. Both Harris and Randy Weaver lay huddled in the cabin for nine more days with the Weavers' three surviving daughters before they surrendered to the FBI and were charged with Degan's death and other crimes. Their trial the following April attracted national media attention and a dedicated coterie of Christian Patriots and Aryan Nations supporters.

Weaver's lawyer was Gerry Spence, the flamboyant criminal defense attorney from Wyoming. Throughout the proceeding he referred to his client as a "white separatist" and never as the white *supremacist* he truly was. Spence's choice of words was critically important, because they suggested that all Weaver—and by extension, his supporters—wanted was to be "left alone," when their real goal was to purge America of blacks and Jews. The separatist label was an utter false-hood, of course, as Weaver and his wife fervently believed in the superiority of white, Anglo-Saxon Christians—the true people of Israel—over Satanic Jews and subhuman blacks. Weaver's supporters in the courtroom used the same fictitious terminology and before long the media was doing it, too: referring benignly to Weaver and other neo-Nazis, including those responsible for unprovoked and brutal murders, as simple "separatists."

On July 8, 1993, after the longest deliberations in the history of the Idaho federal courts, the jury announced its verdict: Harris was acquitted on all counts and Weaver was convicted of relatively minor offenses, including failure to appear at his earlier trial on the gun charges. He served only sixteen months in jail and was released in December 1993, just in time for Christmas. Two years later, in 1995, the U.S. Department of Justice settled a lawsuit that had been filed by the Weaver family. Although the government refused to admit any wrongdoing, it paid Weaver and his daughters $3.1 million for the deaths of Vicki and Samuel Weaver. Harris received $380,000 in a separate settlement.

The events at Ruby Ridge and their aftermath made Randy Weaver and Kevin Harris heroes in the eyes of the radical right. And the arrests of both men provided a rallying point for racist revolutionaries like Louis Beam, who helped organize United Citizens for Justice—a group that demanded criminal indict-ments against the government agents involved and pressed for Weaver's release from jail.[3] Two months after the standoff on Ruby Ridge, Beam addressed a gathering of 150 Christian Identity believers and other right-wing militants in Estes Park, Colorado. "The federals have by their murder of Samuel and Vicki Weaver brought all of us here together under the same roof for the same reason," Beam told the crowd. "For the first time in the twenty-two years that I have been in the movement, we are all marching to the beat of the same drum."[4]

It was October 1992, and the three-day meeting featured discussions about forming armed militias, reports on the importance of vigilante action, speeches by Identity "ministers," and strategy sessions about how to build a more unified movement to bring about a white Christian Republic. And if the tragedy at Ruby Ridge helped launch the militias, the massacre in Waco provided ample justifi-cation and dozens of martyrs to inspire the new movement.

The trouble began on February 28, 1993, less than five months after the meet-ing in Estes Park, when members of the Branch Davidian religious sect—an ob-scure offshoot of the Seventh-Day Adventist Church—successfully rebuffed federal agents from the Bureau of Alcohol, Tobacco, and Firearms. Four agents were killed and twenty wounded when they stormed the Texas compound—which the Davidians called Mount Carmel—in an effort to arrest David Koresh on gun charges.[5] The fifty-one-day siege that followed ended on April 19, 1993, when the FBI assaulted Mount Carmel and the compound went up in flames. The debacle occurred just five days after the trial of Randy Weaver and Kevin Harris began in Idaho, but Waco was much bigger news. Seventy-six Davidians perished in the fire, including seventeen children. Many of the victims died of gunshot wounds that the government alleged were inflicted by followers of Koresh.

Later that year, on November 30, 1993, President Clinton signed the Brady Bill, imposing a five-day waiting period for handgun buyers.[6] The law became effective in February 1994, while Congress was debating a new crime bill which contained language banning certain assault weapons.[7] Right-wing activists seized on Ruby Ridge, the tragedy at Waco, and the passage of new gun-control legislation as confirmation of their worst fears: If religious dissenters like the Weavers and the Davidians could be murdered by federal agents, it was only a matter of time before other Christian Patriots would be killed, too. And the Brady Bill was clear proof that federal bureaucrats intended to disarm Americans in preparation for a communist-style takeover by the New World Order.

Several weeks before the final government assault on the Davidian compound, a militia enthusiast named Linda D. Thompson—who also was a former soldier and an army reservist—distributed leaflets at an Indianapolis gun show urging that "everyone between seventeen and forty-five" should converge on Waco as members of the "unorganized militia."[8] Thompson was forty-one years old, a mother of three, and a self-proclaimed "dumpy nobody from Indianapolis." She also was a lawyer who had once worked for the ACLU and she had tried— unsuccessfully—to establish herself as David Koresh's attorney.[9] Failing at legal intervention, she instructed supporters to come to Waco and bring "long arms, vehicles (including tracked and armored), aircraft, and any available gear for inspection for fitness and use in a well-regulated militia . . ."[10] Two days later a tiny band of Thompson's "unorganized militia" brandished unloaded semiautomatic weapons as they milled about in a field adjacent to a Dairy Queen several miles from Mount Carmel. "Based on our observations this morning, they have definitely lived up to their title," quipped one ATF official.[11] There were no jokes from the ATF two weeks later, however, when the Waco compound went up in flames. Thompson was quick to take advantage of the tragedy and produced a series of videotapes claiming, among other things, that the government had deliberately set fire to the compound using tank-mounted flamethrowers. At least one of those tapes, *Waco, The Big Lie*, attracted the attention of Timothy McVeigh (who had visited Waco before April 19, selling patriotic bumper stickers and expounding his antigovernment beliefs) and Terry Nichols.[12]

Waco, Ruby Ridge, and the Brady Bill were the dominant themes at meetings organized in 1994 by John Trochman, founder of the Militia of Montana and cochair of Louis Beam's United Citizens for Justice. Two years earlier, Trochman had proclaimed himself a "free white Christian man, Republic of Montana State Citizen," and asserted he had never "knowingly been a citizen of the United States."[13] Though Trochman spoke the language of white supremacy, he understood the importance of delivering a political message more suitable for a broader audience. As he crisscrossed Montana in 1994 from February to May, lecturing to hundreds of potential recruits, he warned ominously about invasions by U.N. troops in black helicopters and spoke about the violent government clashes in Idaho and Texas. Trochman also extolled the glory of the Second Amendment and announced that American soldiers were being trained in "special operations" in preparation for the New World Order assault on civilians. "This federal government has rendered the several states defenseless by taking away their organized militia . . . and is now in the process of disarming the unorganized militia—that's you and me—by laws which are unconstitutional," Trochman warned. "A government which turns its tanks upon its own people for any reason is a government with a taste for blood. . . . We are on the brink of invasion, surrender, annihilation [and] population reduction. Plans are now about to swing into high gear. Will you be left alive, unmutilated? Or will you be part of the 'reduction process'?" he asked.[14] Trochman acted on these fears a year later when he and six other Montana militiamen were arrested after allegedly wearing concealed weapons and intimidating officials at the Musselshell County jail. Equipped with weapons, radio equipment, plastic handcuffs, and $80,000 in cash, gold, and silver, the men were suspected of planning to kidnap a local judge whose rulings had angered Christian Patriots, but charges were never brought against them.[15]

On April 19, 1994, the first anniversary of Waco, Linda Thompson issued an inflammatory call to arms. Titled *Ultimatum* and signed "acting adjutant general" of the "Unorganized Militia of the United States," the document could have been lifted verbatim from the phony indictment issued by Bill Gale's Committee of the States a decade earlier. Among other things, Thompson charged the government with treason for violating states rights, enforcing the "unlawful federal income tax," usurping the rights of "sovereign citizens," and permitting the existence of the Federal Reserve. Mailed to every member of Congress, the declaration demanded abolition of the Fourteenth, Sixteenth, and Seventeenth Amendments; repeal of the Brady Bill and the North American Free Trade Agreement; repudiation of the United Nations; and nullification of all debts owed to the Federal Reserve. "If you do not personally and publicly attend to these demands, you will be identified as a Traitor, and you will be brought up on charges for Treason before a Court of the Citizens of this Country [*sic*]," Thompson threatened. Then, in an accompanying *Alert*, Thompson ordered all militia units to assemble "armed and in uniform" in Washington, D.C., on September 19, 1994, to enforce her demands.[16] Fellow patriots were divided in their response to Thompson's call. Most accused her of aiding the "conspiracy" by openly inciting violence that was sure to get scores of patriots killed, while others praised her courage or agreed with the need for a show of force. "Thompson's proposed armed coup is either utter nonsense, or the deliberate leading of conservatives over a cliff," warned the John Birch Society with predictable timidity.[17] One month before the supposed showdown, Thompson backed off. The *Ultimatum* had merely been a ploy to mobilize militia members for future action, she explained. "God bless us all. Death to the New World Order," she wrote.[18] Notwithstanding cancellation of the scheduled rebellion, militia members remained on high alert—continuously exchanging faxes, phone calls, electronic messages, and listening to short-wave radio broadcasts for news of the imminent invasion by the New World Order.

By the fall of 1994, rising fears had spawned militia groups in more than a dozen states, and some overanxious recruits were eager to engage the enemy. On September 8, three men were arrested on weapons charges after police in the small town of Fowlerville, Michigan, found them with loaded rifles and handguns, armor-piercing ammunition, night-vision goggles, gas masks, two-way radios, and survival knives. Dressed in camouflage, they said they were on "night maneuvers."[19] And early in 1995, members of a Detroit-area militia plotted to raid a National Guard base, Camp Grayling, and blow up decommissioned Soviet tanks stored there. The tanks had been captured during the Persian Gulf War and were used for training purposes, but the militiamen were convinced that invading communist armies would commandeer them.[20]

Formed two months after the Montana group, the Michigan Militia claimed some ten thousand members in sixty-three of the state's eighty-three counties by the fall of 1994. Though these figures were exaggerated, the militia movement was far larger than the Posse Comitatus ever had been and it attracted tens of thousands of supporters nationwide. In Missouri, militia groups expanded from four to forty of the state's 114 counties from 1994 to 1995.[21] And in Montana, where some observers took solace in the fact that 68 percent of people polled said they "actively opposed" the views of the militia, as many as 20 percent declared their support—a huge number for a supposed fringe group.[22] By 1996 the Southern Poverty Law Center counted 370 active militia groups nationwide.

Just as Bill Gale had inspired Linda Thompson's "indictment" of Congress, his instructions for forming citizens' grand juries were revived by militia activists who convened "common-law courts" in the 1990s. Beginning in 1993, disgruntled Christian Patriots used such proceedings to manufacture fake indictments and issue "citizen's arrest warrants" against judges and other enemies.[23] One survey found that 55 percent of 431 state and local judges reported encountering common-law advocates who challenged their authority with physical threats, bogus lawsuits, and common-law liens. The U.S. Marshals Service reported that threats against federal judicial officials rose from 271 in 1996, to 612 in 1997.[24] Some court activists charged opponents with "capital crimes" and announced that the militia would enforce their edicts.[25] In 1994, a Missouri highway patrolman, Corporal Bobbie J. Harper, helped arrest a common-law court activist, Robert N. Joos Jr., for simulating the legal process. Three months after the arrest, Corporal Harper was standing in the kitchen of his rural home, spooning ice cream into a bowl, when a bullet fired from a high-powered rifle slammed into his chest, lodging one-sixteenth of an inch from his heart. Harper retired from the highway patrol but died the following April during heart surgery. Harper's suspected assailant, a Christian Patriot by the name of Timothy T. Coombs, is still a fugitive eight years later.[26]

By 1998, threats and other confrontations had spurred twenty-seven states to either pass or consider new laws to punish or outlaw common-law court activities. While many court enthusiasts were new to the right-wing movement, there were others—like former AAM activist Gene Schroder—who had been deeply immersed in Posse Comitatus doggerel for years. Instead of extolling the virtues of parity, Schroder was now crisscrossing the country warning that America had been in an official state of emergency ever since 1933 because of Depression-era declarations issued by President Franklin D. Roosevelt. Schroder convened his own common-law courts, which "found" that all civil liberties had been suspended and concluded that the Republic was in dire need of rescuing. He toured the country—and the Internet—issuing his clarion cry of warning to anyone who would listen, and he sold plenty of books and videos along the way to worried Christian Patriots who were eager to find out more.

In addition to their pretended jurisprudence (as well as their frequent target practice and night maneuvers) militia activists sought legislative allies to advance their political agenda. In Montana, a so-called "sheriff empowerment" bill passed the legislature but was vetoed by the governor. The measures would have required all federal law enforcement agents to register with the local sheriff before pursuing a suspect in their jurisdiction. Another bill urged all Montanans to have "the proper weapons for service in the militia." And although this measure was more a product of the Christian Right than the militias, the Montana Senate passed legislation requiring lifetime state registration of gays and lesbians, along with murderers and rapists. "This type of action [homosexuality] is even worse than a violent sex act," explained State Senator Al Bishop.[27]

In neighboring Idaho, a coterie of high-ranking elected officials flirted with the militia, including the secretary of state, the superintendent of public instruction, the lieutenant governor, the attorney general, and freshman Republican congresswoman Helen Chenoweth, whom the state's leading newspaper dubbed "the poster child" for the militias.[28] Founded in January 1994, the Idaho-based United States Militia Association was led by Sam Sherwood, a forty-four-year-old sometime computer consultant. Like many in the movement, Sherwood enjoyed delivering long-winded speeches to rapt audiences of eager followers who hung on his every word. A devout Mormon who falsely claimed Israeli citizenship (he spent five weeks on a kibbutz when he was twenty-one and praised the Jewish state), Sherwood wasn't the anti-Semite that other militia leaders were, but his obsession with conspiracies attracted an extremist following of haters nonetheless.[29] Feeding the paranoia common in the movement, one of Sherwood's militia brochures predicted that American gun owners would soon be disarmed by Chinese police:

"Bill Clinton is bringing up to 100,000 Hong Kong Chineese [sic] to America to be his federal police. Bill Clinton is planning to seize every gun in America

with his Chineese [*sic*] police!" And in terms surely offensive to Jews, the bro-
chure accused the president of killing "more babies than Hitler."[30] The president's crime bill did call for one hundred thousand new police officers, but the
fantasy about Hong Kong patrolmen had its origins, ironically, in a Republican-
sponsored amendment (that was inspired by fears of "Asian gangs") that tried to
add a feasibility study to the bill to examine the possible use of a small number
of Hong Kong police as federal law liaisons to Asian communities. (The proposal
was dropped from the final bill).[31]

Idaho provided an especially receptive audience for Sherwood's polemics
against gun control. On July 3, 1994, an estimated fifteen hundred people gathered at the state capitol for a "Citizens Rally for Constitutional Rights" to declare
their fealty to the Second Amendment. Sherwood addressed the crowd, then
solicited $10 monthly memberships while presiding over a table flanked with a
large banner that read IDAHO MILITIA INFORMATION.[32] The following month he
claimed five hundred members across the state and declared that half of Idaho's
sheriffs supported his efforts. At least sixteen lawmen took the time to formally
disagree. "[We] give absolutely no support to the idea of a militia," announced
Greg Moffat, president of the Tri-County [Sheriffs] Association.[33] The state adjutant general also had little patience with Sherwood. "Further evidence of the
fallacy of forming local government militia units as preached by the U.S. Militia
Association, is found in the Idaho law which declares that *only* the governor may
organize the *unorganized militia*," explained Commanding General Darryl Manning in an October 1994 memo.[34] Criticism notwithstanding, Sherwood claimed
one thousand members across twenty counties by November and said he mobilized many of them on behalf of political candidates. State school superintendent
Anne Fox returned the favor when she addressed eighty camouflage-clad members of the U.S. Militia Association at the state capitol in February. Fox had been
invited to speak about education issues but when she compared the negative press
she had received during her first six weeks in office to the persecution of Anne
Frank by the Nazis, condemnation was swift. Appropriately, it came from Daniel
Yurman, director of Community Relations for the two hundred families that
comprised the Jewish Community of Eastern Idaho. Yurman was a staunch opponent of the militias and arguably the most knowledgeable person in the state
about their activities.[35] In a letter to the governor, Yurman said: "It is an outrage
for Anne Fox to on the one hand speak to citizens' militia members dressed up
like Gestapo storm troopers and on the other claim she has been persecuted the
same as the six million Jews who died in the Holocaust." Fox apologized privately
to Jewish leaders but declined to distance herself publicly from the militia.[36] The
same was true for Idaho secretary of state Pete Cenarrusa who had shared the
platform with Fox. At first Cenarrusa tried to put himself at arms' length from
Sherwood's organization but then he thought better of it and told the *Idaho
Statesman* that the militias were a good group of people whom he would address
again.[37] Less than a month later, Lieutenant Governor C. L. "Butch" Otter spoke

to Sherwood's members. But instead of delivering his standard stump speech, Otter was forced to answer questions from militia members who demanded to know how he planned to resist enforcement of federal environmental laws. Otter's answers didn't satisfy the group, but according to news reports, Sherwood had a definite idea of what to do. "Go up and look legislators in the face, because someday you may be forced to blow it off," he allegedly told his members on March 2, 1995.[38] Sherwood later said he had been misquoted. An outraged legislature unanimously denounced the statement, but not Congresswoman Helen Chenoweth. Two weeks later—and less than three months after arriving in Washington, D.C.—she convened an all-day hearing in Boise, *Excessive Use of Government Force*, at which Sherwood spoke. Flanked by Lieutenant Governor Otter and Secretary of State Cenarrusa, Chenoweth, fifty-seven, declared her yardstick for measuring a democracy: "[W]hen the government is afraid of the people."[39] Talk of "black helicopters," state sovereignty, Second Amendment rights, the Endangered Species Act, and other forms of government tyranny dominated the session, but Sherwood was neither questioned nor criticized about his remarks suggesting violence. Even after the Oklahoma City bombing, Chenoweth stuck to her rhetorical guns. "I am not willing to condemn militias," she told the *Statesman*. "While we can never condone [the bombing,] we still must begin to look at the public policies that may be pushing people too far."[40] Among other things, Chenoweth concluded that a federal version of Montana's "sheriffs' empowerment" legislation was needed.[41] Despite enthusiasm in militia ranks for Chenoweth's proposed "Civil Rights Act of 1995," the Idaho Police Chiefs Association overwhelmingly refused to endorse the measure. The proposal also went nowhere on Capitol Hill.[42]

The idea of requiring federal agents to obtain written permission from local authorities before pursing law enforcement actions at the county level may have been a political non-starter, but that didn't prevent some local lawmen from siding with the militia when it came to enforcing the Brady Bill. One of them was Sheriff Jay Printz of Ravalli County, Montana, who successfully challenged the Brady Bill in federal court. The top lawman in the remote Bitterroot Valley, Printz was criticized for taking a go-slow approach when it came to dealing with area tax protesters and other militia supporters. "People are pretty conservative in this area and some of the issues [militia leaders] bring up, I'm concerned about, too," the sheriff acknowledged.[43] Printz acted on these sympathies early in 1995 when he filed a lawsuit asserting it was unconstitutional for Congress to compel local law enforcement officials like himself to conduct criminal background checks on would-be gun buyers. His case was consolidated with that of another sheriff who had similar views, Richard Mack of Graham County, Arizona, a sparsely populated jurisdiction with just 28,000 residents.[44] By a vote of five to four, the United States Supreme Court agreed with the sheriffs. The majority opinion, written by Justice Antonin Scalia, was a triumph for states' rights and gutted the requirement that local law enforcement assist the federal government in screening out felons, juveniles, those convicted of domestic violence, and others deemed similarly dangerous from purchasing handguns. Printz's legal bills were paid by the National Rifle Association.[45] After filing his lawsuit, Sheriff Mack joined the Christian Patriot speaking circuit where he gave passionate speeches about his devotion to constitutional government and hawked his two books: *From My Cold Dead Fingers: Why America Needs Guns!* and *Government, GOD, and Freedom: A Fundamental Trinity.* Mack had won office in 1992 with 57 percent of the vote, but all his traipsing out-of-state became a campaign issue and he was defeated in the Democratic primary after just one term in office.[46]

Activists like Sheriff Mack came and went, but militia enthusiasts continued to push their agenda by emphasizing states' rights and the supposed supremacy of the Tenth Amendment. Beginning in 1994, at least twenty state legislatures considered or passed resolutions championing states' rights and condemning the federal government.[47] Instead of relying on the dated—and more explicitly racist—arguments offered by segregationists in the 1960s, these proclamations denounced "unfunded federal mandates" and hailed the importance of the Tenth Amendment. Long a rallying point for opponents of the federal government, the Tenth Amendment reserved to the states any powers "not delegated to the United States [nor prohibited] by the Constitution. . . ."[48] There wasn't much difference between these militia-inspired resolutions and the language found in the platform of the Republican Party. After all, many of the seventy-three Republicans who had helped the GOP seize control of Congress in November 1994, had done so by denouncing federal environmental laws, gun control, the Department of Education, civil rights statutes, and other "intrusions" by Washington, D.C.[49] But despite these similarities, leaders of the Tenth Amendment movement, such as Colorado state senator Charles Duke, saw things in a very different light. According to Duke, House Speaker Newt Gingrich was a "counterfeit Republican" and a "globalist" bent on betraying American sovereignty to international interests. One year before the Oklahoma City bombing, Duke, a fifty-three-year-old former engineer for Hewlett-Packard, introduced a resolution in the state senate asserting the supremacy of state government. The measure lacked the force of law, but its text gave a different impression:

> Whereas, the scope of power defined by the Tenth Amendment means that the federal government was created by the states specifically to be an agent of the states. . . . Be it resolved . . . that this serve as a notice and demand to the federal government, as our agent, to cease and desist, effective immediately, mandates that are beyond the scope of its constitutionally delegated powers.[50]

Duke's resolution passed easily fifty-one to thirteen in the Colorado House, and twenty-five to seven in the Senate, and he became an instant celebrity at militia meetings and on the right-wing talk-show circuit.

Another advocate of the Tenth Amendment movement was Colorado attorney general Gale Norton (who was appointed secretary of the interior in 2001 by President George W. Bush). In August 1996, in a speech for the Independence Institute (a conservative "free-market think tank" based in Golden, Colorado), Norton took pride in the fact that her office was "in the trenches . . . trying to make a difference" on issues of state sovereignty. The remark was innocuous enough, but a digression that followed was revealing. Norton recalled that on a recent trip to Virginia she had wandered through a Civil War graveyard and was struck by a memorial to all the soldiers "who died in defense of the sovereignty of their state."

"Sure, I had been filing briefs and I thought that was pretty brave. [But] we lost the idea that the states were to stand against the federal government gaining too much power over our lives. That is the point I think we need to reappreciate," she explained.[51]

Charles Duke's lead partner in promoting the Tenth Amendment movement was a California state senator, Don Rogers, who won passage of a California version of Duke's Colorado resolution in August 1994. Rogers also was an anti-abortion, pro-gun, pro-business conservative who expressed his contempt for environmental laws and the income tax with personal action as well as words. (In 1992, he had accumulated $140,000 in unpaid taxes and penalties to the IRS.)[52] Rogers's views won him an invitation to address a conference of Christian Identity believers in 1994. The gathering was sponsored by the *Jubilee*, a California hate sheet with a national following that denounced race-mixing, extolled the virtues of "Christian Israelites," and proudly published the writings of men like Louis Beam. Rogers had spoken to the group before and he described it falsely as a meeting of "patriotic Americans who are working to preserve and restore individual rights and freedoms."[53]

The state sovereignty movement had particular appeal in the West, where the Clinton administration's attempted enforcement of environmental laws (particularly the Endangered Species Act) was opposed by corporations, farmers, ranchers, miners, and loggers who believed they were entitled to the region's federally owned natural resources, with minimal interference and expense.[54] Like those early Posse activists in Oregon who opposed land-use planning, and their brethren in Wisconsin who won recruits by vilifying the Department of Natural Resources, Tenth Amendment activists and their militia allies popularized their cause by demonizing the Bureau of Land Management, the U.S. Forest Service, the U.S. Fish and Wildlife Service, and the National Park Service. Conflicts ranged from scuffles between federal environmental workers and angry ranchers to pipe-bomb attacks and death threats.[55] Tensions peaked in Idaho in 1995 after a federal judge closed six national forests to protect endangered salmon. "Please don't shoot me," pleaded one forest supervisor to a group of armed ranchers and miners that descended on his office in protest. Implementation of the ruling was halted by an injunction, but the fears of losing logging, grazing, and mining rights on public lands was enough to drive hundreds of furious Idahoans into the arms of the militia.[56] Speaking to a large crowd in Challis, Idaho, in early March, Sam Sherwood urged everyone to "get a semiautomatic assault rifle and a revolver and a uniform." Sherwood also foresaw "blood in the streets" if the judge's ruling was upheld. "We want a bloodless revolution. But if the bureaucrats won't listen, we'll give them a civil war to think about," he threatened. Secretary of State Pete Cenarrusa predicted civil unrest. "There is going to be a great uprising among the people here," he said. "It's a matter of survival and when these instincts are aroused, anything can happen."[57]

Not all of Sherwood's appearances were enthusiastically received. WE WANT OUR TOWN BACK, and WE STAND AGAINST SEDITION, were two of the signs carried by fifty antimilitia protesters in September 1995 when the Idaho militia leader showed up to address a hundred and fifty people in a local high school.[58] And across the state line, the Montana Human Rights Network launched an aggressive statewide campaign to oppose the militias through grassroots organizing, legislative advocacy, public education, and other means. The militia movement works like "a funnel moving through space," explained Network director Ken Toole, now a state senator:

> At the front end, it's picking up lots and lots of people by hitting on issues that have wide appeal, like gun control and environmental restrictions.... Then you go a little bit further and it's about ideology, about the oppressiveness of the federal government.... Then further in, you get into the belief systems ... it's about the anti-Semitic conspiracy. Finally at the narrowest end ... you get someone like Tim McVeigh popping out.[59]

The Network's job—which it performed admirably with limited resources—was to block the wide funnel opening, waving off all likely sympathizers as loudly and visibly as possible, while pointing to the violence and bigotry issuing from the narrower end. Similar efforts were launched by groups in other states, like the Coalition for Human Dignity in Portland, Oregon, and the Northwest Coalition Against Malicious Harassment, which pulled together antihate activists from across the region. Just as PrairieFire and other rural groups had successfully confronted the radical right during the farm crisis, these organizations played a crucial role in exposing the militia movement by encouraging critical media coverage. They also helped turn public opinion against paramilitary groups and isolated state legislators who chose political equivocation instead of condemnation when it came to antigovernment threats and violence.

While some state elected officials thrilled to talk of the Tenth Amendment, their counterparts at the local level also raised the flag of county secession. Between 1990 and 1992, officials in Catron County, New Mexico, passed a total of twenty-one ordinances that purported to supersede the authority of federal workers managing public lands. Some seventy other counties throughout the West followed suit. Several of the Catron County ordinances defined federal grazing permits as private property—not the public entitlements that they actually were—while others claimed title to all Forest Service roads within the county or arbitrarily gave the county the authority to seize and manage public lands for private use.[60] Similar thinking surfaced in Nye County, Nevada, the largest, and one of the least populated, counties in the nation. Ninety-three percent of the 18,000 square miles that make up Nye County is owned by the federal government and when County Commissioner Dick Carver mounted a bulldozer in July 1994 and careened through a federal barrier blocking access to a wilderness area in the Toiyabe National Forest, a crowd of supporters, some of them armed, cheered. Federal workers chose not to intervene. Elsewhere in Nevada, other would-be secessionists made similar political noise but used explosives instead. Three bombings of federal property in the state targeted the Forest Service and the Bureau of Land Management from 1993 to 1995. Luckily, no one was injured.[61]

Haunted by memories of Ruby Ridge and Waco, the federal government dodged confrontation. Commissioner Carver's actions were clearly illegal, but federal officials declined to arrest him, deciding, lamely, to file a civil suit instead. A federal court eventually ruled in the government's favor—finding, not suprisingly, that public lands belong to the federal government, not the state or county. But Carver already had gained the momentum and fifteen minutes of fame he needed from the showdown, and he joined the Christian Patriot meeting circuit, making a traveling troika with State Senators Duke and Rogers, and spinning the story of the Nye County rebellion to many enthusiastic audiences.[62] Fearing similar confrontations between federal workers and secessionist-inspired county authorities, the Bureau of Land Management instructed its employees to go peacefully if arrested by local officials and then call the nearest U.S. attorney. One Forest Service memorandum even gave employees the option of not wearing their uniforms or traveling in government vehicles if they thought it would jeopardize their safety. And in Idaho, the director of the BLM issued a "County Supremacy Movement Safety Guidance" memo that, among other things, advised employees to "avoid areas with a known potential for conflict."[63]

"The self-conscious timidity of the Justice Department means that no federal employee in the West can do his job of protecting resources and remain confident that his actions will be supported," said Jeff DeBonis, the executive director of Public Employees for Environmental Responsibility, a national organization composed of state and federal employees working in resource management and environmental protection. Criticism by experts like DeBonis and others prompted a House committee to pass legislation requiring more thorough reporting of such incidents, but not all committee members supported the measure.

"People here in the West know they can't mine, they can't log, they can't work, they can't turn their cattle out," said Helen Chenoweth, the militia apologist from Idaho.[64] Other members of Congress lent similar legitimacy to claims of the Tenth Amendment movement.

"The federal government doesn't have a right to own any lands except post offices and armed-forces bases," asserted freshman Congresswoman Barbara Cubin of Wyoming, mindlessly. Unlike Charles Duke's paper-tiger resolutions, this wasn't just a verbal argument about the theoretical apportionment of power in the Republic; vast resources were at stake, including 435 million acres of Western lands managed by federal agencies. The idea that the federal government should cede ownership of this property to the states was ludicrous, but it appealed to both militant local officials and influential conservatives in Washington, D.C. "The whole idea is that this land is within a state; so why is the federal government the owner of the land?" explained one analyst of the Heritage Foundation, a right-wing think tank. The solution was ready-made and simplistic: With the exception of select national parks, Congress would "return" all federal land to the states over five to seven years. But this far-reaching proposal failed to explain how the states would pick up the cost of managing such huge tracts of land; in 1994 the federal government spent almost $1 billion on fire management alone in Western states.[65] Idaho's Pete Cenarrusa seemed blind to such facts when he demanded that "state officials . . . support us in our claim to public lands within our respective states."[66] Such posturing did not impress the state controller, however, who noted that transferring ownership of federal land to the state would be a "financial disaster" that would cost Idaho $90 million a year in federal funds. In Colorado, Governor Roy Romer agreed. Citing a potential $40 million loss of federal payments, Romer announced his opposition to a bill then pending in Congress to return federal land to the states.[67]

By 1995, sixteen states had adopted versions of Duke's sovereignty resolution. "[State] secession is inevitable if we cannot return the federal government to its constitutional box," warned the Colorado senator in typically alarmist terms.[68] Despite the growing popularity of Duke's movement, prominent Republicans like Utah governor Mike Leavitt shrugged off the state sovereignty agenda. "I really believe these people are just a speck in the national picture," Leavitt told the *New York Times*. "What's changed is the technology," he said, suggesting that fax machines and the Internet had exaggerated the political impact of supposed fringe groups.[69] Leavitt's explanation sounded comforting, but it missed the point. The same technology was available to liberal organizations, which were much better funded than Duke and his militia-loving cohorts, but they weren't having nearly as much success coordinating ideological assaults on state legislatures. What politicians like Leavitt did not want to admit was that the Tenth Amendment movement had a real political base and it was composed not only of former Posse Comitatus activists, tax protesters, Identity believers, and other Christian Patriots, but also thousands of otherwise mainstream members of the GOP. Governor Leavitt was forced to acknowledge this political reality when his plans to hold a major national conference of state leaders in Philadelphia were scuttled by the sovereignty movement. The Conference of the States, as the event was called, was due to take place in October 1995 and was sponsored by political heavyweights like the National Conference of State Legislatures and the bipartisan (but GOP-leaning) National Governors Association. As conceived by Governor Leavitt and Nebraska governor Ben Nelson, a Democrat, the conference required the prior approval of at least twenty-six states, but by April 1995 only fourteen had agreed to participate and by July it had been canceled. Charles Duke of Colorado and his California ally, Don Rogers, played key roles mobilizing opposition to the event, claiming it was a stalking horse for a secret "Constitutional Convention" to deliver America into the octopus arms of the New World Order.

Although Leavitt belittled such theories, enough state legislators embraced them elsewhere to derail his gathering. While pundits enjoyed scoffing at the paranoid anxieties of militia members who feared black helicopters and foreign invasions, respectable elected officials echoed many of the same claims, giving the militias political clout. In May 1994, for example, Oklahoma legislators endorsed right-wing conspiracy-mongering when the state House adopted a resolution demanding that Congress "cease any support for the establishment of a 'new world order' [and] refrain from taking any further steps toward the economic or political merger of the United States into a world body or any form of world government."[70]

Oklahoma legislators may only have been putting harmless words on paper, but a similar outlook drove Timothy McVeigh and Terry Nichols to destroy the Alfred P. Murrah Building one year later. After loading more than two tons of fuel oil and fertilizer in the back of a rented Ryder truck, the men detonated their bomb at 9:02 A.M. on April 19, 1995. The blast turned nine floors of the federal building into rubble, killing 168 people and wounding hundreds more. It was the two-year anniversary of Waco. Media hype briefly attributed the blast to foreign terrorists but experts on the militia movement suspected otherwise.

Within ninety minutes of the blast, Timothy McVeigh was pulled over by a highway patrolman outside Perry, Oklahoma, for driving his 1977 Mercury Marquis without a license plate. A Gulf War veteran who quit the military after rejection by Army Special Forces, McVeigh was arrested on traffic charges and for carrying a loaded semiautomatic pistol. Two days later he was charged in the bombing after an FBI inventory of the contents of his car turned up an envelope containing typewritten documents and copies of pages from right-wing magazines and books, including excerpts from *The Turner Diaries*.[71] Even before the FBI uncovered this evidence, watchdog groups were making a connection between the *Diaries* and the bombing.[72] And it didn't take reporters very long to determine that McVeigh and his accomplice, Terry Nichols, were steeped in right-wing ideology.

Two years before the bombing, Nichols had tried to use a "Certified Fractional Reserve Check" to pay off more than $17,000 he owed the Chase Manhattan Bank. Nichols had obtained the check in January 1993, from a Tigerton, Wisconsin, organization called Family Farm Preservation, which was run by veteran Posse activist Thomas Stockheimer.[73] (In May 1996, Stockheimer and eight associates were charged with mail fraud and conspiracy for selling bogus money orders.)[74] In 1993, James Nichols, Terry's brother, was stopped in Michigan for speeding. James was never charged in connection with the Oklahoma City bombing, but, like Terry, he parroted Posse catechism in court. He attempted to argue his case pro se and tried unsuccessfully to assert his "sovereign" status before the judge. Like countless other "freemen" and Christian Patriots, James Nichols also claimed the Constitution granted him a right to travel, so he needed no license to drive.

40

THE ROAD FROM OKLAHOMA CITY

Two months after the carnage in Oklahoma City, Republican senator Arlen Specter of Pennsylvania held a hearing of his Subcommittee on Terrorism, Technology, and Government, to investigate the militia movement. But Specter invited no representatives of watchdog groups or victims of militia harassment to testify. And witnesses from the FBI and the Bureau of Alcohol, Tobacco, and Firearms revealed less than what could be known from reading the daily newspaper. Caught flatfooted by domestic terrorists instead of the foreign ones they had assumed were responsible for the blast, the FBI was still scrambling to get up-to-speed on the militias. Specter's subcommittee did hear strongly worded testimony from several senators, as well as law enforcement officials, but he also invited five militiamen to speak, and they succeeded in turning the hearing into a platform for their beliefs.

A former federal prosecutor and GOP presidential hopeful, Specter was well known for aggressively questioning Anita Hill during the Supreme Court confirmation hearings for Clarence Thomas four years earlier. And he had exhibited considerable gusto during hearings on the mistakes made by the BATF and the FBI in Waco and Ruby Ridge—debacles that had occurred during Bill Clinton's watch. But Specter displayed little of that prosecutorial fervor when he showed up to do battle with militia leaders on June 15, 1995. Instead of confronting them with evidence of bigotry and their ties to hate groups, Specter was poorly prepared and they skillfully seized the ninety minutes he gave them. Instead of an aggressive probe of militia mendacity, the Senate panel heard the militiamen proclaim their patriotism and honest-to-goodness distrust of government.

Denouncing "the increasing amount of federal encroachment into our lives," Michigan Militia leader Norman E. Olson told the subcommittee that the government "needs a good spanking to make it behave." The colorful quote was picked up in the national media, as was Olson's charge that the Senate panel represented "corruption in government." The accusation may have infuriated Specter but it probably played well in Peoria. Montana militiaman John Trochman abandoned his usual rant about Soviet tanks poised to invade America and assumed the role of a beleaguered patriot defending the Constitution when he described his group as "a giant neighborhood watch . . . made up of a cross-section of Americans from all walks of life. . . ." And James Johnson, a black utility lineman from Columbus, Ohio, and spokesman for that state's "unorganized militia," asserted that the movement "is not about guns and skin color. It is about liberty and freedom." Johnson's testimony was ludicrous—especially when he termed militias "the civil-rights movement of the 1990s"—but no less so than Specter's decision to invite him to Washington in the first place. Like the rare black nationalist who appears at a Klan meeting to endorse "separation of the races," Johnson's presence on the panel undermined charges of white supremacy that critics had successfully leveled against the militias. Specter also neglected to challenge Trochman about his link to the Aryan Nations, or the 1992 Posse-style declaration he had filed saying he was a "free, white, Christian . . . Republic of Montana State Citizen."[1]

When they weren't portraying themselves as genuine patriots, the militiamen welcomed the opportunity to digress about the sinister machinations of the New World Order. "There are weather-control techniques, and we have a whole packet on this, so the New World Order will be able to starve people all over the world. We have the documents to prove it," said Trochman's semi-hysterical sidekick, Bob Fletcher. "I think we can leave that behind for a moment," Specter replied dryly. It was one of the hearings few amusing moments. Then, when Norman Olson compared militia conspiracy theories about who bombed the Murrah Building (it might have been the Japanese government or a CIA plot, he speculated) to public skepticism about the "single-bullet theory" of the Kennedy assassination, Specter lost both his temper and control of the proceedings. "I'll be happy to go one-on-one, here, on the record [to debate you]" about the president's death, barked Specter, taking Olson's bait, as the militia leader surely knew that the senator had served as counsel to the Warren Commission that investigated the Kennedy assassination three decades earlier.

Specter was not the only one who lost ground to the militiamen. Senator Dianne Feinstein—a liberal California Democrat—gave Trochman and the others ample opportunity to clear themselves of any political link to the Oklahoma City bombing when she asked, solicitously and without follow-up, whether there were any circumstances in which an individual "would be justified in bombing a building?"

"No!" came the emphatic and unanimous reply. Feinstein then helped the militias put to rest charges of vigilantism. "Do you believe there are situations in which people can take the law into their own hands?" she asked weakly, giving them the opening they needed. "Absolutely not. . . . Unless our families' lives are threatened," they answered. And what sensible American watching the proceedings live on C-SPAN would disagree with *that*? The spectacle was especially painful for militia experts who had cautioned Specter beforehand about how attempts by politicians and others to interrogate the leaders of right-wing groups often backfired. An essay by this author in that morning's edition of the Capitol Hill newspaper *Roll Call* pointed out that past congressional probes of the Ku Klux Klan had boosted the hooded order or left it in no worse shape than before. "Congress gave us the best advertising we ever got," declared Klan Imperial Wizard William Simmons after delivering a theatrical performance on Capitol Hill in 1921. "Congress *made* us," he crowed.[2] The right-wing Liberty Lobby had a similar assessment of the Specter hearing. Militia members simply "stole the show," said the *Spotlight*. Congressman Charles E. Schumer agreed. Specter's hearing had been a "soapbox for the wacky right" according to the New York Democrat.

Specter's witnesses also took advantage of their all-expense-paid trip to Washington to organize a two-and-a-half-hour news conference to promote themselves and share various theories about the bombing. Equipped with visual aids, Olson and others explained how not one, but two bombs were used in Oklahoma City, thereby proving the blast originated *inside* the building and was the work of government agents. Linda Thompson concurred. "[Oklahoma City] is the Clinton administration Reichstag," she explained, comparing the destruction of the Murrah Building to the 1933 fire that destroyed the German parliament and was used as a pretext by Adolf Hitler to brutally suppress his opponents. After all, if the government could kill 76 people in Waco, Thompson argued, it certainly was capable of murdering 168 in Oklahoma City to justify an all-out war against patriotic militias.[3]

Beyond insulting Specter and scoring points with the media, most of Norman Olson's testimony justified the creation of private armies. "Neither the citizens' militia nor the citizens' private arsenal can be an appropriate subject for federal regulation," asserted the Baptist minister and gun-shop owner from northern Michigan. Repeating a popular historical myth, he claimed that it was the "armed militia of the American colonies [that] ultimately led to the establishment of the United States." In truth, many of the state militias were ill-equipped, poorly trained, and performed notoriously badly, and it was the Continental Army led by George Washington—ragged and dispirited though it often was— that won the Revolutionary War. Like most Christian Patriots, Olson couched his arguments in the language of natural rights and disregarded any jurisprudence that contradicted his outlandish claims. Americans could arm themselves without restriction; the right to form militias "existed from antiquity"; and "there is no possible way that a governor or the chief executive of the United States, or any legislative body can 'outlaw' the citizen militia," he declared. However, despite his arrogant pronouncements, every one of his arguments had been thoroughly disposed of in the courts years earlier. In a definitive 1939 case, the United States Supreme Court rejected the argument that the "well-regulated militia" spoken of in the Second Amendment permitted ownership of illegal weapons.[4] In 1977, the Tenth Circuit Court of Appeals reaffirmed that position in the case of a Kansas Posseman who claimed he was entitled to own an unregistered machine gun because he met the state criteria for membership in the militia:

"To apply the [Second] Amendment so as to guarantee appellant's right to keep an unregistered firearm which has not been shown to have any connection to the militia, merely because he is technically a member of the Kansas militia, would be unjustifiable in terms of either logic or policy," the appellate court explained.[5]

And despite Olson's assertion that citizens had an absolute right to form private armies, twenty-four states outlawed the practice and an equal number banned private paramilitary training outright. The authority for the former prohibitions was found in an 1886 United States Supreme Court ruling which observed, in part, that "military operations and military drill are subjects especially under the control of the government of every country. They cannot be claimed as a right independent of law."[6] And a subsequent 1944 case cogently articulated the logic behind the government's authority to restrict the formation of private armies:

> There can be no justification for the organization of such an armed force. Its existence would be incompatible with the fundamental concept of our form of government. The inherent potential danger of any organized private militia, even if never used or even if ultimately placed at the disposal of the government, is obvious. Its existence would be sufficient, without more, to prevent a democratic form of government, such as ours, from functioning freely, without coercion, and in accordance with the constitutional mandate.[7]

But Norman Olson and other militia diehards simply pretended these legal precedents did not exist. Neither did they acknowledge the Dick Act of 1903, which formally established the National Guard as the legal successor to state militias and solidly placed them under government jurisdiction.[8] Perhaps Olson was right to ignore these laws and rulings, however. Because even in the wake of the Oklahoma City bombing, no state attorney general had the courage or the political will to move against a militia group that had illegally established itself as a private army in their state. And in the case of bans on paramilitary training, prosecutors were hampered by the need to show proof of criminal intent. Because many militia groups were content (and smart enough) to practice their military maneuvers without a specific target in mind, it made prosecuting them extremely difficult. But whatever the reason for the failure of states to enforce the law, watchdog groups strongly urged Congress to craft new federal legislation outlawing militias and private armies.[9] Senator Carl Levin voiced these concerns when he declared his disgust at the entire concept of militias, period. "We don't need private armies to protect us from our own government," he said. But Specter had decided not to entertain that discussion, just as he had decided not to run afoul of the gun lobby by challenging the militiamen about their skewed interpretations of the Second Amendment. Coincidentally (or not) House Republicans voted to rescind a ban on armor-piercing bullets on the same day as the Senate inquiry.[10]

Regardless of Specter's reluctance to challenge his witnesses, publicity about the militia movement had plenty of Americans wondering what purpose was served by the existence of private armies unregulated by the state, trained in deadly combat techniques, armed with semiautomatic weapons (or worse), and composed of thousands of trigger-happy conspiracy theorists, many of whom were devoted to the creation of a white, Christian, "Aryan Republic." A Gallup Poll conducted immediately after Oklahoma City found 72 percent of Americans agreeing that the government "should actively investigate and infiltrate [organizations that] have armed and organized themselves to resist the government . . . even if doing so might infringe on their constitutional rights."[11] But supporting "active investigations" was not the same as granting the federal government *more* power to do so. And this point wasn't lost on Specter or other members of Congress. According to another poll, 61 percent of Americans said the government had sufficient investigative powers, and only a third supported the idea of giving authorities *more* leeway to go after antigovernment groups.[12]

Poll results notwithstanding, watchdog groups still pressed Congress to ban private armies. To justify their position that the law could effectively distinguish between militias and groups like the Salvation Army or private gun clubs, supporters of antimilitia legislation pointed to the federal court ruling that shut down Louis Beam's paramilitary Texas Emergency Reserve in 1982. In that case, which had involved violent harassment of Vietnamese fishermen in the Gulf of Mexico, the court found that paramilitary groups cross the line when they create viable military organizations with "command structure, training, and discipline so as to function as a combat or combat support unit."[13] Fraternal groups like the Salvation Army do adopt quasi-military structures but they don't function like combat units. And private gun clubs might practice combat training, but don't set up military "command structures," so neither would they fall under such a ban. But militia groups that regularly drill in combat maneuvers *and* rely on military mechanisms of command, communication, and control *would* violate the law.

"I agree with the sentiment behind that," replied Congressman Schumer when pressed to support such a ban. "But it wouldn't pass the 'sniff test' on Capitol Hill." Given the power of the gun lobby and the tenacity of civil liberties groups like the ACLU, Schumer correctly predicted that Congress would steer clear of trying to negotiate the tricky terrain bounded by the First and Second Amendments, notwithstanding its constitutional obligation to guard against insurrection. And when Schumer's colleague, Representative Jerrold Nadler of New York, proposed a federal ban on paramilitary groups whose training or activities were intended to break the law, the bill went nowhere.[14]

Even necessary measures as innocuous as chemical tagging of explosive ingredients were torpedoed in Congress. One week after the Oklahoma City bombing, the Clinton administration revived a draft of the antiterrorism bill it had prepared after the 1993 World Trade Center bombing in New York. Among other things, it required that certain chemicals used to make explosives—including black powder—be microscopically marked so investigators could more easily trace where bomb components had been manufactured or purchased. But when the gun lobby made the bizarre argument that tagging gunpowder was a form of firearms registration, congressional Republicans instantly gutted the provision by reducing it to a *study*—and one that applied only to plastic explosives, at that.

Less controversial was a proposal that treaded on the margins of the Posse Comitatus Act by authorizing the military to assist civilian law enforcement in the event of nuclear, biological, or chemical attack. Few argued against the measure then, and in light of the anthrax attacks that followed the destruction of the World Trade Center in September 2001, it would be difficult to claim that such preparedness is a bad idea. In fact, just months before the September 11 attacks, a two-day government simulation exercise conducted at Andrews Air Force Base revealed that the United States is woefully unprepared to respond to biological weapons. Called "Dark Winter," the fictional scenario began with two dozen hypothetical smallpox patients arriving at Oklahoma City hospitals and ended less than two weeks "later" with no resolution to the simulated "epidemic" which was projected to claim millions of lives.

President Clinton's antiterrorism proposal, which followed the Oklahoma City bombing, did attract some well-deserved criticism, however, by suggesting looser standards under which suspected criminals and terrorists could be investigated by the FBI. During the reign of J. Edgar Hoover, the Bureau secretly launched probes and smear campaigns against American citizens with impunity. After Hoover's death in 1972 and the Watergate scandal that followed, Senator Frank Church presided over a sweeping inquiry into government intelligence abuses. These developments prompted U.S. Attorney General Edward Levi to impose stricter guidelines on FBI intelligence-gathering. Seven years later, these rules were loosened by the Reagan administration, which was then using the FBI in a large-scale operation against domestic groups that opposed its foreign policy in Central America. It was those rules—issued by Attorney General William

French Smith in 1983—that the Clinton administration was proposing to weaken further. According to the Smith guidelines (which were revised somewhat in 1989), the Bureau was required to have an "objective, factual basis" that a federal crime "has been, is being, or will be committed" before launching a "general crimes investigation." In the case of domestic security and terrorism investigations, the Bureau needed only a "reasonable indication . . . that two or more persons" are engaged in activities "that involve force or violence and a violation of the criminal laws of the United States."[15] Though some critics maintain that the Smith guidelines are overly restrictive, they contain plenty of flexibility for the FBI. For one thing, the "reasonable indication" standard needed to trigger an investigation is substantially lower than the threshold of "probable cause." In the words of one federal appellate court: "[The FBI] need not wait until the bombs begin to go off, or even until the bomb factory is found."[16] The Smith guidelines also allow the FBI to continue an investigation even when the targeted organization "has not engaged in recent acts of violence, nor is there any immediate threat of harm—yet the composition, goals, and prior history of the group suggests the need for continuing federal interest."[17]

The Clinton administration also sought to expand federal powers of electronic surveillance by broadening wiretap authority to include *any* suspected felony, and authorizing so-called "roving wiretaps," permitting authorities to monitor multiple phone lines used by a suspect, instead of requiring court approval for each one. Also included was funding for one thousand new federal agents and prosecutors. While federal authorities had long sought many of these provisions, some of them didn't have much to do with fighting terrorism per se. "They just happened to be on someone's wish list," said Phillip B. Heymann, a former Clinton administration deputy attorney general.[18] Expanded eavesdropping encountered stiff resistance from Senator Daniel Patrick Moynihan, a New York Democrat, who announced that the administration's proposals bothered him "and they ought to bother the Senate." Republican Majority Leader Bob Dole concurred, and worried about "getting caught up with the emotion [of Oklahoma City] and going too far. . . ." Whatever his concerns, they didn't appear to extend to Republican-sponsored provisions that got added to the bill, such as a limit to death-row appeals or restrictions on the rights of habeas corpus (which the Clinton administration strongly supported). Xenophobia and other fears ensured the adoption of language allowing more speedy deportation of suspected foreign terrorists by limiting their access to evidence and the right to confront their accusers. Reflecting some of these changes, the bill was renamed the Anti-Terrorism and Effective Death Penalty Act, and passed in April 1996.

Unfortunately, however, the latter provisions regarding foreigners were not invoked in the case of those terrorists associated with Al Qaeda who managed to enter the United States and plan the deadly attacks of September 11, 2001. Congress may have declined to grant the FBI authority for roving wiretaps in 1996, but in the wake of September 11, the "U.S.A. Patriot Act" made electronic surveillance much easier and less subject to court supervision, especially when it involves the Internet. Given the proven ability of terrorists—both domestic and foreign—to utilize computers, cell phones, and other new technologies to plan mass murder, some of these current changes with regard to electronic surveillance probably are warranted. Among other things, the Patriot Act also expanded the government's authority to detain noncitizens as well as conduct secret searches; allowed broad sharing of information among intelligence agencies; and created a new crime of "domestic terrorism."[19] However, in addition to these changes, U.S. Attorney General John Ashcroft has now weakened the Smith guidelines to allow easier infiltration of suspected groups. As attractive as this move might be to some in light of September 11, it is unclear how such changes will provide much added protection against future terrorist attacks. In fact, some critics (including prominent former FBI officials) have argued that the attorney general's counterterrorism strategy of arresting and jailing hundreds of immigrants and other terrorism suspects without hard evidence has been both counterproductive and ineffective. And looking back on the tragic failure of the FBI to adequately follow up reports by a Minnesota flight school about the suspicious behavior of alleged Al Qaeda trainee Zacarias Moussaoui, it is clear that what was needed then to intercept the terrorist plot was less a loosening of investigative guidelines and simply more old-fashioned common sense.[20]

As with passage of the U.S.A. Patriot Act in 2001, the Clinton administration successfully parlayed anger over Oklahoma City, and fears of future violence, into support for antiterrorism legislation in 1996. However, nothing in that bill had any bearing on the eventual collapse of the militia movement. Though the Clinton administration had complained that the Smith guidelines were too restrictive, they were not loosened and the Justice Department still managed to indict, arrest, and convict dozens of militia activists and others on the radical right during the latter half of the 1990s. According to Robert Blitzer, chief of domestic terrorism and counterterrorism planning for the FBI, the number of domestic terrorism cases investigated by the Bureau after the Oklahoma City bombing hovered around one thousand by the spring of 1998, compared to fewer than one hundred prior to the bombing.[21] And with images of Oklahoma City still fresh in their minds, a few state and local officials finally woke up and moved in a more determined manner against the militias.

When leaders of "the Republic of Texas" shot and took a neighboring couple hostage in April 1997, the Texas attorney general, Dan Morales, denounced the group as "bona fide criminals [and] terrorists" and urged them "to surrender, and surrender quickly." Still, not everyone in law enforcement got or gave that same message early enough. Prior to the arrest of the Texas activists—who claimed to represent the real government of Texas—the group had been regarded as more of a nuisance than a threat. "He's a nut with a fax machine," said the local sheriff about the group's leader four months before the hostage-taking incident.

The showdown ended with one patriot dead, and the rest of the group serving long prison terms.[22]

But even as Oklahoma City prompted a federal crackdown, the ghosts of Waco and Ruby Ridge steered government agents away from confrontation. Such reluctance was graphically illustrated in Montana, where a group of self-described "Freemen" kept the FBI at bay for nearly three months in 1996. Direct ideological descendants of the Posse Comitatus, the Freemen declared their independence from the government and amassed an arsenal of one hundred weapons and more than forty thousand rounds of ammunition on a 960-acre ranch they called "Justus Township," outside Jordan, Montana, population 364. After several years of harassing authorities and ordinary citizens with common-law liens, phony checks, and other forms of paper terrorism, (including death threats), the Freemen were indicted on an array of state and federal charges.[23] Militant believers in Christian Identity, they claimed their assault on the banking system and the courts was justified by God. The standoff began in March 1996, after the FBI lured two of the group's leaders into the open and arrested them without bloodshed. But instead of immediately surrendering, the remaining Freemen played a waiting game for eighty-one days. Regardless of events in Waco and Ruby Ridge, many neighboring ranchers were infuriated by the FBI's go-slow approach. As spring planting neared and the ranch remained cordoned off, some neighbors made noises about forming their own posse to root the Freemen out. Luckily, a Montana legislator convinced the remaining Freemen to surrender. Two years later, six of the men were convicted for a variety of crimes, including issuing false financial instruments, bank fraud, mail fraud, and threatening to kill Jack D. Shanstrom, Montana's chief federal judge.[24]

Though the FBI was criticized for its tactics, the peaceful conclusion to the standoff was a boost to the Bureau. But the FBI still had difficulties penetrating underground groups like the Aryan Republican Army, which was accused of committing at least twenty-two bank robberies across seven states from 1994 to 1996. At first lawmen dubbed the gang "the Midwest Bank Bandits," and it took federal agents more than a year to realize the crimes were politically motivated. Led by two men, Peter Kevin Langan and Richard Lee Guthrie Jr., this group of half a dozen white supremacists stole cars, manufactured explosives, and robbed banks to fund a white-supremacist revolution. As one hallmark of their crimes, they dropped decoy pipe bombs in their wake to slow the police. Militants with an offbeat sense of humor, they taunted lawmen with goofy postcards that Langan signed "Commander Pedro," and sometimes wore caps and windbreakers emblazoned with the letters "FBI." One of the men even donned a Santa suit for one December heist. The men hid out in places like Elohim City, the Christian Identity compound in eastern Oklahoma, and they set up safe houses in Kansas and Ohio. Their luck finally ran out in January 1996, after authorities apprehended Guthrie in Cincinnati and arrested Langan three days later in a fusillade of gunfire. Guthrie eventually pleaded guilty to weapons and bank robbery charges and agreed to testify against his coconspirators, but never did. An apparent suicide, he was found hanging by a bedsheet in his Kentucky jail cell.[25]

Crimes like these justified more aggressive FBI surveillance of the neo-Nazi movement, but law enforcement remained largely powerless in the face of seemingly spontaneous "lone wolf" attacks launched by white supremacists unafraid to die for their beliefs. In April 1996, one week before the first anniversary of the Oklahoma City bombing, Larry Wayne Shoemake, a supporter of the National Alliance, entered an abandoned restaurant in Jackson, Mississippi, and sprayed bullets into a predominantly black neighborhood for forty minutes. Armed with two military-style assault rifles, a pistol, a shotgun, a .357-caliber handgun, and more than twenty thousand rounds of ammunition, he wounded seven African-Americans and killed one before committing suicide. Shoemake was inspired by *The Turner Diaries* and a National Alliance publication titled *Separation or Annihilation*. In a letter found by police, he declared that "Blacks is the problem, Its in their genes [sic]," and proclaimed his need to "kill hundreds of thousands or more."[26]

Shoemake's motivation was similar to that of the three white men who aspired to form a Klanlike group and then savagely murdered James Byrd Jr. near Jasper, Texas, dragging him to death from the back of a pickup truck in June 1998.[27] The same was true of the youths who beat Matthew Shephard because he was gay and left him hanging on a prairie fence outside Laramie, Wyoming, that October. But whether or not organized hate groups were linked to crimes such as these (and usually they were not), the rationale for most such attacks remains the same: Perpetrators of hate crimes see their victims as less than human and the violence is done purposefully to send a message of superiority and social control. Like the festival lynchings of blacks in an earlier era, the victims of hate violence are targeted to remind others like them of their supposed vulnerability and inferior status.

The deaths of Byrd and Shephard were but two of thirteen hate-motivated homicides reported to the FBI in 1998, but the real numbers were no doubt much higher. Reported lethal hate crimes rose to seventeen in 1999, with a series of high-profile incidents that summer. First was a three-day shooting spree over Fourth of July weekend in Illinois and Indiana. The perpetrator, Benjamin Nathaniel Smith, was a member of the quasi-religious hate group, World Church of the Creator. The well-educated son of stable, middle-class parents from the tony Chicago suburb of Wilmette, Smith targeted blacks, Jews, and Asians for death. He wounded nine victims and killed two others before committing suicide. The following month, an Aryan Nations supporter, Buford O. Furrow Jr., opened fire on a Jewish Community Center in Los Angeles, shooting five people and terrorizing dozens of children and day-care workers. After fleeing the scene, Furrow murdered a Filipino-American postal worker before turning himself in.

Although high-profile incidents of hate violence and other crimes kept the far right in the news, the Christian Patriot movement was faltering by the end of the 1990s. Bad press, aggressive opposition from watchdog groups, the crackdown by federal authorities, and civil suits by victims had dampened recruitment or, in some cases, shut groups down entirely.[28] But the approaching millennium and fears of Y2K offered patriot activists a temporary reprieve. The movement had always excelled at profiting from calamity—from the distress of taxpayers, to the financial woes of farmers—and this time paranoia over the anticipated collapse of civilization that was supposed to accompany the new millennium gave patriots a much-needed boost. Advertisements for electric generators, water purifiers, military rations, and extra ammo swelled the pages of right-wing publications and the pockets of those clever enough to unload their merchandise before the survivalist market went bust. But when the millennium came and nothing happened, the movement once again lost recruits.

While it has become easier to appreciate the danger of right-wing violence since the Oklahoma City bombing (and fears of terrorism have certainly heightened after September 11, 2001), many pundits are still hesitant to acknowledge that hate groups also pose a political and social threat. After all, groups like the Posse and the militias have all too often been defined as simply a "fringe element" with an insignificant following. But measuring the influence of the Posse Comitatus and its militia descendants involves more than just counting members; one must also evaluate how successful these groups have been in reaching larger audiences and whether their ideas have attracted a broader following.

Since its founding in 1971, the Posse has demonstrated a remarkable ability to spread bigotry by marrying anti-Semitic and racist ideas to issues that have genuine mass appeal, such as hatred of banks and taxes, and distrust of government. Mike Beach lied when he told reporters he had half a million members in 1974, and even though the FBI estimate of ten thousand followers was closer to the mark, the Bureau's appraisal failed to account for the broader appeal of the Posse's antitax message. And no head count, poll, or survey could accurately assess how many of the tens of thousands of protesting farmers who rallied under the banner of AAM and other groups fell victim to Posse rhetoric during the farm crisis.

By 1983, the IRS tallied fifty-eight thousand illegal tax-protest returns and these numbers counted only those Americans with enough gumption to break the law and tell the government in writing. There is simply no way of knowing how many of these (and other) tax protesters had also attended a scofflaw seminar and come away with an armful of hate literature, a subscription to the *Spotlight*, and an introduction to the Jewish/Marxist plot behind the income tax.[29] But one thing is clear: Fifteen years after the heyday of the tax-protest movement, a bipartisan chorus of congressmen gave credence to the claims of right-wing activists regarding alleged IRS abuses. After hearing testimony from irate taxpayers and agency whistle-blowers in 1997 and 1998, the House and Senate voted nearly unanimously to severely weaken IRS enforcement. Echoing the themes of Senator Arlen Specter's 1995 hearings into Ruby Ridge and Waco, the GOP-controlled hearings focused attention on commando-style raids by armed tax inspectors wearing flak jackets. Absent from the hearings was any testimony about the steep drop in audit rates for wealthy Americans and large corporations after the Republican-controlled Congress sharply cut the IRS budget in 1995. Instead lawmakers chose to emphasize the image of a menacing federal agency out of control.

"The IRS is too big and too mean," said House Majority Leader Dick Armey of Texas in November 1997. Swept up in the heady antigoverment climate of the GOP "revolution," the House voted 426 to 4 to overhaul IRS collection practices, and the Senate enthusiastically followed, 97 to 0. The move resulted in as much as $300 billion in lost tax revenues.[30]

Protecting taxpayer rights was the cry of Congress, but bashing the IRS made for good election-year politics, too. Behind the congressional hearings and political posturing, the underlying goal of conservative Republicans and groups like the seventy thousand–member Americans for Tax Reform was the elimination of the Internal Revenue Code (and the progressive income tax) altogether. Anti-Semitism did not necessarily have anything to do with this agenda, and the vast majority of irate taxpayers and IRS "reformers" knew nothing about the conspiracy theories that had fueled hatred and suspicion of the IRS for decades. But the success of IRS-bashing in the 1990s cannot be separated from the efforts of men like A. J. Porth, Martin Larson, Bill Gale, and others who spent years projecting their message of tax rebellion beyond their own followers and toward the political center.

A similar dynamic has occurred with the radicalization of the gun lobby and its allies in government who have come to embrace a militant interpretation of the Second Amendment that asserts the Constitution provides an unquestionable right to individual gun ownership with minimal regulation. Such ideas were always popular in the political backwaters populated largely by ranting conspiracy theorists and gun fanatics, but they now have become the raison d'être of the gun lobby ensconced in the halls of Washington. And with the appointment of Attorney General John Ashcroft they have found their highest-ranking political champion to date. In a May 2001 letter to the NRA's chief lobbyist, Ashcroft declared his unequivocal belief that the Second Amendment confers an individual right to gun ownership, as opposed to the "collective right" defined by the U.S. Supreme Court in 1939. In offering his opinion, Ashcroft deliberately avoided citing Supreme Court precedent and gave new encouragement to militia enthusiasts and others who have toiled long and hard to insert their radical view of gun rights into law.[31] This point of view was given further credence by the Fifth Circuit Court of Appeals in New Orleans, which ruled in October 2001 that "the Second Amendment does protect individual rights" of gun ownership. Although the Fifth Circuit left the door open to gun controls that were "limited, narrowly tailored, [and] specific," the case still represents the very first instance in which a federal court agreed with the notion that the right to bear arms spoken of in the Second Amendment is something more than a collective one pertaining to the militia.[32]

In 1986, a Harris Poll found that one-third of farmers believed that "Jewish bankers . . . are behind those who overcharge them for farm equipment or jack up the interest on their loans"; but 98 percent of the respondents said they had no direct contact with right-wing groups. The prevalence of Farm Belt anti-Semitism at the time did not mean that every poll respondent who supported the notion of a Jewish conspiracy had been recruited by the Posse Comitatus. But what the numbers do strongly suggest, is that the anti-Semitism espoused by Christian Patriots and others had mass appeal well beyond the twelve to fifteen thousand rural rightists counted by watchdog groups at the height of the farm crisis.

A decade after the farm crisis, researchers sought reliable estimates for the size of the militia movement, but accurate numbers were hard to come by. The Michigan Militia claimed more than ten thousand members in a majority of counties across the state at its height, but this was an exaggeration. According to the Southern Poverty Law Center, the number of antigovernment "patriot" groups peaked at 858 in 1996, after their popularity surged as a result of all the publicity following the Oklahoma City bombing, albeit much of it negative. The critical coverage soon took its toll, however, and militia numbers plummeted. There were plenty of guerrilla warriors in the militia movement that were outraged by Waco and big government, but only the most hard-core were willing to embrace the crackpot notion that the government had used Timothy McVeigh as a patsy to murder its own citizens.[33]

In 1998 between twenty and twenty-five million American adults (12 percent of the population) scored as "unquestionably anti-Semitic" by agreeing with six or more of eleven anti-Jewish statements posed in a comprehensive survey conducted by the Anti-Defamation League.[34] The ADL was correct to hail the 12 percent figure—it represented a sharp decline from the 20 percent measured in 1992—but the data remained troubling nonetheless. Ignorance and age have always been accurate predictors of anti-Semitism, and the ADL survey confirmed this: Twenty-two percent of respondents age sixty-five and older fell into the "most anti-Semitic" category, as did 18 percent of those with no more than a high-school education. Thirty-five percent of African-Americans also were found to be "most anti-Semitic." Although Jews make up only about 2.5 percent of the U.S. population, roughly one in four of respondents surveyed believed that the number of Jews in America was at least ten times that figure. Not surprisingly, those who were more likely to overestimate the Jewish population also scored as "most anti-Semitic." Survey respondents showed even less knowledge of blacks, with a huge 62 percent of those polled saying that African-Americans constituted 25 percent or more of the population, which was double the actual number. And of this 62 percent, approximately one-third thought that the black population was at least half of the United States.[35] Twenty-five percent of respondents admitted they opposed interracial dating.[36] Had the ADL polled only in the South on the last question, the results would have been far worse. For example, more than half a million Alabama voters who cast ballots during the 2000 presidential election voted *against* repealing that state's century-old constitutional ban against interracial marriage. The U.S. Supreme Court had outlawed such bans in 1967, but the provision remained on the books in Alabama. Sixty percent of voters there endorsed removing it in the 2000 referendum, but a majority of whites did not.[37] Likewise, hundreds of thousands of Alabama voters also elected Roy Moore to the post of chief justice of the state supreme court. A conservative Christian ideologue, Moore had made headlines for defying a federal court order to remove a plaque containing the Ten Commandments from his courtroom and for refusing to stop praying before court sessions. And early in 2002, Moore ruled that "homosexual behavior . . . is a . . . crime against nature, an inherent evil, and an act so heinous that it defies one's ability to describe it."[38]

As attractive as it might seem to use election results to evaluate the strength of right-wing social movements, there are pitfalls. One difficulty lies in the practice used by many analysts who apply the same standards to far-right candidates they use when assessing the outcome of "normal" elections. According to the "winner-take-all" logic that governs interpretations of most elections, as long as extremist candidates do not win a significant number of posts, or achieve victory in fewer prominent races, then democracy can be pronounced safe and secure. Hence when David Duke, the former Imperial Wizard of the Knights of the Ku Klux Klan, won 44 percent of the vote against the incumbent Democrat, J. Bennett Johnston, in the 1990 race for the U.S. Senate in Louisiana, Duke's showing was widely (and erroneously) labeled a resounding *defeat*. Yet among white voters, fully 60 percent cast their ballot for Duke—an unabashed racist and self-proclaimed Holocaust denier. And this was after a high-profile campaign during which few voters could convincingly claim that they were not aware of Duke's bigoted beliefs. Though the Ku Klux Klan was an anemic shadow of its former self in 1990, Klan ideology prevailed at the polls nonetheless, and it did so in exactly the form prescribed by Duke when he first exchanged his white robe in favor of a business suit and telegenic image back in 1987, when he entered the Democratic presidential primaries.[39] One year after his loss to Johnston in the Senate race, Duke defeated the incumbent Republican governor, Buddy Roemer, in the gubernatorial primary, but lost the general election to Democrat Edwin W. Edwards after a tremendous outpouring of opposition. And by 1996 Duke still managed to poll 141,000 votes (or 11.5 percent), placing fourth in a crowded field of fifteen candidates in Louisiana's open primary for U.S. Senate.[40] Measured by conventional political standards, Duke was the electoral equivalent of a lost cause, but a closer look at the breadth and depth of support he received throughout his various campaigns reveals a much more disturbing picture of widely held racist beliefs among the electorate. More recently, Pat Buchanan managed to seize the Reform Party and $12.6 million in federal matching funds, but he fared dismally on Election Day, 2000. Nevertheless, Buchanan's recent book, *The Death of the West*, which laments the demise of white Anglo-Saxon culture (and its accompanying gene pool), enjoyed a solid run on the *New York Times* bestseller list.

A similar point can be made regarding the appeal of the Christian Patriot movement. Although its backers will never seize the reins of government, abolish the Federal Reserve, rescind all but the first ten Amendments, repeal the income tax, or round up blacks and Jews, the ideas the movement has espoused over the past thirty years on the subject of states' rights have received more than a fair hearing by the courts they love to hate. During the combined twelve-year tenure of Presidents Ronald Reagan and George Herbert Walker Bush, hundreds of conservative judges were appointed to the federal judiciary. Most importantly, a string of U.S. Supreme Court decisions have endorsed states' rights, based on principles and values quite consistent with those put forth by militia types, though absent the paranoid rhetoric and far-right diatribes. Much like the period of civil rights reversals that followed the collapse of Reconstruction after the Civil War, the Reagan-Bush judiciary has gutted many important legal protections that were won by the civil rights movement in the 1950s and 1960s.

Beginning with its landmark decision in a 1996 case barring the Seminole Indian tribe from suing the state of Florida in federal court, the U.S. Supreme Court began to invoke the Eleventh Amendment to justify a radical interpretation of states'-rights doctrine. Under the Eleventh Amendment, a state is shielded from lawsuits unless it has deliberately waived its sovereign immunity. However, for many years, the Court reasoned that Congress had the power to waive a state's sovereign immunity in order to exercise its authority to regulate interstate commerce. But in the Seminole tribe case and a series of subsequent decisions, the Court overturned years of precedent and ruled that the commerce clause does *not* allow Congress to pass laws giving individuals the right to sue state governments for certain types of discrimination in either federal or state court. The Seminole ruling—and others that followed—was decided by the same 5 to 4 majority of Justices Rehnquist, O'Connor, Scalia, Thomas, and Kennedy that has gutted affirmative action and critical provisions of the Federal Voting Rights Act. In one particularly scathing dissent addressing the decisions of the majority in these recent cases, Supreme Court Justice John Paul Stevens compared the rulings to "a mindless dragon that indiscriminately chews gaping holes in Federal statutes."

"Where there is a right, there must be a remedy," Justice David Souter declared in one of his dissents. The Court allowed political partisanship to triumph over its commitment to states' rights, however, when it anointed George

W. Bush as president and denied the Florida Supreme Court the right to evaluate the fitness of the disputed ballots cast in the 2000 presidential election. Nevertheless, the Rehnquist Court has worked hard to turn back the clock and sharply constrain the ability of the federal government to define and protect the civil rights of Americans. Like the emasculation of federal marshals who once relied on army troops as a posse comitatus to defend the rights of blacks, the Court has enacted its judicial version of the Southern Compromise in the hopes of ushering in another era of states' rights. Such a development surely would have pleased Bill Gale.

Over the past thirty years, the Posse Comitatus and its Christian Patriot descendants have demonstrated remarkable flexibility in the face of both adversity and opportunity. While conventional wisdom holds that "hard times" drive extremist groups, the story that has been told in these pages offers a different point of view. Financial deprivation and economic themes are powerful and sometimes determining forces that motivate far-right groups and their members. But so, too, are the ideas these movements espouse. The phenomenon of Massive Resistance that took place across the South in the 1950s and 1960s was motivated, in part, by economic fears of whites who understood—whether consciously or not—that abolishing segregation would create greater opportunity for blacks which might then lead to more economic competition. But that hardly explains the extent of the visceral fear that gripped so many white Americans—North and South—in the wake of the *Brown* decision. In fact, the tremendous economic expansion of the 1950s and 1960s should have made whites less susceptible to racial fear-mongering, which certainly was not the case. Indeed, as Judge Thomas P. Brady so clearly articulated in *Black Monday*, the war against civil rights was a fight for white racial purity and against the supposed polluting and degenerate influence of blacks. While whites have fashioned and fed such ideas for centuries in order to justify various forms of economic exploitation—especially slavery—it also is true that the beliefs themselves took on a life of their own long ago.

Even less economic motivation can be discerned in the anticommunist and paramilitary movements of the 1960s, which gained momentum by joining tripartite fears of blacks, communism, and Jews, and largely ignored bread-and-butter issues of any kind. And while the tax-protest movement did have a lot to say about money, its opposition to the Sixteenth Amendment probably would not have been nearly as vigorous if federal revenues had been earmarked largely for the betterment of white Christian America.

Of course, the farm crisis was certainly one of those classic historical moments when the threat of economic ruin drove large numbers of people to seek simplistic solutions laced with bigotry. But what of the many equally desperate farmers who chose the liberal politics offered them by PrairieFire or the North American Farm Alliance instead? And can it honestly be said that economics was a major factor driving thousands of Americans to join the militias during the unprecedented economic growth of the mid-1990s, rather than love of guns, hatred of the federal government (especially one presided over by a "liberal" president, Bill Clinton), latent anti-Semitism, fear of nameless international elites, and deep anxiety about the racial character of their Anglo-Saxon and Christian American Republic in a fast-changing, multicultural, and increasingly nonwhite world?

Bill Gale's Posse Comitatus was steeped in gutter-level anti-Semitism and race hatred, but he and others managed to broaden their constituency by disguising bigotry as patriotism and appealing to Americans' long-standing affinity for local control, individual liberty, direct democracy, and the "sovereignty" of the people. And it is precisely because the Christian Patriot movement was able to seize and manipulate these ideas so effectively—and use them to gather support for its bigotry—that the movement remains a challenge and a threat. Of course, America is not, and will not become, some sort of fascist dictatorship. But the radical right has been successful in influencing aspects of mainstream politics and discourse. And if left unchallenged, its ideas and propaganda *will* affect the way people think and act.

If the 1980s showed that hard times could fuel a social movement in the farm belt, the militias of the 1990s are evidence that the Christian Patriot movement is here with us to stay, in one form or another. And the laundry list of issues that will motivate its supporters in the future is quite predictable, and long: immigration, changing demographics, globalism, guns and taxes, environmental enforcement, resource conflicts in the West; and, in the wake of September 11, add resentment of Israeli and American foreign policy in the Middle East, as well as "patriotic" invocations of civil defense and hate-filled diatribes against people of Arab descent to the list.

Luckily, there are plenty of people in the ranks of the radical right who are feckless and incompetent, but that doesn't make the ideas they espouse any less dangerous, nor does it minimize the likelihood their movement will produce another Timothy McVeigh. And neither does the existence of bumbling believers negate the influence of shrewder leaders who are capable of fashioning sophisticated strategies to spread their message, broaden their political base, or incite violence.

The Oklahoma City bombing and its aftermath undercut the militia movement, and that was a good thing. But if the past is prologue, the Christian Patriots will reinvent themselves to suit the next opportunity. Unfortunately, most people—including government authorities—have a habit of disregarding far-right movements until their activities become sufficiently dangerous or disruptive to generate genuine alarm. And by then, instead of having preemptively challenged the ugly ideas and hateful messages that these organizations disseminate, it is usually too late to do anything but react. There is no simple remedy to the challenges posed by the radical right. But as generations of abolitionists, World War II veterans, civil rights activists, and others have demonstrated, many

Americans are eager to courageously embrace democratic values that are the antithesis of hatred and bigotry. The best way to contain—even diminish—the influence of the radical right and its corrosive ideas, is for decent, thoughtful Americans to pursue even more aggressively the full promise of our democracy. For only in the act of advancing pluralism and equality—politically, legally, socially, culturally, and in all its other diverse designs—can the nation move forward and far beyond the reach of those who might try to hold us back.

EPILOGUE

Hallelu-Yahweh! May the WAR *be started!* DEATH *to His enemies, may the World Trade Center* BURN TO THE GROUND! . . . *We can blame no others than ourselves for our problems due to the fact that we allow . . . Satan's children, called jews [sic] today, to have dominion over our lives. . . . My suggestion to all brethren, if we are left alone, sit back and watch the death throws [sic] of this Babylonian beast system and later we can get involved in clean up operations. If this beast system looks to us to plunder, arrest and fill their detention camps with, then by all means fight force with force and leave not a man standing!*

—"Pastor" August B. Kries III, Sheriff's Posse Comitatus[1]

The terrorist attacks of September 11, 2001, focused America's attention on threats from abroad, but even as the World Trade Center towers were collapsing, right-wing hate groups were celebrating in the United States. "WONDERFUL NEWS BROTHERS!!" exulted Hardy Lloyd, the Pittsburgh coordinator of the racist, anti-Semitic World Church of the Creator. In an e-mail message sent to supporters throughout western Pennsylvania, Lloyd crowed that "maybe as many as ten thousand Zoggites [sic] are dead," and he invoked the promise of vigilante street violence. "The war is upon us all, time to get shooting lone wolves!! [September 11] is a wonderful day for us all. . . . Let's kick some Jew ass."

A call to the domestic terrorism unit of the local FBI drew a blank, as neither

Lloyd or his group was familiar to the special agent fielding calls, despite the fact that just four months earlier, outgoing FBI director Louis J. Freeh had told the Senate Select Committee on Intelligence that "formal right-wing hate groups, such as the World Church of the Creator and the Aryan Nations, represent a continuing terrorist threat."[2] Like others on the radical right, Lloyd simultaneously praised and vilified the Al Qaeda terrorists. "My only concern is that we Aryans didn't do this and that the rag-heads are ahead of us on the Lone Wolf point scale."[3] Other neo-Nazis called the attackers "towel-heads" and "sand niggers," yet hailed them as "very brave people [who] were willing to die for whatever they believed in."[4]

"We may not want them marrying our daughters. . . . But anyone who is willing to drive a plane into a building to kill jews [sic] is alright by me. I wish our members had half as much testicular fortitude," observed Billy Roper, the deputy membership coordinator of the National Alliance.[5] Other militants joined in the call to arms. "[T]he current events in Jew York city [sic] have caused me to activate my unit," announced Paul R. Mullet, the Minnesota leader of the Aryan Nations.[6] "We are preparing to strike here in Minnesota and other surrounding areas. Please be advised that the time for ALL ARYANS TO ATTACK IS NOW NOT LATER. Our opportunity may never be the same."

Inspired by the fiction of *The Turner Diaries* and its real-life martyr, Bob Matthews, anti-Semites like Mullet may have been hoping to realize their long-awaited dream of overthrowing the Zionist Occupied Government, but in the aftermath of the terrorist attacks, the targets of vigilante violence were not Jews, but Arabs and others mistaken for Middle Easterners. In the ten weeks following 9/11, the American Arab Anti-Discrimination Committee reported more than five hundred violent incidents including simple assault, arson, shootings, and at least half a dozen murders. And attacks on Asian Americans spiked sharply with about 250 incidents reported in the last three months of 2001, alone. In Phoenix a man went on a shooting rampage, killing a forty-nine-year-old Sikh and firing at a Lebanese-American gas-station clerk. In San Diego, two men on a motorcycle yanked open the car door of a woman they mistakenly thought was of Arab descent and slashed her in the head. In the Chicago suburb of Bridgeview, on each of the three nights following 9/11, hundreds of mostly white youths chanting, "U.S.A.! U.S.A.!" and waving American and Confederate flags marched on a local mosque while white supremacists distributed literature and worked the crowd. Police in riot gear turned them back.[7] Predictably, there was plenty of encouragement from the right. "Dirty Rotten Arabs and Muslims," proclaimed the Web site of the Council of Conservative Citizens—a group once endorsed by former U.S. Senate Majority Leader Trent Lott. "Arab treachery and deviousness have been a scourge since biblical times," the group advised.

Bigotry and intolerance were not limited to criminals, mobs, and hate groups. In Georgia, U.S. Representative Saxby Chambliss, chairman of the House Subcommittee on Terrorism and Homeland Security, suggested that the Sheriff of

Lowndes County be "turn[ed] loose" to "arrest every Muslim that crosses the state line." And in Louisiana, Representative John Cooksey called for racial profiling of anyone wearing "a diaper on his head and a fan belt wrapped around the diaper."[8] In February 2002, U.S. Attorney General John Ashcroft faced mounting criticism for statements he made the previous November disparaging Islam. In a radio interview with Cal Thomas, a conservative pundit and syndicated columnist, the Attorney General reportedly said that, "Islam is a religion in which God requires you to send your son to die for him. Christianity is a faith in which God sends his son to die for you." Thomas published Ashcroft's statements on November 9, but it wasn't until Muslim groups discovered Thomas's column in early February that the resulting controversy reached the pages of *The Washington Post*. Ashcroft's response that his reported statements, "do not accurately reflect what I believe I said" did little to allay Arab American concerns.[9]

The hardened rightists and thuggish blowhards who cheered the attacks of 9/11 did so for several reasons, not least of which was that they relished the sight of mass destruction in the heart of what the Posse's August Kries termed "the Babylonian Beast system" that was "Jew York." Like nineteenth-century Populists who often railed against urban America in an anti-Semitic vein, the haters of today despise New York for its racial, ethnic, sexual, and religious diversity. The devastation at the Pentagon was welcomed for creating pain and confusion in the nation's capital, which has long been regarded by the radical right as enemy-occupied territory. Right-wing hopes for stimulating widespread disorder waned quickly, however, when it became clear that 9/11 was going to prompt more aggressive surveillance of dissidents, including, possibly, them.

"The feds are clamping down with the definition of a domestic terrorist," warned Christopher R. Kenney, the "commander" of "the Republic of Texas," a Posse-type group whose original leaders are serving long prison terms for earlier crimes. "I am sure there will be even more restrictions coming down the pike. We must prepare while we can."[10] August Kries of the Posse Comitatus was more direct: "There has been much talk lately of exchanging Freedom for security by this treasonous federal beast system. We will NOT blindly be led down the road to their jew [*sic*] World Order totalitarian government.... If this so-called security is forced on us we would rather FIGHT and RESIST ALL TYRANNY than surrender as subjects and slaves!"[11]

In addition to praising the carnage, many right-wing leaders pitched a message they hoped might reach beyond their usual audience. The attacks of September 11 "are in need of a fervent and immediate response by White Racial Loyalists everywhere," explained Matthew Hale, thirty, the leader of the World Church of the Creator. Supporters need to "preach [about] the control of the United States government by International Jewry and its lackeys. Perhaps never before have our people been so receptive to our message," Hale observed.[12] William Pierce agreed. In an Internet radio broadcast on September 22, the author of *The Turner Diaries* claimed that America was attacked "because we have been letting ourselves be used to do all of Israel's dirty work in the Middle East." The National Alliance distilled this message into a flyer that pictured the disintegrating towers and asked the rhetorical question, "Is Our Involvement in the Security of the Jewish State Worth This?"[13]

David Duke, the former Klansman who had won 607,000 votes a decade earlier in his unsuccessful quest to become a U.S. senator from Louisiana, denounced the "ultrapowerful Jewish lobby" after 9/11, and explained that "Zionists caused the attack America endured just as surely as if they themselves had piloted those planes." Duke denounced Jews as an "insidious media influence that has pushed white guilt and racial miscegenation." Echoing the anti-Semitic conspiracy theories widely accepted by the Arab press throughout the world after 9/11, Duke also suggested "even if Israeli agents were not the actual provocateurs behind the operation, at the very least they had prior knowledge."

Such comments would never win the support of a majority of Americans, but that is not what they were designed to do. With one out of every five people holding unfavorable views toward Israel, and 22 percent saying the attack on the United States would not have occurred if the two countries were not such close allies, the right-wing line was shrewdly calibrated to bring in new recruits. And according to a May 2002 poll commissioned by the ADL, anti-Semitism has increased markedly in the wake of 9/11, reversing a decade-long trend in declining anti-Jewish prejudice. In 1998, the agency's poll identified 12 percent of adult Americans—representing approximately twenty-five million people—as "most anti-Semitic." But by 2002, this figure had risen to 17 percent, representing some thirty-five million people.[14]

Not content to scapegoat Israel and the Jews, many on the radical right—as well as numerous mainstream conservatives—blamed the tragedy on what they called America's "open door" policy on immigration, and the nation's embrace of pluralism. "America is now drinking the bitter dregs of multiculturalism and diversity," explained the Council of Conservative Citizens on its Web site, along with an essay blaming the September 11 attacks on Abraham Lincoln and America's "[sinful] religion of equality and unity."[15] And according to David Duke, "If the demographics of America were still the same as in the 1960's we would be absolutely secure."[16]

While President George W. Bush promptly declared Osama bin Laden the responsible culprit, leaders of the Christian Right tried to put their own, self-serving spin on the tragedy. With the Pentagon and the Twin Towers still smoldering, Christian Coalition leader Pat Robertson and the Reverend Jerry Falwell, the founder of the Moral Majority, commented on events. "Well, after Tuesday's attacks, many Americans are struggling with grief, fear, and unanswered questions. How should Christians respond to this crisis?" Robertson asked his guest on *The 700 Club*. After encouraging viewers to pray, the duo then got down to business.

"[T]he Lord has protected us so wonderfully these two hundred twenty-five years. And since 1812, this is the first time that we've been attacked on our soil," Falwell observed incorrectly, forgetting Pearl Harbor. "And I fear . . . that this is only the beginning . . . if in fact God continues to lift the curtain and allow the enemies of America to give us probably what we deserve. . . . The ACLU's got to take a lot of blame for this."

"Well, yes," Robertson replied.

"[T]hrowing God out of the public square, out of the schools. The abortionists have got to bear some burden for this because God will not be mocked. And when we destroy forty million little innocent babies, we make God mad." Falwell was on a roll now. "I really believe that the pagans, and the abortionists, and the feminists, and the gays and the lesbians who are actively trying to make that an alternative lifestyle . . . all of them who have tried to secularize America, I point the finger in their face and say, 'You helped this happen.' "

"Well, I totally concur," said Robertson.

The news media instantly picked up on Falwell's remarks, although Robertson had said exactly the same thing earlier in the broadcast when he declared that America had insulted God "at the highest levels of our government" through "rampant secularism [and] occult," pornography, and abortion. As punishment, "God Almighty is lifting His protection from us. And once that protection is gone, we all are vulnerable." Both men spent the next two months trying to undo the damage to their reputations. On December 5, Robertson resigned his Christian Coalition post. Though other factors contributed to his decision, the conversation with Falwell certainly played a part.[17] Months later, on February 21, 2002, Robertson attempted to regain his footing by denouncing Islam, saying—on *The 700 Club*—that it "is not a peaceful religion that wants to coexist. They want to coexist until they can control, dominate, and then if need be, destroy." According to Robertson, U.S. immigration policies are "so skewed to the Middle East and away from Europe that we have introduced these people into our midst and undoubtedly there are terrorist cells all over them."[18]

The terrorist hijackers believed they would be rewarded in heaven. So, too, did American anti-abortion zealots who believed they were doing God's work by sending fake anthrax through the mail. The hoax letters began arriving—more than 280 in the first round—at family-planning and abortion clinics in seventeen states on October 15, 2001, the same day that staffers in the office of Senate Majority Leader Tom Daschle unleashed a plume of real anthrax spores when they opened an envelope sent from a fictitious fourth-grade class in Franklin Park, New Jersey. "You can not stop us. We have this anthrax. You die now. Are you afraid? Death to America. Death to Israel. Allah is great," read the crude block lettering on the note to the senator.

The letters sent to Planned Parenthood clinics and others in October also were sophisticated, though the white powder that wafted out of them turned out to be fake. The envelopes were marked "TIME SENSITIVE" and "URGENT SECURITY

NOTICE ENCLOSED," and printed with the return address of the U.S. Marshal Service or the U.S. Secret Service. The threatening messages they contained were signed by a well-known anti-abortion group, the Army of God. Three weeks later, a second round of more than 270 similar threats began arriving at women's reproductive-health clinics, only this time the packages were delivered via Federal Express; they also contained death threats signed by the Army of God: "You have chosen a profession, which profits from the senseless murder of millions of innocent children each year. . . . We are going to kill you. This is your notice. Stop now or die."

The man who allegedly claimed responsibility and was indicted for sending the threats was Clayton Lee Waagner, a self-described "anti-abortion warrior" and federal fugitive who had escaped eight months earlier from a jail in Illinois where he was awaiting sentencing on federal weapons (and stolen vehicle) charges.[19] The father of nine children, Waagner, forty-five, had once testified that God told him to kill abortion doctors. The first wave of anthrax hoaxes arrived on October 15, but it took two more weeks for the FBI to finally open a national investigation and assign all the cases to its domestic terrorism unit in Philadelphia. Despite demands from abortion advocates and health-care providers, Attorney General John Ashcroft has yet to classify the Army of God, with its twenty-year record of violence and murder, as a domestic terrorist group. In fact, the Justice Department is so wary of political flak for treating crimes against abortion clinics as domestic terrorism that it made no formal announcement of the Philadelphia investigation, leaving abortion providers and women's groups in the bizarre position of holding their own press conference to announce the government probe instead.[20]

Waagner was arrested in early December after he was recognized by an alert employee at a Kinko's copy shop in suburban Cincinnati. It was a lucky break for the FBI, which had missed the chance to nab Waagner a week earlier, had they actually been monitoring the anti-abortion movement. It turned out that Waagner had paid a visit to Neal Horsley in Carrollton, Georgia—a man who collects detailed personal information about anyone he deems responsible for abortions, and posts it on the Internet. (Using different typefaces, Horsley indicates whether the "criminals" have been killed [crossed out], wounded [gray], or still remain unscathed [plain black type].)

According to Horsley it was shortly before noon, the day after Thanksgiving, when the back doorbell rang. After exchanging pleasantries with Waagner— whom Horsley says he did not know—Horsley returned to his desk. Waagner reappeared about an hour later displaying a firearm, demanding to be let inside. "You don't recognize me, do you?" Waagner asked. According to Horsley, Waagner introduced himself and spent the next hour with a pistol in his lap, bragging that he had been the one behind the anthrax threat letters. Then Waagner told Horsley that he had targeted at least forty-two abortion-clinic workers to be killed unless they quit their jobs. According to Horsley, Waagner wanted him to use his anti-abortion Web sites to receive "resignations" from his assassination targets. After agreeing to the scheme, Horsley was allegedly bound with duct tape and Waagner made his escape.[21] Horsley's account begs the question, *Why didn't the FBI have Horsley under close surveillance to begin with, given his close connections to the violent anti-abortion underground?*[22]

Over the years, a variety of right-wing activists have stockpiled small amounts of biological weapons. When law enforcement agents raided the Arkansas compound of the Covenant, the Sword, and the Arm of the Lord in 1985, they found thirty-three gallons of cyanide that some CSA members said had been provided by the former Michigan Klan leader, Robert Miles. In 1995, four members of the Minnesota Patriots Council were arrested and convicted for possessing ricin—an extremely potent toxin derived from castor beans that two of the men had produced several years earlier. The men reportedly planned to use the ricin, which is six thousand times deadlier than cyanide, to kill law enforcement officials by smearing it on doorknobs and car steering wheels. Later that year, an Arkansas survivalist was arrested and charged with possessing ricin that he had smuggled into the United States from Canada two years before. The man, Thomas Lewis Lavy, fifty-four, hung himself in his jail cell the day after his arrest.[23]

Larry Wayne Harris, an Aryan Nations member and microbiologist from Lancaster, Ohio, used his job at a water treatment plant to order bubonic plague through the mail. The bacteria turned out to be inert, but Harris was brought up on wire-fraud charges, pleaded guilty, and was sentenced to eighteen months' probation in 1995. Three years later, Harris was arrested in Las Vegas after bragging that he had enough "military-grade" anthrax to wipe out a city. As it turned out, what he had was a harmless veterinary vaccine, and the charges were dropped. Harris may or may not have known the difference but that didn't stop him from self-publishing a book, *Bacteriological Warfare: A Major Threat to North America*, which the Southern Poverty Law Center termed "an effective do-it-yourself manual for mass destruction."[24] And writing in 1998 in *The Modern Militiaman's Internet Gazette*, the editor, Martin Lindstedt, suggested, "The Resistance needs to develop some of this weaponry in order to deal with the current ruling criminal regime."[25]

The radical right may or may not possess the expertise necessary to launch effective biological attacks here in America, but in the wake of 9/11, there is no shortage of highly charged racial issues for hate groups to inflame and exploit. Long before September 11, large numbers of Americans held negative views of Arabs and immigrants. One ABC News poll conducted in 1991 found majorities of Americans who saw Arabs as "terrorists" (59 percent), "violent" (58 percent) and "religious fanatics" (56 percent). And a Gallup poll conducted two years later found that two-thirds of Americans believed that there were "too many" Arab immigrants in the United States.[26] A *Newsweek* poll conducted in September 2001 revealed that 32 percent of Americans think Arabs should be put under special surveillance similar to the treatment of Japanese-Americans during World War

II. Sixty-two percent of Americans may disagree, but the one-third figure clearly indicates the tremendous untapped potential for anti-immigrant and right-wing groups. True, the radical right suffers from a lack of stable, well-funded organizations as well as an absence of leaders, finances, and organizational vehicles capable of achieving mainstream political success. But in the post–September 11 world, Americans would do well to be on the lookout for more hardened underground activity on the part of hate groups, as well as more efforts by the radical right to recruit and mobilize supporters based on fear and distrust of Arabs, immigrants, Israel, and American Jews.

ACKNOWLEDGMENTS

I began work on this book shortly after the bombing of the Federal Building in Oklahoma City in 1995, and concluded in the wake of the tragedy of September 11, 2001. Although the perpetrators of both attacks lived a world apart, each was motivated by an ideology steeped in bigotry. Timothy McVeigh and Terry Nichols felt justified in murdering scores of fellow Americans in pursuit of their vision of a white, Christian, "Constitutional Republic." The terrorists of Al Qaeda saw all Christians and Jews as infidels and enemies, obstacles to their goal of asserting radical fundamentalist Islam anywhere they wished.

While some people regard this country's radical right as a fringe movement of brutish ne'er-do-wells incapable of threatening the values and institutions of democracy, I do not. Whether the victims of hate are counted one at a time, like Matthew Shepherd and James Byrd, or by the score, the cost is still immeasurable. In the larger sense, consider the damage done to the fabric of democracy by those who promote or silently sympathize with racism, anti-Semitism, gay bashing, hatred of Arabs and immigrants, or similarly bigoted beliefs. Of course, not everyone who has helped me with this book agrees with these assessments, or with the other conclusions and interpretations the reader will find here. But each person who contributed to this effort has my heartfelt thanks, because without their participation this book would be diminished.

I am especially indebted to my longtime friend and colleague Leonard Zeskind who first urged me—nearly twenty years ago—to more closely track the purveyors of hate in order to oppose them more effectively. I am also grateful to my friend and mentor Dave Ostendorf, who joined me in these efforts while we were working on the front lines of the farm crisis during the 1980s; and to those farmers, lawyers, rural advocates, and others who participated in many aspects of the fight to secure economic justice for farmers and defeat the rural radical right. They include: the courageous former North Dakota agriculture commissioner, Sarah Vogel; Randi Roth, Jim Massey, Lynn Hayes, and the staff of the Farmers Legal Action Group; Barb Grabner, Mark Lundgren, and my colleagues at PrairieFire; Roger Allison, Steve Wandro, Merle Hansen, Carol Hodne, Joan Blundell, Denise O'Brien, Gary Lamb, Mark Ritchie, Joe and Mary Jane Weisshaar, George Naylor, Dave Carter, the late Father Norm White, Tam Ormiston, the late Reverend Mac Charles Jones, Jonathan Levine, Rabbi A. James Rudin, David Goldstein, Carol Smith, and many others.

Although I started work on the manuscript in 1995, my agent, Ronald Goldfarb, had been encouraging me to write a book like this for several years. Had it not been for his persistent encouragement and able guidance, this project would still be nothing more than another item on my list of things to do—someday. Likewise, I deeply appreciate the patience and faith of Thomas Dunne and Sean Desmond, my skillful and supportive editors at St. Martin's Press. My appreciation also to Mark Fowler, for his advice and counsel, and to my copyeditor whose precise and diligent hand has greatly improved both my writing and the text.

As a seven-year project, this book would have taken even longer to complete without the financial support I received from various individuals and foundations. I want to especially thank Lance Hill and the Southern Institute for Education and Research at Tulane University for their steadfast personal, institutional, and financial support. Thanks, also to: the Samuel Rubin Foundation, Daniel and Joanna S. Rose, Josephine G. Lindsley, Harriet Barlow and the Blue Mountain Center, Victor and Lorraine Honig and the Limantour Fund, the Lubo Fund, the Hall/Rubinstein Family Fund, and the EMSA Fund.

Any and all mistakes in this manuscript are my own, but it took many people to gather the voluminous material which documents the story I have attempted to tell. Among them are: my colleague Ken Stern at the American Jewish Committee and its always accommodating library staff, especially Cyma Horowitz and her able colleagues: Michele Anish, Charlotte Bonelli, and Steven Z. Koplin; Ken Toole and the staff of the Montana Human Rights Network; Devin Burghart and Justin Massa of the Center for New Community in Chicago; Mark Potok and the staff of the Intelligence Project of the Southern Poverty Law Center; Jonathan Mozzochi, Chuck Tanner and Steve Gardiner, all formerly of the Coalition for Human Dignity; Eric Ward; John Lunsford and Professor Barry Mehler of Ferris State University. Also to those individuals who cannot be named and who took serious risks to penetrate the ranks of the radical right, deep thanks and admiration.

Numerous libraries and archivists have been equally indispensable to my research. Among them: Robert Marshall and Sharon Howe of the Urban Archives Center at California State University, Northridge, whose long-distance help unearthed a trove of terrific material from the files of the Community Relations Committee of the Jewish Federation Council of Los Angeles. In that connection, my warmest thanks go to the late Joseph Roos, who tracked and catalogued the escapades of Hitler sympathizers and other homegrown rightists for decades, beginning in the 1930s. I also wish to thank James Danky, newspapers and periodicals librarian for the State Historical Society of Wisconsin, and Sheryl Williams, Rebecca Schulte, and others on the staff of the Kansas Collection at the Spencer Library at the University of Kansas in Lawrence, which contains unparalleled material on the far right. Complementing this help have been legions of court clerks, administrative assistants, and others who took time away from more pressing tasks to help me find crucial files, documents, or microfilm records on unreasonably short notice. Karen Matthews, the clerk-recorder of Stanislaus County, California, who stood up to the threats of right-wing militants and paid dearly for her courage, helped me further by sharing her personal story.

I owe special thanks to the relatives and descendants of William Potter Gale, who generously shared their memories, thoughts, and reflections. This process was sometimes painful, occasionally humorous, but always revealing. They shared their ideas and reminiscences willingly and I have enormous respect for their honesty and self-disclosure. Time and again, I was heartened by the fact that Bill Gale's bigotry did not survive him particularly well. As Gale's son aptly put it, "If anything, I learned the ill effects of prejudice from a unique perspective."

I am thankful, also, to those who helped me track down genealogical treasures and sort fact from fiction when it came to the riddles of Gale/Grabifker family lore: the late Amy Levinson worked indefatigably in Portland, Oregon; Harvey Kaplan did the same for me in Glasgow, Scotland.

Among those who provided photos, dug up useful facts and background material, or contributed in other ways were: Jenny Warburg, Walter Bell, and Jorge Jaramillo; Carrie Baker, who retrieved important legal documents and case law; Dorothy Dellar Kohanski, whose recollections of the hardships endured by many of the Jewish settlers at Painted Woods, North Dakota, were extremely helpful; Dan Yurman, who helped with last-minute fact-checking on the shenanigans of the Idaho militia and its allies; Fran Pici; and Bill Newnam.

After spending many years being interviewed by reporters and authors it was a pleasure to reverse roles. Among the journalists who shared materials and insights indispensable to my research was my friend and fellow author Jim Corcoran, whose book, *Bitter Harvest*, remains the definitive account of the life of

Gordon Kahl. Thanks also to Scott North, Jim Ridgeway, Beth Hawkins, Dennis King, Bob Lange, Lorraine Jewett, Bruce Maxwell, Kevin Flynn, Gary Gerhardt, and others whose research and writing over the years helped me write this book.

The recollections of those in law enforcement also proved to be extremely helpful, as did many of the documents that some individuals and state agencies released to me. Among those I wish to thank are: Bob Hamilton, Marvin Woidyla, Macil Flye, Sidney Lezak, and Amos F. Rasumussen, all of Oregon. In addition, state officials in Wisconsin, Oregon, and Arkansas were especially cooperative with the release of documents that agencies in other states refused to disclose.

When it came to researching the intricacies of the Posse Comitatus Act, as well as the larger drama of Reconstruction, I am especially grateful to the following scholars who commented on early drafts of the manuscript: military historians Paul Schieps and Robert Coakley, Professor Lawrence N. Powell of Tulane University, and Professor William McFeely, formerly of the University of Georgia.

Thanks to everyone who slogged through pages of rough draft and helped polish later versions of the manuscript: especially my father, whose sharp eye and experienced pen dramatically improved the text, and my mother and brother, whose help was also invaluable. Thanks also to: Joel Howell, Marian Meyers, Brian Spears, Ellen Spears, Elizabeth Beck, Midge Sweet, Bill Berkowitz, Toby Sonneman, and others unnamed whose feedback and support was indispensable throughout. And, finally, I wish to thank my children, who helped greatly in their own special ways.

ANCESTORS AND DESCENDANTS OF WILLIAM POTTER GALE

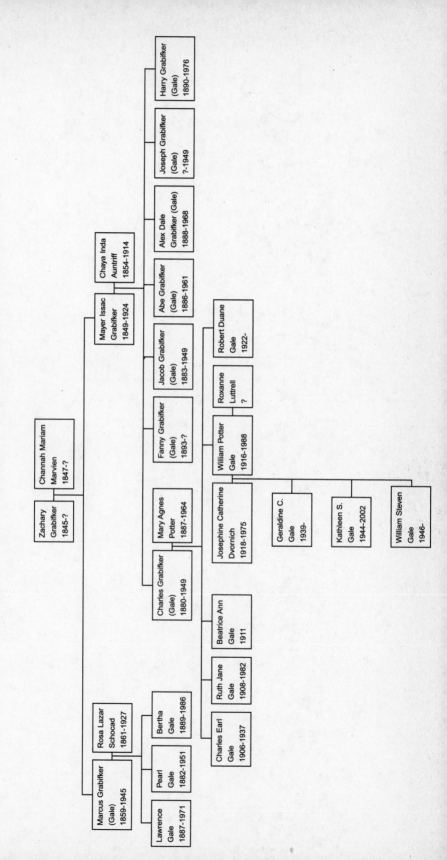

READER'S TIMELINE

CHRONOLOGICAL HIGHLIGHTS OF THE ISSUES, EVENTS, AND INDIVIDUALS FOUND IN *THE TERRORIST NEXT DOOR*

Thirteenth Century

The earliest references to "hue and cry" and the sheriff's posse comitatus appear in several works of medieval jurisprudence. [pp. 383–385]

1649

John Sadler, a Puritan member of the British Parliament, issues what may be the first Anglo-Israelite manifesto, *Rights to the Kingdom: or Customs of our Ancestors*. More than 250 years later, the anti-Semitic ideology of British Israelism will be popularized by American white supremacists. [p. 84]

1776

May 1—Adam Weishaupt establishes the Illuminati to promote Enlightenment philosophy and challenge the entrenched power of conservative Jesuits in Bavarian society. By 1784, Weishaupt's movement has several thousand members but its utopian, liberal ideas are denounced as subversive and it must operate in secret. [pp. 88–89]

1795

Richard Brothers, a Canadian living in England and an early proponent of British Israelism, is declared insane and institutionalized for the next eleven years. Brothers's messianic, millenarian delusions attract a small following and his ideas eventually form the basis for Christian Identity theology. [pp. 84–85]

1797

John Robison writes *Proofs of a Conspiracy Against All the Religions and Governments of Europe, Carried on in the Secret Meetings of Freemasons, Illuminati, and Reading Societies. Collected from Good Authorities.* Also written the same year is *Mémoire pour servir à l'Histoire du Jacobinisme (Memoirs Illustrating the History of Jacobinism)* by a French Jesuit, Abbé Augustin Barruel. These early and influential attacks on Freemasons, the Illuminati, and other secret societies lay the groundwork for two centuries of anti-Semitic conspiracy theories, fear mongering, and hatred, including the infamous *Protocols of the Elders of Zion.* [pp. 89–91]

1798

June 18—Congress passes the first of four Alien and Sedition Acts and Vice President Thomas Jefferson responds with a states' rights manifesto. More than half a century later, Jefferson's argument that a state can "interpose" its "sovereignty" over that of the federal union is seized by slave owners and other Southern secessionists. [pp. 43–44]

1803

February 24—The U.S. Supreme Court decides *Marbury v. Madison*, which boldly asserts the powers and prerogatives of the national government, thus setting the stage for future battles over states' rights versus federal power. [p. 44]

1828

December 19—Vice President John C. Calhoun anonymously publishes his treatise on states' rights, *The Exposition*, as a report to the South Carolina Legislature. Expanding on the doctrine of interposition articulated by Thomas Jefferson, Calhoun's essay outlines a comprehensive theory of state sovereignty, detailing how a state can supposedly make a federal law inoperable within its borders. [pp. 45–46]

1853

The French writer and diplomat Count Joseph Arthur de Gobineau publishes his *Essai sur l'Inégalité des Races Humaines (Essay on the Inequality of the Human Races)*, which greatly advances the notion that Aryans are supreme among the hierarchy of "races." [pp. 86–87]

1854

May 27—Southern demands for aggressive enforcement of the 1850 Fugitive Slave Act prompt Attorney General Caleb Cushing to authorize expanded use of the military as a posse comitatus to pursue escaped slaves. One week later, on June 2, the largest posse in American history (1,600 men) assembles in Boston and forcibly escorts Anthony Burns, an escaped Virginia slave, to the ship that returns him to bondage. [p. 52]

1859

November 1—Marcus Grabifker (Gale), uncle of Charles Gale, the father of the future founder of the Posse Comitatus, is born in the Pale of Settlement near Loitsk (or Lodz), Poland. [p. 13]

1865

A French lawyer, Maurice Joly, writes a satirical political pamphlet attacking Napoleon III. Titled *Dialogue Between Montesquieu and Machiavelli*, the tract is devoid of anti-

Semitism, but is later plagiarized by the authors of *The Protocols of the Elders of Zion* who appropriate Joly's prose describing the authoritarian evils of Napoleon III and attribute them to the Jews. [pp. 407–408 n. 32]

December—Half a dozen former Confederate Army officers establish the Ku Klux Klan in Pulaski, Tennessee. Four months later, former Confederate general Nathan Bedford Forrest is appointed "Grand Wizard." [p. 53]

1871

April 20—Klan violence prompts Congress to pass the first Ku Klux Klan Act, making conspiracies to deprive persons of their civil and political rights a federal crime. The measure aids in the dismantling of the "First Era" Ku Klux Klan, but paramilitary activity by white supremacists helps defeat Reconstruction, nonetheless. [p. 53]

1876

September 14—Anticipating violence during the upcoming presidential election, U.S. attorney general Alfonso Taft reminds federal marshals of their authority to form a posse comitatus of local civilians, militiamen, or federal troops to ensure order at polling places throughout the South. Seven thousand special deputy marshals are dispatched to keep the peace. [pp. 53–54]

1877

January 9—Democrats and former Confederates stage a coup in New Orleans, seizing control of most state offices, including the state arsenal and the supreme court, leaving the Republican governor in control of only the statehouse. [pp. 55–56, 419 n. 4, 420 n. 15, 421 n. 28]

February 23—Rep. John D. C. Atkins (D-Tennessee) introduces an early version of the Posse Comitatus Act to prevent federal troops from protecting Republican governors and legislatures in states where Democrats have asserted victory in the November 1876 election. The measure fails to win final congressional approval. [pp. 55, 58]

March—Disputed returns from the November 1876 presidential election—in which Democrat Samuel J. Tilden won the popular vote against Republican Rutherford B. Hayes, but Tilden's 184 electoral votes were one vote short of what was needed to win the presidency—result in the historic Southern Compromise: Hayes agrees to recognize Democratic administrations in Florida, Louisiana, and South Carolina, if congressional Democrats accept him as president. Republicans withdraw army troops to their barracks, thereby allowing white Democrats free reign to subjugate blacks in the decades that follow. [pp. 53–56]

1878

May 27—U.S. Rep. J. Proctor Knott (D-Kentucky) introduces the Posse Comitatus Act. The bill is approved the following day with all but one of the 130 "yea" votes cast by Democrats. Several weeks later, on June 15, the House of Representatives approves the final version of the act, as Section 29 of the Army Appropriation Bill. The measure hastens the restoration of white supremacy across the South by barring the use of army troops to protect blacks and their Republican political allies. [pp. 57–60, Appendix 1]

1879

As nationalism rises across Europe, Wilhelm Marr, a German anti-Semite, coins the term "anti-Semitism" to describe growing anti-Jewish attitudes that accompany increased Jewish participation in civil society and politics. [pp. 86–87]

1881

April—Shops, synagogues, and homes are destroyed when mobs of Russian peasants and workers launch vicious pogroms against the Jews, whom authorities blame for the assassination of Czar Alexander II. The attacks prompt the first massive wave of Jewish immigration to America. All told, several million Jews flee Russia and Eastern Europe during the next twenty years. [pp. 13–14]

1883

Twenty-three-year-old Russian Jewish immigrants, Marcus and Rosa Grabifker (Gale) arrive at the Jewish agricultural settlement of Painted Woods, some thirty miles east of Bismarck, North Dakota. [p. 11]

1886

The U.S. Supreme Court outlaws private paramilitary armies in *Presser v. Illinois*. [p. 320]

1894

Fleeing persecution and seeking economic opportunity, fourteen-year-old Charles Grabifker (Gale) leaves the Russian Pale of Settlement with his parents and five siblings. The family gets as far as Glasgow, Scotland. Charles continues on to America soon afterward, seeking his uncle Marcus, in North Dakota, only to find that he has moved west to Oregon some four years earlier. [p. 14]

1898

April 28—Four days after the start of the Spanish-American War, Charles Gale, eighteen, lies about his age and place of birth and joins the army. When Gale reenlists seven months later he discloses his Jewish heritage on military papers by stating his parents' nationality as "Hebrew." [pp. 13–14]

1899

Houston Stewart Chamberlain publishes *The Foundations of the Nineteenth Century*, proclaiming the future of Aryan racial redemption through selective breeding. Chamberlain's ideas are praised by British newspapers, endorsed by American President Theodore Roosevelt, and amplified by Nazi propagandists in the decades that follow. [pp. 87–88]

1903

June 17—Henry Lamont "Mike" Beach, a future leader of the Posse Comitatus, is born in Mitchell, Nebraska. Five years later his family moves to Oregon. [p. 117]

August 26–September 7—The earliest known publication of *The Protocols of the Elders of Zion* appears in abbreviated form under the title "Programme for World Conquest by the Jews" in *The Banner*, a newspaper in St. Petersburg, Russia, edited by P. A. Krushevan, an organizer of the murderously anti-Semitic Union of the Russian People, known as the Black Hundreds. [pp. 91, 407–408 n. 32]

1905

Thomas Dixon Jr. writes *The Clansman*, a novel glorifying the post–Civil War KKK that becomes the inspiration for D.W. Griffith's 1915 film, *Birth of a Nation*. [pp. 8, 401 n. 22]

July 24—Charles Gale, twenty-five, marries Mary Agnes Potter, seventeen, in St. Paul, Minnesota. The couple's first child, Charles Earl Gale, elder brother to William Potter (Bill) Gale, is born the following year. [p. 16]

1913

Wesley A. Swift is born in New Jersey. The son of a Methodist minister, Swift will adopt Christian Identity as his religion and become an early mentor to Posse Comitatus founder Bill Gale. [p. 24]

1914

November 4—Chaya Inda Grabifker, sixty, the grandmother of Bill Gale, dies in Glasgow. Her only daughter, Fanny, leaves for America, staying briefly with her brother Charles in Minnesota before joining her uncle Marcus in Oregon. [p. 16]

1915

August 16—Two months after the commutation of his death sentence by the governor of Georgia, Leo Frank is abducted from a prison farm and lynched by a group calling itself "The Knights of Mary Phagan." Two years earlier, Frank had been wrongly convicted for the murder of thirteen-year-old Phagan, an employee at Frank's pencil factory in Atlanta. [pp. 83, 431 n. 24]

November 25—"Colonel" William Joseph "Doc" Simmons inaugurates the "Second Era" Ku Klux Klan by orchestrating a nighttime cross burning atop Georgia's famous Stone Mountain. One month earlier, Simmons had recruited thirty-four supporters, including members of the mob that lynched Leo Frank, to sign an official charter for the "purely benevolent and eleemosynary" Knights of the Ku Klux Klan. [pp. 431–432 n. 24]

1916

November 20—William Potter Gale is born in St. Paul, Minnesota, the fourth child of Charles and Mary Gale. [p. 16]

1920

May 22—Automobile magnate Henry Ford publishes the first of ninety-one articles denouncing Jews and Judaism in his newspaper, *The Dearborn Independent*. The articles are a reconstituted, Americanized version of *The Protocols of the Elders of Zion* and are later compiled into a four-volume set and published as *The International Jew: The World's Foremost Problem*. One year later, on August 16–18, 1921, the *Protocols* are debunked by Philip Graves, the Constantinople correspondent for *The Times of London* in an article in which he notes—among other things—that large sections of the *Protocols* were lifted from Maurice Joly's 1865 satirical critique of Napoleon III. [pp. 28–29, 407–408 n. 27–37]

1924

Ku Klux Klan membership peaks with approximately three to four million members. [p. 74]

March 13—Mayer Isaac Grabifker, Bill Gale's Jewish grandfather, dies in Glasgow, Scotland. [p. 26]

1927

June 30—Faced with mounting criticism, Henry Ford renounces *The Protocols of the Elders of Zion* and claims he is unaware of the anti-Semitic content of his newspaper, *The Dearborn Independent*. [pp. 29, 408 n. 37]

1930

Howard Rand, a Bible scholar, lawyer, and one-time Prohibition candidate for Massachusetts attorney general, becomes one of the early founders of the Christian Identity movement in America when he organizes the first national convention of British-Israelite groups in the U.S. [p. 405, n. 5]

1932

August 8—While still attending high school in Los Angeles, Bill Gale, fifteen, joins the National Guard Reserves. [p. 18]

1933

Fanny Gale, Charles Gale's sister and youngest sibling, arrives in Los Angeles with her husband and infant daughter. Fanny frequently visits Charles Gale, becoming a regular reminder of the Gale family's Jewish roots. [pp. 21, 407 n. 27]

January 31—One day after Adolf Hitler becomes chancellor of Germany, William Dudley Pelley establishes the Silver Shirt Legion of America. [pp. 29, 117]

1934

November 15—Bill Gale enlists in the army after graduating high school and serves as a private with the coast artillery at Fort MacArthur in California. [p. 18]

1937

"Radio Priest" Father Charles Coughlin reaches the peak of his popularity by denouncing President Roosevelt and the New Deal as Communist collectivism, attacking "Reds" in Hollywood, and "exposing" the supposed Jewish financiers of the Bolshevik revolution. Coughlin's weekly "Hour of Power" radio broadcasts reach between five and twelve million listeners, circulation of his newspaper, *Social Justice*, is approximately 800,000, and in 1938 the publication carries excerpts from *The Protocols of the Elders of Zion*. Preaching a similar message, the Rev. Gerald L. K. Smith inaugurates his new organization, the anti-Semitic "Committee of One Million." [pp. 27, 29]

June 7—Bill Gale marries Josephine Catherine Dvornich, the daughter of prosperous Yugoslavian immigrants from San Pedro, California. The couple's first child, Geraldine, is born two years later. [p. 18]

1938

July 30—Henry Ford, seventy-five, is awarded the Grand Cross of the German Eagle by the German Vice-Consul of Detroit. It is the highest honor Hitler can bestow upon a foreigner. [pp. 28–29]

1939

May—Two months after the Nazi invasion of Czechoslovakia, Henry Beach, thirty-six, joins William Dudley Pelley's pro-Hitler Silver Shirts and becomes a leader of the group in Oregon. Two years later, in 1941, Pelley claims 25,000 members and 75,000 sympathizers, but scholars of the movement estimate that membership probably peaked in 1934 at around 15,000. [p. 117]

1942

February 19—President Franklin D. Roosevelt issues Executive Order #9066 authorizing the forced relocation of approximately 120,000 Japanese Americans from California, Washington, and Oregon to ten concentration camps—benignly labeled "relocation centers"—in the western deserts of the United States. The order also authorizes the military to proceed against American citizens and others (especially those affiliated with pro-Hitler groups) it deems dangerous to military security, by banishing them from coastal regions and other militarily sensitive areas. [pp. 118–119]

May—William Dudley Pelley and two associates are indicted by a federal grand jury in Indianapolis for sedition because of antigovernment statements Pelley published in his magazine, *The Galilean*. Pelley and his codefendants are convicted in August and Pelley is sentenced to fifteen years in prison. [pp. 118, 441 n. 38]

1943

February 13—Henry Beach sues the army, claiming he has been "deprived of his rights and liberties" and subjected to an "inquisition" because of his membership in right-wing groups, including the Silver Shirts. [p. 119]

September 9—Bill Gale, a twenty-seven-year-old army major, departs for Southwest Pacific Army headquarters in Brisbane, Australia. Gale is hospitalized soon after he arrives and spends the next two and a half months complaining of abdominal pain. He is flown back to the United States in April 1944 where he spends another month in the hospital with the same symptoms, leading to a diagnosis of "psychoneurosis" and anxiety that is classified as "moderately severe." [pp. 18–19]

1944

The U.S. Supreme Court affirms the government's right to restrict the formation of private armies, ruling that, "There can be no justification for the organization of such an armed force. . . . The inherent potential danger of any organized private militia, even f never used or even if ultimately placed at the disposal of the government, is obvious." [p. 320]

Notwithstanding the war against Nazism, American anti-Semitism reaches an all-time high with 24 percent of Americans saying they regard Jews as a menace to the country, up from 15 percent two years earlier. One year later, 58 percent will say that Jews have too much power compared to 36 percent in 1938. [pp. 29–30]

1945

Wesley Swift leaves his job as an auto-supply salesman to organize for the Ku Klux Klan in southern California. He soon meets Gerald L. K. Smith and the men establish a close relationship. Swift recruits fellow Klansmen as "bodyguards" for his new mentor. [p. 24]

June 30—Marcus Gale, eighty-five, dies of a heart attack while resting quietly in his home in Portland, Oregon. [p. 20]

September 1—Bill Gale, twenty-eight, is evacuated from an army hospital in the Pacific and returned to the United States, complaining of jaundice. [p. 19]

1946

August 15—Bill Gale is sent overseas to work with the staff of General Douglas Mac-Arthur, helping supervise U.S. occupation forces in Japan. Gale is soon joined in Tokyo by Josephine and their three young children, two girls and a newborn boy. [p. 19]

1947

Wesley Swift establishes the "Great Pyramid Club" in Los Angeles to promote Christian Identity theology and recruit for the Ku Klux Klan. [p. 25]

1948

November 2—South Carolina governor Strom Thurmond, a Democrat, carries four southern states and polls 1.1 million votes as the presidential nominee of the segregationist Dixiecrat Party. According to a Gallup poll, 68 percent of Southerners and 42 percent of Northerners believe that the federal government should do nothing to end racial discrimination in employment. [p. 30]

1949

April 25—Bill Gale's Jewish father, Charles, sixty-nine, dies in Los Angeles. [p. 20]

1950

January 21—Alger Hiss, a former State Department officer, is convicted of perjury and sentenced to prison for lying about his connection to a Communist spy ring during the 1930s. The trial and conviction fuel Cold War fears. The following month, on February 9, Sen. Joseph R. McCarthy (R-Wisconsin) tells the Republican Women's Club of Wheeling, West Virginia, that he has a list of 205 members of the Communist Party who "are still working and shaping policy in the State Department." [p. 32]

April 27—After twelve cumulative years of army service, Lieutenant Colonel Bill Gale, thirty-three, is pronounced permanently unfit for military service and classified as disabled due to his repeated hospitalizations for abdominal pain which Gale claims is due to hepatitis, despite repeated medical tests to the contrary. [p. 21]

1951

Retired army colonel John O. Beaty publishes *The Iron Curtain Over America* to expose the role of "Judaized Khazars" in European and American life. The book is embraced strongly by Christian Identity believers and others on the radical right. [pp. 33–34]

1952

Congressman Ralph Gwinn (R-New York) introduces the "Liberty Amendment," which seeks to abolish the federal income tax by repealing the Sixteenth Amendment. By 1964, seven states will endorse Gwinn's proposal but it ultimately fails. [pp. 98–99]

The once prestigious *American Mercury* magazine is acquired by J. Russell Maguire, an oilman and munitions magnate, who soon fills its pages with hard-core anti-Semitic and right-wing propaganda. [p. 82]

July 11—Gerald L. K. Smith and 300 volunteers inundate the Republican National Convention with 150,000 pieces of literature denouncing Dwight Eisenhower as a tool of the Jews. [p. 35]

1954

Bill and Josephine Gale move to West Hollywood, California, and the couple's three children, Geraldine, fifteen; Kathleen, ten; and Billy, eight, attend area public schools. [p. 22]

May 17—The U.S. Supreme Court declares segregation unconstitutional in *Brown v. Board of Education of Topeka*. [pp. 36–37]

July 23—Mississippi circuit court judge Tom P. Brady denounces the *Brown* decision in a ninety-two-page booklet, *Black Monday*. Published by the Citizens' Council movement, the tract inspires scores of Southerners and others to fight integration. [pp. 37–39]

1955

August 28—Fourteen-year-old Emmett Louis Till of Chicago is murdered after being kidnapped from his grandfather's home in Money, Mississippi, for allegedly "wolf-whistling" at a white woman. An all-white jury acquits the two men charged with the crime. [p. 41]

December 1—Speaking before 2,000 Citizens' Council members and forty state legislators, Mississippi's senior senator, James O. Eastland, denounces "political pressure groups bent upon the destruction of the American system of government, and the mongrelization of the white race." The following year, more than a hundred congressmen and senators from eleven states sign the "Southern Manifesto" asserting that the *Brown* decision and its legal progeny are unconstitutional. [p. 40]

Rosa Parks refuses to give up her seat on a bus in Montgomery, Alabama. The yearlong bus boycott that follows thrusts Dr. Martin Luther King Jr., a young pastor at Montgomery's Dexter Avenue Baptist Church, onto the national stage. [pp. 40, 41–42]

1956

FBI Director J. Edgar Hoover authorizes the Bureau's Internal Security Counterintelligence Program. Known as COINTELPRO, its goal is to disrupt and discredit the civil rights movement and leftist organizations and, later, both white supremacist organizations and Vietnam War protest groups. [p. 134]

1957

Tax protesting pioneer Arthur Julius Porth is ordered to pay $4,000 to the IRS after his lawsuit against the government is dismissed. Porth had argued that being forced to withhold money from his workers' paychecks made him an unpaid tax collector, which amounted to slavery and a violation of the Thirteenth Amendment. [p. 98]

May 1—Bill Gale is named state chairman of the California Constitution Party. [p. 22]

August 29—Congress passes the Civil Rights Act of 1957—the first such measure to pass Congress since the adoption of the federal civil rights laws of 1875. [pp. 61–62]

September 2—Three days after a federal judge orders the desegregation of Central High School in Little Rock, Arkansas, Gov. Orval Faubus instructs National Guard troops to prevent black students from integrating the school. Three weeks later, on September 23, President Eisenhower federalizes the Arkansas National Guard and orders army troops to enforce the desegregation orders of the federal court. The next day one thousand troops arrive in Little Rock led by Major General Edwin A. "Ted" Walker. [pp. 48–49]

November—As part of his campaign for governor of California on the Constitution Party ticket, Bill Gale announces the filing of a "criminal indictment" against President Eisenhower for the "flagrantly illegal action [of] invading and occupying [the] sovereign State of Arkansas." Gale's "indictment" pronounces Eisenhower guilty of "high crimes and misdemeanors" and demands the president's immediate arrest and trial for allegedly violating the 1878 Posse Comitatus Act. [p. 50]

1958

Invigorated by the *Brown* decision and the fight to preserve segregation, Ku Klux Klan membership reaches a post-war high of 40,000. [pp. 74]

October 12—The Temple, Atlanta's oldest synagogue, is bombed by white supremacists. From 1954 to 1959, 530 acts of Klan violence are aimed at blacks, integrationist whites, and Jewish targets in Georgia, Florida, Alabama, and Tennessee. [p. 74]

November 4—After the Constitution Party fails to receive the 50,000 votes required to achieve ballot status, Bill Gale runs for governor as a write-in candidate and receives 1,073 votes. [p. 62]

December 9—Robert Welch, sixty-one, establishes the John Birch Society. [p. 68]

1959

Bill Gale leaves the Constitution Party and starts a new, more militant organization, the Christian Defense League, with the help of his friend, the former Klansman, San Jacinto Capt. [p. 66]

1960

After running into conflict with Wesley Swift about the Christian Defense League, Bill Gale starts the California Rangers, "a secret underground guerrilla force" composed of a "complex of organizations" whose goal is to recruit "militant-minded" racists. [p. 66]

June—Robert Bolivar DePugh, thirty-seven, establishes the Minutemen in preparation for an anticipated Communist takeover of the United States. For the next ten years, DePugh and other Minutemen train in military maneuvers, infiltrate leftist groups, campaign noisily against gun control, and stockpile illegal weapons. [p. 72]

1961

April—John Birch Society founder Robert Welch denounces charges of anti-Semitism as "malicious" and "unfair," saying such accusations provoke "anger against Jews in general." Just three years after its founding, the JBS is spending $1 million annually and has at least 24,000 dues-paying members in twenty-seven states and the District of Columbia. Headquartered in Belmont, Massachusetts, it has sixty-three full-time employees. [p. 70]

1962

Bill Gale and a follower, George Joseph King Jr., join American Legion Signal Hill Post 490 to recruit members for Gale's paramilitary group, the California Rangers. It is here that Gale meets Richard Butler, the future founder of the Aryan Nations. After making an anticommunist speech at the Post, Butler, forty-four, is invited by Gale to his home for several all-night indoctrination sessions in Christian Identity. [pp. 67, 110]

Subscriptions to ultra-conservative publications soar in the wake of communist advances abroad, such as the 1959 victory of Fidel Castro in Cuba and the construction of the Berlin Wall in 1961. From 1955 to 1962, the weekly circulation of *Human Events* skyrockets from 13,502 to more than 123,000. Income for the Twentieth Century Reformation Hour, the Christian Anti-Communism Crusade, and the Christian Crusade totals $2,663,900 in 1962, more than triple the figure three years earlier. [p. 68]

April—A. J. Porth begins submitting his tax returns with the following notation: "I plead the Fifth Amendment to the Constitution of the United States." The action wins him the endorsement of the Wichita *Evening Eagle and Beacon* and helps launch his career as a leader of the tax-protest movement. [p. 98]

September 29—After Mississippi governor Ross R. Barnett defies a federal desegregation order, retired major general Edwin Walker, who had commanded the federal troops during the Little Rock crisis, arrives in Oxford, Mississippi, to help rally a white mob opposed to integration at the University of Mississippi. By daybreak on September 30, 160 of 300 federal marshals are wounded—twenty-eight by gunfire—and two bystanders are dead. It takes 12,000 soldiers dispatched by President Kennedy to restore order. [pp. 75–76]

December 4—Bill Gale ends his twenty-five-year marriage to Josephine Dvornich and files for divorce. [pp. 67]

1963

Bill Gale moves to Lancaster, California, on the outskirts of Los Angeles, and publishes *The Faith of Our Fathers*, a fifty-four-page booklet detailing his Christian Identity beliefs. [p. 79]

June 11—President Kennedy federalizes National Guard troops after Alabama governor George Wallace blocks two black students from attending the University of Alabama at Tuscaloosa. Six months earlier, during his inaugural address, Governor Wallace had famously proclaimed "segregation now, segregation tomorrow, segregation forever" and denounced "the false doctrines of communistic [racial] amalgamation." [pp. 76–77]

June 12—NAACP field secretary Medgar Evers, thirty-seven, is gunned down in the driveway of his home in Jackson, Mississippi, by Byron de la Beckwith, a Citizens' Council member. [pp. 77–78]

August—George Joseph King Jr., a friend of Bill Gale and member of Gale's California Rangers, is arrested for selling a 50-caliber machine gun to undercover Treasury agents trying to infiltrate the Rangers. Publicity about the arrest leads to Gale's firing from Waddell and Reed, the securities firm where he and King both work. The arrest also prompts an investigation by American Legion officials, who revoke the charter of Signal Hill Post 490 in October 1964 after concluding that Gale and King used Post meetings for the "dissemination of anti-Jewish and anti-Negro materials." [pp. 66–67]

1964

Bill Gale opens his own securities and insurance firm in Glendale, on the northern outskirts of Los Angeles, and runs unsuccessfully in the GOP primary for Congress in the Twenty-seventh Congressional District. Gale also incorporates his Ministry of Christ Church and tries, unsuccessfully, to revive the dormant Christian Defense League. [pp. 67, 93]

J. Edgar Hoover expands the FBI's COINTELPRO program of surveillance and disruption targeting civil rights activists and left-wing groups to include white supremacist groups and the KKK. [p. 134]

July 2—President Lyndon Johnson signs the Civil Rights Act of 1964, adding to the outrage of segregationists and white-supremacist groups. [p. 95]

1965

Bill Gale marries Roxanne Lutrell who helps him expand the Ministry of Christ Church, which lays the groundwork for the establishment of the Posse Comitatus. [p. 92]

The John Birch Society prints 500,000 copies of a pamphlet by Robert Welch titled *Two Revolutions at Once* attacking the Rev. Martin Luther King Jr. as "a trouble-maker pushing pro-Communist programs." Spurred by the success of the civil rights movement, the 1964 defeat of Barry Goldwater, fears of urban unrest, and other factors, membership in the

John Birch Society approaches 100,000, by mid-year. The JBS staff numbers 220, its budget is $6 million and the number of JBS bookstores rises to 340 from 225 in late 1964. [pp. 70–71]

August 6—President Johnson signs the Voting Rights Bill into law. The measure is upheld unanimously by the U.S. Supreme Court the following year, prompting further segregationist anger and violence against civil rights workers, four of whom are killed during the year. [p. 95]

August 11–16—Riots in Watts, Los Angeles, result in thirty-four people dead (most of them black), nearly 1,000 injuries, and approximately 4,000 arrests. The riots give added impetus to right-wing groups that attempt to capitalize on white fears of civil unrest. [p. 102]

October 21—A. J. Porth is indicted on five counts of tax evasion and his subsequent trial and conviction make him a martyr in the eyes of right-wing tax protesters across the nation. [pp. 99–100]

November—Bill Gale publishes the first issue of *IDENTITY*, the newsletter of his Ministry of Christ Church. [p. 94]

1966

September—Bill Gale publishes the first of a two-part article under the title "Racial and National Identity." Its religious content is similar to his Basic Identity tract, *The Faith of Our Fathers*, but the text also emphasizes Gale's ideas about constitutional government and brings him closer to assembling his doctrine for the Posse Comitatus. [p. 95]

1967

Three years after passage of the federal Civil Rights Act outlawing job discrimination, 63 percent of whites favor leaving the matter of fair treatment in employment up to "states and local communities" instead of the federal government. [p. 95]

Gordon Kahl renounces the income tax in a letter to the IRS, vowing never to "give aid and comfort to the enemies of Christ" and declaring he will no longer tithe to "the Synagogue of Satan." [pp. 192–193, 465 n. 5, 6]

August—Bill Gale begins to discuss the emerging tax protest movement in his *IDENTITY* newsletter. [p. 97]

1968

Nearly fifteen years after the *Brown* decision ruled segregation unconstitutional, only 36 percent of whites nationally, and 20 percent of whites in the South, approve of federal efforts to promote school integration, down from 48 percent (nationally) who approved in 1966. [p. 95]

November 5—Alabama governor George Wallace demonstrates the broad appeal of white racism by winning nearly ten million votes for president on the far-right American Independent Party ticket. [p. 299]

1969

The Eighth Circuit Court of Appeals rules against tax protestor and disbarred attorney Jerome Daly in a landmark decision invalidating the so-called "Porth-Daly Fifth Amendment Return." [p. 100]

July 13—After evading federal authorities for more than a year, Robert DePugh, forty-six, and an associate are arrested in New Mexico. DePugh had become a federal fugitive in February 1968, after his indictment for allegedly plotting a series of bank robberies. [p. 111]

1970

October 8—Wesley Swift, fifty-seven, dies in the waiting room of a Mexican clinic while awaiting treatment for kidney disease and diabetes. [p. 110]

1971

June—Bill Gale's *IDENTITY* newsletter announces the need to form "Christian Posses" across the United States to enforce the principles of a "Constitutional Republic" and repudiate various "unlawful acts" of the federal government, including integration. The undated article titled "The Constitutional Republic" appears sometime between April and July and most of its eighteen pages are devoted to listing various government misdeeds that Gale says justify taking "vigilante action." [p. 108]

September—Bill Gale publishes his *Guide for Volunteer Christian Posses* containing the memorable instruction for how to deal with government officials who "disobey" the Constitution: "He shall be removed by the Posse to a populated intersection of streets in the township and at high noon be hung there by the neck, the body remaining until sundown, as an example to those who would subvert the law." The *Guide* is quickly reprinted in *The National Chronicle*, a tabloid read primarily by Identity believers. [pp. 108, 112]

1972

Tax protester Marvin Cooley authors *The Big Bluff*, which becomes a right-wing bestseller and puts him in high demand on the far-right speaking circuit. Cooley is convicted of tax evasion the following year. [pp. 105]

Bill and Roxanne Gale purchase a hundred acres in rural Mariposa, California, that Gale calls "The Manasseh Ranch" based on his belief that America's Christian founders were descendants of the Lost Hebrew tribe of Manasseh. [pp. 113]

Summer—The far right *American Mercury* magazine devotes half its seventy-page summer issue to "The Great Tax Strike," informing its 9,100 subscribers of the strategies and travails of tax protestors across the nation. [p. 101]

June/July—Bill Gale announces the formation of "The United States Christian Posse Association" and offers to issue charters "upon application by a minimum number of seven Christian citizens, all of who must be residents of the County in which the Posses [sic] is to be organized." [p. 109]

August 31—The FBI in Portland, Oregon, launches the Bureau's first investigation of "an organization calling itself Identity, or alternatively, Portland Posse Comitatus," which it describes as ". . . [an] association of long-time Right Wing extremists . . . preaching hate against the Negroes and the Jews, and calling for the repudiation and overthrow of the existing law enforcement and judicial systems of this nation." [pp. 119–120]

October—Inspired by Bill Gale's Posse *Guide*, supporters of two Michigan tax protestors, George Kindred and James Freed, announce the formation of a citizen's grand jury "in accordance with the Law of POSSE COMITATUS and the CHRISTIAN COMMON LAW [*sic*]" following the arrest of both men on tax charges. Consistent with Gale's recommendations, the unnamed supporters threatened to hang the officials responsible for the arrest of the duo. [p. 111]

November—*Tax Strike News* reprints Bill Gale's *Guide for Volunteer Christian Posses* verbatim but without attribution. [p. 111]

1973

The far-right Liberty Lobby publishes *Tax Revolt: U.S.A.! Why and How Thousands of Patriotic Americans Refuse to Pay the Income Tax*. Written by Martin Larson, the book is the first to report in detail on the tax strike movement. [p. 102]

Inspired by what he has learned from tax protester Marvin Cooley, Robert Matthews (the future founder of The Order), twenty, lists ten non-existent dependents on his W-4 tax form. Matthews is arrested, convicted on misdemeanor charges, and placed on six months' probation. [p. 105]

Henry Beach, seventy, steals the text of Bill Gale's Posse *Guide* and republishes it as his own under the auspices of the "Citizens Law Enforcement and Research Committee," thereby becoming the mythological "founder" of the Posse. [p. 114]

Gordon Kahl becomes involved in the Posse Comitatus and tax-protest activities while living with his wife and children in west Texas where he is working as a mechanic. [p. 193]

March 12—Eight months after opening its first investigation of the Posse Comitatus, the FBI in Portland, Oregon, concludes its probe saying the group's views are simply "unusual" and its members "have never presented a threat to this community." Six weeks later, on April 26, the Bureau launches another investigation on the grounds that the group is "preaching a program of hate . . . and calling for the repudiation and overthrow of . . . law enforcement and judicial systems . . ." [p. 120]

July 27—The FBI justifies its investigation of the Ministry of Christ Church, saying Bill Gale's "Identity Group" is engaged in activities which could "constitute seditious conspiracy and/or could involve assaulting or killing a federal officer." [p. 134]

October 19—One of the first local Posse Comitatus chapters to be chartered by Mike Beach's Citizens Law Enforcement and Research Committee is established in Lane County, Oregon. [p. 115]

1974

After quitting the John Birch Society two years earlier, tax protester Ardie McBrearty establishes the United States Taxpayers' Union. [pp. 106–107]

Richard Butler relocates the dwindling remnants of Wesley Swift's congregation to Idaho where he has purchased twenty acres outside Hayden Lake. The property is the future home of the Aryan Nations. [p. 110]

Roderick "Rick" Elliott begins publishing *The Primrose and Cattleman's Gazette*, a weekly tabloid that turns to anti-Semitism and Posse-style rhetoric to woo farmers. [p. 225]

January—The National Association to Keep and Bear Arms (NAKBA) calls for the "immediate organization of literally hundreds of citizen posses from coast-to-coast." Later in the year, Minutemen founder Robert DePugh seizes control of NAKBA and moves the group's headquarters from Oregon to Missouri. [pp. 116, 135]

Thomas Stockheimer of Mosinee, Wisconsin, establishes the "Little People's Tax Advisory Committee," a tax-protest group that he quickly transforms into a launching pad for the Posse Comitatus. Two months later, Stockheimer and six others charter the Marathon County chapter of the Posse under the auspices of Mike Beach's Citizens Law Enforcement and Research Committee. [p. 123]

May—The Wisconsin Department of Justice, Division of Criminal Investigation, launches a formal investigation of the Posse Comitatus. [p. 133]

June 6—A new FBI assessment describes the Sheriff's Posse Comitatus (SPC) as not "antisemetic [sic] or anti-black in its pronouncements." Though ignoring evidence of racial and religious bigotry, the report does note that local Posse groups might "take such actions as the arrest and trial of federal agents and other citizens, and forcibly intimidate IRS officers." Such actions constitute advocacy of "violence, terrorism, or intimidation of public officers," according to the Bureau. [p. 120]

July—Robert Matthews, twenty-one, leaves Arizona and the tax-protest movement, settling in Metaline Falls, Washington, where he becomes involved with the Aryan Nations. [p. 106]

September 12—Thomas Stockheimer and two dozen Posse activists issue "Christian Citizens' Grand Jury Indictments" against more than fifty state and local officials they accuse of violating their rights. [p. 125]

October 19–20—Approximately 250–300 people from 12–15 states attend the "Midwest-National Tax and Posse Comitatus Convention" in Milwaukee, Wisconsin. [p. 126]

December 13—Thomas Stockheimer is convicted of felony assault for his August 16 attack on IRS agent Fred Chicken at the home of a farmer outside Abbotsford, Wisconsin. [p. 127]

December 18—Richard Butler charters the "Kootenai County Christian Posse Comitatus," in Coeur d'Alene, Idaho. [p. 131]

1975

After moving to Marathon County from Racine, Wisconsin, future Posse leader James Wickstrom is recruited by Thomas Stockheimer and Charles Dodge to attend meetings of the Little People's Tax Advisory Committee. [pp. 127–128, 444 n. 36]

January 27—Three years after the death of FBI director J. Edgar Hoover, and five months after the resignation of President Richard Nixon following the Watergate scandal, Idaho senator Frank Church chairs a bi-partisan committee investigating FBI and CIA intelligence abuses. [p. 135]

February 8–9—Tax protest and Posse celebrities address activists from at least ten states at the "Big Tri-State Tax and Law Rally" in Eureka Springs, Arkansas. On February 9, several hundred people attend the "Northwest Regional Posse Comitatus and Tax Convention" in Seattle to hear Mike Beach and others. [pp. 131–132]

March 12—Richard Butler and about fifty Posse supporters attract media and law enforcement attention when they attempt to "arrest" Roger A. Davis, a local police officer from Post Falls, Idaho, at the Kootenai County Courthouse in Coeur d'Alene. [pp. 130–131]

March 21—FBI director Clarence B. Kelley designates Portland, Oregon, as the FBI "Office of Origin" responsible for coordinating all information on the Sheriff's Posse Comitatus (SPC). Every FBI office is subsequently ordered to open files on all "individual SPC units" and submit reports to Portland. [p. 132]

April 17—The FBI in Little Rock, Arkansas, sends an urgent Teletype to Washington, D.C., warning of a possible threat against Vice President Nelson A. Rockefeller by an individual with links to the Posse Comitatus in Mississippi. [p. 132]

May 6—Reversing some of its earlier assessments, the FBI now classifies the Posse as a "white hate group." [p. 134]

May 7—Herbert S. Breed, fifty-eight, chairman of the Klamath County Posse Comitatus, sends intimidating letters to Oregon legislators warning that citizens' grand juries will try them for treason if they refuse to repeal a landmark conservation measure. [p. 133]

May 21—FBI director Clarence Kelley orders a more thorough investigation of the Posse, due to "an increase of vigilante-type activity coupled with an escalation of violent hate rhetoric." Kelley orders all field offices to "obtain in-depth coverage of each SPC group" using informants instead of secondary sources such as newspaper clippings and other law enforcement agencies. [pp. 136–137]

May 26—In the first major media report on the Posse Comitatus, *Newsweek* magazine carries a full-page article about the group, citing Henry Beach's outlandish claim of 500,000 members. [p. 137]

May 29—The FBI in El Paso, Texas, reports that members of a "tax rebel group" have appeared on local television in the town of Midland, and notes that an "aggressive investigation" of the group (which includes Gordon Kahl) is continuing. Four months later, when the El Paso office reports its plans to close some of its investigations, it is rebuked for failing to develop "a Bureau-operated source . . . in each SPC unit." [p. 132]

June—Fearful of the talk of tax protest and confronting law enforcement officials, Henry Beach resigns from the Portland, Oregon, Posse Comitatus. [pp. 146–147]

September 2—Led by Francis Gillings, forty-four, a group of fifty heavily armed men and women affiliated with the San Joaquin County Posse Comitatus gather in a tomato field outside Stockton, California, to protest union-organizing efforts by the United Farm Workers (UFW). Gillings is arrested after firing his shotgun at a sheriff's deputy. [pp. 139–141]

September 17—The Liberty Lobby publishes the first issue of the *National Spotlight*, saying its goal is to satisfy "a growing hunger on the part of millions of Americans for old-fashioned truth and integrity in the press." The tabloid is replete with racist propaganda and anti-Semitic conspiracy theories, and the lead editorial in its inaugural issue hails the Posse Comitatus as "a heartening sign of public determination." [p. 142]

November 20—The Church Committee releases its report into government intelligence abuses. The revelations lead U.S. Attorney General Edward Levi to impose new restrictions on government spying. [p. 135]

December—Pointedly criticizing some Posse members for acting like "a pack of hoodlums," Mike Beach sends out a mailing criticizing those who have engaged in "stupid actions and fighting with the Sheriff." Beach also chastises Posse leaders who have allied themselves with the tax protest movement or espoused racism and anti-Semitism. Previously, in November, Beach began printing the Posse *Blue Book* without the controversial paragraph calling for public hangings of disobedient government officials. [p. 146]

December 4–6—The "National Tax Strike and Posse Comitatus Convention," in Denver, Colorado, attracts approximately two hundred participants.

1976

Irwin Schiff adds fuel to the fire of the tax protest movement with his antitax bestseller, *The Biggest Con: How the Government Is Fleecing You*. [p. 104]

Wisconsin Posse activist Donald Minnecheske deeds 29 of his 577 acres to the "Life Science Church," a tax dodge set up by the disbarred tax-protesting lawyer, Jerome Daly. The property becomes an armed compound and the state headquarters for the Wisconsin Posse Comitatus. [p. 125]

May 24—Multnomah County, Oregon, Posse Comitatus "Captain" LaVerne Hollenbeck, forty-six, is convicted of unlawful use of a police insignia, stemming from a January 19 incident in which Hollenbeck was stopped for speeding and displayed his Posse Comitatus "badge." [p. 152]

June—After a fifteen-day trial for their role in the Stockton tomato field incident, California Posse leaders Francis Gillings and Norman Brown are convicted of felony assault. [p. 145]

July 19—After losing the appeal of his federal felony conviction for assaulting IRS agent Fred Chicken, Thomas Stockheimer becomes a federal fugitive. [p. 127]

August 25—One day after the Sacramento, California, FBI reports that it is closing its file on the San Joaquin County Posse, five local activists depart for Portland, Oregon, carrying pistols, ammunition, and other equipment in preparation for their takeover of a potato and wheat farm in eastern Oregon. Two days later, the group (which now numbers seven men) seizes Mikami Farms for eight hours before surrendering to a heavily armed contingent of Oregon State Troopers and sheriff's deputies. The incident makes national headlines and reinforces the Posse's reputation as a band of trigger-happy extremists. [pp. 158–163]

September 9—Two weeks after the Posse takeover of Mikami Farms, the Portland FBI requests permission to initiate a full domestic security investigation of the Posse. "The movement's boldness and disregard for the laws of this country demonstrate great potential for violence," says the twenty-two-page FBI report, which also warns that Posse membership does "not appear to be declining." Seventy-eight chapters have been formed over the previous two years in twenty-three states, with California, Oregon, Wisconsin, and Illinois having the most local groups. [p. 164]

October 14—The U.S. attorney general authorizes a full domestic security investigation of the Sheriff's Posse Comitatus, permitting the widespread use of informants. [p. 164]

1977

Richard Butler establishes the Aryan Nations outside Hayden Lake, Idaho. [p. 110]

Inspired by visions of Communist invasion and fears of the endtimes, John R. Harrell, a multimillionaire, establishes the paramilitary Christian-Patriots Defense League (CPDL) on his fifty-five-acre estate outside Louisville, Illinois. [p. 206]

January—Francis Gillings is convicted of tax evasion and sentenced to federal prison.

April 14—While living in Missouri with his wife, Dianne, James Wickstrom forms the "Mission of Jesus the Christ Church" and declares his commitment to tax resistance in a seven-page statement to Wisconsin revenue authorities. [p. 128]

June—Gordon Kahl is convicted of tax evasion, sentenced to one year in jail, placed on five years' probation, and ordered to undergo a psychiatric evaluation at the federal prison hospital in Springfield, Missouri. [p. 194]

September 8—Approximately forty farmers and ranchers form the American Agriculture Movement (AAM) in Springfield, Colorado, and pledge not to buy, sell, or produce any farm supplies or commodities until Congress raises farm prices. [p. 168]

October 5—One year after authorizing its full domestic security investigation of the Posse, the FBI terminates the inquiry due to "a marked decline of SPC chapters and membership and illegal activity" and other factors. [p. 167]

November–December—Bill and Roxanne Gale move from the Los Angeles area to their "Manasseh Ranch" outside Mariposa, California, a 100-acre property that Gale uses for his Identity meetings and paramilitary training. [p. 113]

December 10—American Agriculture Movement protestors roll into Washington, D.C., to highlight the problem of low farm prices. Thousands of farmers simultaneously converge on state capitals across the nation in support of the group's call for "100 percent parity" and a "farm strike" set for December 14. [p 170]

1978

James Wickstrom endorses AAM's call for a farm strike and publishes *The American Farmer: Twentieth Century Slave*, a fourteen-page booklet asserting that Jews are "land-grabbing devils" intent on "financially and morally rap(ing) the WHITE CHRISTIAN AMERICAN PEOPLE [*sic*]." [p. 178]

James Ellison, thirty-eight, launches The Covenant, the Sword, and the Arm of the Lord (CSA), a paramilitary Christian Identity encampment on 224 acres in southern Missouri dedicated to preparing for the coming "race war." [p. 205]

William Pierce, founder and leader of the neo-Nazi National Alliance, publishes *The Turner Diaries* under the alias Andrew Macdonald. The book is a fictional, futuristic diary of thirty-five-year-old Earl Turner, a white racist who helps lead a successful revolution to overthrow the government of the United States. The book inspires a generation of violent white supremacists, including Oklahoma City bomber Timothy McVeigh. [pp. 7, 291]

April 12—The U.S. House of Representatives votes 268 to 150 to defeat the "flexible parity" farm bill sponsored by Senator Bob Dole (R-Kansas). The vote infuriates members of the American Agriculture Movement. [p. 175]

June 28—Signaling the beginning of the white backlash against affirmative action, the U.S. Supreme Court rules that the University of California-Davis Medical School had unconstitutionally discriminated against a white student, Allan P. Bakke. [p. 103]

November 7—Ray Omernick, a Wisconsin potato farmer and former charter member of the Marathon County Posse Comitatus, is elected to the state legislature from the Eighty-sixth Assembly District. [p. 125]

1979

Thomas Stockheimer moves to the Posse Comitatus compound in Tigerton Dells, Wisconsin, after serving time in prison for bail jumping in connection with his 1974 conviction for assaulting IRS agent Fred Chicken. Stockheimer appoints James Wickstrom leader of the Wisconsin Posse Comitatus and Wickstrom pronounces himself the group's "National Director of Counterinsurgency." [p. 128]

Liberty Lobby founder, Willis A. Carto, sixty-three, establishes the Holocaust-denying Institute for Historical Review in Torrance, California. [p. 142]

February 4—The American Agriculture Movement begins its second winter of lobbying for farm relief in Washington, D.C., but its efforts are met with hostility by most policymakers, the media, and others. Disillusioned and frustrated, the farmers leave Washington one month later and the experience leads some followers of AAM to turn sharply to the right. [p. 175]

August—An embittered Gordon Kahl is released from Leavenworth federal prison after serving eight months following his failure to overturn his 1977 conviction on tax evasion charges. [p. 194]

1980

The IRS receives more than 20,000 illegal tax-protest returns, nearly triple the number received two years before. [p. 100]

Following the October 6, 1979, decision of the Federal Reserve Board to raise interest rates in an attempt to curb inflation, the interest rate on many farm-operating loans rises to 20 percent and higher, pushing more farmers to the brink of insolvency. [p. 180]

Tax protester Frederick "Tupper" Saussy III publishes *The Miracle on Main Street*, which denounces the Federal Reserve System, paper money, and promotes the use of bogus "Public Office Money Certificates." The 160-page paperback sells 100,000 copies over the next two years. [p. 202]

Circulation of the far right tabloid, the *Spotlight*, reaches approximately 250,000. Farm and rural residents make up a substantial portion of the paper's readership. [p. 202]

Right-wing conspiracist Lyndon LaRouche runs for president in the Democratic Party primaries. In addition to achieving national name recognition, LaRouche ends his campaign with 185,000 votes and more than $500,000 in federal matching funds—a first for an extremist candidate. [p. 174]

September—Bill Gale joins James Wickstrom during one of several paramilitary training exercises held at the Posse Comitatus compound in Tigerton Dells, Wisconsin. Two months later, Wickstrom receives 16,000 votes out of two million cast in the race for U.S. Senate while running on the Constitution Party ticket. [p. 184]

1981

Spotlight subscriptions climb to 315,000. [p. 142]

Kansas farmer Keith Shive, fifty-nine, starts the Farmers Liberation Army. [p. 186]

An all-points bulletin is issued in North Dakota for the arrest of Gordon Kahl for violating probation in connection with his 1979 parole from prison. [p. 196]

An American Jewish Committee study finds anti-Semitism to be a "serious social problem," with nearly one in four respondents agreeing with the statement that Jews have "too much power in the United States."

1982

Irwin Schiff writes his second popular anti tax book, *How Anyone Can Stop Paying Income Taxes*, which earns him at least $135,000 in royalties over the next two years and another $85,000 in the decade that follows. [p. 104]

January—Gordon Kahl and his family spend the winter in Arkansas, where Kahl attends tax-protest meetings and visits the paramilitary compound of The Covenant, the Sword and the Arm of the Lord (CSA). Kahl meets Leonard Ginter, a former member of the Wisconsin Posse Comitatus, who will later hide him from federal authorities. [p. 194]

March 26–28—According to news reports, American Agriculture Movement founders Jerry Wright and Eugene Schroder attend a three-day paramilitary training session in Weskan, Kansas, led by James Wickstrom and Bill Gale. The gathering is held on land owned by an AAM supporter, Leonard Cox, and features instruction in explosives, guerrilla warfare, knife-fighting, hand-to-hand combat, first-aid, and "useable poisons." [pp. 183–184]

May—North Dakota Posse activist and Christian Identity believer Len Martin, fifty-eight, treks across the state with a stuffed monkey doll on his back symbolizing his feelings about the IRS. The stunt attracts quizzical looks, feature news coverage, and right-wing acclaim. [p. 195]

May 4—Colorado tax protester and Posse activist Charles Norman Howarth is arrested in Colorado Springs after selling ten pipe bombs to undercover police. Raids on his home and office yield bomb components, automatic weapons, ammunition, Klan robes, a library of hate literature and a list of fifty Klan and Posse members across the state. Also arrested is Kansas Posse activist Wesley White and two other men. [p. 185]

June—Dodge City, Kansas, radio station KTTL begins regular broadcasts of the taped sermons and speeches of Bill Gale and James Wickstrom. The hate-filled broadcasts over the 100,000-watt station prompt vigorous protests. [pp. 188–189]

September 6—Bill Gale delivers his first sermon about the Committee of the States, explaining how and why patriots should take control of the federal government. Like his 1971 Posse Comitatus manifesto, the cornerstone of Gale's message is an "indictment" of Congress for "unlawful" and "treasonous" activity. [pp. 286–287]

October—AAM founder Eugene Schroder reportedly organizes the first of two bomb-making seminars on his father's farm outside Springfield, Colorado. About twenty people from five states attend, including fellow AAM leader Alvin Jenkins, according to the *Denver Post*. [p. 186]

Rick Elliott's *Primrose and Cattleman's Gazette* serializes "Who Rules America," an anti-Semitic "expose" that first appeared in the publication of the neo-Nazi group, the National Alliance. Similar articles follow, including those promising "a 'crash course' on Jewish-Communism . . . the 'International Jew' and his Satanic plans to rule the world." [p. 227]

October–December—Liberal farm groups organize non-violent "Penny Auctions" and other "farm gate defenses" to protest farm foreclosures in Minnesota, Missouri, Illinois, and Wisconsin. [p. 190]

November—One hundred and five Kansas sheriffs receive a "Citizens' Grand Jury" indictment ordering them to arrest ten judges and threatening vigilante action if lawmen refuse. [p. 188]

1983

Robert Matthews establishes the Order. Also known as the Brüders Schweigen or Silent Brotherhood, its members will rob banks, counterfeit money, and murder critics and fellow white supremacists, all in pursuit of Matthews's scheme to incite a race war and overthrow the government. [p. 106]

The IRS receives 58,000 illegal right-wing tax-protest returns, up tenfold from five years earlier. The agency launches a special "Illegal Tax Protester Program" and Congress raises the penalties for illegal tax protest. [p. 202]

Legislation to outlaw paramilitary training is pushed by the Anti-Defamation League and its allies in six states: Kansas, Nebraska, Missouri, Idaho, Oregon, and Wisconsin. Six other states already have passed similar measures since 1981. [p. 204]

Larry Humphreys establishes the Heritage Library on his 300-acre ranch outside Velma, Oklahoma. The heir to millions in cash, property, and oil wells, Humphreys spends the next five years promoting Christian Identity and urging farmers to take up arms to fight foreclosures. [p. 265]

Former Klan leader Louis Beam promotes "leaderless resistance" in the first issue of the *Inter-Klan Newsletter and Survival Alert*, a newsletter produced by him and former Michigan Klan leader Robert Miles. In a separate publication titled *Essays of a Klansman*, Beam outlines how "Aryan Warriors" can earn higher "points" for murdering more highly placed government officials. [pp. 292–293]

January 4—A melee erupts in Springfield, Colorado, when several hundred members and supporters of AAM Grass Roots attempt to stop the foreclosure sale of Jerry Wright's farm. Sheriff's deputies use clubs and tear gas to control the crowd. [p. 189]

February 13—Federal marshals Robert Cheshire and Kenneth Muir are killed and three other lawmen are wounded in a shootout with tax protester Gordon Kahl and two other Posse activists including Kahl's son, Yorie. The incident makes the Posse Comitatus front-page news and sets off a nationwide manhunt for Kahl, who evades authorities until he is killed in Arkansas four months later. [pp. 196–198]

The Denver Post runs a front-page article exposing the alleged role of some Colorado AAM leaders in bomb-making seminars and other paramilitary activities. The negative publicity further divides the already fractured farm group. [p. 212]

March—Missouri lawmakers outlaw paramilitary training. A similar ban passes in Idaho this year. [p. 208]

June 3—Gordon Kahl and Lawrence County Sheriff Gene Matthews are killed when twenty-eight local, state, and federal law enforcement agents attempt to arrest Kahl at the home of Leonard and Norma Ginter outside Smithville, Arkansas. Kahl's body is burned beyond recognition when law enforcement agents incinerate the Ginter home in an attempt to drive Kahl from the dwelling. [pp. 218–220]

June 10—James Wickstrom is convicted of impersonating a public official for his role as the self-appointed clerk and judge of a bogus Posse-created township in Shawano County, Wisconsin. Convicted on two counts, Wickstrom is sentenced to the maximum term: a year and a half in jail. [p. 204]

June 15—Denver talk-show host Alan Berg invites Rick Elliott and Colonel "Bud" Farrell on the air for an interview on KOA radio, which quickly turns combative. [pp. 227–228]

September—Leaders of AAM, Inc., write new bylaws authorizing the expulsion of state chapters that support unlawful activity. The Kansas and Colorado AAM chapters withdraw from the national organization in protest. [p. 214]

November 1—Frustrated farmers affiliated with the Grass Roots faction of the American Agriculture Movement declare a nationwide "Farm Revolt" to protest low commodity prices. [pp. 5, 224]

November 12—Ten days after their failed attempt to blow up a natural gas pipeline in southern Arkansas, Richard Wayne Snell and two accomplices rob a Texarkana pawnshop owned by William Stumpp, an Episcopalian who Snell wrongly assumes is Jewish. Snell later receives the death penalty for killing Stumpp and is executed on April 19, 1995, the same day as the Oklahoma City bombing. [p. 221]

December 27—Alden and Micki Nellis announce they are discontinuing publication of the *AAM News* but Alvin Jenkins recommends that readers subscribe to Rick Elliott's anti-Semitic tabloid, the *Primrose and Cattleman's Gazette*, instead. [p. 225]

1984

Christian Identity minister Sheldon Emry publishes *Billions for the Bankers, Debts for the People: The Real Story of the Money-Control Over America*, a thinly veiled anti-Semitic tract denouncing the "debt-usury banking system." The thirty-page primer becomes a popular recruitment tool by the radical right seeking support from farmers. [p. 181]

American Agriculture Movement activist Billy Davis, a Mississippi lawyer and cattleman, becomes the vice presidential running mate for Lyndon LaRouche. [p. 214]

January 2—Delaware tax protestor Traves Brownlee advocates the formation of an armed citizen militia. Convicted for tax evasion later in 1984, Brownlee is sentenced to five years in federal prison. [p. 400 n. 8]

May 23—Posse activist Donald E. Zabawa provides the Kansas Bureau of Investigation (KBI) with a detailed statement about the alleged criminal activities of about twenty men affiliated with the Posse Comitatus, including Mike Ryan. Zabawa later recants, but much of what he tells the KBI about Ryan turns out to be true. [pp. 233]

June 18—Members of the Order murder KOA radio talk-show host Alan Berg in the carport of his Denver home. [pp. 227–228]

June 30—Richard Wayne Snell shoots and kills Louis Bryant, a black Arkansas State Trooper, during a routine traffic stop. Snell flees but is arrested an hour later after being wounded in a shootout with police. [pp. 221–222]

July 4—Bill Gale hosts the founding meeting of the Committee of the States (COS) at his Manasseh Ranch in California. Forty-four people sign the COS declaration proclaiming themselves "the Lords and Masters of this self-governing Republic known as the United States of America," and ordering the dissolution of Congress. Gale proclaims himself the "chief of staff" of the COS "Unorganized Militia." [pp. 287–288]

July 19—Led by Bob Matthews, the Order robs a Brinks armored car outside Ukiah, California, seizing $3.8 million, the largest amount ever stolen in an armored car robbery at the time. [p. 285]

September 17—Colorado authorities issue a nineteen-count indictment charging National Agriculture Press Association founder Rick Elliott, and his wife, Karla, with theft and conspiracy for bilking farmers out of hundreds of thousands of dollars. Both are convicted. [p. 229]

October 23—Armed with an illegal military-style assault rifle, Nebraska farmer Arthur Kirk is shot and killed by a State Highway Patrol SWAT team on his farm. A member of Rick Elliott's National Agricultural Press Association, the financially distressed and emotionally distraught Kirk believed that agents of the Israeli secret police had been sent to kill him. [p. 230]

November 6—James Wickstrom wins 7,721 votes running for governor of Wisconsin, a notable showing given his status as a convicted criminal and well-known Posse leader. [p. 204]

December 8—Order founder Robert Matthews is killed on Whidbey Island, near Seattle, Washington, after a thirty-six-hour machine-gun battle with federal agents. Unable to dislodge Matthews from his safe house, an FBI SWAT team lobs flares and tear gas into the dwelling, setting it ablaze. [p. 106]

1985

Tax protestor Frederick "Tupper" Saussy III is convicted on federal misdemeanor charges for tax evasion. Saussy goes underground and remains a federal fugitive for more than ten years. [p. 202]

Nearly one out of five farms are in severe financial distress, including 93,000 that are technically insolvent, holding $47 billion in debt. [p. 246]

February 25—In one of the largest protests of the farm crisis, approximately 14,000 people led by the liberal advocacy group Minnesota Groundswell, descend on the state capitol to call for higher commodity prices, debt relief, and a moratorium on farm foreclosures.

April—The Iowa Farm Unity Coalition criticizes "the extremist philosophies and actions of those individuals and organizations that promote violence, anti-Semitic, or racist responses to the Farm Crisis. . . ." The declaration becomes the blueprint for dozens of similar statements issued by other groups over the next several years, including the influential National Council of Churches. [p. 246]

April 30—After four days of brutal torture and sexual abuse, twenty-six-year-old James Thimm is murdered by Identity leader Mike Ryan near Rulo, Nebraska. (Five-year-old Luke Stice was killed by Ryan the previous month.) On June 25, lawmen from three states descend on Ryan's Identity encampment and uncover five truckloads of stolen farm equipment, dozens of weapons, and about 150,000 rounds of ammunition. [pp. 236, 240]

June 12—PrairieFire Rural Action, the North American Farm Alliance, issues the first in a series of "Confidential Memorandums" warning about the rural radical right and its efforts to recruit farmers. Among other things, the memo declares that the strategy of "disregarding and isolating extremists by deliberately not responding to their activities [is] no longer effective." [p. 246]

August—Las Vegas police arrest two members of the Committee of the States on misdemeanor traffic violations and uncover a briefcase full of incriminating evidence, which is later used successfully to prosecute them and Bill Gale. [p. 295]

August 15—ABC's *20/20* airs "Seeds of Hate," a twenty-two-minute segment about the attempt by right-wing groups to recruit farmers. The prime time broadcast featuring Geraldo Rivera paints an unflattering portrait of those farmers who have been drawn to the radical right. [p. 243]

August 17—Nebraska authorities unearth the badly decomposed bodies of Luke Stice and James Thimm from unmarked graves on Mike Ryan's eighty-acre Identity encampment outside Rulo. State lawmakers then announce plans to hold hearings on the Posse Comitatus and other paramilitary groups and in January 1986 paramilitary training is outlawed in the state. [pp. 240–242]

September 20—The American Jewish Committee holds a news conference in New York City to highlight the plight of farmers and speak out against farm belt anti-Semitism. [p. 251]

Hate group expert Leonard Zeskind says there are between 2,000 and 5,000 "hard-core activists" and between 14,000 to 50,000 "sympathizers" of the radical right in the Midwest. [p. 252]

November—PrairieFire Rural Action, the North American Farm Alliance, and the Center for Democratic Renewal (formerly the National Anti-Klan Network) begin training farmers, clergy, union members, hotline operators, lawyers, state officials, and others on countering hate group recruitment in rural communities. Over the next several years additional meetings will reach more than 1,000 participants. [p. 247]

November 15—Former Georgia AAM leader Tommy Kersey teams up with Christian Identity promoter Larry Humphreys of Oklahoma to prevent the eviction of Oscar Lorick, a black farmer in Georgia. The event wins Humphreys and Kersey front-page publicity and inspires the men to attempt similar armed confrontations in the Midwest. [p. 266]

December—A federal jury convicts ten members of the Order on racketeering and conspiracy charges for bank robbery, counterfeiting, and murder, including the killing of Alan Berg, as well as other crimes. Thirteen defendants had already pleaded guilty to other charges. [p. 107]

1986

January—A Lou Harris poll commissioned by the ADL reveals that farm and rural anti-Semitism is a "mass phenomenon," with 27 percent of respondents agreeing that "farmers have always been exploited by international Jewish bankers who are behind those who overcharge them for farm equipment or jack-up the interest on their loans." [p. 253]

Tommy Kersey and Larry Humphreys speak to 1,000 farmers in a series of meetings across the upper Midwest. Mixing right-wing strategies with apocalyptic rhetoric, the men exhort farmers to take up arms to resist foreclosures. The tour culminates on January 25 with a gathering outside Kearney, Nebraska, and is vigorously denounced in newspaper editorials and by farm, rural, and religious groups. [p. 271]

March 18—LaRouche followers Mark Fairchild and Janice Hart stun the Illinois political establishment by winning the Democratic Party nominations for lieutenant governor and secretary of state, respectively. [p. 274]

May—Rick Elliott is convicted by a Colorado jury on fourteen counts of theft and one count of conspiracy for bilking farmers and others out of hundreds of thousands of dollars. He is later sentenced to the maximum of eight years in jail and serves four. Elliott's wife receives a deferred sentence. [p. 274]

October—A federal indictment issued in Boston charges Lyndon LaRouche and ten top aides with fraud and obstruction of justice. A subsequent indictment issued in Virginia charges LaRouche and others with conspiracy and more than $34 million in loan fraud. [p. 276]

Jewish groups join with farm organizations to announce a nationwide petition drive for higher farm prices, emergency assistance, and a moratorium on farm foreclosures. [p. 278]

October 23—Federal agents seize Bill Gale, sixty-nine, in California. In a ten-count indictment issued in Nevada on October 9, he and seven others are charged with conspiracy, attempting to interfere with federal tax laws, and mailing death threats to IRS agents. [p. 284]

November 4—Despite his pronounced right-wing views and recent bankruptcy filing, Larry Humphreys wins 28 percent of the vote as the GOP nominee for Congress running against Representative David McCurdy, the popular Democratic incumbent. [p. 274]

December 1—David John Moran, thirty, the "National Education Chairman" of the Committee of the States, cites the arrest of Bill Gale five weeks earlier by "agents of ZOG" as "the proverbial straw that broke the camel's back" before he commits five armed robberies in Northern California. Moran is killed one week later in a shootout with the state highway patrol. [p. 285]

December 15—Federal agents round up eight people associated with the Arizona Patriots and arrest four, charging them with plotting to rob an armored car to fund a white supremacist training camp. [p. 289]

1987
March 11—The Illinois Supreme Court unanimously invalidates the use of "Land Patents," a worthless but popular tactic promoted by Posse Comitatus activists and others as a way for farmers to supposedly nullify their debts. [pp. 260, 482]

April 24—Federal grand juries in Denver, Colorado, and Fort Smith, Arkansas, indict fourteen neo-Nazis for seditious conspiracy and other crimes, but in a stunning defeat for government prosecutors, all of the defendants are acquitted the following year. [pp. 207–208]

May—Backed by funding from Willie Nelson's Farm Aid, lawyers with the Minnesota-based Farmers Legal Action Group win a landmark federal court injunction temporarily halting all government farm foreclosures. [p. 280]

October 2—A federal jury in Las Vegas, Nevada, finds Bill Gale and four codefendants affiliated with the Committee of the States guilty of conspiracy, attempting to interfere with federal tax laws, and mailing death threats to the IRS. [p. 297]

1988
April 28—Bill Gale dies of complications from emphysema at Castle Air Force Base in Merced, California, three months after being sentenced to three one-year concurrent terms in prison for his role in the Committee of the States. [p. 298]

December—Lyndon LaRouche and six aides are convicted of conspiracy and loan fraud. LaRouche spends five years in federal prison, from 1989 to January 1994. [p. 276]

1991
January—Christian Identity believer Randy Weaver is arrested on gun charges after refusing to become an informant following his 1989 purchase of two sawed-off shotguns in a government sting operation. [p. 302]

1992

A comprehensive national survey conducted by the Anti-Defamation League finds one in five American adults—between 35 and 40 million people—hold unquestionably anti-Semitic views. [p. 249]

As evidence of the popularity of right-wing, antigovernment sentiment in the rural West, officials in Catron County, New Mexico, pass twenty-one ordinances from 1990 to 1992 that purport to supersede the authority of federal workers managing public lands. Approximately seventy other counties throughout the West approve similar measures. [pp. 312–313]

July 20—Former Minutemen founder Robert DePugh, sixty-nine, is sentenced to two and one-half years in prison after a raid on his Norborne, Missouri, home turns up an unregistered machine gun, a mortar, and more than one hundred rounds of antiaircraft ammunition. DePugh's home was searched after a police raid on a photography studio he owned in Iowa yielded photographs of nude and seminude underage girls.

August 21—Fourteen-year-old Samuel Weaver—son of Christian Identity survivalists Randy and Vicki Weaver—and Deputy U.S. Marshal William Degan are killed in a shootout in Boundary County, Idaho. An FBI sharpshooter kills Vicki Weaver, forty-two, the following day and Kevin Harris, a family friend, is severely wounded. Harris and the Weaver family surrender nine days later. [p. 302]

October—Inspired by the confrontation between federal agents and the Weaver family in August, a three-day gathering of 150 right-wing militants in Estes Park, Colorado, plants the seeds for the formation of the militia movement with discussions on the importance of vigilante action and strategy sessions led by Christian Identity "ministers" about how to transform America into a "white Christian Republic." [p. 303]

1993

Disgruntled Christian Patriots revive the Posse concept of "Citizens' Grand Juries" with the formation of so-called "Common Law Courts" which they use to manufacture fake indictments and issue "citizens' arrest warrants" against judges and other perceived enemies. [p. 306]

January—Oklahoma City bomber Terry Nichols obtains a bogus "Certified Fractional Reserve Check" which he tries to use to pay off more than $17,000 he owes Chase Manhattan Bank. Nichols gets the check from Family Farm Preservation, a group based in Tigerton, Wisconsin, run by veteran Posse activist Thomas Stockheimer. (Stockheimer and others associated with the scheme later receive long prison terms, as a result of Stockheimer's involvement in Family Farm Preservation.) Meanwhile, Nichols's brother, James, parrots Posse Comitatus rhetoric in court in an unsuccessful attempt to assert his "sovereign" status by arguing that the Constitution grants him a right to travel, so he needs no license to drive. [p. 316]

February 28—Four federal agents are killed and twenty wounded in Waco, Texas, when members of the Branch Davidian religious sect successfully rebuff an attempt to arrest their leader David Koresh on gun charges. A fifty-one-day siege follows. [pp. 303–304]

March—Timothy McVeigh travels to Waco, Texas, where he sells patriotic bumper stickers and expounds his antigovernment beliefs while federal agents lay siege to the Branch Davidian compound. [p. 304]

April 14—Charged in a broad conspiracy indictment for the death of Federal Marshal William Degan and other crimes, Randy Weaver and Kevin Harris stand trial in federal court in Boise, Idaho. The proceeding is a rallying point for many hate groups and neo-Nazi activists. Harris is later acquitted and Weaver is convicted of only minor offenses. [pp. 302–303]

April 19—Fifty-one days after the unsuccessful federal raid on the Waco, Texas, compound of the Branch Davidian religious sect, seventy-six Davidians, including seventeen children, are killed when the FBI attempts to storm the compound and it goes up in flames. The event fuels the growing militia movement and sets Timothy McVeigh on the path that will lead him to bomb the Oklahoma City federal building two years later. [p 304]

1994

The growing "Tenth Amendment Movement" prompts at least twenty state legislatures to consider or pass nonbinding resolutions championing states' rights and condemning the federal government. [pp. 310–311]

January—Sam Sherwood, forty-four, establishes the Idaho-based United States Militia Association and by November claims one thousand members across twenty Idaho counties. [p. 302]

January 30—Karen Matthews, the Stanislaus County clerk-recorder, is assaulted and pistol-whipped in the garage of her California home for refusing to comply with the demands of tax protesters who had confronted her in her office several months earlier. In May 1997, nine members of the tax-protest group, Juris Christian Assembly, are convicted for their role in the felony assault. [p. 166]

February—Militia of Montana leader John Trochman crisscrosses Montana from February to May, speaking to hundreds of potential recruits, denouncing federal gun-control legislation, the events on Ruby Ridge, and the failed government siege in Waco. According to Trochman, Soviet and U.N. troops are poised to invade America. [p. 305]

April 19—Seizing on the first anniversary of the destruction of the Branch Davidian compound in Waco, militia leader Linda Thompson issues an "Ultimatum" charging Congress with treason and calling on "militia units" to assemble "armed and in uniform" in Washington, D.C., on September 19, 1994, to enforce her demands. She later rescinds the call. [pp. 305–306]

May—Oklahoma legislators endorse right-wing conspiracy-mongering with the adoption of a nonbinding resolution demanding that Congress "cease any support for the establishment of a 'new world order' . . . [and] refrain from taking any further steps toward the economic or political merger of the United States into a world body or any form of world government." [p. 315]

July—Nye County, Nevada, commissioner Dick Carver emphasizes his belief in the sovereignty of county authority over federal property by driving a bulldozer through a barrier blocking access to a federal wilderness area in the Toiyabe National Forest. [p. 313]

Unknown opponents of the government take up bombing federal property in Nevada. Three explosions target the U.S. Forest Service and the Bureau of Land Management from 1993 to 1995. No one is injured. [p. 313]

September 16—Three months after helping arrest white supremacist and common law court activist Robert N. Joos Jr., a Missouri Highway Patrol officer, Corporal Bobbie J. Harper, is shot in the chest by a sniper while standing in the kitchen of his rural home. The suspected assailant, Timothy Thomas Coombs, a Christian Patriot activist, escapes and remains a fugitive. Harper later dies of complications related to the shooting. [pp. 306–307]

November 1—Washington State senator Jack Metcalf, the former national cochairman of the right-wing anti–Federal Reserve group Redeem Our Country, is elected to the U.S. Congress. [pp. 263–264]

1995

Three years after the death of white supremacist Vicki Weaver and her teenage son, her husband and three daughters are paid $3.1 million by the U.S. Department of Justice to settle a lawsuit filed by the Weavers. The government does not admit wrongdoing. The Weavers' family friend, Kevin Harris, receives $380,000 in a separate settlement. [p. 303]

Militia groups in Missouri expand from four to forty of the state's 114 counties from 1994 to 1995. [p. 306]

Four members of the Minnesota Patriots Council are arrested and convicted for possessing ricin, a deadly toxin derived from castor beans that is 6,000 times more potent than cyanide. The men had manufactured the ricin and reportedly planned to use it to kill law enforcement officials. [p. 341]

Larry Wayne Harris, an Aryan Nations member and microbiologist from Lancaster, Ohio, pleads guilty to wire fraud charges after using his position at a water treatment plant to order bubonic plague through the mail. The bacteria was inert and Harris is sentenced to eighteen months' probation. [p. 341]

March—After a federal court orders six national forests temporarily closed to logging, grazing, and mining to protect endangered salmon, Idaho militia leader Sam Sherwood urges a crowd in Challis to "get a semiautomatic assault rifle and a revolver and a uniform" and threatens "blood in the streets" if the ruling remains in place. [p. 312]

March 3—Montana militia leader John Trochman and six others are arrested after allegedly wearing concealed weapons and intimidating officials at the Musselshell County jail. Equipped with weapons, radio equipment, plastic handcuffs, and $80,000 in cash, gold, and silver, the men are suspected of planning to kidnap a local judge whose rulings had angered Christian Patriots, but charges are never brought against them. [p. 305]

April 19—A powerful truck bomb manufactured by Timothy McVeigh and Terry Nichols destroys the Alfred P. Murrah Federal Building in Oklahoma City, Oklahoma. One hundred and sixty-eight people are killed. Exactly twelve hours after the bombing, at 9 P.M., Posse Comitatus activist Richard Wayne Snell is executed by Arkansas authorities for the 1983 murder of a pawnshop owner whom Snell had robbed, mistakenly thinking he was Jewish. [p. 315]

April 25—The Clinton Administration proposes legislation requiring certain chemicals used to make explosives—including black powder—be microscopically "tagged" so investigators can more easily trace the manufacture and purchase of bomb components. The measure is vigorously opposed (and ultimately defeated) by the gun lobby, which calls it a form of firearms registration. [p. 322]

April 27—Idaho congresswoman Helen Chenoweth refuses to criticize militia groups in the wake of the Oklahoma City bombing. "I am not willing to condemn militias," she tells the *Idaho Statesman*. [p. 309]

May 2—Rep. Jerrold Nadler (D-New York) introduces legislation to outlaw paramilitary groups whose training or activities are intended to break the law, but the bill goes nowhere in the Republican-controlled Congress. [p. 322]

June 15—Sen. Arlen Specter (R-Pennsylvania) holds a hearing of his Subcommittee on Terrorism, Technology, and Government to investigate the militia movement, but Specter and his colleagues are upstaged by the militia witnesses who succeed in seizing control of the proceeding and turning it into a platform for their beliefs. [p. 317]

August—A poll of Montana residents finds 68 percent say they "actively oppose" the views of militia groups, but as many as 20 percent of respondents declare their support. [p. 306]

1996
The number of active militia groups grows to 370 nationwide. [p. 306]

After three years of Christian Patriot and Common Law Court activity, more than half (55 percent) of 431 state and local judges report encountering common-law advocates who challenge their authority with physical threats, bogus lawsuits, and common-law liens. The U.S. Marshals Service reports the following year that threats against federal judicial officials rose from 271 in 1996 to 612 in 1997. [p. 306]

After leading a group of half a dozen white supremacists called the Aryan Republican Army on a seven-state crime spree since 1994, Peter Kevin Langan and Richard Lee Guthrie Jr. are arrested. The men allegedly committed at least twenty-two bank robberies in their quest to fund a white supremacist revolution. [pp. 325–326]

March 25—After several years of harassing authorities and ordinary citizens with common-law liens, phony checks, and other forms of paper terrorism, (including death threats), LeRoy Schweitzer and Daniel E. Peterson, leaders of the Montana Freemen, are arrested by the FBI. The event prompts an eighty-one-day standoff with the remaining members of the group who have amassed an arsenal of a hundred weapons and more than 40,000 rounds of ammunition on a 960-acre ranch they call "Justus Township," outside Jordan, Montana. [p. 375]

1997

April—Leaders of the "Republic of Texas" (ROT) shoot and take a neighboring couple hostage. Leaders of the Posse/Christian Patriot group insist they represent the legitimate government of Texas, and claim Texas is independent from the United States. The incident ends with one ROT member dead and the group's remaining leaders in prison. [pp. 324–325]

1998

Threats and confrontations with Christian Patriot and militia movement activists over the preceding five years prompt twenty-seven states to either pass or consider new laws to punish or outlaw common-law court activities. [p. 307]

Three years after the Oklahoma City bombing, the number of domestic terrorism cases investigated by the FBI rises to around one thousand, compared to the fewer than one hundred cases under investigation prior to the bombing. [p. 324]

Between 20 and 25 million American adults (12 percent of all adults) score as "unquestionably anti-Semitic" by agreeing with six or more of eleven anti-Jewish statements posed in a comprehensive survey commissioned by the ADL. [p. 329]

May 8—Echoing the antitax sentiments of generations of right-wing tax protestors, the U.S. Senate votes unanimously to overhaul IRS collection practices. The move results in as much as $300 billion in lost tax revenues over the next several years. [p. 327]

June—Three white men who aspire to form a Klan-like hate group savagely murder James Byrd Jr., a black man, near Jasper, Texas, dragging him to death from the back of a pickup truck. [p. 326]

July—Six leaders of the Montana Freemen are convicted for a variety of crimes, including issuing false financial instruments, bank fraud, mail fraud, and threatening to kill Jack D. Shanstrom, Montana's chief federal judge. [p. 325]

October—Matthew Shepherd, a gay youth, is beaten and left hanging from a prairie fence outside Laramie, Wyoming. Like the dragging death of James Byrd Jr. earlier in Texas, the viciousness of the murder provokes national outrage. Despite condemnation of the crime, legislators in Wyoming refuse to pass a hate-crime law in the wake of Shepherd's murder and an effort to add sexual orientation to the list of groups covered in nearby Colorado's hate-crime statute fails. [p. 326]

1999

July 4–6—Benjamin Nathaniel Smith, the well-educated son of stable, middle-class parents from the Chicago suburb of Wilmette, and a member of the white supremacist group,

World Church of The Creator, goes on a two-state, three-day shooting spree, targeting blacks, Jews, and Asians. He wounds eight people and kills two others before committing suicide. [p. 326]

August—Aryan Nations supporter Buford O. Furrow Jr. opens fire on a Jewish Community Center in Los Angeles, shooting five people and terrorizing dozens of children and day-care workers. After fleeing the scene, Furrow murders a Filipino-American postal worker before turning himself in. [p. 326]

2000

September—A lawsuit filed by the Southern Poverty Law Center bankrupts the Aryan Nations when a jury awards $6.3 million to a woman and her son who had been terrorized by guards at the compound. The Aryan Nations property is later seized and sold to satisfy the judgment, sending the already disintegrating hate group into further disarray. [p. 502 n. 28]

November 7—More than half a million Alabama voters oppose repealing the state's century-old Constitutional ban against interracial marriage despite the fact that the U.S. Supreme Court ruled in 1967 that such laws are unconstitutional. The ban is repealed. [p. 330]

2001

May—U.S. attorney general John Ashcroft sends a letter to the chief lobbyist for the National Rifle Association, declaring that the Second Amendment confers an individual right to gun ownership, as opposed to the "collective right" defined by the U.S. Supreme Court. Ashcroft's letter gives new encouragement to militia enthusiasts and others equally wedded to inserting their radical view of gun rights into law. [p. 328]

September 11—Hate groups celebrate the terrorist attacks of 9/11, seizing on public fear to foment both anti-Arab bigotry and anti-Semitism through protests, Internet postings, radio broadcasts, telephone hotline messages, and written propaganda. About 750 incidents of anti-Arab (500) and anti-Asian (250) violence and bigotry, including slurs, threats, assaults, property damage, and homicide, are reported in the weeks immediately following 9/11. [p. 336]

2002

May—A national poll commissioned by the ADL reveals a marked increase in anti-Semitism, reversing a decade-long trend. In 1998, the agency's poll identified 12 percent of adult Americans—representing approximately twenty-five million people—as "most anti-Semitic." But by 2002, this figure had risen to 17 percent, representing some thirty-five million people. [p. 338]

APPENDIX I

THE POSSE COMITATUS: AN ANNOTATED BIBLIOGRAPHY

The concept of "posse comitatus" is rooted in medieval British common law and the ancient tradition of "hue and cry," meaning to "run and cry after the felon." The earliest written references to both terms date back almost eight hundred years, to the thirteenth century. The first reference to "hue and cry" is found in one of the most famous works of medieval jurisprudence, *Bracton De Legibus Et Consuetudinibus Angliae (Bracton on the Laws and Customs of England)*, an early- to mid-thirteenth-century text. Translated from Latin by Samuel E. Thorne, it reads as follows (all brackets in the original):

> We have spoken above of felony committed in public before many by-standers and onlookers, as in gathering of some kind, and of those who are present and can be arrested. [Now we must speak of those] who flee immediately after a felony and cannot be arrested. Let the hue be raised at once against such men and let them be pursued from vill to vill until the malefactors are caught, for otherwise the entire township will be amerced.[1]

Alexander M. Burrill gives the Latin translation for "hue and cry" as *hutesium et clamor* and as *clamor popularis*. And citing *Bracton* he notes that "hue and cry" refers to

The ancient law [which] was that where a felony had been committed, and the felon fled and could not be taken, hue and cry was to be immediately raised, (*statim levetur hutesium*) and pursuit (*secta*) made after him from town to town, (*de villa in villam*) or from one district to another, (*de terra in terram*) until he was taken; otherwise the township (*villata*) where the felony was committed was liable to be amerced.[2]

And speaking of the posse comitatus, Burrill notes that "the most common instances of the use of this power in England, have been in cases where a possession has been kept upon a forcible entry, or any force or rescue used contrary to the command of the king's writ, or in opposition to the execution of justice."[3]

Following *Bracton*, the next work to refer to the concept of "hue and cry" is a late-thirteenth-century manuscript written in French and attributed to Britton, though, like *Bracton*, it is of uncertain authorship. In this text a "hue and cry" "wrongfully raised" or "duly raised and not pursued" is cited as a punishable offense. Writing "Of the Sheriff's Tourns," at which day the sheriff would choose "twelve of the most sage, lawful and sufficient men" to whom would be presented "the wrongs and offences . . . from the townships," the author lists the following offenses: "Of mortal enemies of the king or queen, or their children, and of those consenting to them; of counterfeiters of the king's seal and of his money . . . *of hue and cry wrongfuly raised, or duly raised and not pursued*" (emphasis added).[4]

According to James A. Ballentine, the British statute of "hue and cry" was "enacted in 1285, which provided for immediate hue and cry upon the commission of a robbery or other felony and that the people of the hundred where a robbery was committed should be held liable for it unless they captured the robber. 13 Edw I, chs 1,2; 4 Bl Comm 293."[5] This statute and the meaning of "hue and cry" are discussed in more detail in *Stroud's Judicial Dictionary of Words and Phrases*, where "hue and cry" is defined as

A pursuit of one having committed felony by the high way; for if the party robbed, or any in the company of one that was murdered or robbed, commeth to the constable of the next towne and willeth him to raise hue and cry, or to make pursuit after the offender, describing the party and shewing as neere as he can which way he is gone, the constable ought forthwith to call upon the parish for aide in seeking the felon, and if he be not found there, then to give warning to the next constable, and he to the next to him, until the offender be apprehended, or, at the least, until he be so pursued to the sea-side.[6]

Citing English law, Stroud notes that "the enactment of 3 Edw. 1, c. 9, 'that all generally be ready and apparelled at the commandment and summons of the sheriffs, and at the cry of the country, to sue and arrest felons' was re-enacted by s.8(1) of the Sheriffs Act 1887 (c.55), which imposed 'a fine' on those convicted of being default in answering the summons."[7] And *Bouvier's Law Dictionary and Concise Encyclopedia* provides additional insight into the etymology of "hue and cry":

"The meaning of hue is said to be *shout*, from the Saxon *huer*; but this word also means *to foot*, and it may be reasonably questioned whether the term may not be *up foot and cry*, in other words, run and cry after the felon." Like Ballentine, Bouvier also cites the Statute of Winchester:

> We have a mention of "hue and cry" as early as Edward I; and by the Statute of Winchester, 13 Edw. 1., "immediately upon robberies and felonies committed, fresh suit shall be made from town to town, and county to county, by horsemen and footmen, to the seaside. The constable (the person being described, etc.) is to call upon the parishioners to assist him in the pursuit in his precinct; and to give notice to the next constable, who is to do the same as the first, etc. If the county will not answer the bodies of the offenders, the whole hundred shall be answerable for the robberies there committed, etc."

While *Bracton* contains the first written reference to the practice of "hue and cry," it is in the thirteenth-century work, *Fleta*, where one finds what is probably the earliest reference to a sheriff's posse comitatus. *Fleta* owes much to *Bracton*, is written in Latin, and also is of unknown authorship. Like the work of Britton, it is thought that *Fleta* was written sometime during the last decade of the thirteenth century. Writing about the need for sheriffs to faithfully execute the commands of the king, *Fleta*'s author observes:

> Sheriffs also frequently give a false answer in returning that they could not execute the king's command because of the power of some magnate who resisted them, and since such answers redound to the king's extreme dishonour let sheriffs beware in future of making this return. But as soon as his underbailiffs notify him that they have encountered such resistance, let the sheriff at once put everything aside and, taking with him the posse of his county, execute the king's command personally.[8]

John Bouvier took note of this concern centuries later when he observed that "it has been held to be [the sheriff's] duty to [take the posse comitatus] if he has any reason to anticipate resistance."[9]

The next reference to the posse comitatus after *Fleta* emerges nearly three hundred years later, in a textbook of Elizabethan law penned by William Lambard, "a scholarly barrister with a strong taste for historical and linguistic research." Writing in 1581 about "breaches of the peace," Lambard observes: "That when such forcible entrie should be made into landes or tenementes, or into Benefices, or Offices of the Church, and complaint thereof come to any Justice of the Peace, he should take sufficiet power of the Countie, and go to the place where the forcible entrie was made . . . "[10] Lambard's reference is scant, but Michael Dalton provides a more thorough treatment of the sheriff's posse comitatus in his 1619 volume, *Countrey Justice*.[11] Dalton's work contains numerous references to both "hue and cry" (which he calls "huy and cry") and the posse comitatus. He devotes two full pages to the latter, writing:

> Where the Just. of P., sheriffe, or other officer, is enabled to take the power of the county, it seemeth, they may commaund, and ought to have the ayd and attendance of all knights, gentlemen, yeomen, husbandmen, laboreres, tradesmen, servants, and apprentices, and of all other such persons, being above the age of 15. yeares, and that are able to travell.

According to Dalton, "women, Ecclesiasticall persons, and such as bee decrepit or diseased of any continuall infirmitie," are not required to serve. Dalton tells us that it is up to the sheriff to determine how many men shall make up the posse and how they shall be armed, but that it is not justifiable for the sheriff or any other officer to "assemble *Posse Comitatus*, or raise a power or assembly of people . . . without just cause." Referring to the Statute of Winchester cited previously, Dalton writes that "every Justice of Peace may cause Huy and Cry, fresh suit, & search to be made, upon any Murther, Robbery, Theft, or other felony committed: and this he may do by force of the Commission . . ." The same is true for suppressing riots or in instances of forcible entry. According to Dalton, the authority to take the power of the county is not limited to the sheriff, but extends also to his undersheriffs or bailiffs, as well as the Justice of the Peace. In the case of individuals, however, the authority to assemble a posse is strictly limited: "Every man may assemble his friends and neighbours, to defend his person, &c. (being in his house) against violence, &c. but not to goe abroad with him to a Fayre or Market, &c." (Matthew Bacon takes a slightly different point of view on the rights of individuals to assemble a posse in his *Abridgement of the Law*, noting that "a constable, or even a private person, may assemble a competent number of people, in order, with force, to suppress rebels or enemies, or rioters, and afterward with such force actually to suppress them."[12]

According to Dalton, a posse should never be assembled lightly, and, he admonishes,

> Againe, it is not good for the justices to assemble the power of the county, without certaine information, or knowledge of such riotous assembly; yet if upon false information of a riot, to be at such a place, the justices shall cause

the power of the county to be assembled, the justices shall be excused by reason of the information; and if without information, the justices . . . shall assemble the power of the county to go thither to arrest the riottors . . . and . . .
find no riot there, then shall they be punished for making such an assembly
of their owne heads, without information.

Dalton's *Countrey Justice* and Lambard's *Eirenarcha* provide much of the basis
for William Blackstone's discourse on the posse comitatus in his oft-cited work,
Commentaries on the Laws of England.[13] Published in 1765, Blackstone's *Commentaries* stand, along with Dalton's works, as one of the most frequently cited authorities on the posse comitatus, although Blackstone tells us substantially less
than Dalton, informing us only that

[The sheriff] is also to defend his county against any of the king's enemies
when they come into the land: and for this purpose, as well as for keeping
the peace and pursuing felons, he may command all the people of his county
to attend him; which is called the *posse comitatus,* or power of the county:
which summons every person above fifteen years old, and under the degree
of a peer, is bound to attend upon warning, under pain of fine and imprisonment.

More than two hundred years later, the *Oxford English Dictionary* concisely defined the composition of a posse comitatus in nearly identical terms, as "a body
of men above the age of fifteen . . . and . . . exclusive of peers, clergymen, and
infirm persons."[14]

Although the posse comitatus may have been more significant in medieval
times, it gradually became less commonly used. As John Bouvier has observed of
England, "From the fourteenth to the seventeenth centuries summons and warrants took the place of hue and cry, which practically fell into disuse."[15] According
to Alan Harding, part of the reason for this can be traced to the growing un-
reliability of the posse comitatus. "Horizontal and nationwide class divisions had
by 1700 made the posse comitatus unusable as a police force, since it included
the very classes [that] were prone to riot."[16] Whatever difficulties were encountered in sixteenth-century England, the concept found its way into American law
and tradition, though similar problems surfaced here, both with regard to local
posses and state militias, whom federal authorities sometimes found too sympathetic to protesting farmers, strikers, and other citizens whom militiamen were
called into service to restrain or apprehend. The use of posse comitatus in America was of the most benefit on the sparsely populated Western frontier where
lawmen depended greatly on the additional manpower, and where federal marshals often assembled posses from the ranks of nearby military garrisons to pursue
thieves and bandits.[17]

Notwithstanding the restrictions imposed by the Posse Comitatus Act of 1878, the federal government has sought, since 1980, to employ the military in efforts to interdict the flow of drugs by land, sea, and air, or to provide specialized training to civilian law enforcement in areas where the military is believed to possess unique expertise. Regardless of these slight liberalizations, the core restrictions on use of the military as a civilian police power remain intact.

SUPPRESSION OF INSURRECTION AND CIVIL DISORDER: FROM SHAYS'S REBELLION TO THE CIVIL WAR

Although the Posse Comitatus Act of 1878 was conceived in the bloody and bitterly partisan climate of Reconstruction, the legislative taproot of the Act reaches back more than a century before the end of Reconstruction, to the Constitutional Convention of 1787, when the framers of the Constitution first debated how and under what circumstances, if any, the new federal government might be justified in using force against its own people to further the goal of "a more perfect union." Just one year earlier, in 1786, Daniel Shays, a former captain in George Washington's army, had led two sorties of armed men to prevent the Massachusetts Supreme Court from handing down indictments against small farmers who had rebelled against property seizures for overdue debts and delinquent taxes. Events reached a climax on January 25, 1787, when Shays led fifteen hundred men in an unsuccessful attack on the national arsenal in Springfield, which left four rebels dead.[1]

The specter of Shays's Rebellion loomed large in the thoughts of many of the men who met in Philadelphia four months later to draft America's new Constitution.[2] Writing about the conflict in a letter to James Madison, George Washington observed, "What stronger evidence can be given of the want of energy in our governments than these disorders? If there exists not a power to check them, what security has a man for life, liberty, or property?"[3] Federalists in Philadelphia argued in favor of strengthening the hand of the national government to put down insurrections. Edmund Randolph, governor of Virginia, contended that the existing Articles of Confederation "cannot preserve the particular States against seditions within themselves or combinations against each other."[4] While antifederalists like Elbridge Gerry of Massachusetts were opposed to "letting loose the myrmidons of the U. States on a State without its consent [sic]."[5]

Ultimately, these competing sentiments were embodied in Article I, Section 8, and Article IV, Section 4, of the Constitution. Significantly, Article I grants Congress the power to (among other things) "provide for calling forth the Militia to execute the Laws of the Union, suppress Insurrections and repel Invasions"; and, "To provide for organizing, arming, and disciplining, the Militia, and for governing such Part of them as may be employed in the Service of the United States, reserving to the States respectively, the Appointment of the Officers, and the Authority of training the Militia according to the discipline prescribed by Congress."[6] And Article IV provides that "[t]he United States shall guarantee to every State in this Union a Republican Form of government, and shall protect each of them against Invasion; and, on Application of the Legislature, or of the Executive (when the Legislature cannot be convened) against domestic Violence."[7]

Conflict over the issue of how armed force might be employed *within* the United States surfaced again when the Constitution was presented to the states for ratification.[8] Virginia antifederalists like Patrick Henry and George Mason maintained that peacetime standing armies would lead to tyranny and despotism, while supporters of the new Constitution like James Madison and Alexander Hamilton argued that federal control over state militias in times of civil emergencies, seditions, and insurrections—events which Hamilton described as "maladies as inseparable from the body politic as tumors and eruptions from the natural body"[9]—was essential. But even the most ardent antifederalists conceded that the federal government should have some control over the use of force to quash domestic disorders. Ultimately, what appeared in the Constitution represents "a consensus that the militia would be used by the federal government in only those instances where civil law should completely fail and that . . . the creation and use of a standing army to control the people was the greatest danger to be avoided," according to military historian Robert Coakley.[10] But the way in which the Constitution framed these thorny issues also was "broad, general, and in some cases, a little ambiguous [and it] remained for future Congresses, presidents, and federal courts to determine what it would mean in practice."[11]

The nation's earliest legislation permitting use of the army to suppress civil disorders was passed by the First Congress, with the Judiciary Act of 1789. Although the Act did not explicitly mention the use of the military, it specified the duty of federal marshals and provided, in part, that they "shall have the power to command all necessary assistance in the execution of" their duty.[12] Three years later, in 1792, Congress passed the first law explicitly giving the president the power to use the army to deal with domestic disorders. Known as the "Calling

Forth Bill," the legislation laid the groundwork for use of military personnel by nonmilitary officials.[13] The first section of the law authorized the president to call up the militia to repel invasions and put down insurrections "on application of the legislature of such state, or the Executive (when the legislature cannot be convened). . . ."[14] The second and more controversial section of the Act gave the president additional authority to call out the militia *without* a state's request, "whenever the laws of the United States shall be opposed, or the execution thereof obstructed . . . by combinations too powerful to be suppressed by ordinary course of judicial proceedings, or the powers vested in marshals. . . ."[15] The Act also said that before calling up the militia, the president must first issue a warning commanding the insurgents to disperse and "retire peaceably to their respective homes within a limited time."[16] It was under this statutory authority—and its subsequent iterations—that President Eisenhower justified federalizing the Arkansas National Guard in 1957.

The first occasion the government had to use military force within the country came in 1793 and 1794, when President Washington sought to enforce the government's proclamation of neutrality in the war between England and France.[17] Militiamen also were used when the government successfully, and almost bloodlessly, suppressed the Whiskey Rebellion in 1794. That conflict, in which Washington dispatched the militias of four states to western Pennsylvania to put down resistance to a federal excise tax on liquor, led Congress to make permanent and strengthen the Calling Forth Act of 1792.[18] Presidential authority was further strengthened in 1807, ironically at the behest of President Thomas Jefferson (a staunch antifederalist), with passage of a bill permitting use of the "land and naval force of the United States" to suppress domestic disorders.

In addition to the use of regular troops and militias by the president, Congress, and state legislatures, federal troops were sometimes summoned as a posse comitatus by local civil authorities. This happened in response to slave rebellions like the brief but bloody uprising led by Nat Turner in 1831 in Virginia, and in response to urban riots throughout the 1830s, though in the latter instances local military commanders did not always allow their troops to intercede.[19] The army did intervene in the conflict between antislavery "freestaters" and proslavery forces in the Kansas Territory from 1855 to 1860. There the stakes were high, as each contingent had large numbers of armed supporters and the conflict involved significant rival claims to the land, resources, and political control of the newly opened Kansas Territory. That fierce and bloody conflict in many ways mirrored the national crises of the Civil War and Reconstruction that soon followed.[20]

APPENDIX III

CONGRESSIONAL APPROVAL OF THE POSSE COMITATUS ACT OF 1878

The names of House members listed here are spelled just as they appear in the *Congressional Record* of May 28, 1878, pp. 3877–78. No vote tally is given in the *Record* that lists the party affiliation of each congressman or the state they represent, so party affiliation data was obtained by cross-reference from three sources: *The Biographical Directory of the United States Congress, 1774–1989* (Washington, D.C.: U.S. Government Printing Office, 1989, Bicentennial Edition); *The Biographical Directory of the United States Congress, 1774–1971* (Washington, D.C.: U.S. Government Printing Office, 1971); and *American Leaders 1789–1991: A Biographical Summary* (Washington, D.C.: Congressional Quarterly, Inc., 1991).

According to the *Congressional Record–House*, 45th Cong., 2d sess., vol. 7, part 4 (May 28, 1878), p. 3877, the 130 members who voted in favor of the Knott Amendment which later became known as the Posse Comitatus Act were:

Acklen	(D–LA)	Bland	(D–MO)
Aiken	(D–SC)	Boone	(D–KY)
Atkins	(D–TN)	Bragg	(D–WI)
Banning	(D–OH)	Bridges	(D–PA)
Bell	(D–GA)	Bright	(D–TN)
Bicknell	(D–IN)	Brogden	(R–NC)
Blackburn	(D–KY)	Buckner	(D–MO)

Cabell	(D–VA)	Hart	(D–NY)
Caldwell, John W.	(D–KY)	Hartridge	(D–GA)
Caldwell, W. P.	(D–TN)	Hartzell	(D–IL)
Candler	(D–GA)	Hatcher	(D–MO)
Carlisle	(D–KY)	Henry	(D–MD)
Chalmers	(D–MS)	Herbert	(D–AL)
Clark, Alvah A.	(D–NJ)	Hewitt, Abram S.	(D–NY)
Clark of Missouri	(D–MO)	Hewitt, G. W.	(D–AL)
Clymer	(D–PA)	Hooker	(D–MS)
Cobb	(D–IN)	House	(D–TN)
Collins	(D–PA)	Hunton	(D–VA)
Cook	(D–GA)	Jones, Frank	(D–NH)
Cox, Samuel S.	(D–NY)	Kenna	(D–WVA)
Cravens	(D–AR)	Kimmel	(D–MD)
Crittenden	(D–MO)	Knott	(D–KY)
Culberson	(D–TX)	Landers	(D–CT)
Davidson	(D–FL)	Ligon	(D–AL)
Davis, Joseph J.	(D–NC)	Lockwood	(D–NY)
Dean	(D–MA)	Lynde	(D–WI)
Dibrell	(D–TN)	Mackey	(D–PA)
Dickey	(D–OH)	Maish	(D–PA)
Douglas	(D–VA)	Manning	(D–MS)
Eden	(D–IL)	Mayham	(D–NY)
Eickhoff	(D–NY)	McKenzie	(D–KY)
Elam	(D–LA)	McMahon	(D–OH)
Ellis	(D–LA)	Mills	(D–TX)
Evins, John H.	(D–SC)	Money	(D–MS)
Ewing	(D–OH)	Morrison	(D–IL)
Felton	(D–GA)	Morse	(D–MA)
Finley	(D–OH)	Muldrow	(D–MS)
Forney	(D–AL)	Patterson, T. M.	(D–CO)
Franklin	(D–MO)	Phelps	(D–CT)
Fuller	(D–IN)	Potter	(D–NY)
Garth	(D–AL)	Rea	(D–MO)
Gause	(D–AR)	Reagan	(D–TX)
Giddings	(D–TX)	Reilly	(D–PA)
Goode	(D–VA)	Rice, Americus V.	(D–OH)
Gunter	(D–AR)	Riddle	(D–TN)
Hamilton	(D–IN)	Robertson	(D–LA)
Hardenbergh	(D–NJ)	Ross	(D–NJ)
Harris, Henry R.	(D–GA)	Sayler	(D–OH)
Harris, John T.	(D–VA)	Scales	(D–NC)
Harrison	(D–IL)	Singleton	(D–MS)

Smith, William E.	(D–GA)	Waddell	(D–NC)
Southard	(D–OH)	Walsh	(D–MD)
Sparks	(D–IL)	Warner	(D–CT)
Springer	(D–IL)	Whitthorne	(D–TN)
Steele	(D–NC)	Wigginton	(D–LA)
Stenger	(D–PA)	Williams, A. S.	(D–MS)
Stephens	(D–GA)	Williams, James	(D–DE)
Swann	(D–MD)	Willis, Albert S.	(D–KY)
Throckmorton	(D–TX)	Willis, Benj. A.	(D–NY)
Townshend, R. W.	(D–IL)	Wilson	(D–WVA)
Tucker	(D–VA)	Wood	(D–NY)
Turner	(D–KY)	Wright	(D–PA)
Turney	(D–PA)	Yeates	(D–NC)
Vance	(D–NY)	Young	(D–TN)
Veeder	(D–NY)		

One hundred twenty-nine of these 130 Congressional Representatives were Democrats. The sole Republican was Representative Curtis H. Brogden of North Carolina.

The 117 members of Congress who voted "no" on the Posse Comitatus Act were:

Aldrich	(R–IL)	Cannon	(R–UT)
Bacon	(R–NY)	Caswell	(R–WI)
Bagley	(R–NY)	Clark, Rush	(R–IA)
Baker, William H.	(R–NY)	Cole	(R–MO)
Ballou	(R–RI)	Conger	(R–MI)
Banks	(R–MA)	Cox, Jacob D.	(R–OH)
Bayne	(R–PA)	Crapo	(R–MA)
Bisbee	(R–ME)	Cummings	(R–IA)
Blair	(R–NH)	Cutler	(D–NJ)
Bouck	(D–NY)	Danford	(R–OH)
Boyd	(R–IL)	Davis, Horace	(R–CA)
Brentano	(R–IL)	Deering	(R–IA)
Brewer	(R–MI)	Denison	(R–VT)
Briggs	(R–NH)	Dunnell	(R–MN)
Browne	(R–IN)	Eames	(R–RI)
Burchard	(R–IL)	Ellsworth	(R–MI)
Burdick	(R–IA)	Errett	(R–PA)
Butler	(R–MA)	Evans, I. Newton	(R–PA)
Cain	(R–SC)	Fort	(R–IL)
Calkins	(R–IN)	Frye	(R–ME)
Campbell	(R–PA)	Gardner	(R–OH)

Garfield	(R–OH)	Patterson, G. W.	(R–NY)
Hale	(R–ME)	Phillips	(R–KS)
Hanna	(R–IN)	Pollard	(R–MO)
Harmer	(R–PA)	Pound	(R–WI)
Harris, Benj. W.	(R–MA)	Powers	(R–ME)
Hayes	(R–IL)	Price	(R–IA)
Hazelton	(R–WI)	Pridemore	(D–VA)
Hendee	(R–VT)	Rainey	(R–SC)
Henderson	(R–IL)	Randolph	(R–TN)
Hubbell	(R–MI)	Reed	(R–ME)
Humphrey	(R–WI)	Rice, William W.	(R–MA)
Hungerford	(R–NY)	Robinson, G. D.	(R–MA)
Hunter	(R–IN)	Robinson, M. S.	(R–IN)
Ittner	(R–MO)	Ryan	(R–KS)
James	(R–NY)	Sampson	(R–IA)
Jones, John S.	(R–OH)	Sapp	(R–IA)
Joyce	(R–VT)	Schleicher	(D–TX)
Keifer	(R–OH)	Sexton	(R–IN)
Keightley	(R–MI)	Shallenberger	(R–PA)
Kelley	(R–PA)	Sinnickson	(R–NJ)
Ketcham	(R–NY)	Smalls	(R–SC)
Lapham	(R–NY)	Smith, A. Herr	(R–PA)
Lathrop	(R–IL)	Stewart	(R–MN)
Lindsey	(R–ME)	Stone, John W.	(R–MI)
Marsh	(R–IL)	Stone, Joseph C.	(R–IA)
McCook	(R–NY)	Strait	(R–MN)
McGowan	(R–MI)	Townsend, Amos	(R–OH)
McKinley	(R–OH)	Van Vorhes	(R–OH)
Metcalfe	(R–MO)	Wait	(R–CT)
Mitchell	(R–PA)	Ward	(R–PA)
Monroe	(R–OH)	White, Harry	(R–PA)
Morgan	(D–MO)	White, Michael D.	(R–IN)
Neal	(R–OH)	Williams, Andrew	(R–NY)
Norcross	(R–MA)	Williams, C. G.	(R–WI)
Oliver	(R–IA)	Williams, Richard	(R–OR)
O'Neill	(R–PA)	Willits	(R–MI)
Overton	(R–PA)	Wren	(R–NV)
Page	(R–CA)		

One hundred twelve of these Congressional Representatives were Republicans. The five Democrats were: Bouck (D–NY), Cutler (D–NJ), Morgan (D–MO), Pridemore (D–VA), and Schleicher (D–TX).

The forty-four members of Congress not voting on the Posse Comitatus Act were:

Baker, John H.	(R–IN)	Killinger	(R–PA)
Beebe	(D–NY)	Knapp	(D–IL)
Benedict	(D–NY)	Loring	(R–MA)
Bliss	(D–NY)	Luttrell	(D–CA)
Blount	(D–GA)	Martin	(D–WVA)
Bundy	(R–NY)	Muller	(D–NY)
Camp	(R–NY)	Peddie	(R–NJ)
Chittenden	(R–NY)	Pugh	(R–NJ)
Clafin	(R–MA)	Quinn	(D–NY)
Clarke	(D–KY)	Robbins	(D–NC)
Covert	(D–NY)	Roberts	(D–MD)
Durham	(D–KY)	Shelley	(D–AL)
Dwight	(R–NY)	Slemons	(D–AR)
Evans, James L.	(R–IN)	Starin	(R–NY)
Foster	(R–OH)	Thompson	(R–PA)
Freeman	(R–PA)	Thornburgh	(R–TN)
Gibson	(D–LA)	Tipton	(R–IL)
Glover	(D–MO)	Townsend, M. I.	(R–NY)
Haskell	(R–KS)	Walker	(D–VA)
Henkle	(D–MD)	Watson	(R–PA)
Hiscock	(R–NY)	Welch	(R–NY)
Jorgensen	(R–VA)	Williams, Jere N.	(D–AL)

Of these forty-four, twenty-one were Democrats and twenty-three were Republicans.

ABBREVIATIONS TO SOURCES

ADL	Anti-Defamation League of B'nai B'rith
AJC Archives	Archives of the American Jewish Committee
AJHS	American Jewish Historical Society
ASP, CID	Arkanas State Police, Criminal Investigation Division
ATF	Bureau of Alcohol, Tobacco, and Firearms
Calif. DOJ	California Department of Justice
DCI	Division of Criminal Investigation
FBI	Federal Bureau of Investigation
IEB, WCCA WDC, Nat. Archives	Individual Exclusion Board, Wartime Civil Control Administration, Western Defense Command, Record Group 338, National Archives, Washington, D.C.
KBI	Kansas Bureau of Investigation
LACRC Collection	Jewish Federation Council of Greater Los Angeles' Community Relations Committee Collection, Urban Archives Center, California State University, Northridge

NARA   National Archives and Records Administration

NMPRC   National Military Personnel Records Center

ODJ   Oregon Department of Justice

U.S. DOJ   United States Department of Justice

WCCA   Wartime Civil Control Administration

WDC   Western Defense Command

Wisc. DOJ   Wisconsin Department of Justice

ENDNOTES

1. Hell's Victories

1. Exhibit #3, transcript of National Identity Broadcast, William P. Gale, aired July 12, 1982, 10:15 P.M., on radio station KTTL-FM, Dodge City, Kansas. "Petition to Enlarge" before the Federal Communications Commission, Washington, DC, MM docket no. 85-127; file no. BRH-830201ZY; file no. BPH-830502AY.

2. "Informal Objection of the State of Kansas," *In re: Application of* CATTLE COUNTRY BROADCASTING *for Renewal of License of Station KTTL-FM, Dodge City, Kansas,* file no. BRH-830201ZY, July 15, 1983.

3. Colonel Ben Cameron [William P. Gale], "Armageddon," *IDENTITY* (Glendale, California: Ministry of Christ Church, April 1968), vol. 3, no. 2, pp. 1–12.

4. Newton N. Minow, "There's No Room for Bigotry on the Airwaves," *TV Guide*, Dec. 3, 1983, pp. 51–52. Wayne King, "Kansans Protest Broadcasts of Hate," *New York Times*, May 18, 1983, p. A18.

5. "Kansans Protest Broadcasts of Hate," May 18, 1983, p. A18. Ben Bradlee Jr., "FCC Probes Supremist [*sic*] Broadcasts," *Boston Sunday Globe*, July 28, 1985.

6. See Appendix I.

7. Answering his rhetorical question, "And what if the sheriff doesn't want to call out the posse?" Gale responded simply; "It is not his choice . . ."; Colonel Ben Cameron [William P. Gale], "The Constitutional Republic," *IDENTITY* (circa June 1971), vol. 6, no. 1. p. 16. William P. Gale, "Guide for Volunteer Christian Posses. The Posse Comitatus. By the authority of the Constitution of the United States," *IDENTITY* (circa Sept. 1971), vol. 6, no. 2.

8. Gale was not the only person in right-wing circles to suggest the formation of unorganized militias before the 1990s. In January 1984, Traves Brownlee, a Delaware tax protester, also advocated the formation of armed militias. (See: *Illegal Tax Protester Information Book*, Department of the Treasury, IRS, document 7072 (1–86) p. 30.)

9. Wayne King, "Link Seen Among Heavily Armed Rightist Groups," *New York Times*, June 11, 1983, pp. 1, C2.

10. Investigator Russell Welch, "Interview of Witness: Richard Wayne Snell," Arkansas State Police (ASP), Criminal Investigation Division (CID), Aug. 1, 1984, file no. 46-083-83. Memo of Sergeant Mike Fletcher to Lieutenant Finis Duval, July 4, 1984, Richard Wayne Snell, case file no. 49-997-84. Memo to Lieutenant Duval from Trooper M. Baughman re: Richard Wayne Snell, July 5, 1984, ASP, CID.

11. Report of interview with William Samuel Thomas by Special Agent Bill Hobbs, Bureau of Alcohol, Tobacco, and Firearms (ATF), ASP, CID, May 3, 1985. Kevin Flynn and Gary Gerhardt, *The Silent Brotherhood* (New York: Penguin Books, 1995), pp. 309–10.

12. Report of interview with William Samuel Thomas by Special Agent Bill Hobbs, ATF, ASP, CID, p. 2. Interview of Richard Wayne Snell, Investigator Russell Welch, ASP, CID, file no. 49-997-84, Aug. 30, 1984. Richard Wayne Snell, *The Shadow of Death! (Is There Life After Death?)*, (Boring, OR: CPA Books, undated).

13. "Richard Snell Update," *Taking Aim*, Militia of Montana, vol. 2, no. 1, March 1995, pp. 7, 13.

14. "Richard Snell Update" (March 1995).

15. Judy Thomas, "We Are Not Dangerous, Leader of Separatists Says," *Kansas City Star*, March 17, 1996, pp. A1, 14–15. Associated Press, "White Separatist Leader Dies," June 1, 2001.

16. Michael Daly, "His Hatred Survives," *New York Daily News*, April 23, 1995, p. 6.

17. Jo Thomas and Ronald Smothers, "Oklahoma City Building Was Target of Plot as Early as '83, Official Says," *New York Times*, May 20, 1995, p. 6.

18. Howard Pankratz, "Bombing Was Revenge," *Denver Post*, May 13, 1996. Thomas and Smothers, "Oklahoma City Building Was Target of Plot as Early as '83, Official Says," May 20, 1995, p. 6.

19. In a noon broadcast on WCBS Radio from New York City just two days after the bombing, experts at the Southern Poverty Law Center were quoted as saying the attack was foreshadowed in *The Turner Diaries*; WCBS-AM News 88, CBS Network News, Cynthia Weber reporting, April 21, 1995, 12:00 P.M. ET, radio, TV reports.

20. ABC TV News broadcast, *Day One*, May 18, 1995. In May 1996, Thomas Stockheimer and eight associates were charged with mail fraud and conspiracy for selling bogus money orders. (See: *United States of America v. Thomas Stockheimer et al*, case no. 96-CR-115 TJC, U.S. District Court, Eastern District of Wisconsin, May 14, 1996.)

21. Colonel Ben Cameron [William P. Gale], "The Constitutional Republic," *IDENTITY* (circa June 1971), Vol. 6, No. 1 p. 16. On a few occasions in his taped sermons and writings, Gale claimed that he first wrote about the Posse Comitatus in his church newsletter in 1969, but that is unlikely. A thorough review of every back issue of *IDENTITY* reveals that the first article even mentioning the term "posse comitatus" does not appear until 1971, and the earliest reference in the right-wing press to the concept of "bringing back the posse comitatus" as a method for organizing right-wing groups is in Hal Hunt's *National Chronicle*. In an article reporting on a March 1, 1971, meeting in Topeka, Kansas, of "patriots" affiliated with the "U.S. Constitution Council," Bradley J. Smith of Salem, Wisconsin, reported that the Council was "empowered to draft a circular for general distribution covering the legal and historic interpretation of the term, 'Law and Order.' " This circular would outline "the historic legal terminology [of] 'POSSE COMITATUS.' "

22. Thomas Dixon Jr., *The Clansman: An Historical Romance of the Ku Klux Klan* (New York: Grosset and Dunlap, 1905). Cameron, a wounded Confederate officer, is nursed back to health and becomes a Grand Dragon of the Ku Klux Klan. In the course of leading the hooded order he presides over a lynching that follows the rescue of a white woman from the depredations of a newly freed slave. Dixon dedicated the novel, "To the memory of a Scotch-Irish leader of the South, my uncle, Colonel Leroy McAfee, Grand Titan of the Invisible Empire Ku Klux Klan." In his foreword to the reader, penned December 14, 1904, in Dixondale, Virginia, Dixon wrote:

> In the darkest hour of the life of the South, when her wounded people lay helpless amid rags and ashes under the beak and talon of the vulture, suddenly from the mists of the mountains appeared a white cloud the size of a man's hand. It grew until its mantle of mystery enfolded the stricken earth and sky. An "invisible empire" had risen from the field of death and challenged the visible to mortal combat.
>
> How the young South, led by the reincarnated souls of the clansmen of old Scotland, went forth under this cover and against overwhelming odds, daring exile, imprisonment, and a felon's death, and saved the life of a people, forms one of the most dramatic chapters in the history of the Aryan race.

23. Colonel Ben Cameron [William P. Gale], "The Constitutional Republic," p. 16. Gale is not more specific about the date this issue of *IDENTITY* was published, although it was certainly prior to September 1971. On September 23, 1971, Hal Hunt's *National Chronicle* reprinted the subsequent volume of *IDENTITY* (vol. 6, no. 2) that contained an even more thorough exposition on the Posse Comitatus. Since Gale rarely—if ever—published more than four issues of *IDENTITY* per year, it is unlikely that vol. 6, no. 1, appeared any later than June or July 1971, and may have appeared sooner. Since vol. 5, no. 5—the issue that immediately preceded it—appeared sometime prior to March 1971 (it is reasonable to assume that vol. 6, no. 1, the issue in question, was published sometime between April and July 1971).

24. "Posse Comitatus. Deputies Thwart 'Citizen's Arrest,'" *Spokesman Review*, Spokane, Washington, March 14, 1975. "Officers Thwart Posse 'Arrest,'" *Spokane (Wash.) Daily Chronicle*, March 13, 1975.

25. "Place Mat War Murky," *Everett (Wash.) Herald*, Feb. 16, 1976. "Posse Group Files Flag Suit," *Everett (Wash.) Herald*, April 17, 1976. "Flag Place Mats Draw Protest," *Everett (Wash.) Herald*, Feb. 14, 1976. (For more on the activities of the Snohomish County Posse Comitatus, including its threats to arrest county officials, see: Jim Haley, "County Officials Escape Arrest," *Everett (Wash.) Herald*, July 3, 1975.

2. Family Roots

1. "Marcus Gale," *Who's Who in American Jewry*, (New York: National News Association, 1940), vol. 3, 1938–1939, p. 316. "A Tribute to Marcus Gale—The Gentle Man," Rabbi Phillip Kleinman, April 12, 1947. For more on the history of the Jewish farming settlement at Painted Woods, see: Lois Fields Schwartz, "Early Jewish Agricultural Colonies in North Dakota," *North Dakota History* (Bismarck, ND: State Historical Society of North Dakota, 1965), vol. 32, no. 4, Oct. 1965, pp. 217–32; Dr. W. Gunther Plaut, "Jewish Colonies at Painted Woods and Devils Lake," *North Dakota History* (Bismarck, ND: State Historical Society of North Dakota, 1965), vol. 32, no. 1, Jan. 1965, pp. 59–70; J. Sanford Rikoon, *Rachel Calof's Story: Jewish Homesteader on the Northern Plains* (Bloomington and Indianapolis, IN: Indiana University Press, 1995), pp. 115–17; correspondence of Rabbi Judah Wechsler and others, Baron de Hirsch records, box 64, folder 11, American Jewish Historical Society (AJHS); Mary Ann Barnes Williams, *Pioneer Days of Washburn, North Dakota, and Vicinity* (Washburn, ND: BHG, Inc., 1936), reprinted by the McLean County Historical Society (1995). *Andreas' Historical Atlas of Dakota* (Chicago, IL: R. R. Daniel and Sons, 1884); *McLean County Heritage, McLean County, North Dakota* (Washburn, ND: McLean County Historical Society, 1978), pp. 46–47.

2. Williams (1936), pp. 71–73.

3. Ibid., pp. 18–19

4. Ibid., p. 18.

5. W. Gunther Plaut, *The Jews in Minnesota* (New York: AJHS, 1959), as cited by Lois Fields Schwartz, "Early Jewish Agricultural Colonies in North Dakota," *North Dakota History* (Bismarck, ND: State Historical Society of North Dakota, 1965), vol. 32, Oct. 1965, p. 222. For a detailed history of the agricultural exploits of Jewish immigrants in America, including a discussion of the conditions that sparked their endeavors, and an overview of the groups that came to their aid, see: Leonard G. Robinson, "Agricultural Activities of the Jews in America," *American Jewish Yearbook* (Philadelphia, PA: Jewish Publication Society of America, 1912) pp. 21–115; *Jews in American Agriculture: The History of Farming by Jews in the United States* (Jewish Agricultural Society, 1954); Gabriel Davidson, *Our Jewish Farmers and the Story of the Jewish Agricultural Society* (New York: L. B. Fischer, 1943); Frank D. Hornstein, *Jews and Social Justice: A Contemporary Perspective* (unpublished M.A. thesis, Urban and Environmental Policy, Tufts University, 1985).

6. Quoted in Plaut, *Jewish Colonies at Painted Woods and Devils Lake* (1965), p. 65.

7. Correspondence of A. Axelrod to Mr. Solomons, Esq., May 14, 1891. Baron de Hirsch records, box 64, folder 11, (AJHS).

8. For a self-published account of the westward migration of other contemporary settlers of Painted Woods, see: Dorothy Dellar Kohanski, *The Saga of Solomon Dellar and His Children*, (Laguna Hills, CA: 1985).

9. Alexander Orbach, "The Development of the Russian Jewish Community, 1881–1903," *Pogroms: Anti-Jewish Violence in Modern Russian History*, eds. John D. Klier and Shlomo Labroza (Cambridge, England:Cambridge University Press, 1992), p. 143.

10. Hans Heilbronner, "Pogroms in Russia," *The Modern Encyclopedia of Russian and Soviet History*, Joseph L. Wieczynski ed., (Gulf Breeze, FL: Academic International Press, 1982), vol. 28, p. 162.

11. Heilbronner (1982), p. 163.

12. For an overview of the May Laws and other conditions which led to the massive emigration of Jews from Russia, see: eds. Klier and Lambroza (1992).

13. Correspondence of Ruth Gale, Oct. 10, 1979. Corinne Rosenberg, interview by the author. Mary Pratt, interview by the author. Charlene Davenport, interview by the author. 1920 Federal Population Census, Catalog of National Archives Microfilm, Multnomah County, OR, G400.

14. Correspondence of Ruth Gale, Oct. 10, 1979. Rosenberg, interview. Extract of an entry in a REGISTER OF DEATHS for Isaac Grabifker (no. 65259), District of Govan, County of Lanark, Scotland.

15. In letters and notes to a niece, Charles Gale's oldest daughter, Ruth, acknowledged that Gale had told her he left Glasgow at fourteen and lied about his age to join the army; see: Correspondence of Ruth Gale, Oct. 10, 1979. Rosenberg, interview. Pratt, interview. Military discharge papers of Charles Gale, Oct. 19, 1898, Milwaukee, WI, National Archives and Records Administration (NARA), National Military Personnel Records Center (NMPRC), St. Louis, MO.

16. Military discharge papers of Charles Gale.

17. Form for the physical examination of a recruit for Charles Gale, Feb. 27 and March 5, 1903, NARA, NMPRC.

18. Leonard Dinnerstein, *Anti-Semitism in America* (New York: Oxford University Press, 1994), p. 35.

19. Ibid., p. 57.

20. Ibid., p. 56.

21. Marriage certificate of Charles Gale and Mary Agnes Potter, Ramsey County, State of Minnesota, July 24, 1905. Certified copy of birth register for Mary Agnes Potter, Dakota County, Minnesota, July 20, 1949. Certificate of death for Mary Agnes Gale, State of California Department of Public Health, certificate no. 5383, March 13, 1964.

22. Ruth Jane Gale was born September 3, 1908, and her sister Beatrice Ann was born February 16, 1911. See: Declaration for Pension of Charles Gale. *Report of Separation from the Armed Forces of the United States*, Oct. 21, 1925, NARA, NMPRC. Certificate of Death, William Potter Gale, State of California, Local Registration District 3-88-24, certificate no. 000384, NARA, NMPRC.

23. Rosenberg, interview.

24. Ibid. Extract of an entry in a REGISTER OF DEATHS for Inda Grabifker (no. 65260), District of Gorbals in the Burgh of Glasgow, Scotland. Mayer Isaac died a decade later at age seventy.

25. For a comprehensive history of Portland's Congregation Neveh Zedek/Shalom and Marcus Gale's role in it, see: Gary Miranda, *Following a River, Portland's Congregation Neveh Shalom: 1869–1989* (Portland, OR: Congregation Neveh Shalom, 1989), pp. 53, 80–81, 90.

26. Biography of Marcus Gale, archives of Congregation Neveh Shalom, Portland, OR: John Simons, ed., *Who's Who in American Jewry* (New York: National News Association), vol. 3, 1938–1939, p. 316. George Rubenstein, "1880—Congregation Nevah Zedek Talmud Torah—1908," *Portland (Ore.) Jewish Tribune*, June 14, 1908. "Original Dedication of Neveh Zedek Recalled," *Portland (Ore.) Scribe*, March 20, 1936.

27. In 1931, Charles's youngest sister Fanny finally married. She was thirty-seven years old and had met her husband, Sam Gilbert, a pharmacy-school graduate, through her brother Abe, a hat salesman in Portland. The couple departed Oregon for New York, where they were wed. Fanny reestablished contact with Charles two years later, in 1933, when she arrived in Los Angeles with her husband and infant daughter, Corinne.

28. Enlistment record of Charles Gale, Sept. 20, 1920, NARA, NMPRC. "Who Is William P. Gale?" *Constitution News-Review* (Constitution Party, 1962), p. 12. See also: pp. 34–35.

29. Affidavit of Charles Gale, Monterey County, CA, April 9, 1926, NARA, NMPRC. Medical affidavit of W. A. Naylor, M.D., San Francisco County, CA, July 17, 1928, NARA, NMPRC.

30. *Application for Federal Recognition as a National Guard Officer and for Appointment in the National Guard of the United States*, for William P. Gale, Feb. 16, 1941, and *Request for Records from the Adjutant General*, for William P. Gale, March 8, 1950, NARA, NMPRC. Gale enlisted on August 8, 1932, and was transferred to active duty as a private in Company I of the 160th California Infantry on August 28. Gale was honorably discharged in November 1934 so that he could enlist in the regular Army.

31. Geraldine Bernstein, interview by the author.

32. Roxanne Gale, interview by the author. See also: *William P. Gale v. Josephine C. Gale*, Los Angeles County, CA, Superior Court, case no. D621923, exhibit 1, "Property Settlement Agreement," Jan. 29, 1963. For Gale's discharge date from the army, see: "Official Statement of Service," April 6, 1946, to Chief of Finance, Gravelley Point, VA, from Lieutenant Lenore Beck.

33. Officers and Warrant Officers Qualification Card copy, U.S. Army, NARA, NMPRC. Roxanne L. Gale, "In Memory of Colonel W. P. Gale," June 17, 1988, p. 2.

34. Gale erroneously claimed that he led the entire Filipino Battalion, although he was later promoted to company commander of the First Filipino Infantry regiment at Salinas, California, in July 1942. See: Efficiency report of William P. Gale, July 1, 1941, prepared by Major William

B. Zeller, NARA, NMPRC. Gale, "In Memory of Col. W. P. Gale," June 17, 1988, p. 2. Seymour (1991), p. 39. Memo of Commanding General, Seventh Army Corps, San Jose, California, July 17, 1942, NARA, NMPRC. Efficiency report of First Lieutenant Clarence F. Hauber concerning William P. Gale, July 1, 1941, NARA, NMPRC.

35. Seymour (1991), p. 60.

36. Clinical record brief of William P. Gale, April 14, 1944, O. C. Helming, Jr., NARA, NMPRC. Report of the Disposition Board, 42nd General Hospital, Base Section 3, March 15, 1944, NARA, NMPRC.

37. Efficiency report of William P. Gale, Jan. 1, 1944–June 30, 1944, Brigadier General L. J. Whitlock, July 8, 1944, NARA, NMPRC.

38. Gale, "In Memory of Col. W. P. Gale," p. 3. Seymour (1991), pp. 46–47.

39. Seymour (1991), pp. 50–51.

40. Ibid., pp. 52–54.

41. Ibid., pp. 48–55.

42. Gale, "In Memory of Col. W. P. Gale," p. 3. Seymour (1991), p. 57.

43. Bernstein, interview. See also: Seymour (1991), p. 56.

44. Efficiency report of William P. Gale, July 1, 1947, Colonel Charles R. Hutchinson, NARA, NMPRC. Efficiency report of William P. Gale, Jan. 1, 1947, Colonel Charles R. Hutchinson, NARA, NMPRC.

45. Certificate of Death for Charles Gale, Los Angeles County Health Department, Division of Vital Records, registration district no. 1992, registrar's no. 283. Certificate of Death for Jacob Gale, Multnomah County, OR, May 10, 1949, state file no. 4584, local registration no. 1664. Records of marriages and births, Edinburgh, Scotland. Obituary of Jacob Gale, (*Portland*) *Oregon Journal*, May 3, 1949.

46. Certificate of Death for Marcus Gale, Oregon State Board of Health, Division of Vital Statistics, state file no. 2381, local registrar's no. 2336. Extract of an entry in a REGISTER OF DEATHS for Isaac Grabifker (no. 65259), District of Govan, County of Lanark, Scotland.

47. Proceedings of Army Physical Evaluation Board, April 27, 1950, NARA, NMPRC.

48. Medical records of William P. Gale. Doctor's progress notes, Dec. 3, 1953, and July 2, 1954, NARA, NMPRC. For the ending date of Gale's employment at Hughes, see: letter to William P. Gale from Harold L. George, reprinted in Seymour (1991), p. 78; financial affidavit of William Gale, *United States v. William Potter Gale*, et al., CR86-160-HDM, Oct. 28, 1986.

49. Kathleen Gale, interview by the author. Seymour (1991), p. 79.

50. Seymour (1991), p. 80. For a discussion by Gale of the role of Capt, see: William P. Gale, "A Reply to the National Chronicle," *IDENTITY* (Nov. 1975), vol. 8, no. 1.

51. Bernstein, interview by the author.

52. Correspondence of Joseph Roos to Judge Lester W. Roth, May 11, 1948; papers of the Jewish Federation Council of Greater Los Angeles' Community Relations Committee Collection, University Library, Urban Archives Center, California State University, Northridge (LACRC Collection), record group no. 5, 1948–1954, box 95. "Rites Set for Minister Dr. Wesley A. Swift, Fifty-seven," *Los Angeles Times*, Oct. 12, 1970. "Religion and Hate—IV: The Reverend Wesley A. Swift," *The Facts* (New York: Anti-Defamation League of B'nai B'rith [ADL]), April 1948, vol. 3, no. 4, pp. 6–9. "California Rangers," *Paramilitary Organizations in California* (Sacramento, CA: Calif. DOJ, 1965), p. CR-1.

3. Hollywood Bolsheviks

1. For a brief summary of several theories of how Swift became familiar with Identity doctrine, as well as additional biographical detail about Swift's early involvement in the Klan, see: Michael Barkun, *Religion and the Racist Right: The Origins of the Christian Identity Movement* (Chapel Hill, NC: University of North Carolina Press, 1994), pp. 61–66.

2. "The Home Front," March 1, 1948, file no. 48-180, LACRC Collection. Barkun (1994), p. 64.

3. "Swift Hurt in Accidental Shooting," *Lancaster Ledger*, undated newspaper clipping, LACRC Collection.

4. "Anglo-Saxon Christian Congregation" and "The Great Pyramids," LACRC Collection.

5. In 1924, Davidson and a colleague authored *The Great Pyramid: Its Divine Message*. Davidson's work was embraced by leading Identity figures such as William Cameron and Howard Rand, a Bible scholar, lawyer and onetime Prohibition candidate for Massachusetts attorney general. Rand became one of the founders of the Identity movement in America when he started a small Anglo-Israelite group in 1928. By 1953 his slick, multicolored hate sheet, *Destiny*, was being sent to fifteen thousand subscribers in the United States. See: Ralph Lord Roy, *Apostles of Discord: A Study of Organized Bigotry and Disruption on the Fringes of Protestantism* (Boston, MA: The Beacon Press, 1953), pp. 93–94; E. Raymond Capt, *A Study in Pyramidology* (Thousand Oaks, CA: Artisan Sales, 1986), pp. 7, 37–38.

6. For more on Taylor's work, see: Capt (1986), p. 34. See also: Barkun (1994), p. 13, and John Anthony West, *The Traveler's Key to Ancient Egypt: A Guide to the Sacred Places of Ancient Egypt* (New York: Alfred A. Knopf, 1985), pp. 88–91.

7. Swift's Congregation first began meeting in 1945, though it was not formally incorporated until August 1948. See: "Anglo-Saxon Christian Congregation" and "The Great Pyramids," LACRC Collection. See also: Articles of Incorporation of Anglo-Saxon Christian Congregation, August 31, 1948, California Secretary of State. The first meeting of the board of directors of Swift's Congregation was held July 20, 1948. The other incorporators, besides Swift, were his brother-in-law, E. Clifford Deaville, of Los Angeles, and San Diego attorney Bertrand L. Comparet. Swift incorporated the Congregation the same month he incorporated another organization, "Dr. Wesley Swift's Ministry, Inc." That group filed its papers with the California Secretary of State on August 2, 1948. Swift, Deaville, and Comparet were also listed as the three directors for this group. According to the California attorney general's 1965 report on paramilitary organizations in California, the Congregation was started in 1946. See: Calif. DOJ (1965), p. CR-2.

8. "Wesley Swift Meeting," July 16, 1948, LACRC Collection. Swift subsequently claimed he had not advocated killing Jews, but added that his earlier prediction "must be true and will be fulfilled." See: "Pyramid Club Meeting, Aug. 27, 1948, file no. 48-497," LACRC Collection.

9. "Wesley Swift Meeting," May 14, 1948, cross-reference sheet, file no. 48-266, LACRC Collection. Speaking about the president, Swift also said, "Truman is a poor fellow who . . . is being tutored by the Jews." See: "Memo to Milton A. Senn from Mosher, Great Pyramid Club, Friday, Sept. 24, 1948," LACRC Collection.

10. "Wesley Swift—KOWL," undated memo. Memos of Arthur B. Berman, March 26, 1945, and March 29, 1945. Correspondence of Joseph Roos to Judge Lester W. Roth (1948), LACRC Collection.

11. Originally calling itself the Los Angeles Jewish Community Committee, Roos's group changed its name in 1941 to the Community Relations Committee of the Jewish Federation Council of Greater Los Angeles.

12. Correspondence of Joseph Roos to Judge Lester W. Roth (1948), LACRC Collection.

13. "The Jewish Federation Council of Los Angeles Community Relations Committee Collection. 1933–1982," LACRC Collection. See also: Memo of Victor W. Nielsen to Colonel William A. Boekel, "Report of Investigations in Los Angeles on Source Material Available on Individuals and Organizations," Dec. 7, 1942; HQ Western Defense Command and Fourth Army (WDC), Wartime Civil Control Administration (WCCA); Record Group 338, Individual Exclusion Board (IEB), WCCA, WDC, National Archives, Washington, D.C.

14. "Milton A. Senn, Melvin Nadell, May 28, 1948" and "CROSS REFERENCE SHEET, Wesley Swift Meeting, May 21, 1948, file no. 48-267," LACRC Collection.

15. Comparet was a San Diego native and served as deputy district attorney in San Diego County from 1926 to 1932, and as deputy city attorney from 1942 to 1947. Dr. Bertrand L. Comparet, A.B., J.D., *Your Heritage: An Identification of the True Israel through Biblical and Historic Sources* (Metairie, LA: New Christian Crusade Church, undated).

16. Correspondence of Gerald L. K. Smith to Wesley Swift, June 26, 1958, box 99. Papers of Gerald L. K. Smith, Bentley Historical Library, University of Michigan. A 1948 report of the Jewish Community Relations Committee of Los Angeles had this to say about how the two men first became acquainted:

> When Gerald L. K. Smith came to California the first time in the spring of 1945, one of Jeffers' lieutenants, a "reverend" Jonathan Perkins, organized in Smith's behalf a "Southern California Committee of Christian Clergymen." Under the auspices of this committee, Gerald Smith was presented to Southern California audiences. Perkins, who has a long record . . . claimed that four hundred clergymen were members of the committee, but, in fact, no self-respecting man of the cloth wanted to have anything to do with it, and there were no more than eight to ten so-called ministers on the committee. Wesley Swift was one of them.

See: Correspondence of Joseph Roos to Judge Lester W. Roth (1948), LACRC Collection. Michael Barkun cites an account of Smith's about how he met Swift. This story puts the date sometime in 1946, approximately a year or so later. See: Barkun (1994), p. 64. For a colorful account of Jeffers, see: John Roy Carlson, *Under Cover: My Four Years in the Nazi Underworld of America—The Amazing Revelation of How Axis Agents and Our Enemies Within Are Now Plotting to Destroy the United States* (New York: E. P. Dutton and Co., 1943), pp. 173–74.

17. By 1962, the once-intimate relationship between Smith and Swift had frayed. It ended several years later. See: Leo P. Ribuffo, *The Old Christian Right: The Protestant Far Right from the Great Depression to the Cold War* (Philadelphia, PA: Temple University Press, 1983), p. 177. Correspondence of Gerald L. K. Smith to Wesley Swift, April 6, 1950, box 33. Papers of Gerald L. K. Smith, Bentley Historical Library, University of Michigan. Letter of Gerald L. K. Smith to Wesley Swift, Aug. 3, 1955, box 44. Papers of Gerald L. K. Smith, Bentley Historical Library, University of Michigan.

18. For a definitive biography of Smith, see: Glen Jeansonne, *Gerald L. K. Smith: Minister of Hate* (New Haven, CT: Yale University Press, 1988).

19. Jeansonne (1988), chapter 6, "High Priest of Prejudice," pp. 101–14. Ribuffo (1983), pp. 147–48, 154–55. Ribuffo writes, "There was some basis for Smith's claim that Ford was one of his 'staunchest admirers,' " and that Ford asked friends "to contribute to [Smith's] Committee of One Million and probably gave money himself." For a discussion of the relationship between Ford and other prominent anti-Semites, such as Father Charles Coughlin, see: Donald Warren, *Radio Priest: Charles Coughlin—The Father of Hate Radio* (New York: The Free Press, 1996), pp. 144–48. Both Warren and Ribuffo cite the role of Ernest G. Liebold, Ford's longtime personal secretary, and a "central figure in Ford's infamous campaign against Jewish influence in American business, culture and politics" (Warren, p. 146), in helping to link up Ford with both Coughlin and Smith.

20. Ribuffo (1983), pp. 167, 170.

21. Ibid., pp. 164–66.

22. Smith actually lost by a 2-to-1 margin. See: Jeansonne, (1988), pp. 64–79. Ribuffo (1983) puts the number of votes at 120,000 p. 161.

23. Jeansonne (1988), p. 156.

24. Ribuffo (1983), pp. 175–76; Jeansonne (1988), p. 121.

25. "Gerald L. K. Smith Meeting, Hollywood High School," Nov. 14, 1948, CROSS-REFERENCE SHEET, Nov. 15, 1948, file nos. 48-657, 48-659, LACRC Collection.

26. "Wesley Swift Meeting," June 4, 1948, file no. 48-325, and "Memo to Milton A. Senn from Mosher," June 7, 1948, LACRC Collection.

27. While Cameron was the likely author of the *Dearborn Independent* articles, some attribute them to others. According to historian Robert Lacey, Cameron wrote the columns while Ford's private secretary Ernest Liebold "supplied most of the data and development of the ideas [and] was probably the central driving force of the entire campaign," and hired private detectives to "gather dirt" on prominent Jews. See: Robert Lacey, *Ford: The Men and the Machine* (Boston, MA: Little, Brown and Co., 1986), pp. 205–8. Ribuffo ([1983], pp. 10–12, 157) also maintains that Cameron, "prodded by Ford himself, wrote most of the articles." And Norman Cohn attributes authorship of the series to a Dr. August Muller—a German who Cohn says was "placed" on the staff of the *Dearborn Independent* by Dr. Edward A. Rumely—"a very active member of a German propaganda ring in the United States" who was a close friend of Ford's. See: Norman Cohn, *Warrant for Genocide: The Myth of the Jewish World-Conspiracy and the Protocols of the Elders of Zion* (New York: Harper and Row, 1966), pp. 160–61.

28. *Jewish Activities in the United States—Volume II of The International Jew: A Second Selection of Articles from the* Dearborn Independent (Dearborn, MI: Dearborn Publishing Co., April 1921), "The Jewish Aspect of the Movie Problem," pp. 121, 125.

29. Ibid., p. 119.

30. The four volumes were, respectively: *The International Jew—The World's Foremost Problem: Being a Reprint of a Series of Articles Appearing in the* Dearborn Independent *from May 22 to October 2, 1920* (Dearborn, MI: Dearborn Publishing Co., Nov. 1920); *Jewish Activities in the United States—Volume II of the International Jew: A Second Selection of Articles from the* Dearborn Independent (Dearborn, MI: Dearborn Publishing Co., April 1921); *Jewish Influences in American Life—Volume III of The International Jew—The World's Foremost Problem: A Third Selection of Articles from the* Dearborn Independent (Dearborn, MI: Dearborn Publishing Co., Nov. 1921); and *Aspects of Jewish Power in the United States—Volume IV of The International Jew—The World's Foremost Problem: A Fourth Selection of Articles from the* Dearborn Independent (Dearborn, MI: Dearborn Publishing Co., May 1922).

For a brief but thorough account of Ford's role in publishing the *Independent* and an acerbic critique of the paper's anti-Semitic content, see: Jonathan Norton Leonard, *The Tragedy of Henry Ford* (New York: G. P. Putnam's Sons, 1932), pp. 181–209. See also: George Johnson, *Architects of Fear: Conspiracy Theories and Paranoia in American Politics* (Los Angeles: Jeremy P. Tarcher, Inc., 1983), p. 111.

31. See, for example: "Is the Jewish 'Kahal' the Modern 'Soviet'?"; "The All-Jewish Mark on Red Russia"; and "Jewish Testimony in Favor of Bolshevism"; pp. 163–74, 213–23, and 225–35), chapters 15, 19, and 20, respectively, in *The International Jew—The World's Foremost Problem: Being a Reprint of a Series of Articles Appearing in the* Dearborn Independent *from May 22 to October 2, 1920* (Dearborn, MI: Dearborn Publishing Co., Nov. 1920).

32. For a definitive exegesis on the origins of the *Protocols*, see: Cohn (1966), pp. 60–76; for a discussion of the role of the *Protocols* in Nazi propaganda, see pp. 194–215. For more on the history and origins of the *Protocols*, see: Dr. J. Brutzkus, "The Elders of Zion: History of the forged 'Protocols' " *Jewish Chronicle*, June 22, 1934, p. 28; James Parkes, *Anti-Semitism: An Enemy of the People* (New York: Pelican Books, 1946), chapter 11, "The Protocols of the Elders

of Zion"; Benjamin W. Segel, *A Lie and a Libel: The History of the* Protocols *of the Elders of Zion*, Richard S. Levy, trans. and ed., (Lincoln, NE: University of Nebraska Press, 1995 [translated from *Welt-Krieg, Welt-Revolution, Welt-Verschworung, Welf-Oberregierung*, 1926]).

The history of the *Protocols* is a tortured tale of plagiarisms and preposterous fiction masquerading as fact. It also is a story of substantial political intrigue. The *Protocols* were used by agents of the Russian secret police (the Okhrana) and other anti-Semites for the dual purpose of inciting pogroms and discrediting internal enemies close to the Czar.

According to Cohn, the first version of the *Protocols* appeared from August 26 to September 7, 1903, under the title of "Programme for World Conquest by the Jews," in *Znamia (The Banner)*, a newspaper published in St. Petersburg, Russia. The editor of *The Banner* was Pavolachi A. Krushevan, an organizer of the murderously anti-Semitic Union of the Russian People, otherwise known as "the Black Hundreds." Members of the Union vigorously opposed all attempts to liberalize Czarist rule, and specialized in assassination and pogroms.

Other versions of the *Protocols* were published after 1903, but the forgery gained its greatest momentum after 1917–18, when the Russian civil war began and the imperial family of Czar Nicolas II was murdered by Bolsheviks. Defenders of the Czar blamed Jews for the assassination and named them as the secret force behind the revolution, using the *Protocols* to inspire their anti-Bolshevik forces and carry out vicious pogroms.

When the *Protocols* were first exposed as a fake in 1921 by Philip Graves, the Constantinople correspondent of *The Times* (London), he noted that large sections had been lifted from an 1865 political pamphlet. As explained by James Parkes, author of *Anti-Semitism: Enemy of the People* (pp. 39–42), that tract, entitled, *Dialogue aux enfers entre Montesquieu et Machiavel (Dialogue Between Montesquieu and Machiavelli)* was written by a French lawyer, Maurice Joly, who had intended it as a satirical attack on the authoritarianism of Napoléon III. In Joly's fictional work—which earned him fifteen months' imprisonment—Montesquieu argues for liberalism while Machiavelli (who is meant to represent Napoléon III) endorses despotism. In the *Protocols*, the malevolent designs of Machiavelli become the schemes of the Jews, and the liberal views of Montesquieu are presented as a fig leaf for Jewish tyranny.

Commenting on the convoluted origins of the *Protocols*, Cohn has noted that "there is a cruel irony in the fact that a brilliant but long-forgotten defence of liberalism should have provided the basis for an atrociously written piece of reactionary balderdash which has swept the world." (Cohn: [1966], p. 74).

33. Lacey (1986), p. 218.

34. Lacey (1986), p. 218. Edwin Black, "The Anti-Ford Boycott," *Midstream*, Jan. 1986, pp. 40–41. John Roy Carlson (1943), p. 210. Leonard (1932), chapter 13, "Wall Street and 'The Elders of Zion,' " pp. 181–209.

35. Cohn (1966), p. 138.

36. Black, "The Anti-Ford Boycott," Jan. 1986, pp. 40–41.

37. Marshall is likely the author of the letter, which Ford agreed to sign. See: "Statement by Henry Ford," *American Jewish Yearbook* (New York: American Jewish Committee, 1927), vol. 29, pp. 383–89.

38. The award was presented on July 30, 1938. Lacey (1986), p. 386.

39. For a comprehensive treatment of the activities of Pelley, Winrod, and Smith, see: Ribuffo, (1983). For two contemporary accounts of the activities of American pro-Nazi groups during the late 1930s and early 1940s, see: Richard Rollins, *I Find Treason: The Story of An American Anti-Nazi Agent* (New York: William Morrow and Company, 1941) and John Roy Carlson (1943). The latter book was authored pseudonymously by Avedis Derounian and underwent no fewer than twenty-four printings the year it was published. According to Ribuffo, *Under Cover* led nonfiction best-sellers in 1944. For a briefer account of the activities of the far right during this period, see: David H. Bennett, *The Party of Fear: The American Far Right from Nativism to the Militia Movement* (New York: Vintage Books, Random House, 1995), chapter 13, "To Inverted Nativism and Beyond, 1930–1945," pp. 238–72. For an example of mass-

media coverage critical of Pelley's Silver Shirts and other groups promoting "anti-American propaganda," see "Fascism in America," *Life* magazine, March 6, 1939.

40. As cited by Ribuffo (1983), pp. 61–62.

41. Warren (1996), chart 1, "Coughlin Radio Audience Before and After 'Kristallnacht' Broadcast, November 1938," Appendix, p. 303.

42. Donald Warren, interview by the author. For more on Coughlin's role publishing the *Protocols*, see: Warren (1996), pp. 149–53.

43. For more on Winrod's election results and candidacy, see: Ribuffo (1983), pp. 119–24. Nye made his remark on August 21, 1941, according to Leonard Dinnerstein, *Anti-Semitism in America* (New York: Oxford University Press, 1994). p. 129.

44. Dinnerstein (1994), p. 131. For a thorough treatment of American anti-Semitism during the war years, see chapter 7, "Anti-Semitism at High Tide: World War II (1939–1945)," pp. 128–49. For more on anti-Semitism during the war, see: David S. Wyman, *The Abandonment of the Jews: America and the Holocaust 1941–1945* (New York: Pantheon Books, 1984), pp. 9–15.

45. Howard Schuman, Charlotte Steeh, and Lawrence Bobo, *Racial Attitudes in America: Trends and Interpretations* (Cambridge, MA: Harvard University Press, 1985), p. 12. Taylor Branch, *Parting the Waters: America in the King Years, 1954–1963* (New York: Simon and Schuster, 1988), p. 13.

46. Hodding Carter III, *The South Strikes Back* (Garden City, NY: Doubleday and Co., 1959), p. 14.

47. Schuman, Steeh, and Bobo (1985), p. 17.

48. Arnold Forster and Benjamin Epstein, *Danger on the Right: The Attitudes, Personnel, and Influence of the Radical Right and Extreme Conservatives* (New York: Random House, 1964), p. 103.

49. Clyde Wilcox, *God's Warriors: The Christian Right in Twentieth-Century America* (Baltimore and London: Johns Hopkins University Press, 1992), p. 8. Ribuffo (1983), pp. 259–60. Forster and Epstein (1964), pp. 100–114.

50. For a brief but thorough overview of the blacklist and the political climate in Hollywood during this period, see: William L. O'Neill, *A Better World—The Great Schism: Stalinism and the American Intellectuals* (New York: Simon and Schuster, 1982), chapter 7, "The Blacklist," pp. 219–51.

4. The Enemy Within

1. Quoted in Howard Zinn, *A People's History of the United States* (New York: Harper Colophon Books, 1980), p. 422. See also: Seymour Martin Lipset and Earl Raab, *The Politics of Unreason: Right-Wing Extremism in America, 1790–1977* (Chicago: University of Chicago Press, 1978), second edition, p. 215. In Salt Lake City, McCarthy said the list contained the names of fifty-seven communists; on February 20 he told the Senate the number was eighty-one. For additional, secondary accounts of McCarthy's early speeches, see: David H. Bennett, *The Party of Fear: The American Far Right from Nativism to the Militia Movement* (New York: Vintage Books, Random House, 1995), pp. 293–97.

2. Bennett (1995), p. 290.

3. William L. O'Neill, *A Better World—The Great Schism: Stalinism and the American Intellectuals* (New York: Simon and Schuster, 1982), p. 224.

4. Bennett (1995), pp. 301–2.

5. Sartre quoted in Bennett (1995), p. 291. Leonard Dinnerstein, *Anti-Semitism in America* (New York: Oxford University Press, 1994) p. 164.

6. John Beaty, *The Iron Curtain Over America* (Barboursville, VA: Chestnut Mountain Books, 1960), p. 29.

7. Khazaria occupied a strategic area in Central Asia between the Black and Caspian Seas to the east and west and the Ural Mountains to the north. Protected by the natural barrier of the Caucasus Mountains to the south, Khazaria's powerful rulers fended off both Byzantine Christians and armies of Muslim Arabs, playing an important role in preventing the latter from invading and conquering Eastern Europe from the south. See: Raphael Patai and Jennifer P. Wing, *The Myth of the Jewish Race* (New York: Charles Scribner's Sons, 1975), p. 71.

8. Why this occurred is unknown, but some investigators, including the Jewish writer Arthur Koestler, have theorized that the conversion of the Khazars was carefully calculated to maintain the kingdom's neutrality—and power—in a world sharply polarized by Christianity and Islam. See: Arthur Koestler, *The Thirteenth Tribe: The Khazar Empire and Its Heritage* (New York: Random House, 1976), pp. 58–60). Others have simply noted that the acceptance of Judaism by the Khazars was due to the influence of Jewish merchants (Shelomo Dov Goitein, "The Jews Under Islam—Part One: Six–Sixteenth Centuries," *The Jewish World: History and Culture of the Jewish People*, Elie Kedourie, ed. [New York: Harry N. Abrams, Inc., 1979], p. 182). Although the people of Khazaria did convert to Judaism, what happened after the fall of the empire in the tenth century and its disintegration as a result of Mongol invasions several centuries later is open to dispute. Did the Khazarian converts migrate extensively across the continent, seeding hundreds of settlements and forming the nucleus of Eastern European Jewry, as Koestler and several other Jewish scholars (as well as many anti-Semites) maintain? Or were they merely absorbed into a larger ethnic community of Jews that already were present? (For a thorough and scholarly treatment of the subject, see: D. M. Dunlop, *The History of the Jewish Khazars* [New York: Schocken Books, 1967]).

9. Ironically, it was Arthur Koestler, a Jew, who helped greatly popularize the Khazar theory in his 1976 book *The Thirteenth Tribe: The Khazar Empire and Its Heritage*.

10. Beaty (1960), p. 25.

11. Ralph Lord Ray, *Apostles of Discord: A Study of Organized Bigotry and Disruption on the Fringes of Protestantism* (Boston, MA: The Beacon Press, 1953), pp. 88–89.

12. Beaty (1960), p. 77.

13. Ibid., p. 64.

14. Ibid., p. 74.

15. "Background on Present Anti-Semitic Conditions." Report prepared for the meeting of the investigative and fact-finding committee of the American Jewish Committee, May 25, 1951, *Archives of the American Jewish Committee* (AJC Archives), p. 1.

16. Ibid., p. 2.

17. As quoted in "Background on Present Anti-Semitic Conditions," May 25, 1951, (AJC Archives), p. 9.

18. For a detailed account of the attempt by anti-Semites to enlist Senator McCarthy's help in derailing the nomination of Anna M. Rosenberg as Assistant Secretary of Defense, see: Arnold Forster and Benjamin Epstein, *The Troublemakers* (Garden City, NY: Doubleday and Co., 1952), pp. 25–61. The campaign was orchestrated largely by Gerald L. K. Smith and Wesley Swift and involved Donald Surine, a former FBI agent and staff investigator for McCarthy.

19. "Background on Present Anti-Semitic Conditions," May 25, 1951, AJC Archives, p. 5. For one account of how Jewish groups viewed McCarthy, see: Arnold Forster, *Square One: The Memoirs of a True Freedom Fighter's Lifelong Struggle Against Anti-Semitism, Domestic and Foreign* (New York: Donald I. Fine, 1988), pp. 116–25.

20. Upton Close, "Constitution Party of the United States," *Closer Ups*, vol. 8, no. 16, Aug. 18, 1952, p. 3.

21. *Time* magazine, May 5, 1952, as cited in "The Anti-Semites vs. Eisenhower," *The Facts*, ADL, Sept. 1952, vol. 7, no. 5, p. 5.

22. Arnold Forster and Benjamin R. Epstein, *Cross-currents: The Book that Tells How Anti-Semitism Is Used Today as a Political Weapon* (Garden City, NY: Doubleday and Co., 1956), p. 31.

23. "Operation Chicago," *The Facts*, ADL, Sept. 1952, vol. 7, no. 5, p. 4.

24. Memo to NCRAC Membership and CJFWF Communities from Jules Cohen, national coordinator, *Bigotry in Political Campaigns*, "Anti-Semitism in Connection with the 1952 Presidential Campaign," p. 1, National Community Relations Advisory Council, AJC Archives, July 2, 1952.

25. Quoted in Bennett (1995), p. 301.

26. Quoted in "Balloting by Other Bigots," *The Facts*, ADL, Sept. 1952, vol. 7, no. 5, p. 4.

27. "The Major Political Conventions—and After," 1952, AJC Archives, p. 6.

28. Six years later, Gwinn was still a regular fixture on the right-wing speaking circuit when he addressed a meeting of "prominent businessmen" sponsored by the Citizens' Council of Mississippi, telling them that the Supreme Court's desegregation orders exemplified the "creeping socialism" of the federal government. See: Hodding Carter III, *The South Strikes Back* (Garden City, NY: Doubleday and Co., 1959), p. 96.

29. "Constitution Party (Operation America, Inc.)," Aug. 12, 1952, AJC Archives. See also: "The Constitution Party," *The Facts*, ADL, Sept. 1952, vol. 7, no. 5; and correspondence of Percy L. Greaves Jr., temporary chairman, and Suzanne Stevenson, temporary co-chairman, "Constitution Party of the USA," Sept. 2, 1952, AJC Archives and "Two Leaders Quit Party Over 'Anti-Semitism,' " Sept. 2, 1952, unsourced newspaper clipping, AJC Archives.

30. Correspondence of Percy L. Greaves Jr. (1952), and "Two Leaders Quit Party Over 'Anti-Semitism,' " Sept. 2, 1952, unsourced newspaper clipping, AJC Archives.

31. The cases and states involved were: *Oliver Brown et al., v. Board of Education of Topeka, Shawnee County, Kansas, et al.* on appeal from the U.S. District Court for the District of Kansas; *Harry Briggs Jr. et al., v. R. W. Elliott et al.*, on appeal from the U.S. District Court for the Eastern District of South Carolina; *Dorothy E. Davis et al., v. County School Board of Prince Edward County, Virginia, et al.*, on appeal from the U.S. District Court for the Eastern District of Virginia; and *Francis B. Gebhart et al., petitioners, v. Ethel Louise Belton et al.*, on Writ of Certiorari to the Supreme Court of Delaware. See: *Brown v. Board of Education*, Opinion of the Court, May 17, 1954, Supreme Court of the United States, nos. 1, 2, 4, and 10, October term, 1953.

32. Jim Crow was that amalgam of state and local laws, regulations, and customs purposefully enacted and/or maintained predominantly—though not exclusively—in the American South for the purpose of segregating blacks and systematically depriving them of rights and opportunities.

33. Herbert Brownell with John P. Burke, *Advising Ike: The Memoirs of Attorney General Herbert Brownell* (Lawrence, KS: University Press of Kansas, 1993), pp. 187–96.

34. *Brown v. Board of Education*, 347 U.S. 483 (1954).

35. Like other "respectable" segregationists, Brady had an impressive string of credentials: he was a Yale University graduate; he had served as director of the Mississippi Highway Safety Patrol; he was a member of the University of Mississippi Hall of Fame; and was the vice president of the Mississippi State Bar Association in 1954–55. His efforts on behalf of segregation received recognition from the Mississippi Legislature in 1956, which passed a joint resolution commending him "for work which he had done in behalf of the maintenance of segregation and the Citizens' Councils of various states." See: "Judge Brady Feature Speaker,"

Constitution Party California Bulletin, circa Nov. 21, 1957, "CONSTITUTION PARTY, 1957, Correspondence, Newsclippings, Propaganda," LACRC Collection. Tom P. Brady, *Black Monday: Segregation or Amalgamation—America Has Its Choice* (Winona, MS: Association of Citizens' Councils, 1955). For more on Brady, see: Neil R. McMillen, *The Citizens' Council: Organized Resistance to the Second Reconstruction, 1954–1964* (Urbana, IL: University of Illinois Press, 1971), pp. 17–18. Carter III (1959), p. 27. Wyn Craig Wade, *The Fiery Cross: The Ku Klux Klan in America* (New York: Simon and Schuster, 1987), p. 299.

5. Black Monday

1. "Segregation and the New Hate Groups," *The Facts,* ADL, Sept. 1954, vol. 9. no. 6, p. 21.

2. The immediate practical impact of the *Brown* decision was felt beyond the eleven states of the old Confederacy (Alabama, Florida, Georgia, Louisiana, Mississippi, South Carolina, Texas, Arkansas, North Carolina, Tennessee, and Virginia), in half a dozen border states as well. They were: West Virginia, Maryland, Oklahoma, Missouri, Kentucky, and Delaware. See: Neil R. McMillen, *The Citizens' Council: Organized Resistance to the Second Reconstruction, 1954–1964* (Urbana, IL: University of Illinois Press, 1971), pp. 5–11.

3. Hodding Carter III, *The South Strikes Back* (Garden City, NY: Doubleday and Co., 1959), pp. 21–48, 109. Carter cites a Southern Regional Council publication, *New South*, which quotes Sunflower County, Mississippi, resident Arthur Clark Jr., a Citizens' Council founder, as recommending the "removal" through "the careful application of economic pressure" of "various agitators" who "stir up discontent" and "who cannot be controlled otherwise." For more on the general subject of Citizens' Councils and their use of economic reprisals, see: "The Citizens' Councils and the Desegregation Issue," *The Facts,* ADL, June 1955, vol. 10, no. 4, p. 51; McMillen (1971), pp. 15–40; and Taylor Branch, *Parting the Waters: America in the King Years, 1954–1963* (New York: Simon and Schuster, 1988), p. 138.

4. Tom P. Brady, *Black Monday: Segregation or Amalgamation—America Has Its Choice* (Winona, MS: Association of Citizens' Councils, 1955), pp. 11, 12.

5. Ibid., p. 47.

6. Ibid., pp. 7, 78.

7. Approximately seventy-five to a hundred whites attended the town hall meeting that immediately followed. Carter III (1959), pp. 30–32.

8. Ibid., p. 44.

9. For a thorough discussion of the complexity of Southern lynchings, including a penetrating analysis of the relationship between black population and white violence, see: Stewart E. Tolnay and E. M. Beck, *A Festival of Violence: An Analysis of Southern Lynchings, 1882–1930* (Urbana, IL: University of Illinois Press, 1995). Among their observations was the correlation that black victims "were almost twice as likely to be from cotton-dominant areas." Tolnay and Beck (1995), p. 119.

10. In 1899, 77 percent of the county was black, compared with 53 percent statewide. See: Tolnay and Beck (1995), pp. 41–42.

11. McMillen (1971), p. 211.

12. Carter III (1959), p. 24.

13. Quoted in Carter III (1959), p. 32.

14. The meeting took place on April 7, 1956, in New Orleans. Cited in Carter III (1959), p. 70.

15. Brady (1955), p. 73. In 1957, Brady addressed the Commonwealth Club of California and assured them, "Above all, the Councils are dedicated to nonviolence and have prevented lynchings and mob action in the South." Quoted in Carter III (1959), p. 204.

16. As quoted in "Segregation and the New Hate Groups," *The Facts*, ADL, Sept. 1954, vol. 9, no. 6, p. 21. See also: Carter III (1959), pp. 35, 109.

17. Quoted in Branch (1988), p. 182.

18. Quoted in Carter III (1959), p. 39.

19. Wyn Craig Wade, *The Fiery Cross: The Ku Klux Klan in America* (New York: Simon and Schuster, 1987) p. 299.

20. Henry E. Garrett, Ph.D., "Scientist Explains Race Differences," *The Citizen*, Jan. 1968, vol. 12, no. 4, p. 19. For more about Garrett, see: McMillen (1971), p. 171.

21. Quoted in McMillen (1971), p. 9.

22. For a complete text of the "Southern Manifesto," see Herbert Brownell with John P. Burke, *Advising Ike: The Memoirs of Attorney General Herbert Brownell* (Lawrence, KS: University of Kansas Press, 1993), Appendix C, pp. 359–63.

23. Quoted in Carter III (1959), pp. 60–61. Such sentiments were the norm among the region's most prominent elected officials. Georgia's 1954 Democratic gubernatorial candidate, Marvin Griffen, pledged, "Come hell or high water, races will not be mixed in Georgia schools" (McMillen [1971], p. 9). And in 1961, Mississippi governor Ross Barnett proclaimed October 26 "Race and Reason Day in Mississippi," in honor of Carleton Putnam's book by the same name. Published in 1961, Putnam's text was "a veritable white supremacist's catechism," and sold 60,000 copies in six months. U.S. senators J. Strom Thurmond of South Carolina and Harry F. Byrd of Virginia gave it their unqualified endorsement (McMillen [1971], pp. 167–8).

24. "The Citizens' Councils and Anti-Semitism," *The Facts*, ADL, Jan. 1956, vol. 11, no. 1, p. 67.

25. Reverend William P. Gale, *The Faith of Our Fathers* (Mariposa, CA: Ministry of Christ Church, 1963), p. 53.

26. "Race Relations Law Survey: May 1954–May 1957," *Race Relations Law Reporter* (Nashville, TN: School of Law, Vanderbilt University, 1957), vol. 2, pp. 881–94.

27. Brady (1955), p. 84.

28. Brady (1955), p. 84. See also: Carter III (1959), p. 109.

29. For a brief summary of these actions and a discussion of their constitutionality, see: *Race Relations Law Reporter*, (Nashville, TN: School of Law, Vanderbilt University, 1957), vol. 2, pp. 892–94. See also: Carter III (1959), p. 94, and McMillen (1971), p. 269.

30. Brady (1955), p. 63.

31. Ibid., p. 63–64.

32. Dan Wakefield, "Justice in Sumner: Land of the Free," *The Nation*, Oct. 1, 1955, reprinted in *The Nation: Selections from the Independent Magazine of Politics and Culture*, Katrina Vanden Heuvel, ed. (New York: Thunder's Mouth Press, 1990), pp. 204–8. See also: McMillen (1971), pp. 217–18, and Carter III (1959), pp. 119–20.

33. Lerone Bennett Jr., *Before the Mayflower—A History of Black America: The Classic Account of the Struggles and Triumphs of Black Americans* (New York: Penguin Books, 1985), p. 377.

34. Long before the Montgomery bus boycott, on the eve of the Great Depression, blacks in Chicago launched the "buying power" movement which used pickets, boycotts, and demonstrations to pressure white businesses to hire more black workers. By the mid-1930s the move-

ment had spread to other cities. In New York, future congressman Adam Clayton Powell led a four-year nonviolent direct-action campaign which won 10,000 jobs for Harlem's blacks. Bennett Jr. (1985), pp. 360–61.

6. Philosopher, Statesman and Chief

1. Hodding Carter III, *The South Strikes Back* (Garden City, NY: Doubleday and Co., 1959), p. 56.

2. A total of four Alien and Sedition Acts were passed from June 18 to July 14, 1798. The Alien Act of June 25 gave the president power for two years to deport any alien he deemed dangerous to the safety of the country. The Alien Enemies Act of July 6, provided for apprehension and deportation of "male aliens who were subjects or citizens of a hostile country." And the Sedition Act of July 14 permitted the arrest and imprisonment of any person who "attempted to impede the lawful processes of government, foment insurrection, or write, publish, or utter any false or malicious statement about the president [*sic*], Congress, or government of the U.S." Apart from the stated goal of protecting America from its enemies, the Acts also were used to undermine domestic political opposition to the Federalist Party. In the end, however, the legislation backfired and led to the Party's downfall. Gorton Carruth, *The Encyclopedia of American Facts and Dates* (New York: HarperCollins, 1993, Ninth Edition), p. 118.

3. Jefferson's doctrine became known as the Virginia and Kentucky Resolutions. Page Smith, *The Constitution: A Documentary and Narrative History* (New York: William Morrow and Company, 1978), pp. 113, 308–9.

4. Carruth (1993), p. 126.

5. See, for example, *McCullough v. Maryland* (1819), in which Marshall recognized the doctrine of implied powers and affirmed the right of Congress to create a national bank, even though no such right was expressly granted in the Constitution.

6. Margaret L. Coit, *John C. Calhoun: American Portrait* (Cambridge, MA: The Riverside Press, 1950), p. 3. For more biographical material about Calhoun, see: Irving H. Bartlett, *John C. Calhoun: A Biography* (New York: Norton, 1993). Charles M. Wiltse, *John C. Calhoun* (Indianapolis, IN: The Bobs Merrill Company, 1941–1949), vol. 1–3. John Niven, *John C. Calhoun and the Price of Union: A Biography* (Baton Rouge, LA: Louisiana State University Press, 1988). For a comprehensive summary of Calhoun's most important political writings, see: Ross M. Lence, ed., *Union and Liberty: The Political Philosophy of John C. Calhoun* (Indianapolis, IN: Liberty Fund, 1992).

7. Coit (1950) pp. 4–5.

8. Coit (1950), pp. 7–8. For more on Calhoun's relationship with his father, see: Bartlett, (1993), pp. 21–42.

9. Lacy K. Ford Jr., "Inventing the Concurrent Majority: Madison, Calhoun, and the Problem of Majoritarianism in American Political Thought," *Journal of Southern History* (Southern Historical Association, 1994), vol. 9, no. 1, Feb. 1994, pp. 40–42.

10. Henry Wilson, *Rise and Fall of the Slave Power in America* (Boston, MA: James R. Osgood and Company, 1874), vol. 2, p. 37.

11. Ibid., p. 37.

12. S. G. Goodrich, *Personal Recollections of Poets, Philosophers and Statesmen*, (New York: The Arundel Print, 1856), pp. 470, 785–6.

13. When the essay was widely republished, it was commonly referred to as *The Exposition and Protest* and it contained both Calhoun's essay arguing South Carolina's grievances against the national government (the *Exposition*) and the text of formal resolutions adopted by the South Carolina general assembly opposing protective tariffs and federal power (Lence [1992]). Sum-

marizing the doctrine of states' rights advanced by Calhoun in the *Exposition*, biographer Charles M. Wiltse has written:

> The state rights argument was in essence a defense of minority interests. Its proponents reasoned that the Constitution was a compact between the states, each of which had been sovereign and independent in its own right before the Constitution was ratified. By that compact a general government had been created, but it was a government of limited and specifically delegated powers: a Confederacy rather than an organic state. Since it rested on a compact, the parties thereto had in the last resort the right to judge of infractions and to interpose their own original sovereignty whenever the joint agreement was violated by an unauthorized exercise of power on the part of the general government. The progressively rising tariffs had seriously impaired and now threatened to destroy the economic prosperity of the south. So the Southern leaders applied the state rights formula, declared the tariff to be a violation of the compact, and threatened to interpose to prevent its enforcement if it were not modified by Congress.

See: Charles M. Wiltse, *John C. Calhoun: Nullifier, 1829–1939* (Indianapolis, IN: The Bobs Merrill Company, 1949), p. 65.

14. See, in particular, Calhoun's famous "Fort Hill Letter," to the North, of 1831 (Lence [1992], pp. 367–400) and his letter to South Carolina governor James Hamilton of 1832. For further discussion of these concepts, see: Ford Jr., "Inventing the Concurrent Majority: Madison, Calhoun, and the Problem of Majoritarianism in American Political Thought," p. 26; and Louis Hartz, "The Reactionary Enlightenment" (from *Western Political Quarterly V* [March 1952], pp. 31–50), reprinted in Edward N. Saveth, ed., *Understanding the American Past* (Boston, MA: Little, Brown, 1954), pp. 251–76; and, more briefly, Gordon S. Wood, "The Dialectics of Dixie," *The New Republic*, vol. 210, no. 5, Jan. 31, 1994, pp. 30–35.

15. Coit (1950), p. 188.

16. Initially Calhoun had hesitated to oppose tariffs, having been counseled by advisers that doing so might diminish his chances of winning his lifelong ambition: to become president. He finally took a stand on February 28, 1827, casting the deciding vote in the Senate on the proposed Woolens Bill, defeating the tariff measure. Coit (1950), p. 167.

17. Ibid., p. 167.

18. Ibid., p. 167.

19. This legislation was somewhat ambiguous in its intent. While it reaffirmed the right of the federal government to impose tariffs, it also lessened the burden somewhat. Regardless of its impact, partisans of nullification saw it as a call to arms. Richard N. Current, ed., *Encyclopedia of the Confederacy* (New York: Simon and Schuster, 1993), vol. 3, p. 1160. David C. Roller and Robert W. Twyman, eds., *The Encyclopedia of Southern History* (Baton Rouge, LA: Louisiana State University Press, 1979), p. 932. See also: Wiltse (1949), pp. 86–153.

20. Wiltse (1949), p. 147.

21. Ibid., pp. 86, 88.

22. As quoted by James M. McPherson in "The War of Southern Aggression," *New York Review of Books*, Jan. 19, 1989, p. 16.

7. The Little Rock Crisis

1. "Education: Public Schools—Arkansas," *Race Relations Law Reporter* (1957), vol. 2, p. 931. Herbert Brownell with John P. Burke, *Advising Ike: The Memoirs of Attorney General Herbert Brownell* (Lawrence, KS: University of Kansas Press, 1993), Appendix D, "Brownell Opinion

to Eisenhower on Little Rock School Desegregation," p. 365. Neil R. McMillen, *The Citizens' Council: Organized Resistance to the Second Reconstruction, 1954–1964* (Urbana, IL: University of Illinois Press, 1971), pp. 269–70.

2. McMillen (1971), pp. 271–72.

3. The suit was filed on August 27, 1957 and the injunction secured two days later. *Mrs. Clyde Thomason v. Dr. William G. Cooper et al.*, Chancery Court, Pulaski County, Aug. 29, 1957, no. 108377, as published in *Race Relations Law Reporter* (1957), vol. 2, pp. 931–34.

4. Temporary restraining order, *Mrs. Clyde Thomason v. Dr. William G. Cooper et al.*, Chancery Court, Pulaski County, Aug. 29, 1957, no. 108377, as published in *Race Relations Law Reporter* (1957), vol. 2, pp. 933–34. Regarding the falsity of Faubus's assertions about local gun sales, see: Brownell and Burke (1993), p. 207.

5. Brownell and Burke (1993), p. 209. Robert W. Coakley, Office of the Chief of Military History (OCMH), monograph no. 158M, *Operation Arkansas* (Washington, DC: Histories Division, Department of the Army, 1967), p. 9. McMillen (1971), p. 274.

6. Brownell and Burke (1993), pp. 367–68.

7. McMillen (1971), p. 271. Arkansas was not the first state to use police powers to prevent integration. A year earlier, Texas governor Allan Shivers had used the Texas Rangers to bar black children from entering an all-white public school in Mansfield, near Fort Worth, and the Eisenhower administration did not then intervene. According to Eisenhower's attorney general, Herbert Brownell, the administration was "powerless" because it lacked appropriate jurisdiction. Brownell and Burke (1993), p. 204; McMillen (1971), p. 104.

8. Brownell and Burke (1993), pp. 208–10. According to Brownell, the governor's orders were "in direct derogation of the orders of the Federal Court." Brownell and Burke (1993), pp. 367–68. Governor Faubus's official proclamation ordering the state militia to active duty asserted that "a state of emergency presently exists," and cited "imminent danger of tumult, riot, and breach of the peace . . ." See: "State of Arkansas Executive Department," *Race Relations Law Reporter* (1957) vol. 2, p. 937.

9. McMillen (1971), p. 277. Two years later, in 1959, E. A. Lauderdale Jr., a member of the Little Rock Citizens' Council board of directors, was convicted and sentenced to prison for dynamiting the school board office and several other related targets in Little Rock. After serving only six months of his three-year sentence in 1961, he was pardoned by Governor Faubus. McMillen (1971), p. 284.

10. Presidential proclamation 3204 [22 F.R. 7628], "Obstruction of Justice in the State of Arkansas," as reprinted in *Race Relations Law Reporter* (1957), vol. 2, pp. 963–64.

11. As cited in Brownell and Burke (1993), p. 379.

12. Presidential executive order 10730 [22 F.R. 7628], "Providing Assistance for the Removal of an Obstruction of Justice within the State of Arkansas," as reprinted in *Race Relations Law Reporter* (1957), vol. 2, pp. 964–65.

13. Coakley, *Operation Arkansas* (1967), pp. 63–64.

14. Elizabeth Huckaby, *Crisis at Central High: Little Rock, 1957–58* (Baton Rouge, LA: Louisiana State University Press, 1980), p. 43.

15. Ibid., p. 43.

16. Hodding Carter III, *The South Strikes Back* (Garden City, NY: Doubleday and Co., 1959), p. 84.

17. Harry S. Ashmore, *Hearts and Minds: The Anatomy of Racism from Roosevelt to Reagan* (New York: McGraw-Hill, 1982), p. 284–6. "Major General Edwin Walker: Obituary," *The Times* (London), Nov. 5, 1993.

18. Huckaby (1980), p. 43.

19. "Obituary of Major General Edwin Walker," *Daily Telegraph* (London), Nov. 5, 1993, p. 25.

20. Ashmore (1982), p. 285. Richard Pearson, "General Edwin Walker Dies: Controversial Warrior," *Washington Post*, Nov. 2, 1993, p. B-6.

21. Walker had agreed to command the troops in Little Rock only after President Eisenhower refused his resignation. Associated Press, "General Edwin Walker, Right-Wing Activist, 84," *Newark (New Jersey) Star Ledger*, Nov. 2, 1993.

22. Ashmore (1982), p. 285.

23. Taylor Branch, *Parting the Waters: America in the King Years, 1954–1963* (New York: Simon and Schuster, 1988), p. 656.

24. Huckaby (1980), p. 200.

25. "Constitution Party Ends Meeting Optimistically," *Los Angeles Times*, Dec. 9, 1957. At the May 31–June 1, 1957, Constitution Party rally in San Francisco, Gale was identified as having been "named state chairman to succeed Arthur Case." See: "Constitution Party in San Francisco Hears Russell Maguire at Rally," *American Reporter*, vol. 7, no. 7, Oct. 1957, p. 2. And, in an undated flyer announcing the December 6–8, 1957, meeting presided over by Gale, his biographical sketch stated, "Gale has been state chairman for the Constitution Party since June 1957." See also: William P. Gale, "Reply to the National Chronicle," *IDENTITY* (Nov. 1975), vol. 8, no. 1, p. 5.

In an undated letter soliciting contributions for the Constitution Party from fellow "Patriots," Gale wrote:

> You have been paying for the support of communist and socialist experiments all over the world.
>
> For twenty-five years you have been paying a constantly increasing cost for support of socialist experiments at home.
>
> To these fantastic orgies of bureaucratic waste has been added experiments in one world government via the United Nations, NATO, UNESCO, the International Organization for Control of the Liquor Traffic in Africa, and most recently, the International Atomic Energy Treaty . . . a "constitutional monstrosity." . . .
>
> Every dollar you contribute will help the Constitution Party turn the tide from socialism to Americanism and unequivocable Constitutional government. . . . It is our firm opinion that the efforts of patriotic organizations who disseminate true information and educational media, will come to naught unless their views are subsequently interpreted in the form of political action. The time to do this is now [*sic*].

Undated letter of William P. Gale, CONSTITUTION PARTY, 1957; correspondence, Newsclippings, Propaganda," LACRC Collection.

26. Indictment for high crimes and misdemeanors, "CONSTITUTION PARTY, 1957; correspondence, Newsclippings, Propaganda," LACRC Collection. See also: "Ike Is Indicted as Criminal," *Right: A Monthly Newsletter of, by, and for the American Right Wing*, no. 26. Nov. 1957, p. 1.

27. For the most detailed account of the role of federal troops (and federalized National Guard troops) in Little Rock, see: Coakley *Operation Arkansas* (1967). The army troops of the 101st Airborne Division—and the members of the Arkansas National Guard that had been called into federal service—that Eisenhower sent to Little Rock were not dispatched as a posse comitatus, but ordered there pursuant to a presidential proclamation and an executive order in which Eisenhower invoked his statutory and constitutional authority to suppress insurrection. For the most thorough summary of Eisenhower's justification for using federal troops, and a

response to the argument that his doing so was a violation of the Posse Comitatus Act, see: Brownell and Burke (1993), pp. 365–84.

According to Attorney General Herbert Brownell, Eisenhower could locate his authority to intervene in Title 10, Sections 332, 333, and 334, of the Revised United States Code. Section 332, for example, permitted the president to use "the armed forces of the United States or call into federal service the militia of any state to enforce the laws or suppress rebellion whenever he considers that 'unlawful obstructions, combinations or assemblages, or rebellion' against federal authority make it impossible to enforce federal laws by 'the ordinary course of judicial proceedings'" (Coakley, *Operation Arkansas* [1967], p. 55).

These laws are ultimately grounded in Article I, Section 8, of the Constitution, which grants Congress the power to "provide for calling forth the militia to execute the laws of the Union, suppress insurrections and repel invasions"; and "to provide for organizing, arming, and disciplining the militia, and for governing such part of them as may be employed in the service of the United States, reserving to the states respectively, appointment of the officers, and the authority of training the militia according to the discipline prescribed by Congress" (George Anastaplo, *The Amendments to the Constitution: A Commentary* [Baltimore, MD: Johns Hopkins University Press, 1995], Appendixes and Sources, M-1, "The Constitution of 1787," p. 367).

Additional Constitutional authority for Eisenhower's intervention can be found in Article IV, Section 4, which reads, "The United States shall guarantee to every state in this Union a republican form of government, and shall protect each of them against invasion, and, on application of the Legislature, or of the Executive (when the Legislature cannot be convened), against domestic violence" (Anastaplo [1995], p. 373).

For more on the role of troops in Little Rock, see: unpublished manuscript of Dr. Paul Scheips, *Legal Manners Pertaining to the Use of Troops at Little Rock*, pp. 58–59; and proclamation no. 3204 [22 F.R. 7628], "Obstruction of Justice in the State of Arkansas," by the President of the United States of America, Sept. 23, 1957, as published in *Race Relations Law Reporter* (1957), vol. 2, p. 963.

For a contrary view with regard to Eisenhower's statutory authority to send in the troops, see: remarks of John C. Stennis, "The Multiplying Evils of Bad Law," *Mississippi Law Journal* (Mississippi State Bar Association), vol. 29, no. 5, Oct. 1958, pp. 430–43; and R. Carter Pittman, "The Federal Invasion of Arkansas in the Light of the Constitution," *Alabama Lawyer* (Alabama State Bar Association, 1958), vol. 19, no. 2, pp. 168–71.

28. Stennis "The Multiplying Evils of Bad Law," Oct. 1958, pp. 430–43.

29. Major Clarence I. Meeks III, USMC, "Illegal Law Enforcement: Aiding Civil Authorities in Violation of the Posse Comitatus Act," *Military Law Review*, vol. 70 (1975), p. 85.

30. According to historian C. Vann Woodward, "The Redeemers who overthrew Reconstruction and established 'Home Rule' in the Southern states conducted their campaign in the name of white supremacy." C. Vann Woodward, *The Strange Career of Jim Crow* (London: Oxford University Press, Second Revised Edition, 1966, p. 31).

31. Robert W. Coakley, *The Role of Federal Military Forces in Domestic Disorders, 1789–1878* (Washington, DC: Center of Military History, United States Army, 1988), pp. 128–37.

8. Vicious and Desperate Men

1. Robert W. Coakley, *The Role of Federal Military Forces in Domestic Disorders, 1789–1878* (Washington, DC: Center of Military History, United States Army, 1988), pp. 133–37.

2. See: 6 OP. ATTY GEN. 466, 473 (1854), as cited in Coakley (1988), p. 132; and Major Clarence I. Meeks III, USMC, "Illegal Law Enforcement: Aiding Civil Authorities in Violation of the Posse Comitatus Act," *Military Law Review*, vol. 70 (1975), p. 88.

3. Some scholars of Louisiana Reconstruction put the figure lower, calculating only several hundred deaths. For a critical contemporary account of the situation in Louisiana, see: Speech

of Representative Charles H. Joyce of Vermont (Feb. 9, 1877), *Appendix to the Congressional Record*, 44th Cong., 2d Sess., vol. 5 (1877), pp. 83–101. For a comprehensive history of Reconstruction in Louisiana, see: Joe Gray Taylor, *Louisiana Reconstructed, 1862–1877* (Baton Rouge, LA: Louisiana State University Press, 1975). See also: Eric Foner, *Reconstruction: America's Unfinished Revolution, 1863–1877*, (New York: Harper and Row, 1989).

4. In the bloodiest incident of racial violence since the end of the Civil War, more than one hundred blacks, including several dozen members of a black militia, were massacred by whites in Grant Parish, Louisiana. Most of the killing occurred on Easter Sunday, 1873, when scores of black freedmen were murdered while attempting to keep Grant Parish—which had elected Republicans to office—and the town of Colfax from being forcibly seized by Democrats. Although Governor William P. Kellogg, a Republican, had dispatched federal troops to aid black militiamen, white steamboat captains refused to transport the soldiers, deliberately delaying their arrival. When the federal troops finally arrived, the most they could do was bury the dead. Foner (1989), p. 437; Coakley (1988), pp. 323–24.

Indictments were brought against the murderers, but the U.S. Supreme Court overturned the only three convictions that were secured. The Court's 1876 decision in *United States v. Cruikshank* asserted that the federal government had the right to enforce Reconstruction-era civil-rights amendments only when violations were committed by *states*, not individuals. The judicial backtracking symbolized in *Cruikshank* undermined the legal rationale for many elements of Reconstructionist policy and significantly emboldened the forces of white supremacy.

Three years before announcing its decision in *Cruikshank*, the court had affirmed states' rights in the so-called Slaughterhouse cases of 1873 in which the majority opinion authored by Justice Samuel F. Miller asserted that "primary authority over citizens' rights rested with the states, leading federal courts to limit national jurisdiction over the administration of justice, further weakening civil-rights enforcement," according to historian Eric Foner. For more on these decisions, see: Foner (1989), pp. 529–31.

The massacre at Colfax may have been bloody, but it was a modest military conflict compared to the events of September 14, 1874. On that day about five thousand men, led by ex-Confederate veterans organized under the banner of the White League, staged a violent and temporarily successful coup to unseat Governor Kellogg in New Orleans. During the conflict—which became known as the Battle of Liberty Place—the insurgents captured the chief of police, cut the governor's telegraph line, and took control of the statehouse, state arsenals, and armories. It took a proclamation from President Ulysses Grant ordering the insurgents to disperse, as well as the threat of six infantry companies dispatched from other states, to restore Governor Kellogg to power. See: Coakley (1988), pp. 324–26; Lawrence Powell, "A Concrete Symbol," *Southern Exposure*, vol. 18, no. 1, Spring 1990, pp. 40–43.

5. Joyce, *Appendix to the Congressional Record* (1877), p. 83.

6. In spite of their reluctance to demand army intervention in the South, Republican leaders found their political position fast eroding. By 1874, Democrats held a 168- to 109-seat majority in the House of Representatives (14 seats went to minor parties) and gained 10 seats in the Senate, although they still fell behind the Republicans by a margin of 29 to 45. Gorton Carruth, *The Encyclopedia of American Facts and Dates* (New York: HarperCollins, 1993, Ninth Edition), p. 314.

7. For a detailed account of the Ellenton Massacre, see: *Appendix to the Congressional Record*, 44th Cong., 2d Sess., 1877, "Minority Report on the Condition of South Carolina," p. 235.

8. Grant to House of Representatives, *Use of the Army in Certain of the Southern States* H. Ex. Doc. 30, 44th Cong., 2d Sess. (Jan. 24, 1877), pp. 102–3. Four days later Governor Chamberlain asked Washington for help suppressing the insurrection. (Correspondence of Daniel Chamberlain as cited in *Use of the Army in Certain of the Southern States*, pp. 102–3.) For more detail on the activities of Democrats and the rifle clubs, see: Feb. 21, 1877, remarks of Representative J. H. Rainey, *Appendix to the Congressional Record*, 44th Cong., 2d Sess., pp. 217–19. See also: "Minority Report on the Condition of South Carolina" (H. Rpt. 175, Part 2, 44th Cong., 2d

Sess.), as printed in *Appendix to the Congressional Record*, pp. 221–58. This document also contains the text of the Oct. 17, 1876, proclamation of President Ulysses S. Grant (p. 230).

9. Meeks III, *Military Law Review*, vol. 70 (1975), p. 90.

10. Taft termed the marshal's practice of using federal troops "too well settled for dispute." *Appendix to the Congressional Record*, 44th Cong., 2d Sess. (1877), pp. 224–26.

11. Foner (1989), p. 567.

12. Ibid., p. 567.

13. Ibid., p. 568.

14. Carruth (1993), p. 320.

15. Armed Democrats seized control of most state offices, including the state arsenal and Supreme Court on January 9, 1877. Republican governor Stephen B. Packard, a former United States marshal, controlled only the statehouse. Eventually the army was called in, but the troops just preserved the status quo until congressional committees could investigate the election and return to Washington. Coakley (1988), p. 336.

    In South Carolina, former Confederate general Wade Hampton asserted victory over the incumbent governor, Daniel Chamberlain, and Hampton's rifle club allies threatened a December 7 Inauguration Day coup. Coakley (1988), p. 339. "Recent Election in the State of South Carolina," H. Rpt. 175, Part 2, 44th Cong., 2d sess. (Feb. 21, 1877), pp. 137, 156. Senate Doc. 209, 57th Cong. 2d sess., (March 2, 1903), pp. 137, 156. Frederick T. Wilson, "Federal aid in domestic disturbances, 1787–1903," (1903), p.185.

16. Grant to House of Representatives, *Use of the Army in Certain of the Southern States*, H. Ex. Doc. 30, 44th Cong., 2d Sess. (Jan. 22, 1877), pp. 2–3. Meeks III, *Military Law Review*, vol. 70, (1975), p. 91. Coakley (1988), pp. 342–43.

17. Among other things, the Democrats' report claimed: "The fact of troops being sent to the state was used to overawe the colored people and prevent them from voting the Democratic ticket. They were told that the troops had been sent there to compel the blacks to vote the Republican ticket and to shoot all those who voted for the Democrats." *Report of the Majority of the Select Committee of the House to Investigate the Recent Election in the State of South Carolina*, H. Rpt. 175. Pt. 1. 44th Cong., 2d Sess. (Feb. 21, 1877), pp. 7–8.

18. The bill, H.R. no. 4692, was for the fiscal year ending June 30, 1878. See: Remarks of Representative Atkins, *Congressional Record*, 44th Cong., 2d Sess., vol. 5 (1877), p. 1886. The full text of Section 5 of the Act read as follows:

> That no part of the money appropriated by this Act, nor any money heretofore appropriated shall be applied to the pay, subsistence, or transportation of troops used, employed, or to be used or employed, in support of the claim of Francis T. Nicholls or of S. B. Packard to the governor of the state of Louisiana. Nor shall any of said money be applied in support of the claim of the two bodies claiming to be the legislature of said state, presided over respectively by L. A. Wiltz and Louis Bush; nor of the two bodies claiming to be the legislature of said state, presided over respectively by C. C. Antoine and Michael Hahn; nor in support of the claim of Thomas C. Manning and associates to be the Supreme Court of said state; nor in support of the claim of John T. Ludeling and associates to be the Supreme Court of said state; nor in the aid of the execution of any process in the hands of the United States Marshal in said state issued in aid of and for the support of any such claims. Nor shall the army, or any portion of it, be used in support of the claims, or pretended claim or claims, of any state government, or officer thereof, in any state, until the same shall have been duly recognized by Congress. And any person offending against any of the provisions of this Act shall be deemed guilty of a misdemeanor, and upon

conviction thereof, shall be imprisoned at hard labor for not less than five nor more than ten years.

Congressional Record, 44th Cong., 2d Sess., vol. 5 (1877), p. 2119.

19. Atkins, who had been elected to the Confederate Congress in 1861 and 1863, referred to himself as "one of the untrammeled representatives upon this floor." *Congressional Record*, 44th Cong., 2d Sess., vol. 5 (1877), p. 2113; *Biographical Directory of the United States Congress 1774–1989* (Washington, DC: U.S. Government Printing Office, 1989, Bicentennial Edition), p. 553.

20. Remarks of Representative Atkins (1877), pp. 2111–13.

21. According to Atkins, "Continued wars and standing armies [in Europe] have wasted the resources of the common people, diverted the minds of the masses from habits of frugal economy, blinded the youth with the glare and pomp of military adventure, made the masses tenants at the will of a bonded and landed aristocracy upheld by standing armies made insolent and tyrannical through pampering and the lavish expenditure of gold" (Remarks of Representative Atkins [1877], p. 2112).

22. Ibid., p. 2112.

23. Ibid., p. 2114.

24. *Congressional Record*, 44th Cong., 2d Sess., vol. 5 (Mar. 2, 1877), p. 2120. Remarks of Representative Conger.

25. The bill was passed on a voice vote with the Speaker of the House declaring that two-thirds of the House supported the measure. *Congressional Record*, 44th Cong., 2d Sess. vol. 5 (Mar. 2, 1877), p. 2120. Remarks of the Speaker.

26. On the dilemma of soldiers under these circumstances, see: *Congressional Record—House*, 45th Cong., 2d Sess. vol. 7, (May 20, 1878), pp. 3587–88. Remarks of Representative Humphrey.

27. Hayes was sworn in on Saturday, March 3, but the actual inauguration did not occur until Monday, March 5, because March 4 was a Sunday. Carruth (1993), p. 320.

28. Federal troops withdrew from their positions defending the South Carolina legislature at Columbia on April 10 and the Packard administration ended in Louisiana two weeks later, on April 24.

29. Woodward (1966), p. 6.

30. As quoted in Foner (1989), p. 582.

9. Legislating Redemption: The Posse Comitatus Act Becomes Law

1. *Congressional Record—House*, 45th Cong., 2d Sess., vol. 7 (May 18, 1878), p. 3538. Remarks of Representative Hewitt.

2. Representative Atkins successfully moved for a suspension of the rules so that the entire House could resolve itself into a "Committee of the Whole" for the purpose of debating the Army Appropriation Bill. See: *Congressional Record—House*, 45th Cong., 2d Sess., vol. 7 (May 20, 1878), p. 3578. Remarks of Representative Atkins.

Representative Kimmel argued that the Constitution's framers had intended the militia as a substitute for a standing army, but the militia had "decayed from neglect." See: *Congressional Record—House*, 45th Cong., 2d sess., vol. 7 (May 20, 1878), pp. 3579–81, 3583, 3586. Remarks of Representative Kimmel.

For arguments countering this perspective, see the remarks of Representative William A. Phillips of Kansas, who opined,

But besides this spirit of false economy there is a class of visionaries, and some of them have spoken on this floor, who pretend that a United States Army of any kind is a menace to popular liberty; that any military establishment outside of state militia is pregnant with the overthrow of civil government. Sir, all through our history we have had political theorists holding to a doctrine of a revised, regenerated, well-organized state militia, but it has existed only in training days and speeches.

Congressional Record—House, 45th Cong., 2d sess., vol. 7 (May 20, 1878), p. 3615.

3. Remarks of Representative Kimmel (1878), p. 3582.

4. *Congressional Record—House*, 45th Cong., 2d Sess., vol. 7 (May 20, 1878), p. 3586.

5. Helen Bartter Crocker, "J. Proctor Knott's Education in Missouri Politics, 1850–1862," *Missouri Historical Society Bulletin* (Jan. 1974), no. 30, pp. 105–6.

6. The oath also required Knott to declare his loyalty to the provisional government of Missouri. For a brief but thorough discussion of Knott's political credentials and outlook, see: Crocker, "J. Proctor Knott's Education in Missouri Politics, 1850–1862," pp. 101–16. See also: Edwin W. Mills, "The Career of James Proctor Knott in Missouri," *Missouri Historical Review* (April 1937), no. 31, pp. 288–94.

7. As quoted by Crocker, "J. Proctor Knott's Education in Missouri Politics, 1850–1862," p. 113.

8. *Congressional Record—House*, 45th Cong., 2d Sess., vol. 7 (May 27, 1878), p. 3845. Remarks of Representative Knott.

9. *Biographical Directory of the United States Congress, 1774–1989* (Washington, DC: U.S. Government Printing Office, 1989, Bicentennial Edition), p. 961. *Congressional Record—House*, 45th Cong., 2d Sess., vol. 7 (May 27, 1878), p. 3850. Remarks of Reps. Southard and Ellis.

10. *Congressional Record—House*, 45th Cong., 2d Sess., vol. 7 (May 27, 1878), p. 3851. Remarks of Representative Gardner.

11. See Appendix III.

12. *Congressional Record—Senate*, 45th Cong., 2d sess., vol. 7 (June 7, 1878), p. 4240. Remarks of Senator Kernan. Kernan's amendment also deleted the words "under the pretext or" which appeared in the House version.

13. *Congressional Record—Senate*, 45th Cong., 2d Sess., vol. 7 (June 7, 1878), pp. 4240–42. Remarks of Senators Kernan and Beck.

14. *Congressional Record—Senate*, 45th Cong., 2d Sess., vol. 7 (June 8, 1878), p. 4304. The vote to strike Section 29 in its entirety as amended failed, with 21 voting in favor, 29 opposed, and 26 absent.

15. *Congressional Record—House*, 45th Cong., 2d Sess., vol. 7 (June 15, 1878), p. 4685. Remarks of Representative Hewitt.

In the course of the Conference Committee deliberations the Democrats, led by Hewitt, held defiantly to their principles, threatening to kill all appropriations for the army if the language of the Posse Comitatus Act was not preserved. The same obstinacy had been expressed by Representative Atkins and his Confederate colleagues in the previous session of Congress in 1877, when they insisted on preserving the language of Section 5 of the Army Appropriation Bill, causing the entire bill to fail. This fact was noted during debate on the Knott Amendment when Representative Charles E. Hooker, a Mississippi Democrat, observed that it was Section 5, which barred funding for federal troops in Louisiana and South Carolina, that "was attached to the army bill [the previous year] and defeated it." (See: *Congressional Record—House*, 45th Cong., 2d Sess., vol. 7 [May 27, 1878], p. 3845. Remarks of Representative Hooker.)

16. See: *Congressional Record—House*, 45th Cong., 2d Sess., vol. 7 (June 15, 1878), p. 4686. Remarks of Representative Hewitt.

Concerns in the Senate about the enforceability of the criminal sanctions contained in the Knott Amendment had prompted senators to delete by a margin of just one vote language providing for fines and jail terms. (See *Congressional Record—Senate*, 45th Cong., 2d Sess., vol. 7 [June 8, 1878], p. 4304. Remarks of Senator Blaine.) However, Representative Hewitt proudly reported that this language had been restored by the Conference Committee:

> The House Committee planted themselves firmly on the doctrine that rather than yield this fundamental principle, for which three years the House had struggled, they would allow the bill to fail—notwithstanding the reforms which we had secured; regarding these reforms as of but little consequence alongside the great principle that the army of the United States in time of peace should be under the control of Congress and obedient to its laws.

See: *Congressional Record—House*, 45th Cong., 2d Sess., vol. 7 (June 15, 1878), p. 4686. Remarks of Representative Hewitt. See also the remarks of Senator Sargent (*Congressional Record—Senate*, 45th Cong., 2d Sess., vol. 7 [June 15, 1878], p. 4648), which contain a substantive analysis of the resolution of different versions of the Posse Comitatus Act by both the House and Senate.

17. *Congressional Record—House*, 45th Cong., 2d Sess., vol. 7 (June 15, 1878), p. 4686. Remarks of Representative Hewitt.

18. According to C. Vann Woodward,

> The acquiescence of Northern liberalism in the Compromise of 1877 defined the beginning, but not the ultimate extent of the liberal retreat on the race issue. The compromise merely left the freedman to the custody of the conservative redeemers upon their pledge that they would protect him in his constitutional rights. But as these pledges were forgotten or violated and the South veered toward proscription and extremism, Northern opinion shifted to the right, keeping pace with the South, conceding point after point, so that at no time were the sections very far apart on race policy.

(C. Vann Woodward, *The Strange Career of Jim Crow* [London: Oxford University Press, Second Revised Edition, 1966] pp. 69–70.)

The annals of the Posse Comitatus Act have been of interest to only a handful of military historians. While some have argued that the Act was passed to correct the "gross abuses" committed by federal forces during and after the Civil War, and therefore represented "a shift back to the strict prohibition against such use [of the army] that the Founding Fathers had envisioned," others have presented the history of the Act in the more direct context of Reconstruction-era politics. (For an example of the former, see: Major C. I. Meeks III, USMC *Illegal Law Enforcement: Aiding Civil Authorities in Violation of the Posse Comitatus Act*, a thesis presented to the Judge Advocate General's School, United States Army, 23rd Judge Advocate Officer Advanced Course, April 1975, pp. 5–16. For an example of the latter, see: Robert W. Coakley, *The Role of Federal Military Forces in Domestic Disorders, 1789–1878* [Washington, DC: Center of Military History, United States Army, 1988], pp. 334–48.)

19. Woodward (1966), p. 7. Woodward compares these codes to the "Black Codes" of the previous era and writes: "In bulk and detail as well as in effectiveness of enforcement the [new] segregation codes were comparable with the Black Codes of the old regime, though the laxity that mitigated the harshness of the black codes was replaced by a rigidity that was more typical of the segregation code." The codes of the "old regime" Woodward refers to were enacted by the provisional legislatures established by President Johnson in 1865. These codes established

"systems of peonage or apprenticeship resembling slavery." The Black Codes were on the books "only a short while, however, for they were either disallowed by military government or repealed by subsequent legislatures." Woodward (1966), pp. 23–24.

10. From Jew to Reverend Gale

1. "California Constitution Party News," *American Reporter*, vol. 7, no. 7, Oct. 1957, p. 4, LACRC Collection.

2. "The All-American Platform of William P. Gale," and "The Constitution Party Platform of Principles and Plans: Ten Commandments for Government," circa 1957, "CONSTITUTION PARTY, 1957. Correspondence, Newsclippings, Propaganda," LACRC Collection. See also: "1960 Fact Sheet: William Potter Gale," memo of Charles Wittenstein to Sylvia Edelman, Nov. 30, 1970. AJC Archives.

3. "William T. Gale [*sic*]," undated report, AJC Archives.

4. For brief but excellent summaries of the 1957 legislation, see: Herbert Brownell with John P. Burke, *Advising Ike: The Memoirs of Attorney General Herbert Brownell* (Lawrence, KS: University of Kansas, 1993), pp. 218–26; and Taylor Branch, *Parting the Waters: America in the King Years, 1954–1963* (New York: Simon and Schuster, 1988), pp. 220–22.

5. "WANTED: All Constitutional Californians TO: Register with the Constitution Party," undated, "CONSTITUTION PARTY, 1957. Correspondence, Newsclippings, Propaganda," LACRC Collection. "Constitution Party Hopes to Get on Ballot: Quarterly Parley of Conservative Group in Fresno Ends; Rally in L.A. Planned," *Los Angeles Times*, March 4, 1957. "Right-Wingers Seek Party Status," *Los Angeles Times*, Feb. 24, 1957. See also: "1960 Fact Sheet: William Potter Gale, February 1960," memo of Charles Wittenstein to Sylvia Edelman, Nov. 30, 1970, AJC Archives.

6. Kathleen Gale, interview by the author. "State Headquarters," by Lotty Kilgo Keech, vice chairman, *California Constitution Party Bulletin*, vol. 2, no. 1, Jan. 1958, p. 2.

7. Wittenstein (1970). "Constitution Party Ends Meeting Optimistically," *Los Angeles Times*, Dec. 9, 1957. "California Constitution Party News," *American Reporter* (Sacramento, CA: 1957) vol. 7, no. 7, Oct. 1957, "CONSTITUTION PARTY, 1957. Correspondence, Newsclippings, Propaganda," LACRC Collection.

8. William P. Gale, "A Reply to the National Chronicle," *IDENTITY* (Nov. 1975), vol.8, no. 1.

9. Roxanne L. Gale, "In Memory of Colonel W. P. Gale," June 17, 1988, pp. 3–4.

10. Kathleen Gale, interview. Gale has described his "ordination" as a ceremony involving the "laying-on of hands by three clergymen to consecrate Christ." Cheri Seymour, *The Committee of the States: Inside the Radical Right* (Mariposa, CA: Camden Place Communications, Inc., 1991), pp. 80–81. Whatever may have actually transpired, the ceremony Gale described is not one that is performed in the Episcopal Church. According to Gale, he spent "about four months" preaching at one Episcopalian church before quitting to preach on his own. However, according to the Episcopal Diocese of Los Angeles, Gale never served a pulpit in their jurisdiction. Furthermore, Episcopal clergymen must receive formal seminary training—which Gale did not—and are ordained always as "priests," not as "ministers," the title Gale always claimed for himself. (Interview and author's correspondence with Episcopal Diocese of Los Angeles.)

11. "An Open Letter to the Citizens of Mariposa, California, from the Ministry of Christ Church," *IDENTITY* (Mariposa, CA: Ministry of Christ Church, undated looseleaf volume), p. 1.

12. Although Gale probably was "ordained" by Swift, he derided these reports vigorously after the two men had a falling-out in the early 1960s. "Only JESUS CHRIST 'ordains' His Ministers!" Gale wrote in November 1975. (William P. Gale, "A Reply to the National Chronicle," [1975].)

13. Seymour (1991), p. 83.

14. Ibid., p. 88.

15. Correspondence of Ruth Gale, Feb, 21, 1980, and Oct. 10, 1979.

16. Kathleen Gale, interview.

17. Correspondence of William C. Gale, July 25, 1997.

18. Correspondence of Ruth Gale, Oct. 10, 1979.

19. Correspondence of Ruth Gale, Oct. 10, 1979.

20. Corresondence of Ruth Gale, Feb. 21, 1980, and Oct. 10, 1979.

21. Corinne Rosenberg, interview by the author.

11. Birchers and Minutemen

1. Because Gale was not very reliable when recalling dates, and his account of events often was self-serving, it is not possible to determine when he and Capt actually started the Christian Defense League. Michael Barkun puts the date "at some point between 1957 and 1962," but there is no evidence to suggest that the League came into being before Gale ran for governor in 1958, and other evidence suggests that it was founded before Gale established the California Rangers in 1960. Michael Barkun, *Religion and the Racist Right: The Origins of the Christian Identity Movement* (Chapel Hill, NC: University of North Carolina Press, 1994), pp. 66–68. *Extremism on the Right: A Handbook* (New York: Anti-Defamation League of B'nai Brith, 1983), p. 86. "California Rangers," *Paramilitary Organizations in California* (Sacramento, CA: Calif. DOJ, 1965), pp. CR-1–CR-10. William P. Gale, "A Reply to the National Chronicle," *IDENTITY* (Nov. 1975), vol. 8, no. 1.

2. Cheri Seymour, *The Committee of the States: Inside the Radical Right* (Mariposa, CA: Camden Place Communications, Inc., 1991), p. 94.

3. Calif. DOJ (1965), pp. CR-6, CR-7.

4. "Legion Post Accused of Bigotry Asks Hearing," *Los Angeles Times*, Dec. 21, 1963; Bill Stout, "Hate Mongers in Our Midst," *Beverly Hills Times*, Sept. 6, 1963; Calif. DOJ (1965), p. CR-7.

5. Ibid. See also: Seymour (1991), pp. 89–91.

6. Calif. DOJ (1965), pp. CR-7–CR-8.

7. Seymour (1991) pp. 89–91. "Legion Post Accused of Bigotry Asks Hearing," *Los Angeles Times*, Dec. 21, 1963.

8. Seymour (1991), p. 94.

9. "California's Private Armies: The Muster," *New York Herald Tribune*, April 25, 1965, p. 14.

10. Complaint: Action for a Divorce," *William P. Gale v. Josephine C. Gale*, Los Angeles County, California, Superior Court, case no. D621923, Dec. 4, 1962.

11. "Complaint: Action for a Divorce," *William P. Gale v. Josephine C. Gale*, Los Angeles County, California, Superior Court, case no. D621923, Dec. 4, 1962. "Property Settlement Agreement, Exhibit 1," *William P. Gale v. Josephine C. Gale*, Los Angeles County, California, Superior Court, case no. D621923, Jan. 29, 1963.

12. "Who Is William P. Gale?" *Constitution News-Review* (Constitution Party, 1962), p. 12.

13. Corinne Rosenberg, interview by the author.

14. Of 206 groups in existence in late 1961, 19 had been started in 1960 and 79 in the first ten months of 1961. See: "The John Birch Society," *The Facts*, ADL, Nov.–Dec. 1961, vol. 14, no. 5, p. 226.

15. *Congressional Record*, vol. 108, no. 181, Oct. 4, 1962. Remarks of Senator McGee: "Increasing Tempo of Attack from Ultraconservative and Rightist Publications and Organizations." For 1965 subscription figures, see: Wesley McCune, "The American Right Wing During 1965," (Washington, DC: Group Research, 1966), p. 7, paper delivered at the Annual Conference on the Critics and the Schools, National Education Association, Washington, D.C., Jan. 17, 1966.

In 1962, income for the Twentieth Century Reformation Hour, the Christian Anti-Communism Crusade, and the Christian Crusade totaled $2,663,900. In 1959, the figure was $758,400. For a detailed report on the annual income of thirty select right-wing organizations for 1958–1962, see: Wesley McCune, "The Finances of the Right Wing: A Study of the Size and Sources of Income of Thirty Selected Operations" (Washington, DC: Group Research Reports, Sept. 1, 1964), vol. 4, no. 16.

16. For more on Schwartz's group, which was founded in 1953, see: Wesley McCune, "Christian Anti-Communism Crusade," *Special Reports* (Washington, DC: Group Research Reports, May 1, 1962), vol. 4, no. 2; Fred C. Cook, "The Ultras: Aims, Affiliations, and Finances of the Radical Right," *The Nation*, June 30, 1962, p. 571; Clyde Wilcox, *God's Warriors: The Christian Right in Twentieth-Century America* (Baltimore and London: Johns Hopkins University Press, 1992), pp. 70–85; and Arnold Forster and Benjamin R. Epstein, *Danger on the Right: The Attitudes, Personnel, and Influence of the Radical Right and Extreme Conservatives* (New York: Random House, 1964), pp. 47–67.

17. For a detailed report on the annual income of thirty selected right-wing organizations for the period 1958–1962, see: McCune, "The Finances of the Right Wing: A Study of the Size and Sources of Income of Thirty Selected Operations."

18. "American Hero: John Birch," *New American*, June 16, 1986, p. 56. See also: Wesley McCune, "John Birch Society, Inc.," *Organizations* (Washington, DC: Group Research Reports, May 1, 1962) section 1; Robert Welch, *The Blue Book of the John Birch Society* (Belmont, MA: Western Islands, 18th printing, 1961), p. 146.

19. John F. McManus, "A Program for Responsible Citizenship" (Belmont, MA: The John Birch Society, 1986), p. 4. "The John Birch Society," *The Facts*, ADL, Nov.-Dec. 1961, vol. 14, no. 5, p. 224. Welch (1961), p. 146.

20. The transcript of Welch's remarks at that 1958 session was printed in 1959 as *The Blue Book of the John Birch Society*. For a brief biographical sketch of Welch, see: Welch (1961), pp. 167–68.

21. Welch (1961), p. 1.

22. Ibid., p. 4.

23. Ibid., p. 20.

24. Ibid., p. 19.

25. The ten-point program of Robert Welch included the following: (1) Establish anti-communist "reading rooms" all across America. (2) Expand circulation of conservative publications, such as *American Opinion* (the future house organ of the John Birch Society). (3) "Rebuild the wall of mass opinion" by increasing the reach of conservative media commentators such as Billy James Hargis, Carl McIntire, and other "great Americanists with a huge radio following." (4) Launch a massive letter-writing campaign targeting everybody "whose opinions, actions, and decisions count for anything." (5) Organize fronts: "little fronts, big fronts, temporary fronts, permanent fronts, all kinds of fronts," with names such as "A Petition to Impeach Earl Warren" and "Women Against Labor Union Hoodlumism." (6) Shock people by exposing "highly placed secret communists." (7) Attack anyone who criticizes the anti-communist movement, by asking "embarrassing questions" during their public speeches. (8) Create a speakers' bureau to address church clubs, PTA groups, and others, "not on communism or anti-communism in general, but on specific subjects," where their remarks would be "informative and well-received." (9) Work internationally and help establish "governments-in-exile" com-

posed of "the most respected and solidly anti-communist refugees." (10) "Put our weight on the political scales . . . just as fast and far as we c[an]." Welch (1961), pp. 64–101.

26. Welch (1961), pp. 33–46. For an example of one leading fascist philosophical treatise that invokes Spengler in this vein, see: Ulick Varange (Francis Parker Yockey), *Imperium* (Sausalito, CA: Noontide Press, 1962).

27. Welch (1961), pp. 169–172.

28. Ibid., pp. 103, 107.

29. Ibid., pp. 100, 146–147, 161–62.

30. Ibid., p. 147.

31. Estimates of JBS membership vary widely. Citing the remarks of U.S. Representative Edgar W. Hiestand, himself a Society member, one 1961 ADL report put the figure at 60,000 (40,000 men and 20,000 women). "The John Birch Society," *The Facts*, ADL, Nov.-Dec. 1961, vol. 14, no. 5, pp. 223, 225–226. Several years later, ADL researchers Arnold Forster and Benjamin Epstein observed that this "60,000" figure, "conflicted with the number of members reflected by the dues reported in the Society's financial statements to the Attorney General of Massachusetts. From studies of these official reports, the highest possible estimate of membership at the close of 1962 would have been 24,000." Forster and Epstein (1964), p. 11. Near the end of 1965, the ADL estimated that JBS membership was "pushing toward the 100,000 mark," near-doubling since 1963. See: "The John Birch Society—1966," *The Facts*, ADL, Feb. 1966, vol. 17, no. 1, p. 349. In his 1959 *Blue Book*, Welch stated that his end-of-year goal was to have 30,000 dedicated members and $1 million in "outside" income, beyond Society dues. However, a footnote in the fourth printing of the *Blue Book*, which appeared in February 1961, stated that "we did not get anywhere near either of these goals by the end of 1959." See: Welch (1961), pp. 154, 162. According to these assessments, JBS membership might be safely estimated at approximately 50,000 in 1963, proving unlikely Hiestand's estimate of 60,000 members two years earlier. Therefore, the 1964 estimate by Forster and Epstein of 1961 Birch membership, which put the figure at 24,000, appears to be more accurate.

32. "The John Birch Society," *The Facts*, ADL, Nov.-Dec. 1961, vol. 14, no. 5, pp. 225–26.

33. "The John Birch Society," *The Facts*, ADL, Feb. 1966, vol. 17, no. 1, p. 349. See also: Wesley McCune, "The American Right Wing During 1965" (Washington, DC: Group Research, Inc., 1966), pp. 2, 12, paper delivered at the Annual Conference on the Critics and the Schools, National Education Association, Washington, D.C., Jan. 17, 1966.

34. "Among the major organizations of the Radical Right, only the John Birch Society has a nationwide paid staff of organizers and public-relations men, a membership active and activated, a permanent recruiting program, a tightly controlled and generally efficient centralized direction, and a financial income which enables it to continue to expand its nationwide organizational structure," the ADL noted. "The John Birch Society—1966," *The Facts*, ADL, Feb. 1966, vol. 17, no. 1, p. 349.

35. "The John Birch Society—1966," *The Facts*, ADL, Feb. 1966, vol. 17, no. 1, p. 350.

36. Forster and Epstein (1964), pp. 2–5.

37. For a thorough summary of the charges of anti-Semitism leveled by Jewish groups, see: "The John Birch Society," *The Facts*, ADL, Nov.-Dec. 1961, vol. 14, no. 5, pp. 223–26.

38. John Roy Carlson, *Under Cover: My Four Years in the Nazi Underworld of America—The Amazing Revelation of How Axis Agents and Our Enemies Are Now Plotting to Destroy the United States* (New York: E. P. Dutton and Co., 1943).

39. Forster and Epstein (1964), p. 30.

40. Quoted in Forster and Epstein (1964), pp. 31–32.

41. "The John Birch Society," *The Facts*, ADL, Nov.-Dec. 1961, vol. 14, no. 5, p. 225.

42. Forster and Epstein (1964), p. 37.

43. Robert Welch, *The New Americanism: And Other Speeches and Essays* (Boston and Los Angeles: Western Island Publishers, 1966), pp. 153, 164.

44. Robert Welch, "Two Revolutions at Once," reprinted in *The New Americanism—And Other Speeches and Essays* (Boston and Los Angeles: Western Island Publishers, 1966), p. 203.

45. "The John Birch Society—1966," *The Facts*, ADL, Feb. 1966, vol. 17, no. 1, pp. 352–53.

46. Emphasis from the original, as quoted in "The John Birch Society—1966," *The Facts*, ADL, Feb. 1966, vol. 17, no. 1, p. 352.

47. U.S. National Advisory Commission on Civil Disorders, 1968, as cited by Howard Schuman, Charlotte Steeh, and Lawrence Bobo, *Racial Attitudes in America: Trends and Interpretations* (Cambridge, MA: Harvard University Press, 1985), p. 30.

48. Forster and Epstein (1964), p. 37.

49. For an example of this right-wing critique of Welch and the Birch Society, see: Helen M. Peters, "The Unmasking of the John Birch Society!" reprinted in the *National Chronicle*, vol. 22, no. 32, Oct. 11, 1973.

50. "Who is William P. Gale?" *Constitution News-Review* (Constitution Party, 1962), p. 12.

51. J. Harry Jones Jr., *The Minutemen* (Garden City, NY: Doubleday and Co., 1968), p. 1 (on the origins of the Minutemen, see p. 39).

52. United States Government memo to Mr. W. C. Sullivan, from [deleted], dated April 1, 1965, p. 1 (FBI, Minutemen file no. 62-107261-999). See: Lance Hill Collection—Manuscripts and Rare Brooks, Howard Tilton Memorial Library, Tulane University, New Orleans, Louisiana.

53. Jones Jr. (1968), p. 111.

54. Welch (1961), p. 64. See also: Donald Janson, "DePugh Says He Eluded FBI with Hippie Disguise," *New York Times*, July 18, 1969.

12. Flags, Tents, Skillets, and Soldiers

1. Arnold Forster and Benjamin R. Epstein, *Danger on the Right: The Attitudes, Personnel, and Influence of the Radical Right and Extreme Conservatives* (New York: Random House, 1964), pp. 8, 272–80.

2. On Klan membership see: Daniel Levitas, "Anti-Semitism and the Far Right," *Anti-Semitism in America Today: Outspoken Experts Explode the Myths*, Jerome Chanes, ed. (New York: Birch Lane Press, 1995), p. 176. Historian David Chalmers puts the number of Klan members in the mid-1920s at "more than three million," while author Wyn Craig Wade says, "From 1921 to 1924, Klan membership grew to four million." David M. Chalmers, *Hooded Americanism: The History of the Ku Klux Klan* (Durham, NC: Duke University Press, Third Edition, 1987) p. 291; and Wyn Craig Wade, *The Fiery Cross: The Ku Klux Klan in America* (New York: Simon and Schuster, 1987), p. 183. For estimates of Klan membership in the 1950s, see: Chalmers (1987), pp. 335–42, and Wade (1987), pp. 297, 302.

3. Barbara Patterson, "Defiance and Dynamite," *New South* 18 (May 1963), pp. 8–11, as cited in Chalmers (1987), pp. 349, 351, 356–65.

4. Taylor Branch, *Parting the Waters: America in the King Years, 1954–1963* (New York: Simon and Schuster, (1988), pp. 648–49. Meredith became something of an embarrassment to the civil rights movement years after his successful fight to be admitted to Ole Miss. In 1989, he worked

for North Carolina Republican senator Jesse Helms, an extreme conservative, and he backed former Klansman David Duke's bid for Louisiana governor two years later.

5. Branch (1988), p. 331–35. Barnett was later found guilty in federal court of civil contempt for his attempt to obstruct Meredith's admission.

6. "Obituary of Major General Edwin Walker," *Daily Telegraph* (London), Nov. 5, 1993, p. 25.

7. As quoted in Branch (1988), p. 656–57.

8. Max Freeman, "Negro Student Turned Back," *The Guardian* (London), Sept. 28, 1962, p. T3.

9. As quoted in Branch (1988), p. 656.

10. Branch (1988), p. 663.

11. Lerone Bennett Jr., *Before the Mayflowers—A History of Black America: The Classic Account of the Struggles and Triumphs of Black Americans* (New York: Penguin Books, 1985), p. 567. See also: Harry S. Ashmore, *Hearts and Minds: The Anatomy of Racism from Roosevelt to Reagan* (New York: McGraw-Hill, 1982), p. 286.

12. "Camelot on Tape: No Surprises in JFK Records," *Time* magazine, July 4, 1983, p. 20.

13. Branch (1988), p. 668–69.

14. "Walker Is Facing 4 Federal Counts," *New York Times*, Oct. 2, 1962, p. 1.

15. Stephan Lesher, *George Wallace: American Populist* (Reading, MA: Addison-Wesley, 1994), p. 167.

16. Wallace's speech was written by a notorious Klansmen, Asa "Ace" Carter, who had been retained by Wallace adviser John Peter Kohn, an inveterate racist. Decades later, Carter was exposed as the author, pseudonymously, of the best-selling novels *The Education of Little Tree* and *Rebel Outlaw: Josey Wales*. For more on Carter's notorious reputation and his connection to Wallace, see: Wade (1987), p. 303, and Lesher (1994), p. 174.

More than twenty years after delivering these remarks, Wallace attempted to rehabilitate himself by calling the speech "a very bad mistake," and claiming he never believed blacks were inferior (Lesher [1994], p. 161). Whether or not Wallace was motivated by white supremacy or political opportunism (or both), the governor's pledge to maintain segregation fueled the racist beliefs of countless Southern whites. And whatever his motives, they mattered little to the black citizens of Alabama who had to endure a torrent of indignity and violence that naturally flowed from the governor's segregationist stance.

17. For a detailed account of Wallace's attempt to maintain segregation at the University of Alabama, see: Lesher (1994), pp. 201–66.

18. Lesher (1994), p. 233.

19. Jack Elliott Jr., "Beckwith Lawyers Seek New Trial, Claim Justice Wasn't Swift, Memories Dim," *Memphis (Tenn.) Commercial Appeal*, Mar. 18, 1997, p. B1. Beverly Pettigrew Kraft, "Beckwith Gets Life in Evers Slaying," Gannett News Service, Feb. 5, 1994. Beverly Pettigrew Kraft, "Former Cop Provides Alibi for Beckwith in Evers Shooting," Gannett News Service, Feb. 3, 1994. Mitchell Landsberg, "Defense Opens in White Supremacist's Case; Witnesses Provide Alibi," Associated Press, Feb. 2, 1994. Beverly Pettigrew Kraft, "Evers Wife Describes Finding Body," Gannett News Service, Jan. 28, 1994. "Chronology of Events in Medger Evers Case," Associated Press, Jan. 12, 1994. Jerry Mitchell and Beverly Pettigrew Kraft, "Beckwith's Third Trial in Evers Shooting Set for January," Gannett News Service, Dec. 2, 1993. Jerry Mitchell, "Beckwith Behind Leaflets Aimed at Jurors," Gannett News Service, Aug. 12, 1993. Beverly Pettigrew Kraft, "Family Members Trying to Tone Down Beckwith," Gannett News Service, Jan. 11, 1993. Jack Elliott Jr., "Segregationist's Defense: 1963 Assassination Case Too Old for Trial," Associated Press, Oct. 15, 1992. Frank Fisher, "Beckwith Takes Stand, Says Remembers Nothing of Civil Rights Murder," Associated Press, Aug. 3, 1992. Dan George, "Beckwith

Returned to Mississippi to Stand Trial for Evers Slaying," Associated Press, Oct. 3, 1991. Jay Eubank and Beverly Pettigrew Kraft, "Civil Rights Leader's Body Exhumed for Suspect's Third Trial," Gannett News Service, June 6, 1991. Beverly Pettigrew Kraft, "Mississippi Asks Tennessee to Extradite Beckwith," Gannett News Service, Dec. 19, 1990. "Events Leading to Civil Rights Case Arrest," Associated Press, Dec. 18, 1990. Lee Howard, "Man Tried in Evers Slaying Full of Racial Venom," Gannett News Service, Dec. 17, 1990. "District Attorney Says Case of Slain NAACP Leader Won't be Retried," Associated Press, Aug. 17, 1987.

20. Forster and Epstein (1964), p. 75. Wesley McCune, "Billy James Hargis, His Christian Crusade, His Christian Echoes National Ministry, and Connections with Other Groups," *Special Reports* (Washington DC: Group Research Reports, Oct. 10, 1962), vol. 4, no. 11. Leo P. Ribuffo, *The Old Christian Right: The Protestant Far Right from the Great Depression to the Cold War* (Philadelphia, PA: Temple University Press, 1983), p. 260. Wilcox (1992), p. 9.

21. Billy James Hargis, *The Real Extremists: The Far Left* (Tulsa: Christian Crusade, 1964). "About the Author." For more on the Christian Crusade, see: Forster and Epstein (1964), pp. 68–86.

22. Quoted in Wesley McCune, "Billy James Hargis, His Christian Crusade, His Christian Echoes National Ministry, and Connections with Other Groups" (1962), vol. 4, no. 11, p. 10.

23. Forster and Epstein (1964), pp. 83–84.

24. Paul Greenberg, "Last Appearance in Little Rock for General Walker," *Harrisburg Patriot*, Nov. 12, 1993, p. A15.

13. Anglo-Saxons Triumphant

1. Reverend William P. Gale, *The Faith of Our Fathers* (Mariposa, CA: Ministry of Christ Church, 1963), p. 6.

2. Ibid., pp. 8, 12.

3. Ibid., p. 12.

4. Ibid., pp. 5–7, 9, 13.

5. From Swift's sermon, "God, Man, Nations and the Races," delivered Jan. 27, 1963, in Hollywood, California. Dr. Wesley A. Swift, *God, Man, Nations and the Races* (Lancaster, CA: Church of Jesus Christ Christian, 1963), p. 27. Collection of the Freedom Center, California State College at Fullerton.

6. Gale (1963), p. 19.

7. Ibid., p. 24

8. Ibid., p. 25

9. Ibid., p. 17.

10. Ibid., p. 35.

11. Ibid., p. 27. On the question of the number of tribes of the ancient Israelites, Gale maintains that following their exodus from Egypt, the original twelve tribes increased to thirteen, "because Joseph had given his birthright to his two sons Ephraim and Manassah, splitting the twelfth tribe into two parts." See: Gale (1963), p. 22.

12. Ibid., pp. 29, 31.

13. Ibid., p. 27.

14. Ibid., p. 30.

15. Gale (1963), p. 33. For a classic summary of this argument from an anti-Semite's point of view, see: *Aspects of Jewish Power in the United States—Volume IV of The International Jew—The*

World's Foremost Problem: A Fourth Selection of Articles from the Dearborn Independent (Dearborn, MI: Dearborn Publishing Co., May 1922), pp. 121–31.

16. Gale (1963), p. 40. In Gale's mind, Lincoln was a hero because he had attempted to issue interest-free money and had made plans to ship blacks back to Africa. The president's assassination also was a Jewish plot according to Gale.

17. Elbert O. Kelsey, "Money Made Mysterious, Part V—The Civil War Bankers. For North: Rothschilds' August Belmont and Company. For South: Rothschilds' Erlanger and Company," *American Mercury*, vol. 87, no. 417, Oct. 1958, pp. 89, 92.

18. "The American Mercury and Russell Maguire," *The Facts* ADL, Oct.-Nov. 1959, vol. 13, no. 7, pp. 143–46. H. L. Mencken, *Microsoft Encarta Encyclopedia, 1993–1996. American Mercury*, Fall 1975, volume 111, no. 518.

19. Gale (1963), p. 32 (emphasis from the original).

20. Ibid., pp. 41–42.

21. Criticism of the Federal Reserve is not limited to conservatives, of course. Liberals like author William Greider also have castigated the Fed for what they see as the fundamentally undemocratic way that the Fed manages the nation's economy in favor of banking and corporate interests at the expense of workers and the middle class. See: William Greider, *Secrets of the Temple: How the Federal Reserve Runs the Country* (New York: Simon and Schuster, 1987). For additional liberal critiques of the Fed, see: "Money Out of Control," *Monthly Review*, vol. 36, no. 7, Dec. 1984, pp. 1–12; "Controlling the Fed: Who Holds the Purse Strings?" *Progressive Agenda: A Bi-Monthly Newsletter from the Center for Democratic Alternatives*, no.9, Feb. 1988, pp. 1, 5–9.

22. Gale (1963), pp. 37, 44, 45. For more variations on these themes, see: Eustace Mullins, *Secrets of the Federal Reserve* (Staunton, VA: Bankers Research Institute, 1983); Rev. Charles E. Coughlin, *Money! Questions and Answers* (Royal Oak, MI: The National Union for Social Justice, 1936); Charles S. Norburn, MD., *Honest Money: The United States Note* (Asheville, NC: New Puritan Library, 1983); M.J. Beckman, *Born Again Republic* (Billings, MT: Freedom Church Bookstore, 1981); Paul Stevens and E. O. Kelsey, "Money Made Mysterious," *American Mercury*, vol. 87, nos. 417 and 418, pp. 65–95 and pp. 99–140, respectively.

23. J. J. Goldberg, *Jewish Power: Inside the American Jewish Establishment* (Reading, MA: Addison-Wesley, 1996), pp. 101–4.

24. Leo Frank was the manager of a pencil factory in Atlanta, Georgia, when one of his employees, thirteen-year-old Mary Phagan, was found raped and murdered in the factory basement on April 27, 1913. Although the evidence against him was biased and inconclusive, Frank was convicted of the crime. (Eighty-one years later, on March 11, 1986, Frank was posthumously pardoned by Georgia governor Joe Frank Harris in response to a campaign by a coalition of Jewish groups.)

  After Georgia governor John M. Slaton commuted Frank's death sentence in 1915, Thomas E. Watson, the former congressman and onetime agrarian populist, denounced Frank as a "filthy perverted Jew of New York," and called on Georgians to avenge the death of Phagan, a "working-class Gentile" and "a daughter of the people, of the common clay, of the blouse and the overall . . ." (Wyn Craig Wade, *The Fiery Cross: The Ku Klux Klan in America* [New York: Simon and Schuster, 1987], pp. 144–45.) Frank was abducted from a prison farm on August 16, 1915, and lynched by a mob calling themselves "the Knights of Mary Phagan." For a definitive history on the Frank case, see: Leonard Dinnerstein, *The Leo Frank Case* (New York: Columbia University Press, 1968).

  Just two months after Frank's murder, on October 26, Colonel William Joseph "Doc" Simmons, a former circuit-riding Methodist minister, took note of the widespread support for Frank's lynching when he recruited members of the Knights of Mary Phagan to sign the first charter of the revived Ku Klux Klan. Then, on Thanksgiving evening, Simmons orchestrated a nighttime cross-burning atop Georgia's famous Stone Mountain. Two weeks later, on December 6, 1915, he ordered members of his hooded order to ride on horseback and fire their rifles in the air outside the Atlanta Theater on Peachtree Street where D. W. Griffith's *Birth of a Nation* was making its premiere. Thus the second-era Ku Klux Klan was born.

25. Gale (1963), p. 51.

26. Ibid., p. 54.

27. "How Old Is Anglo-Saxon Truth?" *The Anglo-Saxon World*, p. 39, undated. For more on British "Early Myths of Origin," and Sadler, see: Leon Poliakov, *The Aryan Myth: A History of Racist and Nationalist Ideas in Europe* (New York: Basic Books, 1971), pp. 37–53.

28. According to Rabbi Arthur Hertzberg, Mather wrote his book in "biblical, mythic accents," arguing that the early Puritans had left Europe "not simply to escape persecution. They had come on a messianic journey to bring about the Second Coming of Christ." See: Arthur Hertzberg, *The Jews in America* (New York: Simon and Schuster, 1989), p. 40.

29. Ralph Lord Roy, *Apostles of Discord: A Study of Organized Bigotry and Disruption on the Fringes of Protestanism* (Boston, MA: The Beacon Press, 1953), pp. 92–93. See also: Michael Barkun, *Religion and the Racist Right: The Origins of the Christian Identity Movement* (Chapel Hill, NC: University of North Carolina Press, 1994), p. 6.

30. C. F. Parker, B.A. "A Short History of the Modern Israel-Identity Movement: 1. Early Traces of the Teaching," *The National Message*, Feb. 14, 1948, p. 57.

31. As quoted in Poliakov (1971), pp. 175–77. Hume's 1754 essay was the second edition of this work, which was first published twelve years earlier, in 1742. For more on the Enlightenment roots of twentieth-century racism, see: *Race and the Enlightenment*, Emmanuel Chukwudi Eze, ed. (Oxford, England: Blackwell Publishers, 1997).

32. Opinion cited in Reginald Horsman, *Race and Manifest Destiny: The Origins of American Racial Anglo-Saxonism* (Cambridge, MA: Harvard Business School, 1981), p. 101.

33. Jefferson changed his outlook about black inferiority twenty years after he wrote *Notes on the State of Virginia*, when a French priest and political dissident, Henri Gregoire, sent him a copy of *Literature of Negroes*.

34. Horsman (1981), pp. 54–61, 121–22, 142–46. Stephen Jay Gould, *The Mismeasure of Man* (New York: W. W. Norton and Company, 1981).

35. Raphael Patai and Jennifer P. Wing, *The Myth of the Jewish Race* (New York: Charles Scribner's Sons, 1975), pp. 9, 21–25. Explicitly racial theories about the Jews predate Lassen's thesis, of course. For another perspective on Lassen's contribution to the science of racial typology, see: Poliakov (1971), pp. 196–97.

36. Quoted in Patai and Wing (1975), pp. 9–10.

37. As quoted in Daniel Jonah Goldhagen, *Hitler's Willing Executioners: Ordinary Germans and the Holocaust* (New York: Random House, First Vintage Books Edition, 1997), p. 398. Michael D. Biddis, *Father of Racist Ideology: The Social and Political Thought of Count Gobineau* (New York: Weybright and Talley, 1970), p. 108.

38. Gobineau published his ideas in six books spread out over four volumes from 1853 to 1855. For more on Gobineau and the intellectual roots of European racist thought, see: Patai and Wing (1975), pp. 273–74; *Gobineau: Selected Political Writings*, Michael D. Biddis, ed. (New York: Harper and Row, 1970); Michael D. Biddis, *Father of Racist Ideology: The Social and Political Thought of Count Gobineau* (New York: Weybright and Talley, 1970); and Poliakov (1971), pp. 215–54.

39. Poliakov (1971), p. 212.

40. Poliakov (1971), pp. 313–14; Biddis, *Father of Racist Ideology* (1970), pp. 257–59.

41. Poliakov (1971), p. 319. For more on Shaw's affinity for eugenics, see: Daniel J. Kevles, *In the Name of Eugenics: Genetics and the Uses of Human Heredity* (New York: Alfred A. Knopf, 1985), pp. 21, 57, 63, 86.

42. For more on Stoddard and his affiliation with the Klan, which he denied, see: David M. Chalmers, *Hooded Americanism: The History of the Ku Klux Klan* (Durham, NC: Duke University Press, Third Edition, 1987), p. 270.

43. Lothrop Stoddard, "The Pedigree of Judah," *The Forum*, March 1926, vol. 75, no. 3; undated reprint published by *The Thunderbolt, Inc.*, of Marietta, Georgia, including "A Gallery of Jewish Types: Portrait Drawings by Lionel Reiss." See also: Kevles (1985), note 23, p. 320.

44. For a detailed history of the early eugenics movement, including the widespread popularity of its ideas, see Kevles (1985); also Barry Mehler, *A History of the American Eugenics Society, 1921–1940*, unpublished Ph.D. dissertation, University of Illinois at Urbana-Champaign, 1987.

45. Gould (1981), pp. 42–69.

46. Ibid., pp. 73–107.

47. Richard J. Hernstein and Charles Murray, *The Bell Curve: Intelligence and Class Structure in American Life* (New York: Simon and Schuster, 1994). Critics of *The Bell Curve* are legion. For one of the most thorough compendiums of scholarly (and other) articles critiquing the work of Hernstein and Murray, see: *Anti-Murrayiana* (Washington, DC: Poverty and Race Research Action Council, 1996).

48. As quoted in Kevles (1985), p. 85. For other examples of Roosevelt's affinity for eugenics, see pp. 74, 94. See also: David H. Bennett, *The Party of Fear: The American Far Right from Nativism to the Militia Movement* (New York: Vintage Books, Random House, 1995), pp. 283–84.

49. As quoted in Poliakov (1971) pp. 319–20.

50. In addition to his post as chairman of the Zoological Society, Grant was a trustee of the American Museum of Natural History and a councilor of the American Geographical Society. Madison Grant, *The Passing of the Great Race, or: The Racial Basis of European History* (New York: Charles Scribner's Sons, 1916), p. 16.

51. Membership in the fraternal order of British stonemasons was originally limited to those who practiced the craft, but over time non-masons were attracted by its secret signs and passwords, its ideals of brotherhood, and its knowledge of mathematics and Greek geometers. Non-masons were first admitted as honorary members in the early 1600s, but eventually they came to outnumber actual masons. In 1717, modern Freemasonry was born and the earliest constitution of Masonry was adopted in London in 1723. Women were barred from joining, as were men who were not "freeborn," or those classified as "immoral or scandalous." But because its constitution was nonsectarian (it obliged masons only to believe in "that Religion in which all Men agree"), Jews were not automatically denied membership. The first Jew joined a London lodge in 1732, and by 1793 a Jewish lodge—the Lodge of Israel—had been established. The movement was not immune to anti-Jewish bigotry, however, and Jews were excluded from many lodges. For more on the origins of Masonry, see: Jacob Katz, *Jews and Freemasons in Europe, 1723–1939* (Cambridge, MA: Harvard University Press, 1970); Norman Cohn, *Warrant for Genocide: The Myth of the Jewish World-Conspiracy and the Protocols of the Elders of Zion* (New York: Harper and Row, 1966), p. 26.

52. Cohn (1966), p. 26.

53. Ephraim Radner, "New World Order, Old-World anti-Semitism," *The Christian Century*, Sept. 13–20, 1995, p. 846.

54. George Johnson, *Architects of Fear: Conspiracy Theories and Paranoia in American Politics* (Los Angeles: Jeremy P. Tarcher, Inc., 1983), pp. 47–49.

55. John Robison, *Proofs of a Conspiracy Against All the Religions and Governments of Europe, Carried On in the Secret Meetings of Freemasons, Illuminati, and Reading Societies (Collected from*

Good Authorities) (New York: George Forman, no. 64, 1798; reprint by Western Islands Publishing Company, Belmont, MA, 1967).

56. Quoted in Gerald B. Winrod, *Adam Weishaupt: A Human Devil*, (Boring, OR: CPA Book Publisher, 1996, facsimile reprint), pp. 31–32.

57. There is some dispute as to the actual date Barruel's work was published. Norman Cohn says it first appeared in 1797, shortly after Robison's work. Cohn (1966), p. 25.

58. Cohn (1966), p. 26.

59. Johnson (1983), pp. 51–67.

60. Richard Hofstadter, *The Paranoid Style in American Politics* (New York: Alfred A. Knopf, 1965). Bennett (1995), p. 49.

61. As quoted in Cohn (1966), p. 30.

62. In *Warrant for Genocide*, Cohn notes that the famous historian of anti-Semitism, M. Leon Poliakov, in a private communication to him, "argued convincingly that [the Simonini letter] was fabricated by the French political police under Joseph Fouché with the object of influencing Napoleon against the Jews at the time of 'the Great Sanhedrin.' " See: Cohn (1966), footnote 1, p. 27.

63. Cohn (1966), pp. 22–23.

64. Cohn, (1966), p. 30.

65. The book was written by the German novelist Herman Goedsche, under the pseudonym Sir John Retcliffe. Cohn (1966), pp. 34–35.

66. "For eighteen centuries Israel has been at war with that power which was first promised to Abraham but which was taken from him by the Cross," proclaims *The Rabbi's Speech*, the final literary incarnation of *Biarritz*. Translated by Norman Cohn and reprinted in Appendix 1 of *Warrant for Genocide*, p. 269.

A spate of other works emphasized the same theme. Among the most prominent were: *World Conquest of the Jews*, by Osman-Bey, which was in its seventh edition by 1875; *Le juif: le judaïsme et la judaïsation des peuples chrétiens*, the "Bible of modern anti-Semitism," by Gougenot des Mouseaux, which was published shortly after *Biarritz*; *La France juive*, written by Edouard Drumont in 1886, which greatly popularized the Judeo-Masonic conspiracy myth in France; and *Jewish Fraternities, Local and Universal*, written in 1868 in Russia by Jacob Brafmann, a Jew and a spy for the Russian police, whose writings were often distributed at government expense. See also: Cohn (1966), pp. 41, 51, 54, 57–59.

14. The Ministry of Christ Church

1. Roxanne Gale, interview by the author.

2. John Snell, "FBI Probes Church with Racist Beliefs," *The (Portland) Oregonian*, undated newspaper clipping. Memo of Roy H. Millenson to Milton Ellerin, AJC Archives, May 25, 1964.

3. California Secretary of State documents, corporation no. 479657. See also: letter to Charles Antis of the Ministry of Christ Church, from James T. Philbin, associate tax counsel, California Franchise Tax Board, Oct. 15, 1964.

4. "California Rangers," *Paramilitary Organizations in California* (Sacramento, CA: Calif. DOJ, 1965), p. CR-5.

5. "Notice," *IDENTITY* (circa March 1967), vol. 2, no. 5.

6. Certificate of Death for Mary Agnes Gale, State of California, Department of Public Health, Local Registration District 7053, certificate no. 5383.

7. Roxanne Gale, interview.

8. "Miscegination [sic]," IDENTITY (Nov. 1965), vol. 1, no. 1.

9. "Marxism in Christmas Cards," IDENTITY (Dec. 1965), vol. 1, no. 2, pp. 8–10.

10. "Education," IDENTITY (Dec. 1966) vol. 2, no. 4, p. 13.

11. Tom Hawk, "The D'Andrea Case," IDENTITY (circa March 1966), vol. 2, no. 1, p. 5.

12. Howard Schuman, Charlotte Steeh, and Lawrence Bobo, Racial Attitudes in America: Trends and Interpretations (Cambridge, MA: Harvard University Press, 1985), pp. 87–95.

13. "Education," IDENTITY (Dec. 1966), p. 13.

14. IDENTITY (Sept. 1966), vol. 2, no. 3., p. 11.

15. IDENTITY (Dec. 1966), vol. 2, no. 4, p. 10.

16. IDENTITY (Dec. 1966), vol. 2, no. 4, pp. 10–11.

15. The Conjurer's Circle

1. Tom Hawk, "The Graduated Income Tax," IDENTITY (Aug. 1967) vol. 2, no. 6., p. 4. William P. Gale, aka Colonel Ben Cameron, "The Enemy Within," IDENTITY (circa Fall 1969), vol. 5, no. 1, p. 6. "Tax Rebellion," IDENTITY (circa Feb. 1971) vol. 5, no. 5, p. 20.

2. Porth was convicted in 1967, but his troubles began in 1962, after he submitted a blank tax return to the IRS, citing his Fifth Amendment rights against self-incrimination. In a letter to Kansas revenue authorities, Porth asserted: "Our whole money system and tax structure is a fraud. I cannot aid and abet such unconstitutional behavior." Correspondence of A. J. Porth to Graydon D. Luthey, Department of Revenue, Topeka, Kansas, May 27, 1962, from Why I Do Not Pay Income Tax: Federal or State, by A. J. Porth (self-published and undated booklet).

3. Correspondence of William P. Gale to Hon. George Templar, Judge, U.S. District Court, Topeka, Kansas, Dec. 10, 1970, Spencer Library Kansas Collection, University of Kansas, Lawrence. Correspondence of William P. Gale to Judge Templar, Nov. 16, 1970, as reprinted in the National Chronicle, vol. 19, no. 45, Nov. 26, 1970.

4. Transcript of tape-recording of remarks of A. J. Porth and Jerome Daly, 1969, distributed by Laymen Education Guild at Law, Pinckney, Michigan.

5. Martin A. Larson, Tax Revolt, U.S.A.! Why and How Thousands of Patriotic Americans Refuse to Pay the Income Tax (Washington, DC: Liberty Lobby, 1973), pp. 34–41. Porth, Why I Do Not Pay Income Tax.

6. Transcript of tape-recording of remarks of A. J. Porth and Jerome Daly, 1969.

7. Unsigned editorial, "The Fifth vs. the Revenuers," Wichita (Kans.) Evening Eagle and Beacon, March 26, 1962, p. 46.

8. Constitutional Basis Protests, fact sheet 78–3, Internal Revenue Service, Public Affairs Division, Washington, D.C., April 1978. See also: United States v. Porth, 426 F.2d 519 (10th Cir.), cert. denied, 400 U.S. 824 (1970) and United States v. Daly, 481 F.2d 28 (8th Cir.), cert. denied, 414 U.S. 1064 (1973).

9. From 1931 to 1964, thirty-two state legislatures adopted measures supporting a limit on the percentage of income the government could collect, usually around 25 percent. Forster and Epstein (1964), p. 164. For a discussion of the role of property taxes in the taxpayer revolts of the 1930s, see: David Timothy Beito, Striking Against the State: Taxpayer Revolts During the American Great Depression, 1930–1935, unpublished Ph.D. dissertation, University of Wisconsin–Madison, 1986.

10. Arnold Forster and Benjamin Epstein, *Danger on the Right: The Attitudes, Personnel, and Influence of the Radical Right and Extreme Conservatives* (New York: Random House, 1964), p. 170.

11. Correspondence from A. J. Porth to Graydon D. Luthey, Department of Revenue, Topeka, Kansas, May 27, 1962.

12. Porth, "Official Warrant of Arrest," *Why I Do Not Pay Income Tax*.

13. Correspondence of A. J. Porth to Mr. Bertrand M. Harding, Acting Commissioner, U.S. Treasury Dept., May 18, 1964, p. 3. Porth, *Why I Do Not Pay Income Tax*.

14. Correspondence of A. J. Porth to Mr. J. Marvin Kelley, Regional Counsel, IRS, Dec. 23, 1964. Porth, *Why I Do Not Pay Income Tax*.

15. Larson (1973), p. 38.

16. Transcript of tape-recording of remarks of A. J. Porth and Jerome Daly, 1969.

17. Larson (1973), p. 39.

18. Transcript of tape-recording of remarks of A. J. Porth and Jerome Daly, 1969.

19. Opinion cited by Joseph P. Rocco in "The Tax Protest Cases: A Policy Approach to Individual Constitutional Rights," *California Western Law Review*, vol. 19, no. 2, 1983, p. 355.

20. Twenty thousand eight hundred illegal returns were received in 1980. See: *Illegal Tax Protestors. Reference Guide for Public Affairs Officers*, Dept. of the Treasury, Internal Revenue Service, Washington, D.C. (undated). See also: *Constitutional Basis Protests*, Internal Revenue Service, Public Affairs Division, fact sheet 78-3, April 1978. For data on the number of illegal tax protesters, see: Summary statement of William J. Anderson, Director, General Government Division, United States General Accounting Office, before the Subcommittee on Commerce, Consumer and Monetary Affairs, House Committee on Government Operations on the Internal Revenue Service's Efforts Against Illegal Tax Protestors, June 10, 1981, p. 2. See: "Illegal Tax Protestors Threaten Tax System," *Report by the Comptroller General of the United States*, July 8, 1981.

21. Transcript of tape-recording of remarks of A. J. Porth and Jerome Daly, 1969.

22. Transcript of tape-recording of remarks of A. J. Porth and Jerome Daly, 1969.

23. As cited by Larson (1973), p. 96.

24. Scott founded his group in 1968. He made the Los Angeles speech in February 1972. After encouraging scores of taxpayers not to cooperate with the IRS, and repeatedly goading the government to prosecute him, Scott was convicted for failure to file. Larson (1973), pp. 42–45. Martin A. Larson, *The Continuing Tax Rebellion: What Millions of Americans Are Doing to Restore Constitutional Government* (Old Greenwich, CT: The Devin-Adair Company, 1979), pp. 148–49, 151–52.

25. John Steinbacher, "IRS Gestapo Attacks Patriots," *American Mercury*, Fall 1972, vol. 108, no. 506, pp. 9–10. "Justice for San Diego Ten Banquet," *Tax Strike News*, July 1972, p. 9. Larson (1979), pp. 64–67.

26. "Justice for San Diego Ten Banquet," *Tax Strike News*, July 1972, p. 9.

27. According to the statement of ownership, management, and circulation of January 1964 for the *American Mercury*, 26,927 individuals received the publication by mail subscription on average during the preceding twelve months. By fall 1972, the average number of paid subscriptions during the preceding twelve months was 9,103.

28. "The Great Tax Strike," *American Mercury*, Summer 1972, vol. 108, no. 505, p. 3.

29. Martin A. Larson, Ph.D., "Robert Welch and the Tax Rebellion," *American Mercury*, Fall 1974, vol. 110, no. 514, pp. 5, 6, 11. "Revolution of the Right," *American Mercury*, Spring 1973, vol. 109. no. 508, pp. 3–4.

30. Howard Schuman, Charlotte Steeh, and Lawrence Bobo, *Racial Attitudes in America: Trends and Interpretations* (Cambridge, MA: Harvard University Press, 1985), pp. 87–95.

31. Larson (1973), p. ix.

32. Martin A. Larson, Ph.D., "The Crisis of Race and Culture," *American Mercury*, Fall 1967, vol. 103, no. 486, pp. 7, 11.

33. Ibid.

34. Larson (1979), p. xi.

35. Donald I. Warren, *The Radical Center: Middle Americans and the Politics of Alienation* (Notre Dame, IN: University of Notre Dame Press, 1976).

36. Ibid., pp. 20–21.

37. "The Great Tax Strike," *American Mercury*, Summer 1972, vol. 108, no. 505, p. 3.

38. Larson (1979), pp. ix–x.

39. Despite the backlash against affirmative action, the most overt forms of anti-black racism still continued to fall into disrepute. For example, in 1978 the Mormon Church rescinded its 148-year prohibition on the ordination of black men. Gorton Carruth, *The Encyclopedia of American Facts and Dates* (New York: HarperCollins, 1993, Ninth Edition), pp. 733–34.

40. "The Great Tax Strike," *American Mercury*, Summer 1972, vol. 108, no. 505, pp. 3–4.

41. Mark Sullivan, "Tax Rebel Irwin Schiff Back in Court," Associated Press, May 27, 1980.

42. "Putting the Heat on Tax Protestors," *Time*, April 2, 1984, p. 84. David Cay Johnson, "The Anti-Tax Man Cometh: A Protester Calls Form 1040 a Hoax and Finds a Following," *New York Times*, July 5, 1985, pp. C1–6.

43. Steve Marshall, "Tax Protester Puts Pen to Paper in Pen," *USA Today*, March 13, 1990, p. 2A.

44. Larson (1979), pp. ix–x.

45. W. Vaughn Ellsworth, "Patriots Plan Pressure to Demand Release of Marvin Cooley, Popular Political Prisoner," *Tax Strike News*, vol. 6, no. 3, March 1975, p. 1.

46. Larson (1979), p. 59.

47. Ellsworth, "Patriots Plan Pressure to Demand Release of Marvin Cooley, Popular Political Prisoner" (March 1975).

48. W. Vaughn Ellsworth, "Delinquent Tax-Sale Foiled by Citizen's Arrest," *National Chronicle*, vol. 21, no. 5, March 2, 1972.

49. Ibid. After being convicted in 1973 of failure to file proper tax returns, Cooley was sentenced to prison. Beginning in 1975, he served two years of a three-year sentence, and hundreds of supporters threw a huge party in his honor when he was released in 1977. Unlike other protestors, however, Cooley quickly resumed his activities. A decade later, in 1989, this earned him another two-year sentence for tax evasion. Larson (1979), pp. 57–64. Kevin Flynn and Gary Gerhardt, *The Silent Brotherhood* (New York: Penguin Books, 1995), pp. 463.

50. Flynn and Gerhardt (1995), pp. 43, 52, 55–56.

51. United Press International, Domestic News, Dec. 12, 1984. For a definitive account of the life of Robert Matthews and his activities, see: Flynn and Gerhardt (1995).

52. As quoted by James Ridgeway, *Blood in the Face: The Ku Klux Klan, Aryan Nations, Nazi Skinheads, and the Rise of a New White Culture* (New York: Thunder's Mouth Press, 1990), p. 96.

53. Ardie McBrearty, "An Open Letter to Robert Welch: A Member of the John Birch Society Contradicts His Leader," *American Mercury*, Fall 1972, vol. 108, no. 506, pp. 18–19.

54. "Greetings from 'Big Brother,' " *Tax Strike News*, July 1972, p. 11. Inaugurated by Congress with passage of "The Intergovernmental Cooperation Act of 1968," regionalism was established in 1972 by President Richard Nixon when he signed an executive order creating ten Federal Regional Councils. The federal government's move towards "regionalism" was motivated by a desire to promote greater cooperation among different branches of government and to improve the administration of grants to the states. Public Law 90–577, 90th Congress, S. 698, Oct. 16, 1968. Presidential executive order no. 11647, Feb. 12, 1972. For more examples of right-wing attacks on regionalism, see: "Regional Governance Conspiracy," *Bulletin*, Committee to Restore the Constitution (Fort Collins, CO: 1973), July 1973. "Move to Blank Out the Constitution!" *National Chronicle*, vol. 21, no. 8, March 23, 1972, p. 1.

55. Flynn and Gerhardt (1995), pp. 323–24.

16. Volunteer Christian Posses

1. Colonel Ben Cameron (William P. Gale), "The Constitutional Republic," *IDENTITY* (circa June 1971), vol. 6, no. 1, p. 16.

2. Gale often claimed that he wrote his Posse "Guide" in 1969, but his first text calling for creation of county posses did not appear until 1971. Colonel Ben Cameron (William P. Gale), "The Constitutional Republic" *IDENTITY* (circa June 1971). William P. Gale, "Guide for Volunteer Christian Posses," *IDENTITY* (circa Sept. 1971).

3. William P. Gale, "Guide for Volunteer Christian Posses" (circa Sept. 1971), p. 1.

4. Ibid., p. 11.

5. Ibid., p. 4.

6. Ibid., p. 10.

7. William P. Gale, "United States Christian Posse Association," *IDENTITY* (circa June/July 1972), vol. 6 no. 4.

8. Ibid., p. 13.

9. "Dr. Swift Called," *National Chronicle*, vol. 19, no. 39, Oct. 15, 1970, p. 1. "Rites Set for Minister Dr. Wesley A. Swift, 57," *Los Angeles Times*, Oct. 12, 1970. Michael Barkun, *Religion and the Racist Right: The Origins of the Christian Identity Movement*, (Chapel Hill, NC: University of North Carolina Press, 1994), p. 68.

10. William P. Gale, "A Reply to the National Chronicle" *IDENTITY* (Nov. 1975), vol. 8, no. 1.

11. Ibid., (1975).

12. Journalists Kevin Flynn and Gary Gerhardt put the date of Butler's arrival in Idaho at 1974, while Michael Barkun says it was 1973. Kevin Flynn and Gary Gerhardt, *The Silent Brotherhood* (New York: Penguin Books, 1995), pp. 64, 72–75; Barkun (1994), p. 70. Swift established his congregation around 1945 and formally incorporated it in 1948 in California, under the name Anglo-Saxon Christian Congregations. Eight years later, in 1956, he changed the name to Church of Jesus Christ, Christian. It was this latter congregation that Richard Butler took over after Swift's death, until he changed the name again, giving it the official title Church of Jesus Christ Christian, Aryan Nations. Butler was not the first emissary of the Church of Jesus Christ, Christian, to arrive in Idaho. More than a decade before Butler had transplanted what was left of Swift's congregation there a Reverend R. L. Wendler of Boise had registered with the Idaho Department of State as the congregation's official representative. To what extent this earlier foray by Swift into Idaho had figured in Butler's decision to relocate there is not known, but it may have played a role. Certificate of Qualification of Foreign Corporation, "Church of Jesus Christ, Christian," State of Idaho, Dec. 23, 1963.

13. "Elder Statesman: A Life of Hate and the Future in the Balance," *Intelligence Report* (Montgomery, AL: Southern Poverty Law Center), Summer 1998, p. 24. According to journalists Flynn and Gerhardt, Butler formally designated the compound the home of the Aryan Nations in June 1978. Flynn and Gerhardt (1995), p. 76.

14. Cheri Seymour, *The Committee of the States: Inside the Radical Right* (Mariposa, CA: Camden Place Communications, Inc., 1991), pp. 81–82. William P. Gale, "A Reply to the National Chronicle" (1975). Exactly when Gale recruited Butler to Identity and introduced him to Swift is difficult to say, but it was likely in 1962. In a letter to a supporter written in 1986, Butler says he "had the good fortune and honor" to meet Swift "in 1961 or '62." See: Correspondence of Richard G. Butler to Jack Rader, May 15, 1986, author's files. Flynn and Gerhardt (1995), pp. 68–69.

15. DePugh spent four of his eleven-year sentence in prison, during which time the organization was inactive. "DePugh of Minutemen Paroled," *New York Times*, May 1, 1973.

16. Transcript of tape-recorded remarks of George Kindred, panelist, "Solution: The County Posse," presented at the Liberty Lobby Bi-Centennial Celebration, July 2, 3, 4, 1976, in Washington, D.C.

17. Robert B. DePugh, "The Minutemen Speak! A Message from the Underground," *The Patriot*, May 1968, p. 3. "Survive!" *The Patriot*, Oct. 1968, vol. 2, no. 1. James W. Freed, "Spitfire," *The Patriot*, Oct. 1968, vol. 2, no. 1. James W. Freed, "Spitfire: Second Installment," *The Patriot*, Nov./Dec. 1968, vol. 2, no. 2.

18. "The Michigan Story," *IDENTITY*, March 1973, vol. 7, no. 1, pp. 3–4; and June 1973, vol. 7, no. 2, pp. 1, 3.

19. Ibid. "Michigan Story," *National Chronicle*, May 3, 1973, vol. 22, no. 14, pp. 1, 3. Transcript of tape-recorded remarks of George Kindred (1976).

20. "The Posse Comitatus," *Tax Strike News*, Nov. 1972, pp. 16–17.

21. "Posse Comitatus," *National Chronicle*, Sept. 23, 1971, vol. 20, no. 35, pp. 1, 3.

17. The Posse *Blue Book*

1. According to Gale and other Identity believers, the origins of all the "white, Christian" European nations, as well as America, could be traced to a corresponding tribe of Israel. Denmark was populated by the descendants of the tribe of Dan, Germany by the tribe of Judah, the descendants of Ephraim populated England, et cetera. According to conventional Bible scholars, however, the tribe of Manasseh settled in land east of the Jordan river. Colonel Ben Cameron (William P. Gale), "Dilemma of the Republic," *IDENTITY*, March 1970, vol. 5, no. 3. William H. Gentz, ed., *The Dictionary of Bible and Religion* (Nashville, TN: Abingdon Press, 1986), p. 1064.

2. *IDENTITY*, vol. 10, no. 1 (circa Nov.-Dec. 1977).

3. William P. Gale, "A Message for 1973," tape-recorded sermon no. 73001b (Ministry of Christ Church, Mariposa, California).

4. "Tape Ministry," *IDENTITY* (circa Feb. 1972), vol. 6, no. 4 p. 18.

5. In a further nod to the tax-protest movement, Beach extended the advice given by Gale in his *Guide for Volunteer Christian Posses*, that people interested in more information should contact Minnesota tax protester Jerome Daly. "Sheriff's Posse Comitatus" (Portland, OR: Citizens Law Enforcement and Research Committee), p. 10.

6. Following are the most pertinent articles and newsletters published by Gale which discuss the Posse Comitatus that were plagiarized by Mike Beach: Colonel Ben Cameron (William P. Gale), "The Constitutional Republic" (circa June 1971). William P. Gale, "Guide for Christian Posses" (circa Sept. 1971). William P. Gale, "Guide for Christian Posse Comitatus," *IDENTITY*

(circa April–May 1972), vol. 6, no. 3, pp. 10–12. William P. Gale, "United States Christian Posse Association" (circa June–July 1972), vol. 6, no. 4.

7. "Sheriff's Posse Comitatus" (Portland, OR: Citizens Law Enforcement and Research Committee), p. 15.

8. Ibid.

9. "Application for Charter, United States Christian Posse Association," for Josephine County, Oregon, vol. 24, pp. 865–66, recorded July 26, 1974.

10. Undated letter of H. L. Beach, Spencer Library Kansas Collection, University of Kansas, RH, WL, Eph, 1215.

11. "Price List: Sheriff's Posse Comitatus," Citizens Law Enforcement and Research Committee, Spencer Library, Kansas Collection, University of Kansas, RH, WL, Eph, 1215.

12. "Dear Patriot" letter (circa 1974). Correspondence of H. L. Beach, Spencer Library Kansas Collection, Ephemera.

13. Lane County, Oregon, Posse Charter, Oct. 19, 1973; filed Nov. 2, 1973.

14. Doug Bates, "The Posse Rides," *Eugene (Ore.) Register-Guard*, Feb. 22, 1976, pp. 1D, 3D.

15. Lane County, Oregon, Posse Charter, Oct. 19, 1973; filed Nov. 2, 1973.

16. Margaret Bentson, "Posse Comitatus Will Seek Out Constitution Violaters," *(Eugene, Ore.) Valley News*, Nov. 7, 1973; reprinted in *Armed Citizen News* (National Association to Keep and Bear Arms, Feb. 1974), no. 72, p. 2. "Sheriff's Posse Comitatus: Extremist Matter," FBI, Portland, Oregon, June 6, 1974, p. 9.

17. Dean Kennedy, "The Need is Now: An Alternative to Compromise—Posse Comitatus," *Armed Citizen News* (Dec. 1973). "Sheriff's Posse Comitatus: Extremist Matter," FBI, Portland, Oregon, June 6, 1974, p. 11.

18. "People's Posse," *Washington Observer* (Torrance, CA.), Feb. 15, 1974.

19. Undated, unsigned correspondence to David Burks.

20. Ibid.

21. Kennedy, "The Need Is Now: An Alternative to Compromise—Posse Comitatus" (Dec. 1973).

22. Dave Tutwiler, "NAKBA to Support Posse Comitatus Nationwide!" *Armed Citizen News* (Jan. 1974), no. 71, p. 1. "Sheriff's Posse Comitatus: Extremist Matter," FBI, Portland, Oregon, June 6, 1974, p. 16.

23. "NAKBA's Speaker's Bureau," *Armed Citizen News* (Aug. 1972), no. 54, p. 4.

24. Audiotape sermon of William P. Gale, "The Committee of the States" (Mariposa, CA: The Ministry of Christ Church, Sept. 6, 1982).

25. Roxanne Gale, interview by the author.

26. Transcript of tape-recorded remarks of George Kindred, panelist, "Solution: The County Posse," presented at the Liberty Lobby Bi-Centennial Celebration, July 2, 3, 4, 1976, in Washington, D.C.

27. "Problems of the Posse Comitatus," *National Chronicle*, Jan. 8, 1976, vol. 25, no. 1, p. 4.

28. Beach was born on June 17, 1903, in Mitchell, Nebraska. See: Questionnaire, Headquarters Western Defense Command and Fourth Army, Individual Exclusion Hearing Board, Presidio of San Francisco, Feb. 3, 1943. National Archives, Suitland Reference Branch, box no. 5, location 6/37/48/1, files of the Western Defense Command, Civil Affairs Division, Individual

Exclusion Board, Non-Japanese Exclusion Board Hearings (hereinafter referred to as "WDC files, National Archives").

29. Testimony of Henry Lamont Beach before the Individual Hearing Exclusion Board of the Western Defense Command of the Fourth Army, October 2, 1942, had WDC files, National Archives.

30. Report of C.B. Aug. 29, 1939, files of the author.

31. Leo P. Ribuffo, *The Old Christian Right: The Protestant Far Right from the Great Depression to the Cold War* (Philadelphia, PA: Temple University Press, 1983), pp. 48–58. Karen E. Hoppes, *William Dudley Pelley and the Silvershirt Legion: A Case Study of the Legion in Washington State, 1933–1942*, Ph.D. dissertation, City University of New York, Graduate School and University Center, New York City, 1992.

32. Ribuffo (1983), p. 57.

33. "Chief Pelley's Silver Program: How Far Do You Endorse It?" unsourced pamphlet, Record Group 338, WCCA, WDC, National Archives, Washington, D.C. (hereinafter referred to as "WCCA files, National Archives).

34. Pelley's circular was distributed April, 2, 1938. Memo of Lieutenant Colonel Boris T. Pash, Chief, Counter-Intelligence Branch, Military Intelligence, to AC of S, Civil Affairs Division, Nov. 18, 1942, p. 1, Record Group 338, WCCA files, National Archives.

35. Dick Cockle, "Founder of Posse Comitatus Decries Radicals, Lives Quietly," *(Portland) Oregonian*, June 23, 1985, p. B1.

36. "Investigation of Henry L. Beach, Portland, Oregon, made by Martin F. Hayes, Assistant Investigator, Feb. 16, 1943, WDC Files, National Archives.

37. Opinion cited in memo of Lieutenant Colonel Boris T. Pash, Chief, Counter-Intelligence Branch, Military Intelligence, to AC of S; Civil Affairs Division, Nov. 18, 1942, p. 5, WCCA files, National Archives.

38. Pelley and two others, Lawrence A. Brown and Agnes Marian Henderson, were indicted in Indianapolis in May 1942 along with the Fellowship Press, which Pelley controlled. *United States of America v. William Dudley Pelley, et al., in the U.S. District Court for the Southern District of Indiana, no. 7391 Cr.*

39. Opinion cited in "An Exact Copy of the Pelley Indictment for Sedition," pp. 8, 47, Jan. 19, 1942. "Silver Shirt Legion of America," p. 8, WCCA files, National Archives.

40. Ibid. Ribuffo (1983), p. 188.

41. Transcript of testimony of Henry L. Beach before the Individual Exclusion Hearing Board, Oct. 2, 1942, Exhibit C, p. 21, WDC files, National Archives.

42. Correspondence of Lieutenant Colonel Frank E. Meek to Henry L. Beach, Sept. 22, 1942, WDC files, National Archives.

43. Memo of Victor W. Nielsen to Colonel William A. Boekel, Oct. 26, 1942. WCCA files, National Archives.

44. Presidential executive order no. 9066 was issued Feb. 19, 1942. Lieutenant Colonel H. W. Schweitzer, "History of Japanese Program, Office of the Provost Marshal General," Japanese-American Branch, Headquarters, Army Service Forces, Presidio of San Francisco, California, Sept. 25, 1945, WCCA files, National Archives, pp. 4–6.

45. *Henry L. Beach v. Lieutenant General John L. DeWitt, et al.*, no. 23803, National Archives—Pacific NW Region, record group no. 21, USDC, Ore., Portland, Civil and Criminal, 1922–1943, box no. 785, folder no. 1811.

46. "Mechanic Asks U.S. Court to Restrain Control Board, Allegedly Restricting His Rights as American Citizen," *(Portland) Oregonian*, Feb. 14, 1943.

47. For a summary of the legal challenges to presidential executive order no. 9066, see: "Paraphrase of Confidential Radio to CG, EDC [Commanding General, Eastern Defense Command]," of CG, WDC-4A (Commanding General, John L. DeWitt, Western Defense Command and Fourth Army), Feb. 23, 1943, WCCA files, National Archives.

48. Phil Hunt, " 'They're Calling Us Kooks,' Leader of the Posse Complains," *(Portland) Oregon Journal*, Feb. 18, 1974, p. 6. "Sheriff's Posse Comitatus," FBI, field office file no. 157-1432, June 6, 1974, p. 6.

49. Jerrold K. Footlick with William J. Cook, "Return of the Posse," *Newsweek*, May 26, 1975, p. 54.

50. "Identity, Also Known as Posse Comitatus," FBI, April 26, 1973.

51. Ibid.

52. "Sheriff's Posse Comitatus: Extremist Matter," FBI, Portland, Oregon, June 6, 1974, p. 11.

53. Ibid., p. B (cover page).

54. Ibid., pp. B (cover page), P.

55. Ibid., pp. 10–11.

56. "Posse Chief Calls Korean War His Turning Point," *Milwaukee Journal*, July 29, 1980. RECORD OF PRISONER, Shawano County Jail, Feb. 19, 1980. Memo of Ernest V. Smith, Special Agent, to SA-159 file, "Sheriff's Posse Comitatus," Jan. 30, 1975.

18. The Posse Rides Wisconsin

1. "Posse Chief Calls Korean War His Turning Point," *Milwaukee Journal*, July 29, 1980. Testimony of Fred M. Chicken, document 42, Dec. 11, 1974, *United States of America v. Thomas F. Stockheimer*, U.S. District Court, Western District of Wisconsin, 74-CR-72.

2. Martin A. Larson, *Tax Revolt, U.S.A.! Why and How Thousands of Patriotic Americans Refuse to Pay the Income Tax* (Washington, DC: Liberty Lobby, 1973), pp. 42–45. Martin A. Larson, *The Continuing Tax Rebellion: What Millions of Americans Are Doing to Restore Constitutional Government.* (Old Greenwich, CT: The Devin-Adair Company, 1979), pp. 148–49, 151–52.

3. Affidavit of Steven C. Underwood, U.S. Attorney, *Thomas F. Stockheimer v. Fred Chicken et al.*, U.S. District Court, Western District of Wisconsin, civil no. 74-C-293, Dec. 5, 1974. RECORD OF PROCEEDINGS IN CRIMINAL CASES, document 5, *United States of America v. Thomas F. Stockheimer*, U.S. District Court, Western District of Wisconsin, 74-CR-72, Aug. 23, 1974.

4. Report of Ernest V. Smith, "Sheriff's Posse Comitatus," Wisc. DOJ, Oct. 11, 1974.

5. Airtel to SAC, Milwaukee, from Director, FBI, "Sheriff's Posse Comitatus, aka," Sept. 9, 1974.

6. "Sheriff's Posse Comitatus," case no. SA-159, Oct. 11, 1974, Wisc. DOJ. Stockheimer filed articles of incorporation for the committee on January 10, 1974, with the Wisconsin Secretary of State and on January 15 with the Wood County REGISTER OF DEEDS. "Sheriff's Posse Comitatus," case no. SA-159, Oct. 14, 1974, Wisc. DOJ.

7. "Sheriff's Posse Comitatus," FBI, Milwaukee, Wisconsin, Nov. 7, 1974, p. 18.

8. Jerrold K. Footlick with William J. Cook, "Return of the Posse," *Newsweek*, May 26, 1975, p. 54.

9. Letter of John R. Wagner to Mr. David Neeb, May 1, 1974, Wisc. DOJ. "Complaint of John R. Wagner to Assistant Attorney General David Neeb," Wisc. DOJ, DCI–Operations, May 3, 1974. The five counties were Marathon, Manitowoc, Taylor, Shawano, and Winnebago. Thomas Stockheimer formally registered his "non-profit" Sheriff's Posse Comitatus, Inc., with the state in early June 1974.

10. Memo of David W. Neeb to Frank Meyers, "The Posse Comitatus," Wisc. DOJ, DCI, May 1, 1974. Memo of Frank A. Meyers to Russell J. Nelson, "The Posse Comitatus," Wisc. DOJ, DCI, May 8, 1974.

11. Wisconsin Legislative Reference Bureau, *1975 Blue Book*, pp. 829–31.

12. Omernick ran in the Eighty-sixth Assembly District. Wisconsin Legislative Reference Bureau, *1975 Blue Book*, pp. 829–31.

13. "1974 American Party State Platform," Wisconsin Legislative Reference Bureau, *1975 Blue Book*, pp. 761–64.

14. Ibid.

15. Pat Rupinski, "The Posse Arrived in '74," *Wausau (Wisc.) Daily Herald*, Feb. 21, 1980, pp. 1, 10. Pat Rupinski, "Omernick Says Posse Groups May Be Necessary to Protect Property," *Wausau (Wisc.) Daily Herald*, undated newspaper clipping. Wisconsin Legislative Reference Bureau, *1979–1980 Blue Book* (State of Wisconsin, Madison, 1979), pp. 78, 79, 908, 928.

16. Wisconsin Legislative Reference Bureau, *1975 Blue Book* (State of Wisconsin Madison, 1975), pp. 829–31. Wisconsin Legislative Reference Bureau, *1979–1980 Blue Book*, p. 78.

17. Wisconsin Legislative Reference Bureau, *1975 Blue Book*, p. 819.

18. The next-highest vote-getter in the Senate race won just 5,396 votes, less than one-half of one percent of the nearly 1.2 million votes cast, while McFarren received 2 percent of the total. Wisconsin Legislative Reference Bureau, *1975 Blue Book*, p. 819.

19. McFarren won 5.86 percent of the vote total in Manitowoc County, 6.14 percent of the vote total in Marathon County, and 6.5 percent of the vote total in Shawano, compared with his 2 percent vote total statewide. And he won 4.3 percent in both Taylor and Chippewa Counties. Wisconsin Legislative Reference Bureau, *1975 Blue Book*, pp. 819–22.

20. "Posse Comitatus: A Danger to Democracy," remarks of the Honorable David Obey of Wisconsin, *Congressional Record—Extensions of Remarks*, March 4, 1980, p. E1021.

21. Ibid.

22. "Subpoena to Testify Before Christian Citizens' Grand Jury," Sheriff's Posse Comitatus of Wisconsin, to Robert McConnell, Sept. 9, 1974.

23. Remarks of the Honorable David Obey of Wisconsin (March 4, 1980), p. E1021. John Welter, "The Posse's Out Up North: Some Sheriffs Run Scared," *Madison (Wisc.) Capital Times*, Oct. 16, 1974, pp. 1, 5. Warren Wolfe, "Wisconsin Posse Files Many Suits," *Minneapolis Tribune*, Dec. 15, 1974, as reprinted by the *National Chronicle*, March 13, 1975, p. 1.

24. George Kindred, "Posse Comitatus; What Is It?" *IDENTITY* (Nov. 1975), vol. 8, no. 1.

25. "Undercover Operations/Surveillance," report of Agent Dillingham, case no. SA-159, Sept. 16, 1974, Wisc. DOJ, DCI. "Surveillance" report of Ernest V. Smith, Special Agent, case no. SA-159, Sept. 16, 1974, Wisc. DOJ, DCI.

26. In 1972, Minnecheske was taken to court for illegally dumping sand in a local river, but the case was eventually dismissed. That same year he pleaded guilty to three counts of selling liquor to a minor. Bill Stokes, "What's He Up To? It Puzzles Many," *Milwaukee Journal*, Feb. 4, 1979.

27. Ibid. "Posse's Minnecheske Paroled After 11 Months," *Green Bay (Wisc.) Press Gazette*, March 19, 1984. Associated Press, "Posse Leader Gets 2-Year Term," *Madison (Wisc.) Capital Times*, April 30, 1983.

28. Warren Wolfe, "Wisconsin Posse Files Many Suits," *Minneapolis Tribune*, Dec. 15, 1974, as reprinted by the *National Chronicle*, March 13, 1975, p. 1.

29. Memo to file SA-159 from Special Agent Ernest Smith, Wisc, DOJ, DCI, Sept. 18, 1974.

30. "Lineup for Sept. 20, 1974, State Office Building," Eau Claire Police Department (Wisconsin).

31. Complaint Report of Officer Richard Dahnert, "State Office Building, Eau Claire, Wisc.," Department of Administration, State Protective Service, Sept. 23, 1974.

32. Complaint Report of Officer M. J. O'Donohue, Department of Administration, State Protective Service, Wisconsin, Sept. 24, 1974.

33. D. Backstrom, "Supplementary Investigation Report," Police Department, City of Eau Claire, Wisconsin, case no. 74-101156, Sept. 24, 1974.

34. Memo of Robert M. Ankenbrandt to file SA-159, DCIR "Cross-Reference Check," Wisc. DOJ, DCI, Oct. 15, 1974.

35. Memo of Robert M. Ankenbrandt to Russell J. Nelson, Wisc. DOJ, DCI, Oct. 10, 1974.

36. The man behind the meeting was Charles Dodge, the co-founder of Stockheimer's Little People's Tax Advisory Committee who was later convicted of tax evasion. Remarks of the Honorable David Obey of Wisconsin (March 4, 1980). Case activity report of Robert M. Ankenbrandt, "Undercover Operation," Wisc. DOJ, DCI, Oct. 10, 1974. Memo to file no. SA-159(15) from Robert M. Ankenbrandt, Wisc. DOJ, DCI, Feb. 23, 1981. FBI teletype to Director, FBI, from Milwaukee, Wisconsin, Oct. 20, 1974.

37. FBI teletype to Director, FBI, from Milwaukee, Wisconsin, Oct. 20, 1974.

38. "Sheriff's Posse Comitatus," FBI, Milwaukee, Wisconsin, Nov. 7, 1974, p. 22.

39. Ibid., pp. 24, 28. "The First Gathering of the Clans! Americans for Constitutional Government and Law," *National Chronicle*, vol. 23, no. 12, July 25, 1974. "Sheriff's Posse Comitatus," case no. SA-159, Wisc. DOJ, DCI, Oct. 24, 1974.

40. "Posse Chief Calls Korean War His Turning Point," *Milwaukee Journal*, July 29, 1980. RECORD OF PRISONER, Shawano County Jail, Feb. 19, 1980. Memo of Ernest V. Smith, special agent to SA-159 file, "Sheriff's Posse Comitatus," Jan. 30, 1975.

41. "Sheriff's Posse Comitatus," FBI, Milwaukee, Wisconsin, Nov. 7, 1974, pp. 30–31. Stockheimer also used the Milwaukee Posse Convention to drum up support for his upcoming trial for assaulting Fred Chicken. The chairman of his legal defense fund was Ralph David Pennings, a charter member of the Marathon County Posse who was convicted of filing false income tax returns and later became known for his role in manufacturing Laetrile, a medically worthless drug derived from chemicals found in the pits of fruit that was illegally sold as a cure for cancer. Remarks of the Honorable David Obey, Wisconsin (March 4, 1980).

42. Warren Wolfe, "Wisconsin Posse Files Many Suits," *Minneapolis Tribune*, Dec. 15, 1974, as reprinted by the *National Chronicle*, March 13, 1975, p. 1.

43. United States District Court, *United States v. Thomas F. Stockheimer*, criminal docket 74CR72.

44. Stockheimer was sentenced February 19, 1975. United States District Court, *United States v. Thomas F. Stockheimer*, criminal docket 74CR72. "60-Day Term for Stockheimer," Associated Press, undated newspaper clipping.

45. The United States Court of Appeals affirmed Stockheimer's conviction in May 1976. Stockheimer was ordered to report to the U.S. marshal's office in Madison, Wisconsin, on July 19, 1976, to begin serving his sixty-day sentence but he never showed up. A warrant was issued for his arrest later that year. Stockheimer was finally picked up by authorities on November 10, 1977, in Grafton, West Virginia.

46. *U.S. District Court v. Thomas F. Stockheimer*, criminal docket 76CR90, April 7, 1978.

47. ABC-TV News broadcast, *Day One*, May 18, 1995. *United States v. Thomas Stockheimer et al.*, case no. 96-CR-115 TJC, U.S. District Court, Eastern District of Wisconsin, May 14, 1996.

48. Military record of James Paul Wickstrom, NARA, NMPRC.

49. Report of Herbert E. Bobeck, special agent, "Interview with James P. Wickstrom," Wisc. DOJ, DCI, Sept. 13, 1984.

50. Don Bradley and Jenny Deam, "Shooting Near Extremist Church Stirs Fears," *Kansas City Star*, Nov. 2, 1986, p. 37A. "U.S. Leads Bloody Raid on Church While Foes of Regional Rule Pray," *The Spotlight*, July 12, 1976, p. 3.

51. Report of Herbert E. Bobeck, special agent, "Interview of James P. Wickstrom," Wisc. DOJ, DCI, SA-159, Nov. 21, 1984.

52. Ibid.

53. Larry Cortese, "Posse's Check of Bomb Shelters Shows Deplorable Conditions," *Shawano (Wisc.) Evening Leader*, Feb. 23, 1980. Affidavit of James P. Wickstrom, State of Wisconsin, County of Shawano, Feb. 27, 1980.

19. The Posse and the FBI

1. Affidavit of Leonard Wilmer Brabham, *Leonard Wilmer Brabham vs. Roger A. Davis, et al.*, District Court of the First Judicial District of the State of Idaho in and for Bonner County, Mar. 10th, 1975.

2. Affidavit of Leonard Wilmer Brabham, March 10, 1975. Richard Mauer, "Controversy Cloaked Posse Comitatus," *Idaho Statesman*, Sept. 18, 1980, pp. 1A, 5A. Associated Press, "Posse Comitatus: Deputies Thwart Citizen's Arrest," *Spokane (Wash.) Spokesman-Review*, March 14, 1975. Jay Shelledy, "The Posse Comitatus Rides Again! 'Vigilante' Groups Want Power Returned to Counties—or Else," *Tribune*, undated newspaper clipping. "Officers Thwart Posse 'Arrest,'" (Spokane, Wash.) *Daily Chronicle*, March 13, 1975. Criminal complaint, *State of Idaho v. Leonard W. Brabham*, case no. F10768, Jan. 27, 1975. Judgment, *State of Idaho v. Leonard W. Brabham*, Dec. 17, 1975.

3. A decade later Cutler was sentenced to twelve years in federal prison for attempting to hire a hit man to decapitate Thomas Martinez, an FBI informant. Associated Press, "Man Held by FBI in Idaho linked to Aryan Nations," *Seattle Times*, Aug. 19, 1985. See also: Kevin Flynn and Gary Gerhardt, *The Silent Brotherhood*, (New York: Penguin Books, 1995), p. 463.

4. Unclassified report of the FBI, Butte, Montana, March 1, 1976.

5. Mauer, "Controversy Cloaked Posse Comitatus," pp. 1A, 5A. Associated Press "Posse Comitatus: Deputies Thwart 'Citizen's Arrest' " (March 14, 1975). Jay Shelledy, "The Posse Comitatus Rides Again! 'Vigilante' Groups Want Power Returned to Counties—or Else," *Tribune*, undated newspaper clipping. "Officers Thwart Posse 'Arrest,' " (*Spokane Wash.) Daily Chronicle*, March 13, 1975. "Gestapo Methods of Our Law Enforcement Officers," *National Chronicle*, March 27, 1975, vol. 24, no. 12, pp. 1, 4.

6. "Atty.-Gen. to Hear Both Law and Posse," *Spokane (Wash.) Spokesman-Review*, March 28, 1975, as cited in the *National Chronicle*, April 3, 1975, vol. 24, no. 13.

7. "Notify Atty.-Gen. Kidwell," *National Chronicle*, March 27, 1975, vol. 24, no. 12.

8. As cited in the *National Chronicle*, March 20, 1974, p. 4.

9. "L. Brabham Not Guilty," *National Chronicle*, vol. 24, no. 50, Dec. 18, 1975. Criminal complaint, *State of Idaho v. Leonard W. Brabham*, case no. F10768, Jan. 27, 1975. Judgment, *State of Idaho v. Leonard W. Brabham*, Dec. 17, 1975.

10. Airtel from SAC, Little Rock, to Director, FBI, "Sheriff's Posse Comitatus, aka Posse Comitatus, Americans for Constitutional Government and Law," Jan. 29, 1975. Airtel from SAC, Little Rock, to Director, FBI, "Sheriff's Posse Comitatus, aka Americans for Constitutional Government and Law, Carroll County, Arkansas," Feb. 24, 1975. Flyer of "Little People's Tax Advisory Committee." Memo of SAC, Milwaukee, to Director, FBI, Oct. 23, 1974.

11. Airtel from SAC, Sacramento, to Director, FBI, Jan. 9, 1975. Teletype from Portland, FBI, to Director, Feb. 11, 1975. Airtel from Director, FBI, to SACs, Los Angeles, etc., "Northwest Posse Comitatus Convention, February 8–9, 1975," Jan. 7, 1975. Airtel from SAC, Sacramento, to Director, FBI, "Northwest Posse Comitatus Convention, February 8–9, 1975," Jan. 9, 1975.

12. Sheriff's Posse Comitatus Charter, DuPage County, Illinois, Dec. 19, 1974. "Posse Wants Judge Arrested," *Chicago Daily News*, March 31, 1975, as cited in memo of SAC, Chicago, to Director, FBI, April 8, 1975. See also: Neil Goldstein, "Sheriff's Posses Formed," *Suburban Week*, supplement to the *Chicago Sun-Times* and the *Chicago Daily News*, Feb. 26 and 27, 1975, pp. 1, 8.

13. Goldstein, "Sheriff's Posses Formed," Feb. 26 and 27, 1975, pp. 1, 8.

14. "Posse Leader Was Betrayed," *National Chronicle*, undated clipping.

15. Correspondence of Director, FBI, to SAC, Portland, "Sheriff's Posse Comitatus," March 21, 1975. Memo of Director, FBI, to SAC, Portland, "Sheriff's Posse Comitatus," April 17, 1975.

16. Memo of SAC, Portland, to Director, FBI, "Sheriff's Posse Comitatus," March 7, 1975.

17. Memo of Director, FBI, to SAC, Portland, "Sheriff's Posse Comitatus," March 21, 1975.

18. Memo to Director, FBI, from SAC, Portland, "Sheriff's Posse Comitatus," April 17, 1975.

19. Teletype from FBI, Little Rock, to Director, April 17, 1975.

20. The fourteen states were: California, Oregon, Washington state, Idaho, Wyoming, Arizona, Minnesota, Wisconsin, Iowa, Illinois, Missouri, Ohio, Texas, and Arkansas. Teletype of FBI, Dallas, to Director, "Citizens for Constitutional Compliance," Feb. 13, 1975. Memo of SAC, Cleveland, to Director, FBI, "Sheriff's Posse Comitatus," Feb. 19, 1975. Memo of SAC, St. Louis, to Director, FBI, "Sheriff's Posse Comitatus," March 13, 1975. Memo of SAC, Minneapolis, to Director, FBI, "Sheriff's Posse Comitatus," May 5, 1975. FBI teletype from Denver to Director, June 5, 1975.

21. Airtel from SAC, El Paso, to Director, FBI, "Sheriff's Posse Comitatus, aka (SPC), Citizens Law Enforcement and Research Committee: Extremist Matter—White Hate Group," May 13, 1975. Memo from SAC, Dallas, to Director, FBI, May 19, 1975. Memo from J. G. Deegan to W. R. Wannal, "Sheriff's Posse Comitatus, aka (SPC)," May 22, 1975. Teletype from FBI, El Paso, to Director, May 29, 1975.

22. For an account of Kahl's activities in Texas during this period, see: James Corcoran, *Bitter Harvest: Gordon Kahl and the Posse Comitatus—Murder in the Heartland* (New York: Viking, 1990), pp. 52–55.

23. Teletype from FBI, El Paso, to Director, May 29, 1975.

24. Masthead, *Armed Citizen News*, June 1971, no. 41, p. 2. Russell Struve, "Getting Around," *Armed Citizen News*, Jan. 1972, no. 47, p. 7. "NAKBA Speakers Bureau," *Armed Citizens News*, Aug. 1972, no. 54, p. 4. Herbert Breed, "Countering the Nullifiers," *Armed Citizen News*, Oct.

1973, no. 68, p. 7. Clark E. Mears, "Investigation Report," Oregon Department of Justice, case/file no. SI-75-012, Posse Comitatus–Oregon, June 4, 1975, pp. 4–5.

25. Correspondence of Herbert S. Breed to State Representative Mary W. Rieke, May 7, 1975.

26. "'Posse' Threatens Senator with Death," *Salem (Ore.) Capital Journal*, May 15, 1975, p. 1. See also: "Members of Legislature Complain about Letters from Citizens Group," *(Portland) Oregonian*, May 16, 1975.

27. "Is There Anything that Can Be Done about This?" asked Representative Ralph Groener, a Democrat from Oregon City. "If this kind of action proliferates, 'mobacracy' [sic] will rule rather than reason. I feel it is my responsibility to mip [sic] this in the bud if I can." Correspondence of Ralph Groener to Lee Johnson, May 14, 1975.

28. Correspondence of Cecil L. Edwards to Lee Johnson, May 13, 1975.

29. For more on the history of the Klan in Oregon, see: David A. Horowitz, "Social Morality and Personal Revitalization: Oregon's Ku Klux Klan in the 1920s," *Oregon Historical Quarterly*, Winter 1989, vol. 90, no. 4, p. 369. Lawrence J. Saalfeld, *Forces of Prejudice: The Ku Klux Klan in Oregon, 1920–1925*, (Portland, OR: University of Portland Press, 1984). David A. Horowitz, "Order, Solidarity, and Vigilance: The Ku Klux Klan in La Grande, Oregon," *The Invisible Empire in the West: Toward a New Historical Appraisal of the Ku Klux Klan in the 1920s*, Shawn Lay, ed. (Urbana, IL: University of Illinois Press, 1992).

30. As of June 1975 there were chartered Posse chapters in at least the following Oregon counties: Multnomah, Marion, Lane, Douglas, Josephine, Jackson, Klamath, Baker, and Umatilla.

31. Both the Klamath County district attorney and the U.S. attorney in Portland also declined to bring any charges against Breed. "Investigation Report of Clark E. Mears," case file no. SI-75-012 Posse Comitatus–Oregon, June 4, 1975.

32. Correspondence of Lee Johnson to Cecil L. Edwards, undated.

33. Memo of John E. Moore, Chief Counsel, Criminal Justice Special Investigation Division, to Lee Johnson, Attorney General, "Posse Comitatus Investigation," May 19, 1975. "Investigation Report of Clark E. Mears," June 4, 1975.

34. Memo from SAC, Milwaukee, to Director, FBI, "Sheriff's Posse Comitatus," May 6, 1975. "Sheriff's Posse Comitatus: Extremist Matter," FBI, Portland, Oregon, June 6, 1974, p. B (cover page).

35. Memo from SAC, Milwaukee, to Director, FBI, "Sheriff's Posse Comitatus," May 6, 1975.

36. Ronald Kessler, *The FBI* (New York: Pocket Books, 1993), pp. 2–3.

37. "The Complete Collection of Political Documents Ripped Off from the FBI Office in Media, PA, March 8, 1971," *WIN Peace and Freedom thru Non-violent Action*, March 1 and 15, 1972, vol. 8, nos. 4 and 5, respectively.

38. David M. Chalmers, *Hooded Americanism: The History of the Ku Klux Klan* (Durham, NC: Duke University Press, Third Edition, 1987), p. 398.

39. Ibid., p. 398.

40. Wyn Craig Wade, *The Fiery Cross: The Ku Klux Klan in America* (New York: Simon and Schuster, 1987), p. 361.

41. Patsy Sims, *The Klan* (New York: Dorset Press, 1978), pp. 119–24. Wade (1987), pp. 361–64. Chalmers (1987), pp. 398–400. Taylor Branch, *Parting the Waters: America in the King Years, 1954–1963* (New York: Simon and Schuster, 1988), pp. 420–22.

42. In 1965 the testimony of Klan informant Gary Thomas Rowe helped convict three Klansmen for the murder of Viola Gregg Liuzzo. Liuzzo, a forty-year-old Detroit housewife and

the mother of five, had traveled to Alabama to help civil-rights activists prepare for the famous Selma-to-Montgomery march. Although Rowe helped bring Liuzzo's murderers to justice, numerous questions persist about his role as an agent provocateur and the larger failure of the FBI to use its inside information to prevent civil-rights workers from being attacked, often brutally. Branch (1988), p. 421.

43. Kessler (1993), p. 4. Gorton Carruth, *The Encyclopedia of American Facts and Dates* (New York, HarperCollins, 1993, Ninth Edition), pp. 702, 704, 708.

44. Kessler (1993), p. 471. Final report of the Senate Select Committee to Study Governmental Operations with Respect to Intelligence Activities, S. Rep. 755, 94th Cong., 2d Sess. (1976).

45. As reprinted in *Armed Citizen News*, Jan. 1975, no. 62 (incorrectly numbered; should be no. 82), p. 8.

46. Ibid.

47. Ibid.

48. "DePugh of Minutemen Paroled," *New York Times*, May 1, 1973. DePugh was taken to the Federal Penitentiary at Leavenworth, Kansas, to start his jail term in July 1969, after being apprehended by federal agents. *New York Times Abstracts*, July 24, 1969, pp. 34, C2.

49. Correspondence of Charles L. Adams to Mr. Scott Stanley Jr. and Mr. Robert Welch, reprinted in *Armed Citizen News*, Dec. 1974, no. 81, p. 4.

50. "Profits for Patriots," *Armed Citizen News*, Jan. 1975, no. 8, p. 4.

51. "A Further Report on the Patriots Leadership Conference," *Armed Citizen News*, Jan. 1975, no. 83, p. 8. Rod Rose, "Patriots Leadership Conference," *Armed Citizen News*, Dec. 1974, no. 81, p. 9.

52. *Armed Citizen News*, May 1975, no. 86, p. 23. See also: *Armed Citizen News*, Nov. 1975, no. 90, p. 15.

53. Jack Marlow, "The FBI and the Ku Klux Klan," *Armed Citizen News*, Nov. 1975, no. 90, p. 3.

54. Ibid.

55. Correspondence of Director, FBI, to SAC, Albany, "Sheriff's Posse Comitatus (SPC), aka Citizens Law Enforcement Research Committee (CLERC)," April 21, 1975.

56. William W. Turner, *Hoover's FBI* (New York: Thunder's Mouth Press, 1993), pp. 324, 326. Kessler (1993), pp. 470–71.

57. Airtel from Director, FBI, to SAC, Albany, May 21, 1975.

58. "Dear Patriot" letter (circa 1974). Correspondence of H. L. Beach. Spencer Library Kansas Collection, University of Kansas. Jerrold K. Footlick with William J. Cook, "Return of the Posse," *Newsweek*, May 26, 1975, p. 54.

59. Footlick and Cook, "Return of the Posse," *Newsweek*, May 26, 1975, p. 54

60. Airtel from SAC, Portland, to Director, FBI, May 27, 1975.

61. Correspondence to SAC, Butte, from Director, FBI, "Kootenai County Christian Posse Comitatus, Coeur D'Alene, Idaho," Sept. 18, 1975.

62. The Bureau named as "non-functioning" chapters in Baker, Umatilla, and Clatsop Counties. The inquiry into the Washington County Posse chapter was closed because the group had limited itself to appearing before county commission meetings, according to the FBI. Similarly, the activities of the Multnomah County group in Portland "no longer sustain[ed] the statutory basis for the investigation. Memo from SAC, Portland, to Director, FBI, "Sheriff's Posse Comitatus," March 7, 1975.

63. In Wisconsin, the FBI closed its files on all eight Posse chapters and their leaders within a year of the assault on Fred Chicken. Memo from SAC Milwaukee to Director, FBI, "Sheriff's Posse Comitatus," May 6, 1975.

20. The Spirit of Vigilantism

1. "An Eye Witness at Tracy," *National Chronicle*, Sept. 25, 1975, vol. 24, no. 38. Associated Press, "Posse Comitatus: God, Guns and the Constitution," *Salem (Ore.) Capital Journal*, Nov. 19, 1975, Section 5, p. 4.

2. "This Is the Week That Was," *Focus* magazine from the *Stockton (Calif.) Record*, Oct. 5, 1975. Walt Wiley and Steve Duscha, "Armed 'Posse' Blocks UFW; Deputy Injured," *Sacramento Bee*, Sept. 2, 1975, p. 1.

3. Jerrold K. Footlick with William J. Cook, "Return of the Posse," *Newsweek*, May 26, 1975, p. 54.

4. Wiley and Duscha "Armed 'Posse' Blocks UFW; Deputy Injured," Sept. 2, 1975 p. 1.

5. "Emergency Order Adopting Emergency Regulations of the Agricultural Labor Relations Board," chapter 9, "*Access to Workers in the Fields by Labor Organizations*," Aug. 29, 1975, California Agricultural Labor Relations Board. Ronald L. Goldfarb, *Migrant Farm Workers; Caste of Despair* (Ames, IA: Iowa State University Press, 1981), pp. 198–99.

6. Wiley and Duscha, "Armed 'Posse' Blocks UFW; Deputy Injured," Sept. 2, 1975, p. 1.

7. Ibid. Raul Ramirez, "Tomato Field Game: Posse 1, the UFW 0," undated, unsourced newspaper clipping.

8. "Farm Field 'Showdown': Deputies vs. 'Posse' " *Stockton (Calif.) Record*, Sept. 2, 1975, pp. 1, 2. "Gillings Arrested in Tomato Field," *Tracy (Calif.) Press*, Sept. 3, 1975, pp. 1, 2.

9. Gillings had failed to appear in court on an $18 speeding ticket. "Gillings Arrested after Shot Fired," *Stockton (Calif.) Record*, Sept. 2, 1975. "Canlis, Gillings, Differ On Arrest Versions," *Stockton (Calif.) Record*, Sept. 3, 1975, pp. 1, 2.

10. *State of California v. Francis Earl Gillings*, appellant's opening brief, "Appeal from the judgment of the Superior Court of the State of California for the County of Merced," 5 crim. no. 2885, July 20, 1977. *The People, v. Francis Earl Gillings*, "Opinion," 5 crim. no. 2885 (Super. Ct. no. 8622), in the Court of Appeal of the State of California, Fifth Appellate District, July 10, 1978.

11. Sheriff Deputy Sues Gillings for $1 Million," *Stockton (Calif.) Record*, Nov. 20, 1975. "Gillings Arrested in Tomato Field," *Tracy (Calif.) Press*, Sept. 3, 1975, pp. 1, 2.

12. "An Eye Witness at Tracy," *National Chronicle*, vol. 24, no. 38, Sept. 25, 1975.

13. "Unions Push Election Efforts; 'Posse' Pulls Out of Fields," *Stockton (Calif.) Record*, Sept. 3, 1975, pp. 1, 2. "Gillings Claims McDaniel Ousted," *Stockton (Calif.) Record*, Sept. 5, 1975, pp. 1, 2.

14. Irwin Suall, "The Vigilantes Are Comin' If you Don't Watch Out . . ." *ADL Bulletin*, Nov. 1975, p. 3.

15. Associated Press, "Posse Comitatus: God, Guns, and the Constitution," *Salem (Ore.) Capital Journal*, Nov. 19, 1975, section 5, p. 4.

16. "Editorial from Stockton Paper," *National Chronicle*, vol. 24, no. 39, Oct. 2, 1975, p. 4.

17. "Editorial," *National Spotlight*, vol. 1, no. 1, Sept. 17, 1975, p. 11.

18. Ibid., p. 1.

19. Paul W. Valentine, "Carto Testifies Two Groups Exchange Mailing Lists," *Des Moines Sunday Register*, May 23, 1971, p. 6-G. "Liberty Lobby and the Carto Network of hate," *The Facts*, ADL, Winter 1982, vol. 27, no. 1, p. 9. "Carto, Willis A." Group Research, Inc., section 2—INDIVIDUALS, July 1, 1964. "Liberty Lobby," Group Research, Inc, section 1—ORGANIZATIONS, Aug. 10, 1965.

20. Mark Lockman, "Tax Fighters, Posse Charting Joint Course at Picnic in Forest," *National Spotlight*, Sept. 17, 1975, vol. 1, no. 1, p. 13.

21. Ibid.

22. John George and Laird Wilcox, *American Extremists: Militia, Supremacists, Klansmen, Communists, and Others* (Amherst, NY: Prometheus Books, 1996), p. 216.

23. Confidential memo to Jack R. Winkler, Chief Assistant Attorney General, from Gregory W. Baugher, Deputy Attorney General, "Legal Status of Posse Comitatus," California Office of the Attorney General, Sept. 5, 1975.

24. Larry Stammer, "Posse Comitatus: New Vigilante Groups Form," *Los Angeles Times*, as reprinted in the *Salem (Ore.) Capital Journal*, Sept. 12, 1975, p. 5. *People of the State of California v. Francis Earl Gillings*, San Joaquin County, "Order Holding to Answer and Commitment," Oct. 9, 1975. Associated Press, "Posse Comitatus: God, Guns, and the Constitution," *Salem (Ore.) Capital Journal*, Nov. 19, 1975, section 5, p. 4. Associated Press, "Three in Vigilante Group Arrested in Workers-Growers Dispute," *Salem (Ore.) Statesman*, Sept. 3, 1975, section 2, p 17. "An Eye Witness at Tracy," *National Chronicle*, vol. 24, no. 38, Sept. 25, 1975, pp. 1, 4. Susan Sward, "Those 'Stepped On by Big Brother' Are Joining Posse," Associated Press, *Houston Chronicle*, Aug. 27, 1976, section 4, p. 22. Bill Richards and Joel Kotkin, "Frontier 'Justice' Rides in West," *Washington Post*, Sept. 18, 1976, pp. A1, A8. For a description of the early court proceedings against Gillings and Brown, see: "First Hearing of Posse Concerning the Deputy Confrontation at Tracy, California," *National Chronicle*, vol. 24, no. 42, Oct. 23, 1975, p. 1; "Gillings Arrested in Tomato Field," *Tracy (Calif.) Press*, Sept. 3, 1975, p. 1.

25. Transcript of testimony of George Everett Hill, *State of Oregon v. Cummings*, Feb. 17, 1977. U.S. DOJ, Identification Division, FBI record of George Everett Hill.

26. "Gillings Claims McDaniel Ousted," *Stockton (Calif.) Record*, Sept. 5, 1975, pp. 1, 2.

27. Thorne Gray, "Pistol Packer Is Sheriff Candidate," reprinted in *Tax Strike News*, April 1974, vol. 5, no. 4, p. 10.

28. Ibid. "Posse Comitatus Questions Americans Must Answer," *Tax Strike News*, Nov. 1975, vol. 6, no. 11, p. 14.

29. "Gillings for Sheriff," *Armed Citizen News*, June 1974, no. 76, p. 3. San Joaquin County Registrar of Voters, interview by the author.

30. "Gillings' Group Files Suit," *Tracy (Calif.) Press*, Nov. 15, 1974.

31. "Gillings Loses Appeal on Sales Tax Conviction," *Tracy (Calif.) Press*, March 24, 1975, p. 2.

32. "The Day Gillings Was Evicted: Deputies Arrive—No Fuss," *Tracy (Calif.) Press*, Mar. 28, 1975. "Gillings Loses Appeal on Sales Tax Conviction," *Tracy (Calif.) Press*, March 24, 1975, p. 2. "Gillings Ordered to Pay Sale Violation Fine," *Tracy (Calif.) Press*, April 14, 1975. "A Gillings 'Posse' to 'Fight Crime,' " *Stockton (Calif.) Record*, March 19, 1975, p. 13. Francis E. Gillings, "Gillings Explains," undated letter to the editor, *Stockton (Calif.) Record*.

33. "A Gillings 'Posse' to 'Fight Crime,' " *Stockton (Calif.) Record*, March 19, 1975, p. 13. "Gillings Forming a 'Citizens' Posse': Enforce Constitution 'to the Letter,' " *Tracy (Calif.) Press*, March 17, 1975. "Gillings Forms Citizens' Posse," *Lodi (Calif.) News-Sentinel*, March 15, 1975, p. 9. Michael Taylor, "Posse Riding in the Valley," *San Francisco Chronicle*, April 28, 1975, p. 1. Editorial, "Self-Acclaimed Law Enforcers Are Hazard to Public Peace," *Stockton (Calif.) Record*,

March 23, 1975. FBI report, Sacramento, California, "San Joaquin County Sheriff's Posse Comitatus (SPC)," May 30, 1975.

34. Goldfarb (1981), p. 192.

35. Francis Gillings, "Other Posse News," *National Chronicle*, Sept. 11, 1975, vol. 24, no. 36, p. 1.

36. "Posse Comitatus Questions Americans Must Answer," *Tax Strike News*, Nov. 1975, p. 14. "Gillings and Hill Speak," *National Chronicle*, Oct. 2, 1975, vol. 24, no. 30, p. 1.

37. *United Farm Workers of America v. Superior Court*, 14 C.3rd 902;-Cal.Rptr.-/-P.2d., pp. 910, 919.

38. Associated Press, "Three in Vigilante Group Arrested in Workers-Growers Dispute," *Salem (Ore.) Statesman*, Sept. 3, 1975, section 2, p 17.

39. Stanley P. Klevan, "Posse Will Keep Badges, Leader Says," *Stockton (Calif.) Record*, Sept. 13, 1975.

40. Memo to Deputy District Attorney Frank Dean from Harry E. Sexton, Supervising Investigator, Office of the District Attorney, San Joaquin County, California, Sept. 17, 1975.

41. Thomas D. Elias, "Posse Chief's Threat: Group Will Use Force to Oppose Gun Control," *Sacramento (Calif.) Bee*, Oct. 30, 1975, p. A18.

42. "Tax Tea Party '74," *Tax Strike News*, vol. 5, no. 2, Feb. 1974, p. 15. "Gillings, Wife, Face Tax Trial in March," *Stockton (Calif.) Record*, undated news clipping.

43. "Gillings Court Dates," *Stockton (Calif.) Record*, Nov. 18, 1975, p. 16. "Gillings Indicted on Tax Counts," *Tracy (Calif.) Press*, Nov. 14, 1975. "Gillings Is Indicted: Income Tax Evasion," *Modesto (Calif.) Bee*, Nov. 13, 1975.

44. Howard Zinn, *A People's History of the United States* (New York: Harper Colophon Books, 1980), p. 545.

45. Ibid.

46. William Grieder, *Secrets of the Temple: How the Federal Reserve Runs the Country*, (New York: Simon and Schuster, 1987), pp. 90. John W. Wright, ed., *The New York Times 1998 Almanac* (New York: Penguin Reference Books, 1997), p. 78.

47. Zinn (1980), p. 545.

48. "Affidavit of Probation Violation and Motion for Issuance of Bench Warrant," *State of California v. Francis Earl Gillings*, Merced County, no. 8622. dept. 2, Aug. 6, 1979.

49. "Problems of the Posse Comitatus," *National Chronicle*, vol. 25, no. 1, Jan. 8, 1976, pp. 1, 4.

50. "Posse Reorganization," Citizens Law Enforcement and Research Committee, undated letter.

51. Susan Sward, "Those 'Stepped On by Big Brother' Are Joining Posse," *Houston Chronicle*, Aug. 27, 1976, section 4, p. 22.

52. Certificate of Involuntary Dissolution, "Citizen's Posse Comitatus," State of Oregon, Department of Commerce, Corporation Division, Feb. 16, 1979.

53. Dick Cockle, "Founder of Posse Comitatus Decries Radicals, Lives Quietly," *Sunday Oregonian*, June 23, 1985, p. B1.

54. Suall, "The Vigilantes Are Comin' If You Don't Watch Out..." Nov. 1975, p. 3.

55. Richards and Kotkin, "Frontier 'Justice' Rides in West," Sept. 18, 1976, p. A1.

56. Stammer, "Posse Comitatus: New Vigilante Groups Form," Sept. 12, 1975. p. 5.

57. Ibid. Jerrold K. Footlick with William J. Cook, "Return of the Posse," *Newsweek*, May 26, 1975, p. 54.

21. Badges and Stars

1. Spencer Heinz, "Freewheeling Vigilantes Want to Lock Up 'DA, Few Judges,'" *(Portland) Oregon Journal*, March 9, 1976, p. 6.

2. Obituary of Sylvester P. Ehr, *(Portland) Oregonian*, Feb. 11, 1984, p. D12. Richard Ehr, interview by the author.

3. Sylvester P. Ehr, *Bearers of the Pall* (Portland, OR: Syl Ehr, 1978), p. 386. "The Sheriff's Posse Comitatus: Good or Bad," KATU-TV, News, Portland, Oregon, broadcast segment, 1976.

4. Ehr (1978), pp. 95, 103.

5. Ibid., pp. 1, 95, 103.

6. Richard Ehr, interview.

7. Obituary of Sylvester P. Ehr, *(Portland) Oregonian*, Feb. 11, 1984, p. D12. Richard Ehr, interview.

8. *Tax Strike News*, vol. 6, no. 3, March 1975, p. 2. In 1978, Ehr was listed as one of seven trustees of the United States Taxpayers Union. Among the seven members of the USTU governing board, which was a separate body, were Posse activists Francis Gillings and Vernon Edwin Essig, who later played a role in the Oregon "potato shed" takeover in 1976. See: *USTU Victory News and Handbook*, vol. 2, no. 1, Jan.-Feb. 1978, p. 2.

9. *United States of America vs. Sylvester P. Ehr*, no. CR 78-59, U.S. District Court, District of Oregon, March 15, 1978. "Government Blunder Brings Mistrial," *(Portland) Oregonian*, June 9, 1978, p. C7. "U.S. Dismisses Tax Case Against Posse Leader Ehr," *(Portland) Oregon Journal*, Aug. 5, 1978, p. 14.

10. "Jury Finds Tax Fraud," *(Portland) Oregon Journal*, April 25, 1975, p. A5.

11. Transcript of proceedings, *United States of America v. Glen L. Lundy*, no. CR 75–23, United States District Court, District of Oregon, April 21 and 22, 1975.

12. "Jury Finds Tax Fraud," *(Portland) Oregon Journal*, April 25, 1975, p. A5.

13. Heinz, "Freewheeling Vigilantes Want to Lock Up 'DA, Few Judges,'" March 9, 1976, p. 6.

14. Biography of Lee P. Brown, Office of the Mayor, City of Houston, Texas, Jan. 4, 1999.

15. Gordon DeMarco, *A Short History of Portland* (San Francisco: Lexikos, 1990), pp. 144–46.

16. Heinz, "Freewheeling Vigilantes Want to Lock Up 'DA, Few Judges,'" March 9, 1976, p. 6.

17. "Sheriff's Posse Comitatus," nonprofit articles of incorporation, State of Oregon, Department of Commerce, Corporation Division, July 28, 1975. "Citizens Law Enforcement and Research Committee," nonprofit Articles of Incorporation, State of Oregon, Department of Commerce, Corporation Division, July 28, 1975.

18. Affidavit of Russell Arsenault in support of arrest warrant, *State of Oregon v. LaVerne Donald Hollenbeck*, C 76-06-86-72, Jan. 19, 1976.

19. "Posse Leader Found Guilty Second Time," *(Portland) Oregonian*, Sept. 4, 1976, p. A11.

20. Heinz, "Freewheeling Vigilantes Want to Lock Up 'DA, Few Judges,'" March 9, 1976, p. 6.

21. Gary Miranda, *Following a River: Portland's Congregation Neveh Shalom, 1869–1989* (Portland, OR: Congregation Neveh Shalom, 1989), p. 75.

22. Though the judge suspended the fine and jail term, Hollenbeck insisted on appealing, which resulted in 240 hours of community service and a doubling of his earlier sentence of one year's parole. Complaint court record and judgment order of Judge Donald H. Londer, *Multnomah County v. LaVerne Donald Hollenbeck*, no. DA 119892, May 24, 1976. "Posse Man Found Guilty," *(Portland) Oregonian*, May 25, 1976, p. A11.

23. Ronald A. Buel, Dave Collins, and Phoebe Friedman, "Portland's Neo-Nazi Cult," *Willamette Week* (Portland, Oregon), May 2, 1977, p. 3.

24. "The Sheriff's Posse Comitatus: Good or Bad," KATU-TV News, Portland, Oregon, broadcast segment, 1976. Heinz (1976).

25. Marvin Woidyla, interview by the author; Macil Flye, interview by the author.

26. Ibid.

22. The Hoskins Estate

1. Larry King, Clark Hilden, G. H. ("Joe") Searl, Kate Simon, *Uniquely Oregon* (Dubuque, IA: Kendell/Hunt Publishing Company, 1992), pp. 104–105. Robert D. Hagan, *Totally Oregon* (Salem, OR: Oregon Pride Publications, 1989), p. 242.

2. Bob Woehler, " 'Forgotten Man' Tells of Feuds Over Mikami Land," *Tri-City (Ore.) Herald*, Sept. 23, 1976, second p. 1.

3. Hoskins had died in 1925, but according to his son, Bill, the estate had never been properly probated and one of Bill's brothers had sold off pieces of the farm without permission from the remaining heirs.

4. Testimony of Everett Thoren, *State of Oregon v. Cummings*.

5. Report of Trooper Michael E. Hays, OSP, Nov. 22, 1971. Report of Trooper Donald R. Bergin, OSP, Jan. 14, 1972.

6. Letter to Captain Shelton from Holly V. Holcomb, Superintendent, Criminal Division, General Headquarters, OSP, Feb. 12, 1974.

7. *Armed Citizen News*, June 1971, no. 41, p. 2. Russell Struve, "Getting Around," *Armed Citizen News*, Jan. 1972, no. 47, p. 7. "NAKBA Speakers Bureau," *Armed Citizen News*, Aug. 1972, no. 54, p. 4. Herbert Breed, "Countering the Nullifiers," *Armed Citizen News*, Oct. 1973, no. 68, p. 7.

8. Correspondence of Thomas R. Braun to Gilbert Petteys, April 6, 1974.

9. Letter to Captain Shelton from Holly V. Holcomb, Superintendent, Criminal Division, General Headquarters, OSP, Feb. 12, 1974.

10. "Vigilante Posse Charges Judges, DA, with Treason," unsourced newspaper clipping, Oct. 14, 1975.

11. UPI, "Six On List of 'Posse,' " *Salem (Ore.) Capital Journal*, Oct. 14, 1975. Jim Eardley, "Investigation Asked of Complaints Against Umatilla County DA, Judges," *Pendleton (Ore.) East Oregonian*, Oct. 14, 1975. "State Asked to Investigate 'Treason' Case," *(Portland) Oregonian*, Oct. 15, 1975. Spencer Heinz, "Freewheeling Vigilantes Want to Lock Up 'DA, Few Judges,' " *(Portland) Oregon Journal*, March 9, 1976, p. 6.

12. "Sheriff Says Posse Must Cease Operation," *Salem (Ore.) Capital Journal*, Oct. 25, 1975, section 2, p. 17.

13. Memo to Sheriff McPherson from Sam M. Porter, Dec. 17, 1974.

14. "Posse Comitatus Member Asks for Jury," Oct. 15, 1975.

15. Jerry F. Boone, "Birch Society Denies Posse Comitatus Link," *Tri-City (Ore.) Herald*, Oct. 29, 1975.

16. "Affidavit Notice of Felony, State of Oregon, in Matters of Public Concern," Josephine County, Feb. 13, 1976.

17. Ibid.

18. " 'Posse' files suit," *Salem (Ore.) Capital Journal*, June 9, 1976.

19. Allen Morrison, " 'Posse of Oregon' Petitions Court to Block Candidates," *(Salem) Oregon Statesman*, March 20, 1976, p. 9. "Petition for writ of Original Jurisdiction," *Posse of Oregon v. Secretary of State Clay Meyers, Lee Johnson, Candidate*, case no. S1-75-012, March 19, 1976. Correspondence of David Gernant to Everett Thoren, Sept. 21, 1976. "Posses Want Ultimate Power," *(Salem) Oregon Statesman*, March 27, 1976, section 1, p. 4.

20. "Oregon Officials Sued," *National Chronicle*, July, 22, 1979, vol. 25, no. 9. "Comitatus Sues Officials," *(Salem) Oregon Statesman*, April 23, 1976, pp. 1–2. AP, " 'Posse' Organization Sues State Officials," *Salem (Ore.) Capital Journal*, April 23, 1976, p. 1B.

21. *Sam M. Porter Sr. v. Robert S. Nichols et al.*, Clackamas County, Oregon, no. 76-8-1, July 31, 1976. Exhibit A, pp. 1–4, "Minutes of the Oregon Association of Posse Comitatus."

22. "Portlander Owns Priceless Scriptural Treasure," *Portland* magazine, February 1975, pp. 54–55.

23. "Goodwill Convicted," *(Portland) Oregonian*, Oct. 14, 1981. "New Prosecutor Ordered in Case," *(Portland) Oregonian*, Aug. 26, 1981. "Hyperthermia Said Death Cause," *(Portland) Oregonian*, Oct. 19, 1982, p. B1. Richard Read, "Potato Shed Case Leader Goodwill Found Dead," *(Portland) Oregonian*, Oct. 14, 1982, p. F7. Affidavit of Donald Allen Goodwill, in the Circuit Court for Multnomah County, June, 11, 1977. Testimony of Donald Allen Goodwill, *State of Oregon v. Cummings*, Feb. 18, 1977.

24. "Bearer Guilty of Refusing Gun Check," *(Portland) Oregonian*, July 1, 1976.

25. Report of John Gard, officer ID no. 06782-97, case no. 2363-76, July 19, 1976.

26. Report of the FBI, Portland, Oregon, Aug. 16, 1976, "Unknown Subject Sheriff's Deputies and Oregon State Troopers Umatilla County, Oregon; Donald Goodwill, Ronald Sellers, Aldis Weaver, Everett J. Thoren, Ervin Haring—Victims." See also: Testimony of Everett Thoren, *State of Oregon v. Cummings*.

27. Jerrold K. Footlick with William J. Cook, "Return of the Posse," *Newsweek*, May 26, 1975, p. 54. Affidavit of Donald Allen Goodwill, in the Circuit Court for Multnomah County, June, 11, 1977.

28. Testimony of George Everett Hill, *State of Oregon v. Cummings*.

29. Ibid.

30. Testimony of Everett Thoren, *State of Oregon v. Cummings*.

31. Testimony of George Everett Hill, *State of Oregon v. Cummings*.

32. Ibid.

33. Custody report of Trooper Richard J. Harp for Robert David Cummings, OSP, Aug. 31, 1976.

34. Vehicle report, Corporal Glenn Youngman, Umatilla County Sheriff's Department, Aug. 27, 1976. Custody Report of Jim Carey for Robert David Cummings, case no. 1859-76.

35. Testimony of Donald Goodwill, *State of Oregon v. Cummings*. Testimony of George Hill, *State of Oregon v. Cummings*.

36. Interview with Dale Clifford Madsen, by Trooper Richard Harp, Sept. 7, 1976.

37. Affidavit of Donald Allen Goodwill, in the Circuit Court for Multnomah County, June, 11, 1977.

23. Spud Shed

1. Additional documentation for the events described at Mikami Farms, beyond the endnotes to this chapter, can be found in police records, court transcripts, newspaper articles, and other sources—including, but not limited to the following: "Portlander Owns Priceless Scriptural Treasure," *Portland* magazine, Feb. 1975, pp. 54–55. Jerry F. Boone, " 'Posse' Suspects Silent in Court," *Tri-City (Ore.) Herald*, Sept. 2, 1976. " 'Posse' Seven Arraigned for Seizure of Potato Shed," *(Portland) Oregonian*, Sept. 2, 1976. "Judge Grants Continuance to Jailed 'Posse' Members," *(Portland) Oregonian*, Aug. 31, 1976. "Posse Legal Process to Be Redone," unsourced news clipping, Sept. 20, 1976. "Posse to Enter Pleas Next Week," unsourced news clipping, Sept. 22, 1976. Jerry Boone, "Maximum Sentences Sought in Posse Case," Aug. 30, 1976. Kip Cady, "County Expects Seven Trials to Be Very Expensive," *Pendleton (Ore.) East Oregonian*, Oct. 13, 1976. United Press International, "Prejudice Charged," *(Portland) Oregon Journal*, Sept. 14, 1976, p. 6. Ann Sullivan, "Occupation of Spud Shed: Portlander Denies Role in Incident," *(Portland) Oregonian*, Sept. 1, 1976. Testimony of Donald Ray Cooper, *State of Oregon v. Cummings*. Report of Frederick John Eastlick, Umatilla County Sheriff's Department, Oct. 26, 1976. Transcript of court proceedings, *State of Oregon v. Essig*, Hood River, Oregon, Dec. 7, 1976. Case no. DA-76-033, interview with Daniel Judd, Deputy Sheriff, Umatilla County, Nov. 8, 1976; date of interview, Oct. 28, 1976. Information report of Trooper Richard J. Harp, OSP, 9/8/76. Custody report of Trooper Richard J. Harp for Farrell Anthony Griggs, OSP, Aug. 31, 1976. Secret indictment, *State of Oregon v. Farrell Anthony Griggs*, no. CR 6293, Umatilla County Circuit Court, Sept. 8, 1976. "Order" of Clifford B. Olsen, Circuit Judge, Umatilla County, *State of Oregon v. Donald Allen Goodwill*, no. 6324, Nov. 9, 1976. "Order," *State of Oregon v. Vernon Edwin Essig*, no. CR 6289, Sept. 20, 1976. Secret indictment, *State of Oregon v. Donald Allen Goodwill*, no. CR 6324, in the Circuit Court of the State of Oregon for Umatilla County, Sept. 21, 1976. Affidavit in Support of Motion for a Change of Venue, *State of Oregon v. Ervin Rolland Haring*, Circuit Court, Umatilla County, Oregon, no. CR 6288, Sept, 18, 1976.

2. Bob Hamilton, interview by the author.

3. Interview with Margarito Saldena Gonzales, October 27, 1976, Oregon Department of Justice (ODJ) files. Interview with Benjamin Brian Harvey by Trooper Richard J. Harp, OSP, Nov. 21, 1976, ODJ files.

4. Transcript of testimony of Sach Mikami, *State of Oregon v. Vernon Edwin Essig*, Umatilla County Circuit Court, Hood River, Oregon, Dec. 6, 7, 8, 1976, p. 6.

5. Interview of Sachiheko Mikami by Trooper Richard Harp, Oct. 23, 1976, ODJ files. Transcript of interview with Debbie Furakawa, case no. 1859-76, Aug. 29, 1976, ODJ files.

6. "Special Report" of Fred Martin, Umatilla County Sheriff's Department, Sept. 5, 1976.

7. "Posse Commetatus [sic] Disturbance, Mikami Bros. Farm," Senior Trooper Phillip B. Underwood, Aug. 27, 1976, ODJ files. Interview with Farrell Anthony Griggs, Aug. 28, 1976, ODJ files. Interview with Margarito Saldena Gonzales, Oct. 27, 1976, ODJ files.

8. Interview with Harvey Furukawa by Trooper Richard Harp, Oct. 27, 1976, ODJ files. Transcript of interview with Debbie Furakawa, case no. 1859-76, Aug. 29, 1976, ODJ files.

9. Transcript of testimony of Amos F. Rasmussen, *State of Oregon v. Vernon Edwin Essig*. Amos F. Rasmussen, interview by the author.

10. Ibid.

11. Transcript of interview with Debbie Furakawa, case no. 1859-6, Aug. 29, 1976.

12. Jerry Boone, "Newsman Recalls the Night the Posse Rode into Town," *(Portland) Oregon Journal*, July 10, 1982, pp. 3, C1.

13. Memo from SAC, Sacramento, to Director, FBI, "Subject: San Joaquin County Posse Comitatus (SJCPC)," Aug. 24, 1976.

14. Transcript of interview with George James Cameron, Oct. 25, 1976, ODJ files. Special report of Corporal Glenn Youngman, Umatilla County Sheriff's Department, Aug. 26, 1976, ODJ files.

15. Report of Trooper Richard J. Harp, OSP, Sept. 23, 1976, ODJ files.

16. Transcript of Everett Thoren, *State of Oregon v. Cummings*.

17. "Crime Report," of Lieutenant Bob Oliver, Oregon State Patrol, Aug. 27, 1976.

18. Jerry Boone, "Posse Comitatus Surrenders Peacefully," *Tri-City (Ore.) Herald*, Aug. 29, 1976. Amos Rasmussen, interview by the author.

19. Information report of Ross E. Patrick, Senior Trooper, OSP, Sept. 1, 1976, ODJ files.

20. Custody report of Trooper Richard J. Harp for Donald Allen Goodwill, Department of State Police, Aug. 30, 1976, ODJ files. Case no. 1859-76, vehicle report, Corporal Glenn Youngman, Aug. 27, 1976, ODJ files.

21. Report of Lieutenant Bob Oliver, Oregon State Patrol, undated, ODJ files. Paul Pintarich, "Real Police Face Down 'Posse' at Shed," *(Portland) Oregonian*, Aug. 28, 1976. "Land Fight Led to Takeover," *Tri-City (Ore.) Herald*, Aug. 29, 1976.

22. "Special Report" of John Campbell Jr., Umatilla County Sheriff's Office, Aug. 31, 1976, ODJ files. "Special Report" of Karin Howard, Umatilla County Sheriff's Office," Aug. 31, 1976, ODJ files.

23. Correspondence of Everett Thoren to Donald Goodwill, undated.

24. Ann Sullivan, "Stanfield Arrestees Said Part of 'Security Force,' *(Portland) Oregonian*, Aug. 31, 1976.

25. Correspondence of Sue Cooper and Velma Griggs to "Don, Geo, and Bob," Sept. 2, 1976, ODJ files.

26. Teletype from Portland FBI to HQ, Aug. 28, 1976.

27. "Seven Comitatus Members Charged with two Felonies," Aug. 31, 1976, unsourced newspaper clipping.

28. Correspondence of Sean M. McWeeney, Assistant Special Agent in Charge, Portland FBI, to Clark E. Mears, Chief Investigator, Criminal Justice Special Investigations Division, Oct. 12, 1976, p. 1.

29. Bill Richards and Joel Kotkin, "Frontier 'Justice' Rides in West" *Washington Post*, Sept. 18, 1976, pp. A1, A8.

30. Ibid. Bill Richards and Joel Kotkin, "Far-Rightists Rustle Up Visions of the Old West," *New York Post*, Sept. 20, 1976, p. 22. Bill Richards and Joel Kotkin, "Posse Comitatus Claims 'Highest Law,' " *Sunday Oregonian*, Sept. 26, 1976, p. A18.

31. "Affidavit of Probation Violation and Motion for Issuance of Bench Warrant," *State of California v. Francis Earl Gillings*, Merced county, no. 8622, dept. 2, Aug. 6, 1979.

32. "Sheriff's Posse Comitatus (SPC), aka Citizens Law Enforcement and Research Committee (CLERC)," airtel to SAC, Albany, from Director, FBI," Oct. 26, 1976. Memo to Stephen H. Keutzer, Chief Counsel, Oregon Department of Justice, from Clark E. Mears, Chief Investigator, "Pending Activities, Posse Comitatus," Sept. 14, 1976.

33. "Affidavit and CONSTITUTIONAL ORDER, in Matters of Public Concern of Abuse of Process," *State of Oregon v. Umatilla County Court*, Umatilla County Circuit Court, Sept. 13, 1976. Correspondence of David Gernant to Everett Thoren, "Re: State ex rel *Haring v. McPherson*," Sept. 21, 1976. "Public Notice" of Everett Thoren, Sept. 14, 1976.

34. Jim Eardley, "Confrontation 'Could Have Become Bloodbath,' " *Pendleton (Ore.) East Oregonian*, Aug. 20, 1977.

35. Jerry Boone, "Newsman Recalls the Night the Posse Rode into Town," *(Portland) Oregon Journal*, July 10, 1982, p. 3, C1. "Security Lid Clamped on Potato Shed Trial," unsourced news clipping, Dec. 9, 1976, vol. 71, no. 51, pp. 1, 10.

36. Teletype from Portland FBI to Director, Dec. 29, 1976.

37. "Order for Pre-sentence Investigation," *State of Oregon v. Vernon Edwin Essig*, Hood River Circuit Court, no. 1516, Dec. 9, 1976. "In Potato Shed Takeover: Jury Finds First Defendant Guilty," *(Portland) Oregonian*, Dec. 9, 1976, p. A17.

38. Correspondence of Don Cooper to Vern Essig, Jan. 3, 1977.

39. Correspondence of Ruth Gillings, "To Whom It May Concern," Jan. 1977.

40. "Court Upholds Verdict of Man in Shed Takeover," *(Salem) Oregon Statesman*, Nov. 16, 1977.

41. Robert Hamilton, interview. Cummings received two concurrent six-month jail terms. He also was ordered to reimburse Umatilla County $2,000 in attorneys' fees and pay $500 in fines.

42. State court records clerk, Pendleton, Oregon, interview by the author.

43. Transcript of testimony of Karen Matthews, Rayburn House Office Building, Washington, D.C., July 11, 1995.

44. Karen Matthews, interview by the author.

45. Karen Matthews, "The Terrorist Next Door," *New York Times*, June 1, 1997, Op-Ed. Serge F. Kovaleski, "Officials at Forum Describe Alleged Militia Threats," *Washington Post*, July 12, 1995. Transcript of testimony of Karen Matthews, Rayburn House Office Building, Washington, D.C., July 11, 1995. "Indictment in Karen Matthews Beating," news release, U.S. DOJ, United States Attorney, Eastern District of California, June 26, 1995.

46. Bob Hamilton, interview.

47. "Sheriff's Posse Comitatus," U.S. DOJ, FBI, Portland, Oregon, Sept. 9, 1976.

48. "Sheriff's Posse Comitatus (SPC) Also Known as Citizens Law Enforcement and Research Committee (CLERC)," U.S. DOJ, FBI, Portland, Oregon, Sept. 12, 1977.

49. Airtel from Director, FBI, to SAC, Albany, re: "Sheriff's Posse Comitatus (SPC), Domestic Security," Oct. 5, 1977.

24. Farm Strike!

1. Donald P. Baker and Blaine Harden, "Tractors Leave Capitol Hill; Farmers Vote to Stay, Fight," *Washington Post*, Jan. 22, 1978, p. A1. Charles J. Cannon, "American Agriculture Movement Tactics Switch from Confrontation to Education," United Press International, May 1, 1983.

2. Gerald McCathern, *From the White House to the Hoosegow* (Canyon, TX: Staked Plains Press, 1978), p. 7.

3. Baker and Harden, "Tractors Leave Capitol Hill; Farmers Vote to Stay, Fight," Jan. 22, 1978, p. A1. Bill Curry, "A Strike Down on the Farm," *Washington Post*, Nov. 14, 1977, p. A1. Associated Press, Springfield, Colorado, P.M. cycle, July 20, 1978.

4. Baker and Harden, "Tractors Leave Capitol Hill; Farmers Vote to Stay, Fight," Jan. 22, 1978, p. A1. Curry, "A Strike Down on the Farm," Nov. 14, 1977, p. A1. New York Times Company Abstracts, *New York Times*, Dec. 15, 1977. "Bud Bitner Killed in Pickup Crash," *AAM News*, vol. 6, no. 21, Nov. 29, 1983, p. 3.

5. "Farmers Protests in Carter's Hometown," *Facts on File World News Digest*, Dec. 3, 1977, p. 916, D1. Don Kendell, Associated Press, Dec. 11, 1977, Mead Data Central. Curry, "A Strike Down on the Farm," p. A1.

6. "Striking Farmers Talk with Carter," *Facts on File World News Digest*, Dec. 31, 1977, p. 1002, E3.

7. *Hen House Hash*, undated AAM newsletter published in Corning, Iowa, circa April 1978.

8. Curry, "A Strike Down on the Farm," Nov. 14, 1977, p. A1.

9. McCathern (1978), pp. 19–26.

10. According to AAM, the protest drew 11,742 tractors and 30,000 farmers, while mainstream-media reports put the number of tractors at 4,000. McCathern (1978), p. 29.

11. "Farmers Protest in Carter's Hometown," *Facts on File World News Digest*, Dec. 3, 1977, p. 916.

12. Curry, "A Strike Down on the Farm," Nov. 14, 1977, p. A1. Don Kendell, Associated Press, Dec. 11, 1977, Mead Data Central.

13. Wilson Morris, "Farmers Vow Food Power Fight to Get Demands," *Washington Post*, Dec. 11, 1977, p. A1.

14. Ibid. (1977), p. A1.

15. Mike Christensen, "Georgia Protest Leader's Rhetoric Is Drifting to the Right," *Atlanta Journal-Constitution*, Jan. 12, 1986, pp. 1B, 6B. Larry Batson, "Hard Times Turn Farmers Away from Plowshares to Swords," *Minneapolis Star Tribune*, Dec. 29, 1986, pp. 1A, 4A–5A (Metro).

16. McCathern (1978), p. 40.

17. Appearing the same day on CBS-TV's *Face the Nation*, Agriculture Secretary Bergland said the federal government should guarantee farm prices at cost of production levels, but that was "about as far as the government should go." Although this pledge fell far short of 100 percent parity, it was a rhetorical concession, given that current federal price floors were far lower. But Bergland also predicted that farm protests would not force any changes in government policy. Don Kendell, AP, Dec. 11, 1977, Mead Data Central.

18. "The Daily Diary of President Jimmy Carter," Dec. 24, 1977: http://carterlibrary.galileo.peachnet.edu/diary/1977/d122477t.pdf. "Striking Farmers Talk with Carter," *Facts on File World News Digest*, Dec. 31, 1977, p. 1002, E3.

19. If loan rates were too low, however (or if other factors discouraged farmers from cutting production), the result was often huge surpluses and falling prices. Without enough grain tied to the government program, the loan rate functioned more like a price ceiling, instead of the floor it was designed to be. Even with low participation, successive years of surpluses and low market prices drove up the cost of farm programs because those farmers who had signed up for the program invariably opted to turn their grain over to the government and keep the loan.

20. Darrell Smith, "The Free Market's Biggest Fan: Earl Butz Still Loves Farmers and Hates Controls," *Farm Journal*, 1999.

21. Ibid. Dan Morgan, *Merchants of Grain* (New York: Penguin Books, 1980), pp. 201, 349. Wendell Berry, "Failing Our Farmers," *New York Times*, July 6, 1999, p. A21: Smith (1999).

22. Accompanied by the country/gospel singer Pat Boone on a flight back from the Republican National Convention in Kansas City, Boone asked Butz why blacks were so rare in the Re-

publican Party. "I'll tell you what coloreds want," the Agriculture Secretary quipped. "It's three things: First, a tight pussy; second, loose shoes; and third, a warm place to shit." Butz's remarks were reported in *Rolling Stone* magazine and The Associated Press picked up the story, but hardly any newspapers were bold enough to run the quotation uncensored. Instead they printed the supposed punch line with the euphemisms "obscenity" and "vulgarism" appearing between ellipses. But Butz's political fate was sealed and he resigned. According to the *Columbia Journalism Review*, only two newspapers printed the joke verbatim: the *Madison Capital Times* in Wisconsin, and the *Toledo Blade* in Ohio. When the *Lubbock Avalanche-Journal* announced that readers could see the original statement in the newspaper office, more than two hundred people reportedly did so. And when the *San Diego Evening Tribune* offered to mail Butz's remarks to anyone who asked, the paper received more than three thousand requests. Two years earlier, President Gerald Ford had forced Butz to apologize for an offensive anti-Catholic joke he told to newsmen regarding the pope's opposition to birth control. For more on Butz's remarks, see: www.urbanlegends.com/celebrities/butz_racistremark.html. Charles Schutz, "The Sociability of Ethnic Jokes," *Australian Journal of Comedy*, vol. 1, no. 1, 1995, www.ozcomedoy.com/journal/11schutz/htm. James F. Klumpp and Thomas A. Hollihan, "Debunking the Resignation of Earl Butz: Sacrificing an Official Racist," *Quarterly Journal of Speech*, 1979, vol. 65, pp. 1–11. Gorton Carruth, *The Encyclopedia of American Facts and Dates* (New York: HarperCollins, 1993, Ninth Edition) p. 722. "U.S. Farmers Association Pickets Butz," *AAM News*, vol. 6, no. 4, April 5, 1983, p. 1. David Bird and Albin Krebs, Notes on People; "Not a Happy Ending for Earl Butz," *New York Times*, July 3, 1981, p. C12.

23. For a definitive account of the role of multinational grain companies in setting farm prices and influencing farm policy, see: Morgan (1980).

24. Kevin Ristau and Mark Ritchie, "The Farm Crisis: History and Analysis," *Shmate*, no. 16, Fall 1986, p. 12.

25. Don Kendell, Associated Press, Dec. 11, 1977, Mead Data Central.

26. Curry, "A Strike Down on the Farm," Nov. 14, 1977, p. A1.

27. Smith, "The Free Market's Biggest Fan: Earl Butz Still Loves Farmers and Hates Controls," *Farm Journal*, 1999.

28. Lynn Darling and Dan Morgan, "Farmers' Plight: Profits and Shrinking Political Clout," *Washington Post*, March 16, 1978, p. A3.

29. Daniel Levitas, "A Crisis of Dignity: The Emotional Costs of Going Under," *Rural America*, July–Aug. 1983.

30. Ristau and Ritchie, "The Farm Crisis: History and Analysis," Fall 1986, pp. 10–20.

31. Carruth (1993), pp. 723–24.

32. Ibid., pp. 725, 733.

33. Baker and Harden, "Tractors Leave Capitol Hill; Farmers Vote to Stay, Fight," Jan. 22, 1978, p. A1.

34. Morgan (1980).

35. William Grieder, *Secrets of the Temple: How the Federal Reserve Runs the Country* (New York: Simon and Schuster, 1987), p. 339. Boosting exports became even more important to federal policymakers and the grain cartel several years later when the Carter administration embargoed all grain exports to the Soviet Union in response to the 1979 invasion of Afghanistan.

36. This was not a rally in support of organic farming, however. "If Mexico is allowed to use DDT, and Americans eat the vegetables, let U.S. farmers use DDT also. Then we can compete with the imports," AAM explained. "Striking Farmers Block Mexican Imports," *Facts on File World Digest*, March 10, 1978, p. 163, F1. Blaine Harden, "Farmers 'Working' Washington in

Shifts as They Lobby for Parity," *Washington Post*, March 9, 1978, p. A6. *Hen House Hash* (circa March 1978).

37. David Senter, interview by the author.

38. *Hen House Hash* (circa March 1978).

39. Jack Anderson, "Leader of the Agricultural Rebels," unsourced news clipping, Dec. 27, 1978.

40. "Agriculture Leader Plans to Sell Part of His Farm," AP, Dec. 11, 1979.

41. Batson, "Hard Times Turn Farmers Away from Plowshares, to Swords," Dec. 29, 1986, p. 4A (Metro).

42. Darling and Morgan, "Farmers' Plight: Profits Pinch and Shrinking Political Clout," March 16, 1978, p. A3.

43. *Hen House Hash* (circa March 1978).

44. "American Agriculture Movement Accomplishments," undated flyer, circa 1982–83.

45. Blaine Harden, "Farmers 'Working' Washington in Shifts as They Lobby for Parity," *Washington Post*, March 9, 1978, p. A6.

46. McCathern (1978), p. 116.

47. Darling and Morgan, "Farmers' Plight: Profits Pinch and Shrinking Political Clout," March 16, 1978, p. A3.

48. Richard L. Lyons, "House Votes Down Farm Price Rises by 268 to 150; House Votes to Kill Farm Bill as Protesting Farmers Look On," *Washington Post*, April 13, 1978, p. A1.

49. Ibid. Democrats outnumbered Republicans, 292 to 143.

50. Associated Press, Springfield, Colorado, July 20, 1978.

51. William R. Ritz, "Farm Militants Study Bomb-Making: U.S. Probing Guerrilla 'Seminars,' " *Denver Post*, Feb. 13, 1983, pp. 1A, 14A.

52. American Agriculture Movement (AAM) newsletter, published in Bertrand, Nebraska, May 1978.

53. "News from Springfield, Colorado," AAM newsletter, Corning, Iowa, circa April 1978.

25. Tractorcade

1. Dan Morgan, "Drive to Increase Farm Income Expected to Be Harder this Year," *Washington Post*, Feb. 5, 1979, p. A1. "Tractors Invade Washington," *Facts on File World News Digest*, Feb. 16, 1979, p. 109, C2.

2. Ken Ringle, "In the Aftermath of February; Farmers Leave City, $1 Million Mall Damage," *Washington Post*, March 4, 1979, p. B1.

3. "Tractors Invade Washington," *Facts on File World News Digest*, Feb. 16, 1979, pp. 109, C2.

4. Ibid.

5. Blaine Harden, "Farmers Dig In for Long Siege," *Washington Post*, Feb. 8, 1979, p. A1.

6. David Pauly with Richard Manning, "A Harvest of Ill Will," *Newsweek*, Feb. 19, 1979, p. 61.

7. Harden, "Farmers Dig In for Long Siege," Feb. 8, 1979, p. A1.

8. Morgan, "Drive to Increase Farm Income Expected to Be Harder This Year," Feb. 5. 1979, p. A1.

9. Wesley McCune, "Radical Right Courts the Farm Protest Drive," *Group Research Report*, Feb. 28, 1979.

10. Ibid.

11. "To the Congress of the United States. Notice and Demand. . . . Served Upon Every Member of the Congress by Members of the American Agriculture Movement on February 14, 1979. . . . Done at Springfield, Colorado, December 30, 1978," undated flyer.

12. James Wickstrom, *The American Farmer: Twentieth Century Slave* (Wisconsin Posse Comitatus), circa 1978.

13. Liza Bercovici, "Final Tractorcade Brings Harmony," *Washington Post*, March 2, 1979, p. B1.

14. Ringle, "In the Aftermath of February; Farmers Leave City, $1 Million Mall Damage," p. B1. Tom Hallman and Ann Wead Kimbrough, "A Farm Union in Georgia? Labor Leader Says AFL-CIO Would Welcome Affiliation," *Atlanta Journal-Constitution*, April 7, 1985, p. K1.

15. Sharon Conway, "D.C. Police Evict Campers, Other Farmers' Vehicles," *Washington Post*, March 7, 1979, p. C2.

16. Jack Eisen, "U.S. Funds Sought for D.C. Costs in Curbing Farmers," *Washington Post*, March 14, 1979, p. C1.

17. Associated Press, Washington Dateline, March 28, 1979. Associated Press, Washington dateline, April 1, 1979.

18. Carl Hilliard, "Today's Focus," Associated Press, July 2, 1979.

19. Ibid. Associated Press, Domestic News, Aug. 4, 1979. Scott Kraft, "Strike Is Dead, But Frustration Continues," Associated Press, Dec. 14, 1979.

20. Gorton Carruth, *The Encyclopedia of American Facts and Dates* (New York: HarperCollins, 1993, Ninth Edition), p. 743. William Grieder, *Secrets of the Temple: How the Federal Reserve Runs the Country* (New York: Simon and Schuster, 1987), p. 361.

21. Sheldon Emry, *Billions for the Bankers; Debts for the People* (Phoenix, AZ: Lord's Covenant Church, 1984), p. 6.

22. Ibid., p. 19.

23. Reverend William P. Gale, *The Faith of Our Fathers* (Mariposa, CA: Ministry of Christ Church, 1963), p. 44. For more variations on this theme, see: Eustace Mullins, *Secrets of the Federal Reserve* (Staunton, VA: Bankers Research Institute, 1983). The Reverend Charles E. Coughlin, *Money! Questions and Answers* (Royal Oak, MI: The National Union for Social Justice, 1936). Charles S. Norburn, M.D., *Honest Money: The United States Note* (Asheville, NC: New Puritan Library, 1983). M. J. Beckman, *Born-Again Republic* (Billings, MT: Freedom Church Bookstore, 1981). Paul Stevens and E. O. Kelsey, "Money Made Mysterious," *American Mercury*, vol. 87, nos. 417 and 418, pp. 65–95 and pp. 99–140, respectively.

24. Emry (1984), p. 21.

25. The early and withering effects of the gold standard were especially evident during the economic panic of 1873. More than twenty years later, Bryan's famous "cross of gold" speech closed debate on the Democratic Party platform in Chicago in 1896 and helped win him the Party's presidential nomination. For the complete text of the speech, see: Ronald F. Reid, *Three Centuries of American Rhetorical Discourse* (Prospect Heights, IL: Waveland Press, 1988), pp. 601–6. A. Craig Baird, *American Public Address* (New York: McGraw-Hill, 1956), pp. 194–200.

26. "Speak Out," *AAM News*, Feb. 26, 1980, vol. 3, no. 3, p. 7.

27. Ibid., p. 3. See also: Charles J. Cannon, "American Agriculture Movement Tactics Switch from Confrontation to Education," United Press International, May 1, 1983.

28. "On Collective Farms," *AAM News*, vol. 5, no. 25, Jan. 11, 1983, p. 7.

26. No Substitute for Knowledge

1. "Militant Farmers Group Prepares for 'Revolution,' " United Press International, Kansas Regional News, July 26, 1982.

2. Betty Luman, "Posse Comitatus—A Belief Authority Stops at County Level: Is Paramilitary Antitax Group a Threat to Law and Order?" United Press International, Domestic News, April 2, 1983. John Petterson, "Paramilitary Instruction Under Fire," *Kansas City (Mo.) Times*, Feb. 15, 1983, pp. A1, A10.

3. William R. Ritz, "Farm Militants Study Bomb-Making: U.S. Probing Guerrilla 'Seminars,' " *Denver Post*, Feb. 13, 1983, pp. 1A, 14A. "Ecological Seminar," informant's report, 99-55879, March 29, 1982. According to the August 24, 1982 edition of *AAM News*, Leonard Cox gave the opening prayer at the Northwest District AAM meeting in Colby, Kansas, on August 3, and spoke out challenging a move that had been made by AAM, Inc., to abandon *AAM News* as the organization's official publication.

4. "Ecological Seminar," informant's report, 99-55879, March 29, 1982. "Farmers Liberation Army Emerges," *AAM News*, Aug. 24, 1982, vol. 5, no. 24, p. 2.

5. "Militant Farmers' Group Prepares for 'Revolution,' " United Press International, Kansas Regional News, July 26, 1982. "Ecological Seminar," informant's report, 99-55879, March 29, 1982.

6. "Interview—James P. Wickstrom," Wisc. DOJ, DCI, case no. SA-159, Sept. 26, 1984. "Ecological Seminar," informant's report, 99-55879, March 29, 1982.

7. "Ecological Seminar," informant's report, 99-55879, March 29, 1982.

8. Robert M. Ankenbrandt, "Undercover Activity," Wisc. DOJ, DCI, SA-159-8, Aug. 4, Sept. 11, and Sept. 18, 1980.

9. Frank Ryan, "Capitol Commentary," United Press International, May 26, 1981.

10. Barbara Cotter, "Neighbors of Howarths Shocked by Bomb Arrests," *(Colorado Springs) Gazette Telegraph*, May 6, 1982, p. A2.

11. Charles N. Howarth, "The Constitution of the Posse Comitatus," circa 1980.

12. Supplementary affidavit of Thomas Harris, *People of the State of Colorado v. Wesley Ray White*, 83CR389, District Court, El Paso County, State of Colorado, Feb. 22, 1983. "Militant Farmers' Group Prepares for 'Revolution,' " United Press International, Kansas Regional News, July 26, 1982. UPI, Colorado Regional News, Aug. 1, 1982. Jack Cox, "Right-Wing Posse Comitatus Increases Activity in Colorado," *Denver Post*, Aug. 1, 1982. Barbara Cotter, "Bomb Sales Ring May Be Cracked; Grand Jury to Question Suspects Tonight," *(Colorado Springs) Gazette Telegraph*, May 6, 1982, pp. A1, 5.

13. Cotter, "Bomb Sales Ring May Be Cracked; Grand Jury to Question Suspects Tonight," May 6, 1982, pp. A1, 5. Barbara Cotter and Joyce Trent, "Grand Jurors to Investigate Illegal Bombs," *(Colorado Springs) Gazette Telegraph*, May 5, 1982, p. A1. Joyce Trent, "Four Springs Residents Charged in Bomb Sales," *(Colorado Springs) Gazette Telegraph*, May 7, 1982, p. A2.

14. Howarth was sentenced to two years in prison and denied probation, while White received a year in jail on one charge and was granted supervised probation on another. Howarth was paroled after serving one year. Two other Colorado Springs men, Salvador Parisi, twenty-nine, and Donald Dorey, thirty-nine, were given deferred sentences after pleading guilty to illegal possession of explosives. "Klan Leader Howarth Is Released on Parole," *(Colorado Springs) Ga-*

zette Telegraph, Feb. 8, 1984, p. B3. Judgment of conviction: sentence: and Order to Sheriff (Mittimus) *People of the State of Colorado v. Wesley Ray White*, 83CR389, District Court, El Paso County, State of Colorado, April 6, 1984. Judgment of Conviction: Sentence: and Order to Sheriff (Mittimus), *People of the State of Colorado v. Charles Norman Howarth*, 82CRO787, District Court, El Paso County, State of Colorado, Feb. 25, 1983.

15. Jack Cox, "Candidate for Sheriff Vows Big Cleanup; Posse Comitatus Member 'Thorough,' " *Denver Post*, Aug. 2, 1982.

16. Ritz, "Farm Militants Study Bomb-Making; U.S. Probing Guerrilla 'Seminars,' " pp. 1A, 14A.

17. Ibid.

18. Ibid.

19. Ibid.

20. Ibid.

21. "Militant Farmers' Group Prepares for 'Revolution,' " United Press International, Kansas Regional News, July 26, 1982.

22. Ibid.

23. Ibid.

24. Born in 1744 in the German Jewish ghetto of Frankfurt am Main, Mayer Amschel Rothschild was a coin dealer who became prominent in banking. After his five sons established offices in London, Paris, Naples, and Vienna, the family executed financial transactions for governments and leading members of the European aristocracy with amazing efficiency. Rothchild's grandsons, in turn, became prestigious members of British and French society. By the mid–nineteenth century, the family was enormously influential across Europe.

25. A spirited disagreement exists among historians and others who interpret Midwestern Populism and its nineteenth-century roots as either largely reactionary or essentially progressive. For more on the extensive debate about the anti-Semitic content of Populism and the nineteenth-century Populist movement, see: Edward Flower, "Anti-Semitism in the Free Silver and Populist Movements and the Election of 1896" (M.A. thesis, Department of History, Columbia University, 1952), as cited by Lipset and Raab (1978), p. 95. Frederic Cople Jaher, "Were the Populists Anti-Semitic?" *Anti-Semitism in the United States*, Leonard Dinnerstein, ed. (New York: Holt, Rhinehart and Winston, 1971), pp. 78–86. Norman Pollack, "Hofstadter on Populism: A Critique of the Age of Reform," *Journal of Southern History*, vol. 26 (1960), pp. 478–500. William F. Holmes, "Whitecapping: Anti-Semitism in the Populist Era," *American Jewish Historical Quarterly*, March 1974, no. 63, pp. 244–61. Richard Hofstadter, *The Age of Reform: From Bryan to FDR* (New York: Vintage, 1960). Richard Hofstader, *The Paranoid Style in American Politics* (New York: Knopf, 1965). Norman Pollack, "The Myth of Populist Anti-Semitism," *American Historical Review*, Oct. 1962, pp. 76–80. William C. Pratt, "Using History to Make History? Progressive Farm Organizing During the Farm Revolt of the 1980s," *The Annals of Iowa*, vol. 55 (Winter 1996), State Historical Society of Iowa, p. 31.

26. Bruce Maxwell, "Far-Right Group Ready to Fight for Farmers," *Rochester (Minn.) Post-Bulletin*, Nov. 12, 1984, p. 6.

27. Alden Nellis, "To Protest or to Revolt," *AAM News*, vol. 5, no. 24, Aug. 23, 1982, pp. 2, 7. "Cryts Spends Weekend in Fort Smith Jail," *AAM News*, Aug. 24, 1982, vol. 5, no. 24, p. 1. "Jury Finds Cryts Not Guilty," *AAM News*, June 14, 1983, vol. 6, no. 9, pp. 1, 8.

28. The 1982 AAM convention was held in Minot, North Dakota. "Senter Hired as Director of National Office," *AAM News*, vol. no. 3, Feb. 26, 1980, p. 1. "Around the Countryside," *AAM News*, vol. 5, no. 24, Aug. 24, 1982, p. 3. Alden and Micki Nellis, "Why We Weren't at

the Convention," *AAM News*, vol. 5, no. 36, Jan. 25, 1983, p. 12. David Senter, interview by the author.

29. "Around the Countryside," *AAM News*, vol. 5, no. 24, Aug. 24, 1982, p. 3.

30. Memo of Supervisor Williams, "Posse Comitatus," KBI, Nov. 4, 1982.

31. Jolene Hoss, " 'Citizens' Grand Jury' Calls for the Jailing of Ten Judges,' " *Salina (Kans.) Journal*, Nov. 21, 1982. Annette Galluzzi, "Posse Comitatus Threatens Judges," *Garden City (Kans.) Telegram*, Nov. 20, 1982. "Request for Information—Kansas Bureau of Investigation," Case Activity Report, case no. SA-159, Wendell A. Harker, Special Agent, Wisc. DOJ, DCI, Dec. 10, 1982.

32. The notices were mailed on November 13, 1982, from Topeka. Hoss, "Citizens' Grand Jury Calls for the Jailing of Ten Judges," Nov. 21, 1982. Galluzzi, "Posse Comitatus Threatens Judges," Nov. 20, 1982. "Request for Information—Kansas Bureau of Investigation," Case Activity Report, case no. SA-159, Wendell A. Harker, Special Agent, Wisc. DOJ, DCI, Dec. 10, 1982. United Press International, Regional News, Kansas, Jan. 21, 1983, A.M. cycle.

33. "Request for Information—Kansas Bureau of Investigation," Wendell A. Harker, Special Agent, Wisc. DOJ, DCI, Dec. 13, 1982.

34. Transcript of KTTL broadcast, Nov. 30, 1982.

35. Dodge City Citizens for better Broadcasting, "Petition to Enlarge" before the Federal Communications Commission, Washington, D.C., MM docket no. 85-127. File no. BRH-830201ZY. File no. BPH-830502AY, p. 4. Janet Cawley, "High-Noon Showdown for Radio Racism," *Chicago Tribune*, May 22, 1983. Associated Press, "Kansas Radio Broadcaster Jailed after Contempt-of-Court Citation," *Kansas City (Mo.) Times*, Nov. 16, 1983, pp. D1–2. Alan S. Katchen, "The Station that Broadcasts Hate," *ADL Bulletin*, Feb. 1985, p. 4. Wayne King, "Kansans Protest Broadcasts of Hate," *New York Times*, May 18, 1983, p. A18. Pat Remick, United Press International, Regional News, Kansas, July 15, 1983. Pat Remick, United Press International, Kansas Regional News, Aug. 4, 1983. Gene Smith "Posse Problems—Real or Imaginary?" *Topeka Capital-Journal*, March 27, 1983. Bill Hirschman, "KTTL Resumes Anti-Semitic Broadcasts," *Wichita (Kans.) Eagle-Beacon*, undated.

36. Naomi Gunderson, interview by the author.

37. King, "Kansans Protest Broadcast of Hate," May 18, 1983, p. A18. Ben Bradlee Jr., "FCC Probes Supremist [*sic*] Broadcasts," *Boston Sunday Globe*, July 28, 1985.

38. "Informal Objection of the State of Kansas," *In re: Application of* CATTLE COUNTRY BROAD-CASTING *for Renewal of License of Station KTTL-FM, Dodge City, Kansas*, file no. BRH-830201ZY, July 15, 1983. "FCC Accused of Procrastinating," *Electronic Media*, Oct. 25, 1984. Jim Drinkard, Associated Press, July 12, 1983. Angelia Herrin, "Broadcast Slurs Ruled Not Cause to Seize License," *Wichita (Kans.) Eagle-Beacon*, Apr. 27, 1985, pp. 1D, 13D. The Babbses separated in September 1983 after seventeen years of marriage. Two months later Nellie Babbs was jailed on contempt-of-court charges after she refused to answer questions about her failure to pay $4,000 in back taxes owed by KTTL to Gray County, Kansas. "Controversial Owner of Radio Station Returned to Jail," Associated Press, Nov. 17, 1983. "Kansas Broadcaster Answers Second Contempt Citation," Associated Press, Nov. 16, 1983.

39. "Farm Sale Draws Crowd; Sheriff Won't Let Farmers Bid," *AAM News*, vol. 5, no. 35, Jan. 11, 1983, pp. 1–4. "Farmers Tried in Springfield," *AAM News*, vol. 6, no. 15, Sept. 6, 1983, pp. 1, 4–9.

40. John Toohey, "Farmer Sues for $100 Million, Calls Federal Officials Maggots," *Denver Post*, Nov. 2, 1983. "Jerry Wright's Case Accepted by Supreme Court," *AAM News*, vol. 6, no. 6, May 3, 1983, p. 1. "Supreme Court Decides Not to Hear Jerry Wright's Case," *AAM News*, vol. 6, no. 10, June 28, 1983, p. 1. Jerry Wright Files Suit on FmHA, Federal Land Bank," *AAM News*, vol. 6, no. 20, Nov. 15, 1983, p. 1.

41. Report of Wendell A. Harker, "Attend Seminar—Kansas," Wisc. DOJ, DCI, Feb. 14, 1983. John Chambers, "Right-Wing Posse Spans U.S. Counties," *Topeka (Kans.) Capital-Journal*, Feb. 15, 1983, pp. 1, 3. "Lawmen Quiet about Secret Meeting on Secret Organizations," *Hays (Kans.) Daily News*, Feb. 10, 1983.

42. United Press International, Kansas Regional News, Feb. 9, 1983.

43. Report of Wendell A. Harker, "Attend Seminar—Kansas," Wisc. DOJ, DCI, Feb. 14, 1983.

27. Tax Protester

1. For definitive biographical material on Gordon Kahl, see: James Corcoran, *Bitter Harvest: Gordon Kahl and the Posse Comitatus—Murder in the Heartland* (New York: Viking, 1990), pp. 43–68.

2. Transcript of notes of FBI interview with Miss Lonnie Kahl, Feb. 19, 1983, Minneapolis, file no. 89B-388 sub C-81.

3. Corcoran (1990), pp. 45–49.

4. Videotape, *Gordon Kahl Was* . . . Death and Taxes Uncensored Ministries, Country People Productions, Venice, California, 1996.

5. Videotape, *Gordon Kahl's Texas Tax Trial*, Country People Productions, 1993. *Kahl Meets U.S. Marshal Bud Warren*, undated audiotape, circa 1981.

6. *Kahl Meets U.S. Marshal Bud Warren*.

7. Len Martin, *Why "They" Wanted! to Get Gordon Kahl* (Boring, OR: CPA Book Publisher, 1996), p. 8.

8. Videotape, *Gordon Kahl's Texas Tax Trial*, Country People Productions, 1993. "Dakota Dragnet; Two U.S. Marshals Are Slain," *Time* magazine, Feb. 28, 1983, p. 25. Joanne Omang, "North Dakota Militant Eludes Lawmen," *Washington Post*, Feb. 16, 1983, p. A3. Transcript of notes of interview with Joan Kahl, by Special Agent J. P. Hufford, FBI, Feb, 17, 1983, Mpls. file no. 89B-388 sub C-313.

9. "Fugitive Was Known in Texas for Eccentric Views," Associated Press, Domestic News, Feb. 14, 1983. Omang, "North Dakota Militant Eludes Lawmen," Feb. 16, 1983, p. A3.

10. Videotape, *Gordon Kahl's Texas Tax Trial*." Teletype from El Paso, Texas, FBI to headquarters, May 29, 1975; memo from FBI director to El Paso, Special Agent in Change, Sept. 11, 1975.

11. Videotape, *Gordon Kahl's Texas Tax Trial*.

12. Corcoran (1990), p. 54. United States Department of Justice, FBI record no. 209-851-R4, for Gordon Wendell Kahl.

13. Audiotape, *Kahl Meets U.S. Marshal Bud Warren*. Corcoran (1990), p. 54.

14. Opinion of Circuit Court Judge Donald Ross; appeals from the United States District Court for the District of North Dakota; *United States of America v. Scott Faul et. al*, United States Court of Appeals for the Eighth Circuit, May 14, 1984 (filed Nov. 7, 1984), p. 3. Corcoran (1990), p. 55. U.S. DOJ, FBI record no. 209-851-R4, for Gordon Wendell Kahl.

15. *Kahl Meets U.S. Marshal Bud Warren*. U.S. DOJ, FBI record no. 209-851-R4, for Gordon Wendell Kahl.

16. *Kahl Meets U.S. Marshal Bud Warren*. *Scott Faul et al. v. United States of America*, petition for a Writ of Certiorari, U.S. Supreme Court, October Term, 1984, nos. 84-1373, 84-6332, and 84-6350, May 30, 1985, p. 3.

17. *Scott Faul et al. v. United States of America*, petition for a Writ of Certiorari (May 30, 1985), p. 3. "Fugitive Was Known in Texas for Eccentric Views," Associated Press, Domestic News, Feb. 14, 1983. Correspondence of Michael V. Anderson, revenue officer, to Gordon W. Kahl, c/o Joan Kahl, March 28, 1983.

18. Audiotape, *Kahl Meets U.S. Marshal Bud Warren.*

19. Ibid.

20. Ibid. Corcoran (1990), pp. 56–58.

21. Corcoran (1990), pp. 63–65.

22. "Notice of Ex-Communication," correspondence of Yorie Von Kahl, "Bishop of the Gospel Doctrine Church of Jesus Christ," to Joan Kahl, Aug. 27, 1982. "Motion to Renew Motion to Sever, Motion for Psychiatric Examination, and Motion to Continue," and "Affidavit [of Joan Kahl] in Support of Motion," *United States of America vs. Scott Faul et al*, in the United States District Court for the District of North Dakota, Southeastern Division, C3-83-16, May 4, 1983. Bruce Maxwell, "Far Right Group Ready to Fight for Farmers," *Rochester (Minn.) Post-Bulletin*, Nov. 13, 1984, p. 6.

23. Corcoran (1990), pp. 63–68.

24. Martin (1996), pp. 4–5. Corcoran (1990), p. 60. "Farmer Liberation Army Goals Listed," *Bismarck (North Dak.) Tribune*, March 20, 1983.

25. Martin (1996), pp. 4–5. Corcoran (1990), pp. 79–80, 156–57.

26. Martin (1996), p. 19. Transcript of notes of interview with Leonard Paul Martin, by USMS Inspector Larry Homenick, FBI, Feb. 18, 1983, Minneapolis file no. 89B-388 sub C-38.

27. Martin (1996).

28. Memo of Daniel Levitas and the Reverend David L. Ostendorf to Key Farm and Rural Contacts, "Rural Radical Right Update," PrairieFire Rural Action, April 20, 1988, pp. 4–6.

29. Transcript of notes of interview with Byron C. Dale, FBI, Feb. 18, 1983, Minneapolis file no. 89B-388 sub C-133. Transcript of notes of interview with Fred Richter, Feb. 18, 1983, Minneapolis file no. 89B-388 sub C-73. Corcoran (1990), pp. 24–26.

30. Corcoran (1990), pp. 77–80. Transcript of notes of interview with Ester Graff, by Special Agent Scott T. Johnson, FBI, Feb. 22, 1983, Minneapolis file no. 89B-388 sub C. Transcript of notes of interview with Gottlieb Maier, by Special Agent Scott T. Johnson, FBI, Feb. 22, 1983, Minneapolis file no. 89B-388 sub C. Summary of prosecutive interview of Vernon Alan Wegner, by Special Agent Kenneth M. Aldridge, FBI, Fargo, North Dakota, March 16, 17, 1983.

31. Transcript of notes of interview with Robert Dick, by Deputy Glenn Whaley, Inspector Mark Sorenson, and Inspector Don Lamb, U.S. Marshals Service, FBI, March 30, 1983, Minneapolis file no. 89B-388 sub C-375. Transcript of notes of interview with Clarence S. Martin, by Supervisory Special Agent John E. Shimota, FBI, Feb. 22, 1983, Minneapolis file no. 89B-388 sub C-47.

32. Opinion of Circuit Court Judge Donald Ross (filed Nov. 7, 1984), pp. 3–7. Gerald Kopplin, " 'Bloodshed Could Have Been Avoided'—Friends," United Press International, Feb. 19, 1983.

33. Leeanne Spigner, "Fugitive's Body Identified; Couple Moved," *Jonesboro (Ark.) Sun*, June 7, 1983.

34. Opinion of Circuit Court Judge Donald Ross (Nov. 7, 1984), p. 4.

35. "I, GORDON KAHL," handwritten letter, author's collection, circa Feb. 1983, p. 3. Opinion of Circuit Court Judge Donald Ross (Nov. 7, 1984), pp. 3–7. "Rough Draft 302," FBI, Special

Agent Ivan W. Nicholson, March 4, 1983, transcription of North Dakota State Radio Communications for Feb. 13, 1983, Section III, Channel 3, 4:46 P.M.–6:20 P.M. (pp. 16–31).

36. Opinion of Circuit Court Judge Donald Ross (Nov. 7, 1984), pp. 3–7. "I, GORDON KAHL," p. 4.

37. July 9, 1982 broadcast, Exhibit 1, Dodge City Citizens for Better Broadcasting, "Petition to Enlarge" before the Federal Communications Commission, Washington, D.C., MM docket no. 85-127. File no. BRH-830201ZY. File no. BPH-830502AY.

38. H. C. Davids, "Ruger's Mini-14 Is no Mattel Toy: Weapons Specialist Says It's a Well-Built Bargain," *Soldier of Fortune*, Dec. 1980, pp. 1, 46–50, 83–84.

39. "I, GORDON KAHL," p. 7.

40. Report of Special Agent Larry C. Brubaker, March 31, 1983, Minneapolis file no. 89B-388 sub C-368. Transcription of North Dakota State Radio Communications for Feb. 13, 1983, Section III, Channel 3, 4:47 P.M.–6:19 P.M. (p. 30).

41. Autopsy report for Gordon Wendell Kahl, State of Arkansas, Department of Public Safety, State Crime Laboratory, Medical Examiner Division, case no. MEA-275-83, June 4, 1983, p. 4.

42. "Autopsy Results," transcript of report by Special Agent Ivan W. Nicholson, FBI, Bismarck, North Dakota. Autopsy report by Merritt D. Moon for Kenneth Muir, Autopsy Protocol A-83-8, Bismarck Hospital, March 15, 1982. AP, "Dakota 'Fanatic' Hunted in Slaying of 2 Marshals," *New York Times*, Feb. 15, 1983, p. 14.

43. Transcript of notes of interview with Dr. Kenneth R. Mattheis, by Special Agent Ivan W. Nicholson, FBI, March 2, 1983, Minneapolis file no. 89B-388 sub C-255.

44. "Autopsy Results," transcript of report by Special Agent Ivan W. Nicholson, FBI, Bismarck, North Dakota.

45. Transcript of interview with Dr. Ardashir Mardirosian, by Special Agent Brent H. Frost, FBI, March 2, 1983, Minneapolis file no. 89B-388 sub C. Corcoran (1990), pp. 1–3.

46. Transcript of interview with Mary Lou Stanoch, by Special Agent Lester L. Davis Jr., FBI, Feb. 28, 1983, Minneapolis file no. 89B-388 sub C. "I, GORDON KAHL," p. 8. Corcoran (1990), pp. 2, 98.

47. Transcript of interview with Attorney Irvin Nodland, by Special Agent Ivan W. Nicholson, FBI, Feb. 19, 1983, Minneapolis file no. 89B-388 sub C. Transcripts of notes from interview with Charles Miller, Assistant United States Attorney, by Special Agent Ivan W. Nicholson, Feb. 20, 1983.

48. Appeal, "Appendix of Scott Faul," *United States of America v. Scott Faul*, United States Court of Appeals for the Eighth Circuit, CR no. 83-1912-ND, pp. 14–15. Corcoran (1990), p. 131.

49. "Posse Comitatus Offers Letter Allegedly Penned by Fugitive," Associated Press, March 6, 1983. "Group Yields Letter, Not Fugitive," Associated Press, March 8, 1983. Domestic News, Associated Press, March 9, 1983.

50. "I, GORDON KAHL," p. 1.

51. "I, GORDON KAHL," p. 16.

52. Corcoran (1990), p. 100. "Autopsy Results," transcript of report by Special Agent Ivan W. Nicholson, FBI, Bismarck, North Dakota. Autopsy report by Merritt D. Moon for Robert Cheshire Jr., Autopsy Protocol A-83-7, Bismarck Hospital, March 15, 1982. Opinion of Circuit Court Judge Donald Ross (filed Nov. 7, 1984), p. 6.

53. "I, GORDON KAHL," pp. 11, 14.

54. "I, GORDON KAHL," pp. 12–13.

55. Associated Press, "Dakota 'Fanatic' Hunted in Slaying of 2 Marshals," *New York Times*, Feb. 15, 1983, p. 14.

56. "Authorities Guarantee Kahl's Safety if He Surrenders," United Press International, March 10, 1983. "Dakota 'Fanatic' Hunted in Slaying of 2 Marshals," *New York Times*, Feb. 15, 1983, p. 14. Domestic News, United Press International, Feb. 15, 1983. Domestic News, Associated Press, March 9, 1983. Opinion of Circuit Court Judge Donald Ross, (filed Nov. 7, 1984), pp. 28–29.

57. Gordon Hanson, Associated Press, Feb. 14, 1983. Kent Flanagan, Associated Press, Feb. 16, 1983.

58. Ibid. (see also:) United Press International, Feb. 15, 1983. Transcript of report by Special Agent Dewely L. Cady, FBI, Feb. 19, 1983, Minneapolis file no. 89B-388 sub C-63.

59. "Kahl Home Still Heavily Damaged," Associated Press, June 1983, ASP, CID, file no. 46-083-83.

60. Omang, "North Dakota Militant Eludes Lawmen," Feb. 16, 1983, p. A3.

61. Gerald Kopplin, United Press International, Domestic News, Feb. 17, 1983.

62. Ibid. See also: Kent Flanagan, "Police Convoy Seals Off Town, But Finds No Kahl," Associated Press, Feb. 17, 1983. Kent Flanagan, "Marshal Service Offers $25,000 Reward for Tax Protester," Associated Press, Feb. 18, 1983.

63. Flanagan, "Police Convoy Seals Off Town, But Finds No Kahl," Feb. 17, 1983.

28. Civil Disorder

1. United Press International, Feb. 15, 1983.

2. Lee Mitgang, "More Tax Protesters, But Tougher IRS Penalties," Associated Press, March 5, 1983. Orr Kelly with Michael Bosc, "Tax Rebels Multiply—and Collectors Act," *U.S. News and World Report*, Aug. 7, 1983, p. 39. For a more detailed assessment of the problem of illegal tax protesters, see: Comptroller General of the United States, "Illegal Tax Protesters Threaten Tax System," United States General Accounting Office, GGD-81-83, July 8, 1981. Barbara Rosewicz, Washington News, United Press International, Jan. 31, 1984.

3. F. Tupper Saussy, *The Miracle on Main Street: Saving Yourself from Financial Ruin* (Sewannee, TN: Spencer Judd, Publishers, 1980). For more on Saussy, his criminal record, and his political activities, including his relationship with James Earl Ray, see: J. Patrick Shannan, *I Rode with Tupper* (Boring, OR: CPA Book Publisher, 1992). John Branston, "The Amazing Tupper Saussy," *The Memphis Flyer*, no. 482, May 20, 1998. John Branston, "The Missing Link," *The Memphis Flyer*, no. 480, May 6, 1998. Jim Lewis, "Ye Shall Pay Coins, Gold and Silver: U.S. Constitution," United Press International, Regional News, Virginia, March 12, 1983. "Tax Protester Tupper Saussy Says He Can Prove Innocence," United Press International, Regional News, Tennessee, March 26, 1985. Pat Shannan, "Tupper Saussy Arrested in L.A.," *The Jubilee*, Nov.-Dec. 1997, vol. 10, no. 2, pp. 1, 9. "Fugitive Warrant Issued for Tax Protester," United Press International, Regional News, Georgia and Tennessee, April 14, 1987. "Appeals Court Upholds Conviction of Tax Evader," United Press International, Regional News, Tennessee, Oct. 4, 1986. William C. Trott, "Ray Gunning for Publisher," United Press International, Sept. 18, 1987. "Fugitive Autographed Copies of James Earl Ray's Biography," United Press International, May 17, 1987. "Saussy Tip Received in California," United Press International, Regional News, California, June 13, 1988. See also: www.tuppersaussy.com/tennwaltz.html.

4. Nolan Waters, "Militias Emerging in Midwest," *Wichita (Kans.) Eagle-Beacon*, April 3, 1983.

5. Bill Prochnau, "For the Posse, Ready Arms Hold Hostile World at Bay," *Washington Post*, June 21, 1983, p. A1. By 2002 standards, those same readers would be earning $50,000 per year.

NOTES TO PAGES 203–205

6. Statement of William J. Anderson, Director, General Government Division, "Internal Revenue Service's Efforts Against Illegal Tax Protesters," U.S. General Accounting Office. Comptroller General of the United States, "Illegal Tax Protesters Threaten Tax System," United States General Accounting Office, GGD-81-83, July 8, 1981.

7. United Press International, Feb. 15, 1983.

8. *Donahue* transcript no. 02233, Multimedia Program Productions, Cincinnati, Ohio, Feb. 23, 1983.

9. "Posse Strength Tested with Leader in Jail," *Rochester (Minn.) Post-Bulletin*, Nov. 15, 1984, p. 14. "Anti-Federalist Group Claims to fight for Law and Order," United Press International, Feb. 15, 1983.

10. "Highway Patrol Request for Rifles Not Direct Link to Posse Group," United Press International, Regional News, Feb. 18, 1983.

11. Patrick Kelly, "Farm Group Says It's Not Affiliated with Posse Comitatus," United Press International, Regional News, Feb. 15, 1983. Gene Smith, "Posse Problems—Real or Imaginary?" *Topeka (Kans.) Capital-Journal*, March 27, 1983.

12. The first six states were: California, Connecticut, North Carolina, Florida, Rhode Island, and Pennsylvania. Gene Smith, "Posse Problems—Real or Imaginary?" March 27, 1983. John Petteson, "Paramilitary Instruction Under Fire: Missouri, Kansas Bills Would Combat Civil Disturbances," *Kansas City (Mo.) Times*, Feb. 15, 1983. United Press International, June 28, 1983. United Press International, April 9, 1983. Mark Shenefelt, United Press International, March 19, 1983.

13. Transcript of testimony of Delwin Goheen, president of the Kansas Sate Rifle Association, Inc., before the House Judiciary Committee, February 21, 1983.

14. Roger Verdon, "Paramilitary Training Bill Moves Through Legislature," *Hutchinson (Kans.) News*, Feb. 27, 1983. Minutes of the House Committee on the Judiciary, Feb. 21, 1983, p. 2. Richard Tapscott, "Futile Effort to Revive Civil Disorder Bill," *Kansas City (Mo.) Times*, March 19, 1983.

15. Associated Press, "Paramilitary Bill Foe Held on Traffic Charge," *Kansas City (Mo.) Times*, Feb. 22, 1983. Lew Ferguson, Associated Press, *Topeka (Kans.) Capital-Journal*, March 1, 1983. *Citizen's of Osage County, Kansas Newsletter*, undated, circa Feb. 1983. Patrick Kelly, "Hearings Open on Paramilitary Bill; Man Arrested Outside Hearing Room," United Press International, Regional News, Feb. 21, 1983.

16. Journal of the Kansas House of Representatives, March 2, 1983, pp. 318–19. Roger Myers, "Paramilitary Ban Killed in House," *Topeka (Kans.) Capital-Journal*, March 3, 1983, pp. 1, 2. Editorial, "For All the Wrong Reasons," *Topeka (Kans.) Capital-Journal*, March 6, 1983. "Paramilitary Bill Has Carlin Cautious," *Topeka (Kans.) Capital-Journal*, March 4, 1983. Associated Press, "Panel Narrows Scope of Paramilitary Bill," *Kansas City (Mo.) Times*, March 15, 1983. "Revived Posse Bill Draws Same Objections," *Topeka (Kans.) Capital-Journal*, March 15, 1983. "Paramilitary Bill Killed," *Topeka (Kans.) Capital-Journal*, March 16, 1983. AP, "Panel Kills Paramilitary Bill; Measure Too Broad, Critics Say," *Kansas City (Mo.) Times*, March 16, 1983.

17. Originally Ellison had been affiliated with the Christian church (Disciples of Christ), a mainline Protestant denomination.

18. Letter of Kent Yates to Jim Ellison, Aug. 27, 1984, ASP, CID.

19. Judy Thomas, "We Are Not Dangerous, Leader of Separatists Says," *Kansas City (Mo.) Star*, March 17, 1996, pp. A1, 14–15. Born August 16, 1925, Millar, seventy-five, died of a heart attack on May 28, 2001. Associated Press, "White Separatist Leader Dies," June 1, 2001.

20. "Interview with Bruce Gibson," ASP, CID, May 7, 1985.

21. Report of interview with William Samuel Thomas, by Special Agent Bill Hobbs, Bureau of ATF, ASP, CID, May 3, 1985, p. 1.

22. Zarephath-Horeb/CSA. Holy Convocation, Schedule of Classes, Oct. 7, 1983–Oct. 9, 1983, ASP, CID.

23. Ibid.

24. Bruce Maxwell, "Paramilitary Group Began After 'Divine Meeting,'" *Rochester (Minn.) Post-Bulletin*, Nov. 12, 1984, pp. 1, 4. James Coates, *Armed and Dangerous: The Rise of the Survivalist Right* (New York: Hill and Wang, 1987), pp. 145–48, 152.

25. *Extremism on the Right: A Handbook*, (New York: Anti-Defamation League of B'nai Brith, 1983), pp. 5–6.

26. Testimony of Michael Lieberman on Legislative Bill 772, hearings before the Judiciary Committee, Lincoln, Nebraska, Jan. 21, 1986.

27. John Harrell, "ATTENTION: An OPEN LETTER to All Those Interested in the Christian-Patriots Defense League," undated. Bruce Maxwell, "Defense League Had One Encounter with Law," *Rochester (Minn.) Post-Bulletin*, Nov. 12, 1984. Deborah Singer and Roger Moore, "Preparing for the Day of Disorder," *Kansas City (Mo.) Star*, July 26, 1982. Deborah Singer and Roger Moore, "Leaders Share Views on Supremacy, Calamity Ahead," *Kansas City (Mo.) Star*, July 26, 1982. *Extremism on the Right* (1983), pp. 5–6.

28. Deborah Singer and Roger Moore, "Leaders Share Views on Supremacy, Calamity Ahead," *Kansas City (Mo.) Star*, July 26, 1982.

29. "Senate Quickly Passes Paramilitary Crime Bill," United Press International, March 2, 1983. *Missouri Revised Statutes*, chapter 574, "Offenses Against Public Order," section 574.070 (L.1983 S.B. 72 section 3). Smith, "Posse Problems—Real or Imaginary?" March 27, 1983. Jim Willis, "Threats Reported in Proposed Curbs on Paramilitary Groups," Associated Press, Feb. 24, 1983.

30. List of explosive materials and destructive devices and *Evidence Control Logs*, ASP, CID, Apr. 20–25, 1985. Indictment, *United States of America v. James D. Ellison, Gary Richard Stone, Timothy Wayne Russell, Kerry Noble, Rudy Loewen, David Giles*, June 6, 1985.

31. Report by Sergeant Irby, ASP, CID, April 29, 1985. Ellison was convicted on a RICO indictment and conspiracy to commit arson on July 17, 1985 (report by Sergeant Irby, ASP, CID, July 19, 1985). On August 12, Ellison and seven others entered guilty pleas on a variety of federal charges stemming from their possession of illegal firearms (report by Sergeant Irby, ASP, CID, Aug. 15, 1985). On September 4, 1975, Ellison and seven others were sentenced by Judge Oren Harris in Hot Springs, Arkansas. In addition to his twenty-year sentence, Ellison received four separate five-year sentences to run concurrently with the twenty-year sentence (report by Sergeant Irby, ASP, CID, Sept. 6, 1985).

32. Thomas, "We Are Not Dangerous, Leader of Separatists says," March 17, 1996, p. A15.

33. United Press International, Regional News, Idaho, April 9, 1983. Mark Shenefelt, United Press International, Regional News, Idaho, March 19, 1983.

34. Legislative bill 42, Legislature of Nebraska, 88th Legislature, 1st Session, Jan. 6, 1983. Nebraska Codes 28-1480 and 28-1481. Legislative Bill 772, Legislature of Nebraska, 89th Legislature, 2d Session, Jan. 8, 1986.

29. AAM Split

1. *Parity Not Charity: U.S. Farmers Movement in the 1980s* (undated document, circa 1984).

2. Ibid.

3. William R. Ritz, "Farm Militants Study Bomb-Making. U.S. Probing Guerrilla 'Seminars,' " *Denver Post*, Feb. 13, 1983, pp. 1A, 14A.

4. Patrick Kelly, "Group Says It's Not Affiliated with Posse Comitatus," United Press International, Regional News, Feb. 15, 1983. "Jenkins Sues Denver Post," *AAM News*, May 31, 1983, vol. 6, no. 7, p. 3. "Denver Post Sued for $5 Million," *Denver Post*, May 12, 1983. "Lawsuit Against the *Denver Post* Dismissed," *Denver Post*, Oct. 4, 1984. See also the following documents filed in connection with *Alvin Jenkins v. the Denver Post*, Civil Action no. 83-CV-22, District Court, County of Baca, State of Colorado: "Complaint," May 11, 1983; "Motion by defendants for a more definite statement and to strike the second cause of action," June 7, 1983; "Memorandum of points and authorities in support of defendants' motions to strike and for more definite statement," June 7, 1983; "Motion to dismiss for failure to prosecute," Sept. 10, 1984; Dismissal Order [for failure to prosecute], Sept. 24, 1984. Linda Gibson, Baca County District Court, interview by the author.

5. John Chambers, "Right-Wing Posse Spans U.S. Counties," *Topeka (Kans.) Capital-Journal*, Feb. 15, 1983, pp. 1, 3.

6. "Message from Darrell Ringer," *AAM News*, vol. 6, no. 2, March 8, 1983, p. 3. Kelly, "Group Says It's Not Affiliated with Posse Comitatus," Feb. 15, 1983. "Grass Roots Reunion," *AAM News*, vol. 6, no. 14, Aug. 23, 1983, pp. 3, 7. UPI, *Hutchinson (Kans.) News*, Feb. 16, 1983. Attorney General Stephan vigorously opposed the Posse, but he also was sympathetic to farmers' plight—and mindful of the power of the rural vote—so he went out of his way to mend fences. Although Stephan may have been sensitive to the pitfalls of unfairly tarring everyone in AAM with the broad brush of the Posse Comitatus, others in law enforcement easily confused the two. "[One] organization active in Colorado is reported to be the Farmers Liberation Army, aka the American Agriculture Movement," wrote a Wisconsin lawman after comparing notes with fellow officers at a seminar in Kansas. Report by Wendell A. Harker, "Attend Seminar—Kansas," Wisc. DOJ, DCI, Feb. 14, 1983.

7. "Alvin Jenkins Reports," *AAM News*, vol. 6, no. 3, March 22, 1983, pp. 1, 2.

8. Ibid., p. 8.

9. "AAM, Inc., Distances Themselves from Grass Roots," *AAM News*, vol. 6, no. 2, March 8, 1983, p. 6.

10. "Senter Hired as Director of National Office," *AAM News*, Feb. 26, 1980, vol. 3, no. 3, p. 1.

11. "AAM Will Demonstrate at Federal Reserve Banks," *AAM News*, vol. 5, no. 36, Jan. 25, 1983, p. 7. "Alvin Jenkins," *AAM News*, vol. 6, no. 14, Aug. 23, 1983, p. 3. Alden Nellis, "AAM Must Clean House," *AAM News*, vol. 6, no. 14, Aug. 23, 1983, p. 8. Micki Nellis, "Why Publish PAC Figures Now?" *AAM News*, vol. 6, no. 3, March 22, 1983, p. 6.

12. Patrick O'Reilly, interview by the author.

13. Dennis King, interview by the author.

14. For the most thorough analysis of Lyndon LaRouche, see: Dennis King, *Lyndon LaRouche and the New American Fascism* (New York: Doubleday, 1989). King's account of the 1980 presidential campaign appears on pp. 90–91.

15. LaRouche made repeated attempts to project his message to farmers. During the 1980 Texas primaries, LaRouche held a news conference at the Alamo to call attention to the farmers' plight. "NCLC Gains Support among Farmers; LaRouche Cult Changes Gears," *The Hammer*, no. 4, Aug. 1983, p. 12. *The Independent Democrats' 1984 Platform: Five Crises Facing the Next President* (New York: Independent Democrats for LaRouche, 1984), pp. 413–15.

16. David Senter, interview by the author.

17. Lawrence Freeman, "AAM, Inc., Tried to Thwart Federal Reserve Protests," *AAM News* vol. 6, no. 3, March 22, 1983, p. 5.

18. Keith Shive, "Let's Take Our Half and Go," *AAM News*, vol. 6, no. 4, April 5, 1983, p. 7.

19. "Summary of New AAM, Inc, Bylaws," *AAM News*, vol. 6, no. 14, Aug. 23, 1983, p. 8. "Around the Countryside," *AAM News*, vol. 6, no. 16, Sept. 20, 1983, p. 7.

20. "Alvin Jenkins," *AAM News*, vol. 6, no. 14, Aug. 23, 1983, p. 3. Alden Nellis, "AAM Must Clean House," *AAM News*, vol. 6, no. 14, Aug. 23, 1983, p. 8.

21. Alvin Jenkins, "On Rights, Freedoms, and Responsibilities," *AAM News*, vol. 16, no. 15, Sept. 6, 1983, pp. 9–10.

22. "Farm Revolt Set to Begin Nov. 1," *AAM News*, vol. 6, no. 15, Sept. 6, 1983, p. 1.

23. Leonard Zeskind, "Gordon Kahl on the Run," *The Hammer* (Kansas City: Institute for Research and Education on Human Rights, Inc., 1983), no. 4, Aug. 1983, p. 8.

24. "Witness Got $25,000 in Kahl Case," United Press International, Oct. 12, 1983.

30. Kahl and His Courier

1. "Government Will Call 17 Witnesses for Kahl Trial," United Press International Oct. 11, 1983. Opinion of Judge Donald Ross. (Appeals from the United States District Court for the Western District of Arkansas, *United States of America v. Ed Udey et al.*, United States Court of Appeals for the Eighth Circuit, no. 83-2655, Nov. 7, 1984, pp. 3–4. James Corcoran, *Bitter Harvest: Gordon Kahl and the Posse Comitatus—Murder in the Heartland* (New York: Viking, 1990), pp. 233–41.

2. Associated Press, July 2, 1983. Corcoran (1990), p. 179.

3. Jim Neumann, "Yorie Kahl's Gun Believed to Be Found," *(Fargo, ND) Forum*, p. A1. Opinion of Judge Donald Ross (Nov. 7, 1984), pp. 22–25.

4. *Scott Faul et al. v. United States of America*, petition for a Writ of Certiorari, U.S. Supreme Court, October Term 1984, nos. 84-1373, 84-6332, and 84-6350, May 30, 1985, pp. 2–3. Opinion of Judge Donald Ross (Nov. 7, 1984), pp. 2–3. Jeff Meyer, "Slain Fugitive's Son Sentenced in Slayings of Marshals," Associated Press, June 24, 1983. Tom Uhlenbrock, "Court Affirms Conviction in Gordon Kahl Shootout," United Press International, Nov. 8, 1984. The verdicts were read on May 28, 1983 (Corcoran [1990], pp. 231–32).

5. Opinion of Judge Donald Ross (Nov. 7, 1984), pp. 3–4. Corcoran (1990) pp. 233–41.

6. "Shootout Leaves Town's Residents Fearful," Associated Press, June 12, 1983. Memo from Wendall A. Harker, Special Agent, General Investigations Bureau, to Russell Nelson, Director, General Investigations Bureau; Wisc. DOJ, DCI, June 6, 1983, file no. SA-159. United Press International, Regional News, June 8, 1983.

7. "Government Will Call 17 Witnesses for Kahl Trial," United Press International, Oct. 11, 1983.

8. The details and circumstances of the attempt to apprehend Kahl, and his subsequent death and that of Lawrence County Sheriff Gene Matthews, are found in the following documents: Associated Press, Oct. 11, 1983. Leeanne Spigner, "Hundreds Pay Final Tribute to Sheriff," *Jonesboro (Ark.) Sun*, June 6, 1983, p. 1. Jan Tyler, "Death of Sheriff Mourned by Man," *Jonesboro (Ark.) Sun*, June 5, 1983. Janet Kesterson, "Lawman Describes Shootout Scene," *Jonesboro (Ark.) Sun*, June 5, 1983, p. 1. Paul Holmes, "Shootout Shotgun in House," undated, unsourced newspaper clipping. Arkansas State Police, CID, file no. 46-083-83. Statement of Tom Barden, Lawrence County Sheriff's Department, June 29, 1983. Statement of Norma Ginter, Lawrence County Sheriff's Department, June 9, 1983. Steve J. Cox, criminalist, "Report of Laboratory Analysis," June 10, 1983. Statement of Thomas W. Lee, "Ginter Resident" [*sic*]. "Gordon Kahl

Shootout," statement of Perry Webb, Deputy Sheriff, Lawrence County, undated, file no. 46-083-83. Statement of Warren Williams, Lawrence County Deputy Sheriff. Statement of Ivan Raymond Wade, June 28, 1983. Bob Tomlinson, "Ref: MEA report MEA-275-83," Lawrence County Sheriff's Department, June 28, 1983. "Assisting Federal Authorities—Ref: Gordon R. Kahl [sic]," memo of Tfc. G. S. Huddleston, Arkansas State Patrol, June 8, 1983. "Assistance in Serving a Federal Warrent (Gorden Kahl) [sic]," memo from Sergeant G. D. Coggin, Arkansas State Patrol, June 8, 1983. "Crime Scene Search," report by Sergeant Mike Coy, ASP, CID, June 8, 1983. "Interview of suspect, Norma Leona Ginter," report by Sergeant Mike Coy, ASP, CID, June 8, 1983. "Leonard George Ginter, Description of Subject" ASP, CID. "Search Warrant Return," Sergeant Mike Coy, ASP, CID, June 3–4, 1983. "Shootout in a Sleepy Hamlet: Wanted for Murder, a Militant Tax Evader Is Slain in Arkansas," *Time* magazine, June 13, 1983, p. 16. Corcoran (1990), pp. 241–51.

9. The Ginters were both convicted on felony charges of harboring Kahl for which Leonard Ginter was sentenced to five years in prison. Ginter's wife had her sentence suspended for all but the six months she had been in prison and she received an additional five years' probation. Also accused of murder by the State of Arkansas, Leonard Ginter pleaded guilty to a lesser charge and was sentenced to eight more years in jail. Opinion of Judge Donald Ross (Nov. 7, 1984), pp. 2–3. "Four Sentenced for Hiding Gordon Kahl," United Press International, Nov. 29, 1983. Inv. E. A. Fitzpatrick, status report, Aug. 30, 1984, ASP, CID.

10. Wayne King, "Link Seen Among Heavily Armed Rightist Groups," *New York Times*, June 11, 1983, pp. 1, C2.

11. Russell Carollo, "A Look Back at Suspect's Lifestyle," *Texarkana (Ark.) Gazette*, July 2, 1984, p. 1. Lyle McBride and Bill Webb, "Suspect in Shooting Described as Survivalist," *Texarkana (Ark.) Gazette*, July 1, 1984, pp. 1A, 15A.

12. Report of interview with William Samuel Thomas by Special Agent Bill Hobbs, Bureau of ATF, ASP, CID, May 3, 1985, p. 8.

13. Ibid., p. 2. See also: Interview of Richard Wayne Snell, by Investigator Russell Welch, ASP, CID, file no. 49-997-84, Aug. 30, 1984.

14. Robert Davis, "Slain Trooper Laid to Rest; Many Mourn," *Texarkana (Ark.) Gazette*, July 6, 1984, p. 1. Report by Investigator Charles Lambert, ASP, CID, July 6, 1984. Report by Trooper M. Baughman regarding Richard Wayne Snell, July 5, 1984. Invoice to Farmers First National Bank from Alert Recovery, Inc., Aug. 15, 1983.

15. Memo from Sergeant Mike Fletcher to Lieutenant Finis Duval, July 4, 1984, re: Richard Wayne Snell, case file no. 49-997-84. Memo to Lieutenant Duval from Trooper M. Baughman re: Richard Wayne Snell, July 5, 1984, ASP, CID.

16. Richard Wayne Snell, *The Shadow of Death!* (undated booklet), p. 23.

17. Mary Snell, "An American Patriot to Be Executed by the Beast," *Taking Aim: The Militiaman's Newsletter*, vol. 1, no. 10, Dec. 1994, p. 1.

18. Statement of Officer Allen Edmond Calvin, June 30, 1984.

19. Report by Broken Bow, Oklahoma, patrolman Bill E. Huckaby, June 30, 1984, re: "Shooting on June 30, 1984," ASP, CID.

20. Report of Investigator Russell Welch, ASP, CID, Aug. 30, 1984, p. 5.

31. Snake Oil for Sale

1. Associated Press, "Airmen Won't Be at Rites," undated, unsourced newspaper clipping. ASP, CID, file 46-083-83.

2. Mike Dorsher, "Kahl Euologized as Modern-Day Paul Revere," United Press International, June 10, 1983. Jeff Meyer, Associated Press, Domestic News, Heaton, North Dakota, June 11, 1983.

3. "Posse Leader Goes on Trial," Associated Press, June 9, 1983. United Press International, July 5, 1983. "Tax Rebel Brands Trial a Total Sham," *Atlanta Journal-Constitution*, June 12, 1983. Timothy Harper, "Posse Leader Boasts of Increased Membership," Associated Press, June 12, 1983. Bill Prochnau, "For the Posse, Ready Arms Hold Hostile World at Bay," *Washington Post*, June 21, 1983, p. A1.

4. For more on the founding of NAFA, see: Andrew H. Malcolm, "Farmers and Unions Joining to Fight Economic Hardship," *New York Times*, June 5, 1983, pp. 1, C1. "North American Farm Alliance Will Meet," *AAM News*, vol. 6, no. 6, May 3, 1983, p. 1. *Parity Not Charity* (undated document, circa 1984). "North American Farm Alliance Formed," *AAM News*, vol. 6, no. 5, April 19, 1983, pp. 1, 3.

5. "Waterloo Rally Draws 2,500 on Revolt Day," *AAM News*, vol. 6, no. 20, Nov. 15, 1983. *Parity Not Charity* (undated document, circa 1984).

6. "Jesse Jackson Speaks in Kansas," *AAM News*, vol. 6, no. 23, Dec. 27, 1983, p. 1.

7. Alden and Micki Nellis, "Farewell," *AAM News*, vol. 6, no. 23, Dec. 27, 1983, p. 4.

8. U.S. DOJ, FBI record no. 47-382-A.

9. Correspondence of J. Barbara Coopersmith, Associate Director, Mountain States Regional Office, Anti-Defamation League, to R. F. and Karla J. Elliott, Dec. 23, 1981.

10. R. F. Elliott, "Bureaucratic Doughfeet," *Primrose and Cattleman's Gazette*, vol. 8, no. 48, Nov. 29, 1982, p. 1.

11. *Primrose and Cattleman's Gazette*, Dec. 27, 1982, p. 125.

12. Bruce Maxwell, "Farm Group Head Has Supporters, Detractors," *Rochester (Minn.) Post-Bulletin*, Nov. 14, 1984, p. 5.

13. Bryan Abas, "Last Roundup for the *Cattlemen's Gazette*?" *Columbia Journalism Review*, Jan.-Feb. 1985, pp. 8–9.

14. Notes of Larry Miller, investigator, Marion, Alabama, District Attorney's Office.

15. "Cattlemen's Gazette Promotes Anti-Semitism One of Many Phoney Solutions to a Real Problem," *The Hammer*, Spring 1984, no. 6, p. 25.

16. Abas, "Last Roundup for the *Cattlemen's Gazette*?" Jan.-Feb. 1985, pp. 8–9.

17. Frederick J. Simonelli, *American Fuehrer: George Lincoln Rockwell and the American Nazi Party* (Champaign, IL: University of Illinois Press, 1999), p. 124. Vincent Carroll, "The Steady Persistence of Small Ideas," unsourced news clipping, circa June 1983. Ben Kreigh, "Under the Flatirons," *Primrose and Cattleman's Gazette*, Jan. 10, 1984, p. 19. Ben Kreigh, "Under the Flatirons," *Primrose and Cattleman's Gazette*, June 7, 1983, p. 15. Wes Blomster, "A Bum Steer: Pressing Prejudice at the *Cattleman's Gazette*," *Westword*, (Denver, Colorado), Jan. 13, 1983.

18. Colonel "Bud" Farrell, "Open Letter to . . . the Goyim (Gentiles)," *Primrose and Cattleman's Gazette*, March 15, 22, 29, April 15, 19, 1983.

19. Colonel Farrell, "Open Letter to . . . the Goyim (Gentiles)," March 22, 1983, p. 16.

20. For a thorough account of Berg's career on *KOA*, including his murder, see: Stephen Singular, *Talked to Death: The Life and Murder of Alan Berg* (New York: Beech Tree Books, William Morrow, 1987).

21. Transcript of KOA radio interview with Alan Berg, Bud Farrell, and Rick Elliott, June 15, 1983.

22. Wayne King, "Links of Anti-Semitic Band Provoke Six-State Parley," *New York Times*, Dec. 27, 1984, p. B7.

23. Rick Elliott claimed that Bud Farrell had hired David Lane, not him. Elliott also said that he didn't know that Lane even worked at the NAPA office until Farrell fired Lane one day for showing up with a holstered gun. John C. Ensslin, "Publisher Says Clash with Berg Fateful," *Denver (Colo.) Rocky Mountain News*, July 13, 1986, p. 20.

24. National Agricultural Press Association (NAPA), Colorado Membership List (by cities).

25. "The Death of the White Race," *Primrose and Cattleman's Gazette*, May 17, 1983, p. 19.

26. "Direct from Gordon Kahl—Accused of Slaying Federal Marshalls in North Dakota [*sic*]," *Primrose and Cattleman's Gazette*, May 17, 1983, p. 8. "Gordon Kahl, Victim of Federal Ambush Attempt and Massive Manhunt, Tells His Side in North Dakota Slaying of Two Federal Marshalls," *Primrose and Cattleman's Gazette*, May 24, 1983, p. 5. "Gordon Kahl, Victim of Federal Ambush Attempt and Massive Manhunt, Tells His Side in North Dakota Slaying of Two Federal Marshalls," *Primrose and Cattleman's Gazette*, May 31, 1983, p. 20. "Gordon Kahl, Victim of Federal Ambush Attempt and Massive Manhunt, Tells His Side in North Dakota Slaying of Two Federal Marshalls," *Primrose and Cattleman's Gazette*, June 7, 1983, p. 2.

27. Henry Ford Sr., "How the 'Jewish Question' Touches the Farm," *Primrose and Cattleman's Gazette*, May 24, 1983, p. 11.

28. "Georgia: Two Main Ideas Surface at Meeting," *AAM News*, Nov. 29, 1983.

29. Bartell Nyberg, "Arrest May End Publisher's Plan to Help Farmers," *Denver Post*, Sept. 30, 1984. James Houtsma, "Promoters of 'Common-Law Liens' Organize in State," *Mankato (Minn.) Free Press*, March 15, 1984.

30. Maxwell, "Farm Group Head Has Supporters, Detractors," Nov. 14, 1984, p. 5.

31. The jurist, U.S. District Judge Warren Urbon of Nebraska, handled more than forty pro se lawsuits from 1983 to 1985. "United States District Court: Pro Se Litigation," author's files.

32. Houtsma, "Promoters of 'Common-Law Liens' Organize in State," (Mar. 15, 1984): Abas, "Last Roundup for the *Cattlemen's Gazette*?" (Jan.-Feb. 1985), pp. 8–9.

33. Affidavit of Gary Clyman, investigator, *People of the State of Colorado v. Roderick F. Elliott, Karla J. Elliott, and National Agricultural Press Association, Inc.*, District Court, Weld County, Colorado, case no. 84-CR-581, Division 4, Sept. 17, 1984, pp. 8, 9.

34. Interview transcript, Rick Elliott, Buck Chavers, Larry Miller: Marion, Alabama, District Attorney's Office, p. 3.

35. Nyberg, "Arrest May End Publisher's Plan to Help Farmers," Sept. 30, 1984. Affidavit of Gary Clyman (Sept. 17, 1984). John C. Ensslin, "Two Farmers Testify $50,000 Lent Publisher Not Repaid," *Denver (Colo.) Rocky Mountain News*, Jan. 30, 1985. John C. Ensslin, "Jury Convicts Former Publisher of Theft over Unpaid Farm Loans," *Denver (Colo.) Rocky Mountain News*, May 28, 1986, p. 10.

36. Nyberg, "Arrest May End Publisher's Plan to Help Farmers," Sept. 30, 1984. Bartell Nyberg, "Fort Lupton Publisher Files Bankruptcy Papers," *Denver Post*, May 3, 1985, pp. 1, 7C. *People of the State of Colorado v. Roderick F. Elliott, Karla J. Elliott, and National Agricultural Press Association, Inc.*, District Court, Weld County, Colorado, case no. 84-CR-581, Division 4, Sept. 17, 1984.

37. Letter of Milt Bigalk, NAPA Regional Office, Rushford, Minnesota, circa July 1984.

38. Bruce Maxwell, "Farmers Increasingly Drawn to Extremists," *Rochester (Minn.) Post-Bulletin*, Nov. 10, 1984, p. 12.

39. "Seeds of Hate," ABC-TV News, *20/20*, August 15, 1995.

40. The assessment of Kirk's mental state was made by Dr. Emmet M. Kenney, a psychiatrist at Omaha's Creighton University. See: Correspondence of the Honorable Samuel Van Pelt, Special Investigator to the Honorable Robert Kerrey, Governor, State of Nebraska, and Senator Chris Beutler, Chairman, Judiciary Committee, Dec. 1, 1984, p. 7. For other accounts of the Arthur Kirk incident, see: Daniel Levitas, "Violence on the Rise," *Catholic Rural Life*, Nov. 1985, pp. 16–17. Bruce Maxwell, "Radical Right Wing on the Rise in the Midwest," *Rochester (Minn.) Post-Bulletin*, Nov. 10, 1984, pp. 1, 12. "Seeds of Hate," videotape, ABC-TV News, *20/20*, August 15, 1995.

41. Following the incident, Rick Elliott spoke at a news conference organized by Kirk's widow to denounce the actions of police. Maxwell, "Radical Right Wing on the Rise in the Midwest," (Nov. 10, 1984), p. 12.

42. Letter of Larry Jones, "Dear Friend and Partner," Oct. 1987. Letter of Larry Jones, Nov. 12, 1987. Financial summary of Feed the Children, Sept. 30, 1986. Levitas and Ostendorf, memo, "Rural Radical Right Update," April 20, 1988, pp. 6–7.

43. "Retired Judge Alarmed," United Press International, Regional News, Dec. 16, 1984.

32. Jim Wickstrom's Main Man

1. James Ridgeway, "Posse Country: Murder and White Supremacy in the Farm Belt," *Village Voice* (New York), Oct. 22, 1985, pp. 1, 13–17. Sean Holton, "One of Two Rulo Bodies Believed to Be Child," *Kansas City (Mo.) Star*, Aug. 19, 1985. Paul Wenske and Dan Gillmor, "Raid Confirmed Her Worst Fear: Grandson's Dead," *Kansas City (Mo.) Times*, Aug. 20, 1985, pp. A1, A12. "Slaying by Alleged Farmer-Survivalists Stun Rural Nebraskans," *Des Moines Sunday Register*, Aug. 25, 1985, p. 2A.

2. Jack Croft and Kevin Collison, "Many Strange Turns Taken in Life of Jailed Survivalist Michael Ryan," *Omaha (Neb.) World-Herald*, Aug. 25, 1985, pp. 1, 12.

3. Rod Colvin, *Evil Harvest: The True Story of Cult Murder in the American Heartland* (Omaha, NE: Addicus Books, 2000), pp. 9–17.

4. Statement of Donald E. Zabawa, May 23, 1984, p. 2.

5. KBI report, by Dave Schroeder, March 7, 1983, case no. 99-55879.

6. KBI report by James E. McCubbin, March 8, 1983, case no. 99-55879. KBI report by Dave Schroeder, March 7, 1983, case no. 99-55879. Sean Holton, "One of Two Rulo Bodies Believed to Be Child," *Kansas City Star*, Aug. 19, 1985.

7. KBI report by James E. McCubbin, March 8, 1983, case no. 99-55879.

8. United Press International, Regional News, July 12, 1984. United Press International, Regional News, June 13, 1984. Affidavit of James Malson, Special Agent for the KBI, State of Kansas, County of Franklin, May 18, 1984. Investigation report by Special Agent John E. McElroy, KBI case no. 29-72461, May 15, 1984. "Holton Man Guilty in Threat Case," *Topeka (Kans.) Capital-Journal*, July 13, 1984.

9. Investigation report, by G. K. Welch, Special Agent, KBI, "Posse Comitatus," March 23, 1984.

10. Statement of Donald E. Zabawa, May 23, 1984, p. 1. According to Zabawa he was advised by Christian-Patriots Defense League founder John Harrell to contact Shive.

11. Zabawa statement (May 23, 1984), pp. 5, 6.

12. Paul Wenske and Dan Gillmor, "New Evidence Links Farm to Posse Comitatus," *Kansas City (Mo.) Times*, June 29, 1985, pp. A1, A16.

13. Terry Hyland and Jack Croft, "Son of Suspect Is Third Charged in Slaying of Man at Rulo Farm," *Omaha (Neb.) World-Herald*, Aug. 20, 1985, pp. 1, 11. Associated Press, "Teen Sentenced

to Life in Rulo Torture-Slaying," *Des Moines Register*, May 10, 1986, p. 22A. Paul Wenske, "Cult Leader's Son Raised for 'Holy War,' " *Kansas City (Mo.) Times*, March 27, 1986. Transcript of the direct testimony of David Andreas, *State of Nebraska v. Dennis Ryan, also State of Nebraska v. Michael Ryan*, Douglas County Nebraska, March 13, 1986.

14. Associated Press, "Pistol tied to Nebraska Murders Located on Norton County Farm," *Topeka (Kans.) Capital-Journal*, Aug. 21, 1985.

15. Wenske and Gillmor, "Raid Confirmed Her Worst Fear: Grandson's Dead," (Aug. 20, 1985), pp. A1, A12.

16. "Names of Twenty-five Tied to Group on Rulo Farm," *Omaha (Neb.) World-Herald*, Aug. 25, 1985.

17. Larry Fruhling, "Tales of Horror Emerge from Nebraska Cult Farm," *Des Moines Register*, March 16, 1986, pp. 1A, 12A.

18. Colvin, (2000), p. 201.

19. Wm. Byron Foster, "Inquisition Held into the Whereabouts of Cheryl Gibson and Her Five Children," *Hiawatha (Kans.) Daily World*, Dec. 14, 1984, p. 1. Croft and Collison, "Many Strange Turns taken in Life of Jailed Survivalist Michael Ryan," (Aug. 25, 1985), pp. 1, 12; Dan Gillmor and Paul Wenske, "Finding Children Brings Father's Yearlong Search to End," *Kansas City (Mo.) Times*, July 1, 1985. Bob von Sternberg, "Father Seeks His Missing Family, Says Posse Comitatus Responsible," *Wichita (Kans.) Eagle-Beacon*, Jan. 2, 1985. "Omaha Group Helps in Search for Gibsons," United Press International, Regional News, Kansas, Dec. 25, 1984. Colvin (2000), p. 149.

20. Fred Thomas, "Lawman Links Killings to Religion; Says Farm Leader Called Himself Instrument of God," *Omaha (Neb.) World-Herald*, Aug. 20, 1985, pp. 1, 11. Hyland and Croft, "Son of Suspect Is Third Charged in Slaying of Man at Rulo Farm," (Aug. 20, 1985), pp. 1, 11.

21. Testimony of David Andreas (March 13, 1986), pp. 8, 9, 12.

22. Ibid., pp. 3–7, 28. See also: Croft and Collison, "Many Strange Turns Taken in Life of Jailed Survivalist," (Aug. 25, 1985), pp. 1, 12. Larry Fruhling, "Cult Appealed to Despair and Found Farmers Easy Prey," *Des Moines Register*, Sept. 2, 1985. Colvin (2000), pp. 178–79.

23. Wenske and Gillmor, "Raid Confirmed Her Worst Fear: Grandson's Dead," (Aug. 20, 1985), pp. A1, A12. Paul Wenske, "Man Tells of Helping Cult Members Torture His 5-year-old Son," *Kansas City (Mo.) Times*, undated news clipping, circa March 26, 1986.

24. Colvin (2000), pp. 180–85.

25. Fruhling, "Tales of Horror Emerge from Nebraska Cult Farm," (Mar. 16, 1986), pp. 1A, 12A. Colvin (2000), p. 217.

26. Fruhling, "Tales of Horror Emerge from Nebraska Cult Farm," (Mar. 16, 1986), pp. 1A, 12A. David Cazalet, "Father Details Son's Torture," *Hiawatha (Kans.) Daily World*, March 26, 1986, p. 1. Wenske, "Man Tells of Helping Cult Members Torture His 5-year-old Son," circa March 26, 1986. Colvin (2000), p. 237.

27. Testimony of David Andreas (March 13, 1986), pp. 64–68.

28. Ibid., pp. 74–78.

29. Ibid., pp. 78–80.

30. Fruhling, "Tales of Horror Emerge from Nebraska Cult Farm," (Mar. 16, 1986), pp. 1A, 12A. Cazalet, "Father Details Son's Torture," Mar. 26, 1986), p. 1. Wenske, "Man Tells of Helping Cult Members Torture His 5-year-old Son," circa March 26, 1986.

31. Testimony of David Andreas (March 13, 1986), p. 149.

32. Fruhling, "Tales of Horror Emerge from Nebraska Cult Farm," (Mar. 16, 1986), pp. 1A, 12A. Associated Press, "Prosecutor Says Torture Victim Skinned Alive," *Des Moines Register*, March 11, 1986, p. 5A.

33. Colvin (2000), pp. 267–68.

34. Testimony of David Andreas (March 13, 1986), p. 129.

35. Associated Press, "Witness: Ryan Told Victim God 'Wasn't Fooling Around,' " *Des Moines Register*, March 19, 1986. Fruhling, "Tales of Horror Emerge from Nebraska Cult Farm," (Mar. 16, 1986), pp. 1A, 12A.

33. A Domestic Dispute

1. Wm. Byron Foster, "Inquisition Held into the Whereabouts of Cheryl Gibson and Her Five Children," *Hiawatha (Kans.) Daily World*, Dec. 14, 1984, p. 1.

2. David Cazalet, "U.S. Attorney Said 'Unaware' of Facts," *Hiawatha (Kans.) Daily World*, Aug. 22, 1985, p. 1. Fred Thomas, "FBI Denies Rebuffing Man Who Sought Farm Probe," *Omaha (Neb.) World-Herald*, Aug. 20, 1985, p. 11.

3. Dennis Whelan, interview by the author.

4. Cazalet, "U.S. Attorney Said 'Unaware' of Facts," (Aug. 22, 1985), p. 1. Thomas, "FBI Denies Rebuffing Man Who Sought Farm Probe," (Aug. 20, 1985), p. 11.

5. Whelan, interview.

6. For a thorough account of these and other events concerning Rulo, see: Rod Colvin, *Evil Harvest: The True Story of Cult Murder in the American Heartland* (Omaha, NE: Addicus Books, 2000).

7. Paul Wenske and Dan Gillmor, "Man's Search for Family Leads to Survivalists," *Kansas City (Mo.) Times*, June 27, 1985, pp. A1, A16, Wenske and Gillmor, "New Evidence Links Farm to Posse Comitatus," June 29, 1985, pp. A1, A16. David Thompson, "Agent Says Guns on Farm Came from Dealers in 4 States," *Omaha (Neb.) World Herald*, Aug. 23, 1985, p. 11. Testimony of David Andreas (March 13, 1986), p. 44.

8. Paul Wenske and Dan Gillmor, "Kansas Farm Searched in Survivalist Probe," *Kansas City (Mo.) Times*, Aug. 21, 1985, pp. A1, A9. Kevin Collison, "Kansas Says Discovery of Bodies Is Shocking," *Omaha (Neb.) World-Herald*, Aug. 22, 1985, p. 13. Fred Thomas, "Pistol Found in Kansas Suspected in Rulo Death," *Omaha (Neb.) World-Herald*, Aug. 21, 1985, pp. 1, 8.

9. Paul Wenske and Dan Gillmor, "Finding Children Brings Father's Yearlong Search to End," *Kansas City (Mo.) Times*, July 1, 1985. Dennis Whelan, interview by the author.

10. Wenske and Gillmor, "New Evidence Links Farm to Posse Comitatus," (June 29, 1985), pp. A1, A16.

11. Paul Wenske and Dan Gillmor, "Alarm Slow to Sound about Survivalist Camp," *Kansas City (Mo.) Times*, Aug. 23, 1985.

12. Foster, "Inquisition Held into the Whereabouts of Cheryl Gibson and Her Five Children," (Dec. 14, 1984), p. 1. James Ridgeway, "Posse Country: Murder and White Supremacy in the Farm Belt," *Village Voice* (New York), Oct. 22, 1985, pp. 1, 13–17.

13. Ridgeway, "Posse Country: Murder and White Supremacy in the Farm Belt," (Oct. 22, 1985), pp. 1, 13–17.

14. David Cazalet, "Father Details Son's Torture," *Hiawatha (Kans.) Daily World*, (Mar. 26, 1986), p. 1.

15. Ridgeway, "Posse Country: Murder and White Supremacy in the Farm Belt," (Oct. 22, 1985), pp. 1, 13–17. "Tape 62: The Death of Farmer Arthur Kirk by state senator Ernie Cham-

bers. This talk was delivered in Omaha at the NAPA meeting shortly after Mr. Kirk's death," undated circular of Paul Johnson, VHS/Beta videotapes, Red Oak, Iowa, circa 1986.

16. Steven Stingley, "Kerrey Lauds Lawmen Involved in Rulo Probe," *Omaha (Neb.) World-Herald*, Aug. 24, 1985. Dennis Whelan, interview by the author.

17. Wm. Byron Foster, "Michael Ryan Charged with Murder of 5-year-old," *Hiawatha (Kans.) Daily World*, (Aug. 19, 1985), pp. 1, 7. Wm. Byron Foster, "No Bond for Murder Suspects," *Hiawatha (Kans.) Daily World*, Aug. 22, 1985, p. 1. Wenske and Gillmor, "Kansas Farm Searched in Survivalist Probe," Aug. 21, 1985, pp. A1, A9. Associated Press, "Ex–Cult Leader Sentenced to Death in Torture Killings," *Des Moines Register*, Oct. 17, 1986. AP, "Rulo Cult Member Gets Life Sentence," *Des Moines Register*, May 9, 1986, p. 4A, AP, "Ryan Given Life Term in Child's Murder," Aug. 29, 1986. Colvin (2000), pp. 348–55.

18. Mike Ryan was tried separately in April 1986 in the killing of Luke Stice. "Teen Sentenced to Life in Rulo Torture-Slaying," Associated Press, *Des Moines Register*, (May 10, 1986), p. 22A.

19. Associated Press, "Holocaust Victims Weren't Jews, Cult Head's Wife Says," *Des Moines Register*, March 22, 1986, p. 11A.

20. Stingley, "Kerrey Lauds Lawmen Involved in Rulo Probe," Aug. 24, 1985.

21. Eric Adler, "Legislators Plan Hearing to Study Extremist Groups," *Omaha (Neb.) World-Herald*, (Aug. 24, 1985), p. 2.

34. Neoconservatives and the Grand Wazir

1. "Seeds of Hate," ABC-TV News, *20/20*, August 15, 1995.

2. Jewish Telegraphic Agency, "TV Program Reveals Radical Right Exploiting Farm Crisis," *Kansas City (Mo.) Jewish Chronicle*, Aug. 16, 1985.

3. "Seeds of Hate," ABC-TV's *20/20*, August 15, 1995.

4. "Whole Truth Takes a Backseat on ABC's *20/20*," *NFD (National Federation of Decency) Journal*, Oct. 1985, p. 15.

5. Tom Shales, "Hatred in the Heartland," *Washington Post*, Aug. 15, 1985.

6. Kay Gardella, "Harvest of Hate: *20/20* Segment Is Inflammatory Reporting," *New York Daily News*, Aug. 14, 1985. Monica Collins, "Geraldo Rivera: *20/20* Reporter Is in the Fray, But Not Frayed," *USA Today*, Aug. 15, 1985.

7. Shales, "Hatred in the Heartland," Aug. 15, 1985.

8. John Peterson, "Guns, Hatred, and Farmers," *Iowa Farmer Today*, (Aug. 24, 1985), p. 8B.

9. Michael A. Hoffman II, "One-sided Look at Farmers," *The Spotlight*, Sept. 2, 1985, p. 7.

10. Correspondence of Roderick F. Elliott, National Agricultural Press Association, to "Mr. James Duffy, Pres., ABC Television," August 19, 1995.

11. The Midwest Office of Rural America changed its name in January 1985 to PrairieFire Rural Action.

12. For similar examples of the response of churches to the rural radical right, see: Marilyn Murphy, "Statement Rejects Extremism as Answer to Rural Crisis," *The Globe*, Feb. 6, 1986. "Statement on Extremism and Extremist Philosophy Relative to Rural Crisis," Ecumenical Rural Concerns Committee of Northwest Iowa, Jan. 29, 1986. "On Behalf of Caution, Justice, and Hope," Iowa Inter-Church Forum, Jan. 20, 1986. "Statement Issued on the Farm Crisis and the Threat of Hate Groups in Rural Illinois," Princeton, Illinois, Nov. 17, 1987. "A Statement on the Exploitation of the Rural Crisis by Extremist Organizations," Rural Life Commission, Archdiocese of Omaha, undated, circa 1987. Father Norm White, "In My Opinion," *The Witness*, Catholic Archdiocese of Dubuque, Iowa, April 10, 1988. Jason Petosa, "Conference

Ministers Plan Counter-right-wing Efforts in Nation's Farm Belt," *United Church News*, United Church of Christ, Sept. 1986, vol. 2, no. 7, pp. 1, 6. "The United Methodist Church Seeks Peaceful Solutions to the Farm Crisis," *Kearney (Neb.) Daily News*, Jan. 23, 1986. "The Exploitation of the Rural Crisis by Extremist Organizations: A Resolution," Consultation of Co-operating Churches in Kansas, Dec. 16, 1985. For the text of the National Council of Churches statement, see: "Action on the Exploitation of the Rural Crisis by Extremist Organizations," Nov. 8, 1985, as reported in *D.H.P. Exchange Domestic Hunger and Poverty*, National Council of Churches of Christ in the U.S.A. Inc., New York, no. 57, Nov. 1985, p. 4.

13. Daniel Levitas, Memo to Jewish Community Leadership, "The Growth of Anti-Semitic Extremists in Rural Iowa," PrairieFire, June 12, 1985.

14. USDA Economics Research Service, as cited in, *Who Is Behind the Farm Crisis?*—a pamphlet jointly published by the Center for Democratic Renewal (Atlanta), the Institute for Research and Education on Human Rights (Kansas City), and PrairieFire Rural Action (Des Moines), 1985.

15. National Farm and Power Equipment Dealers Association, as cited in, *Who Is Behind the Farm Crisis?* 1985.

16. Howard Shoemaker, "TV Sensationalism," *Omaha (Neb.) World-Herald* letter to the editor, Aug. 23, 1985. For related comments, criticism, and coverage of the *20/20* segment, see: Doug Hughes, "There's No Place for Bigotry," *Kansas City (Mo.) Star*, letters, Aug. 25, 1985, p. 3E. Jewish Telegraphic Agency, "TV Program Reveals that Radical Right Exploiting Farm Crisis," *Kansas City (Mo.) Jewish Chronicle*, Aug. 16, 1985. Kay Gardella, "Harvest of Hate: *20/20* Segment Is Inflammatory Reporting," *New York Daily News*, Aug. 14, 1985.

17. Letter from Justin J. Finger to Alfred Schneider, Aug. 16, 1985.

18. Daniel Levitas, "Anti-Semitism in the United States," *Year 2000 Grolier Multimedia Encyclopedia* (Grolier Interactive, 1999).

19. The rise of Jewish neoconservatism was fueled by several factors: fear and distrust of blacks following the arrival of a more militant Black Power movement, the 1968 assassination of the Reverend Dr. Martin Luther King Jr., and a rise in black anti-Semitism; the influence of Cold War thinking which dictated that the Jewish community subordinate its traditionally liberal agenda to the cause of combating communism and the "Evil Empire" that was the Soviet Union; and the belief that it was necessary to form alliances with ultraconservative Christian evangelicals who opposed the separation of church and state but supported Israel. Most liberals deplored the deterioration of black-Jewish relations, but a handful of Jewish intellectuals saw it as an opportunity to advance their conservative political agenda. By the mid-1970s, neoconservatives like Nathan Glazer, Irving Kristol, and Norman Podhoretz had managed to parlay Jewish racism, fears of multiculturalism, and distrust of quotas (which had once been used to exclude Jews from colleges and universities) into full-scale opposition to affirmative action. Inspired by Glazer's 1975 book, *Affirmative Discrimination: Ethnic Inequality and Public Policy*, the ADL and other Jewish groups sided against the University of California in the *Bakke* case, which outlawed the use of quotas to promote diversity in higher education. (See: *Regents of the University of California v. Bakke* 438 U.S. 265, June 28, 1978.) Neoconservatives were also staunch anti-communists and they tried—with less success—to manipulate Jewish support for Israel into advocacy for the Reagan administration's military buildup against the Soviet Union, which, among other things, was an aggressive backer of some of Israel's Arab enemies.

20. Pat Robertson, *The New Millennium: Ten Trends that Will Impact You and Your Family by the Year 2000* (Dallas, TX: Word Publishing, 1990), as quoted by Michael Lind, "Reverend Robertson's Grand International Conspiracy Theory," *New York Review of Books*, Feb. 2, 1995, p. 23. Robertson's subsequent book, *The New World Order* (Dallas, TX: Word Publishing, 1991), contained even more disturbing anti-Jewish themes and relied on century-old conspiracy theories about Jewish bankers and communist subversives, promoted by long-standing bigots like Nesta Webster and Eustace Mullins, a Holocaust denier. Among those who criticized Robertson

for this was Michael Lind, a former neoconservative intellectual. "Not since Father Coughlin or Henry Ford has a prominent white American so boldly and unapologetically blamed the disasters of modern world history on the machinations of international high finance in general and on a few influential Jews in particular," wrote Lind in the *New York Review of Books* (Feb. 2, 1995, p. 25).

Robertson countered Lind's criticism by invoking his support of Israel and reaffirming his faith in anti-Semitic sources: "[*The New World Order*] was carefully researched and contains seven single-spaced pages of bibliography from original historical sources," Robertson wrote. "I have lobbied for Israel and donated hundreds of thousands of dollars to Jewish interests and organizations," he added (Gustav Niebuhr, "Pat Robertson Says He Intended No Anti-Semitism in Book He Wrote Four Years Ago," *New York Times*, March 4, 1995). However, it took several years for the ADL to finally take the Christian Coalition founder to task, with the publication of *The Religious Right: The Assault on Tolerance and Pluralism in America* (New York: Anti-Defamation League of B'nai Brith, 1994), pp. 11–26. Then the agency quickly reversed course and pursued rapprochement with Robertson and his Republican benefactors. See: Daniel Levitas, "Jews and the Right: The Anti-Defamation League's Deal with the Christian Coalition," *The Nation*, vol. 260, no. 24, June 19, 1995, pp. 882, 884, 886, 888. For a thorough but concise analysis of the relationship between certain eschatological beliefs and Christian alliances with Jewish groups in support of Israel, see: Donald Wagner, "Evangelicals and Israel: Theological Roots of a Political Alliance," *Christian Century*, Nov. 4, 1998.

21. What Smith said was this: "It is interesting at great political rallies how you have a Protestant to pray, a Catholic to pray, and then you have a Jew to pray. With all due respect to those dear people, my friends, God Almighty does not hear the prayer of a Jew." As quoted in: William Martin, *With God on Our Side: The Rise of the Religious Right in America* (New York: Broadway New York, 1996), p. 215.

22. Irving Kristol, "The Political Dilemma of American Jews," *Commentary*, (New York: American Jewish Committee, 1984) vol. 78, no. 1 pp. 24–25, as quoted by Michael Lind, "Reverend Robertson's Grand International Conspiracy Theory," *New York Review of Books*, Feb. 2, 1995, p. 21.

23. Eric Pace, "Nathan Perlmutter, Top Executive of Anti-Defamation League, Dies," *New York Times*, July 14, 1987, p. D27.

24. Ibid. See also: Levitas, "Jews and the Right: The Anti-Defamation League's Deal with the Christian Coalition," June 19, 1995, p. 884. Nathan Perlmutter, *The Real Anti-Semitism in America* (New York: Arbor House, 1982).

25. Eric Pace, "Irwin J. Suall, Fierce Fighter of Bias for ADL, Dies at 73," *New York Times*, Aug. 20, 1998, p. D20.

26. Pace, "Nathan Perlmutter, Top Executive of Anti-Defamation League, Dies," July 14, 1987, p. D27.

27. Dr. Ellen Isler and Rabbi A. James Rudin, "Anti-Semitism, Extremism, and the Farm Crisis: A Background Memorandum," American Jewish Committee, Sept. 18, 1985.

28. John Peterson, "Guns, Hatred, and Farmers," *Iowa Farmer Today*, Aug. 24, 1985, p. 8B. Bishop Maurice Dingman, "Bishop Dingman Speaks Out," guest editorial, *Des Moines Register*, undated, circa Sept. 1985.

29. Crystal Nix, "Extremists in Farm Belt Are Assailed," *New York Times*, Sept. 21, 1985.

30. "Anti-Semitic Activity Rising in Midwest; Jews Prime Target for Hate," *Kansas City (Mo.) Jewish Chronicle*, Dec. 13, 1985, p. 40. Wayne King, "Right-Wing Extremists Seek to Recruit Farmers," *New York Times*, Sept. 20, 1985.

31. Dan Gillmor, "Jews Will Counter Anti-Semitism with New Alliances," *Kansas City (Mo.) Times*, Oct. 11, 1985.

32. For more on the Harris Poll, see: Louis Harris, "A Study of Anti-Semitism in Rural Iowa and Nebraska," Feb. 1986, p. 7. David Siedenberg, "Behind the Statistics," *Genesis*, Apr.-May 1986, p. 11. "Farm Belt False Alarm," *Inside B'nai B'rith*, June-July 1986, p. 46. Memo from Nathan Perlmutter to National Commission, "Harris Poll on Anti-Semitism in the Farm Belt," Feb. 27, 1986. Diane Wolkow, "Another Look Taken at Midwest Anti-Semitism," *Kansas City (Mo.) Jewish Chronicle*, April 18, 1986. Joseph Aaron, "How Americans View Israel and the Jews," *Jewish Week*, July 18, 1986. Alan S. Katchen, "ADL Director Says Farm Belt Crisis Not as Severe as Represented," *Columbus (Ohio) Jewish Chronicle*, Dec. 12, 1985, pp. 2, 17. "ADL, AJC Differ on Extent of Farmer Anti-Semitism," *Intermountain Jewish News*, March 14, 1986, pp. 1, 6. "Extremist Group Outreach to Rural Americans," *Anti-Defamation League Special Edition*, June 1986. Sheldon Engelmeyer, "ADL's Supposed Shift to the Right: Is It No Longer a 'Clear Voice'?" *Kansas City (Mo.) Jewish Chronicle*, Aug. 23, 1991.

33. Louis Harris, "A Study of Anti-Semitism in Rural Iowa and Nebraska," Feb. 1986, p. 7.

34. Anti-Defamation League news release, March 3, 1996.

35. Aaron, "How Americans View Israel and the Jews," July 18, 1986.

36. *The Grass-Roots Courier*, vol. 1 no. 1, Jan. 7, 1985. Memo from Daniel Levitas, "Update on the Activities of Far-Right Individuals and Organizations and Constructive Programs of Counteraction," PrairieFire, Aug. 1986.

35. Soft-pedaling Hate

1. For more on land patents, their promotion, and related legal rulings, see: Letter of Michael L. Zaleski, Assistant Attorney General, Wisc. DOJ, to Conrad LeBeau, *Patriots Information Network*, May 7, 1985. Conrad LeBeau, " "Hilgeford v. People's Bank," *Patriots Information Network*, Nov. 1985, p. 5. Conrad LeBeau, " "Hilgeford v. People's Bank," *Patriots Information Network*, Sept. 1985, p. 7. Conrad LeBeau, "Land Patents: Attorney General Replies," *Patriots Information Network*, Aug. 1985, pp. 2, 3. Conrad LeBeau, "Land Patents Under Attack," *Patriots Information Network*, May-June 1985. Chuck Walters, "Land Patent Values and Shortfalls an *Acres U.S.A.* Conference Topic," *Acres U.S.A.*, Nov. 23, 1985. Chuck Walters, *Land Patent! Will America Rediscover the Safeguards the Founding Fathers Constructed to Save the Nation from a Landed Aristocracy?* undated circular.

2. *Britt v. Federal Land Bank Association*, 153 Ill. App. 3rd 605.

3. "Nebraska Assembly of Barrister's at Law Presents George Gordon," *Penny Press*, Jan. 28, 1986. *George Gordon School of Common Law*, undated circular, circa Nov. 1986. William Robbins, "Self-Help Advisers Profiting from Farmers' Woes," *New York Times*, Feb. 18, 1986, pp. A1, B9.

4. *George Gordon School of Common Law*, undated circular, circa Nov. 1986. "Tutoring," *George Gordon School of Common Law*, undated circular, circa 1987.

5. Robbins, "Self-Help Advisers Profiting from Farmers' Woes," (Feb. 18, 1986), pp. A1, B9.

6. George Gordon, "Greetings, Friends," *George Gordon's Barrister's Inn*, undated circular, circa 1985.

7. George Gordon, "Why Our Decline," *George Gordons [sic] School of Common Law*, undated booklet, circa 1987.

8. Robbins, "Self-Help Advisers Profiting from Farmers' Woes," (Feb. 18, 1986), pp. A1, B9.

9. Conrad LeBeau, "The PIN Report Discontinues Publication," *Patriots Information Network*, undated, circa Dec. 1987, p. 3.

10. Dennis McCann, "Franklin Man Eager to Tackle Farm Debt Crisis," *Milwaukee Journal*, Dec. 20, 1987, pp. 1B, 4B.

11. Conrad LeBeau, "News Summary," *Patriots Information Network*, July 1985, p. 1. Conrad LeBeau, "Rift Grows Between International Bankers and Communists: The Single Conspiracy Theory Crumbles," *Patriots Information Network*, Aug. 1986, p. 10.

12. Conrad LeBeau, "You Can Fight Back Against Foreclosure Actions," *The Spotlight*, Feb. 29, 1983, pp. 20–21.

13. Keith Schneider, "Economics, Hate, and the Farm Crisis," *New York Times*, Dec. 7, 1987.

14. Conrad LeBeau, "Editorial on Kol Nidre," *Patriots Information Network*, Feb.-March 1986, p. 7.

15. Conrad LeBeau, "Eustace Mullins Supports CCS," *The PIN Report*, July-Aug. 1987, p. 5. Ed Schwartz (1996), pp. 96–98.

16. Conrad LeBeau, "What Are Fractional Reserve Checks?" *Patriots Information Network*, Dec. 1984, no. 31, p. 3.

17. Jim Lewis, " 'Ye Shall Pay Coins, Gold and Silver': U.S. Constitution," UPI, Regional News, Virginia, March 12, 1983.

18. For an early version of the radical right's justification for the use of Fractional Reserve Checks, see: LeBeau, "What Are Fractional Reserve Checks?" (Dec. 1984).

19. Charles Walters Jr., *Holding Action* (Kansas City, MO: Halcyon House, 1968), p xiii. "Author's Biography," Charles Walters Jr., *Angry Testament* (Kansas City, MO: Halcyon House, 1969). *Acres U.S.A.* (Kansas City, Mo.), April 1988, pp. 29–30. Levitas and Ostendorf memo, "Rural Radical Right Update," April 20, 1988, pp. 7–9. "Farm Law Experts Say Bad Advice Puts FmHA Borrowers at Risk," news release, Farmers Legal Action Group, Inc. (St. Paul, Minn.), January 24, 1989.

20. Not all of Common Title's promoters suffered legal consequences for their actions. One Kansas Posseman who took $14,000 from a Wichita tire salesman as payment for sight drafts "worth" more than $750,000, won acquittal on a multiple-count indictment for fraud. For more on Common Title Bond and Trust, see: Levitas and Ostendorf memo, "Rural Radical Right Update," April 20, 1988, pp. 2–3. Michael Whiteley and R. Robin McDonald, "Ownership of Farmland is Clouded; Fraud Probe Extends to 8 States, Canada," *Wichita (Kans.) Eagle-Beacon*, July 18, 1987, pp. 1, 6A. R. Robin McDonald and Michael Whitely, "Tax Protester Feels 'Trapped' by the System,' " *Wichita (Kans.) Eagle-Beacon*, July 26, 1987, pp. 1, 6C. Rogers Worthington, "Farmer Sight-Draft Schemes," *AgriFinance*, Nov. 1987, pp. 48–49. "Hartigan Sues over Farm Fraud," public information from Neil F. Hartigan, Attorney General, State of Illinois, Sept. 11, 1987. Preliminary injunction order, *People of the State of Illinois v. Common Title Bond and Trust et al.*, State of Illinois, Fourth Judicial Circuit, Fayette County, no. 87-CH-41. *United States of America v. James E. Patterson*. Pam Davidson, "Farmer Indicted over Bank Note," *Dayton (Ohio) Daily News and Journal Herald*, Apr. 29, 1987, p. 32. "Statement of Attorney General Robert T. Stephan re: Lawsuit against Common Title and Trust," July 6, 1987. *State of North Dakota ex rel. v. Common Title Bond and Trust et al.*, preliminary injunction, civil no. 88-175, State of North Dakota, District Court, Cass County, East Central Judicial District, April 25, 1988. Charles Walters, "Common Title: Kill the Club, or Kill the Law," *Acres U.S.A.*, Sept. 1987.

21. See: "Statistics of the Presidential and Congressional Election of November 3, 1992," found at: http://clerkweb.house.gov/elections/1992/Stat.htm#47. Also: "Statistics of the congressional election of November 8, 1994," http://clerkweb.house.gov/elections/1994/Stat.htm#47. 1999–2000 "eProfile," Representative Jack Metcalf, http://www.opensecrets.org/politicians/index/N00007895.htm. "About Jack Metcalf," http://www.evergreen.edu/user/library/govdocs/metcalf/about.html.

22. Memo of Jim Townsend, ROC National Chairman, to members of Redeem Our Country (ROC), April 1985. Jim Townsend, "New FRB Exposé! Foreigners Control Federal Reserve," *National Educator*, vol. 13, no. 1, June 1981. Jim Townsend, "A Federal Mafia: Monopoly of

Dollars Rules U.S.," *National Educator*, vol. 13, no. 1, June 1981. "James Townsend," *Extremism on the Right* (1983), pp. 139–40.

23. Alan Murray, "Washington State Legislator Wants to Abolish Fed, and He Has Convinced Some People He Has a Point," *Wall Street Journal*, July 16, 1987. "Jack Metcalf: A Chenoweth at Heart? 'Banking Conspiracies' and Native Americans Targeted," *The Dignity Report* (Seattle, WA: Coalition for Human Dignity), no. 19, undated. Jack Metcalf, "Metcalf Sees Hope for U.S. Dollar," *National Educator*, Nov. 1984, p. 1.

24. Jack Metcalf, "Federal Reserve Update," *Honest Money for America*, vol. 4, no. 4, p. 1.

25. Leonard Zeskind, "Background Report on Racist and Anti-Semitic Organizational Intervention in the Farm Protest Movement," (Atlanta: Center for Democratic Renewal, 1985), pp. 8, 9. AP, "Claims of Anti-Semitism Put Populist Party on the Defensive," *Waterloo (Ia.) Courier*, Feb. 9, 1986, p. A8.

26. "Senator Metcalf on the Stump in Minnesota and the Dakotas," *Honest Money for America*, Feb. 1986, vol. 3, no. 1, p. 2.

27. Coalition for Human Dignity, Seattle, WA, "Jack Metcalf: A Chenoweth at Heart?"

36. The Deadfall Line

1. Larry Humphreys, *Heritage Library Broadside*, undated tabloid, p. 1.

2. Lawrence Humphreys Jr., "Vacation," *On Point '86* (Velma, OK: Heritage Library), vol. 2, no. 1, Jan.-Feb. 1986, p. 7.

3. Townsend was from Los Angeles and two of his propaganda works caught the attention of the federal government during World War II: *Seeking Foreign Trouble* and *The High Cost of Hate*. He pleaded guilty to being an unregistered Japanese agent. See: "Publications. German-American. Italian-American, American. Russian. Miscellaneous," *Individual Exclusion Board Subversive Information Manual* (Civil Affairs Division, Western Defense Command and Fourth Army, 1942), pp. 5, 6, 17, WCCL, National Archives. Memo from David Lowe to Irwin Suall, "Heritage Library," Anti-Defamation League, Dec. 3, 1985, p. 2. James Ridgeway, "Farm Country's New Right Knight," *Village Voice* (New York), Feb. 4, 1986, p. 32. *Heritage Library Broadside*, undated newsletter, p. 3.

4. Lawrence L. Humphreys Jr., "Letter to Governors," undated correspondence, circa Dec. 1985.

5. Judy Gibbs, "Bleckley Farm Protester Is Banker's Son Who's Using His Wealth to Fight the Banks," *Macon (Ga.) Telegraph and News*, Nov. 24, 1985. "Banking Laws Critic Files for Liquidation," *Daily Oklahoman*, Aug. 6, 1986, p. 17. Larry Batson, "Hard Times Turn Farmers Away from Plowshares, to Swords," *Minneapolis Star Tribune*, Dec. 29, 1986, pp. 4–5A (Metro).

6. *Lawrence Lewis Humphreys, Appelant, v. State of Oklahoma, Appellee*, no. M-85-133. June 10, 1987, *Oklahoma Bar Journal*, pp. 1767–68. Larry Humphreys, "Common Law Travel," *Heritage Library Broadside*, undated tabloid, p. 3.

7. *Lawrence Lewis Humphreys, Appelant, v. State of Oklahoma, Appellee*, no. M-85-133. June 10, 1987, *Oklahoma Bar Journal*, pp. 1767–68. Gibbs, "Bleckley Farm Protester Is Banker's Son Who's Using His Wealth to Fight the Banks," Nov. 24, 1985.

8. John Lancaster, "Extremists Are Linked to Farm Protest: State, Local Law Officers Brace for More Conflicts," *Atlanta Journal-Constitution*, Dec. 8, 1985, p. A1. Conrad LeBeau, "Nov. 15, 1985," *Patriots Information Network*, Dec. 1985, pp. 1–2.

9. David Beasley, "Activist Kersey Will Close Farm Pricing Union Office, Sell Insurance," *Atlanta Journal-Constitution*, May 10, 1987, p. B4.

10. By Kersey's own estimate fewer than one thousand farmers nationwide ever took his advice. Tommy Kersey, "Farmers Still Planting Themselves into the Grave," *National Farm Products Minimum Pricing Union Newsletter*, vol. 5, May 1985. David Beasley, "More Georgians Now Farming on Paper: Some Finding Brighter Financial Future in Agricultural Commodities Markets," *Atlanta Journal-Constitution*, Feb. 22, 1987, p. B10.

11. "Farmers Stage Capitol Protest," *Atlanta Journal-Constitution*, Feb. 26, 1985, p. C1. *Iowa Farm Unity Coalition 10-Year Anniversary*, Iowa Farm Unity Coalition, Des Moines, Iowa, Nov. 21, 1992.

12. Tom Hallman and Ann Wead Kimbrough, "A Farm Union in Georgia? Labor Leader Says AFL-CIO Would Welcome Affiliation," *Atlanta Journal-Constitution*, April 7, 1985, p. K1. "Fifty Protest Foreclosures on Two Farms," *Atlanta Journal-Constitution*, March 5, 1985, p. A22. "Foreclosures Sale Stymied by Farmers," *Atlanta Journal-Constitution*, Feb. 6, 1985. Tom Hallman, "Protesters Fail to Halt Auction of Farms," *Atlanta Journal-Constitution*, July 3, 1985, p. E5.

13. "Up in Arms," *On Point '85: Heritage Library's Action Newsline*, vol. 1, no. 6, p. 1. Memo from David Lowe to Irwin Suall, "Heritage Library," Anti-Defamation League, Dec. 3, 1985. Pat Powers, "Bleckley Farm Showdown Postponed . . . for a While," *Macon (Ga.) Telegraph and News*, Nov. 16, 1985, pp. 1A, 9A. Audrey Post, "This is the Dead-fall Line, Man with Gun Said," *Macon (Ga.) Telegraph and News*, Nov. 16, 1985, pp. 1A, 9A. John Lancaster, "Cochran Farmer's Ordeal Has Happy Ending: Pair to Buy Farm, Lease It to Him for $1 a Month," *Atlanta Journal-Constitution*, Nov. 23, 1985, p. A1.

14. Post, "This Is the Dead-fall Line,' Man with Gun Said," (Nov. 16, 1985), pp. 1A.

15. Lancaster, "Extremists Are Linked to Farm Protest: State, Local Law Officers Brace for More Conflicts," (Dec. 8, 1985), p. A1.

16. Powers, "Bleckley Farm Showdown Postponed . . . for a While," (Nov. 16, 1985), p. 9A.

17. Post, " 'This Is the Dead-fall Line,' Man with Gun Said," (Nov. 16, 1985), p. 9A.

18. Doug Giesbracht, "Coverage of Farm Protest Called Distorted," *Macon (Ga.) Telegraph and News*, letter to the editor, Nov. 20, 1985.

19. Wendell Cochran, "Georgian Leads Fight on Farm Foreclosures," *Des Moines Sunday Register*, Jan. 19, 1986, pp. 1B, 4B. Lancaster, "Extremists Are Linked to Farm Protest: State, Local Law Officers Brace For More Conflicts," (Dec. 8, 1985), p. A1. Powers, "Bleckley Farm Showdown Postponed . . . for a While," Nov. 16, 1985, pp. 1A, 9A. Post " 'This Is the Dead-fall Line,' Man with Gun Said," (Nov. 16, 1985), pp. 1A, 9A. "What Iowa Doesn't Need," *Des Moines Register*, editoral, Jan. 23, 1986, p. 6A.

20. William E. Schmidt, "Armed Men Delay Eviction of a Georgia Farmer," *New York Times*, Nov. 16, 1985, p. 9. Pat Powers, "Farmer Won't Be Evicted," *Macon (Ga.) Telegraph and News*, Nov. 23, 1985, pp. 1A, 4A.

21. Batson, "Hard Times Turn Farmers Away from Plowshares, to Swords," Dec. 29, 1986, pp. 1A, 4A (Metro). Powers, "Bleckley Farm Showdown Postponed . . . for a While," (Nov. 16, 1985), pp. 1A. Associated Press, "Threatened Farmer Gets Many 'Bitty' Cash Gifts," *New York Times*, Nov. 18, 1985.

22. John Lancaster, "Cochran Farmer's Ordeal Has Happy Ending: Pair to Buy Farm, Lease It to Him for $1 a Month," *Atlanta Journal-Constitution*, Nov. 23, 1985, p. A1. Associated Press, "Farmer's 'Samaritan' Held on Theft, Forgery Charges," *(St. Louis, Mo.) Post-Dispatch*, Nov. 26, 1985.

23. David Goldberg, "The Farming Shakeout in Georgia: Man Activists Defended Isn't Farming Again," *Atlanta Journal-Constitution*, Feb. 4, 1990, p. A9. David Beasley, "Farmer's Benefactor Identified: College Park Man Leads Effort to Get Land Back," *Atlanta*

Journal-Constitution, Dec. 4, 1985, p. A1. "Drowning victims are sons of farmer," *Atlanta Journal-Constitution*, April 21, 1992, p. C4.

24. Gibbs, "Bleckley Farm Protester Is Banker's Son Who's Using His Wealth to Fight the Banks," Nov. 24, 1985. Powers, "Farmer Won't Be Evicted," Nov. 23, 1985, pp. 1A, 4A. Associated Press "Farmer's 'Samaritan' Held on Theft, Forgery Charges," Nov. 26, 1985.

25. "Race Relations," *Heritage Library Broadside*, undated, p. 8. "Making Bricks without Straw," *Heritage Library Broadside II*, undated tabloid, p. 4.

26. Batson, "Hard Times Turn Farmers Away from Plowshares, to Swords," Dec. 29, 1986, p. 4A (Metro). Karen Harris, "Extremist Ideas Can Take Root in Troubled Farms," *Atlanta Journal-Constitution*, Oct. 7, 1985, p. E1. Mike Christensen, "Georgia Protest Leader's Rhetoric Is Drifting to the Right," *Atlanta Journal-Constitution*, Jan. 12, 1986, pp. 1B, 6B.

27. Batson, "Hard Times Turn Farmers Away from Plowshares, to Swords," Dec. 29, 1986, p. 4A (Metro).

28. Cochran, "Georgian Leads Fight on Farm Foreclosures," Jan. 19, 1986, pp. 1B, 4B. "What Iowa Doesn't Need," editorial, *Des Moines Register*, (Jan. 23, 1986). Ray Locker, "Officials Wary of Farm Activist," *Montgomery Advertiser*, pp. 1–2A, undated clipping.

29. Gibbs, "Bleckley Farm Protester Is Banker's Son Who's Using His Wealth to Fight the Banks," Nov. 24, 1985.

30. "Up in Arms," *On Point '85: Heritage Library's Action Newsline*, vol. 1 no. 6, p. 1.

31. Michael Collins Piper, "Heir to Banking Millions Champions Farmers' Cause," *The Spotlight*, Jan. 6 and 13, 1986, p. 12.

32. Susan Mattson Halena, "Farmers Urged to Take Up Arms," *(St. Cloud, Minn.) Daily Times*, Jan. 17, 1986, p. 1C.

33. Lee Egerstom, "Farm Activists Issue Call for Militant Stand," *St. Paul (Minn.) Pioneer Press Dispatch*, Jan. 13, 1986, p. 4A. Betsy Burkhard, "Farm Activists Plan Sioux City Rally," *Sioux City (Ia.) Journal*, undated clipping, Jan. 1986.

34. Conrad LeBeau, *Patriots Information Network*, Aug. 1985, p. 3. Egerstom, "Farm Activists Issue Call for Militant Stand," Jan. 13, 1986, p. 4A. Betsy Burkhard, "Holstein, Sioux City Still on Farm Activists' Itinerary," *Sioux City (Ia.) Journal*, undated clipping, pp. A1, 12.

35. Halena, "Farmers Urged to Take Up Arms," Jan. 17, 1986, p. 1C.

36. Egerstom, "Farm Activists Issue Call for Militant Stand," Jan. 13, 1986, p. 4A.

37. Ibid. See also, Cochran, "Georgian Leads Fight on Farm Foreclosures," Jan. 19, 1986, pp. 1B, 4B. David Beasley, "Macon Evangelist Is Convicted in Farmer Trust Plan," *Atlanta Journal-Constitution*, Nov. 22, 1986, p. B7. David Beasley, "Macon Evangelist Is Indicted Again over Trusts Plan," *Atlanta Journal-Constitution*, Sept. 30, 1986, p. D9. Conrad LeBeau, "A Preacher Is Accused," *Patriots Information Network* newsletter, vol. 2, no. 3, 1986. Randall Mikkelsen, "Evangelist's Lien Plan Sparks Threat of Legal Action in North Dakota," *Agweek*, Feb. 10, 1986. Associated Press, "North Dakota Farmers Told to Take Up Arms," *Des Moines Register*, Jan. 16, 1986, "Midwest Briefs." Halena, "Farmers Urged to Take Up Arms," Jan. 17, 1986, p. 1C.

38. Daniel Levitas, memo to NJCRAC Committee on Midwest Extremism and Farm-Belt Anti-Semitism, "Inroads, Infiltration, and Influence of Anti-Semitic Elements on the Mainstream Farm Protest Movement," PrairieFire, April 10, 1986, p. 4.

39. Craig Spencer, "Farm Meeting Moves to County," *Kearney (Neb.) Daily Hub*, vol. 98, no. 68, p. 1.

40. Bob Davis, "Church Leaders Condemn Radical Right," *Iowa Farmer Today*, reprinted in *Catholic Charities Reports*, vol. 7, no. 2 Feb. 14, 1986, Sioux City, Iowa. See also: Rev. William

Skinner, et. al., "Statement on Extremism and Extremist Philosophy Relative to Rural Crisis," Ecumenical Rural Concerns Committee of Northwest Iowa, Jan. 29, 1986.

41. Kathy Hoeschen, "Siouxland Shuts Out Activists," *Sioux City (Ia.) Journal*, Jan. 1986. Betsy Burkhard, "Holstein, Sioux City Still on Farm Activists' Itinerary," *Sioux City (Ia.) Journal*, Jan. 1986. Lyn Zerschling, "Farm Activists Rally Near Hull," *Sioux City (Ia.) Journal*, undated clipping, Jan. 1986.

42. "What Iowa Doesn't Need" editorial, *Des Moines Register*, Jan. 23, 1986.

43. Daniel Levitas and the Reverend David L. Ostendorf, memo to to key rural contacts, fall training participants and invitees, "Rural Radical Right Update," *PrairieFire*, Jan. 27, 1986.

44. C. David Kotok, "Banking, IRS Attacked at Rally; Farmers Told to Bear Arms," *Omaha (Neb.) World-Herald* circa Jan. 26, 1986, p. 1. Ridgeway "Farm Country's New Right Knight," (Feb. 4, 1986), p. 32. Lawrence L. Humphreys Jr., "Kearney Conference," *On Point '86*, vol. 2, no. 1, Jan.-Feb. 1986, p. 3.

45. "The United Methodist Church Seeks Peaceful Solutions to the Farm Crisis," *Kearney (Neb.) Daily Hub*, Jan. 23, 1986.

46. "Motel Shuts Doors to Crisis Group," *Kearney (Neb.) Daily Hub*, vol. 98, no. 67, p. 1. Associated Press, "Farm Activists Met in Storage Building," *Lincoln (Neb.) Star*, Jan. 27, 1986. Associated Press, "Kersey's farm group heads to Nebraska," Jan. 23, 1985. "January 25 Convention Planned," *On Point '85*, p. 8.

47. Kotok, "Banking, IRS Attacked at Rally; Farmers Told to Bear Arms," circa Jan. 26, 1986, p. 1.

48. Richard Kelly Hoskins, "The Unique West," *Western Destiny*, Oct. 1964, pp. 6, 7. Richard Kelly Hoskins, "Two Controversial Ideas: A Glance At Yockey," *Western Destiny*, July 1964, pp. 5, 15. Richard Kelly Hoskins, *War Cycles, Peace Cycles* (Lynchburg, VA: The Virginia Publishing Company, 1985). Richard Kelly Hoskins, *Vigilantes of Christendom* (Lynchburg, VA: The Virginia Publishing Company, 1990).

49. Kotok, "Banking, IRS Attacked at Rally; Farmers Told to Bear Arms," circa Jan. 26, 1986, p. 4.

50. Associated Press, "Farm Activists Met in Storage Building," Jan. 27, 1986.

51. Kotok, "Banking, IRS Attacked at Rally; Farmers Told to Bear Arms," circa Jan. 26, 1986, p. 1.

52. Ibid.

53. Levitas memo, "Inroads, Infiltration and Influence of Anti-Semitic Elements on the Mainstream Farm Protest Movement," April 10, 1986, p. 4.

54. Larry Fruhling, "Speakers Urge Armed Resistance to Save Farms," *Des Moines Register*, Jan. 26, 1986, p. 6A. Dr. Everett Sileven, *The Story of America's First Padlocked Church and Its Jailed Pastor* (Houston, MO: Faith Baptist Ministries, 1983). Robert L. Thoburn, *The Christian and Politics* (Tyler, TX: Thoburn Press, 1984). Leonard Zeskind, "Undercutting Extremism: Activists Put Damper on Missouri Christian Identity Meeting," *Kansas City (Mo.) Jewish Chronicle*, vol. 79, no. 24, June 11, 1999, pp. 1, 7.

55. The GOP primary was held May 13, 1986. Neal Erickson, Nebraska Assistant Secretary of State for Elections, interview by the author.

56. Daniel Levitas, memo to key farm and rural contacts, "Update on the Activities of Far-Right Individuals and Organizations and Constructive Programs of Counteraction," *PrairieFire*, Dec. 10, 1986, pp. 2, 3.

57. Ibid.

58. Craig Spencer, "Farm Meeting Moves to Country," *Kearney (Neb.) Daily Hub*, vol. 98, no. 68, p. 1.

59. Batson, "Hard Times Turn Farmers Away from Plowshares, to Swords," Dec. 29, 1986, p. 4A (Metro).

60. News release, National Farm Products Minimum Pricing Union, Inc., April 7, 1986.

61. David Beasley, "Activist Kersey Will Close Farm Pricing Union Office, Sell Insurance," *Atlanta Journal-Constitution*, May 10, 1987, p. B4.

62. "Banking Laws Critic Files for Liquidation," *Daily Oklahoman*, Aug. 6, 1986, p. 17. "Bank Buys Humphreys' Farm: But Heritage Library Founder Still in Possession" (reprinted from the *Daily Oklahoman*) *Justice Times*, July 1987, p. 13. Memo from Daniel Levitas to key farm and rural contacts, "Farm Foreclosure, Marital Problems Plague Oklahoma's Larry Humphreys," *PrairieFire*, Aug. 1, 1987, p. 4.

63. Michael Collins Piper, "Candidate for Seat in House Campaigns for Real Money," *The Spotlight*, Oct. 6, 1986, p. 22. Piper, "Heir to Banking Millions Champions Farmers' Cause," Jan. 6 and 13, 1986, p. 12.

64. Dallas L. Dendy Jr., Donald K. Anderson, *Statistics of the Congressional Election of November 4, 1986* (Washington, DC: U.S. Government Printing Office, 1987), pp. 32, 33. Humphreys won 28.3 percent of the overall vote in the Fourth Congressional District, compared to 21.9 percent and 36.5 percent of the votes won by the GOP nominees in the Second and Third Districts. Levitas memo, "Inroads, Infiltration and Influence of Anti-Semitic Elements on the Mainstream Farm Protest Movement," April 10, 1986, p. 4.

65. John C. Ensslin, "Former Publisher's Wife Gets Deferred Sentence," *Denver (Colo.) Rocky Mountain News*, June 14, 1984, p. 41. John C. Ensslin, "Jury Convicts Former Publisher of Theft Over Unpaid Farm Loans," *Denver (Colo.) Rocky Mountain News*, May 28, 1986, p. 10. Associated Press, "*Primrose* Editor Elliot Receives 8-Year Sentence," undated newspaper clipping.

66. Such views were not uncommon in the *Spotlight* and the *Primrose and Cattleman's Gazette*, but Elletson somehow managed to convince the Wyoming Trial Lawyers Association to devote four pages of its newsletter to his correspondence decrying Europeans as "emasculated marionettes unknowingly manipulated into the service of international finance," and warning lawyers that they risked being turned into "men and women compelled to worship at the feet of Mammon for whatever meager pittance the bankers and the subservient judiciary may deign to give them." As of 2001, Elletson was still selling the same ideological wares, only this time over the Internet, where he gave himself the title of "chancellor" of a non-accredited "virtual university," dedicated to advancing his theories of "parapometrics." See: Roger C. Elletson, *Highlights of the Power Parameters of Money*, (Wilson, WY: Christian International Publications, 1979), pp. 2, 9, 19, 23, 24, 29. Roger C. Elletson, "Open Letter to Jack Stanfield," *The Coffee House* (Cheyenne, WY: Wyoming Trial Lawyers Association, 1985), vol. 6, no. 1, p. 21.

67. Kathleen Best, "Farm Pitch: LaRouche Cultivates Rural Support," (*St. Louis, Mo.) Post-Dispatch*, April 7, 1986, pp. 1, 6. Andrew Malcolm, "LaRouche Illinois Drive Focused on Rural Areas," *New York Times*, March 31, 1986. Tom Johnson, "A Report on 'the LaRouche Factor' in Selected Downstate Counties in the 1986 Illinois Primary Election," *American Jewish Committee*, March 31, 1986, p. 9. Farm Credit System borrowers in Illinois were saddled with tremendous debt, with the most burdened borrowers—those with debt-to-asset ratios of more than 70 percent—still paying more than 13 percent interest. And according to senior officials with the Farm Credit Banks of St. Louis, the banks were "approaching marginal" financial condition, with 25 to 30 percent of its farm loans destined for "nonviability" in the coming twelve to twenty-four months. See: Jerri Stroud, "Farm Credit Banks Here Near 'Marginal' Condition," (*St. Louis, Mo.) Post-Dispatch*, April 2, 1986.

68. For a detailed assessment of the March 1986 primary, see: Dennis King, *Lyndon LaRouche and the New American Fascism* (New York: Doubleday, 1989), pp. 103–11. See also: Robert B. Albritton, "The LaRouche Victory in Illinois: An Analysis of the 1986 Democratic Primary Election Returns," *American Jewish Committee*, June 1986. Johnson, "A Report on 'the La-Rouche Factor' in Selected Downstate Counties in the 1986 Illinois Primary Election," March 31, 1986.

69. "Stevenson to Seek to Run as Independent," *Des Moines Register*, March 28, 1986, p. 7A. Andrew H. Malcolm, "Stevenson Bars Right-Wing Running Mates," *New York Times*, March 21, 1986, pp. 1, 13.

70. King (1989), p. 103.

71. Associated Press, "Other LaRouche Backers Win Election," *Belleville (Ill.) News-Democrat*, March 23, 1986, p. 8A. Levitas, "Inroads and Influence of Far-Right Individuals and Organizations," memo to key farm and rural contacts, *PrairieFire* May 8, 1986, p. 2.

72. "ADL and KGB Network Run 'Neo-Nazi' Deception in Farm Belt," *New Solidarity*, circa 1986.

73. Caryle Murphy, "LaRouche Convicted of Mail Fraud," *Washington Post*, Dec. 17, 1988, p. A1. King (1989), p. 377.

74. Martha A. Miles and Caroline Rand Herron, "LaRouche Aides Face New Charges," *New York Times*, Dec. 21, 1986, section 4, p. 4. Peter Pae and Leef Smith, "LaRouche Back in Loudoun after 5 Years in Prison," *Washington Post*, Jan. 27, 1994, p. A11. Caryle Murphy, "LaRouche Convicted of Mail Fraud," *Washington Post*, Dec. 17, 1988, p. A1.

37. Farmers Abandoned

1. Goldstein's campaign included farm tours for Jewish community leaders, letter-writing campaigns to legislators, public forums on the rural crisis for urban Jews (one July 1986 session drew more than six hundred Jews and farmers to a Kansas City synagogue), and social services for families who had lost their farms. Mark Belingloph, "Tour Gives Jews Insight into Rural Communities," *Kansas City (Mo.) Jewish Chronicle*, vol. 90, no. 32, Aug. 8, 1986, pp. 1, 18. Associated Press, "Jews Mount Campaign to Help Farmers," *St. Joseph (Mo.) Gazette*, Sept. 2, 1986. Judy Goldberg, "Jewish Farm Activist Analyzes Ag Situation," *Kansas State Collegian*, Sept. 4, 1986. Ann Toner, "Jews Offer Support to Farmers," *Kansas City (Mo.) Star*, Aug. 4, 1986. Diane Wolkow, "JCRB, ORT Join Forces to Aid Distressed Farmers," *Kansas City (Mo.) Jewish Chronicle*, vol. 90, no. 20, May 16, 1986. Elizabeth Kaplan, "Forum Addresses the Roots of Farm Anti-Semitism," *Kansas City (Mo.) Jewish Chronicle*, July 18, 1986. Daniel Levitas, memo to key farm and rural contacts, "Inroads and Influence of Far-Right Individuals and Organizations," *PrairieFire*, May 8, 1986, p. 5.

2. Daniel Levitas, memo to key farm and rural contacts, "Update on the Activities of Far-Right Individuals and Organizations and Constructive Programs of Counteraction," *PrairieFire*, Dec. 10, 1986, pp. 2, 3. Naomi Godfrey, "Jewish Groups to Aid Midwest Farmers," unsourced news clipping, Oct. 1986.

3. Peter Hernon, " 'On Our Side:' Jackson Preaches Hope for Farmers," *St. Louis (Mo.) Post-Dispatch*, April 7, 1986, pp. 1, 6.

4. "Jewish Bureau Rallies with Protesting Farmers," *Chillicothe (Mo.) Constitution-Tribune*, Aug. 4, 1986. Ann Toner, "Jews Offer Support to Farmers," *Kansas (Mo.) City Star*, Aug. 4, 1986.

5. See: "Tom Harkin Member Profile," www.cnn.com/ELECTION/CQ.profiles/IA00SE NATEHARKIN.html#biographical.

6. "Farm Bankruptcies," *The Continuing Crisis in Rural America: Fact vs. Fiction*, (Des Moines, IA: PrairieFire, 1987), May 15, 1987, p. 3.

7. Democrats gained a 53- to 47-seat majority in the 1986 elections. Rural activists attributed the increase to the depth of the rural crisis and those rural voters who supported Senators Tom Daschle (D–South Dakota), Kent Conrad (D–North Dakota), and Wyche Fowler (D–Georgia). Iowa senator Tom Harkin's Senate victory in 1984 also was attributed in a large measure to the rural crisis.

8. *George M. Britt v. Federal Land Bank Association of St. Louis*, 2nd District, no 86-0248. See also: memo from Daniel Levitas to key farm and rural contacts, "Update on the Activities of Far-Right Individuals and Organizations and Programs of Counteraction," *PrairieFire*, Aug. 1, 1987, pp. 3–4.

9. Conrad LeBeau, "The *PIN Report* Discontinues Publication," *Patriots Information Network*, undated, circa Dec. 1987, p. 3. Once an enthusiastic member of the Populist Party of Wisconsin—he had been appointed "communications director" for the group—LeBeau eventually soured on organizational efforts. "Various attempts to unite monetary reform leaders have failed because the individual leaders themselves cannot agree on what should constitute an honest and constitutional money system," he wrote.

10. Keith Schneider, "Economics, Hate, and the Farm Crisis," *New York Times*, Dec. 7, 1987.

11. LeBeau, "The *PIN Report* Discontinues Publication," circa Dec. 1987, p. 3.

12. Conrad LeBeau, "The *PIN Report* to Be Discontinued," *PIN Report*, Dec. 1987.

13. Conrad LeBeau, "Hydrogen Peroxide Therapy: New Hope for Incurable Diseases," *PIN Report*, PIN no. 54, July-Aug. 1987, p. 9. See also: *United States of America v. Conrad E. LeBeau*, United States Court of Appeals for the Seventh Circuit, no. 92-2724, Jan. 28, 1993. *United States of America v. Conrad E. LeBeau*, Eastern District of Wisconsin, no. 91-C-3563. "Hydrogen Perioxide Sales Stopped," *NCAHF News* (National Council Against Health Fraud), vol. 15, no. 6, Nov.-Dec. 1992, found at http://www.ncahf.org/nl/1992/11-12.html.

14. "Farm Debt Stress Remains Concentrated among Family-Size Farms," *The Continuing Crisis in Rural America: Fact vs. Fiction*, May 15, 1987, p. 5.

15. "Loss of Farms," *The Continuing Crisis in Rural America*, May 15, 1987, pp. 2–3.

16. "Farm Credit System," *The Continuing Crisis in Rural America*, May 15, 1987, p. 6. The federally sponsored Farm Credit System (FCS) had two arms: the Federal Land Bank (FLB) and the Production Credit Association (PCA). Both were among the nation's largest agricultural lenders. With nearly one thousand local, cooperatively owned associations, the FCS provided farmers and ranchers with more than one-third of their total financing—well over $30 billion a year by the mid-1970s. For a thorough history of the origins of the Farm Credit System, and its activities through the mid-1970s, see: W. Gifford Hoag, *The Farm Credit System . . . A History of Financial Self-Help* (Danville, IN: The Interstate, 1976).

17. "Agricultural Implement Manufacturing," *The Continuing Crisis in Rural America: Fact vs. Fiction*, May 15, 1987, p. 8.

18. "Farmers Home Administration," *The Continuing Crisis in Rural America*, May 15, 1987, pp. 6–7.

19. Testimony of Rabbi David Saperstein, Director of the Religious Action Center, Union of American Hebrew Congregations, Washington, D.C., hearing on Mandatory Production Controls, Wheat, Feed Grains and Soybeans Committee, Agriculture Committee of the U.S. House of Representatives, March 31, 1987.

20. Charles Walters, Jr. *Acres U.S.A.*, Nov. 1987, pp. 30, 37.

21. Peter T. Kilborn, "Bit by Bit, Tiny Morland, Kansas, Fades Away," *New York Times*, May 10, 2001, p. 1.

38. An Enemy Government

1. Richard J. Pocker, "Portion of Jury Trial, Closing Argument," *United States of America v. William P. Gale et al.*, U.S. District Court, District of Nevada, Las Vegas, Nev. CR-S-86-160-LDG, Sep. 30, 1987, p. 34.

2. See: *United States of America v. Gale et al.*, Oct. 9, 1986. Maria L. La Ganga, "FBI Seeking Link Between Tax Protester, Pipe Bombs," *Los Angeles Times*, March 12, 1987, p. 1. Associated Press, *Des Moines Register*, Oct. 31, 1986. United Press International, Sept. 17, 1987. Portion of jury trial—Day 1, transcript of opening statements, *United States of America v. Gale et al.*, pp. 11, 21–22.

3. Closing argument of Richard J. Pocker, *United States of America v. Gale et al.*, p. 46.

4. John K. Van De Kamp, Attorney General, State of California, Department of Justice, *Annual Report to the California Legislature: Organized Crime in California 1986*, p. 25. Joel Davis, "Manhunt Figure Linked to Extremist Group," *Davis (Calif.) Enterprise*, Dec. 18, 1986, as quoted in Cheri Seymour, *The Committee of the States: Inside the Radical Right* (Mariposa, CA: Camden Place Communications, Inc., 1991), p. 15.

5. United Press International, Regional News, Arizona-Nevada La Ganga. "FBI Seeking Link Between Tax Protestor, Pipe Bombs," March 12, 1987, p. 1.

6. "Rev. W. P. Gale, 'Committee of the States,' " audiotape 82-049 (Mariposa, CA: Ministry of Christ Church, 1982).

7. Portion of jury trial—Day 1, transcript of opening statements, *United States of America v. Gale et al.*, p. 10.

8. Zabawa first came to the attention of authorities in March 1984, after neighbors reported hearing weapons fire coming from property where Zabawa lived. The previous month he had purchased a Ruger Mini-14 rifle with a folding metal stock and two thirty-round banana clips. Zabawa gave his statement following his arrest on May 20, 1984, which stemmed from actions he took in response to the May 11 arrest of Wiley and Reineking. See: Associated Press, "Sentencing Delayed," *Garden City (Kans.) Telegram*, Sept. 15, 1984. United Press International, Regional News, July 12, 1984. United Press International, Regional News, June 13, 1984. Affidavit of James Malson, Special Agent for the KBI, State of Kansas, County of Franklin, May 18, 1984. Investigation report of Special Agent John E. McElroy, KBI, case no. 29-72461, May 15, 1984. "Holton Man Guilty in Threat Case," *Topeka (Kans.) Capital-Journal*, July 13, 1984.

9. "Contract (Compact) of 1777–1778," *Mariposa County (Calif.) Recorder*, July 13, 1984, vol. 262, 340, p. 13.

10. Gale also took the title of "Secretary of War" in companion documents filed in Nebraska proclaiming the establishment of the "Dejour Government" of the United States. Portion of jury trial—Day 1, transcript of opening statements, *United States of America v. Gale et al.*, pp. 13–14.

11. Gale also tried to give himself an "out" on paper, with regard to the militia, by claiming that its primary mission was "defensive in nature and . . . not to be confused with any local law enforcement authority, or duties and responsibility of any county posse functioning under authority of the Law [of] Posse Comitatus . . . nor in support of any personal vendettas of any kind." Portion of jury trial—Day 1, transcript of opening statements, *United States of America v. Gale et al.*, pp. 50–51.

12. Portion of jury trial—Day 1, transcript of opening statements, *United States of America v. Gale et al.*, p. 15. Closing argument of Richard J. Pocker, *United States of America v. Gale*, Sept. 30, 1987, pp. 33, 37.

13. Mike Martindale, "Cops Link Suspect to Militia Units; Arizona Man Is 1 of 2 Held in Alleged Oakland Kidnap Plot," *Detroit News*, Oct. 14, 1999. James Coates, *Chicago Tribune*, p. 19. United Press International, Regional News, California, Jan. 16, 1998.

14. After the meeting, Kuhman returned to Kansas with Emil Wiley and helped him concoct a bogus lawsuit against sixteen Kansas banks and other creditors. The lawsuit, which was filed in November 1984 on behalf of twenty plaintiffs, sought federal class-action status for five thousand farmers and accused bank officials of usury, mail fraud, stock fraud, extortion, and racketeering. Predictably, the suit was based on tired Posse theories about "money creation," and was dismissed. See: Mike Anton, " 'Savior' to Farmers Takes on Legal, Banking Systems," *Kansas City (Mo.) Star*, Jan. 19, 1986, pp. 1, 8A. United Press International, Regional News, Kansas, Nov. 13, 1984.

15. For an example of the litigation, see: United Press International, Regional News, Arizona, Nevada, Aug. 5, 1984. United Press International, Regional News, Arizona, Nevada, Nov. 10, 1984. Fred Smith, "Group Opposes Laws, Taxes; Sees Enemies Everywhere," *Arizona Republic*, circa Dec. 1985. Anton, " 'Savior' to Farmers Takes on Legal, Banking Systems," Jan. 19, 1986, pp. 1–8A.

16. "Paranoia as Patriotism: Far-Right Influences on the Militia Movement" (New York: ADL, 1995) May 24, 1995. United Press International, Regional News, Arizona-Nevada, March 8, 1987. Mark Shaffer and Andy Hall, " 'Patriots' Mortar Owner Says He's Victim of Organized Smear Campaign," *Arizona Republic*, Dec. 27, 1986. United Press International, Regional News, Arizona-Nevada, April 15, 1987. Smith, "Group Opposes Laws, Taxes; Sees Enemies Everywhere," circa Dec. 1985.

17. William F. Rawson, "Guns, Ammunition, Explosive Devices Seized at Ranch," Associated Press, Dec. 17, 1986. United Press International, Regional News, Arizona-Nevada, Feb. 10, 1987. Steve Daniels and Andy Hall, "Blueprints of Dams Found at Radical Group's Place," *Arizona Republic*, Dec. 19, 1986, p. A16. Associated Press, "Right-Wing Group Member Found Guilty of Weapons Possession," March 18, 1987. United Press International, Regional News, Arizona Nevada, California, Idaho, Montana, Oregon, Utah, Washington, Feb. 4, 1987. Feb. 24, 1987.

18. For a concise but incisive examination of Magna Carta, see: Samuel E. Thorne, William H. Dunham Jr., Philip B. Kurland, and Sir Ivor Jennings, *The Great Charter: Four Essays on Magna Carta and the History of Our Liberty* (New York: Pantheon Books, 1965).

19. Magna Carta contains sixty-one independent clauses, and its contents have long been debated by kings, barons, popes, scholars, jurists, parliaments, governments, lawyers, historians, and especially by varying brands of American and English revolutionaries. But in the words of Harvard legal historian Samuel E. Thorne, Magna Carta actually reveals "no comprehensive or unifying design. It puts forth no single doctrine, says nothing of any constitutional plan or scheme of government" (Thorne et al. [1965], p. 3). Yet Magna Carta has risen, phoenixlike, through centuries of legal scholarship and judicial opinion to become a rallying point for countless political factions, including and especially those who have chosen to see in it the legal roots of individual liberty and the collective right of rebellion against tyranny. Commenting in this vein, Erwin N. Griswold, the Dean of Harvard Law School, explains that "the fact remains that Magna Carta is not primarily significant for what it was, but rather for what it was made to be" (Thorne, et al. [1965], p. viii). And so, through its original text as well as centuries of misinterpretation and outright fiction, Magna Carta, in its "most expansive form [became] the concept of the sovereign power of the people to impose their will on government, so that government became the servant rather than the master of the people. [It also became] the notion that the expression of the will of the people about the fundamental rights that were retained by them was to be itemized in a written document [;] the idea that the written document would be superior to the legislative power as well as the executive power [; and] the proposition that the written document, though specifying the limits of governmental power, was merely a recording of rights that existed prior to the promulgation of the charter and,

insofar as the writing was deficient in stating all those rights, those not stated were nonetheless retained . . ." (Thorne, et al. [1965], pp. 58–59). As expansive as the meaning of Magna Carta has become, it is relevant in the present day only because the *concepts* outlined above have been incorporated in judicial rulings and documents (such as the Constitution) that currently are in effect. But Roger Elvick and Bill Gale were incapable of making such a distinction.

20. Notes of Special Agent Kelly P. Hemmert and Special Agent William H. Deily, Coeur D'Alene, Idaho, July 16, 1984, p. 1. Notes of Special Agent Kelly P. Hemmert, July 17, 1984, p. 1.

21. Notes of Special Agent Dale E. Willis and Special Agent J. F. Biederstedt, FBI, July 18, 1984.

22. Notes of Special Agent J. F. Biederstedt and Special Agent Dale E. Willis, FBI, July 19, 1984.

23. Andrew Macdonald (aka William Pierce), *The Turner Diaries* (Arlington, VA: National Vanguard Books, 1978, Second Edition), p. iii.

24. A decade after writing *The Turner Diaries*, Pierce authored *Hunter* (Hillsboro, WV: National Vanguard Books, 1989), a novel that chronicles the homicidal exploits of a one Oscar Yeager who makes a career of murdering interracial couples, Jews, non-whites, and other minorities. Pierce dedicated the book to the serial killer Joseph Paul Franklin, whom he praises as "the Lone Hunter, who saw his duty as a White man and did what a responsible son of his race must do, to the best of his ability and without regard for the personal consequences." Beginning in 1979, Franklin went on a killing spree, targeting black men, interracial couples, and white women he suspected of having sex with blacks. In addition to bombing Jewish synagogues, Franklin seriously wounded National Urban League president Vernon Jordan in 1980. Two years earlier he had shot and paralyzed Larry Flynt, the publisher of *Hustler* magazine.

25. Macdonald [Pierce] (1978), pp. 29, 34, 35, 118, 210.

26. Ibid., pp. 42, 79.

27. Ibid., p. 62.

28. Ibid., pp. 160–61, 168.

29. Ibid., pp. 160, 173, 175.

30. Ibid., 180–81, 191, 198, 202, 209, 210.

31. Louis R. Beam Jr., *Essays of a Klansman* (Hayden Lake, ID: AKIA Publications, 1983), pp. 23, 27, 45.

32. Notes of Special Agent Kelly P. Hemmert, FBI, July 19, 1984, pp. 1, 3.

33. The school bus bombing occurred in Pontiac, Michigan. In addition to his time in federal prison, Miles spent six months in jail for tarring and feathering a high-school principal. See: Affidavit of Farris L. Genide, Special Agent, FBI, *In the matter of Application of the United States of America for an order authorizing the interception of wire communications*, United States District Court, Eastern District of Michigan, Southern Division, misc. no. 86-0343, pp. 18, 20.

34. Bob Miles, "Racial Comrades in Chains," *Liberty Bell*, vol. 4, no. 6, Feb. 1977, pp. 13–14, 27–28.

35. *Extremism on the Right: A Handbook* (New York: Anti-Defamation League of B'nai Brith, 1983), p. 113.

36. Notes of Special Agent Kelly P. Hemmert, FBI, July 19, 1984, pp. 5–6. Notes of Special Agent Norman C. Brown and Special Agent James Davis, FBI, July 19, 1984, p. 2.

37. Louis Beam, "Leaderless Resistance," *Inter-Klan Newsletter and Survival Alert*, reprinted in *The Seditionist*, no. 12, Feb. 1992, also found at: http://www.louisbeam.com/leaderless.htm.

38. Ulius "Pete" Louis Amoss (1895–1961) was an American businessman who became an expert in espionage after reporting for military service in 1942. The Director of Intelligence for the Office of Strategic Services Near Eastern Desk, Amoss held various army posts until 1946. After the war he founded a nonprofit intelligence service. Whether Amoss, who died in 1961, ever actually wrote the treatise on "Leaderless Resistance" that Beam attributes to him is unknown. What is clear is that Amoss died in 1961, so he could not have written about Leaderless Resistance the following year, as Beam claims, though whatever he did write, if anything, might have been published posthumously. For more information on Amoss, see: Ulius L. Amoss Papers, 1941–1963, University of Oregon, Special Collections, Collection 5.

39. Notes of Special Agent Dale E. Willis and Special Agent J. F. Biederstedt, FBI, July 20, 1984, p. 2; July 21, 1984, p. 2. Dietz was a self-proclaimed former member of the Hitler Youth and the publisher of the *Liberty Bell*, a monthly magazine he produced in Reedy, West Virginia. He was the perfect partner for Beam. Six years before Beam articulated his strategy for Leaderless Resistance, and a year before *The Turner Diaries*, Dietz advised his fellow National Socialists to adopt a "uniform" of blue jeans and denim shirts. The movement should have no designated leader so "the enemy won't know whom to strike," he explained. Dietz came to the United States in 1957, became a naturalized citizen, and joined the John Birch Society in 1974. He then broke with the group, calling JBS founder Robert Welch "a Talmudic tool for the destruction of the White people of America." For more on Dietz, see: "Dear Liberty Bell Supporter," insert to the *Liberty Bell* vol. 3, no. 7, March 1976. George Dietz, "National Socialists: What They Were Really Like," *White Power Report*, Sept. 1977, pp. 28–32. Letter from George P. Dietz to Thomas N. Hill, John Birch Society, reprinted in the *Liberty Bell*, Nov. 1976, p. 21. George Dietz, "Letter to the *Liberty Bell* Supporters," March 1976. "John Birch: Betrayed Again!" *Liberty Bell*, vol. 3, no. 10, June 1976, pp. 3–4, 37–38.

40. Notes of Special Agent Norman C. Brown, FBI, July 17, 1984, p. 1. Notes of Special Agent Norman C. Brown and Special Agent John McAvoy, FBI, July 18, 1984, pp. 2, 3. Notes of Special Agent J. F. Biederstedt and Special Agent Dale E. Willis, FBI, July 22, 1984, pp. 2–3.

41. Notes of Special Agent J. F. Biederstedt, FBI, July 17, 1984, p. 1.

42. Notes of Special Agent J. F. Biederstedt and Special Agent Dale E. Willis, FBI, July 22, 1984, p. 1.

43. John C. Ensslin, "Publisher Says Clash with Berg Fateful," *Rocky Mountain News*, (Denver, CO), July 13, 1986, p. 20.

44. Portion of jury trial—Day 1, transcript of opening statements, *United States of America v. Gale et al.*, p. 15. Portion of jury trial—closing argument of Richard J. Pocker, *United States of America v. Gale et al.*, Sept. 30, 1987, pp. 33, 37.

45. Portion of jury trial—closing argument of Richard J. Pocker, *United States of America v. Gale et al.*, Sept. 30, 1987, p. 26.

46. Portion of jury trial—closing argument of Richard J. Pocker, *United States of America v. Gale et al.*, Sept. 30, 1987, pp. 10–12. Seymour (1991), p. 273, 306–9.

47. Portion of jury trial—Day 1, transcript of opening statements, *United States of America v. Gale et al.*, p. 61.

48. Susan Birnbaum, "Five Right-Wing Extremists Convicted of Threats against IRS Agents," *Jewish Telegraphic Agency*, Oct. 6, 1987.

49. United Press International, Regional News, Oct. 3, 1987. "Five Extremists Convicted for Threats against IRS," *Des Moines Sunday Register*, Oct. 4, 1987, p. 2A. Seymour (1991), p. 347.

50. Portion of jury trial—Day 1, transcript of opening statements, *United States of America v. Gale et al.*, pp. 7, 11, 28.

51. Ibid., pp. 32, 34, 66.

52. Portion of jury trial—closing arguments by Frank J. Cremen and Thomas F. Pitaro, *United States of America v. Gale et al.*, Oct. 1, 1987, pp. 16, 22.

53. Ibid., p. 27.

54. United Press International, Regional News, Oct. 3, 1987.

55. Letter from Roxanne Gale, circa Nov. 1987, p. 3.

56. United Press International, Regional News, Oct. 3, 1987.

57. Letter from Roxanne Gale, "Dear Friends," Feb. 20, 1988.

58. Letter from Joann K. Bischoff, Major, USAF, MC, Chief, Internal Medicine Clinic, Department of the Air Force, Castle Air Force Base, to Thomas F. Pitaro, Attorney-at-Law, Las Vegas, Nevada, Sept. 9, 1987.

59. Letter from Roxanne Gale, "Dear Friends," Feb. 20, 1988. Judgment and probation/commitment order for William P. Gale, *United States of America v. Gale et al.*, Jan. 24, 1988.

60. Letter from Roxanne Gale, circa Nov. 1987.

61. Martindale, "Cops Link Suspect to Militia Units; Arizona Man is 1 of 2 Held in Alleged Oakland Kidnap Plot," Oct. 14, 1999. Mike Martindale, "Plot Suspects Face Trial," *Detroit News*, Oct. 26, 1999. Mike Martindale, "Murder Plot Baffles the Experts," *Detroit News*, July 17, 2000. Mike Martindale, "Couple Defends Suspect," *Detroit News*, Oct. 15, 1999. Mike Martindale, "Kidnap Bid Tied to Trial," *Detroit News*, Oct. 27, 1999.

62. Order of Judge Lloyd D. George, *United States of America v. Patrick McCray*, CRS-86-160-LDG, April 29, 1988.

39. Militia Madness

1. For more on the militia movement, see: Ellen M. Bowden and Morris S. Dees, "An Ounce of Prevention: The Constitutionality of State Anti-Militia Laws," *Gonzaga Law Review*, vol. 33, 1997. Morris Dees and James Corcoran, *Gathering Storm: America's Militia Threat* (New York: HarperCollins, 1996). Thomas Halpern and Brian Levin, *The Limits of Dissent: The Constitutional Status of Armed Civilian Militias* (Amherst, MA: Aletheia Press, 1996). R. J. Larizza, "Paranoia, Patriotism, and the Citizen Militia Movement: Constitutional Right or Criminal Conduct?" *Mercer Law Review*, vol. 47, 1996. Joelle E. Poelsky, "The Rise of Private Militias: A First and Second Amendment Analysis of the Right to Organize and the Right to Train," *University of Pennsylvania Law Review*, vol. 144, 1996. Kenneth Stern, *A Force Upon the Plain: The American Militia Movement and the Politics of Hate* (New York: Simon and Schuster, 1996).

2. For a detailed account of the shootout and events that led to it, see: Jess Walter, *Every Knee Shall Bow: The Truth and Tragedy of Ruby Ridge and the Randy Weaver Family* (New York: HarperCollins, 1995).

3. The federal government declined to prosecute the FBI sharpshooter, Lon Horiuchi, but the Boundary County prosecutor went ahead and charged him with felony involuntary manslaughter in 1997. After four years of legal wrangling, a June 2001 decision by the U.S. Ninth Circuit Court of Appeals gave the county the authority to proceed. However, shortly thereafter the newly elected Boundary County prosecutor, Brett Benton, announced he would not continue the prosecution. Evelyn Nieves, "FBI Agent Can Be Charged in Idaho Siege, Court Rules," *New York Times*, June 6, 2001. Associated Press, "FBI Sniper Won't Stand Trial for Ruby Ridge," June 14, 2001.

4. Transcript of the remarks of Louis Beam, "1992 Rocky Mountain Rendezvous," p. 20. Leonard Zeskind, "Armed and Dangerous: The NRA, Militias and White Supremacists are Fostering a Network of Right Wing Warriors," *Rolling Stone*, Nov. 2, 1995, pp. 55, 58, 59–60, 84, 86, 87.

5. A lengthy Treasury Department report dissecting the raid cited numerous failures on the part of ATF. See: *Report of the Department of the Treasury on the Bureau of Alcohol, Tobacco, and Firearms Investigation of Vernon Wayne Howell, also know as David Koresh* (Washington, DC: U.S. Government Printing Office, 1993). Stephen Holden, "Waco: The Rules of Engagement," *New York Times*, June 13, 1997.

6. Ann Devroy, "Brady Bill Is Signed into Law," *Washington Post*, Dec. 1. 1998, p. A8.

7. See: Dan Peterson, "Our Second Amendment Under Fire," *American Legion Magazine*, vol. 135, no. 1, Jan. 1994, pp. 24–26.

8. United Press International, "Lawyer Says Koresh Has a Right to His Guns," Regional News, Texas, March 29, 1993.

9. Roy Bragg and Stefanie Asin, "Two Protests Fizzle; Koresh Faithful Stymied as Passover Nears," *Houston Chronicle*, April 4, 1993, p. A5.

10. Thompson posted her instructions in an e-mail to supporters on April 1, 1995. "Fatal Decision," *Indianapolis Star*, Aug. 8, 1995, p. A4.

11. Bragg and Asin, "Two Protests Fizzle; Koresh Faithful Stymied as Passover Nears," April 4, 1993, p. A5.

12. *Waco: The Big Lie* (Indianapolis, IN: American Justice Federation, circa 1993). R. Joseph Gelarden, "Local Militia Leader Is Losing Credibility, Some Experts Think," *Indianapolis Star*, May 12, 1995, p. E1. Richard A. Serrano, *One of Ours: Timothy McVeigh and the Oklahoma City Bombing* (New York: W. W. Norton and Co., 1998), pp. 65–79.

13. "Declaration of John Ernest Trochmann, Republic of Montana State, Sanders County," Jan. 26, 1992. "Affidavit of Facts Opposing Venue, Republic of Montana State, Sanders County," undated.

14. Videotape, "Militia of Montana Info." (Noxon, MT: Militia of Montana, circa 1995). "A Season of Discontent: Militias, Constitutionalists, and the Far Right in Montana" (Helena, MT: Montana Human Rights Network, May 1994).

15. The incident occurred on March 3, 1995. Some of the militiamen who were arrested responded by filing a civil suit against county officials. Matt Bender, " 'Freemen' Packed Firepower," *Billings (Mont.) Gazette*, March 5, 1995, pp. 1, 9A. Statement of John Bohlman, Mussellshell County Attorney, Subcommittee on Terrorism, Technology, and Government Information, June 15, 1995.

16. Linda Thompson, *Alert*, and "Ultimatum" (Indianapolis, IN: American Justice Federation April 19, 1994). Don Plummer, "Propagandist: I Have Made a Difference,' " *Atlanta Journal-Constitution*, May 18, 1995, p. C3.

17. Gelarden, "Local Militia Leader Is Losing Credibility, Some Experts Think," May 12, 1995, p. E1.

18. Gerry Lanosga, "Thompson Cancels Assembly of Militia," *Indianapolis News*, Sept. 2, 1994, p. B4.

19. Statement of Senator Carl Levin, U.S. Senate Judiciary Committee, Subcommittee on Terrorism, Technology, and Government Information, June 15, 1995.

20. Allen Lengel, "FBI Investigates Suspected Plot to Destroy Camp Grayling Tanks," *Detroit News*, March 10, 1995, p. B1. Statement of Robert M. Bryant, Assistant Director, National Security Division, FBI, U.S. Senate Judiciary Committee, Subcommittee on Terrorism, Technology, and Government Information, June 15, 1995.

21. Testimony of Colonel Fred M. Mills, Missouri State Highway Patrol, Senate Committee on the Judiciary, Subcommittee on Terrorism, Technology, and Government Information, June 15, 1995.

22. Bill Hall, "Is the Militia as Unpopular in Idaho as in Montana?" *Lewiston (Mont.) Morning Tribune*, Aug. 6, 1995, p. 1F.

23. For a thorough treatment of the revival of common-law courts, see: Devin Burghart and Robert Crawford, *Guns and Gavels: Common-Law Courts, Militias and White Supremacy*, (Seattle, WA: Coalition for Human Dignity, 1996). "High-Profile Patriots Are Getting Their Day in Court: Prosecutors Targeting Common-Law Activists," *Klanwatch Intelligence Report* (Montgomery, AL: Southern Poverty Law Center, 1996), Nov. 1996, no. 84, p. 1 and pp. 5–9. Jerry Nagle, "The Rise of Common-Law Courts in the United States: An Examination of the Movement, the Potential Impact on the Judiciary, and How the States Could respond" (Williamsburg, VA: National Center for State Courts, 1996), Feb. 14, 1996.

24. " 'Common-Law' Victims: 'Paper Terrorism' Isn't Just On Paper," *Intelligence Report* (Montgomery, AL, Southern Poverty Law Center, 1998), Spring 1998.

25. *St. Petersburg (Fla.) Times*, Aug. 10, 1994, as cited by Burghart and Crawford (1996), p. 29.

26. Stephan Braun, "Their Own Kind of Justice: The Common-Law Movement's Rogue Courts Let Those Alienated by America's Legal System Play Judge and Jury for a Night," *Los Angeles Times*, Sept. 5, 1995. "Shooting of Corporal Bobbie J. Harper," testimony of Colonel Fred M. Mills, Missouri State Highway Patrol, Senate Judiciary Committee, Subcommittee on Terrorism, Technology, and Government Information, June 15, 1995. Jim Burrows, "Joos Wants Sentence Vacated," *Neosho (Mo.) Daily News*, Sept. 1, 1998.

27. Bob Anez, "Senate Favors Law Requiring Gays to Register with Law Enforcement," Associated Press, March 22, 1995. Letter of the Montana Human Rights Network, circa March 1995. Shannon Tangonan, "Montana Bill Seeks Registration of Gays," *USA Today*, March 24, 1995.

28. Sidney Blumenthal, "Her Own Private Idaho," *The New Yorker*, July 10, 1995, p. 29.

29. Lawrence Cohler, "Rocky Mountain High Anxiety," *Jewish Week*, June 2, 1995, p. 26.

30. Michelle Cole, "For Sherwood, Militias Are About Freedom," *Idaho Statesman*, May 1, 1995, p. A1.

31. Associated Press, "U.S. Officials Reject Blackfoot Man's Gun Claims," *Idaho Statesman*, circa Aug. 1994.

32. Associated Press, "Large Crowd Rallies for Constitutional Freedom," (Blackfoot, Idaho) *Morning News*, July 4, 1994. Tom Stetson, "Second Amendment Rally Successful," *Jubilee* (Midpines, Calif.), July-Aug. 1994, p. 20. Cole (May 1, 1995), p. A1.

33. Associated Press, "Sixteen Idaho Sheriffs Oppose Formation of Local Militia," *Idaho Statesman*, Aug. 15, 1994.

34. Memo from CG, [Commanding General Darryl Manning] Idaho, Office of the Adjutant General, State of Idaho, Military Division, Oct. 7, 1994.

35. "General Purpose of February Meeting," United States Militia Association, Feb. 11, 1995. Michelle Cole and Marty Talahasse, "Militias Find Allies in Idaho Leaders," *Idaho Statesman*, April 27, 1995. Michelle Cole, "Cenarrusa Says Militias Deceived Him, Disavows Link," *Idaho Statesman*, April 27, 1995. Correspondence from Daniel J. Yurman to Governor Phil Batt, Feb. 11, 1995. Correspondence from Marvin Stern, Anti-Defamation League, to Anne Fox, Feb. 23, 1985.

36. Jim Fisher, "Who Needed Bombing to See Militias Aren't Kiwanis?" *Lewiston (Mont.) Morning Tribune*, April 25, 1995, p. 10A.

37. Cole, "Cenarrusa Says Militias Deceived Him, Disavows Link," April 27, 1995.

38. "Promoting Panic, Sherwood Mostly Promotes Himself," editorial, *(Twin Falls, Idaho) Times-News*, March 14, 1995. Michelle Cole, "For Sherwood, Militias Are about Freedom,"

Idaho Statesman, May 1, 1995, p. A1. Jim Fisher, "Give Militiaman What Hurts Him Most—a Platform," *Lewiston (Mont.) Morning Tribune*, Sept. 23, 1995, p. 10A.

39. Blumenthal, "Her Own Private Idaho," July 10, 1995, p. 28. Nancy Mathis, "Sitting Right on the Edge: U.S. Representative Chenoweth's Views Mirror Those of Some Militias," *Houston Chronicle*, May 7, 1995, p. 1.

40. Cole and Talahasse, "Militias Find Allies in Idaho Leaders," April 27, 1995. Timothy Egan, "Trying to Explain Support From Paramilitary Groups," *New York Times*, May 2, 1995.

41. "What Chenoweth's 'Civil Rights Act of 1995' Says," *Idaho Statesman*, June 11, 1995.

42. Associated Press, "Police Chiefs Reject Idea of Disarming Feds," *Idaho Statesman*, July 1, 1995.

43. Jim Nesbitt, "Extremist Groups Gain Ground in Montana," *Cleveland (Ohio) Plain Dealer*, April 16, 1995, p. 7A. Carol Bradley, "Housebound Fugitives Test Legal System," *Great Falls (Mont.) Tribune*, May 21, 1995, pp. 1, 6A.

44. *Sheriff Richard Mack, Plaintiff, vs. United States of America, Defendant.*, No. CV 94-113-TUC-JMR.

45. Pat Rhodes and Carlotta Grandstaff, "Sheriff Jay Printz: Eight Seconds on a Bull in 26 Years. 'I'm a Conservative Independent with a Radical Bent,' " *Bitterroot (Mont.) Star*, unknown date; see: http://www.bitterrootstar.com/backissues/A Backups/Dec02_30/pgone16.html.

46. Mack's books were co-authored with Timothy Robert Walters and published by Rawhide Western Publishing of Safford, Arizona. Paul Hall, "Patriot Sheriff Loses Job over Constitutional Stand," *Jubilee*, Sept.-Oct. 1996, vol. 9, no. 1, pp. 1, 11.

47. Cheryl Phillips, "GOP Taking Up Arms to Fight for Property Rights," *Great Falls (Mont.) Tribune*, Jan. 15, 1995, p. 7B.

48. The full text of the amendment reads as follows: "The powers not delegated to the United States by the Constitution, nor prohibited by it to the states, are reserved to the states respectively, or to the people."

49. Nancy Mathis, "Sitting Right on the Edge: U.S. Representative Chenoweth's Views Mirror Those of Some Militias," *Houston Chronicle*, May 7, 1995, p. A1.

50. Dirk Johnson, "Conspiracy Theories' Impact Reverberates in Legislatures; Extreme Right's Outcry Scuttles Conference," *New York Times*, July 6, 1995, p. A1.

51. Transcribed remarks of Gale Norton, the Stevinson Center's Annual Summer Symposium, August 24, 1996, Vail, Colorado, found at: http://www.i2i.org/Centers-StevinsonCenter/Stevinson/Vail96.htm#Norton.

52. An oil geologist by profession, Rogers began his twenty-year political career in 1973 with a stint on the Bakersfield City Council. He was elected to the state senate in 1986. Josh Meyer, "Legislator Files for Bankruptcy to Forestall IRS Auction of Plane," *Los Angeles Times*, p. B3. Sam Enriquez, "Financial Woes Aside, Rogers Is Optimistic," *Los Angeles Times*, Oct. 25, 1992, p. T16.

53. Cynthia H. Craft, "Rogers Plans Talk to Group Termed Racist," *Los Angeles Times*, Aug. 27, 1994, p. B1. Cynthia H. Craft, "Senator Rogers Defends Talk to Group Accused of Racism," *Los Angeles Times*, Aug. 25, 1994, p. 1A. Cynthia H. Craft, "Black and Latino Groups Scold Rogers," *Los Angeles Times*, Sept. 1, 1994, p. B1.

54. These were not necessarily new demands. In the late 1970s, conservative activists with a large grassroots following had banded together to demand that Washington "return" federal land to the states. The movement, which was called the Sagebrush Rebellion, planned for the states to privatize most natural resources (timber, water, grazing rights, etc.), or simply turn all

the land over to commercial interests at a profit. As a presidential candidate, Ronald Reagan had espoused their cause and after the election he appointed James Watt as Secretary of the Interior to advance the Rebellion's agenda. But the movement lost momentum when the states were unable to establish a plausible claim that public property held by the government to benefit all citizens, including future generations, could be legally handed over to the states. Twenty years later, similar issues were used by the militia movement to fuel talk of armed rebellion.

55. Robert E. Taylor, "Vitriol and Violence," *National Journal*, July 1995.

56. *Idaho Falls Post Register*, Jan. 22, 1995, p. A8; as cited by Dan Yurman, "Militia Movement Enters State Right," *The Progressive Populist*, 1995–1996.

57. Dan Yurman, "Visions of Blood and Fishes Swim in Political Circles; Militia Leader Takes a Blood Oath Against the Endangered Species Act," Econet Western Lands Gopher Service, Oct. 9, 1995.

58. David Johnson, "Militiaman Sherwood Greeted by Protesters; Sherwood Says He Could Find Some Common Ground with Them," *Lewiston (Mont.) Morning Tribune*, Sept. 14, 1995, p. 1A.

59. Cohler, "Rocky Mountain High Anxiety," June 2, 1995, p. 26.

60. Testimony of Susan Schock, Director of Gila Watch, Silver City, New Mexico, "Hate Groups Under the Gun: The Militia Movement and Hate Groups in America," Washington, D.C., July 11, 1995. Robert Longsdorf Jr., "Land Grab: Claims on Federal Lands," *Trailer Life*, Sept. 1995, vol. 55, no. 9, p. 38.

61. Taylor, "Vitriol and Violence," July 1995. Longsdorf Jr., "Land Grab: Claims on Federal Lands," Sept. 1995, p. 38.

62. http://www.cnn.com/US/9603/sagebrush/.

63. Longsdorf Jr., "Land Grab: Claims on Federal Lands," Sept. 1995, p. 38. For more on the harassment of federal environmental workers and land managers, see: Statement of Jeff De-Bonis, Executive Director, Public Employees for Environmental Responsibility, Public Forum, "American Under the Gun: The Militia Movement and Hate Groups in America," Washington, D.C., July 11, 1995.

64. Taylor, "Vitriol and Violence," July 1995.

65. Longsdorf Jr., "Land Grab: Claims on Federal Land," Sept. 1995, p. 38.

66. Keith Erickson, "Cenarrusa: Best Government Is at 'Local Level,' " *Coeur d'Alene (Idaho) Press*, April 24, 1994.

67. Dan Yurman, "States Say 'No Thanks' to BLM Lands," e-mail correspondence, Oct. 1, 1995.

68. Associated Press, "States Conference in Jeopardy," April 16, 1995. Johnson, "Conspiracy Theories' Impact Reverberates in Legislatures; Extreme Right's Outcry Scuttles Conference," July 6, 1995, pp. A1, 10.

69. Johnson, "Conspiracy Theories' Impact Reverberates in Legislatures; Extreme Right's Outcry Scuttles Conference," July 6, 1995, pp. A1, 10.

70. House Resolution 1047. See: http://www.hoboes.com/pub/Politics/Events/Tenth%20Amendment%20Resolution.

71. Serrano (1998), pp. 33–45, 153, 175–82, 217–20.

72. In a noon broadcast on WCBS Radio from New York City just two days after the bombing, experts at the Southern Poverty Law Center were quoted as saying the attack was foreshadowed in *The Turner Diaries*. *WCBS-AM News 88*, CBS Network News, Cynthia Weber reporting, April 21, 1995, 12:00 P.M. ET, radio-TV Reports.

73. ABC-TV news broadcast, *Day One*, May 18, 1995.

74. *United States of America v. Thomas Stockheimer, et. al*, Case No. 96-CR-115 TJC, U.S. District Court, Eastern District of Wisconsin, May 14, 1996.

40. The Road from Oklahoma City

1. News release of Senator Arlen Specter, "Senator Specter Holds Hearing on Militia Groups," June 15, 1995. Michael Janofsky, "Five Paramilitary Leaders Tell Senate They Pose No Threat," *New York Times*, June 16, 1995, p. A12. Statement of Senator Arlen Specter, Chairman, Subcommittee on Terrorism, Technology, and Government Information, June 15, 1995. Dave Eisenstadt, "Militias Try to Put Fix on Bad Rap," (*New York*) *Daily News*, June 16, 1995, p. 26. Scott Shepard, "Militias, Senators in War of Words," *Atlanta Journal-Constitution*, June 16, 1995, p. A7. Sam Vincent Meedis, "Congress Face-to-face with Militias," *USA Today*, June 16, 1996. Testimony of John E. Trochman and Bob Fletcher, Militia of Montana, Senate Committee on the Judiciary, Subcommittee on Terrorism, Technology, and Government Information, June 15, 1995. Daniel Levitas, "Militia Forum," *The Nation*, July 10, 1995, p. 42. Katharine Q. Seelye, "House Panel Reverses Vote Banning Cop-Killer Bullets," *New York Times*, June 16, 1995, p. A12. Testimony of Colonel Fred M. Mills, Missouri State Highway Patrol, Senate Committee on the Judiciary, Subcommittee on Terrorism, Technology, and Government Information, June 15, 1995. Statement of James L. Brown, Deputy Associate Director for Criminal Enforcement, Department of the Treasury, Bureau of Alcohol, Tobacco, and Firearms, Subcommittee on Terrorism, Technology, and Government Information, June 15, 1995. Statement of Robert M. Bryant, Assistant Director, National Security Division, FBI, Subcommittee on Terrorism, Technology, and Government Information, June 15, 1995. Statement of John Bohlman, Mussellshell County Attorney, Subcommittee on Terrorism, Technology, and Government Information, June 15, 1995. "Declaration of John Ernest Trochmann, Republic of Montana State, Sanders County," Jan. 26, 1993. Laurie Kellman, "Militias Decry Oklahoma Bombing; Government Is Real Enemy, Senate Told," *Washington Times*, June 16, 1995, p. A10.

2. Simmons was a former circuit-riding minister who revived the Klan in 1915 with a nighttime cross-burning atop Stone Mountain, Georgia. Similar hearings conducted twenty-one years later by Congressman Martin Dies focused more on communists than Klansmen and Dies, an archsegregationist from Texas, made his prejudices clear when he urged Klan Imperial Wizard James A. Colescott in 1942 to lead his followers "back to the original objectives of the Klan." See: Daniel Levitas, "Senate Hearings on Militia Groups Could Foster Hate," *Roll Call*, June 15, 1995, p. 5.

3. R. Joseph Gelarden, "Government Behind Oklahoma Blast, Claims Militia Advocate," *Indianapolis Star*, April 25, 1995, p. A8.

4. *United States of America v. Miller*, 307 U.S. 174 (1939).

5. *United States of America v. Oakes*, 564 F. 2d 384 (1977). For a nearly identical case from Ohio in which the defendant claimed his membership in the "sedentary militia" exempted him from federal firearms laws, see: *United States of America v. Francis T. Warin*, 530 F. 2d 103 (1976) cert denied 96 S. Ct. 3168 (1976). And a more recent case (*U.S.A. v. Hale* 978 F. 2d 1016 [8th Cir. 1992]) summarizes these arguments well: "Since the Miller decision, no federal court has found any individual's possession of a military weapon to be "reasonably related to a well-regulated militia." "Technical" membership in a state militia (e.g., membership in an "unorganized" state militia) or membership in a non-governmental military organization is not sufficient to satisfy the "reasonable relationship" test (*Oakes*, 564 F. 2d at 387). Membership in a hypothetical or "sedentary" militia is likewise insufficient. See: *Warin*, 530 F. 2d 103.

6. Seven states had adopted both paramilitary training and militia bans. The U.S. Supreme Court case outlawing private armies was *Presser v. Illinois*. Morris Dees and Philip Zelikow, "Ban Private Military Groups," *New York Times*, May 7, 1995.

7. *Application of Cassidy*, 268 App. Div. 282, 51 N.Y.S. 2d 202, 205 (1944), affirmed, 296 N.Y. 926, 73 N.E. 2d 41 (1947). Dees and Zelikow, "Ban Private Military Group's," May 7, 1995.

8. Militia proponents cited the Second Amendment and Article I, Section 8, of the Constitution, which gave Congress the authority to organize, arm, discipline, and "call forth" the militia in order to "suppress insurrections and repel invasions." Subsequent legislation expanded presidential authority to use state militias and more clearly delineated the role and responsibility of the states and the federal government in equipping, training, and authorizing use of the militias. For a thorough, scholarly treatment of the history and evolution of the militia, see: Jerry Cooper, *The Rise of the National Guard: The Evolution of the American Militia, 1865–1920* (Lincoln, NE: University of Nebraska Press, 1997); and Patrick Todd Mullins, "The Militia Clauses, the National Guard, and Federalism: A Constitutional Tug-of-War," *George Washington Law Review*, vol. 57, 1988, p. 328. For a trenchant critique of the rationale of militia proponents, see: Garry Wills, "To Keep and Bear Arms," *New York Review of Books*, Sept. 21, 1995.

9. Andrea Klausner, Esq., "Memorandum in Support of Proposed Federal Legislation to Bar Unauthorized Military or Paramilitary Organizations," American Jewish Committee, July 19, 1995.

10. Seelye, "House Panel Reverses Vote Banning Cop-Killer Bullets," June 16, 1995.

11. Dana R. Gordon, "The Politics of Anti-terrorism," *The Nation*, May 22, 1995, p. 726.

12. "Issues and Controversies: Anti-terrorism Polices," *Facts on File, World News CD-Rom: Issues and Controversies on File*, Aug. 16, 1996, found at: http://www.facts.com/cd/i00010.htm#I00011_a.

13. *Vietnamese Fisherman's Association v. The Knights of the Ku Klux Klan*, 543 F. Supp. 198, 210 (S.D. Texas 1982). Among the supporters of militia bans were the American Jewish Committee, the Southern Poverty Law Center, the Institute for Research and Education on Human Rights, Inc., and others.

14. H.R. 1544, "A Bill to Prohibit the Formation of Private Paramilitary Organizations," introduced by Representative Jerrold Nadler (D–New York), May 2, 1995.

15. Statement of Robert M. Bryant, Assistant Director, National Security Division, FBI, Subcommittee on Terrorism, Technology, and Government Information, Judiciary Committee, United States Senate, June 15, 1995. Harvey Berkman, "Much Debated: The Domestic Intelligence Guidelines," *National Law Journal*, May 8, 1995, p. A28.

16. In that opinion, the court also noted that "[the FBI] may not investigate a group solely because the group advocates [an unpopular cause]; but it may investigate any group that advocates the commission, even if not immediately, of terrorist acts in violation of federal law." See: *Alliance to End Repression v. City of Chicago*, 742 F. 2d 1007, 1015 (7th Cir. 1984), as cited in: Letter from Marc Rotenberg, Director, and David L. Sobel, Legal Counsel, Electronic Privacy Information Center, to Senator Arlen Specter, April 26, 1995.

17. Berkman, "Much Debated: The Domestic Intelligence Guidelines," May 8, 1995, p. A28. *Alliance to End Repression v. City of Chicago*, 561 F. Supp. 575, 578 n. 5 [N.D. Ill 1983] (quoting internal FBI memorandum), as cited in: letter from Marc Rotenberg, Director, and David L. Sobel, Legal Counsel, Electronic Privacy Information Center, to Senator Arlen Specter, April 26, 1995.

18. Stephen Labaton, "Data Show Federal Agents Seldom Employ Surveillance Authority Against Terrorists," *New York Times*, May 1, 1995.

19. American Civil Liberties Union, "U.S.A. Patriot Act Boosts Government Powers while Cutting Back on Traditional Checks and Balances," Nov. 1, 2001. Jason Zengerle, "What the FBI Is Doing Wrong," *New Republic Online*, Dec. 31, 2001.

20. Zengerle, "What the FBI Is Doing Wrong," Dec. 31, 2001. Jim McGee, "Ex–FBI Officials Criticize Tactics on Terrorism; Detention of Suspects Not Effective, They Say," *Washington Post*, Nov. 28, 2001, p. A1.

21. "Fighting Terrorism: Leading FBI Official Discusses Domestic Terrorism," *Intelligence Report* (Montgomery, AL: Southern Poverty Law Center, 1998), Fall 1998, pp. 8–9.

22. Laura Tolley (*San Antonio Express-News*), "Texan Wants Separatists 'Punished,'" *Atlanta Journal-Constitution*, April 30, 1997, p. A3. Michele Kay, "Anger Simmers at Republic of Texas Camp," *Austin American-Statesman*, Jan. 19, 1997, p. A8. Associated Press, "FBI Nabs Texas Separatist Keyes Near Houston," *Lubbock (Tex.) Avalanche-Journal* Sept. 19, 1997.

23. Becky Bohrer, "Montana Town Healing Rifts Five Years after Freemen Standoff," Associated Press, June 12, 2001.

24. The men were convicted in July 1998. See: James Brooke, "Anti-government Freemen Are Found Guilty of Fraud," *New York Times*, July 3, 1998, p. A12. James Brooke, "Anti-government Militants Are Convicted of More Charges," *New York Times*, July 9, 1998, p. A19.

25. Indictment, *United States of America v. Mark William Thomas, Peter Kevin Langan, Scott Anthony Stedeford, Kevin William McCarthy, Michael William Brescia*, in the U.S. District Court for the Eastern District of Pennsylvania, Jan. 30, 1997. Application and affidavit for search warrant from William A. Deal, Special Agent, FBI, U.S. District Court, Western District of Missouri, Feb. 13, 1996. Richard Leiby, "The Saga of Pretty Boy Pedro," *Washington Post*, Feb. 13, 1997, p. B1. Judy Pasternak, "Did Bandits Bankroll Extremists?" *Los Angeles Times*, March 30, 1996, pp. A1, A12.

26. Jerry Mitchell, "Battle by the Book: Pierce's Novels Inspire Slaughter," *Intelligence Report* (Montgomery, AL: Southern Poverty Law Center, 1999), Winter 1999, no. 93, pp. 12–13. *Explosion of Hate: The Growing Danger of the National Alliance* (New York: Anti-Defamation League, 1998). *Intelligence Report*, May 1996, p. 7.

27. Charisse Jones, "Race Killing in Texas Fuels Fear and Anger," *USA Today*, June 11, 1998, p. 1A. "Second Man Convicted in Dragging Death," *New York Times*, Sept. 21, 1999, p. A16.

28. One notable example of the latter occurred in September 2000, when the Southern Poverty Law Center bankrupted the Aryan Nations by winning a $6.3 million judgement on behalf of a woman and her son who had been terrorized by guards at the compound. Bill Morlin, "Writ Signed to Seize Aryan Nations Assets; Sheriff Allowed to Post Guard 'to Make Sure Nothing Leaves,'" *Spokane (Wash.) Spokesman-Review*, Sept. 13, 2000. Chris Stetkiewicz, "Tech Millions May Save Battered White Supremacists," Reuters News Service, Sept. 8, 2000. "Jury Awards $6.3 Million to Woman, Son in Aryan Nations Case," *Washington Post*, Sept. 7, 2000. David Foster, "Demolition Clears Symbols of Hate," Associated Press, undated.

29. Lee Mitgang, "More Tax Protesters, But Tougher IRS Penalties," Associated Press, March 5, 1983. Orr Kelly, with Michael Bosc, "Tax Rebels Multiply—and Collectors Act," *U.S. News and World Report*, Aug. 7, 1983, p. 39.

30. Daniel Levitas, "Untaxing America," *Intelligence Report* (Montgomery, AL: Southern Poverty Law Center, 2001), Winter 2001, no. 104, pp. 40–45. Richard W. Stevenson, "Senate Votes 97–0 to Overhaul IRS after Complaints," *New York Times*, May 8, 1998, pp. A1, A12. Richard W. Stevenson, "Legislation Reining in the IRS Clears House on Vote of 426 to 4," *New York Times*, Nov. 6, 1997, pp. A1, 18. Rob Wells, "Horror Stories about IRS Mount," *Atlanta Journal-Constitution*, April 30, 1998. Robert D. Hershey Jr., "IRS Admits Taxpayers' Rights Are Abused by Improper Tactics," *New York Times*, Dec. 13, 1997, pp. A1 A9. "Reforming the Tax Collector," *New York Times*, Sept. 28, 1997, p. A18. David Cay Johnston, "Behind IRS Hearings, a GOP Plan to End Tax Code," *New York Times*, May 4, 1998. "Oklahoma Lawmaker Says Tax Code Must Go," *The Spotlight*, Oct. 13, 1997, p. 8. David Cay Johnston, "IRS Figures Show Drop in Tax Audits for Big Companies," *New York Times*, April 12, 1999, pp. A1, 20.

31. Fox Butterfield, "Ashcroft Supports Broad View of Gun Rights," *New York Times*, May, 2001.

32. William Glaberson, "Court Says Individuals Have a Right to Firearms," *New York Times*, Oct. 17, 2001; Brian Levin, "Surprise Ruling Backs Gun Rights," *Intelligence Report* (Montgom-

ery, AL: Southern Poverty Law Center, 2001), Summer 2001, Issue 102, pp. 61, 64; "Both Sides Claim Victory in Gun-Rights Ruling," *Join Together Online*, Oct. 26, 2001.

33. "The Rise and Decline of the 'Patriots,'" *Intelligence Report* (Montgomery, AL: Southern Poverty Law Center, 2001), Summer 2001, no. 102, p. 8.

34. *"Highlights from a November 1998 Anti-Defamation League Survey on Anti-Semitism and Prejudice in America,"* (New York: Anti-Defamation League, 1998).

35. Approximately 12.3 percent, or 34.6 million, of the nation's 281 million people are counted as black. An additional 1.7 million or 0.6 percent identified themselves as black or African-American in combination with other races. See: Elizabeth M. Grieco and Rachel C. Cassiday, "Overview of Race and Hispanic Origin," *Census 2000 Brief* (C2KBR/01-1), March 2001, p. 8.

36. *"Highlights from a November 1998 Anti-Defamation League Survey on Anti-Semitism and Prejudice in America,"* (New York: Anti-Defamation League, 1998), p. 4.

37. In 1998, 38 percent of South Carolina voters had opposed a similar repeal measure. See: http://www.sos.state.al.us/downloads/election/2000/general/2000g-amend.pdf, and http://www.sos.state.al.us/election/2000/general/president.htm.

38. Laura Douglas-Brown, "Alabama Chief Justice: Gay Is 'Inherent Evil,'" *Southern Voice* (Atlanta, Ga.), Feb. 22, 2002, p. 3.

39. Leonard Zeskind, *Ballot Box Bigotry: David Duke and the Populist Party* (Atlanta: Center for Democratic Renewal, 1989). Leonard Zeskind, *The Populist Party: A Fraud by America's Racists and Anti-Semites* (Atlanta: Center for Democratic Renewal, 1984).

40. Thomas B. Edsall, "David Duke to Seek Livingston's Seat," *Washington Post*, Dec. 21, 1998, p. A19. As a presidential candidate on the anti-Semitic Populist Party ticket, Duke polled nearly 50,000 votes across eleven states in 1989. He then narrowly won election to the Louisiana House of Representatives.

Epilogue

1. See http://aryan-nations.org/posse/mainpagenews/WTC.zhtm. 'Reaping the Whirlwind,' *Intelligence Report* (Montgomery, AL: Southern Poverty Law Center, 2001), Winter 2001, no. 204, p. 19.

2. Louis J. Freeh, Director, FBI, "Statement for the Record on the Threat of Terrorism to the United States," United States Senate Committees—Appropriations, Armed Services, and Select Committee on Intelligence—Washington, D.C., May 10, 2001. For more on the World Church of the Creator, its background and beliefs, see: "Expert Report of Daniel Levitas," *Reverend Stephen Tracy Anderson v. Matthew F. Hale, World Church of the Creator et al.*, United States District Court, Northern District of Illinois—Eastern Division, case no. 00C2021.

3. "Wonderful News Brothers," e-mail message from "Master Hardy" to Pittsburgh-Creators@yahoogroups.com, Sept. 12, 2001.

4. "'Reaping the Whirlwind,'" *Intelligence Report* (Montgomery, AL: Southern Poverty Law Center, 2001), Winter 2001, no. 204, p. 18.

5. Devin Burghart, "Stateside," *Searchlight* magazine, Jan. 2002, no. 319, p. 34.

6. "'Reaping the Whirlwind,'" *Intelligence Report* (Montgomery, AL: Southern Poverty Law Center, 2001), Winter 2001, no. 204, p. 18.

7. *ADC Fact Sheet: The Condition of Arab Americans Post-9/11*, American Arab Anti-Discrimination Committee, Washington, D.C., Nov. 20, 2001. Laura Mecoy, "Hate Crimes Often Tough to Prosecute," *Sacramento (Calif.) Bee*, Nov. 24, 2001. Testimony of Dr. James J. Zogby, Submission to the United States Commission on Civil Rights, Arab-American Institute Foundation, Oct. 12, 2001. Michael Pena, "Hate Crime Investigations Yield Arrest of S.F.

Man," *San Francisco Chronicle*, Sept. 20, 2001. Dana Milbank and Emily Wax, "Bush Visits Mosque to Forestall Hate Crimes," *Washington Post*, Sept. 17, 2001. Lou Grieco and James Cummings, "Hate Crimes Reported in Valley; Residents Facing Threats, Vandalism," *Dayton (Ohio) Daily News*, Sept. 13, 2001. Associated Press, "Arab-Americans Fearful of Attacks," Sept. 14, 2001. Janelle Brown, "Anti-Arab Passions Sweep the U.S. Despite Bush's Calls for Tolerance; Firebombings, Shootings, and Other Acts of Violence Strike Islamic Worshippers," *Salon.com*, Sept. 13, 2001. Hanna Rosin, "For Arab-Americans, a Familiar Backlash," *Washington Post*, Sept. 12, 2001. "More Insulted and Attacked After September 11," *New York Times*, March 11, 2002, p. A12.

8. "Lawmaker Tries to Explain Remark," *Washington Post Online*, Nov. 21, 2001.

9. Cal Thomas, "Men of Faith in Washington, D.C., Need Our Prayers," Crosswalk.com News Channel, Nov. 9, 2001 found at: http://crosswalk.starwire.com/partner/Article_Display_Page /0,,PTID74088 I CHID194343 I CIID1117654,00.html. Dan Eggen, "Ashcroft Invokes Religion on U.S. War on Terrorism," *Washington Post*, Feb. 20, 2002, p. A02. "Justice Officials Deny Ashcroft Insulted Islam," *Los Angeles Times*, Feb. 16, 2002.

10. "Republic of Texas," *Terrorism Strikes America: What They Are Saying*, ADL, Oct. 11, 2001, http://www.adl.org/terrorism_america/saying_101101.asp.

11. www.posse-comitatus.org, October 16, 2001.

12. "Marching Orders," electronic mail from Matthew Hale to AryanNews@yahoogroups.com, Sept. 13, 2001.

13. Burghart, "Stateside," Jan. 2002, p. 34.

14. Jerusalem Post Staff, "*Post* Poll: American Support for Israel at All-Time High," *Jerusalem Post*, Oct. 26, 2001. Press release, "ADL Poll: No Increase in Anti-Semitism in Wake of September 11 Attacks," Anti-Defamation League, Nov. 2, 2001. According to one Jewish Telegraphic Agency article, when asked the likely cause of the recent terrorist attacks on the United States, 64.3 percent of Americans blamed the growing number of Arab terrorist groups and the countries that harbor them, while 20.1 percent blamed American support for Israel. Young people and those with incomes over $75,000 were more likely to blame American support for Israel. See: Sharon Samber, "Israel Rates High Marks in Polls in Wake of Terror Attacks on U.S.," *Jewish Telegraphic Agency*, Sept. 25, 2001. Meanwhile a *Time*/CNN poll taken September 13 reported that "only 10 percent of respondents said they feel more favorably about Israel as a result of the attacks, and 21 percent feel less favorably. Some 42 percent of respondents in this poll said they feel less favorably toward Palestinians after the September 11 events." Gallup reported the same thing, saying: "While it's possible that sympathy for Israel could increase as a result of this tragedy, for now, only 10 percent say they feel more favorably about Israel as a result of the attacks and 21 percent feel less favorably." So according to Gallup, twice as many respondents (21 percent) say they feel less favorably toward Israel since 9/11, as compared to those who say they feel more so. See: Jeffrey M. Jones, "Poll Analyses: The Impact of the Attacks on America—Americans Expect a Long and Difficult War," Gallup News Service, Sept. 25, 2001. News Release, "Anti-Semitism on the Rise in America—ADL Survey on Anti-Semitic Attitudes Reveals 17 Percent of Americans Hold 'Hardcore' Beliefs" (New York, NY: Anti-Defamation League, June 11, 2002); *Anti-Semitism in America 2002. Highlights from a May 2002 survey conducted by Marttila Communications Group and SWG Worldwide for the Anti-Defamation League Including Poll Results from 1992 and 1998* (New York, NY: Anti-Defamation League, 2002), June 11, 2002.

15. "Council of Conservative Citizens," *Terrorism Strikes America: What They Are Saying*, Anti-Defamation League, Sept. 25, 2001 (http://www.adl.org/terrorism_america/saying_ 092501.asp)

16. Letter from David Duke, Oct. 13, 2001.

17. Transcript of Pat Robertson's interview with Jerry Falwell, Sept. 13, 2001, *The 700 Club* (http://www.pfaw.org/issues/right/robertson_falwell.html); Associated Press, "Pat Robertson Resigns from Coalition" Dec. 5, 2001; Peter Carlson, "Jerry Falwell's Awkward Apology: What Did He Mean and When Did He Mean It? Huh?" *Washington Post*, Nov. 18, 2001, p. F1.

18. Alan Cooperman, "Robertson Calls Islam a Religion of Violence, Mayhem," *Washington Post*, Feb. 22, 2002, p. A2.

19. "Clayton Lee Waagner Named to FBI 10 Most-Wanted Fugitive List," news release, FBI, Sept. 21, 2001. "Clayton Lee Waagner," news release, FBI, Nov. 29, 2001. Tamar Lewin, "Suspect Named in Fake Anthrax Mailings to Abortion Clinics," *New York Times*, Nov. 30, 2001. Frederick Clarkson, "Abortion Terrorism Intrigue: The Nuremberg Files' Neal Horsley Says Fugitive Abortion Foe Clayton Waagner Took Him Hostage, Claimed Credit for an Anthrax Hoax—and Promised to Kill 42 Clinic Workers If They Don't Resign; Skeptics Say They're in Cahoots," *Salon.com*, Nov. 28, 2001.

20. "Clinic Groups Urge Ashcroft to Broaden Anthrax Investigation," *U.S. Newswire*, Nov. 29, 2001. Maurice Tamman and Ron Martz, "FBI Probing Anthrax Threats to Abortion Clinics in 17 States," *Atlanta Journal-Constitution*, Oct. 30, 2001. News conference transcript, "Attorney General Ashcroft Announces Responsible Cooperators Program," U.S. Dept. of Justice, Nov. 29, 2001. Vicki Saporta, interview by the author.

21. Clarkson, "Abortion Terrorism Intrigue: . . ." Nov. 28, 2001.

22. Todd Spangler, "Accused Anthrax Hoaxer Lived Well on the Run, Police Say," *AP Online*, Dec. 8, 2001.

23. Jo Thomas, "U.S. Groups Have Some Ties to Germ Warfare," *New York Times*, Nov. 2, 2001, p. B8. John Kifner, "Anti-terrorism Law Used in Poison Smuggling Case; Man Had Enough Powder for Mass Killing," *New York Times*, Dec. 23, 1995, p. 7. John Kifner, "Man Arrested in Poison Case Kills Himself in Jail Cell," *New York Times*, Dec. 24, 1995, p. 16. "Crossing the Threshold: The Increasing Threat of Biological Terrorism Has Security Experts on High Alert," *Intelligence Report* (Montgomery, AL: Southern Poverty Law Center, 1997), Winter 1997, no. 85, pp. 7–9.

24. James Ridgeway, "Aryan Nations Follower Had Anthrax, Bubonic Bacteria: White Supremacists and the Means of Biowar," *Village Voice*, (New York) Oct. 17–23, 2001.

25. Thomas, "U.S. Groups Have Some Ties to Germ Warfare," Nov. 2, 2001, p. B8.

26. Jeffrey M. Jones, "Americans Felt Uneasy Toward Arabs Even Before September 11, Majority Supports Increased Security Measures Even for Arabs Who Are United States Citizens," Gallup News Service, Sept. 28, 2001, found at: http://www.gallup.com/poll/Releases/Pr010928.asp.

Appendix I. The Posse Comitatus: An Annotated Bibliography

1. According to Thorne, "The date at which work on the *De Legibus* ceased is generally agreed to be 1256 or 1257," and some scholars note that work on the treatise may have begun as early as the 1220s and 1230s and that Bracton may not have been the original author. Samuel E. Thorne, *Bracton on the Laws and Customs of England*, vol. 2 (Cambridge, MA: Harvard University Press, 1968), p. 350.

2. Alexander M. Burrill, *Burrill's Law Dictionary* (New York: Baker, Voorhis and Co., Second Edition, 1867, as reprinted by Fred B. Rothman and Co., Littleton, Colorado, Second Edition, 1987), vol. 2, pp. 33–44.

3. Burrill (1867 and 1987), vol. 2, pp. 311–12.

4. Translation by Frances Morgan Nichols, M.A., *Britton* (Homes Beach, FL: Wm. W. Gaunt and Sons, Inc., 1983), p. 179.

5. James A. Ballentine, *Ballentine's Law Dictionary*, Third Edition, William S. Anderson, ed., (Rochester, NY: Lawyers Co-operative Publishing Company, 1930, 1948; reprint, San Francisco: Bancroft-Whitney, Co., 1969), p. 1213 (page citation is to the reprint edition).

6. John S. James, *Stroud's Judicial Dictionary of Words and Phrases* (London: Sweet and Maxwell, Ltd., 1986), p. 1970 (page citation is to the reprint edition).

7. James (1986), p. 1196.

8. H. G. Richardson, and G. O. Sayles, ed. and trans., *Fleta*, vol. 2, book 2, (London: Selden Society, 1955), p. 232.

9. John Bouvier, *Bouvier's Law Dictionary and Concise Encyclopedia* (Kansas City, MO: Vernon Law Book Company and St. Paul, Minnesota, West Publishing Co., 1914), pp. 2634–35.

10. William Lambard, *Eirenarcha, or Of the Office of Justices of Peace*, P. R. Glazebrook, ed. (London: Professional Books, Ltd., 1972), p. 147.

11. Michael Dalton, *Countrey Justice*, P. R. Glazebrook, ed. (London: Professional Books, Ltd., 1973), pp. 65, 101, 117, 265, 313–15, 317.

12. Matthew Bacon, *A New Abridgement of the Law* [with large additions and corrections, by Sir Henry Gwyllim and Charles Edward Dodd, Esq., and with the notes and references made to the edition published in 1809, by Bird Wilson, Esq., to which are added notes and references to *American and English Law and Decisions*, by John Bouvier], (Philadelphia: T. and J. W. Johnson, Law Booksellers, 1854), vol. 3, pp. 695–96.

13. Sir William Blackstone, Esq., *Commentaries on the Laws of England*, book 1 (London: Dawsons of Pall Mall, 1966), p. 332.

14. *Oxford English Dictionary*, Second Edition, vol. 12 (Oxford, England: Clarendon Press, 1989), p. 171.

15. Bouvier (1914), p. 1463.

16. As quoted in: Bryan A. Garner, *A Dictionary of Modern Legal Usage* (New York: Oxford University Press, Second Edition, 1995), p. 673. Garner cites Alan Harding, *A Social History of English Law* (Middlesex, England: Penguin Books, Ltd., 1966), p. 270.

17. *The New Encyclopaedia Britannica*, Fifteenth Edition, vol. 9 (Chicago:Encyclopaedia Britannica, Inc., 1991), p. 637.

Appendix II. Suppression of Insurrection and Civil Disorder: From Shays's Rebellion to the Civil War

1. Robert W. Coakley, *The Role of Federal Military Forces in Domestic Disorders, 1789–1878* (Washington, DC: Center of Military History, United States Army, 1988), pp. 4–6.

2. Ibid., p. 7.

3. Ibid., p. 7.

4. Ibid., p. 8.

5. According to the notes of James Madison as quoted in Coakley (1988), p. 11.

6. George Anastaplo, *The Amendments to the Constitution: A Commentary* (Baltimore, MD: Johns Hopkins University Press, 1995), p. 367.

7. Anastaplo (1995), p. 373. Coakley (1988), p. 12.

8. For a partisan yet interesting historical summation of these issues as they surfaced during the Virginia ratification debate, see the remarks of Representative Kimmel: *Congressional Record—House*, 45th Cong., 2d Sess. vol. 7, part 4 (May 20, 1878), pp. 3579–81.

9. Quoted in Coakley (1988), p. 17.

10. Ibid., p. 19.

11. Ibid., p. 19.

12. Major Clarence I. Meeks III, USMC, "Illegal Law Enforcement: Aiding Civil Authorities in Violation of the Posse Comitatus Act," *Military Law Review*, vol. 70 (1975), p. 88.

13. Ibid. The Calling Forth Bill was introduced in the House on April 16, 1792, and became law on May 2 that year. Coakley (1988), p. 19.

14. Coakley (1988), pp. 19–20.

15. Ibid., p. 20.

16. Ibid., p. 22.

17. Ibid., pp. 21–28.

18. The law that was passed on February 28, 1795, contained certain revisions which enhanced the president's powers. Coakley (1988), pp. 43–68. See also the remarks of Representative Banning: *Congressional Record–House*, 44th Cong., 2d Sess. (1878), p. 2116.

19. Coakley (1988), pp. 92–93. Requests were made (but troops not deployed) during anti-Mormon pogroms in Missouri in 1834, and during the 1842 Dorr Rebellion in Rhode Island, where competing state legislatures claimed civil and judicial authority. Coakley (1988), pp. 119–27.

20. The 34th Congress convened in December 1855 and placed restrictions on the use of the army in the Territory of Kansas in response to armed conflict between pro-slavery and Free State forces, each of whom asserted their claim to the governorship and territorial legislative authority. For a detailed account of these events, see: Coakley (1988), pp. 145–93. Senate Doc. 209, 57th Cong. 2d sess., pp. 137, 156, March 2, 1903: Frederick T. Wilson, "Federal Aid in Domestic Disturbances, 1787–1903."

INDEX